THE AESTHETICS OF HATE

THE AESTHETICS OF HATE

Far-Right Intellectuals, Antisemitism, and Gender in 1930s France

SANDRINE SANOS

Stanford University Press • Stanford, California

Stanford University Press
Stanford, California

This book has been published with the assistance of the Claudia Clark–Rebecca Gershenson–Megan McClintock Memorial Fund of the History Department of Rutgers, the State University of New Jersey–New Brunswick, and the Joe B. Frantz History Enhancement Fund at Texas A&M University—Corpus Christi.

Printed in the United States of America on acid-free, archival-quality paper

Library of Congress Cataloging-in-Publication Data

Sanos, Sandrine, author.
The aesthetics of hate : far-right intellectuals, antisemitism, and gender in 1930s France / Sandrine Sanos.
pages cm
Includes bibliographical references and index.
ISBN 978-0-8047-7457-4 (cloth : alk. paper)
1. Right-wing extremists—France—History—20th century. 2. Radicalism—France—History—20th century. 3. Antisemitism—France—History—20th century. 4. Masculinity—France—History—20th century. 5. Fascist aesthetics—France—History—20th century. 6. Politics and literature—France—History—20th century. 7. France—Intellectual life—20th century. 8. France—Politics and government—1914–1940. I. Title.
HN440.R3S26 2012
303.48'40944—dc23

2012014036

Typeset by Bruce Lundquist in 10/14 Minion Pro

À mes parents, Louise et Serge Sanos,
à qui je dois tout et sans qui rien n'aurait été possible.

CONTENTS

	Acknowledgments	ix
	Introduction	1
1	"The Crisis Is in Man": The Nation, the Self, and Cultural Politics in the 1930s	15
2	A Genealogy of the Far Right	43
3	"Will We Get Out of French Abjection?" The Politics and Aesthetic Insurgency of the Young New Right	75
4	The Absent Author: Maurice Blanchot and the Subjection of Politics	118
5	"Negroid Jews Against White Men": Louis-Ferdinand Céline and the Politics of Literature	158
6	The Race of Fascism: *Je Suis Partout*, Race, and Culture	194
	Conclusion	245
	Notes	261
	Bibliography	333
	Index	355

ACKNOWLEDGMENTS

This book took many years to bring to fruition, and because of this, it bears the traces—some visible, some not—of the conversations that have shaped and inflected it. Among other things, it stands as a testament to those whose friendship has sustained me. Whatever remains of failings and weaknesses are, inevitably, of my own doing.

To write, one needs not only a place but time and comfort, and I have been fortunate to receive material support that helped in the making of this book. While at Rutgers University, I benefited from the generous institutional support of its history department, grants from the Vidal Sassoon International Center for the Study of Antisemitism at Hebrew University, residence as a fellow at the Center for the Critical Analysis of Contemporary Culture (Rutgers University), and later a research grant from Earlham College. Finally, a summer stay at the Institute for Advanced Study in Princeton gave me the precious time, resources, and peace needed to complete this work. At the same time, I am indebted to many individuals who, in both small and important ways, have encouraged me and helped with this project. I would like to thank the archivists at the Bibliothèque de documentation internationale contemporaine in Nanterre, especially Grégory Cingal. At Earlham College, the late Bob Southard's faith in my project and his boundless knowledge of Jewish history, JoAnn Martin's incisive comments, and Anupama Arora's astute questions, generous encouragement, and rigorous editorial eye helped me begin revising. I am also grateful for the support afforded me by my colleagues in the history department at Texas A&M University–Corpus Christi. I would especially like to warmly thank the anonymous readers whose sharp and thoughtful comments were crucial in shaping the final manuscript into an intelligible and cogent book. I am also thankful to Chloe Piene for allowing me to use her work for the book cover, and to William Schmiechen, who introduced me to it. Last, but not least, I am grateful to Norris Pope for taking an interest in this project and for being a most supportive and insightful editor, as well as to Sarah Newman and Carolyn Brown for expertly shepherding the book through, and to Jan McInroy for her impeccable work.

Like most, I have turned to networks of affinities and friendships that have sustained me and, at every moment, pushed me to become a better thinker, colleague, and friend. This project was still in its infancy when Francine Muel-Dreyfus agreed to work with me at the École des hautes études en sciences sociales, and her conviction that such an analysis must be undertaken mattered. I cherished my time at Rutgers, and I could not have hoped for a more congenial and lively atmosphere than that of its history department. I would like to thank those faculty and students who provided that vibrant intellectual environment, as well as those who over the years—whether they read portions, parts, chapters, or just discussed this project with me, sometimes on a minute detail—proved tirelessly generous: Belinda Davis, Omer Bartov, and Nancy Hewitt, as well as my peers Brady Brower, Amy Forbes, Kate Keller, Max Likin, Marc Matera, and Michal Shapira. I have been fortunate to learn about intellectual history from Donald R. Kelley, whose erudition and wise advice were precious. Outside Rutgers and at different times, Mary-Lou Roberts, Geoff Eley, Jonathan Judaken, Denis Provencher, and especially Judith Surkis provided much-needed encouragement and insights on different aspects of the book. Especially warm thanks are due to Lou Roberts, Dagmar Herzog, and Todd Shepard, whose works have inspired me.

The web of friends who have always provided a home for me is wide. Their warmth and love have made the travails and times spent revising and revisiting this project all the more bearable. Seema Prabhu and Somkid Kingman offered me a refuge in order to begin a substantial part of revisions, and Seema has remained an indispensable presence despite our geographical distance from each other. In New York and New Jersey, Brian Connolly, Saïd Gahia, Stuart Gold, Rebecca Hartman, David Hogg, Jennifer Milligan, Gautam Sarin, and Todd Shepard all offered cheer, wine, and endless provocative discussions. In Indiana, Anupama Arora and JoAnn Martin made all the difference, and still do. In South Texas, Laura Muñoz and Natasha Crawford, Glenn Tiller and Florence Garcia-Tiller, and David and Janet Blanke welcomed me with their hospitality and friendship. In Paris, London, and Berlin, I owe my wonderful times to Laure Beaufils, Vanessa Benoit, Flora Bernard, Charlotte Bigg, Fabian Chappuis, and Hélène Marineau. Together, all these friends have provided me with the kind of affective and intellectual community without which one cannot thrive or survive. I hope they will forgive my silences, absences, and chronic obsession.

My greatest debt is to those who welcomed and trained me, and offered models of intellectual and professional engagement. This work would not have materialized without the unfailing support and rigorous training of Bonnie G. Smith and Joan W. Scott. I came to the United States to study gender and women's history, and both have guided and inspired me to become a better scholar and thinker. Bonnie Smith's attention to rigor, her boundless energy, and her wit have been invaluable. Her timely and incisive questions always challenged me to avoid the banal and the commonsensical and sharpened my thinking, while encouraging me to think broadly and expansively. She saw how my work mattered before I did. Her enduring support of this project (as I struggled) and her insistence on writing well (as well as many wonderful dinners in New York and Paris) have sustained my work. Joan W. Scott has also been a most generous, attentive, and supportive mentor, always reminding me what it means to do history with passion. She prompted me to question my assumptions, to think differently, and to reflect on the nature of historical writing. Her patience while I tried to think through the various issues at the heart of this project and her faith that I could work it out—while reading entire drafts—still amaze me. I have cherished our many conversations about most things French and feminist. I am ever grateful to her for offering me the gift of a stay at the Institute for Advanced Study, which allowed me to complete this book.

Finally, my family has been an enduring source of love, strength, and affection. My sister, Stéphanie, has always reminded me how important it is to remain steady and joyful. Over the years, she knew to come and drag me away from work when I needed it. My parents, Louise and Serge Sanos, first encouraged me to ask questions and take different and unusual paths (as they had) while always trusting my choices. They taught me to love books, offered wise advice, advocated patience when I was restless, and encouraged me to pursue what mattered most. For this and so much more, I dedicate this book to them, a small measure of what I owe them.

THE AESTHETICS OF HATE

INTRODUCTION

There is meaning in what seems not to have any meaning,
something enigmatic in what seems self-evident, a spark
of thought in what appears to be an anodyne detail.
—Jacques Rancière, *The Aesthetic Unconscious*, 2009

In a little-examined episode of the controversial 2006 novel *Les bienveillantes*, the author, Jonathan Littell, sketches a fairly accurate portrait of the French intellectual far right.[1] The episode is brief: only a few pages in this almost thousand-page novel. Yet, to most readers, it appears to offer an interesting—and informative—glimpse into the world of the French far right during the Vichy years. The novel's fictional hero, a Nazi officer named Maximilien Aue, visits occupied Paris in 1943 and socializes with two of the most famous French fascists and collaborationists, Robert Brasillach and Lucien Rebatet. Aue, whose obsession with perversion and abjection, we learn, is matched by his love of classical literature and impeccable erudition, remembers meeting Brasillach at the École normale supérieure, and Brasillach brought him to meet the "bitter" Charles Maurras at the Action française offices, who was "always eager to pour his bile onto Marxists, bourgeois, republicans, and Jews."[2] Aue then joined the young far right, made up of Thierry Maulnier, Jean-Pierre Maxence, and Georges Blond. He also recalls going to a classical concert with Céline and "feverishly discuss[ing] whether there could be a 'fascist' literature" with those young French men late at night in student restaurants.[3]

Here, Littell's portrayal of Aue's 1943 visit veers away from careful historical accuracy, instead borrowing the tropes that have haunted depictions of the interwar intellectual far right especially since 1945, namely, the associations between fascism, masculinity, homosexuality, and perversion. Hatred of the "other"—the Jew, the Communist—is bound to a secret or shameful love of the "same"—male homosexuality. As historian Carolyn Dean has shown, "from 1930 to 1970," there was a "stubborn" and "persistent" "association between [Nazi] fascism and homosexuality."[4] A similar phenomenon has occurred in France, especially around the figure of Robert Brasillach.[5] In the novel, Aue explains to his friend Lucien Rebatet (author of the 1942 antisemitic and far-right pamphlet *Les décombres*) that Brasillach will now refuse to acknowledge him because when both were young Parisian students, Aue had lost patience with Brasillach's inexperienced desire.[6] Littell presents us with a familiar opposition: Brasillach is the "Romantic" fascist whose love of poetry stands in for his inadequate masculinity and a desire for other men that he dare not fully consummate. He is an aspiring Nazi. In contrast, the "true" Nazi Aue embraces his own desire. He revels in bodily fluids and chance encounters with young men who are "taciturn and available."[7] During this Paris visit, Aue also goes to a "faggot bar" with Rebatet and Pierre-Antoine Cousteau, whom he has met earlier at the offices of *Je Suis Partout*, the most famous collaborationist newspaper of the Vichy years.[8] But, again, the easy homosociability of these devoted far-rightists is, through Aue's eyes, nothing more than a mask for shameful homosexual desire. Aue despises Rebatet and Cousteau because, he explains, they would "not hesitate to denounce someone as homosexual, if one could not denounce them as Jew."[9] Antisemitism, fascism, homosexuality, masculinity are woven together in this Parisian interlude.

Another opposition runs through the entire Parisian episode, just as it does the rest of the novel: the juxtaposition of pure aesthetic taste with fantasies and acts of "perversion" (as Aue recalls it). While meandering on the quays of the Seine, Aue chooses to buy not the obvious and crude pamphlet by his friend Rebatet (which had been a huge best seller), but instead the more abstract and purely literary collection of essays penned by Maurice Blanchot, a "critic whose pre-war writings [Aue] had enjoyed."[10] Rather than teasing out the meaning of the juxtaposition of the crass political and the abstract aesthetic, Littell echoes the familiar characterization of Nazi masculinity. The joining of the sublime (the aesthetic) and the abject (the bodily and the sexual) resonated in postwar fictional portrayals of Nazis.[11] In this vein, Aue describes Rebatet, the rabid antisemite and enthusiastic fascist, as a man "always afraid of his own shadow, [afraid] of men just as he was of women, [afraid] of the presence of his very flesh, [afraid] of everything except for those abstract ideas that could never offer any resistance."[12] Littell's portrayal of the French intellectual far right—like conventional historical accounts—explains these men's choices and writings as the consequence of fantasies of perversion and abjection. Here, a "powerful link" is made between "a pathological politics and a pathological homosexuality," in turn tied to a pathological and improperly regulated self and deficient masculinity.[13] In this book, I argue that this characterization has obscured serious engagement with the ways in which twentieth-century far-right, antisemitic, and fascist ideologies actually mined and used a language of perversion, gender, and sexuality as foundations for their politics. Just like Littell's contemporary literary fictionalization, historians have too easily avoided interrogating those images and metaphors. But this episode—which few have commented on even though the novel was awarded two prestigious prizes—illustrates how the history of the interwar intellectual far right and of French fascism still requires our attention.[14] And the novel itself—and its attending controversy—reminds us that literature in modern France is a political matter. In order to challenge the historiographical conventions that have dominated this topic, a different reading is called for, one that pays attention to the particular vision that these far-right intellectuals articulated. For that reason, this book offers a synthetic approach that reads both literary and political writings, examining the themes they engaged and how these were expressed. Only then can we begin to develop a view that fruitfully revisits enduring interpretations of the interwar far right and French fascism.

The Aesthetics of Hate: An Intellectual Movement

"Toward a lost purity."

—Thierry Maulnier, *La crise est dans l'homme*, 1932

This intellectual far right that I examine was a small and heterogeneous group composed of men such as novelist Robert Brasillach, essayist Thierry Maulnier, music and film critic Lucien Rebatet, and editors Jean de Fabrègues and Jean-Pierre Maxence. Alongside lesser-known but no less important journalists such as Pierre-Antoine Cousteau, they were a motley collection, most of whom have traditionally been known as the Jeune Droite (or Young Right). They emerged out of the intellectual and political circles of the right-wing, nationalist, and monarchist group Action française. After 1936, they could be found in two distinct groups, each attached to a newspaper: on the one hand, Catholic neo-Maurrassian nationalists created the monthly magazine *Combat* (Struggle) while, on the other hand, a group of polemical and virulent fascist sympathizers came together in the pages of the newspaper *Je Suis Partout*

(I Am Everywhere).[15] Despite their small numbers and their avowed differences, these men had a wide intellectual and political influence and formed a loose network of like-minded, engaged intellectuals.

The two groups evolved differently in response to the events that shook the latter part of the decade. Still, both articulated a reactionary nationalist and antisemitic politics as the remedy for a contemporary world that they believed to be beset by decadence, crisis, and contamination. Despite their differences and their trajectories from the early 1930s to 1939, when some explicitly turned to fascism and others did not, I argue, this group formed an intellectual movement tied together by their definition of Frenchness through the language of gender, sexuality, and race. In order to grasp the extent of their redefinition of far-right and fascist politics, I explore the logic by which gender, sex, race, and empire structured and underscored their particular vision of the nation. They translated that vision through the rhetoric of abjection (a pervasive feeling of disgust and a state of being characterized by lack and ambivalence), in turn displaced onto figures deemed different and, ultimately, unassimilable. These figures (the Jew and colonial subjects) were imagined to threaten and contaminate self and nation. That logic helped sustain the fantasized recovery of a normative masculinity said to have been under assault. I argue that one of the distinctive features of this intellectual group is that they offered a vision in which the political, the intellectual, and the aesthetic were mutually imbricated to produce a solution to the loss and "crisis" they experienced. A different formulation of the relationship of aesthetics and politics lay at the heart of their vision of the nation and citizenship. They conceived of the aesthetic—art and literature—as a site of political expression, even claiming it as the highest form of politics. In response to abjection, they imagined the aesthetic as a site of purity and regeneration, defined through the exclusion of particular groups of people deemed foreign and unassimilable to the French nation. This is what I term the "aesthetics of hate."

Seeing these intellectuals as part of an intellectual movement that emerged at a particular moment and developed a distinctive rhetoric of the nation has determined the organization of this book. This intellectual far right has usually been divided into two groups: on the one hand, those associated with *Combat*, who, on the surface, stayed close to their Maurrassian and Catholic origins (that I call the Young New Right); on the other hand, those associated with the newspaper *Je Suis Partout*, which became infamous because of its fascist and collaborationist stance during the Vichy years. This historiographical convention is largely the result of these intellectuals' portrayal of their own interwar involvement, and of an ideological "split" that occurred in 1938.[16] But even if newspapers were distinct and ideological differences did emerge around the issues of antisemitism and fascism, it does not mean that collaboration, conversations, debates, and affiliations ended. Instead, I show that these men were far more involved with one another than has been assumed and that their affinities and exchanges (around their vision of the nation) endured. Attending to these intellectuals as part of a movement requires reading some of the most famous proponents not as authors divorced from their context (as some literary scholars have done) nor as journalistic hacks with little claim to the literary (as some historians have done). Many scholars have already explored different aspects of this group and some of their writings, but I suggest here a more synthetic analysis of their ideas. I show (in Chapter 1) how these young intellectuals were very much of their time and understood their place as a political avant-garde in relation to their contemporaries, such as the surrealists. They were consumed by similar concerns but translated them differently.[17] While these far-right writers belonged to the same intellectual and political tradition (a fact that some historians have already examined), that of Maurrassian nationalism and Catholic politics, they also departed from that tradition in significant ways (Chapter 2). I analyze how each group defined its politics throughout the 1930s in relation to the others, and how those definitions evolved over time in order to highlight both affinities and divergences, especially around issues of masculinity, antisemitism, and fascism (Chapters 3 and 6).

Last, two famous figures epitomize the different political and aesthetic strategies embraced by far-right intellectuals in those years: the literary critic Maurice Blanchot and the novelist Louis-Ferdinand Céline (Chapters 4 and 5). Both are celebrated representatives of the post-1945 literary canon. Yet, in the interwar era, both were involved in far-right politics, albeit in radically different ways—a fact that has been the topic of many scholarly discussions and heated polemics. Like the journalists and critics they associated with in the 1930s, Blanchot and Céline provided an answer to the supposed Jewish contamination of the nation and the self by arguing that aesthetics was not just a privileged realm for political battles but could operate *as* politics. Specifically, they called for the dehistoricization of literature. Through their embrace of the literary as an autonomous realm outside the contingencies of history and politics, both men offered particular instances of literature in order to provide a solution to a cultural and political crisis. That position also allowed them to later refuse publicly discussing and acknowledging their interwar writings after 1945. These repudiated writings are exemplary of the "aesthetics of hate" articulated by this group of far-right intellectuals, even though they have not usually been read within the context of the far-right network in 1930s France.

Aesthetics and Politics

> Poetry brings out for us those indefinitely novel pleasures [*jouissances*] of a world that is forever virgin.
>
> —Thierry Maulnier, *Introduction à la poésie française*, 1939

I term the reflections of these far-right intellectuals the "aesthetics of hate" because they found a solution to a political crisis in the realm of aesthetics. This solution did not take the form of either an aestheticization of politics or a politicization of aesthetics—an opposition that has conventionally structured historical debates on fascism; rather, it offered aesthetics *as* politics. For them, the aesthetic—the realm of beauty, art, and literature—was the only site where the sublime could be attained. This is not to say that certain forms of art or literature can be identified as inherently reactionary, but that, for these intellectuals, only certain aesthetic forms answered their search for a political resolution. The aesthetic alone offered a resolution to the abjection of the corrupt social body, and the possibility of a simultaneous binding and transcendence that enabled the recovery of a whole bounded and normative masculine self.

Their political discourse made visible and was expressed through a "dimension of revulsion, attachment, and psychic violence" that, historian Carolyn Dean explains, has usually been "implicit in social regulation" since the late nineteenth century.[18] But the affective dimensions—always at work in portrayals of those deemed deviant and foreign in far-right politics—of this particular discourse began to function as overt political categories only when harnessed to the realm of aesthetics. Some argued that this required a different form of writing, as Blanchot suggested and Céline attempted, while others suggested that particular forms of literary production could function as a politics and thus bring about a regeneration of the nation. They hoped some form of classicism, inflected by their interest in the modern, might provide redemption. That is why, in order to understand how aesthetics served as a politics for these far-right intellectuals, we must take seriously the narrative and rhetorical strategies they developed in their journalism *and* in their literary writings.

Thinking about how they conceived of aesthetics illuminates the themes that infused their particular political vision of the nation. As critic Andrew Hewitt has reminded us in his excellent study of fascist modernism, "It is not enough simply to insist that aesthetics and politics are indistinguishable" and, subsequently, consider only the ideological work of politics.[19] Following the many incisive and illuminating works on the relation of fascism and modernism, my analysis has also been influenced by philosopher Jacques Rancière's astute and persistent engagement with politics and aesthetics.[20] For Rancière, the aesthetic should be viewed as "a mode of thought that develops with respect to things of art and that is concerned to show them to be things of thought."[21] Rancière has explained that we should leave behind the assumption that politics and aesthetics are separate realms. Instead, since politics is a form of "distribution of the sensible which define[s] the common of a community," an operation that echoes the aesthetic, then understanding that relationship means understanding the "way in which the practices and forms of visibility of art themselves intervene in the distribution of the sensible and its reconfiguration, in which they distributed spaces and times, subjects and objects, the common and the singular."[22] Rancière's purpose is not to examine that intractable object of far-right or "fascist" aesthetics—the politicization of the aesthetic—nor critic Walter Benjamin's 1930s reflections on the aestheticization of the politics.[23] His interrogation suggests ways we can think about and explore how aesthetics could function as politics (since both are involved in thinking a community, its objects, and its subjects) and how these intellectuals claimed the purity of aesthetics against the abjection of the political.

This book offers a different interpretation of the French far right by attending to the question of the relationship of aesthetics and politics. On the one hand, historians have paid scant attention to the literary or aesthetic claims of the far right, or have read them as mere expressions of their politics—a politicization of the aesthetic where, ultimately, only the political matters. On the other hand, literary theorists have tended to pay little attention to the larger historical context.[24] While this work follows the insights of many literary theorists, my purpose is to historicize this intellectual movement while taking seriously its claim to be a political *and* aesthetic avant-garde.[25] If we read these intellectuals back into the 1930s, we can see how their fantasies and obsessions echoed contemporary anxieties around the self, the boundaries of the social body, and the borders of the nation. They addressed postwar modernity in order to imagine another future. They looked to Italian fascism, Nazi myth-making, triumphant American modernization, and those considered "less civilized" in order to define their place within a European and world order. In tracing how the Young New Right and *Je Suis Partout* groups were enmeshed, we can explore how their divergences were also *both* political and aesthetic divergences. Importantly, at the center of their thought was a concern with "civilization"—an idea embedded within a colonial imaginary. Once attention is paid to their civilizational rhetoric, one can illuminate how they defined the relationships between nationalism, antisemitism, and fascism, and explain how, for them, aesthetics could act as politics.[26]

The Gender of Politics, the Sex of Race: The 1930s

> Today, we demand virility.
>
> —Thierry Maulnier, *La crise est dans l'homme*

That these intellectuals were antisemitic, fiercely nationalist, and that they came close to or embraced fascism is a well-known fact. On the surface it might not seem to warrant further analysis. But little attention has been devoted to the ways colonial racism and antisemitism were imbricated rather than parallel in this far-right discourse. Considering this larger "racial" and civilizational imaginary sheds a different light on their politics. In turn, analyzing how the categories of gender, sexuality, and race have structured their political and aesthetic vision illuminates the topic in new ways. Indeed, scholars have examined either France's colonial past or its antisemitic history, but little consideration has been given to the manner in which these functioned together at specific moments. My book addresses those gaps and suggests a different approach.

The ways in which the intellectual far right defined its "aesthetics of hate" come to light only if this movement is reinserted into the particular context of the 1930s. This demands an examination of the categories of difference—gender, sexuality, race—that historians have tended to ignore but that figured obsessively in these years and the ways in which these categories structured these writers' nationalism and antisemitism and inflected the ideological routes they took after 1938. As much excellent scholarship has shown, gender, sexuality, and race operate as privileged signifiers of difference and have provided markers for the delineation of modernity and civilization in the European context. In French history, scholars have illuminated how citizenship was constituted as normatively masculine, and how those assumptions have structured in different ways and at different times the manner in which the nation and republican universalism, as well as ideas regarding the community—civilization, assimilation, immigration—were conceived.[27] Yet few have examined the ways in which the French far right defined French citizenship—and embraced antisemitism and fascism—in relation to a historically specific imagination of normative heterosexual masculinity. In fact, political and intellectual histories of the far right have remained largely immune to any consideration of how sexual difference figured in their discourse. This has been the case even of the most recent French and Anglo-American works on intellectuals and the far right that have been strikingly rigorous and yet analyzed these intellectuals within the confines of conventional political categories.[28] The few exceptions to this methodological "blindness" have mostly been the work of literary theorists and scholars who have sought to engage the manifold ways in which far-right and fascist thought was expressed in twentieth-century France.[29] Still, these analyses only punctuate the field; they have not been "absorbed" into mainstream scholarship.

That antisemitic portrayals and theories of race have been articulated through categories of gender and sexuality is a fact now commonly known. The scholarship on antisemitism has been less resistant than that of other fields to serious analysis of the ways these function as discursive categories. The rhetoric deployed in modern European history to identify, denounce, and exclude Jews has been articulated through normative ideals of gender. Historian Sander Gilman fruitfully explored how political discourse and cultural notions of European identity fantasized a Jewish body imagined to embody all that was deemed antithetical to European civilization.[30] The associations made between Jewishness and effeminacy, deviant sexuality, and perverse homosexuality, as well as a number of other non-normative practices and identities, has long infused European antisemitism, resurfacing at particular moments with great force while often forming the staple of stereotypes circulating in nineteenth- and twentieth-century Europe.[31] That antisemitism is a gendered discourse is an assertion few would contest. But rather than tracing the ways in which these stereotypes seemed to endure despite the vagaries of history, it is especially important to examine *how* they were mobilized in specific ways and arranged so as to analyze the vision that far-right intellectuals offered.

Like many French authors and critics writing in the wake of the aftermath of World War I, the young far-right intellectuals I examine in this book were concerned with the dissolution of the boundaries of the nation, the status of the male self, and the future of French culture and civilization. The male body and male self—imagined to be porous and under assault—figured largely in their political ideals. It is therefore important to examine how the far right imagined Frenchness through categories of difference and how it articulated fantasies of abjection in an interwar context of heightened anxieties around gender, sexuality, race, and nation.[32] For these were not rhetorical flourishes. They were part and parcel of the way these young intellectuals understood nation, self, and bodies. The constitutive role of masculinity in visions and ideals of citizenship and nationalism has a long history in modern France, dating back to the French Revolution. Similarly, gender and sexuality have often been deployed in order to map out the boundaries of inclusion, assimilation, tolerance, and equality.[33] As Robert Nye has argued, throughout the nineteenth century, the embodiment and performance of specific masculine qualities allowed bourgeois men to mark their legitimacy and superiority.[34] Yet masculinity has been an inherently unstable category, requiring normative definitions that tied manliness and virility to visions of political autonomy, citizenship, and moral superiority, especially designed in the fin-de-siècle to regulate and domesticate those who might deviate, such as the "bachelor" or the "homosexual."[35] Christopher Forth has shown how the modern antisemitism that erupted around the Dreyfus Affair must be situated within a larger normative discourse on masculinity and Jewishness and how depictions of "deficient manhood" and "effeminacy" functioned to point to the suspect origins of French Jews.[36] Similarly, the manliness of intellectuals appeared ambiguous, for some associated with effeminacy while others sought to recast it in terms of manly virility.[37] After World War I, critics, intellectuals, and journalists built upon these long-standing tropes in order to delineate the nation and the social body. Far-right intellectuals who had not experienced the war also articulated their critique through the prism of gender, race, and class.

To understand the particular manner in which these intellectuals invested literature and politics in those years, one must understand how the major concern troubling most writers and critics across the political spectrum was none other than the question of the *self*. In the wake of the trauma of World War I, its mutilated bodies, and brutalized men, could one still think of the self and of "man" as stable, bounded, and driven by reason? The postwar decade had been not just the age of music-hall jazz, cinema, and mass newspapers, but also, for many, a time when, as Céline wrote in his celebrated 1932 novel, *Voyage au bout de la nuit*, "shattered courage, demolished reflexes, and broken arms" recalled the atrocities and experience of the bloody war.[38] This revealed masculinity—the unspoken and normative foundation of citizenship—to be fragile, contested, and in need of restoration.[39] The question was how best to define the boundaries of normative masculinity.

At the same time, did the turn to the question of the self, namely subjectivity—best exemplified by psychoanalysis and surrealism—not upset the self's very foundations? Had not the postwar decade unleashed the disorder of civilization? For many on the right and the far right, war, technology, mass culture, and the popularity of socialism and communism signaled a more troubling decadence than they had denounced in previous generations. If such instability was embraced and celebrated by some, it was especially troubling and unsettling to others. Since, as far-right intellectuals believed, the nation was both the expression and the foundation of the self, how could it provide substance to its citizens in the current context? The nation—a long-standing far-right obsession—required determining who was worthy of civilization, embodied the moral values of Western civilization, and could be assimilated or civilized into the imperial project. The boundaries that upheld the French (imperial) nation were now porous, or so it seemed to these men. They had been overtaken by unfettered capitalism, "internationalism," and communism, while the empire seemed under assault from within. As the far-right author Thierry Maulnier loudly proclaimed in the early 1930s, "Crisis is in *man*."[40] Those were the pressing anxieties that this generation of intellectuals had inherited from their conservative forefathers. Young far-right intellectuals manufactured a rhetoric of "crisis," which allowed them to articulate their anxieties. These young men were convinced of the need for action against the "enigma of the contemporary disorder" (as Maurice Blanchot described it in 1937) that they hoped to not only eradicate but fundamentally escape.[41] At stake was the question of French civilization and, at its heart, of the meaning of French masculinity.

This book argues that in order to apprehend the nature of the political reformulation produced by far-right intellectuals, we need to engage with their vision not in terms of the narrow political categories that have dominated histories of the French right but in terms of the ways in which their ideological commitment reflected their normative vision of the self. Race and sexual difference provided phantasmic spaces where the integrity and the boundedness of the individual could be restored. These bodies and boundaries were articulated through a discourse of nation and empire. The desire of far-right intellectuals for an undifferentiated self and a whole nation that were organically fused relied on fantasized notions of racialized and gendered Frenchness. I show how we must take seriously this vision of the self, the nation, and Frenchness to explore how such ideas, in turn, determined the aesthetic choices and strategies these men mapped out. Such an analysis may elucidate the nature of that elusive object "French fascism," for it allows us to map the paradoxical logic as well as the fascination it held for these intellectuals (as opposed to others on the traditional far right).

The Question of French Fascism

> The young fascist [man emerges] from his race and from his nation, proud of his strong body and of his lucid mind, disdainful of what the world will think of him.
>
> —Robert Brasillach, "Introduction à l'esprit fasciste," *Je Suis Partout*, 1938

This book is not explicitly about French fascism, though some of these intellectuals have been deemed "fascist" by some historians. However, it necessarily reflects on the meaning, presence, and expression of fascism in the French interwar years, since it speaks to the understanding among these men of the relationships between civilization, nation, and the individual, and between bodies, race, and identities. I contend that we may better grasp the decision of these intellectuals to support, embrace, or refuse fascism if we pay greater attention to the complex ways in which they reimagined Frenchness and their place within it.[42] I read these writers' texts as symptomatic of a culturally fraught moment when questions of belonging, identity, and difference were being redefined with great urgency. Through the analysis of such materials as newspapers, magazines, literature, and political pamphlets, my work offers an interpretation of the traditional subject matter of political and intellectual history. It engages the essential but complex relationship of aesthetics and politics that is at stake in histories of modern antisemitism, colonialism, fascism, and Nazism. These questions still haunt the history of the modern twentieth century, for they address the particular ways aesthetics and politics were entwined—in this case, by far-right intellectuals seeking to reimagine French masculinity, nationalism, and citizenship. They have been the enduring subject of historiographical debates on the question of French fascism—a topic I return to in my conclusion.

To better understand the relationship of aesthetics and politics and the "turn to fascism," I begin with one particular theme, *abjection*, which at the time was not mere rhetoric of affect. It tied together self and bodies to the social and nation in a political discourse clamoring for regeneration. I argue that we need to historicize the very meaning of abjection, which has, usually, figured until now only as a theoretical model, by Julia Kristeva especially, Judith Butler, and even tangentially by Giorgio Agamben.[43] Kristeva's work is exemplary in this respect. In her theorization, abjection helped make sense of the relation of bodies, culture, and subjectivity. It offered a vision of the self founded in a constitutive repression that always haunted it. The abject, as Kristeva defines it (in an ahistorical and purely psychoanalytic manner), is a "fallen object" and can never be fully expulsed since it is the reminder of the unstable nature of the subject "opposed to the I." As such it is both necessary to found a subject, for which "the abject and abjection are my safeguards. The primers of my culture," yet always threatening as "the abject never ceases challenging its master."[44] Yet few have noted the ways in which Kristeva's use of abjection relies on a notion first delineated in the 1930s.

Abjection is itself a *historical* product that specifically emerged in the wake of World War I. It consumed many French critics and authors throughout the interwar years as they tried to find a solution to a fragmented and unstable self haunted from within by (sexual) difference. Both Georges Bataille and Maurice Blanchot sought in the 1930s to find a resolution to abjection, from different political vantage points. Bataille tried to tease out its meanings in an unpublished 1936 essay. While reflecting on the social order, he explained that "human abjection was the result of the material inability to avoid contact with abject 'things.'"[45] He then added—in a manner that Kristeva would echo—that these "abject things can be defined . . . as the objects of an imperative act of exclusion."[46] Bataille did not further theorize that exclusion (Kristeva did in relation to the subject), though many of his endeavors can be read as attempts to provide an answer to this issue. He produced a "literature of transgression," while Blanchot embraced "the sublime." Louis-Ferdinand Céline fictionalized abject bodies in order to restore a discourse of masterful heterosexuality (it is not a surprise that Kristeva turns to Céline as especially symptomatic of this particular functioning of abjection). Thierry Maulnier, whose obsession with decadence, depletion, and abjection infused his insurgent nationalism, found a solution in his return to a more conventional right-wing politics. The use of abjection was more than a linguistic cliché. It translated a larger concern with the relation of the self, bodies, and nation and inquiry into the very conditions of the individual.

I show that abjection and dissolution constituted pervasive cultural terms in the 1930s that allowed far-right critics to make sense of their experience. Because abjection bound together affect and bodies and gave meaning to "crisis" and decadence, it allowed these authors to provide an origin and an explanation for the problems they identified, namely the assault from within by those very bodies deemed irredeemably different and thus irreducibly foreign. (While abjection disavowed any possibility of recovery, the rhetoric of dissolution suggested a return made possible by an appeal to the law.) An attention to the manner in which abjection figured in far-right political discourse illuminates the logic of its obsession with wholeness, purity, and regeneration and how it was anchored through a grammar of sex, gender, and race and found a solution in aesthetics—the realm of the sublime. Fantasies of abjection, dissolution, and dissociation were translated in a particular aesthetics where young far-right intellectuals reimagined nation, race, and bodies articulated in a gendered and sexual discourse of male identity, citizenship, and civilization.

1

"THE CRISIS IS IN MAN"

The Nation, the Self, and Cultural Politics in the 1930s

Those were years exemplary of paradox and surprise.
—Jean-Pierre Maxence, *Histoire de dix ans*, 1939

We were eighteen; our minds were somewhat confused,
we felt rather disgusted with the modern world—
and had a certain innate bent to anarchy.
—Robert Brasillach, *Notre avant-guerre*, 1941

Cultures of the Anxious Modern

In 1937, far-right essayist and intellectual Thierry Maulnier boldly declared: "We must win back our universe!"[1] Maulnier was, in the mid-1930s, a well-respected literary and political critic. A graduate of the prestigious École normale supérieure, he had begun his journalistic career—as many on the far right did—in the pages of Charles Maurras's monarchist and ultra-nationalist *L'Action Française*. By the time he penned this heartfelt call, Maulnier was regarded by many as the natural heir to Maurras: he was a young man whose wide-ranging literary culture matched his reactionary political commitment. His articles appeared in a far-right magazine he had helped create the previous year and coedited with Catholic conservative Jean de Fabrègues, who shared his revulsion at the decadence the postwar era had unleashed. The magazine's name, *Combat* (Struggle), proclaimed its editors' intent. By 1937, when the Spanish Civil War dominated the news and the Popular Front had come to power, Maulnier had already published several collection of essays that took literature and politics as their central topic. Their titles hinted at the radical discontent he experienced: his essays claimed "The Crisis Is in Man," pondered "Socialist Myths," and announced "France, Tomorrow."[2] Maulnier devoted much of his energy in the 1930s to offering a critique of the chaos and decadence he claimed to have observed around him. Such critique infused his insistent call for a revolution of a particular nature, an aesthetic as well as cultural and political revolution that would come from a new generation of far-right intellectuals.

Thierry Maulnier was not alone in this endeavor. His words formed the rallying cry for a group of young men who, in the years 1930 to 1935, expressed themselves in more or less short-lived journals and magazines of high intellectual caliber but little readership, with rather austere names that hardly hinted at their content.[3] They were trained in the ideas of far-right and conservative nationalism and aspired to cultural and political prominence. Ranging from ultra-Catholic journalists Jean de Fabrègues and René Vincent to novelists Robert Brasillach and Georges Blond, music and film critic Lucien Rebatet, energetic polemicist Jean-Pierre Maxence, and the lesser-known but no less dedicated Pierre-Antoine Cousteau and Pierre Monnier, they were a motley collection united in their disgust with the postwar world in which they had come of age. They sharpened their words in little-read newspapers and magazines: *Les Cahiers* (the Notebooks), *Réaction pour l'Ordre* (Reaction for Order), *La Revue Française* (the French Journal), *La Revue du Siècle* (the Journal of the Century). These young men achieved intellectual and political recognition in the late 1930s with the polemical newspapers they created: from the intellectual magazine *Combat* (Struggle) to the controversial *L'Insurgé* (the Insurgent), and the refashioning of weekly newspaper *Je Suis Partout* (I Am Everywhere). They explained that, in this decade, the 1930s, it was necessary—urgent even—to find a solution to the "confused search" that had pervaded the postwar years and had consumed their youthful undertakings.[4]

It was the memory of a youth influenced and troubled by the political disorders and cultural effervescence of the 1920s that fueled this young intellectual generation's search for a dissident politics that they conceived as an irrepressible desire for *truth*. As one of its leading figures, Catholic writer Jean de Fabrègues, observed, "When faced with the poverty of what the modern world has to offer us, we find ourselves gripped by a tragic sense of uneasiness."[5] With similar language, fellow journalist René Vincent explained in 1935 that their desire for a radical (far-right) politics had emerged out of the disconcerting and confused postwar years:

> The uneasiness of 1920 was born under the sign of the post-war disorder; it was, in a certain way, the product of this disorder; it nonetheless expressed a loud dissatisfaction with this very disorder, [and] a categorical refusal of this unfair state of affairs[; it was] a confused search whose troublesome nature some

> were dangerously inclined to, but in any case, a true search, an unconscious and sometimes blind undertaking, but an undertaking [geared] toward higher values [that were] truer than the ones celebrated by this century.[6]

In the face of the "tragic sense of uneasiness" brought about by the modern world, these young intellectuals claimed action must be urgently undertaken. The modern (namely, the "crazy 20s"), as they experienced it, had produced a pervasive anxiety.

Why did they experience the modern—postwar culture and aesthetics—with such anxiety? (For the words "anxiety" and "disquiet" reappeared obsessively in their writings on the topic of the "après-guerre."[7]) The war had been a momentous event that had decimated the generations of fathers and older brothers they paid homage to and yet were haunted by. They had not experienced the Great War, as most had been born at the beginning of the century. But its long-lasting cultural, social, and political effects convinced them that a "new order" was necessary. Their elders spoke about it as an event that marked a radical rupture: nothing would ever be the same. The war, though, had not just brought about death, mutilation, and violence. The years of conflict had also brought about seemingly unstoppable social, technological, and cultural change. This young generation met these changes with an "uneasy" anxiety tinged with excitement. They did not simply reject the modern, but felt a profound ambivalence toward it.

As they said repeatedly in the pages of the numerous magazines and newspapers they wrote for, the anxiety lay in the dangers of losing oneself and succumbing to the temptation of the disorder of decadence. They explained their "categorical refusal" as an instinctive reaction to such disorder, an almost "unconscious" undertaking, rather than as the rational and reasoned programmatic reaction of oppositional far-right politics. The "unconscious and sometimes blind" endeavor that drove their political engagement had infused their own politics: it had done so because, they argued, it had allowed them to *experience* the "tragic" urgency of their undertaking. They had begun their political reflection "from their own very concrete and immediate anxieties."[8] They wrote and acted out of intimate knowledge rather than distant observation. In short, the foundations of their sense of *self* were at stake in this changing world.

Historians have usually explained the "anxiety" and "refusal" that this generation of far-right intellectuals evoked as the expression of their political analysis: those terms were simply the affective responses of writers and journalists who were steeped in a long-standing far-right politics and who, like their elders, railed against socialism, capitalism, democracy, and parliamentarism. In doing so, they denounced a "bourgeois age" that was corrupt and decadent and that had given the nation a "sordid face" and a "motionless and fixed mask."[9] Yet, as has also been noted, the denunciation of bourgeois "capitalist lies" was not confined to this far-right generation but permeated the atmosphere of interwar France. The very terms of these writers' arguments and analyses must therefore be taken seriously, for the sentiments they articulated were rooted in the cultural and political discourse of the 1930s. We do not fully grasp the significance of their expressions of disgust and refusal unless we situate these intellectuals not just within a political genealogy of far-right ideas but also within the larger context of 1930s French cultural and aesthetic debates. This chapter provides an overview of how categories of civilization, race, gender, and sexuality infused contemporaries' debates and discussions and how these young intellectuals engaged and responded to them.[10] From the beginning, they conceived of this moment as unstable, uncertain, and "in crisis." In turn, that rhetoric of "crisis"—admittedly a recurring feature of French political debates—was infused with a different emphasis and legitimated their literature and political endeavors, allowing them to craft a place in conversation with their political forefathers and, more strikingly, against and with their contemporaries.

The Interwar Period: The Fate and Future of French Civilization

The young far right experienced the novelty of the postwar years paradoxically.[11] While modernity seemed to embody, for them, the uncanny experience of dislocation and displacement, at the same time some of them eagerly partook of its most seductive symptoms. In short, they were engaged with what the modern offered in those years, even as many felt ambivalent or condemned its most egregious manifestations. Many loved the cinema and were passionate consumers of its weekly showing, as Brasillach nostalgically recounted in his 1941 memoir, *Notre avant-guerre*.[12] One of *Je Suis Partout*'s most dedicated journalists, Lucien Rebatet began his journalistic career as a film and music critic, an occupation he continued under the pseudonym of François Vinneuil in the pages of *Je Suis Partout*. He reviewed American films, from Charlie Chaplin to westerns, René Clair, and Abel Gance, but also Leni Riefenstahl and most of the Russian cinematic production of those years. Brasillach, who has been characterized by historians as the quintessential "Romantic Fascist," penned the first encyclopedia of cinema with his brother-in-law Maurice Bardèche, which was translated and distributed by the Museum of Modern Art in 1938.[13] Their fellow polemicist and editor Jean-Pierre Maxence, who often lamented how, in these postwar years, "people drank cocktails just for the sake of it and practiced nudism out of snobbishness rather than hygiene [while] celebrating that new God, America," also fondly recalled in 1939 how "cinema had widened horizons."[14] For this far-right critic enamored with both literature and politics, cinema "changed the art of story-telling by giving it speed and immediate punctuation."[15] Soon, though, he berated this craze for the cinema as a misguided desire for "scandal," where everyone in Paris "ran to watch every surrealist film."[16] As another explained, cinema was truly the expression of "the age of the contingent."[17]

Even when they did not necessarily celebrate those symptoms of modernity, they still participated in the cultural conversations occurring around the seemingly endless proliferation of new cultural forms and activities. They listened to the TSF radio, while participating in Action française's demonstrations in the Latin Quarter.[18] They eagerly commented on the cultural events of their day. Journalist Lucien Farnoux-Reynaud, one of the 1937 far-right *Insurgé*'s regular contributors of a column titled "The New World," had written ten years earlier about the new musical form called "jazz" that had swept through Paris. For him, "the epoch of the jazz band" meant, as historian Jeffrey Jackson has noted, a "broader cultural shift," which he found disturbing.[19] Jazz was the kind of novelty, according to Farnoux-Reynaud, that signaled the worrisome dominance of "knee-length skirts, neck-length hair, women with men's coats and cigarettes." In short, a "confusion of the sexes, an anguish of living, and a feverishness in everyday pleasure."[20] While men like Farnoux-Reynaud felt ambivalent about jazz (as did quite a few critics in those years), many others of these young political journalists were music critics, such as Lucien Rebatet and René Vincent (under the pseudonym Hughes Favart).[21] Hardly the traditionalists that the older ultra-nationalist far-right generation were when it came to art and culture, these young men were indeed of their time and enthusiastic critics of the cultural politics they saw unfolding before them.

In the early 1920s, celebrating modernity seemed all the rage. It offered a welcome distraction and challenge to the war years, which had shaken the foundations of Western civilization. Strikingly, attention to modernity was marked by an enthusiastic interest in "black culture." The exoticizing fascination with "blackness"—dubbed in France "negrophilia"—found its way into the work of avant-garde artists as well as into the dance halls, clubs, and bars of nighttime Paris. Artists like Pablo Picasso, Francis Picabia, and Constantin Brancusi turned to African art as a means to *authentically* access life (they were following in the footsteps of poet and collector Guillaume Apollinaire). Paris salons seemed enthralled by "*l'art nègre*," displaying it on their walls and in their furniture.[22] French artists turned to "blackness" as the quintessential embodiment of difference in order to reinvent an exhausted Western civilization, while others returned from colonies with tales and impressions and Parisians met those "members of the African diaspora" who "flourish[ed]" there.[23] And far-right writers like Maxence bemoaned the fact that, indeed, in the 1920s, "differences were being excessively cherished and nursed."[24] New cultural forms were yearned for, and "negrophilia" fulfilled that need, especially for bohemians, artists, and youth eager to experience something different and radically new. Nowhere was this more apparent than in Paris, which since the late nineteenth century had been the refuge of artists, writers, and political exiles. Paris—that "fundamentally imperial city"—offered a vibrant cultural scene: jazz clubs were all the rage. As Michel Leiris described in his 1939 autobiographical narrative, *L'âge d'homme*,

> In the midst of this era of incredible licentiousness that followed the conflict, jazz acted as a rallying cry, an orgiastic banner. . . . [Jazz] acted magically and its influence can be likened to that of possession. It was the best way to provide parties with their true meaning, a kind of religion with communion through dancing, latent or manifest eroticism, and alcohol, the most effective way to level the gap that separates individuals in whatever gathering.[25]

For men like Leiris, jazz embodied the promise of new, unmediated experiences. For young conservatives like Jean de Fabrègues, the same jazz clubs were spaces where Parisians sought "jazz and cocktails to drown their despair."[26] The music played in these clubs was, from the beginning, associated with something different, and most of all with blackness. This cultural scene was one where blackness came to signify the *exotic* and the *primitive*, with little curiosity about its historical and cultural specificities.[27] This is best epitomized by the enduring public fascination with Josephine Baker, who first found fame with her performance in the *Revue Nègre* music-hall show. In the 1934 film *Zouzou*, Baker gave a rare performance that epitomized the ways in which race, blackness, and difference fascinated French audiences: cinemagoers could revel in her barely covered body as she sang—dressed in a birdlike outfit and standing in a life-size cage—a melancholic song of her long-lost homeland, Haiti. Baker's

African Americanness was conveniently erased so as to present her as the enticing and eroticized figure of the mulatto woman, now lost in metropolitan France. She yearned for Haiti, whose association with slavery and colonial violence was silenced so as to offer the vicarious consumption of exotic sexualized racial difference.[28] Baker, who was made queen of the 1931 Colonial Exposition, was "transformed" into a "colonial woman."[29] Audiences flocked to her shows. The fascination with foreignness and (racial) difference that permeated these Parisian years spoke to a certain obsession with the foundations of civilization, since it posed the questions of what it meant to be French and what infused French culture. Excitement pervaded many of the responses to these queries and even young far-right authors recognized that a certain "fever" and new "appetites" had consumed the 1920s.[30]

For young critics equally interested in politics, culture, and literature, what was happening beyond the borders of the nation was also significant and, for some, both troubling and exciting. The nation's boundaries appeared to have been abolished by the century's most brutal war and its technological advances.[31] In the 1930s, this permeability was no longer the trauma of boundaries erased by the tanks and planes of European armies while men were battling in the muddy trenches of northern France. Borders had been made porous by the development of capitalism, industrialization, and modernity. Ethnography was enthusiastically embraced as French officials found it necessary to manage their colonial territories with greater interest and under the rubric of a reinvigorated "colonial humanism."[32] Travels outside of France meant that artifacts and commodities were brought back to the metropole. While "colonial soldiers, workers, professors, and students [who] were not simple immigrants" but embodied French imperial rule came in greater numbers to the metropole, they were not as welcome as the many foreigners who came to settle in Paris.[33] Especially for right-wing nationalists, the issue of borders became a matter of anxiety as immigration came to figure more prominently in policy debates and political discussions.[34] Immigrant workers and German and Central European refugees were the backdrop to this craze for travel and border crossing.

This is best illustrated by Louis-Ferdinand Céline's celebrated and immensely popular first novel, *Voyage au bout de la nuit* (Journey to the End of the Night), whose epigraph stated: "Travel is useful, it exercises the imagination. All the rest is disappointment and fatigue."[35] His main hero, Ferdinand Bardamu, having survived the paralyzing fear and horror of the war as a foot soldier, embarks on a series of trips across continents, to Africa as a colonial officer, and to America as an immigrant who tries his hand at factory work in Detroit, before returning to metropolitan France, where he is able to move between Paris and the south of France. The metaphor of the ship—the colonial cruiser that takes him to West Africa, the "slave ship" that transports him from Africa to New York, and his last vision of a barge on the river Seine in the midst of the capital—reinforces the ability to cross boundaries that westerners could now enjoy and the pleasures of the ethnographic gaze and of tourism, but also the possible "contamination" that it implied for some of its practitioners. As Maxence noted, "Never had Paris been so curious about foreign places."[36]

But young far-right critics were ambivalent. On the surface, cosmopolitanism seemed be the new fashion, yet for many (especially conservative and nationalist critics), the threats of heterogeneity, contamination, and dilution were very much present. Robert Brasillach, for example, enthusiastically celebrated the pleasures of travel and tourism in his memoirs and fondly told of how, with his far-right companions, he had "discovered foreign countries" in the early 1930s.[37] Tourism had become their passion as they visited Spain, Belgium, the Netherlands, and especially Morocco, which, to him, embodied the "homeland [*patrie*] rediscovered" and offered them the vision of "the land of the nation's youth."[38] Others, like Jean-Pierre Maxence, recalled that this new desire for travel even pervaded literary accounts; he wrote that in the late 1920s, "one travels a lot. . . . One travels in order to discover novel scenery, something quaint that has been renewed, [to give] life a younger flavor. One travels like a romantic. They demand sceneries, a secret, a lesson, a voice. Cruise ships, trains, palaces have become fetishes."[39] Travel could therefore be dangerous because, according to Maxence, it served not "knowledge" but "new emotions" that provided only a "sentimental encyclopedia." Travel had become sterile "escapism" in order "to avoid oneself."[40]

To the far right, no one better epitomized the seduction and dangers of travel and modernity than novelist André Gide, the towering figure who dominated the French literary scene (and was at once respected and reviled by this far right). Gide had already become a prominent author before the outbreak of the First World War, with the publication of such works as *Les nourritures terrestres* (1897), *L'immoraliste* (1902), and *Les caves du Vatican* (1914). Cofounder of the literary magazine that ruled the French literary world, *La Nouvelle Revue Française*, he achieved recognition with the publication of works focused on the interrogation of the nature of the self and through his desire to challenge the very nature of the "novel." In the interwar years, Gide—who had first traveled and stayed in Tunisia in the 1890s—notoriously charted the foundational experience that his trip to Africa had been in an account simply titled *Voyage au Congo* (1927) and offered a critique of French colonial practices. He inaugurated his political engagement when he publicly embraced communism in the early 1930s and attended the 1932 Congress for World Peace. He caused another scandal when, against the grain, he publicly renounced his attachment to communism by publishing a disillusioned account of his 1936 trip to Soviet Russia, titled *Retour de l'U.R.S.S.* (1936). By the mid-1930s, Gide was undeniably one of the most celebrated French novelists.

Yet, he came to represent, for the far right in the 1930s, the quintessential purveyor of inauthentic literature misguidedly obsessed with corrupt values whose very political choices embodied the threats to their fantasized French civilization. Most of the far-right authors paid homage to Gide, only to stress, as Maxence did, that he had brought about "immorality," which had subsequently "triumphed in the most widespread habits and desires" and embodied an "aestheticism" that was now obsolete. Such was Gide's presence that Maxence devoted an entire section to "the case of André Gide" in his 1939 memoirs.[41] Others, in the Catholic mold, more forcefully claimed that a particular "Gidian concern continued to bring about the fruits of anarchy, materialism, and death."[42] Gide's own trajectory, choices, and literary works reminded them that boundaries and borders no longer held the same meaning. Accordingly, to break off from Gide meant breaking off from a particular era that had been filled with "paradoxes" and "contradictions"—Maxence's favorite characterization of the postwar years.

While the new could be exciting, it was also symptomatic of the "profound wound of the times."[43] The paradox, as Maxence, like many others in the early 1930s, was fond of explaining, was that this search for novelty, and these expressions of the modern, signaled not an age that had overcome its contradictions but instead the perfect expression of the "crisis" that pervaded the postwar years. "Crisis" was a trope of far-right discourse (Henri Massis had spoken of a "crisis of the mind" in 1920), but in these young men's writings it meant something at once more profound and somewhat different. "Crisis" was everywhere, in literature, art, politics, they claimed, and featured in many of the articles of the first half of the decade. Maxence summed it up in his memoirs when he explained that "the literary crisis, the political crisis, and the social crisis about to come reveal and imply a crisis of culture."[44] Maxence here repeated almost word for word what others, like his friend the prominent far-right intellectual Thierry Maulnier, had argued several years before. Maulnier had titled his 1932 collection of literary and political chronicles "The Crisis Is in Man." The crisis, they believed, was that those values and ideas that the postwar era had brought forth had left their generation only an "empty and desolate plain." It was a "huge, implacable, and tragic abortion."[45] That "profound wound of the times" was nothing more than the echo of the "wound of man."[46]

The Postwar (Masculine) Self

Inquiries into the nature of the self resurfaced in the interwar period. The *fragile self* became a widespread concern as the very foundation of "man" seemed to have been uprooted by four years of brutal and bloody conflict.[47] The self, as nineteenth-century critics had defined it, owed much to the Romantic notion of the individual. Men as diverse as Émile Durkheim and Maurice Barrès had pondered the nature of the self as they engaged the question of "rising individualism" and attempted to explain it.[48] Others, like Victor Cousin, had attempted to draft the conditions for a willful and unified bourgeois and masculine self.[49] Selfhood was not a new public and intellectual concern, but it seemed to be infused with greater urgency in the early twentieth century. Indeed, after World War I, critics, thinkers, and artists were consumed by the idea that this (necessarily masculine) self was fundamentally unstable and fragmented, with precarious and porous boundaries. As historian Carolyn Dean has argued, "[Writers'] formulation of decentered subjectivity [was] part of a cultural crisis in interwar years in which all the criteria defining what makes a self and what gives it legitimacy were perceived as having dissolved."[50] As another historian has noted, that conflict as well as the rise of new political ideologies seemed to confirm the "devastating failure of individual Man (and Man the species) to come to terms with the world he inhabited," and thus posed the question of humanism as a "project, as a mode of life."[51] A most pressing question was therefore how then to conceive of the self?

Reformulating the self was deemed urgent by many contemporaries.[52] This was far from arcane philosophical reflection, for it posed the question of the nature of civilization, culture, art, and even politics. Yet, as the 1930s unfolded, theoretical and literary attempts to "rescue the self" did not necessarily yield firm or expected responses and in fact often served to dislodge assumptions regarding the unified and rational underpinnings of subjectivity and, thus, of selfhood. The realization of the self's instability had allowed avant-garde artists to express a "critique of Western civilization" and proved productive in the realm of aesthetics.[53] Those on the anticolonial left redefined the relationship of the self and the world. The surrealists' turn to a "tactile aesthetics" furthered their attempt to disrupt the hegemonic colonial visual iconography that had been popularized during the 1931 Colonial Exposition.[54] Catholic thinkers, following the lead of Jacques Maritain, called for a humanism freed from the trappings of "materialism," the chaos unleashed by war, and the seductive dangers of communism.[55] Far-right critics were steeped in those larger concerns: Maxence recalled that, after all, "what other way to escape this malaise, this anxiety than to turn to oneself and to know oneself?"[56] But for men like Maxence, Maulnier, and other young conservatives, "the crisis [that] is in man" posed a different set of questions. This mattered especially as Maurice Barrès's "cult of the self," though a profound inspiration, had become a problematic quest. If the dangers hovering around the subject were to be found *within* it, not outside, how could far-right critics argue for a return to order and discipline as the means to a bounded masculinity in harmony with its social expression and with the nation? As they asked, how then was one to restore a "life" that was "more complete and more virile"?[57]

After all, defining the self determined how the individual was imagined. The individual had different meanings for authors and artists across the political spectrum, depending on whether they celebrated or bemoaned the instability and fragmentation besetting the self. The surrealists especially fictionalized in their art how the self had never been a whole and distinct entity. Everyone, they claimed, was a prisoner of the unconscious. The "unconscious" had become a theme of particular interest in those years, especially to those in the realm of art and literature.[58] The insights of psychoanalysis were becoming increasingly popularized, though controversial, and they underscored artists' turn to the unconscious. It seemed that this burgeoning field of knowledge only reiterated the vision of a self beyond one's control. Sigmund Freud's writings were more widely read and disseminated, even though they were still viewed with suspicion by many. Freudian insights were readily embraced by the artistic avant-garde and those involved in challenging conventions: archivist and author Georges Bataille pondered psychoanalytic principles in order to define the social and the sacred.[59] Novelist Louis-Ferdinand Céline, himself a doctor and hygienist, was aware of Freud's principles, having read some of his works in the late 1920s. Like Freud, he offered a vision of human life ruled by the governing principles of Eros, the life drive, and Thanatos, the death drive.[60] In the name of these conflictual principles, he depicted narrators on the verge of psychosis and in the throes of unconscious desires. His second novel, *Mort à crédit* (Death on the Installment Plan), may even, according to a biographer, "be seen as an ironic transposition of Freud's theories."[61] In literature and in art, the unconscious was now in the open, an unsettling reminder of the fragmentation experienced by the self. As Brasillach wrote in 1941, young men like him had then "discussed Freudism with just as much enthusiasm as they would Léon Daudet's [books]."[62] But to those like Brasillach and Maulnier, psychoanalytic insights especially expressed the reversal of "normal values" in a postwar age.

Interestingly, some young far-right intellectuals recognized that "Freudism" (as they called it) was intuitively correct in its diagnosis, but they ultimately derided its insights and denounced the fragmentation typical of the interwar period.[63] Maxence characteristically explained that "the Freudian method" was symptomatic of misguided and "suspect" attempts to interrogate an "unbearable" anxiety that had first begun in the 1920s.[64] While Jacques Lacan drafted the premises of his theory of identification with the "mirror stage" in 1936, which called for a radically new conception of the self, Catholic editor Jean de Fabrègues wrote the same year in the magazine *Combat* that far-right and conservative critics concerned with the state of contemporary man should erase the "horror of a distorted hierarchy."[65] Young conservative Catholics who were involved in energetic debates regarding the renewal of Catholic theology condemned any psychoanalytically inclined reflection in especially strong terms.[66] Similarly, for Thierry Maulnier, "during the postwar years, we had seen [our contemporaries] revel in the extreme pleasures [*jouissances*] of analytical knowledge, sensations, ideas, and other dissociated activities."[67] Those temptations should be fought and mastered, he and others argued.[68] They argued against the celebration of fragmentation. But they were also trying to resolve Lacan's own insight in 1938: how to avoid "the *self* as the site of illusion and the source of error."[69] For only a restored sense of self allowed the eradication of perversion and provided a remedy for the dissolution of the sexual difference deemed necessary for a harmonious social order.

Fragmentation, narcissism, and deviance were the terms that, far-right intellectuals clamored, needed to be overcome. This was urgent because, as Maulnier explained, "there is otherwise little difference between the castration of thought and its prostitution."[70] In the editorial that opened the first issue of the *Revue du XXe Siècle*, Jean de Fabrègues, Thierry Maulnier, Jean-Pierre Maxence, and his brother, aspiring novelist Robert Francis, argued that only politics would overcome the inherent narcissism of the individual's ego: for them it was obvious that "human nature tends to retreat upon itself, [it] is satisfied with the present, [it] only thinks of itself."[71] They refuted the kind of individualism that, they thought, encouraged only self-absorption and self-delusion. The narcissistic individual could not, they argued, overcome his peculiarities in order to surrender to the needs of the nation and generate that organic bond necessary for a true national polity. The proper individual should not be lost in the throes of narcissism but instead should exhibit the *will* to overcome his inherent weaknesses. Strikingly, their analysis often presumed that such weakness existed within the self itself, rather than being the product of the disorder and chaos they encountered. It was because the self was unbounded that it was necessarily subjected to the precariousness of its nature. This was hardly a novel argument: republican critics and social hygienists of the nineteenth century had themselves argued for the regulation of the male republican citizen in order to produce a properly moral republican self.[72] But the argument took on a new force and urgency in the 1930s. Political events at home and around Europe seemed to demand a certainty and firmness that apparently had been lost. Here, as one contributor to the *Revue du XXe Siècle*, Georges Verdeil, argued, the "individual was strong enough to enact its law, which quickly becomes the law of instincts and whims." To let the individual will (in the form of the law) unfold unchecked meant only "disorder and anarchy."[73] And, as Maulnier added barely a year later, "the disorder of individualism has threatened to disorganize communal life."[74] As a result, only a strong authoritarian state could guarantee a contained and properly regulated self in harmony with the nation. In 1935, balance, unity, and harmony were the recurring tropes that far-right critics invoked against disorder, chaos, and anarchy.

Thus, when debating the nature, meaning, and substance of the nation, critics and intellectuals (especially those on the far right) always assumed that the self was at stake: "he" needed to participate in a harmonious, unbroken, and organic relation with the nation (represented by the figure of Marianne, recuperated from the republican glossary of symbols).[75] But this political order needed to be grounded in the social. Far-right critics thus interrogated the relationship of the self to the social body. Only "a certain selfishness would maybe provide the last resource for a disoriented and unrooted humanity in the face of decadence."[76] That "selfishness" (which Maulnier, for instance, distinguished from mere narcissism and claimed was necessary) must be rooted in an inherited social order.[77] The self was not an abstract entity, but a gendered notion that involved delineating the proper masculinity of the French citizen in a social order underpinning the nation.

In the course of articulating that relationship, they found and bemoaned the unseating of the appropriate gendered and sexual underpinnings of the social order. The unbounded self—understood as belonging to the realm of deviance, abnormality, and therefore amorality—was symptomatic of a sick nation, as it reflected deviant practices and challenged the necessary foundations for an orderly, stable, and bounded society.[78] It seemed that the proper terms of sexual difference ensuring the reproduction of French citizens had been undone. The contemporary crisis was a gendered one, and in this diagnosis, far-right critics were not alone. As historians have shown, gender and sexuality acted as powerful signifiers of a fantasized social body, and were central to the ways in which people gave meaning to the postwar world.[79] Concerns over the very nature of masculinity—irredeemably tainted by the experience of the war—meant a renewed obsession with the regulation of gender roles where "the French woman acted as the privileged symbol of postwar crisis and restoration."[80] If some bemoaned the seeming visibility of the middle-class "New Woman," her short-clipped bob, fashion-crazed ways, cigarette smoking, and independence from traditional domestic femininity, others focused on the "Mother" as the redemptive figure, tying together both past and present and offering a possible solution to concerns about depopulation, natalism, and its unspoken origin, "devirilization."[81] This obsessive public focus on women and femininity spoke to and echoed the anxieties about the very substance of French masculinity.

While the 1920s and 1930s saw a renewed "injunction [for men] to be productive and reproductive citizens," many mused about the need to secure a normative heterosexual masculinity which had been undone by four years of war and whose fragility and instability needed to be erased. Staging the contradictions of masculinity—as the subversive and imaginative surrealists did in their art, for instance—served to reaffirm such elusive boundaries. As Leiris pondered the meaning of the ancient Egyptian form of suicide in his autobiographical recollections, he suggested it involved "becoming at once oneself and the other, male and female, subject and object, that which is killed and that which kills—the only possibility of communion with oneself."[82] According to this account, only certain extreme experiences allowed the restoration of a whole self that had not been split by sexual difference. Since a bounded heterosexual masculinity acted as both the foundation and the expression of the national and social body, certain forms of male identity were marked as deviant. The interwar period saw a proliferation of narratives of perversion that argued for the restoration of a proper social order. The state and the law were harnessed in the service of a discourse of sexual and social hygiene "embodying an erosion of boundaries and corporeal permeability" that sought to regulate and contain the threat of psychological perversion and physiological deviance among its citizens and subjects.[83] As historian Carolyn Dean has explained, the interwar period constituted a moment in which most, in France, sought in the same movement to preserve, recover, and restore a presumably endangered and "frail social body," "through the elaboration of fantasies of the body-violating qualities of pornography and homosexuality."[84] These state efforts and cultural fantasies overlapped in efforts to delineate and solidify the substance of French masculinity and the boundaries of the social body.

According to far-right critics, the perceived erasure of gender distinctions and visibility of "deviant" sexualities threatened the basis of the male subject. How could one be a (male) citizen if his cultural and social foundations were no longer? René Vincent characteristically lamented in *Réaction pour l'Ordre* that "morbid fetishism, cult of the abnormal, confused disquiet . . . have all [now] become the dominant *paternal* values [*valeurs pères de famille*]."[85] The familial metaphor alluded to the fundamental perversion of a traditional social, sexual, and domestic order, which he and others deemed lost. As Maulnier added in the same 1932 issue, "In order to make sense of the world, one needs first to get out of the bar or the bedroom."[86] Paris had become a dangerous and uncertain place where "everything can be seen, everything is said," as onlookers strolled "Saint-Germain-des-Prés with its pederasts, its voyeurs, its crypto-Communist morass of three-trousered sexes, its filthy exhibitionism, its dubious aestheticism, and its foreign [*métèque*] cosmopolitanism!"[87] Sexual deviance called up images of Jewish intellectuals, communists, and foreigners invading the streets of Paris and corrupting the city. Obviously, to men like Catholic conservative critic and editor Henri Massis, such disorder was best epitomized by the pernicious and widespread influence of André Gide, whom he accused of destroying the foundation of moral order when he published his defense of homosexuality in his 1924 essay *Corydon*, subtitled *Four Socratic Dialogues* (and in which he discussed Léon Blum's essay on marriage in rather critical terms).[88] Gide had "seduced" young minds, Massis bemoaned, because his work suggested the possibility of "revolt against a fake world [and] against a moral universe defined only through an architecture of conventions and words."[89] The figure of Gide embodied those dangers that, by the 1920s, seemed to have become widely accepted and tolerated. Of course, Gide's popularity—and his Protestant origins—further undermined the religious (and necessarily Catholic) underpinnings of French society. This led Brasillach to recall in 1941 that "the true master of this paganism expressed in the cult of drugs was André Gide who [turned] to communism as the final means of destruction."[90] Accordingly, for the far right, the 1930s cultural scene was characterized by those "extreme attempts at fragmentation."[91] Deviance and dislocation, which were but symptoms of the self's inherent instability, had to be contained and overcome. Most importantly, the individual should be inseparable from his location within a social body that exists *through* and *in* the nation.

No phenomenon epitomized deviance and contamination more glaringly for far-right critics than the increasing public visibility of homosexuality.[92] It was at once less "ashamed and less covert," while, at the same time, "homosexuals looked and acted like other men," thus unmooring the presumed foundations of masculine identity.[93] The interwar period was, as some of these writers saw it, a narcissistic age intent on disrupting the bourgeois liberal world: had not young men eager to assert themselves as "men of letters" embraced homosexuality (or "inversion") in order to find recognition? asked conservative writer Marcel Arland. Such aesthetic experiments threatened the bourgeois moral subject, by uprooting the apparent foundations of the sexual order, the heterosexual body, and the delineation of a national spirit, and thus replacing order by "anarchy" and "inversion." Brasillach wrote in the early 1940s that the postwar decade had seen the emergence of jazz, sexless women whose story had been told in the "ridiculous" and scandalous Victor Margueritte novel *La garçonne*, the exuberant and erotic "Africanness" of Josephine Baker, the cosmopolitan and bohemian crowds of Montparnasse but also the ostentatious Jewishness of a transformed Paris. In these years, he explained, "[people] discovered drugs, homosexuality, travel, Freud, flight and suicide."[94] Though he wrote this a few years later, Brasillach's memories echoed his fellow critics' staple description of the interwar years. These critics necessarily saw the crisis also manifested in literature, which they took to be the privileged expression of the nation's culture.

Literature had not been immune to such interrogations.[95] The concern with the proper cultural definition of gender and sexual order fueled literary endeavors. The surrealists, André Gide's publication of *Corydon*, André Malraux's heroic epics, and Mary Louise Roberts's feared "*Femme Moderne*—This Being Without Breasts, Without Hips" all seemed to confirm the increasing anxiety among far-right intellectuals regarding what was perceived as the loss of sexual difference. The state of the masculine self appeared to them to be at stake.[96] Novelist Marcel Arland (admired by many of these young far-right critics) recalled in an early 1930s far-right publication that

> [the postwar era] produced true anarchy in both the ethical and aesthetic realms; for the best [of our authors, it signaled] a disdain for literature or a lack of confidence in its powers; it signified an impotence in escaping one's self, a unique horizon, a prison without love; [it was] a search—a culture even—of sexual and mental anomalies (I know of a young writer who could be said to be "inverted" as is fashionable nowadays, another one who called for attention in the name of his mentally retarded state). It was also the quest for extreme experiences; a taste for novelty, whatever it may mean, for the colorful, the out of the ordinary, the unstable, the aborted, the monstrous; a satanism, that we would have happily suggested, means that the worst books are made with such bad sentiments.[97]

This obsession with the self became symptomatic, according to Henri Massis, of a "refusal of life, a wish for escapism, a crisis of anxiety, a spirit of revolt" that characterized the period between 1918 and 1930. In unusually harsh words, he explained:

> Everything was sinking, and rotting in this psychological swamp under the guise of the search for the *human person* [*personne humaine*], a search that looked where the "person" obviously could not be found, where it could not exist. Had it been discovered, it would have appeared in such a mediocre light and [shown itself to be] of so little consequence that it might as well not have existed.[98]

Massis opposed the image of the lowly (stench, filth, and decay) to that of the higher (and purer) transcendent power of the "personalist" vision of the individual. Such a misguided search—which Massis deemed a sterile aesthetic endeavor obsessed with the psychology of the individual—could only produce, he added, "literature [that belonged] to inadequate deviants and monsters."[99]

The principles that Massis denounced were thought to be the direct consequence of the individualism unleashed by republicanism, democracy, and unfettered capitalism: the materialism and commodification characterizing the postwar years. The atomized individual was the product of misguided political principles: one journalist had explained in the *Revue du Siècle* that "the Rousseauan individual—that mathematical unity—frees himself from any social link [and] from any yearning for a community."[100] Indeed, as Fabrègues had explained a few years earlier, individualism meant nothing more than the "old heresy [that was this] sacralized notion of Man from which [they] were dying."[101] In this, Fabrègues showed himself to be steeped in the doctrine of personalism that was articulated in these years and was rather popular from left to right.

This denunciation of the individual—denounced for being an "abstract entity"—should be combated in favor of the "person"—the only being, they argued, able to help the emergence of a nation embodied in and bound to every single one of its citizens.[102] Some, in the early 1930s, claimed that their contemporaries should not embrace the individual but conceive of the "person," a term that captured the innate connection the individual held with its culture, history, and nation. Celebrating the "person" was the province of a number of Catholic thinkers intent on providing an antidote to the rampant individualism and social disorder of the postwar years. In this, they took their cue especially from noted leading Catholic intellectual Jacques Maritain, for whom it was not so much the self that was at stake but the question of the place of the individual within society.[103]

Just like Maurrassian authors and conservative critics, Catholic intellectuals criticized what they perceived to be the dissolution of the individual in the modern world. Whether it be Jacques Maritain, the Thomist philosopher close to *L'Action Française*, Henri Massis, his fellow editor of *La Revue Universelle*, or Emmanuel Mounier, the young "non-conformist" with leftist sympathies, Catholic writers called for an alternative to the ambient materialism—which, for the more right-leaning ones, was obviously equated to socialist ideals and communist philosophy.[104] Emmanuel Mounier, who like his far-right interlocutors was engaged in an attempt to rethink the order of the world, declared in 1932: "A person is more than a well-adapted economic cog or well-defined life: he is a center of freedom, creation, and love. This is the original calling that society must develop in all its distinctiveness. Every man, without exception, has the right and duty to develop his entire personality."[105] The Catholic philosophy of personalism held that the "person was the ontological ultimate," so that only the person could provide a metaphysical foundation to society.[106] Mounier thus helped further define in the journal he created in 1932, *Esprit* (Thought), that new philosophy, which put the person at the center of the world and centered the self in ways that proved widely influential among French Catholic writers of different political persuasions. Those ideas were attractive to young conservatives, especially those immersed in the vibrant Catholic discussions of the period. Even Maulnier explained in 1932 that "Man implies selfishness because he is a person."[107] Before he took on the mantle of far-right thought in the second half of the 1930s, his ultra-Catholic colleague Jean de Fabrègues, fellow companion of Maulnier, Brasillach, and Blanchot, directly echoed Mounier's words, lamenting: "Man is but the standardized cog of a gigantic mechanical force which crushes him."[108] He added in 1931 that, at the moment, "the individual is nothing and the person [should be] everything."[109] The individual represented the horrifying consequences of modern alienation and materialism, while the notion of "person" embodied the individual's vital social integration into a larger body politic. Emphasizing the person provided the opportunity for these men to stress the spiritual substance of the individual and his indissoluble ties to a larger social body. Only strong institutions like the church, the state, and family could bind the individual and allow "him" to be the self-fulfilling "person" that would productively maintain the unity of the nation.

At first, the seduction of the philosophy of personalism answered the desire of young far-right intellectuals to redefine the masculine self. After all, as their elder Massis had written in 1927, "the notion of personality implies . . . an intelligible universe, [that is] shared by all."[110] The personalist ideas appropriated by Fabrègues and many of the Young New Right critics in the first half of the 1930s directly borrowed from Mounier's emphasis on the centrality of the "person" (though they soon disagreed with *Esprit*'s politics). In its concern with the binding together of the self to the social body and the nation, this philosophy of the person echoed integral nationalism's emphasis on the individual's rootedness in history and soil. In the early 1930s, the far right opposed the individual to the person: the individual epitomized the commodified, fetishized, and atomized being that was celebrated and enshrined by capitalism and democracy.[111] In a 1934 article specifically devoted to the question of the "individual and the person," Marcel Desrois explained that it was "the modern world [which] has exalted the individual to the point of idolatry and ruined the individuals who exist now."[112] According to these intellectuals, the individual could not be the valid basis for a nation since it denied the organic relationship between the self and the nation and the way every French man was embodied in the social body. They saw the citizen as a misguided effect of this conception of "man" because "he" was no longer "man, father, brother" and instead was only an "abstraction, a number, . . . and a consumer."[113] The "person" was a mantra for the young far right in the early 1930s because it offered a remedy to disorder and deviance. Massis had first explained it when he argued that contemporary literature's "asphyxiating bubble" housed only "the degradation of life, the dissociation of beings, . . . depraved confessions, criminal desires, devilish and perverse enjoyments." Against this, he contended, "It was the person that one sought to rebuild on the ruins of a devastated self, it was the human that one wished to save from the gutters when he lay as in quicksand."[114] The young and promising far-right critic Thierry Maulnier summed it up when he concluded: "The very nature of the post-war years [*l'après-guerre*] is to have heralded the abnormal as the rule, and the insignificant as essential."[115] For him, "this is serious and it must be said."[116] In 1932 he wrote: "Man must be the first idea to be restored."[117]

The Shadow of Surrealism: A Far-Right Avant-Garde

As a literary and political movement the far right is not usually read alongside surrealism, since the two have been radically at odds politically. Yet there is no denying that both emerged from the same discursive context and expressed the obsession of interwar France with culture, race, and sexual difference. In many ways, the burgeoning intellectual far right was concerned with the same issues that drove the subversive and anticolonial surrealists. Both were firmly committed to an anti-bourgeois politics and culture and thought of themselves as a cultural avant-garde. Both attempted to engage with the question of the precarious male self, but within radically distinct intellectual genealogies. Surrealist art and politics epitomized the "culture of the anxious modern" that young far-right intellectuals were so intent on combating. As Jean-Pierre Maxence explained in *Histoire de dix ans*, published in 1939, surrealism embodied "the attempt to reconquer through a dispossession of the self, through abandonment of oneself into the automatisms of instincts to ghosts, and the larvas of the unconscious."[118] Still, surrealism's attempt at aesthetic and political revolution (that led some to communism) could not be ignored by these young men who also thought of themselves as "non-conformists." In fact, Brasillach recognized that "this time [the postwar era] was also the time of Surrealism."[119] Brasillach, Maulnier, Bardèche, and Maxence read surrealist texts and, throughout the 1930s, devoted quite a few articles to this movement. We must therefore pay attention to the ways in which these far-right critics engaged, questioned, and ultimately derided surrealists in an effort to affirm their political diagnosis and legitimate themselves as the only "true" avant-garde.

Surrealism was the literary and artistic movement that far-right intellectuals most actively contested. It had swept through the Parisian cultural scene in the 1920s. The surrealists had questioned the nature of human subjectivity and the fundamental roles of sexual difference and the unconscious in the postwar world. They had questioned the very foundations of the bourgeois self and family and felt they could achieve a more radical and more authentic subjectivity through the performance of a creative self. In doing this, the surrealists sought no less than to revolutionize art. They "were concerned with the imbrication of the sexual in the visual, of the unconscious in the real."[120] They embraced the modern, even if at times their engagement was tinged with "ambivalence" and "nostalgia."[121] Though led by the charismatic and authoritarian author André Breton, the surrealists hardly constituted a homogeneous group. Before the subsequent splits and strifes, Louis Aragon, not yet the celebrated French Communist poet and novelist that he later became (who parted bitterly from Breton), poet Paul Éluard, artist Philippe Soupault, but also painters Max Ernst, Marcel Duchamp, and Yves Tanguy, feverishly engaged in automatic writing—"*les cadavres exquis*"—and produced hybrid art: collages, automatic drawings, photographic experiments. Surrealists' enthusiastic embrace of communism also signaled their involvement in a creative politics.[122] The artist, for them, represented a revolutionary avant-garde intent on remaking the real. Aragon explained that if "reality is the apparent absence of contradiction, the marvelous is the eruption of contradiction in the real."[123] As artists committed to the destruction of the bourgeois order, the surrealists perfectly embodied that subversive and imaginative spirit that was said to characterize the 1920s. In short, their "politics sought to maximize the disruptive forces unleashed by the quest to recover the lost potential of human experience."[124]

As Hal Foster has shown, surrealism in the interwar years sought to disrupt the real and unveil the forces hidden by the conventions of an exhausted colonial bourgeois world. While the surrealists had not necessarily attached themselves to Freud's psychoanalysis (Breton and Freud disagreed), their work confronted the contradictions revealed by the war and modernization, and it was the idea of the *uncanny*—articulated by Freud in 1919 but translated into French only in 1933—that structured their aesthetic politics.[125] The uncanny—the return of the familiar that has been repressed and that, through virtue of its repression, now appears strange and troubling—in many ways provided the frame for surrealists to work through the fragmentation of the self, their desire to transgress borders and (racial) boundaries, the unleashing of sexuality, and the challenge to gender norms, all of which had come in the wake of the Great War. This, according to Foster, is best epitomized by the work of German artist

Hans Bellmer, in which the "psychic shattering (the convulsive identity) of the male subject may depend upon the physical shattering (the compulsive beauty) of the female," so that, in Bellmer's broken dolls, "the ecstasy of one may come at the cost of the dispersal of the other."[126] This aesthetic allowed surrealists to apprehend the relationship of desire, sex, primal fantasies of origin and wholeness, and the law founding the subject in ways that caused great anxiety to their peers, the young far-right intellectuals emerging then, who read these contradictions not as the uncanny—the familiar made strange—but as the abject—the "violent, dark revolt of being."[127]

To the intellectuals trained under the imposing shadow of Action française leader Charles Maurras, surrealism epitomized both disorder and a sterile aesthetic search for a new kind of "man." Up-and-coming far-right critic Thierry Maulnier conceded that surrealism addressed "issues that are [indeed] also ours." But, he added, it was nothing more than "a logical and external Romanticism."[128] It did not emanate from man's "true" nature. And Romanticism had always been reviled in the pantheon of far-right thought, by Maurras especially. Maulnier agreed that as a movement concerned with the most primeval of authenticity, "it had wanted to break the framework of language where it had rightly identified a signifying system, a relatively arbitrary creation, [in short] a discipline."[129] He had recognized surrealism's existence as the direct outcome of a period when young generations were seeking answers. Already, in a 1932 essay on the "discovery of Man," Maulnier had explained that "all these attempts—even old-fashioned ones like Dadaism and surrealism—were a surprising and sometimes dramatic effort to know, [and] find a stable and firm foundation in the real."[130] Maulnier, however, saw the surrealists' call for self-abandonment as misguided, and ultimately disruptive. They had fictionalized the porous boundaries of the Western masculine self but did so, far-right critics accused, by embracing the dissolution of the self.[131] Maulnier insisted instead on discipline and self-containment. He argued, "In the realm of reason, in the realm of mysticism, in the realm of heroism, nothing can be made greater without a harsh and difficult victory over oneself." He concluded: "To abandon oneself could never constitute for man a valid mode of living."[132] As Fabrègues had noted a few years earlier, surrealism, which had "triumphed in Paris' salons," had turned a most urgent affair into a "literary subject and a game." To Fabrègues, Maulnier, and their fellow writers, this was a most serious affair: the existence of Western civilization was at stake. They must restore "virile reason."[133] They concluded that "true revolt is first within ourselves. Man recognizes himself when he rebels against the weight of things pressing against him."[134] Only then could "the average man be forgotten."

Aesthetics and Politics

In the face of cultural changes that they interpreted as chaos, far-right critics saw engagement within the public sphere as a necessity. Acting as intellectuals (as the previous generation had done around the Dreyfus Affair) was no longer a luxury or a choice; it was a demand. The involvement of young far-right critics in the contemporary interrogation of the self and civilization meant taking a place within the Republic of Letters, one that was explicitly devoted to the restoration of the self-governing and rational bounded subject.[135] As Maxence explained it, in the postwar years "the world had seized [them], swept [them], [and] forced [them] to reject it."[136] With the coming to power of the Popular Front in June 1936, cultural politics became a matter of utmost importance. Culture had become a highly contested terrain, especially the question of who had the right to speak in the name of all French citizens.[137] It is precisely because of the Popular Front cultural effervescence and initiatives that it mattered for far-right journalists to reappropriate the cultural scene and decide what "French literature meant." Literature, it was widely believed, was a privileged cultural form, allowing access to truth and beauty but also acting as an unflinching mirror to contemporaries. The relationship of literature and politics took on special urgency as artists and writers increasingly declared their political and ideological allegiances. Again, the trajectory of André Gide seemed exemplary. Left-wing politics and intellectuals who had embraced communism played a particularly significant public role as the Popular Front laid claim to French culture. Indeed, as historian Julian Jackson has explained, the Communist Party was central "in defining the relationship between the intellectuals and the masses, culture and politics." In those years the former surrealist and avowedly Communist writer Louis Aragon claimed: "Our French novel is French because it expresses the profound spirit of the French people."[138] The left claimed that it could best divine the true meaning of Frenchness, but that claim was contested as various left- and right-wing sensibilities battled over who could pretend to represent the French "people" (*le peuple*). Street demonstrations, electoral battles, newspaper headlines—all were the sites of these contests for legitimacy in speaking for the French nation.[139]

To far-right writers, it was obvious that their era had seen the artificial alienation of culture from the citizenry, a culture—broadly defined—that they did not recognize as "truly French." They found it particularly important to take a place in the cultural and literary scene and lay claim to a renewal of French culture. Because they saw literature, between 1925 and 1930, as a "place of intimate struggles, [and of] the author's fight against his own demons," they believed it was urgent for them to weigh in on the debates traversing the literary world.[140] Many of their writings involved both literary and political commentaries, just as Maxence's 1939 memoir recaptured the "anxiety" and unease of the interwar period by following the fate of both literature and politics.

It is widely known that the interwar literary world was shaped by intense debates regarding the role of literature and the ways intellectuals should participate in the public sphere—something that contemporaries incessantly commented on. As a new relationship emerged between literature, the market, and politics in the 1930s, the boundaries of the "public" were redefined.[141] The publishing world saw its market expand as more commercial literature was released and as the work of a greater number of foreign writers was translated. As Henri Massis explained in 1932, "We read a lot more than before 1914," adding that "this new and ill-defined consumer public" seemed to be looking for something "new."[142] Denoël and Steele, a recently created publishing house, found itself at the forefront of the innovative literary trends, inaugurating its list with the huge popular success of Eugène Dabit's working-class account of Paris, the 1929 novel *L'hôtel du nord*. Writers who had redefined the genre of the novel, such as André Gide, Marcel Proust, and Paul Valéry, were widely celebrated. For instance, in one of his first major collections of essays, Maulnier devoted several essays to Valéry (as well as to Emmanuel Berl, André Malraux, Georges Bernanos, and Jean Guéhenno). They were the canonical and towering figures in an overflowing market. As a wider number of literary prizes attempted to map and order this bustling literary landscape, authors like André Malraux, Louis-Ferdinand Céline, Georges Bernanos, Jean Cocteau, and Jean Giraudoux found themselves thrust forward as the proclaimed new literary generation.[143] Malraux's *La condition humaine* was celebrated with the award of the prestigious Prix Goncourt in 1933, a year after Céline had been awarded the Prix Renaudot for his first novel, the epic and bleak *Voyage au bout de la nuit*. The literary canon itself was the subject of intense discussions and reshufflings, and the subject of many of Maulnier's literary chronicles.

At the same time, the literary scene bristled with discussions regarding the fate of literature, its appropriate content, and its desirable form, thus carrying on the many debates that had raged since the late nineteenth century. The novel—as literary form—was said to be in crisis.[144] Writers and critics discussed the merits of the novel—as genre and commodity—and whether it could be salvaged from the abysses of superficiality and ideology. A recurring concern for many was that of the autonomy of literature, namely its independence from political allegiances. This debate had begun with the resounding critique that the author Julien Benda had initiated in 1927 with the publication of an essay concerning the "treason of the intellectuals." Benda was intent on castigating those like Maurice Barrès, who had called for an involvement of authors in the dirty world of politics. Benda refused such a position, which he saw as a direct and unfortunate consequence of the Great War. Setting the parameters of the debate, he argued that "intellectuals," that is, men of letters, should not and could not engage in the base game of politics but rather should act as "the defenders of universal values."[145] Even then, Benda, a fierce anti-Maurrassian and opponent of nationalist politics, argued that the intellectual might occasionally become involved in politics when "an abstract injustice had been committed," citing the Dreyfus Affair as an example. Yet in 1937 he again returned to his belief in the necessary "monastic isolation" of the intellectual.[146] This intense debate was never settled. It reverberated throughout the decade and was a favorite theme (as was Benda) of young far-right intellectuals.

The issue of the "politicization of literature" came back to the fore when the Spanish Civil War broke out in 1936 and brought about new challenges to all French intellectuals, irrespective of their ideological inclination. The political forces of communism and fascism had already become the increasing focus of debate in France and necessitated that each person take a position and situate France within a rapidly changing international order. Right-wing critics and authors accused left-leaning ones of being enslaved to their politics, mere puppets of a communist ideology rather than the critical and lucid witnesses to their society. They often resorted to the example of Gide, who had published a pamphlet renouncing his earlier espousal of communism. It was not just the way politics shaped the content of literary works that obsessed these critics; it was also the ways in which debates about literary form, style, and aesthetics unfolded.

All of these debates seeped into the pages of newspapers as the interwar press found itself enjoying a wider audience. The 1930s saw the proliferation of mass newspapers, such as *Paris-Soir* and *Le Matin*, daily newspapers whose circulation averaged 750,000.[147] A great number of newspapers, magazines, and weekly publications were created. Some were pure literary endeavors and others were more programmatic; the *Nouvelle Revue Française* (the New French Journal) enjoyed a widespread literary influence—everyone in Paris read it and referred to it—though its impact was not as significant as that of other, more popular publications: *Candide* and *Gringoire,* reaching between 400,000 and 600,000 issues in 1936. Left-wing magazines such as *Marianne* and *Vendredi* were set up amid a sense of hope and urgency and enjoyed relative success.[148] Indeed, the "interwar years witnessed the creation of a great number of literary weeklies," or literary and political publications that reached a greater audience than simple magazines but were narrower in focus than newspapers.[149] The publishing house Fayard created *Candide* in the 1920s and its twin publication, more focused on foreign affairs and politics, *Je Suis Partout*, in 1930. *Gringoire*, which came to prominence for its "extreme brand of far-right populism," hatred of England, unrepentant antisemitism, and verbal violence, was set up in 1928. Novelists published extracts of their new works in these newspapers: François Mauriac's *Les anges noirs* was serialized in *Candide*. Readers in interwar France found themselves with an incredible wealth of press publications to choose from and engage with.

Literature and politics were the dominant themes in those journals. Literary critics across the political spectrum were read every week: Léon Daudet's reviews of recent novels, Robert Brasillach's literary criticism every Thursday in *L'Action Française*, Claude Roy's literary column, which he penned in a number of newspapers. The prestigious *Nouvelle Revue Française* had become the unavoidable platform for great novelists and authors. Readers also avidly followed the various—often heated—discussions that took place, for instance, between André Gide and Henri Massis, or Julien Benda and his critics. These were the discussions that young far-right intellectuals eagerly joined. In the eyes of the older rightist generation, these young men alone offered "the desire to rebuild, [and] the return to balance, that preoccupies those minds mindful of the future of our literature."[150]

Politics and the Meaning of "Frenchness"

The obsessive concern of these young men with the relationship between the self and culture, and its privileged expression, literature, infused their vision of their political role as intellectuals. In keeping with the politics articulated by Daudet and Maurras, the budding far-right critics hoped, in the 1930s, to offer a new definition of the nation and the meaning of "Frenchness." Not since the late 1880s and 1890s had a generation so forcefully and self-consciously called for a "new" order. Their critique was hardly original, but the claim to novelty was a staple of emerging political and cultural movements of the interwar period. The originality lay elsewhere, in their conception of the relationship between aesthetics and politics within a far-right ideology. For the men born at the outset of the twentieth century, such a search and, at times, "blind undertaking," was fueled by the sense of a world turned upside down after the cataclysmic First World War. Unlike the men who had "trained" and influenced them, they were this time intent on freeing themselves from the illusions that they asserted others had succumbed to. As the 1920s drew to a close, they clamored for a "non-conformist" intellectual politics.[151]

In 1931, the up-and-coming literary critic and novelist Robert Brasillach penned a brilliant literary coup: in the pages of the conservative newspaper *Candide*, he heralded the "end of our post-war years."[152] For many, the 1930s thus began in 1931, when this young critic announced that they had entered a different era. He repeated, ten years later, that "this was really the end of an era," and, indeed, there was the pervasive sense of a new age emerging.[153] The men who came of age in the early 1930s saw themselves as a new "generation."[154] Many of them across the political spectrum sought to provide a different practice and ethos of politics, and advocated a new society: Catholic thinker Emmanuel Mounier, the energetic editor of the magazine *Esprit*, sought to ground "man" in a "personalist" vision of the world based on the harmonious complementarity of the heterosexual couple and the family.[155] Prominent Catholic philosophers such as the elderly Jacques Maritain attempted a "spiritualist revolution," while the novelist Pierre Drieu La Rochelle tried to define, in publication after publication, the terms for a new nationalism. Within far-right circles, young critics (such as novelists Robert Brasillach and Georges Blond, the literary critic and journalist Maurice Blanchot, the Catholic critic Jean de Fabrègues, the journalist Pierre-Antoine Cousteau, intellectual Thierry Maulnier, "iconoclast" Jean-Pierre Maxence, the polemicist Lucien Rebatet, and many more) found socialism and communism to be the twin expressions of a decadent modern age. They discussed the promise of fascism, while deriding the dangers of a pro-German fascination with Hitler, but they also had no illusions regarding a French political system that, they argued, had corrupted the substance of the nation. They claimed that "for the last ten years, France has lived in a state of spinelessness."[156] These years have been "disgusting to the point of throwing up."[157] Disgust was symptomatic of the overarching crisis that they denounced. The rhetoric of "crisis" infused their writings on the self, literature, and politics.[158] As in politics, literature "sought today the way toward more profound passions, less fanciful sufferings, and more virile emotions." As Maulnier explained, "It is virility that we demand today."[159]

Frenchness thus needed to be reaffirmed and nationalism redefined. These writers and journalists upheld the "integral nationalism" inherited from the organization Action française, an absolute commitment to a soil born out of years of history, tradition, and civilization. But, at the same time, they attempted to go further than their forefathers. The French nation was to embody the essence of Western civilization, and was defined through the prism of colonialism and antisemitism. Whereas Action française had remained within the framework inherited from its late-nineteenth-century birth, the critics of the Young New Right produced a far-right politics fueled by a concern with the male subject. They wanted to give substance to a decentered and disorderly self. The "nameless, faceless anxiety" of the age was thus given substance in a rhetoric of civilization, nation, race, and bodies.[160]

2

A GENEALOGY OF THE FAR RIGHT

> If we now interrogate the past, it is in order to further shed light on the present, and to better respond to what tomorrow will demand of us. And the time will come when our younger brothers will demand that we answer them and will judge us!
>
> —Jean-Pierre Maxence, *Histoire de dix ans*, 1939

As these young men—who were budding novelists, critics, essayists, and journalists—came of age in the early 1930s, they attempted to rejuvenate a nationalist, xenophobic, and monarchist politics. As one historian has very aptly described it, they harnessed "languages of decadence and renewal" in order to claim their place within a Republic of Letters that they scorned and berated. They claimed they were part of a generation of "non-conformist" and "revolutionary" intellectuals.[1] For some, ideological position was guided by an attachment to the doctrine of personalism, while others attempted to define a new conservative Catholic politics, or even turned to the European fascist regimes that emerged in those years. Infused with a strong sense of the historical moment, they claimed it was time for a radical political renewal (a renewal that they rarely specifically elaborated in their writings), neither fascism nor communism but nonetheless a violent "refusal" of the democratic regime, a forceful and relentless critique of capitalism and its effects, and the rejection of indistinct forces that had brought about this decadence: the disorder of modernity and its symptoms—a dissonant culture, a literature emptied of all substance, and the incarnation of all these ills, the Jew.

The tumultuous events of 1930s France offered these intellectuals the opportunity to come together as a self-defined "generation" of refusal, dissidence, and oppositional politics. Two moments were especially significant: First, February 1934, when popular and far-right leagues rioted against the government in a night that culminated in civilian deaths, provided both hope and disappointment and convinced them of the need for a "different" form of political opposition. Then, when the Popular Front finally won the 1936 May elections, these far-right critics wrote of the urgency of their time and the need to subvert the status quo, now embodied by the Socialist Jewish head of government, Léon Blum. These two moments punctuated a decade that seemed especially prone to at once exciting and urgent political developments, such as the 1933 rise of "Nazi Hitlerism" (as the far right called it) in Germany, the triumph of Italian fascism as Mussolini invaded Ethiopa in 1935, and the violence of the Spanish Civil War in the latter half of the 1930s, while France was beset by riots, demonstrations, and street violence and transformed by the emergence of new political parties and organizations. While they had actively contributed to a variety of conservative and far-right newspapers and magazines since 1930 (and would continue to do so), they now created magazines especially devoted to the denunciation of the chaos and disorder of their world. They took over newspapers in which they warned of the demise of French culture and civilization. In the years following the Popular Front government, and amid the familiar resurgence of widespread antisemitism, they called for the radical resurrection of the French nation, the restoration of French civilization, and the rebirth of its "sons." They looked toward a "new" age, which would leave behind the evils they had witnessed in their youth. They would then emerge as intellectuals leading in the public sphere of letters and culture, heralding the "New Humanism" that Jean de Fabrègues had promised in 1932.[2]

Essential to their "dissident" politics was their self-assertion as men of letters driven by the innate connection that they argued they had with French national culture and history. They wanted to redefine the boundaries of the public sphere in a manner appropriate to the character of French civilization. Political journalism held a central place for these men of letters involved in literature and criticism: it provided the space for the public delineation of a new politics and imagination of the nation. It gave them the opportunity to comment on the world at large. The national tradition they invoked was by no means a novel invention. Instead, in claiming a new politics, they were redefining principles long characteristic of far-right proponents of the infamous and virulent monarchist, nationalist, xenophobic, and antisemitic organization Action française—principles that, day after day, were proclaimed in the pages of its newspaper of the same name.[3] The fierce battles that had emerged a generation ago around the late-nineteenth-century Dreyfus Affair and the fated figure of its unwilling hero, Captain Alfred Dreyfus, were taken up by these young men eager to speak as "intellectuals" for a French nation in need of salvation from Jewish, communist, and foreign contamination. The Dreyfus Affair had constituted a foundational moment for their forefathers: it had allowed them to state publicly the reactionary principles driving their political stance for the decades to come. It had crystallized their refusal and contestation of the republican model, and in the process they had defined themselves as "right-wing intellectuals."[4]

A generation later, the young men coming of age in the early 1930s appealed to this right-wing tradition, but they also adapted it to new times. They were influenced by and borrowed from a long tradition of far-right thought and aesthetics, but they also differed from their elders—such as Charles Maurras—most notably in relation to their conception of modernity and the legitimation strategies they used. Understanding the distinctiveness of these 1930s writers and journalists requires paying attention to the subtle and important ways in which they reinvented the tradition of far-right ultra-nationalism that had shaped them. This was not simply a continuation of Maurrassian nationalism, as some political historians have suggested. Conventional readings of the influences of interwar far-right intellectuals have offered a truncated analysis of their political discourse; we can better trace the themes and obsessions that were reworked by Thierry Maulnier, Robert Brasillach, and others if we consider the multiple and overlapping influences—the ideological mentor Charles Maurras, the polemicist Léon Daudet, and the Catholic intellectual Henri Massis—that bore upon them. While it was Maurras who was most often publicly celebrated by these authors seeking legitimacy, he remained a distant intellectual figure whose aesthetics seemed to be of another age and little attuned to the vagaries of modernity. Instead, it was Daudet and Massis who offered the most pertinent models for intellectuals and journalists at once immersed in the world of politics while also being critics of aesthetic modernity.[5] Recognizing these networks, affiliations, and affinities of 1930s intellectuals with their elders helps us to grasp the circulation of common themes—dissolution, disgust, abjection—from 1931 to 1936, but also allows us to trace the ideological differences that emerged after 1938, which coalesced around the questions of gender, sex, race, and French civilization. These differences emerged most strikingly around the place and role of antisemitism in a larger French ultra-nationalism and in the decision to refute or embrace the title of "French fascists."

L'Action Française: A Coming of Age

Young far-right intellectuals in the 1930s never forgot the intellectual and political debt they owed Charles Maurras, and even when differences emerged, they always celebrated the formative influence he had on them.[6] Maurras was a towering figure for far-right political pamphleteers and writers, and he remained so even after his political influence waned. In the 1960s, Catholic critic and editor Jean de Fabrègues wrote of Maurras: "The man that I knew, loved and admired while still barely a child, from the ages of nineteen to twenty-three, this man is Charles Maurras." He added:

> At an age when passions are strong and often confused, he embodied for *us* intelligence, the ability to give oneself over, the willingness to rebuild an order where the mind would find itself, [and] where the values of truth would be best served, that we thought could be crowned with the highest service: that of divine truth.[7]

Novelist and far-right journalist Robert Brasillach also wrote that "[he] had welcomed us, [in 1930,] in the same way he welcomed all young men, namely with the smile and trust that I have witnessed in him only."[8] That debt was regularly invoked by many. The *Combat* journalists wrote in 1936 when celebrating the publication of Maurras's first literary work: "They know all too well what they owe Mr. Charles Maurras and with them—before them—[those principles] *Thought* and *Homeland* that he has honored." They explained that they wanted to provide the "testimony of young men born in a world forever transformed by his work."[9] In the same spirit, Brasillach's first-time front-page article in *Je Suis Partout* was devoted to the influence of Maurras, where he recalled again—in words almost identical to those of *Combat*—that they "were, everywhere, a certain number who know what [they] owe Maurras."[10] Maurras was a regular presence in *Je Suis Partout*, and "the extraordinary unity and richness of his life" was still celebrated in a 1938 issue of *Combat*, in which René Vincent concluded that "Charles Maurras' greatness is undeniable because he is one of the few without whom life would have been otherwise."[11]

Most, if not all, young far-right journalists—whether members of the self-titled Jeune Droite (Young New Right) or in the pages of the fiercely reactionary newspaper *Je Suis Partout*—had begun their career at the newspaper *L'Action Française*, Maurras's political platform and extension to the political organization created in 1899 in the midst of the turmoils of the Dreyfus Affair.

Maurras was an unavoidable reference for any rightist young man committed to oppositional politics, and he had shaped their entry into the world of literature and politics. They had come of age through the prism of the monarchist organization, which "held a significant place in their intellectual life, *whatever their [political] opinions*."[12] As Fabrègues poignantly asked in his moving and personal introduction to his intellectual biography of Maurras:

> Is it possible for a man who has, at the onset of his life, owed some of his original ideas to a master, then broken off from him in a rather violent conflict that was followed by some kind of armistice . . . which maintained a distance but nonetheless illuminated their differences—is it possible for this man to attempt to chart the life line of the one to whom he is attached by a debt of recognition, then opposition, and finally a profound and never discarded interest?[13]

Fabrègues's summary of his intellectual relationship to Maurras illustrates the ways in which Maurras would inevitably be spoken about through the trope of the master shining light onto his disciples, thus helping to tear the veil of illusions under which they lived. They invoked the ways in which Maurras had exemplified "order and unity" in his life and work: he was at once "a poet, an author, and a political critic . . . whose life and thought had been entirely driven by an immense passion for order. His commitment to classicism in poetry, his reaction against Romanticism, like his political opinions—against revolution and against Jean-Jacques Rousseau—fundamentally embodied a claim for order."[14] Amid the chaos and disorder of the modern, Maurras showed that "Art, like Politics . . . is, by nature, the practice of *order*."[15]

The cultural and political resonance of this monarchist, anti-republican, far-right, antisemitic, and anti-German political movement was not reflected by its circulation numbers. As historian Eugen Weber has noted, "The literary and political influence of the *Action Française* was immense. . . . It had one of the finest literary pages, and the most pungent, venomous and Rabelaisian among polemicists [Léon Daudet]."[16] Its literary columns were widely read and Maurras's fellow editor, Daudet, was especially well known as an astute literary critic. For Charles Maurras, born in Martigues in 1868 and classically trained, the organization Action française helped redraft the traditional nineteenth-century nationalism articulated by Louis de Bonald and Joseph de Maistre.[17] This constituted Maurras's lifelong work, and he devoted all of his energies to it. It was instrumental in the elaboration and dissemination of its Catholic, monarchist, and anti-republican "integral nationalism." But, as has recently been noted, contrary to the prevailing myth of a literary sensibility devoid of ideological concerns, *L'Action Française*'s literary pages were infused with politics and displayed a constant attention to the ways in which the worlds of letters and politics engaged one another.[18]

According to those who knew him, Maurras was a charismatic leader, full of contradictions, who nonetheless exercised a huge influence on the many disciples and "dissidents" that he introduced to politics and to his unique vision of French civilization and history. The importance and influence of Action française cannot be underestimated since, for many far-right critics of the interwar years, it "constituted [their] sole political involvement."[19] Many of the younger far-right critics were first politically trained and "enlightened" by Action française. Historian Raoul Girardet—himself one of the organization's young recruits in the 1940s—remembered that "L'Action française always defined itself as a training-ground."[20] The newspaper *L'Action Française*, under the strict rule of Maurras, offered a place for many young men to hone their writing skills while engaging in the public world of intellectuals. Maurras, who had celebrated the "contagious charm of youth," welcomed every new generation of eager and aspiring intellectuals.[21] They were introduced to a vibrant world of oppositional and reactionary politics, trained in the subtleties of polemical political journalism, and offered the opportunity to explore their talent for literary or cultural criticism. In this world, men like Maurras and Daudet were not afraid to go to prison or suffer exile for their ideas and words.[22]

Maurras's organization thus served as a foundational rite of passage for many far-right intellectuals who emerged in the 1930s and 1940s: it was one of the ways they asserted their autonomy as journalists, if not their independence. According to "fellow traveler" Henri Massis, "Against the many doctrines [that preached] dissolution and death and [which] found their way to confused minds and hearts, and the disaggregation of institutions and mores, the Action française offered a rampart."[23] Maurras's organization was often metaphorically described as the only solid and impenetrable fortification against the dangers assailing the French nation and culture. Lucien Rebatet explained that "like many of the young men of his age, I had upon the end of my studies, found in Maurras, in Daudet, and their disciples, both the explanation and the confirmation of many of our instinctive repulsions."[24] To the many young men attracted to its far-right oppositional politics, Action française provided the terms for both the means and the content of a sustained critique of contemporary French society. The man and the organization provided a coherent language that could be translated into political action. Indeed, "thanks to Maurras," they wrote, "we had found a method and a purpose."[25]

Action française's Ideology of the Nation

The organization Action française emerged around the infamous and momentous Dreyfus Affair, in 1899.[26] The Dreyfus Affair constituted the foundational moment for an engagement with politics, while simultaneously providing these men with a mythic figure, that of Jewish captain Dreyfus, whom they never ceased denouncing as the reminder of the dangers assailing the French nation. The organization was originally created by two men, Maurice Pujo and Henri Vaugeois, who were severely disappointed with the outcome of the Dreyfus Affair and its political repercussions. With the help and energetic contribution of the young Charles Maurras, who soon joined the enterprise, it began developing into the monarchist, xenophobic, reactionary, and antidemocratic organization that would influence generations of young men and resonate throughout most of the century. Indeed, "what brought these men together was an overriding love of France, a great respect for order, and faith in the orderly process of reason."[27]

Action française placed order at the center of its system of thought, a doctrine premised on a definition of the ancient historical nation as the "real country" (*pays réel*), the one that must be distinguished from its "legal incarnation" (*pays légal*), embodied by the democratic republican regime that Maurras and his fellow far-right journalists deemed abhorrent and contrary to the nature of French character. It was concerned with the fate of the culture of civilization, since French civilization represented the product of centuries of evolution rooted in French history. Both "conservative and extremist," Maurras gradually took over the organization until it became the emanation of his own doctrine of "integral nationalism."[28] For him, the greatest dangers were "the socialist plague and democratic gangrene."[29] He denounced what he called the "four confederate states—Protestants, Jews, Freemasons and *métèques* [foreigners]"—internal threats to France that he deemed responsible for its decadence, since they were foreign to its essence. Decadence had followed the anomaly and historical deviation that the French Revolution had been. In a 1922 study, *Romantisme et révolution* (Romanticism and Revolution,) Maurras recalled that the French Revolution had "derived from the Jewish spirit and from those varieties of independent Christianity that had raged either in the oriental deserts or the Germanic forest, that is in the various roundabouts of barbarism."[30] French civilization must be defended and saved, and that was Maurras's mission.

According to Eugen Weber, Action française saw the years following its creation until the outbreak of the First World War as a "time of affirmation," while "the war and postwar years [were] a time of exhilaration."[31] The 1920s and 1930s signaled a different era as the organization and its undisputed head, Maurras, found themselves declared renegades by the Catholic Church. The Vatican was suspicious of Maurras's "pagan" sensibilities and his affirmation of the primacy of the political. In 1926 it officially condemned the organization, denying it the possibility of calling itself an emanation of the Catholic Church.[32] This was a major blow for an organization whose audience was in great part made up of traditionalist and conservative Catholics.[33] But it soon recovered, and its influence did not substantially wane. The events of February 6, 1934, inflicted a much more devastating blow to the organization, which was perceived by many of its younger followers as having failed to seize the opportunity to overthrow a democratic regime they deemed corrupt and illegitimate. To them, this was "a lost victory" that, this time, seriously undermined Action française's claim of being an oppositional force of "insurgents" waiting for the right time to undo the regime.[34] Still, in the 1930s, "Maurrassian politics" held meaning for a large number of young men attracted to the organization and the man.

To Maurras, what mattered most was politics: "politics first!" (*politique d'abord!*) and the preservation of "this 'miracle' of order and equilibrium."[35] This motto inspired Maurrassian followers because, as one *L'Action Française* journalist explained, it meant that "the political order is the *primordial* natural order to which [their] temporal life is attached, [it is] the *positive* order which ensures all forms of life, even the highest."[36] The individual, according to Maurras, found an unbroken and organic expression in the social order, which, in turn, found its natural political manifestation in monarchy. The political was essential to the simultaneous binding and enshrining of the limits of the individual and the national community. Anything else—by that Maurras meant a politics and regime that ignored these historical relations and was blind to the conservative nature of "man," more specifically the republican and parliamentary regime inaugurated by the Third Republic—was artificial, inauthentic, and foreign to the true essence of the nation. Maurras's refusal of the republican and parliamentary regime and his hatred of communism was such a powerfully seductive ideology that it led some to argue, in 1938, that he could be considered the "father of Fascism." They claimed that "it was obvious what Italian fascism or the Portuguese state's antidemocratic experiments owed to the master of French nationalism." Maurras's alleged influence thus "offered a resounding rebuttal to those who pretend they can refuse to recognize the universality of Maurrassian thought."[37] Against arguments that Action française was obsolete, young far-right intellectuals argued in the late 1930s that contemporary affairs and history had confirmed the truth and universality of Maurras's influence.

While the organization attempted to subvert republican and parliamentary politics, notably through its pseudo-militia, the Camelots du roi (as well as its student organization, "Étudiants d'Action française"), the newspaper every day reminded its followers of these principles. The "daily organ of integral nationalism," where Maurras and Daudet had written since its creation in 1908, served as the bearer of truth—a common far-right rhetorical device adopted by most 1930s far-right newspapers and magazines. For Daudet, its editorialist, only *L'Action Française* could be trusted, "because we are the only truly independent newspaper, the only one who tells the truth to the entire country fooled by you and your ignorant, greedy, and cowardly colleagues—[we are the] only ones amongst the Parisian press, Maurras, Bainville and your servant [myself]."[38] To celebrate in 1936 the twenty-ninth year of its existence, he explained that it had been founded "in order to restore, along with monarchy, the honor and safety of all Frenchmen [and it had] operated during this time as the great means for the eradication of the shameful horrors of the [parliamentarian] regime."[39] *L'Action Française* then still saw itself as a force to be reckoned with.

In order to understand the force of Maurras's "integral nationalism," one must not forget that the royalist and reactionary organization had come into being as a reaction to the Dreyfus Affair, a birth that was far from peripheral in its ideological development. Antisemitic rhetoric always figured at the center of this nationalism. The best-selling author of the late-nineteenth-century pamphlet *La France juive*, Édouard Drumont was one of the benevolent figures invoked by Action française: his presence loomed large in the development of a radical far-right antisemitic ideology. Drumont was celebrated not as a fierce polemicist but as a brave and lucid "historian."[40] Since the organization's emergence, antisemitism had therefore always infused its far-right politics: its imagination of the nation involved deriding Jews, whom they perceived to be the privileged bearers of decadence and modernity. Antisemitism constituted one of the essential articulations of Action française's idea of the nation, since it had been essential to its emergence in the wake of the Dreyfus Affair—which Maurras referred to as a "revolution."[41] As one historian has explained, its "integral nationalism [had] presumed, implied [and] called for antisemitism in order to exist."[42] Antisemitic remarks figured prominently in the pages of the nationalist and monarchist newspaper and it displayed disparaging and open discussions of the Jewishness of political and intellectual figures throughout most of its existence.

Maurras argued for what he called a "state-based antisemitism" (*antisémitisme d'état*), which he opposed to a "purely racial" antisemitism, associated with nineteenth-century "racial theoretician" Joseph Arthur de Gobineau—and which, for far-right activists, characterized German antisemitism.[43] He explained that an exclusive attention to racial questions was misguided as it subsumed all questions under that of the "Jewish question" and therefore categorized German antisemitism as "racism"—a distinction that became common among French far-right nationalists in the 1930s. Maurras's own suspicion and hatred of Germany determined this description since, still haunted by the 1871 Franco-Prussian War and later the 1914–1918 conflict, he considered Germany to be the French nation's archenemy, and its culture and ideals antithetical to everything that was French. He saw the German brand of antisemitism as too extreme, an unthinking and vulgar form of racism: throughout the pages of *L'Action Française*, Hitler was described as the "racist propagandist turned head of government."[44] In 1938, René Vincent celebrated in Maurras his refusal to embrace the "racist Myth"—a reference again to Nazi racial antisemitism.[45] Despite such criticisms of the German "racist" brand of antisemitic politics, Maurras nonetheless affirmed in 1933 "that there is everywhere a Jewish question, nothing can be less unsure."[46] In fact, claims that French antisemitism was fundamentally different from its German variant did not mean Maurras and his organization were any less so, but articulated its terms in ways that referred to their own ideological principles and nationalist emphasis on culture, soil, and tradition.

Antisemitism was a matter of civilization. To Maurras, French antisemitism as he advocated it recognized that the Jews could never be truly French since they could not be the emanation of the French soil, of centuries of accumulated tradition. "Jews," Maurras explained, had shown their duplicity and the fact that they made a "nation within the nation" with the Dreyfus Affair. Even if he conceded that French Jews who were veterans of the Great War had shown their commitment to the nation, they remained the exception and could never be considered anything but foreign: for him, they were "Judeo-foreigners"

(*Judéo-métèques*).[47] His refusal to conceive of Jewish individuals as members of the French citizenry derived from his vision of the nation, conceived in reference to an opposition between civilization and barbarism.

One of the fundamental tenets of Maurrassian philosophy was a return to an *authentic* nation, defined by centuries of accumulated tradition, habits, and lives. The French nation was an organic and lived entity: according to one of his former followers turned dissident, Maurras "believed that France could never just be an idea which has bloomed on a pile of corpses." He insisted that it was first and foremost constituted "by living Frenchmen."[48] The French people, a collection of individuals born and bred on French soil, formed the essential component of a nation in need of protection. History, as told by Maurras, had thus shown that the French nation should be upheld as a whole and untouched entity. This faith in the necessity of a nation underscored Maurras's fierce xenophobic politics and unrelenting anti-German sentiments inherited from the Franco-Prussian conflict and the trauma of the First World War.[49] The nation was also and fundamentally an imperial nation, upholding the beauty of French civilization through its mastery of other populations. Upholding a proud and pure imperial nation kept "barbarism" at bay—a barbarism that Maurras saw everywhere, but especially in German civilization and culture.[50] Yet the French nation had been degraded by the emergence and resilience of the republican regime, which had, in the early twentieth century, embodied itself in the figure of Marianne, the female symbolization of the national body. And "Maurras shone light on Marianne's face in order to reveal a bloody puppet . . . with grotesque traits and colors."[51]

Maurras's imagined nation was as much an aesthetic as a political embodiment of his version of Frenchness. Tradition, the bedrock of an authentic nation, was nothing more than "an ancient civilizing capital."[52] Civilization's essence was best translated in art and literature, and especially poetry, a form that Maurras loved and never ceased celebrating.[53] As literary critic David Carroll has noted, "In Maurras' view, the nation is a work (*oeuvre*) whose unifying principles were determined in history and thus supported by tradition in the same way that classical aesthetic criteria determine the laws governing the unity and life of the poem."[54] Though one might doubt that the nation constituted a work of art, nonetheless Maurras's classical aesthetic preferences had much to do with his fantasy of a French nation. Such correspondence between the aesthetic and the political is especially flagrant in a series of essays Maurras published in 1927 on "female Romanticism." Maurras loathed Romanticism, which he deemed "opaque" and "vaporous"—as he characterized Baudelairean poetry.[55] Romanticism, which he explained had come about with (the French) revolution, signified "a moment of disintegration in the history of poetry."[56] In his study, Maurras argued that the four female authors he had chosen (Renée Vivien, Madame de Régnier, Madame Lucie Delarue-Mardrus, and the Countess of Noailles) had all too naturally become Romantic authors because these "young métèques" were not of "very pure French blood."[57] In a chapter titled "From Strangeness to Perversions," he explained that Romanticism was "foreign." As such, "it loved what was strange."[58] In fact, Maurras concluded that it made sense for Romanticism to be embraced by women, since it was feminine in nature: "had it not feminized" and made literature effeminate?[59] The logic was evident: those who were not properly French perverted the nation and its privileged embodiment, literature.

Maurras's unflinching belief in the relationship between politics and aesthetics, culture and civilization, shaped these young authors' relationship to the republican regime and its cultural politics. Maurrassian nationalism meant uncovering a privileged relationship between language, tradition, and culture. Pierre Monnier, who later abandoned Action française politics and attempted his own brand of radical political action, explained that "within the Action Française, I discovered what I had not been able to understand until then . . . , the relation between language and thought, the beauty of words and their combination, [and] the attractiveness of dialectical speech."[60] Monnier, who had been a mediocre student and quickly lost interest in his law degree, found himself entranced by the love of the French language exhibited by Maurras, and his desire to enact French culture within the pages of the newspaper *L'Action Française.*

Maurras was indeed a mythical figure. Brasillach explained that, in 1936, he wished to speak of Maurras not "in the name of those following his doctrine" but rather in order to remind readers of the "radiance [and] the halo surrounding any entire work and great thought where so many live without even realizing it." Admiration and affection surrounded Maurras: he had attracted so many young men to his organization because, Brasillach explained, of the "violent sincerity that could be heard in his writings."[61] Generations of young men found themselves fascinated by this uncompromising figure in a mix of admiration and deference, but also ambivalence especially displayed by those who became "dissenters," the renegades excommunicated by Maurras's own intransigent position. Brasillach summed it up in the same 1936 article: Maurras was their master. But "a master is not a man that others blindly follow in everything he says; a master is the one who has taught us something essential and to whom we are forever indebted."[62] Maurras, the intellectual and political master, provided the official seal for those engaged in a far-right vision of French interwar society.

Léon Daudet, a Cultural Critic of the Far-Right

Charles Maurras had always been invoked as a towering figure for the young generation of far-right critics and writers—by the young writers themselves as well as by historians—but that is an incomplete story. If Maurras was a "master," one may discern that it was the "Rabelaisian" figure of Léon Daudet who served as a model for the kind of journalism young far-right writers practiced and the type of cultural critic they sought to become. Daudet, day after day, oversaw the articles of *L'Action Française*, alongside Maurras and Jacques Bainville, Colonel Larpent, Jean Delebecque, and Georges Gaudy. Yet he is hardly mentioned in histories of the far right.[63] He is presented as a secondary figure despite his regular presence in the pages of *L'Action Française* and has rarely been acknowledged as an intellectual in his own right by historians—the effect of these young far-right critics' own accounts of the period.

Daudet, the son of beloved populist storyteller Alphonse Daudet, was a polemicist and literary critic who had turned to journalism after abandoning the medical career he had first envisaged. He hardly fits conventional political categories. His reactionary politics, unabashed hatred for the republican regime, and fierce xenophobic and antisemitic rhetoric seem to historians at odds with his rather incisive literary sensibility, which allowed him to champion many of the great authors of the modern literary canon. Daudet's presence disrupts narratives of *L'Action Française* as Maurras's sole creation and enterprise, and complicates accounts of French far-right politics, for one may argue that Daudet actually exerted a more pervasive influence: he was at once literary critic and political chronicler, always immersed in the world around him.

Daudet offered a particularly attractive model of a public intellectual—admittedly less rigorous than Maurras or Bainville but livelier and, in the words of many contemporaries, more "truculent"—one at home in the world that he felt it his duty to deride. He had come to political journalism at what he described as a foundational moment in his life, the Dreyfus Affair, and through the years, he proved a constant proponent of antisemitism in *L'Action Française*, where he went on to denounce "Blum" as he had "Dreyfus."[64] Like

Maurras, Daudet was, above all, committed to a harmonious order, which he saw to be especially manifest in the realm of literature. As Henri Massis explained it, it was undeniable that "underneath an apparent spontaneity of action and lively appetites, Léon Daudet possessed a no less instinctive aspiration for harmony, equilibrium, order, a desire for human perfection which, for him, was embodied in the ideal he had of the superior artist."[65] Daudet's conception of the artist was essential to his philosophy and his prolific journalistic activities. He has been described as "the most formidable pamphleteer of his generation."[66] Literary critic Kléber Haedens, who had been a discreet but involved contributor to many of the young far-right publications, explained in his preface to Daudet's writings:

> Léon Daudet was a man so extraordinary that we can only barely today . . . imagine his life and work. It would warrant a great fire of words, in the manner of Rabelais—whom he loved so much—in order to hint at what he was. [He was] journalist, novelist, orator, polemicist, speaker, critic, essayist, biographer, memorialist, doctor, parliamentary representative, traveler, philosopher, etc.[67]

His presence was central in the Maurrassian political paper.

Literature had always been Daudet's passion. A legitimate cultural critic who was at ease in the world of letters, Daudet considered that "literary and theater criticism is extremely important in a well-made newspaper."[68] He had ferociously defended Marcel Proust, Georges Bernanos, and Louis-Ferdinand Céline (authors whom Maurras mostly ignored) and contributed to their literary recognition. Despite some oversights motivated by his fierce politics—he hated Émile Zola for his republicanism and vocal defense of Dreyfus's innocence—Daudet always proved willing to defend the works he—often rightly—considered to belong to the realm of literature. He had famously stated that he cared for nothing except for his homeland (*patrie*). Yet he was said to have also exclaimed, upon defending Louis-Ferdinand Céline's first novel, *Voyage au bout de la nuit*, against accusations of a betrayal of patriotic sentiments: "The homeland can piss off when it comes to literature!"[69] In contrast, Maurras was always too conservative for Daudet's literary taste, finding solace and beauty only in classical literature and, throughout his long career, remaining impervious to the calls of literary modernity. As Massis once lamented, Maurras was more likely to "judge through the prism of what disgusted him" and had never read Gide, Proust, or any of the novelists who became prominent after 1914.[70] While Maurras celebrated turn-of-the century poetry, Daudet read and engaged with contemporary literature, most notably as a sitting member of the Prix Goncourt selection committee.

Still, Daudet was above all a chronicler, a commentator, and a journalist. He explained in 1936 that he had provided a daily article in the pages of *L'Action Française* for twenty-nine years. "For many years, [he] had acted as the newspapers' editor-in-chief, a publication concerned with both ideology [*doctrine*] and action [*combat*]."[71] From the moment he espoused the nationalist, royalist, and anti-democratic cause, he remained *L'Action Française*'s faithful and tireless editorialist. Journalism was Daudet's passion, for he "had discovered it to be a career [characterized] by freedom and recreation where one can just give one's own opinion devoid of any constraints."[72] Journalism provided the necessary complement to political action: for Daudet, it *was* political action. And it could not afford to be tepid or moderate. Polemics represented "the soul of journalism" because "polemics is indispensable to life and movement. It requires a doctrine and a purpose."[73] Polemics meant a certain violence in tone, which Daudet argued was necessary and should be characterized by repetition: it was one of the tools a "fighting journalist" should use, a lesson he unashamedly practiced in his own writings, and one that many young far-right intellectuals later put to use.[74]

Daudet was also a chronicler with a vicious tongue whose harsh words were often stronger than Maurras's own: his contemporaries called him a "brilliant writer, rough polemicist carried away by his verve which serves to confound those men of letters he dislikes and the politicians who disgust us."[75] He appeared as the most prominent signature on the front page of *L'Action Française*, penning the daily editorial, while Maurras contributed under the rubric of politics and "Doubts and Questions."[76] If Action française's "integral nationalism [had] presumed, implied, and called for antisemitism in order to exist," Daudet proved to be its most vocal and unabashed proponent.[77] Daudet was vociferously antisemitic, even if one Maurrassian critic claimed that "he had never held any specific animosity toward the Jews."[78] Édouard Drumont, the author of the best-selling antisemitic pamphlet *La France juive*, published in 1886, was a longtime friend of the Daudet family and one of Léon's formative influences.[79] Just as it had for Maurras, the Dreyfus Affair signified a foundational moment for Daudet, crystallizing his belief in the nefarious influence and foreign nature of Jews within the French nation. His 1930s editorials still regularly featured discussions of the injustices of the Dreyfus Affair and warned of the pernicious influence of Jews—described as foreign to the French spirit—on French culture and politics.

Daudet thus provided the model of a far-right critic committed to French culture and literature while upholding conservative, fiercely nationalist, and antisemitic opinions. He was driven by one principle (which his wife laid out in one newspaper article and which also drove the following generation), namely: "How can propaganda for healthy, sound . . . ideas be exercised?"[80] One might argue that Daudet represented the ultimate nonconformist: "he taught [young far-right critics] the freedom of judgment regarding men and their activities." Daudet showed these young men that "the press is a powerful organism of incredible influence especially in troubled and critical times" where "the verb is struggle and battle."[81] Most of all, he incarnated "insolence" and the need to challenge authority, whatever its form or shape.[82]

Henri Massis: Civilization, Race, and Thought

Henri Massis was also an important mentor and influential model to some of the Young New Right intellectuals.[83] As the author of well-known essays and pamphlets in the 1900s and 1920s and the editor of the respected conservative *Revue Universelle* from 1936 onward, Massis offered the respectability of Catholic reactionary and nationalist politics. Though *La Revue Universelle*—created in 1920 under the editorship of Catholic intellectual Jacques Bainville—had been conceived as a "philosophical, literary, and social space of national and international propaganda," it was explicitly designed as a more moderate version of *L'Action Française*.[84] Massis never contributed to *L'Action Française* but was one of the most prominent intellectuals of the early-twentieth-century far-right literary scene. His concern was primarily the defense of (French) civilization—the title of one of his most provocative essays published in 1927. In fact, as Christine Foureau has noted, "during his entire life, Massis ceaselessly devoted himself to the defense of a Christian and humanist West." Western civilization's most distinguished representative could only be France, which "alone could oppose the barbarians now at the borders of Europe."[85] The fate of Western civilization and of the French nation—its exemplary embodiment—formed both the foundation and the driving principle of Massis's political and literary career (and would echo and further Maurras's own obsession with civilization and barbarism).

One of the enduring motifs of Massis's essays on politics was the possible and dangerous demise of Western civilization—an essence he understood in cultural, aesthetic, ethical, and racial terms. This was made especially striking in perhaps his most famous essay, *Défense de l'Occident* (Defence of the West), published in 1927. While Massis wrote prolifically and was known for the manifestos and petitions he oversaw (especially the 1935 "Manifeste des intellectuels français pour la défense de l'Occident et la paix en Europe" [French Intellectuals' Manifesto for the Defence of the West and European Peace] in support of Mussolini's expansionist policy and colonial ambitions), it was this book in defense of French civilization that resonated most and that still is what he is known for—since it won him the Grand Prix de Littérature de l'Académie Française.[86] This essay tied together the Great War, the ills of modernity, the vagaries of political ideologies, and those "Eastern"—Asian, German, and Eastern European—temptations that threatened to undo the very foundations of the French imperial nation. The danger was made clear as Massis opened his essay: he explained that "the fate of western civilization, the fate of man . . . are today in danger. This is not a case of imaginary threat, nor of pessimistic forebodings by those weak-minded [who] like to immerse themselves [in this idea] in order to fuel their disgust fearful of any effort."[87]

The origin of contemporary decadence lay in the perversion of modernity and the trauma of the Great War. He asserted that Europe had been "wounded" (by the war), "corrupted by mechanical progress," and, as a result, is "currently in a state against nature where it cannot remain."[88] Such a wound to the organic body of the nation, and corruption of what Massis held to be Europe's "natural" destiny, had led only to dissolution and the abyss. Massis warned that the political necessarily implied a metaphysical—theological even, since Europe was, first and foremost, Christian—fall. He somberly noted that language, culture, "ideas were no longer our own." The Western Christian *man* had been dispossessed of what marked him as civilized and superior: in fact, "man is encouraged to lose his boundaries, that he has developed over the ages through a methodical and persevering effort."[89] European unity had been broken by World War I—and this "inhuman and hideous division" had, in turn, undermined the very existence of European civilization, especially as—according to Massis—a new conflict was emerging between West and East.[90] Massis rendered the meaning of the Great War and of postwar modernity in terms that made it possible for those young men (who had neither fought nor experienced it) to appropriate its haunting presence in very personal and powerful terms and to put it in the service of their insurgent politics.

Massis singled out "the East" as the origin and cause of Western decadence. For him, "Asia"—an indiscriminate category including both India and China—

embodied all that was antithetical to the Western character: "Asia" was characterized by a misguided devotion to the irrational and the mystical. It was thought lacking in order, hierarchy, and direction. He pointed to the anarchy and disorder of Hinduism, berating the effects of a "Rousseauan ashram" and of a thought that refuses a "hierarchy of concepts" and that has "broken the link between the mind and the real."[91] Especially struck by what he called the "awakening of Asia and Africa," whose "fever" had been roused by "bolshevism," he singled out Indian leader Mohandas Gandhi and poet Rabindranath Tagore as exemplars of this phenomenon. Lest a reader refuse to believe him, Massis added, "This has resulted in an increased movement in this immense ocean of Asiatic speculation [which is nothing more than] a vast day-dream where all penetrates, all embraces, and blends, only to sink into a chasm of indeterminacy and to a return to the peace of the abyss."[92] Massis fantasized a sinuous and formless Asian "spirit" that would inevitably corrupt the Western mind.

The threat was especially urgent because it had already begun to infiltrate the West: Massis warned that "the East's poison is most assimilable by us because it slides subtly and almost invisibly through German idealism and Slavic mysticism."[93] Massis tied his imperial and civilizational rhetoric of race to the anti-German nationalism of the traditional French far right. Such foreign and corrupting influence could be found in Europe itself—as not all Europe was civilized. In fact, he warned against the return of "barbarism" from those within the European continent who were less evolved. Like Maurras before him, he denounced Germany for its irrational spirit, "Slavism," and the perversion of communism unleashed by the "Bolshevik revolution."[94] Echoing Maurras, Massis especially berated Germany because it was a strange blend of "Asian mysticism and Latin character."[95] For instance, in a discussion of Oswald Spengler's *Decline of the West*, published barely a decade earlier, Massis exclaimed:

> How can we even name that strange revelation, this horrible blend of Kantian idealism, Bergsonism, Freudism [that] attempts to empty the mind of all objective content, [that] extols the priority of the psychical and the individual, [that] reduces truth to emotional effectiveness only, [that] consecrates the ecstasy of flesh, [and that] unleashes vital forces it had pretended to make more spiritual?[96]

Massis remarkably ascribed the disorder of the postwar years and its worrisome obsession with the self to this perverse German influence that, in his mind, was but the mask for the corruption of the "East." (Though antisemitism did not appear in this essay, the common cliché was that the Jew was a particular exemplar of Asiatic barbarism and may thus be said to hover in Massis's narrative.)

Massis—a figure most historians have usually relegated to a secondary role when it comes to far-right rhetoric—showed here how much his vision of Western civilization concerned at once race, culture, and aesthetics. While citing racial thinker Gobineau, Massis spends much of the essay warning of the impending danger not just of "Asian" invasion but of the loss of Western empires in the face of "Asian" nationalism. The fate of colonies was indeed a pressing issue in France, a measure of the greatness of the decadence of the nation—as would be evidenced by the incredible popularity of the 1931 Colonial Exposition. Here, Massis informed his readers that these "Eastern peoples" who had been "subjugated by Europe" now displayed a worrisome tendency to rebellion: after the "easy and ancient submission of the past, [they now] show a silent hostility and sometimes even, a true hatred that is just waiting for the right moment to turn into action."[97] With the challenge to Western imperialism came a challenge to Western civilization. Again, Massis spoke of impending gloom. He predicted, "Asia is not only looking to bring about the natives' revolt in order to deprive our impoverished continent of the incredible resources that is possesses. It actually wants to undermine the Western soul."[98] The political danger of a challenge to (French) imperial rule was both the consequence and the cause of Western loss of its proper character. Such logic drove Massis's enduring commitment to imperialism as a foundation for European political rule. He again displayed his belief in the naturalness of European imperialism less than ten years later as he engineered a "petition for the defense of the West." Written and published in 1935, this petition defended Mussolini's invasion of Ethiopia. In it, Massis proclaimed that "colonizing work is founded upon an idea of the West . . . , [and for] France, . . . and England, it will remain one of the highest and most fertile expressions of their vitality."[99] Massis's nostalgia for a golden imperial age and his "defense" of a (racialized) West are themes that, as one historian has noted, "will run the course of the interwar," and yet have rarely been explored for the central role they had in tying together far-right nationalist and antisemitic politics.[100] Indeed, Massis held that, above all, what characterized the West was a "balance of mind and action" sustained by a clear and firm hierarchy—presumably of peoples and nations.[101]

In many ways, Massis's civilizational rhetoric distinctly shaped the particular nationalist politics of the Young New Right—especially when it came to Thierry Maulnier, Robert Brasillach, and Pierre-Antoine Cousteau, all of whom had been journalists at the *Revue Universelle*. As historian Paul Mazgaj has shown, Massis was crucial in "bridg[ing] the generational gap" that existed between the great figures of Action française—Maurras especially—and these aspiring intellectuals.[102] As Maxence recalled in his late 1930s memoir of the interwar years, they admired him because "Massis was one of the warmest, . . . most able to display such generous understanding. With his pen in his hand, he would go into the fray to fight systems."[103] Brasillach cowrote an essay with him in 1936, *Les cadets de l'Alcazar*, on the Spanish Civil War, that sold rather well. His obsession with Western civilization and the impending corruption by "barbarism" had undergirded his belief in the unique and special nature of Frenchness. In another set of "civilizational essays," published in 1940, he forcefully claimed that "*we alone* possessed what cannot be invented: namely, *thought*, *order*, *style*—all of which could only be found in *our race* and nowhere else."[104] This was the war that must be waged, according to him. It was the war that the young generation of far-right intellectuals inherited and made their own.

The Emergence of a "New" Far Right

Just like their mentors, the "new" far right that came into being in the 1930s was an intellectual movement steeped in an unflinching belief in the intimate relation between aesthetics and politics. They formed a network trained in Catholic, conservative, and Maurrassian traditions with clear political and cultural affinities. While historians have traditionally emphasized—and carefully analyzed—the differences that may have existed between the most prominent of these young far-right intellectuals, it is also important to pay attention to the affinities they demonstrated: these illuminate the manner in which they were drawn together by certain themes—only partly inherited from their mentors—to which they provided a new force, and sometimes even a new meaning, all the while echoing the concerns of their time. Throughout the 1930s, they acted out of a commitment to their simultaneous involvement in the literary and the political.[105] That involvement, in both realms, emerged out of the belief that these were imbricated and essential to one another. As Maurras, Daudet, and Massis had asserted for years, the fate of French civilization lay in the redemption of French culture and the restoration of a truly French political regime.

L'Action Française, unsurprisingly, figured large in their political and professional coming-of-age, for it had answered their indistinct dissatisfaction with the world they found themselves in when "they were eighteen, were somewhat confused, quite disgusted with the modern world and with a fundamental tendency to anarchy."[106] Robert Brasillach and Thierry Maulnier had begun their journalistic career in its pages as literary critics. At *L'Action Française*, Brasillach met Lucien Rebatet, who had begun his career as the cinema critic "François Vinneuil."[107] Jean de Fabrègues had (briefly) held the envied position of secretary to Maurras. Monnier had begun as a contributor to *L'Étudiant Français*—its student newspaper—and as a Camelot du Roi.[108] Though they often wrote elsewhere, most had *L'Action Française* in common (Maurice Blanchot remains a glaring exception to this) and first started writing there (and often continued well into the 1940s, as did Maulnier). Robert Brasillach was, from the age of twenty-two, in charge of a literary chronicle, "*causerie littéraire*," while Maulnier contributed to literary and cultural debates. Many also wrote in a number of right-wing publications, from *Candide* to *Gringoire*. Most, like Fabrègues, Maulnier, and Brasillach, were welcomed as regular contributors by Massis in his highly regarded conservative and Catholic journal, *La Revue Universelle*. Their contributions were numerous and diverse, yet turned to one similar purpose: to oppose and denounce the decadence of their world as their mentors has done—a task made more urgent as the decade unfolded.

Their initial endeavors had begun as offshoots of the Maurrassian world. As they emerged in the early 1930s, they first sought authority and legitimacy by emphasizing what they owed to this French far-right tradition. As René Vincent, an important figure of the Young New Right group, remarked, "We have very naturally followed them [Barrès, Péguy, Maurras, Bernanos, Mauriac]; we immediately espoused their *severe* but *necessary* discipline, out of instinct and reason. We have tried to *prolong* and *echo* their great voices."[109] But they were not the uncritical descendants of these "great voices," even less mere auxiliaries to the doctrine of Action française. They were not as adamantly monarchist as their forefathers had been.[110] Neither were all of them the self-proclaimed descendants of a French nationalist Catholicism. As time went on, these groups sought to distinguish themselves as an avant-garde of sorts that was politically revolutionary and possessed its own aesthetics.[111] They were a loosely connected group involved with similar issues, eager to engage with "politics, literature, mores, theatre, cinema . . . anything that appeared on the horizon."[112] The various far-right newspapers that came into existence—from *Réaction* to *La Revue du Siècle*, to their later incarnations, *Combat*, *L'Insurgé*, and *Je Suis Partout*—were representative of this network of conservative and far-right intellectuals eager to define the meaning of Frenchness, the bounds of citizenship, and the substance of male identity. These were underscored for many by a tradition (at first implicit) of antisemitism and imperial nationalism.

The Young New Right has traditionally been seen to embody, at the beginning, *two* distinct trends, identified around the figures of Jean de Fabrègues and Jean-Pierre Maxence.[113] Fabrègues founded, with René Vincent and Christian Chenut, the first attempt that they could call their own: *Réaction pour l'Ordre* (Reaction for Order). With little financial or material means and a rather simple format, it was a monthly review first published in 1930 under the authority of Georges Bernanos, prominently featured in its first issue, whom they dubbed a "visionary."[114] This newspaper, which devoted articles to the need for the restoration of a spiritual order, still spoke within traditional Maurrassian terms, citing him on "human unity [they] once held" and had lost, in its first programmatic editorial.[115] After its demise, two years later, Fabrègues and Vincent reiterated the experience with *La Revue du Siècle* (Journal of the Century). Meanwhile, Jean-Pierre Maxence—the pseudonym adopted in 1928 by Pierre Godmé—had been in charge of *Les Cahiers* (the Notebooks), an obscure far-right publication, before taking over the editorship of *La Revue Française* in 1930 (where Maulnier also collaborated). Neither *Réaction* nor *Les Cahiers* exceeded a circulation of five hundred issues.[116] Only the creation in 1933 of *La Revue du XXe Siècle* (Journal of the Twentieth Century)—the follow-up to *La Revue du Siècle*—would fuse these different groups. It was an austere publication of eighty pages that offered a number of long articles on politics, arts, and culture. It differed little in format from its predecessors but already prefigured the emergence of *Combat*, the Young New Right mid-1930s shorter and more explicitly political magazine. Its editorial proudly and unabashedly announced their program: "What exists today is not always what we want. We must do what it takes for what we want to come into being."[117] Still, Young New Right intellectuals have been described as parallel but distinct groups in the early 1930s before merging in the wake of February 1934 and then splitting three years later with the emergence of the more radical and fascist-leaning newspaper and group of *Je Suis Partout*.[118]

In 1936, Fabrègues and Maulnier begun a monthly journal titled *Combat*, and a year later Maulnier teamed up with Maxence to publish the polemical weekly newspaper *L'Insurgé*. Brasillach, on the other hand, had taken over the editorship of *Je Suis Partout* that same year and, with a number of other young far-right journalists, undertook a radical reorientation of the newspaper. But their interwar intellectual involvement was a more entangled affair than these critics' and journalists' later fates (and accounts) suggest. The "split" that occurred at the end of the decade should not obscure the complex ties that connected these men, and the profound affinities they expressed. While it is important not to flatten their ideological trajectories, grasping the ways in which these networks endured allows a more sustained exploration of the shared obsessions—civilization, nation, self, bodies—that consumed them in this decade.

Most have portrayed the Young New Right as a movement expressing itself, from 1936 onward, in content-driven and sophisticated journals under the aegis of Fabrègues, Maxence, and Maulnier (even if some historians concede that some of its publications displayed a rather violent rhetoric). This depiction has required distinguishing *Combat* contributors from the writers involved in *Je Suis Partout*—such as its editor, novelist Robert Brasillach, pamphleteer and journalist Lucien Rebatet, polemicist Pierre-Antoine Cousteau, and writer Georges Blond. But this story of the far right has largely been the result of these men's postwar fates and the degrees of literary talent ascribed to each, rather than ideological differences only. While Brasillach, Rebatet, Cousteau, and a few others were prosecuted for treason on the basis of their collaborationist stance at the end of the war, Maulnier was subsequently elected to the prestigious Académie française, which also rewarded Fabrègues with a prize for his philosophical work *Christianisme et Civilisations* (Christianity and Civilizations), in 1966, as it had Maulnier a few years earlier.[119] As a result, historians have portrayed *Je Suis Partout* as the extreme and vulgar version of the interwar French far right while *Combat* represented its more respectable and serious version. Describing *Je Suis Partout* as the world of ideologically driven "mediocre writers" has allowed depicting the unproblematic association of *Combat* with the fate of that generation of young conservative and personalist intellectuals untainted by an admiration for the fascist politics of their day and the shame of collaboration. Such an explanatory model erases the ambiguity of their involvement and ignores the fact that in the 1930s both groups displayed a similar concern with founding a restored and bounded sense of self and nation.[120]

Far-right intellectuals were more involved with one another than is usually assumed, even at the beginning of the decade.[121] Their texts and articles echoed one another as they all—somewhat differently—sought a radical "new" politics. Furthermore, they had always written in each other's publications. Fabrègues's *Réaction* published an article by Thierry Maulnier, which addressed the question of the "end of the post-war years" in response to Brasillach's "*enquête*" in *Candide.*[122] Maxence also provided a long piece on Bernanos's influence, "Bernanos ou la fidélité totale."[123] Thierry Maulnier on Nietzsche, Maurice Blanchot on foreign affairs, Émile Vaast, René Vincent (sometimes under the pseudonym of Hugues Favart) on cinema and literature, and Jean Loisy were still to be found in Fabrègues's short-lived *La Revue du Siècle.*[124] But it was the publication of its follow-up magazine, *La Revue du XXe Siècle,* begun in 1933, which announced the emergence of a distinct movement that came to fruition in 1936. The first editorial was jointly signed by Jean-Pierre Maxence, Robert Francis, Jean de Fabrègues, and Thierry Maulnier. Maurice Blanchot, who collaborated on foreign politics for *Le Journal des Débats* (Journal of Debates)—a conservative paper hospitable to many Young New Right critics—provided a regular chronicle. Vincent, Loisy, and Vaast, Fabrègues's intellectual companions, were also regular contributors, as was Claude Roy, the youngest of this generation, who appeared as reviewer under the pseudonym of Claude Orland. Finally, Jean Saillenfest, who was an important participant in the 1937 *L'Insurgé,* completed "the group." Georges Blond, whom Brasillach and Maulnier had met through their longtime school friend José Lupin, managed to carry on writing in all of those publications.[125]

Their professional and political affinities were evident in the articles they wrote. They often referred to one another, rather disingenuously for their readers since they all knew one another: for instance, Fabrègues told his *Revue du XXe Siècle* readers that the journal had been favorably reviewed and was heralded as the enterprise of committed young intellectuals by the conservative right-wing publications *Le Journal des Débats* and *Aux Écoutes* (the Attentive and Suspicious Listener)—where Maurice Blanchot was an important figure and Thierry Maulnier occasionally provided articles. He similarly noted the complimentary notices in *Candide,* another right-wing newspaper—where Brasillach had contributed his literary "report" on the postwar years—that belonged to the loose network of widely distributed far-right newspapers where these young men wrote.[126] Their ties were undeniable, as was their common desire to depart from the more conservative publications they participated in. Yet a common and distinctive voice emerged only after these men were able to set up platforms they felt were truly theirs. But that would not happen for another few years, when political events energized them into action.

The year 1936 proved decisive: *Combat* was created and others flocked to *Je Suis Partout.* But that did not mark the end of these young men's collaborations—far from it. Contrary to the depiction of the Young New Right as radically distinct from *Je Suis Partout*'s writers, mutual contributions and ongoing conversations carried on until the outbreak of the war. *Combat*, the joint venture of its editors Maulnier and Fabrègues, welcomed a roster of names eerily similar to that of the *Revue du XXe Siècle*: Blanchot, Loisy, Maxence, Roy, Saillenfest, Vaast, Vincent, and Jean Le Marchand, who had been a writer at *Réaction*. They were joined by François Gravier, theater and literary critic Kléber Haedens, Louis Salleron—who occasionally wrote in *Je Suis Partout*—and the far-right activist now divorced from Action française, Pierre Monnier.[127] Ties between *Combat*, *L'Insurgé*, and *Je Suis Partout* remained, albeit more informally after 1938. Robert Brasillach was a regular presence in *Combat* from its very first issue (a fact often understated by historians), and remained so throughout 1937 when he ceased altogether to contribute his biting and ironic articles, as he replaced *Je Suis Partout*'s editor, the older Pierre Gaxotte. *Combat* thus represented Brasillach's training ground as political commentator long before his editorship at *Je Suis Partout*. The first *Combat* issue also announced to its readers the forthcoming contribution of another *Je Suis Partout* journalist, Lucien Rebatet (but it never appeared). René Vincent, Georges Blond, and Claude Roy were found in all three papers until 1939.[128] In fact, Robert Francis—the brother of *L'Insurgé* coeditor Jean-Pierre Maxence—also occasionally provided small articles to *Je Suis Partout*.[129] Even Pierre Gaxotte penned an article in *Combat*, titled "France's Destiny," as late as April 1937,[130] while Maulnier carried on writing throughout the 1930s, although less frequently, in the pages of *Je Suis Partout*.[131] What is striking is that, despite some ideological differences, and the growing tensions between those at *Je Suis Partout* and those at *Combat*, they were all intent on acting as the elite vanguard of a "new" far-right politics and remained acutely aware of being part of the same oppositional intellectual elite, even as they disagreed and debated. They not only reviewed each other's work (often in a very complimentary manner) but responded to one another. René Vincent, for instance, reviewed Robert Brasillach's second novel in *La Revue du XXe Siècle*.[132] They initiated debates and engaged in various literary ventures together. They discussed the role and nature of literature, the fate of culture and civilization, and similarly bemoaned the invasion of politically biased literary criticism of leftist inclination, and the decadence of the world they lived in. Affinities remained, despite the vagaries of the decade's politics.

These men were not only intellectual companions but were often tied by strong bonds of friendship that had flourished in several distinctive Parisian social and institutional spaces. This was a world of "brothers," a "fraternity" bound together by unacknowledged homosocial ties. Their "converging ideas" owed much to their coming of age in a political and literary culture shaped by the same references: Action française and the interwar conservative landscape, which included Charles Maurras and Léon Daudet, but also Jacques Maritain, and especially Henri Massis.[133] The new generation had mostly emerged from the same circles: "Out of these came those nights of good and heated discussion which led us from the École normale supérieure to the Groupes d'étudiants catholiques, from the Cercle des étudiants protestants to the political members of various rightist organizations . . . in order to engage in those fruitful dialogues where conversational pleasure was never the aim, but only [provided] a taste for truth."[134] A few—Maulnier, Brasillach, Bardèche—had met while at the Parisian Louis-le-Grand *lycée* where, away from their native provinces, they had experienced "so many joys, the discovery of the world, discovered Paris, [enjoyed endless] discussions, the fever of youth, friendship."[135] Most significantly, a number of them found their intellectual awakening within the walls of the prestigious École normale supérieure, where they indulged in pranks and experimented with writing while discovering the pleasures of Paris's culture and nightlife.[136]

L'École normale supérieure (ENS), one of the foremost French educational institutions, provided a formative environment, which helped shape these young men's literary tastes and political allegiances. There, as Brasillach explained, they learned "the inextricable tie between writing and politics [and] the insistence of the literary signature within political [and] legal authority."[137] Some of the most renowned leaders of this far-right literary generation emerged from ENS in the early 1930s.[138] In 1928 Thierry Maulnier—a pseudonym he had adopted at the beginning of his journalistic career instead of his own clunky "Jacques Talagrand"—was friend and classmate with Robert Brasillach. With Maurice Bardèche—Brasillach's devoted companion and later brother-in-law—and José Lupin, they formed a tight-knit group. The young men engaged in various literary experiments, creating the short-lived magazine *Fulgur*, a satire of their teenage cinema heroes—all instances that Brasillach narrated with some nostalgia in his 1941 memoir.[139] Their ties of friendship, forged in a shared love of literature, affection for rebellious acts, and desire for a revolutionary politics, were, for quite a few of them, made within the ENS walls.

Convergence was hardly a coincidence. Unlike its leftist reputation (then and now), ENS also harbored in the early twentieth century a very strong right-wing culture.[140] They had already been trained at Louis-le-Grand by the influential Maurrassian French and Latin professor André Bellessort, who wrote for a number of right-wing journals and later became one of *Je Suis Partout*'s regular chroniclers.[141] According to Brasillach, Bellessort was also a "non-conformist," "disrespectful of established authorities," who introduced "backward provincial" young men like himself to the delights of Maurras's prose and thought.[142] This is how many were introduced to a lively and unapologetic right-wing culture that appeared (at least as they recalled it) at once transgressive, enlightening, and full of possibilities.[143]

ENS provided many young recruits, who later made their way through a web of conservative and far-right institutions and networks. Pierre Gaxotte, for instance, the Maurrassian historian and former secretary to Maurras, who edited *Je Suis Partout* from its creation until Robert Brasillach took over, was himself an ENS graduate.[144] Similarly, the playwright Jean Giraudoux and the polemicist and *Gringoire* editor Henri Béraud had also attended it. These young men found at ENS a right-wing tradition in which they gladly immersed themselves—and where antisemitism was both respectable and essential to nationalism. Brasillach always referred to his "passion for Virgil," which he had written about during his years there. Maulnier, who had chosen to speak on Nietzsche for his thesis, was known among his interwar far-right companions as an expert on the German philosopher—and he published on this topic in 1925.[145] Maulnier's success and recognition among his far-right peers as a "dialectician" owed much to the knowledge garnered from his training at this prestigious institution. When Maulnier met Fabrègues, he had (briefly) occupied the celebrated position of secretary for Maurras, which afforded him a certain aura, while Maurice Blanchot hardly seemed a novice in this work either, since he had been engaged in nationalist and monarchist politics since his student days in Strasbourg.[146] It was Jean-Pierre Maxence, still a small publisher and the editor of the unsuccessful *Les Cahiers* when they met him, who then proved a central figure in this loose group of similarly inclined far-right critics. He helped create a space where most came together: *L'Insurgé*.[147]

It is not a surprise that many of these young men had received early training in literature and philosophy. Fabrègues and Blanchot were both trained in philosophy at the Sorbonne, while some, like Georges Blond, were aspiring novelists. Others, who were politically active like Maxence, were nonetheless infused with a strong and wide-ranging literary culture. Maxence recalled that even his earliest (and unsuccessful) venture, *Les Cahiers*, was "concerned especially with literature, and avant-garde literature."[148] He also fondly recounted how he had been moved by Maurice Bardèche's discovery of Paul Claudel's *Le partage de midi*, which was then, in 1930, difficult to find. Bardèche had brought him a copy. The four copies went to Bardèche himself, Maxence, Maulnier, and Brasillach. In fact, Pierre Monnier twice remarked in his memoirs that he and an *Insurgé* friend, Guy Richelet, had been the only ones on the newspaper's team who were not university educated.[149] While they were embedded in the Republic of Letters and enamored of literature, and often philosophy, they found that politics was tied to this love, and being an avant-gardist required intervening in both. In this matter, they followed Pierre Gaxotte's Maurrassian principle that "there can be no dissociation between politics and the arts, force and mind."[150] Five years after they had officially begun their journalistic careers, Jean de Fabrègues warned his readers of their purpose: "The avant-garde has broken through; but the first battalions have only just begun their march, amidst the granite boulders falling on them."[151]

The Shattered Hopes of February 1934

Maxence wrote, in 1939, that "what was at first among [them] nothing more than a confused disquiet, a spontaneous mistrust, an almost instinctive protest, grew to become a motivated refusal, an explicit critique, a violence founded in reason."[152] That "explicit critique" finds its roots in the publications and newspapers they wrote, edited, and participated in during the early 1930s. Already these journalistic and literary ventures simultaneously furthered Maurrassian principles, were inspired by a Catholic commitment (especially for Fabrègues, Vincent, and Maxence), and sought to formalize a "refusal" that other "non-conformists" who were politically at odds with them also tried to articulate. Historians have mined the themes that circulated in the early 1930s, which constituted the pool of ideas that later drew these intellectuals together—from *Réaction* to *La Revue du XXe Siècle*.[153] Those themes—crisis, corruption, decadence, reaction, and revolt—became obsessions after 1934 and urgent preoccupations after 1936.

Revolt—the shape of which they did not elaborate—was confined to the pages of their magazines in the early 1930s. It suddenly seemed possible in early 1934. As one historian has described it, "On 6 February 1934, Paris experienced its bloodiest night of political violence since the Commune of 1871."[154] Large numbers of Parisian citizens, and activists from a number of disparate nationalist and right-wing organizations gathered facing the Palais-Bourbon, on the other side of the Seine. Action française, the Jeunesses patriotes, the Croix de feu, the Solidarité française, and several veterans' associations (including a Communist-leaning one) had called for demonstrations. There were rumors of a takeover of the government by these right-wing groups. These organizations and a large crowd—mostly right-wing people but also citizens disenchanted with the government and critical of its recent policies—had gathered in order to protest the lack of resolution to the Stavisky affair, the forced resignation of the right-wing police prefect Jean Chiappe, and more generally the government's corruption and impotence. Then the police charged. Riots followed. In the morning, fifteen people were dead—including one policeman—and more than a thousand Parisians had been wounded. On February 9, the Communists organized demonstrations protesting the danger of fascism in France. For the left, this was a moment of particular importance as the Comité de vigilance des intellectuels anti-fascistes (the Anti-Fascist Intellectuals' Watchdog Committee), founded in March 1934 in order to "defend democracy," inaugurated a unique mobilization that led to the emergence of the Popular Front coalition.[155] Indeed, these few days were retrospectively seen by both left and right to have been a foundational moment, when all realized the need for a different political regime.

A series of "affairs" can be said to have led to the Parisian riots. The Third Republic had been in the last ten years marred by scandals involving politicians and other high-powered figures. None would prove as damning as the Stavisky affair, which came to epitomize how "rotten parliamentarians" were duping the "good people of Paris."[156] The scandal erupted upon the news of Alexandre Stavisky's suicide on January 8 in his hideout of Chamonix, after his attempt at evading police authorities.[157] Stavisky was a naturalized Jewish immigrant of Russian origin who had managed to con a number of reputable French institutions into fraudulent banking with the benevolent silence (and, at times, ignorance) of some high-ranking government officials. His "suicide" sent ripples through French public opinion. The newly appointed head of government, the Radical Édouard Daladier, decided to fire the right-wing Paris police prefect Jean Chiappe on February 2, avowedly for having failed to pass on important documents regarding the Stavisky affair. The decision was perceived as an outright declaration of war by a number of right-wing leagues and far-right newspapers such as *L'Action Française*. In the days leading up to that fateful February event, the far-right press ceaselessly called for the people of Paris to demonstrate in order to "bring down the parliamentary dictatorship."[158] For Daudet, it was obvious that the French must be rid of the government: he wrote that "he would give fresh news of the parliament's 'rotten men' and of the good people of Paris['s reaction] until the demise of the regime [he] thought was impending, a regime called the republic (or 'democracy' if you will), and made up of thieves, pimps of both sexes and murderous policemen."[159] In the next few weeks, *L'Action Française* called repeatedly for the "expulsion of the thieves" and for active demonstrations—until after February 6, when the thieves became "assassins."[160] The government fell, and another right-leaning one came to power. But confidence was never restored.

But for the far right, and even more so for its young generation, the revolution never came about. Brasillach reminisced that "this had maybe been the first time that we felt directly influenced by external events and that we directly suffered their consequences. . . . All of this was now woven into the very fabric of our lives."[161] For Brasillach, the February protests had not provided a coherent and specific political program, but "all of this": a diffuse yet pressing sense of anger and need for revolt in ways that the traditional right had refused to do. He called it the "failed revolution." Maurice Blanchot explained, one year after the riots, that these days had "proved magnificent by their eagerness, devotion and some sublime actions."[162] Though the demonstrations had displayed a "confused power of revolt and disgust," they had incarnated, as Blanchot stated, "the symbols of *our* hopes."[163] Maxence echoed both authors' accounts when he wrote that the "February days" had "crystallized the bitterness of the post-war decline," revealing that "amongst the young at least, [there was] a shared disgust with the situation, a shared will for change, a shared desire for revolution."[164] Yet, to Blanchot—as to most young men who had once hoped for an overthrow of the regime—these few days had, unfortunately, "ended in a mediocre manner." Ultimately, only bitterness and disappointment dominated in their wake, since this surge of protest had not prevented the return of "retarded men, compromised characters, traitors, and moderates" as representatives of the nation.[165] Those who had failed were, beyond the usual culprits—the government and politicians—those like Maurras and François de La Rocque, leader of the far-right veterans' organization Les Croix de feu, who had not been able to harness the promise and energy of youthful disgust and impatience and had proved to be made of the same cloth as those in power.

According to Brasillach, February 6 had been a "bad conspiracy, but [it was] a superb and instinctive revolt, it was a sacrificial night that has remained in our memories with its smell, its cold wind, its pale figures running, its human groups on the side of pavements, its invincible hope for a National Revolution, the precise birth of a social nationalism in our country."[166] These young intellectuals identified the fateful days in February 1934 as a foundational moment when they learned that "revolution is not born from a wise decision by the impetus of hope."[167] As they told it, it had decisively shaped their commitment to radical oppositional politics because it had showed them that far-right "leagues' leaders . . . did not really wish for a revolution."[168] They had "duped" their followers and had been a "cause of the apparent stillness of France in the face of loud and tragic events."[169] Their age needed a new politics.

While young far-right intellectuals saw the February 6 riots as a foundational experience that they read later as the "origin" of their turn to radical opposition, to many others—and historians after that—the riots had seemed close to a civil war. The left claimed it was a fascist attempt at a coup. The right claimed it had been the expression of people's disgust with a corrupt regime. Many contemporaries saw it as symptomatic of the "moral crisis" that characterized France in those years.[170] The parliamentary report commissioned to investigate the causes and origins of these riots ominously concluded: "How is it possible to still believe in truth, beauty and good, when lying and hatred reign amidst the spectacle of such bloody horrors?"[171]

The February events were momentous, in retrospect, because they seemed to have briefly embodied the hopes of a new generation. In his wartime memoir, Brasillach emphasized a collective and generational feeling: "This era may have been different than what we have called the post-war years [*l'après-guerre*]. It is our youth, it is our own pre-war era [*l'avant-guerre*]."[172] But they were also momentous because they allowed a reviled government to emerge in the following years: as Monnier summed it up, "the great event of the years 35 and 36 was the Popular Front, born out of a social situation made of injustices and the great fear of February 6, 1934."[173] In 1936 they were finally able to identify the causes of decadence in the abjection of the nation and the divided nature of the subject. As the decade unfolded, their resolve to offer a political alternative to the decaying order of the world only strengthened. *L'Action Française* published an editorial in the first weeks of the year 1936 announcing the fate of France for the year to come: "Year 1936, what good will you provide France? You were born under somber skies, in the midst of a mentally confused Europe and shaken with the sounds of war; you will most certainly be a difficult year, and a year of political struggles because the time when all is due has come, when all these false ideas will come suddenly crashing down against a harsh reality."[174] The Young New Right's principles of traditional nationalism, anti-capitalist, anti-socialist, and anti-democratic positions soon expanded beyond the confines of Maurrassian rhetoric and right-wing personalism, for the failure of the February protests had also made them realize that only "insurgency" and "dissidence" should be embraced for "revolution" to come about. The young Claude Roy had provided the answer a year earlier: "Let us be fighters rather than victims, insurgents rather than martyrs."[175] Another added, "And thus began this surprising year of 1936 where we [would witness] so many changes."[176]

3

"WILL WE GET OUT OF FRENCH ABJECTION?"

The Politics and Aesthetic Insurgency of the Young New Right

> To think, to write, that is the primary way we
> have to fight: the first and the only one.
>
> —Thierry Maulnier, *La crise est dans l'homme*, 1932

In his 1936 essay on "socialist myths," the undisputed intellectual leader of the Young New Right, Thierry Maulnier, wrote that both "idealism and materialism are the mind's temptations when realism has been lost, and when the harmonious agreement between thought and the world, between speculation and action, has been broken." He concluded, "These are the unavoidable temptations contemporary intellectuals are torn between."[1] Further reflecting on the role of the intellectual, Maulnier warned that "what is terrible for the man wedded to ideas is not taking sides—he must take sides—[. . .] nor acting upon reality, but it is to be subjected to that reality, to renounce mastering his object."[2] What did Maulnier's elusive and abstract pronouncements mean in terms of a far-right politics? He provided an answer in the front-page article of the polemical weekly newspaper he helped create a year later. In the January issue of *L'Insurgé*, Maulnier boldly announced: "France must be won back."[3] Six months later, while he argued against the Popular Front, which he claimed was determined to take France to war, the *Insurgé* editorial—next to a satiric anti-parliamentarian and antisemitic caricature—berated "the government of the Jew Blum which is a dishonor for all of us, and is a terrible danger in and of itself for every Frenchman."[4]

The men who made up the Young New Right were obsessed with the fate of the subject (and the status of the masculine self) whom they perceived to have been tainted by the degradation and decadence of their age. After 1936 they understood the nation to be abject, not just decadent. Abjection—which they diagnosed and denounced—was a horrifying state, for it undid the possibility of the plenitude they yearned for. Their fantasy of a whole, bounded, and pure nation relied on a civilizational rhetoric founded upon a familiar series of oppositions: civilized against barbarian, French against foreign, free against colonized. Far-right tradition had always upheld that France was the greatest exemplar of Western civilization. For these intellectuals, the French nation was neither geography (like Great Britain) nor race (as Nazi Germany claimed), but found its expression in an aesthetics of culture—a notion of culture assumed to provide the essence of civilization. Maulnier had summed it up, reminding his readers that "our homeland only has worth insofar as it embodies a certain idea of civilization."[5] Since the self and the nation mutually defined each other, in their eyes, the nation's abjection meant that each and every French citizen—themselves included—was also in the throes of this pervasive sense of abjection. Their writings examined this pressing problem: how could they emerge as autonomous and bounded citizens in a world that was forever and always abject?

Abjection had not just been the consequence of the victory of capitalist parliamentary regimes—or *idealism*, as they usually referred to it—and socialist authoritarianism—or *materialism*, as it was common practice to refer to socialism and communism. After 1936 they found an explanation for this unbearable state in the fantasized figure of "Léon Blum," the Jewish Socialist leader of the left-wing Popular Front coalition. In order to find a solution to their (and the nation's) abjection, they called for "dissidence," the radical separation from the traditional realm of politics, and for "insurgency," a suspended state of radical oppositional politics that contested the power of the law, the democratic regime, and its authority to found citizenship. It seemed that only an "insurgent" politics, outside of the law, offered an attractive alternative to the dangers of "left and right-wing totalitarianism" and allowed for the possible resolution to this conundrum. Insurgency was a founding act. It went beyond the oppositional politics of the traditional far right from Charles Maurras to Colonel de La Rocque's militant organization, the Croix de feu. Insurgency required "revolution before reconciliation" (*pas de réconciliation sans révolution*). This was the ominous title of one of Maulnier's editorials.[6] Only the destruction *from within* of the established social, cultural, and political order could, for the Young New Right in 1937, allow for the emergence of a new society, the restoration of a lost nation, and a bounded sense of self steeped in a pure culture and distinctively French civilization. As the only ones aware of the fundamental contradiction produced by abjection, they called upon their fellow citizens to "redo France." "Remaking the nation and society" was the only solution sought by these intellectuals: "The cause of civilization is inseparable from the cause of revolution."[7] Their publications, the magazine *Combat* and especially the short-lived polemical newspaper *L'Insurgé*, were the public expression of their insurgency, and served as their revolutionary weapons.

Their firm belief in the distinctiveness of French civilization—a somewhat racialized concept that they had inherited from the prominent Catholic intellectual Henri Massis, who had denounced the "barbarians" threatening to invade France—undergirded their nationalism. They were without doubt as to the naturalness of a French empire and had inherited its rhetoric from Maurras and Daudet. Antisemitism figured prominently in this vision of abjection. It also offered a convenient explanation for the ills and dangers they decried. Yet the Young New Right's antisemitic rhetoric has been systematically downplayed by historians who have exclusively relied on a piece published in a 1938 issue of *Combat* by then editor Maulnier on the nature and relevance of the "Jewish Question." Historians have argued that Maulnier's article confirms the Young New Right's refusal of antisemitism and that they were distinct from the more virulent *Je Suis Partout*, though they usually—and briefly—acknowledged an "underlying antisemitism" that was, they say, confined to the pages of *L'Insurgé*.[8] The few "isolated allusions" that can be found in *L'Insurgé*, according to one historian, should certainly not be confused with the repetitiveness, violence, and proliferation typical of *L'Action Française*'s anti-Jewish hatred.[9] While it is true that Maulnier and his acolytes rarely engaged in the obsessive denunciations that characterized Maurras's newspaper and even *Je Suis Partout* after 1936, the Young New Right's vision of the nation in the 1930s and its obsession with the abject nature of the self nonetheless depended upon its articulation within the racialized imaginary of Western civilization where mastery over "natives" helped shore up the greatness of France. It was, furthermore, anchored in relation to the familiar antisemitic fantasy of the "Jew" that circulated widely in the interwar period. Such ideas can be found not just in the explicit content of their writings but in the allusions, tropes, and rhetoric mobilized to figure the citizen, the nation, and the need for a revolutionary action.

The question of a proper politics of culture and race and the definition of a French nationalism—namely, who constituted proper French citizens and subjects and therefore, what type of antisemitism should be espoused—were favorite topics of conversation among far-right intellectuals in those years (even more so now that Nazi Germany offered its own model of nationalism and antisemitism). The fact that the role of antisemitism in a politics of the nation would be an issue around which Maulnier and Brasillach would part is itself indicative of its importance. But this political split did not publicly occur until 1938, when *Je Suis Partout* contributors moved to a more explicitly "racial antisemitism," while *Combat* journalists focused instead on its "cultural" version—a disagreement symbolized by Robert Brasillach's simultaneous retreat from *Combat* and assumption of *Je Suis Partout*'s editorship in 1937. Maulnier returned to this issue in his 1938 political essay on the future of (French) nationalism, in which he discussed the limitations of democracy, communism, and fascism.[10] The terms of a proper antisemitism—could there be and, indeed, was there a specifically "French antisemitism"?—were actually debated in the pages of *Combat*. Its editor asked whether antisemitism would constitute a political tool or a philosophical position. Should it form the centerpiece of a dissident politics? Indeed, what kind of nationalism should be championed? In what ways were the Young New Right "neither left nor right," neither socialist nor conservative, neither communist nor fascist? The Young New Right's foremost intellectuals pondered the desirability of antisemitism as one of their driving political tenets, and argued over what conception of "man" derived from and supported it. Restoring France meant upholding an imperial nation sustained by its unchallenged rule over colonial subjects, and its prominence as a leader among the concert of Western nations. Antisemitism, for them, was to be the expression of this larger civilizational racist imaginary. Civilization was necessarily Western, the only achievement of history, and France was one of its greatest representatives—but only if it escaped decadence and abjection.[11] Exploring how obsessions with Jewishness and "Blum" anchored the Young New Right's nationalism requires addressing the ways in which their rhetoric relied upon fundamental but somewhat implicit terms—"culture," "civilization," and "man." In 1937, it became inseparable from the political and aesthetic alienation they experienced—in the form of *abjection*—and how they chose to explain it.

The Dissidence of Journalism and Authorship.

Heirs to the fiercely nationalist, monarchist, reactionary, and antisemitic organization Action française, Young New Right intellectuals proclaimed in the 1930s that they were "dissident"—a term publicized by one of its most prominent journalists, Maurice Blanchot—and revolutionary. They were the uncompromising dissenters and lucid rebels against a perverted and decaying social and political order.[12] According to Pierre Monnier, an *Insurgé* journalist, dissidence had originally named "the desertion of some minds that have suddenly become dissonant" and who found themselves no longer harmoniously in tune with the monarchist organization's charismatic leader, Charles Maurras, and his official doctrine. Monnier invoked former prestigious dissidents who had abruptly split from Maurras (such as the Catholic and conservative writer Georges Bernanos) in order to explain, legitimate, and argue for the necessity of an oppositional politics that parted ways with *L'Action Française*.[13] The familiar metaphorical language of organic unity running through the prose of these intellectuals helped legitimate their departure from traditional Maurrassian politics. Dissidence had been an irrepressible demand rather than a political strategy. Already, several years earlier, Jean de Fabrègues had explained that his magazine, *Réaction pour l'Ordre*, was the necessary, unavoidable, and salutary "reaction" to the modern world in disarray, "democratic decadence," "individualism, the rule of the state, and class struggle."[14] Then, some of these Young New Right intellectuals explained, nationalism was the only possible "reaction in the face of despair."[15] In 1934, they still insisted that "disorder is such today that revolt erupts by itself in the face of this society."[16] Three years later, they attempted to define and affirm a different kind of nationalism in the face of abjection. As Monnier faithfully recounted in his little-read memoir, the youthful dissidence of *Combat* and *L'Insurgé*'s far-right writers had been the natural consequence of their need for independence that was "without compromise."[17]

Dissidence was the only politics available. It gave direction and purpose to the critique they had been leveling at their contemporaries, the nation, and the world since the early 1930s. If the February 1934 protests had proved momentous for their understanding of the possibilities for a regime overthrow, it was the election of the Popular Front in 1936 that allowed these far-right critics to define their "dissidence" and embrace insurgency. To be a dissident, though, did not necessarily entail storming the streets—as in 1934—or donning fascist-style garb—as followers of Marcel Bucard's Franciste movement did—or attending political rallies and speeches—as followers of La Rocque's Parti social français (PSF) enjoyed doing. In fact, many tried political activism, but these attempts were short-lived, often yielding disappointment and disenchantment: Maxence joined the quasi-fascist Solidarité française league in 1935 but left after a year. It was former Communist Jacques Doriot's party, the Parti populaire français, founded in June 1936, that attracted most Young New Right intellectuals: Fabrègues joined it and contributed to its publication, while Jean Le Marchand from *Combat* as well as Maurice-Yvan Sicard and Jean Fontenoy from *L'Insurgé* also became members.

Maulnier, Brasillach, and Maxence were tempted but never fully committed.[18] Political activism did not yield the promised revolution. Action meant little "without ideas."[19] It simply entailed being a different kind of intellectual.

The assumption of the mantle of intellectual—a recurring theme in the French literary world—drove far-right writers' articulation of the form of their political commitment. But that position held a specific meaning for Young New Right critics. They, of course, refuted Julien Benda's accusation that intellectuals had betrayed their role. They defined themselves against those "left-wing Tartuffes" who displayed such "intellectual hypocrisy."[20] As a result, French intellectuals, they explained in *Combat*'s first editorial, were misled and mistaken because they were prone to demagoguery and illusion: "These lowly compromises have been made possible because, upon penetrating the world of social and political realities, intelligence has forgotten itself and served them rather than govern and organize them."[21] An intellectual should rule, not be ruled, and thus form an avant-garde ready to denounce the status quo in his writings. Indeed, "intelligence"—the defining characteristic of the intellectual—"should not put itself in the service of the masses but inform and guide them; it should not follow the course of history but make history."[22] In order to achieve such a role—which constituted the natural purpose of "intelligence"—it should "govern the social world without submitting to it, dominate it without compromising itself."[23] Mastery and control were essential—and a dominant theme of Maulnier's prose. The purpose of *Combat*, as its editors defined it, was to offer a "new synthesis," in which "intelligence and the real would be reconciled in their necessary union and in their true relations," which had been corrupted and broken.[24]

One became an intellectual in print. Young New Right writers formed their authorial selves through the papers they edited, the articles they wrote, the debates they initiated, the insults they hurled at politicians, and the violence they endorsed. Essential to their ability to act as an intellectual elite was the fact that these newspapers represented their own unmediated voice, as opposed to the world of (parliamentary) politics that they felt did not represent them, the general and popular press they despised, and the old guard of which they were now critical. The written word was to be their weapon, and their ability to write forcefully and persuasively defined their identity as intellectuals. Maulnier, one of the most successful and well regarded of these young far-right critics, attained recognition and respect through his ability to write like a "true" intellectual: "To [them] he was the most intelligent. He wrote according to a specific purpose whose dialectical logic came to an irreproachable demonstration."[25]

According to his contemporaries, Maulnier's writing displayed an impressive mastery of rhetoric and philosophical rigor. These "qualities"—and the recognition he had already garnered with the 1935 Grand Prix de la Critique for his essay on Racine—meant that he had rapidly become known as one of the interwar period's leading far-right intellectuals and celebrated as such by his peers.[26] Maulnier epitomized the model of an intellectual whose intelligence could "govern" and "dominate" rather than succumb to "political sentimentality, personal passion, or class hatred."[27]

At a time when newspapers were proliferating, the belief that the press should "not [be] following history but guiding it" sustained these men.[28] As the young conservative novelist Georges Blond explained, "The majority of intellectuals ignore, fail to recognize, or simply deny the influence of the contemporary press."[29] Such an attitude, they felt, was misguided, since many right-wing papers—like the rabidly conservative weekly newspapers *Candide* and *Gringoire*—performed great services, while others (usually left-wing or left-leaning), they maintained, merely pandered to a debased public opinion. Robert Brasillach said with force that "[he] had nothing but contempt for the majority of [his] country's press."[30] But within the pages of *Combat* and *L'Insurgé*, they could enact their dissident and insurgent politics sustained by a commitment that they repeatedly stressed was independent from political parties or obscure financial support. In this way they were distinct from other traditional right-wing newspapers.[31] As the names of their publications indicated, young far-right critics no longer saw themselves as "reacting" as they had in the early 1930s but, instead, as actively engaging in the realm of politics. The prosecution by the Popular Front government of *L'Insurgé* in March and April 1937 for "incitement to murder and violence" seemed to prove that their words in print could be powerful political tools.[32] *Combat*, one of the emerging voices of far-right journalism, as its name indicated, fought "conformism" and sought ways to restore unity and harmony, and its authors did not separate "thought from action, nor culture from political action."[33]

From *Combat* to *L'Insurgé*: Intellectuals as Revolutionaries

In 1939, Jean-Pierre Maxence, one of the leading Young New Right intellectuals who had migrated from Catholic-inspired magazines to the coeditorship of *L'Insurgé*, explained in his "chronicle of the 1930s" that "[they] had not had an innate taste for refusal." But "refusal"—in other words, dissidence and insurgency—had become the only position available, because they would have needed otherwise "to renounce [who they were] or refuse [who they professed to be.]"[34] Like his fellow journalists, he explained this absolute and unconditional refusal of the status quo not only in terms of a political position but as a quasi-metaphysical stance. Their attempt to rejuvenate the political and aesthetic legacy of Action française meant a wholesale renewal of the terms of society, culture, and civilization. In the mid-1930s, Young New Right intellectuals articulated their position as one of a revolutionary avant-garde—more politically uncompromising and engaged in the experience of modernity, even as they criticized its most egregious effects.[35] This principle drove their trajectory as they moved from *Combat* to *L'Insurgé*. While *Combat* was ambitiously designed to "try and grasp main contemporary issues in all their complexity, and to try and assemble the real and coherent principles for a solution," it would do so through a systematic analysis of all issues, whether they be "intellectual debates, literary or aesthetic controversies, or even contemporary political issues, or on the subject of social economics."[36] *Combat* would engage with everything that made up life. *L'Insurgé*, which became the flagship of their revolutionary attempt, had emerged because of the belief that it would "shape the ideas it articulated into forces able to influence the course of events."[37] Words were no longer idle but, in response to what they perceived to be the grave urgency of the situation, should directly act upon the social world.

Combat was born in January 1936 and quickly became a noted intellectual and political reference in the constellation of far-right journalistic publications. One of its editors, Maulnier, described it as a magazine "partly devoted to ideas and partly in the format of a pamphlet," published once a month.[38] Its mission statement insisted that it was "a forum of ideas where young writers express themselves, united by the common desire both to oppose a realist doctrine and to critique contemporary idealism and materialism."[39] It closely followed the format of former journalistic experiments such as *La Revue du XXe Siècle*, albeit in less austere form. Its format was more modern. As its editorial stated in 1939, it aimed to be a "research tool" and "a laboratory of ideas."[40] Although never attaining a wide readership (barely two thousand subscribers), it proved influential, while contrasting with many of the populist and polemical newspapers that usually characterized far-right politics. René Vincent confirmed this in 1943, when he claimed that *Combat* had "first and foremost been a political act."[41]

Combat was a unique venture, in which the forces of "Maurrassism and Catholicism, divorced since 1926, lived together side by side in complete friendship," as one of its contributors was fond of recalling.[42] Those intent on drafting a right-wing personalism and those trained within the Maurrassian fold found a common purpose that *Combat* helped bring to life. According to Monnier, "Thierry [Maulnier] was, alongside [Catholic] Jean de Fabrègues, the founder and editor of *Combat*, a magazine of tabloid format . . . the quickest and the most intelligent of the publications in the years 1936 and 1940."[43] The essayist Maulnier held a prominent role in the development and success of *Combat*, since "from 1930 to 1940, a large number of young Maurrassians [saw] Thierry [Maulnier] as Maurras's successor [and intellectual heir]." According to one of his far-right companions, "[they] read [his articles] in the *Revue du XXe Siècle*, in the *Revue Française*, in *Combat*, the main attempt to define some kind of neo-Maurrassism." Maulnier, he added, quickly came to prominence because "he was able to express our cherished principles in simple and direct terms and with a provocative dialectical force."[44] *Combat*'s contributors were the life and force of the magazine, providing it its distinctive identity and politics, since "[it] did not have a structured editorial team. [It was made up] of a group of whimsical friends with a tendency to anarchy, [who] agreed on many points and [whose ethos was defined] by their opposition to democracy, and reading of Maurras." Its main characteristic—hardly a novel claim—was its "great freedom" in "saying whatever [they] wanted to say."[45] Again, friendship, freedom, convergence, and dissidence were the terms they invoked to speak of their engagement.

Combat's politics was, according to its participants, defined by an ideal "uniting an anti-democratic spirit to an anti-conservative spirit" but where, Brasillach explained, some had insisted that "racism [be] proscribed" in the tradition of Maurrassian integral nationalism.[46] Despite the fond recollections of many of its contributors, its rhetorical violence was undeniable (though always in the form of more essay-like and reflective pieces). Monnier explained that "*Combat* was made up of [both] differences and convergences. Our tastes, origins and training were diverse . . . , [we were able] to express contradictory judgments as in the case of Louis-Ferdinand Céline [but] there was agreement on what mattered most: the noxiousness of the democratic regime and of its opposite, right-wing (Nazi) or left-wing (Stalinist) totalitarianism."[47] In short, *Combat* enabled them to become political authors intent on reestablishing the proper relation between "mind and the world, intelligence and politics, man

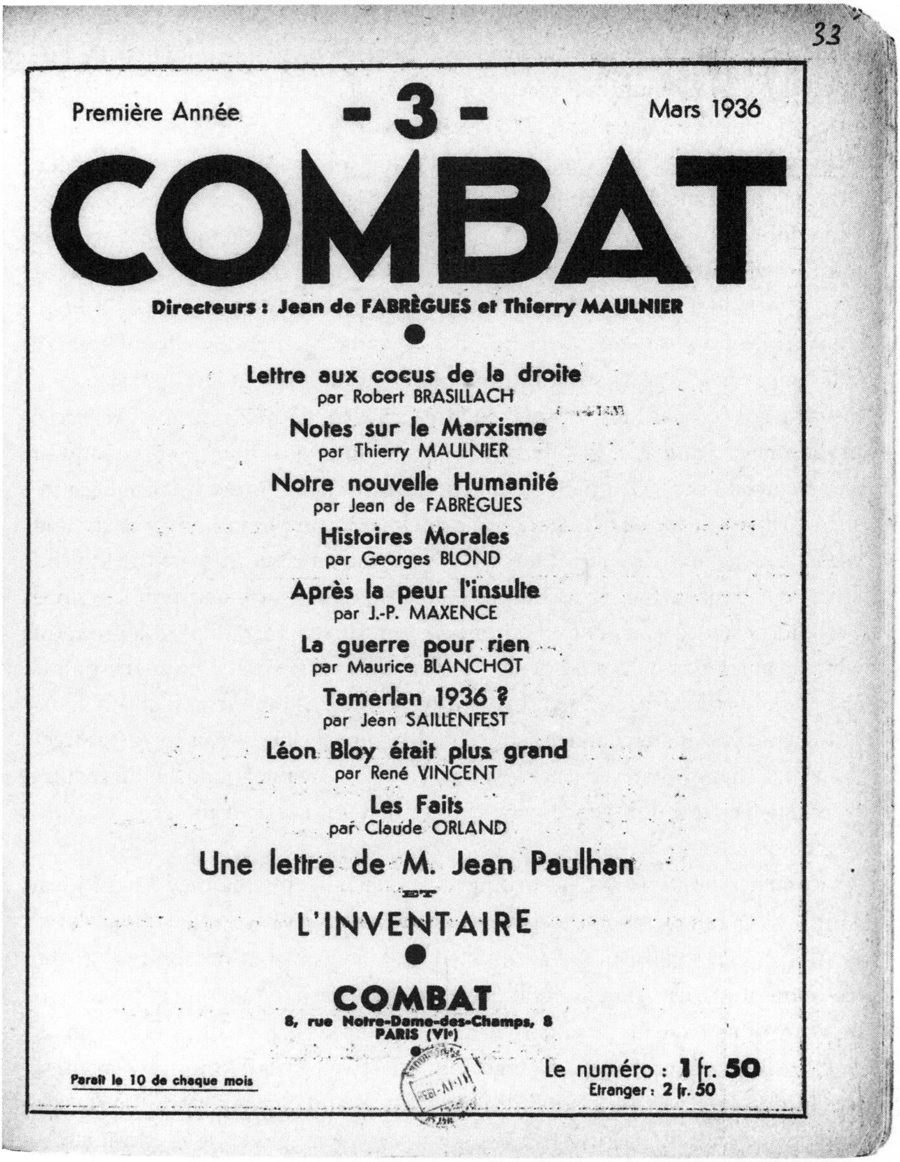

Première Année — 3 — Mars 1936

COMBAT

Directeurs : Jean de FABRÈGUES et Thierry MAULNIER

Lettre aux cocus de la droite
par Robert BRASILLACH

Notes sur le Marxisme
par Thierry MAULNIER

Notre nouvelle Humanité
par Jean de FABRÈGUES

Histoires Morales
par Georges BLOND

Après la peur l'insulte
par J.-P. MAXENCE

La guerre pour rien
par Maurice BLANCHOT

Tamerlan 1936 ?
par Jean SAILLENFEST

Léon Bloy était plus grand
par René VINCENT

Les Faits
par Claude ORLAND

Une lettre de M. Jean Paulhan

ET

L'INVENTAIRE

COMBAT
8, rue Notre-Dame-des-Champs, 8
PARIS (VIe)

Paraît le 10 de chaque mois

Le numéro : 1 fr. 50
Etranger : 2 fr. 50

Combat, March 1936, front page. Courtesy of Bibliothèque nationale de France.

and society in their true subordination and unity."[48] They were an elite brotherhood motivated by the same desires, the same disgusts.

Barely a year later, however, in the wake of the Popular Front victory, the emergence of a new mass politics, and the ravages of the Spanish Civil War at the borders of the country, *Combat* seemed too limited an outlet for these engaged intellectuals.[49] A number of them decided to create a more ambitious venture: a polemical weekly newspaper that they named *L'Insurgé*. Its format borrowed from traditional weeklies such as *Candide* and *Gringoire* but was more modern in its presentation, with bold illustrations and provocative headlines. In one issue, large black headlines were accompanied by a striking and dark representation of a familiar figure drawn in stark and stylized lines. Smiling enigmatically, sitting on a coffin that suggested many others to come, presumably in remembrance of those "martyred" during the February 1934 protests, Léon Blum, head of the French government, sat entrenched and defiant, staring at the reader, his body well defined, one hand on his knee, the other holding a menorah, the vivid reminder of his Jewishness.[50] This caricature (created by Ralph Soupault) was only one of many that graced the front pages of this short-lived polemical newspaper. Usually the centerpiece of the *Insurgé* front pages, a caricature of this kind immediately evoked the fantasized threat of Jews to the French nation, feeding on a lively tradition of right-wing political cartoons in the pages of the far-right press.[51] Such caricatures illustrated the virulent political tone that the newspaper had been designed to showcase. Headlines screamed disgust at an all-pervasive corruption, berated the betrayal of workers, denounced the shameful subjection of Blum to Stalin, and incessantly called for revolt.

Fantasies of abjection finally found unrestrained expression not in the magazine "devoted to ideas" but in the polemical newspaper devoted to "violence." While *Combat* was designed to be a more serious and measured venue for their conception of culture and politics, *L'Insurgé* represented its obscene supplement. *L'Insurgé*'s existence disrupted the image of *Combat* as a respectable forum immune to the vicissitudes of daily politics.[52] The themes (the nation, the individual, society, and civilization) were almost identical, but the manner in which they were addressed differed. Maulnier, "the doctrinarian," had this time teamed up with the colorful and energetic far-right figure Jean-Pierre Maxence, who became *L'Insurgé*'s true "orchestrator and master-mind."[53] Aside from those close to Jean de Fabrègues, who declined to participate in such a politically charged enterprise, the editorial team was strikingly similar to that of

PREMIERE ANNÉE. — N° 5. — PARAIT TOUS LES MERCREDIS

L'INSURGÉ

POLITIQUE ET SOCIAL

31, rue Caumartin, Paris-9e
Tél. : OPERA 20-51.

Le numéro : 1 franc

UN GOUVERNEMENT D'AFFAMEURS

LES FRANÇAIS IMPROVISÉS

par Thierry MAULNIER

Augmentation des salaires 15 %
Augmentation du coût de la vie de 25 à 35 %

Mangerons-nous demain ?

Vers l'écrasement des classes moyennes

DU PAIN ! DU PAIN !

par Jean-Pierre MAXENCE

LIBÉREZ LA PRESSE

PATENOTRE continue à corrompre

Le Komintern recommande *L'Ami du Peuple*

UN PROJET DE CORPORATION DES ASSURANCES

par Louis GUESCLIN

LE POPULAIRE DE PARIS
ORGANE CENTRAL DU PARTI SOCIALISTE (S. F. I. O.)
6 Février
L'acte de naissance du Front Populaire porte une date authentique : 6 FÉVRIER 1934

L'Insurgé, February 10, 1937, front page. Courtesy of Bibliothèque nationale de France.

Combat (with a few prominent exceptions).[54] The same names could be found on both mastheads: Maurice Blanchot, Georges Blond, François Gravier, Jean Loisy, Claude Roy, Hugues Panassié, and Jean Saillenfest. Especially attuned to current affairs and politics, it displayed a virulence and a willingness to denounce and accuse that were more akin to populist far-right political rags, and more reminiscent of other interwar populist far-right newspapers.[55] Polemics and violence ruled *L'Insurgé*.

L'Insurgé was designed to act as *Combat*'s polemical voice: it emerged out of the desire to appeal to a wider and more militant readership. According to its contributors, it was meant to be a "satirical, virulent weekly newspaper, [characterized by] drawings, caricatures, excessively violent polemical articles, willing to exaggerate and even come close to vulgar farce if that generated laughter [and] which would contrast with the restraint and dignity of a daily newspaper or a serious weekly magazine."[56] *L'Insurgé* offered a unique opportunity to enact the politics they were calling for. It was recognized by its fellow far-right peers as the daring and provocative polemical publication that it aimed to be: six months after its creation, Brasillach praised it in his weekly *Je Suis Partout* chronicle, "Lettre à une provinciale." He portrayed it as the exemplar of the new vibrant and nonconformist press that had emerged in the 1930s and was intent on disrupting the status quo. *L'Insurgé* was an "*orphéon*," according to Brasillach (quoting nationalist writer Maurice Barrès), describing in those terms the "young and ephemeral literary journals where the future was being prepared" and which brought an undeniable "passion to politics, economy, [and] social and moral problems."[57] He specifically singled out *L'Insurgé*, whose success, he explained, reflected the fact that it perfectly translated that "certain disquiet, [and] the need to unite the national and the social, felt somehow everywhere around Europe which has spurred the creation of young and novel movements of ideas."[58] If some of them were "excessive," even sometimes "mistaken," Brasillach considered that they—and *L'Insurgé* especially—embodied the kind of revolutionary spirit that had fueled the beginnings of *L'Action Française*, "one the most illustrious of these *orphéons*."[59] Though some historians have stressed that *L'Insurgé* was not representative of the politics of these intellectuals, and was simply an anecdote in their long political journey, it was constitutive of the Young New Right's identity and was claimed as such by its participants.[60] *L'Insurgé* allowed them to create a "counter-public," a political space where they called upon their readers to act with them—the "we" that formed the motif of their writings and included both journalists and their readers against the others whom they denounced and derided—as rebels, revolutionaries, "agitators"—so that they would be "victorious."[61] Both more radical and more conventional, *L'Insurgé* emerged as a direct contestation of the far-right genealogy that these young critics felt they needed to disrupt.

Its title—the *Insurgent*—announced its place. It was a pointed reference to republican and socialist Jules Vallès's novel of the same name, which charted the trials and tribulations of a politically engaged and anti-bourgeois young writer and journalist who had participated in the 1871 Commune. This reference hinted at the insurgency of brave Communards, while also reminding readers of the failed February 1934 protests, which seemed to have signaled to this generation the limits of traditional far-right politics. It was actually a direct borrowing from Léon Daudet, who had written in his 1936 musings on journalism that "Vallès had been, alongside Proudhon, one of the most eloquent of the rebels," and the names of those two figured on the front page of the newspaper.[62] In an early *Combat* article, Maurice Blanchot had explained that Young New Right intellectuals needed to see themselves as the "inheritors of the first insurgents of the postwar years."[63] *L'Insurgé* thus proudly announced that it was to be a more explicit revolutionary conscience than what had come before. Its purpose was intentionally polemical and violent, so that "from the very first issue, [readers] are able understand who [they] are, what [they] want, what [they] defend, what [they] are fighting, without any ambiguity."[64] For Maulnier, Blanchot, and Maxence—three of its main organizers—to be revolutionary meant finding a way to disrupt:

> No one is allowed to live outside of the regime. But we can live either as the privileged ones or the resigned: or, we can on the contrary behave as a foreign and destructive body, like a charge of dynamite in a conflict. The only one truly capable of an efficacious revolutionary action is the one who is already a revolutionary in mind, already an outlaw.[65]

They described themselves as outside of the law and disruptive to traditional political forces. In the first issue of *Combat*, Thierry Maulnier had ominously announced that the "true violence of ideas, the power of rupture lay in the manner in which we never cease fighting present society, even in its political forms."[66] Finally, a year later, *L'Insurgé* allowed them to move closer to the outright "disobedience to laws" that was necessary for the liberation of France from corruption, degradation, and abjection.

The Nation's Abjection

As Maulnier sternly noted in 1939, "France must save what makes her different from other nations; France must not only save itself as a nation, but *as a civilization*."[67] That enduring anxiety regarding the fate of French civilization had always been present among the Young New Right. Already, in 1932, Maulnier had claimed—rather predictably—that "the current crisis—which we must affirm is not only yet another crisis, but the beginning of a final crisis—is a crucial crisis and does not allow for the subtle and puerile games we have found ourselves losing for the last ten years."[68] This crisis implied the nation itself was compromised and the social order in disarray. Émile Vaast had explained it well:

> France has become *contradictory to her own sons*. It opposes one against the other, writers, workers, veterans. It divides churches, "grandes écoles," the University and even the government's cabinets. Some react like their ancestors and build their hopes under the umbrella of the homeland [*patrie*]. Others, who have been convinced that the existence of France as an autonomous political entity is in decline, are trying to find her a replacement; some substitute the kingdom of God, others a mere administrative board, and finally, the greatest number embrace the name of Europe.[69]

Confusion was the rule. The nation was divided, its integrity threatened in the same ways that the individual citizen was lost and disoriented. *Réaction*'s 1930 manifesto had warned that "in order to fill in the immense emptiness of our soul, we are being offered either dubious Oriental asceticism or invited to regenerate thanks to Social Revolution."[70] But that rhetoric of decadence and division took on a new tone from 1936 onward: now, absolute disgust, instinctive nausea, and the undeniable degradation of the social body, the nation, and its citizens were what these intellectuals railed against.

For these far-right critics, the nation was an abject entity that must urgently be purified because it elicited only disgust and revolt. Traditional Maurrassian rhetoric occasionally resorted to this vocabulary of abjection to express the horror and disgust experienced in the face of the republican regime. Disgust was also a common feature of far-right discourse. But, for this younger generation, abjection was not merely a rhetorical figure. Abjection operated as the organizing principle of reactionary politics and the redefinition of a revolutionary nationalism. Unlike the leaders of Action française, they saw abjection as constitutive of the modern world and of their own relationship to it—as it was an affective, almost physical, reminder of what was unstable within the borders of the nation and was lacking in the social body and in each and every citizen (or subject). Historians have noted the striking and repeated use of the register of disgust in Young New Right writings in 1936 and 1937 but rarely examined it.[71] In fact, tracing how they moved from decadence to abjection and then insurgency illuminates how "the abject" functioned politically. It displaced the long-standing anxieties regarding uncontained threats to the self, nation, and civilization and gave those threats shape and meaning—this pervasive disgust legitimated the violence advocated by the Young New Right, made their task urgent, and identified those threats to their normative vision of the bounded male self.

Most Young New Right intellectuals usually bemoaned decadence: they wrote about it, pondered over it, debated it, and most of all, attempted to find solutions to it.[72] Though a common trope with a long history across the political spectrum and especially among the far right, it took on a more ominous meaning. Their story of the nation, of course, lamented the loss of a golden age.[73] The present state of decadence was a fantasized one, a lost quality "[which] emerged only at its very moment of its alleged loss."[74] In the 1930s, though, it was now literally everywhere, manifest in the degradation and decay of social norms, cultural forms, and political regimes. For instance, Maulnier pointed to the fact that it would be difficult for French citizens to admit that "Parisian suburbs have been a disgrace to civilization [and] that, for the last fifteen years, we have allowed our Congolese populations to suffer from hunger, leprosy, and destitution."[75] Decadence was visible in the miserable poverty within the borders of the nation, and abroad in its colonies, where France had failed at its great "civilizing mission." Degradation was one of the manifestations of this decadence, undermining the greatness of France as an imperial nation from within. It signified more than the demise of France's place within the international order but was mostly an issue that plagued the nation *within its borders*. For Maulnier, "If every ever-so-proud young Frenchman can experience this sentiment of degradation when he sees the place of his country within the world, he experiences it just as acutely when he turns his gaze to its internal problems."[76] The nation's true character had been lost, so that every young Frenchman found only "a degraded and fallen condition within a diminished nation."[77]

"Decadence," "degradation," "decrepitude," "debasement": those are the words that appeared most often, almost compulsively, in the prose of *Combat* and *L'Insurgé* journalists. The conditions that these words described could be found within the nation and at the heart of French society. The dissolution of the social body was of course a pressing danger, since it threatened the symbolic borders of the nation.[78] It was inseparable from the degradation affecting the community and civilization and, the journalists explained, was confirmed by the fact that "the French people have been debased and rendered stupid."[79] The "natural" hierarchy that should uphold the social body and sustain the French people had been undone. René Vincent highlighted another glaring sign of degradation, namely contemporary political beliefs in racial equality. For him, the antiracist politics claiming racial equality "between blacks and whites" so prevalent in democratic regimes perverted the natural order of things. This "simplistic" claim for equality in democracy risked undermining Western civilization.[80] Since "democracy has degraded us," disgust was the only feeling one could experience when witnessing such a state of the nation.[81] It was all the more unbearable because, unlike the traditional far right, who had usually expressed disgust in the face of forces seen to be "external" to France, the danger was now internal, and therefore unavoidable.

Combat journalists experienced disgust at everything. They were "sickened" by what they saw. This was one of the most striking and recurring motifs of a prominent *Insurgé* writer, Maurice Blanchot. It figured largely in Maxence's 1939 memoirs of the interwar period. Disgust also formed the leitmotiv of Georges Blond's *Combat* articles, in which he explained he found that even that most sacred of institutions, the family, "had become disgusting."[82] Decadence was held by these critics to constitute both origin and expression of this abjection. Disgust pervaded everything, the family as much as the nation, its collective emanation. Disgust was the only *rational* response, according to these critics bemoaning in an editorial that they refused "a France disgusting us."[83] They explained that it was not only leftist politicians and writers who "had ruined the French" that disgusted them, but the way France had been degraded, debased, and transformed.[84] "France is being assassinated," they cried.[85] This defilement provoked uncontrollable disgust: "France disgusted [them]," as they affirmed in an editorial in April 1936; and another journalist explained, "The current state of the country" was "repugnant."[86]

The nation's state of abjection, as featured in the pages of *L'Insurgé*, had emerged as the product of alienation, resulting from an irreconcilable divorce between the "real," authentic nation, and the legal, artificial one embodied in the democratic regime that harbored both left- and right-wing forces. This classic Maurrassian distinction was, in *Combat* and *L'Insurgé*, both affirmed and reinvented, and the usual denunciation of Socialists, Radicals, and conservatives took on added force. For the members of the traditionalist Action française, only the republican and democratic regime was "abject," as it was composed of "traitors, thieves, and assassins."[87] Maurras had often explained that democracy was the cause of the "nation's intellectual and moral abjection," which he measured according to the degree of admiration expressed in France for Hitler's decisions and acts.[88] But in *L'Insurgé*, corrupt and morally bankrupt politicians had done more than govern badly. All politicians were "rotten" and "retarded" "laughable ghosts" who had, since 1936 especially, "fooled" and "swindled" the French people.[89] The left had perverted the nation—and conned its workers—because it followed an unnatural and foreign ideology, while the right (since 1935) had "castrated" the national body through its impotence and passivity.[90] Some events, like the violent and bloody Clichy riots of March 16, 1937, confirmed this belief: Communist and Socialist militants gathered to protest a Parti social français film screening in this working-class suburb. By then, La Rocque's party was probably the largest in France. After the police fired upon the crowd of almost 9,000 leftist demonstrators, leaving five dead and two hundred wounded (and leading to the most striking caricatures of Léon Blum), they proclaimed that "all of the regime's politicians have French blood on their hands."[91] To these intellectuals, the political regime was but one instance of abjection: the nation and its citizens were also contaminated—and it was this fact that must be remedied.

Even the terms of their political critique referred to the manner in which contemporary ideologies—the familiar scapegoats of far-right politics—had tainted the nation. Their arguments, whether in the pages of *Combat* or *L'Insurgé*, centered around a definition of the French citizen saved from the evils of external and "foreign" ideological forces such as "materialism." Both "idealism" (which, according to Maulnier, had mistakenly produced democracy) and "materialism" could lead only to the degradation of the individual lured by the utopian possibilities of these political regimes: indeed, these "only transform the French people into a degenerate, lifeless, and spineless people."[92] Having "witnessed day after day the growing danger of an enslavement of intelligence [and] faced the idealist failure and the materialist danger," they explained, "it [was] time to restore a new realism."[93] They were unanimous in insisting that Marxism necessarily threatened the very conditions of existence of the individual. Maulnier repeatedly explained in his articles that he felt this political vision was detrimental to "man." He disagreed with this "strange enterprise that pretends to enslave 'man' just enough for him to know how to serve his master." He confessed that he preferred "[those] externally imposed disciplines to those internal hatreds." Fear of confusion and disorder sustained their concern regarding the viability of a political regime. Communism, unsurprisingly, was one of the graver dangers these men felt they faced because it epitomized a vision of the individual and "his" relation to the social that was fundamentally perverted. Indeed, anti-communism was a prominent aspect of the Young New Right, spearheaded by Maulnier, who was known within far-right circles as a specialist on the matter—having actually read Marx and penned some "notes on Marxism."[94] As they would for Blum and Jews, the Young New Right claimed communism was both symptom and origin of the nation's degradation.

The French nation had thus been emptied of its substance, they claimed. It no longer possessed its own spirit: "France has been dispossessed." In the pages of *Combat* and *L'Insurgé*, Maulnier explained that they—the French people—were now "citizens of an absent city."[95] France's substance had been tainted, and thus hollowed because it had been "left to foreign hands," which meant that there was no longer a correspondence between culture and politics, the essence of the nation and its embodiment. Indeed, "being in someone else's hands" was a recurring reference. Since the nation was hollow, absent from itself, it was vulnerable to a "claim to possession."[96] France was now an abject body because it had been "invaded, colonized, subjected to foreign laws."[97] The nation had lost its ability to impose the law on its citizens, its colonial subjects, and even foreigners, and had thus become enslaved, akin to a colonized country. The proof of such degradation lay in the fact that one could witness, according to Maulnier again, "an empire that is crumbling"—France—while another was "being born"—Mussolini's fascist Italy.[98] And it meant that within the European concert of nations, France no longer held its primary place. For literary critic and novelist Robert Brasillach, obsessed with restoring masculine virility, those "masters of France [*matamores gonflés de mot*] have made her fall to the level of a dependent nation, crying throughout the whole of Europe, begging for her candy and her whip."[99] The taint of abjection was the result of this degradation. In fact, theirs was a circular argument. What had rendered the nation hollow was what would befall it if it remained abject.

The nation had been slowly depleted—under the weight of decadence—and that had only been made easier by the most horrifying instance of perversion, namely the election of the left-wing Popular Front coalition led by Jewish Socialist Léon Blum. The sudden confluence of the Republic, Socialism, Communism, and Jewishness was truly unbearable and, to them, represented the pinnacle of the nation's debasement:

> Sordid greed, cowardice, impudence, swindling, and to finish it off, this atrocious betrayal: this is the face of France in 1936. This is the face that has been bestowed on France. Every Frenchman who is somewhat lucid now realizes that he belongs to a nation that has been slowly debased to the extent that it not only suffers the unanimous contempt of civilized peoples, but even begins to deserve it. We must now decide whether the France which has built the most beautiful cathedrals and won the greatest wars, that France of Saint-Louis, of the crusades, of Versailles, will be transformed into a nation of crooks, eunuchs, and thugs.[100]

That ancient Catholic soil that had produced the best in culture was "debased." Such were the characteristics of "French abjection." The compulsive references to this abject nature of the national body were almost ritualistic. The abject symbolized the limits of the bearable and the assimilable: "It [was both] very near and yet inassimilable."[101] The state, the regime, and the national body were all abject occurrences of a horrifying phenomenon, the disruption of the limits of the subject, that is, the individual male self. Abjection helped them define the social body as, in their writings, it acted as a reminder of what could not be and was not bearable. For them the abject was not specifically located—in a government, an institution, a political party—but everywhere, so that everything and everyone was tainted by it. This generalized sense of abjection had to be fought because, as Maxence claimed, "everything that relates to the abject state opposes [us]."[102]

Abjection was such an obsessive concern that it formed the motif of one specific page in *L'Insurgé*, titled "French abjection." "This page's purpose was pure outlet," confessed Monnier. It denounced everything and everyone, because they were

> murdered by a despicable politics subjected to foreign masters, and enraged by French citizens' inept inability to revolt and do nothing else but complain while accepting everything; [they] wanted to show [their] dual reaction with such a provocative title: [a reaction] of disgust in the face of the country's debasement, and of revolt against those responsible for this debasement.[103]

They did not hesitate to denounce the regime and its representatives and, above all, everyone in France who was necessarily corrupted by abjection because they were subjected to the same degrading forces. But this apocalyptic vision was not shared by other far-right pundits; they vehemently rejected it, as it foreclosed the possibility of a return to an authentic nation (*pays réel*) that had survived in the face of the forces of republicanism and modernity. The return to a true untainted national spirit had been both tenet and guiding force of Maurrassian nationalism. Maurras was shocked by *L'Insurgé*'s argument: "Page four's title, 'French abjection,' had [indeed] irritated Maurras. For him, [political figures such as] Herriot, Caillaux, Blum, Malvy, Paul-Boncour, Briand and all the others would be abject, but never France. The juxtaposition of the words 'abjection' and 'French' was more than a rhyme [for him]: it was a mistake."[104] For Maurras, the nation was untainted. But not for the Young New Right. "L'abjection française" also troublingly echoed Maurras's own organization, Action française, the young generation hinting in this manner at the impotence and failure of their elders.[105] Maurras could not abide such an attack; he was extremely critical of *L'Insurgé*, going so far as writing to his beloved protégé, Maulnier, from the confines of prison, urging him to abandon his misguided folly. Page four disappeared soon after, but the denunciations and vitriolic attacks on the nation's abjection did not cease.[106] In fact, the Young New Right called for a "purification" of the nation rather than just a "return," as Maurras and his acolytes had demanded. Restoration was not enough because the community and its members had been tainted in a manner impossible to efface. *Combat*/*L'Insurgé* writers mobilized instead a politics of absolute and radical violence, the only possibility, as they saw it, for a renewal of the nation and of "man."

Their obsession came out of their belief that once the Popular Front had come to power, no one was immune from the forces of degradation. Far-right intellectuals had always held that there was a natural and indissoluble relation between "man"—the male citizen—and the nation. That relation, in turn, was the foundation for a harmonious and flourishing social order. This was a historical relationship; as Maulnier replied when asked whether the French people could "escape this French abjection," "the nation justifies its existence in the effort it makes for the accomplishment of man."[107] Since man should identify with the nation, the nation's corruption inevitably affected every citizen. If the nation was abject, then so was every citizen. No one was immune. The nation could no longer provide political identification for its citizens because it was divided; this meant the nation's citizens were also no longer whole. Abjection was within; in an article "indicting France," Blanchot asserted "we" are the abject.[108] He continued to do so week after week.

How then could individuals emerge as autonomous and whole subjects in a world that was forever and always abject? The self was experienced as alien and divided, a state of being that these young far-right critics adamantly refused, for it revealed the fundamental instability of the human person and undid the relationships between culture, identity, and politics that they held sacred. One of *Combat*'s contributors had insisted that "it no longer suffices to know or even realize what the political conditions of such a degenerate France are, yet we must recognize that [France] must be rebuilt in each of us."[109] That concern became an obsession as they relentlessly told their readers. Since "the life that is imposed on [him] is increasingly dispersed and fragmented," it is obvious that "man today feels the need to rebuild himself."[110] But rebuilding was not an easy task. As one's own degradation could not easily be severed from one's self, only radical action might help one to emerge out of this untenable state. In fact, "we must kill it . . . in every single one of us."[111]

Politically, noxious ideological forces needed to be fought and eradicated, and these intellectuals' rhetorical violence translated such feelings. Many of the *Combat* and *L'Insurgé* authors observed that their contemporaries perceived "order as that which frees" and yearned "to provide man with his center, to offer him a worldview where he can harmoniously establish himself, his thoughts, his activities, his suffering in his rightful place."[112] Maulnier, who edited both publications, concluded that Marxism, and even fascism, had attempted to do this, but failed. Consequently, *L'Insurgé* loudly affirmed that it was clear that "the Communist danger must be fought everywhere. It might be necessary to fight it tomorrow in the streets."[113] The appeal to revolution drove their arguments, since "revolution can only be vanquished through revolution." As intellectuals committed to a radical oppositional politics, "it is not a case of self-defense; it means attacking."[114] Only action would allow the renewal they hoped for: "Once again, nothing is more sterile than to try and grant a reprieve to the regime, to be so obstinate in trying to give some appearance of life for a year, for two years, for ten years."[115] For they claimed that nothing could be saved: "In Hamlet's kingdom, there was something rotten, [but] in the Third Republic, EVERYTHING is rotten."[116] In the face of a putrid regime, all they could see now was "society's body decomposing before [their] eyes." The conclusion was obvious, but they reiterated it nonetheless: "A storm troop is what is needed, a troop whose purpose is to overthrow what is rather than keep it," and "finally irrevocably vanquish."[117] The call for radical and revolutionary violence—the "terrorism" Maurice Blanchot had suggested might constitute the only "method of public salvation"—rested upon a realist engagement with politics. It was because they claimed they had rightly perceived what was at stake in this decadent state that they could "realistically" propose a solution: insurgent politics.[118]

The insurgency they advocated depended on a revolutionary state intent on reinstating order, hierarchy, and authority as a means of reasserting the national boundaries that had dissolved. The paradox of the Young New Right's proposed political solution lay in the fact that they offered revolution as the only possible political alternative to the reestablishment of a social, cultural, and political order. That order was to be founded upon a bounded sense of self guaranteed by harmonious relations between the citizen, the community, and civilization. They redefined revolution in their own terms, explaining that revolution would be achieved if the reigning order was subverted, for "this subversion did not come solely out of the realm of ideas. Neither should it emerge solely from the realm of force, misery, and anger." Refusing either a sterile intellectual position divorced from the reality of politics or the desire for change, which was called for by the masses as well as political parties and groups, a subversive position required "two violences," inspired by the twin figures of Georges Sorel and Charles Maurras. Maulnier told his readers: "It is up to us to unite them."[119] But what did that indeterminate call to insurgency involve? It meant uprooting the political status quo: "We are not saying that the words left and right no longer have any meaning. We are saying they still have meaning but that meaning needs to be done away with" in "the only struggle possible."[120] Most of all, they asserted over and over, it meant displaying "the courage of one's ideas, disrespect and independence from the established order, and the willingness to embrace rupture," so that a true will to rupture meant "fighting contemporary society as it is without sparing its political forms."[121]

Such exhortations never acquired any precise political or pragmatic meaning, because Young New Right intellectuals were in some sense unable to do so: what they wished for was purification and transcendence in order to define the rightful boundaries of the citizen and the community. Maulnier endlessly cried for a "restoration" of order that would allow for a harmonious whole undisturbed by its own tendency to disruption.[122] He explained that while both Marxism and fascism had attempted such a project, Marxism had "taken away the individual's desire and power to think of himself as an autonomous being."[123] Fascism, on the other hand, had oversimplified "man," as it had mistakenly believed that "order [alone] appeared as that which freed."[124] This prospect, as he repeated throughout the years, "horrified [him]."[125] Order should not constitute the sole purpose of mankind; it should be one of its fundamentally guiding principles. He argued that unity (of man) should be restored and that a "new synthesis" was needed that would "attempt to reestablish the mind and the world, intelligence and politics, man and society in their . . . true unity."[126] Only unity could enact a renewal of France, because "a valid French order is possible only if no Frenchman is excluded from it."[127] To avoid confusion and turmoil, it was therefore important to establish order and enforce an understanding of society that would generate a harmonious whole. This was, for far-right critics, the price for the emergence of a full French citizenry. Maulnier never tired of repeating—in what would constitute his one recurring concern—that "what needs to be done is this: we need [an] authority, we need [a] hierarchy, we need a harmonious, coherent and noble society."[128]

Now that it was diagnosed, abjection must be eradicated. That was urgent, Young New Right intellectuals claimed, and was the condition for revolution. But abjection of the divided self was figured as both inside and outside, "an ambiguous opposition" that survived from within.[129] At the same time, the abject also lay beyond the community's "borders," so that the outside was perceived to be both cause and cure of internal abjection.[130] That idea permeated their imagination of the nation. In their writings, this unbearable state of abjection was projected onto the figure of the Jew, at once inside and outside, perceived to hold the invisible obscene power and knowledge that were corrupting France. Maxence had explained it simply: "More than any other government, the Blum government is guilty."[131]

Fantasies of the "Jew": Borders, Boundaries, and Civilization

If the nation was abject in 1936, it was because it had been tainted by one who was abject: for the far-right, that was embodied by the figure of the "Jew." The nation could no longer provide political identification for its citizens because "Blum" prevented far-right critics from imagining a whole and bounded national community. Since the nation was revealed to be lacking—its essence corrupted, its soil tainted—the metaphorical social body could be restored only through the symbolic expulsion of an "object" identified as abject. They had argued that abjection was everywhere, but they also insisted it could be identified: abjection was located in the figure of the "Jew"—perceived to hold both power and the knowledge that had corrupted France.[132] Antisemitism allowed them to produce themselves as a whole and tied together the terms of their virulent and all-encompassing political and social critique. The abject, which was an "impossible object, still part of the subject," was contained within the fantasized figure of "Léon Blum."[133] Maulnier confessed it in one article: "Blum's person does not exist"—and yet Blum was everywhere and—albeit for a brief moment—contained all that they found repugnant.[134] In 1937 it was obvious to far-right critics that the "Jew" was embodied in the menacing and disruptive character of "Blum," for "Léon Blum rightly provoked [among us] reactions of rejection as well as stupid manifestations of rancor."[135]

Contrary to the conventional depiction of the Young New Right as immune from anti-Jewish rhetoric, the group was never shy of identifying Jews—and more specifically a fantasy of the "Jew"—as the cause and exemplar of French decadence and degradation. *L'Insurgé* was from the outset infused with antisemitic rhetoric. Such references had already surfaced in the pages of *Combat*, where journalists mentioned, for instance, the way "French workers know only now to bring flowers to a scorched Jew and adore foreign militarism."[136] Blum and socialism were routinely denounced in the pages of *Combat*. One of the magazine's first issues had announced a forthcoming article by unapologetic antisemite Lucien Rebatet, who was offering his "re-reading [of] Drumont," the most celebrated antisemitic pamphleteer of the nineteenth century.[137] The article never materialized—and Rebatet never contributed to *Combat*—but, in January 1938, readers could enjoy a selection of excerpts from his works. There were excerpts from his famous best seller, *La France juive*, as well as extracts from *La fin d'un monde*, stating that "the Bourgeoisie exploiting the People was itself robbed by the Jew."[138] Their critique of capitalism was best served by Drumont's antisemitic arguments. *L'Insurgé*, after all, had been created under Drumont's benevolent shadow, thereby signaling an allegiance to a vision of the world that took the Jew as the cause of decadence and symptom of modernity. Drumont was quoted on the front page on the meaning of "*insurgé*": the revolutionary [*insurgé*] was one who "violently forced fate's hand." According to Drumont, insurgents were "men ready to do anything, even risk death."[139] The great antisemitic author of *La France juive* served as overarching reference. One contributor revealed years later that within the pages of *L'Insurgé*, the "word 'Jew' and some Jews would appear in the guise of caricatures or [were] inserted in polemical articles."[140] Jewishness actually figured prominently in their anxieties regarding French politics and civilization.

Since the substance of the nation was at stake, it was crucial to determine and legitimate who could claim to be French. In one of his editorials, Maulnier disingenuously pointed out that he was "not questioning our masters' race nor their—often recent—date of entry into the national community." Yet, he added, he "only [asked] how long they had been French, through consent or will."[141] By invoking the specter of naturalized foreigners (like the infamous Stavisky) or immigrants (like the German-Jewish political refugees who were imagined to be invading France in the 1930s), Maulnier pointed to the importance of ancestry in determining who could be French, was truly so, and had been for generations—the Barrèsian soil that had carefully nurtured a French character and where civilization had flourished. The pernicious presence of foreigners—read "Jews"—had brought about disorder, they often intimated, "within our borders."[142] Of course, these foreigners had been anti-fascist Italians, republican Spanish refugees, and "the magma of Communist Germans thrown out by Central Europe." But more often, the most dangerous were these "Men from Nowhere invading the nation, monopolizing every situation, appropriating every power," who would leave French people only "the freedom to wait on them."[143] Here, the usual antisemitic litany of Jews who were stateless, bizarrely dressed, speaking strange gibberish, and infesting capitalism, politics, and culture conflated foreigners, refugees, and Jews in order to paint a nation threatened from without and within by unassimilable individuals.[144] Brasillach, of course, did not mince his words, exclaiming in *Combat* that it was outrageous that men like Louis Louis-Dreyfus were not denounced for "who they were" because they were an "emigrant's grand-son who had the nerve to invoke the old virtues of [his] ancesters the Gauls."[145] In 1937, though, this rhetoric became especially visible in *L'Insurgé* when saving the nation seemed a most urgent task.

Most of all, the figure of Blum provided a convenient focus for the violence and hatred that these critics wished to express. Caricatures thus appeared beneath striking and virulent headlines that defamed the "assassins," "corrupt" and "criminal" members of the political regime and the government "who starve" the people. As long as Blum held his tenure, caricatures featured him.[146] Pages constantly reflected on the fate of the French nation. Former heads of government and Radical politicians Édouard Herriot, Joseph Paul-Boncour, and Camille Chautemps were regularly ridiculed, but it was Léon Blum who figured almost obsessively in the pages of the far-right press, often clad in feminine clothes, as a prostitute, or as the exemplar of the "wandering Jew." Those tropes would have needed little elaboration, since they were familiar to a far-right readership. A week after the "Blum with menorah" issue (and nearly six months before his resignation), Blum could again be seen on the front page: he stood erect, a mock and menacing Bismarck in Germanesque soldierly garb, wearing the sign of freemasonry, a fierce look in his eyes, both feet simultaneously squashing Alsace and Lorraine.[147] It was no longer his hands, but his feet that symbolically destroyed the French nation, signaling an obsession with body parts typical of the modern antisemitic imaginary. In another issue, the "towering outline" of Léon Blum could be seen firing on the tiny resigned figures of Tunisian men. The Jew, the image suggested, would even endanger defenseless "natives" in French colonies who needed protection. The drawing, in shades of black, unmistakably echoed the headline sarcastically thanking Blum for prosecuting them: "Blum is prosecuting us, THANK YOU."[148] The analogy was clear; according to caricaturist Ralph Soupault, Blum the tyrannical despot oppressed *L'Insurgé* journalists and colonial subjects alike, bringing unfettered violence to the nation and its empire. They were the victims of his hunger for power and desire to pervert a "true France."[149] Blum was a monstrous figure constantly threatening the fate of the nation, a belief echoed by far-right writers and journalists through editorials, news reports, and opinion pieces in *L'Insurgé* and in other newspapers.

At the end of March, after the infamous Clichy events, the journalists at *L'Insurgé* called for the "assassins" of government to resign since "some are shot at, others are dissolved." They claimed that they lived in a world turned upside down, where civilians were being killed and legitimate (far-right) political leagues were being outlawed—this, they explained, was the government's doing. Underneath the headline, once again the centerpiece of the *Insurgé* front page, stood a gaunt, specterlike Blum with an elongated body, "[both] hands hanging and dripping with [black] blood," his feet emerging out of a pool of the same blood, which belonged, readers were made to understand, to the French people. The image was striking: red and black had replaced the blue traditionally used by the editors on the front page.[150] Blum stood like a vampiric creature staring back at *L'Insurgé* readers, and the caption read as if he were directly addressing them: "Who can say now that I don't possess any French blood?"[151] Moreover, as Kléber Haedens warned, "it was in Blum's destiny to unleash catastrophes."[152]

PREMIERE ANNEE. — N° 6. PARAIT TOUS LES MERCREDIS 17 FEVRIER 1937.

L'INSURGÉ

POLITIQUE ET SOCIAL

31, rue Caumartin, Paris-9e
Tél. : OPERA 20-51.

Le numéro : 1 franc

L'ALSACE-LORRAINE AURA BLUM

NOUS NE VOULONS plus être HUMILIES

par Thierry MAULNIER

La grande presse française est passée toute entière aux mains de trois ou quatre puissants groupes financiers qui se font en outre les distributeurs de subventions étrangères : ce qui fait que le plus puissant moyen d'information, d'éducation politique et même de culture du peuple français se trouve consacré tout entier à grossir les bénéfices de quelques hommes d'affaires et à servir les desseins politiques de nations voisines.

Le gouvernement Blum manque à la parole de la France en fournissant des armes aux gouvernementaux espagnols pendant qu'il propose la neutralité au monde. Il manque à la parole de la France en s'attaquant aux libertés des Alsaciens et des Lorrains, qu'en 1918 nous avions promis de respecter.

Au moment où tous les peuples du monde retrouvent leur âme nationale, proclament unanime leur volonté d'indépendance et de grandeur, cherchent tous à donner l'exemple de l'union, de la force et de la fierté, nous montrons le spectacle notre mesquinerie, notre anxiété, notre désordre, notre économie paralysée : et au moment de fixer la ligne de notre politique extérieure, nos ministres hésitent s'ils feront la politique de l'Allemagne, celle de l'Angleterre ou celle des Soviets, sans que jamais il soit question de faire la politique de la France.

Nous sommes gouvernés par de petits politiciens associés à de gros financiers : le ministère Blum va mendier aux guichets des banques d'Amsterdam ou de Londres la permission de durer. Nous sommes un peuple vassal. Nous sommes un peuple diminué. Nous avons fait trembler l'Europe : l'Europe se moque de nous. Et les négociations au sujet des anciennes colonies allemandes ont lieu entre Londres et Berlin, sans qu'on songe même à nous demander notre avis.

La déchéance

Ce sentiment de la déchéance, que tout jeune Français un peu fier éprouve quand il considère la place de son pays dans le monde, il l'éprouve au même degré lorsqu'il tourne ses regards vers les problèmes intérieurs.

Les ouvriers ont tenté d'échapper au servage honteux qui soumettait le salaire, le travail, le pain de chacun d'eux au *bon plaisir* de l'employeur : mais, *loin d'avoir* conquis le droit à une vie *indépendante*, ils sont maintenant astreints au contrôle des chefs politiques de leurs organisations syndicales, et les moins dociles d'entre eux risquent de se voir réduits au chômage pour délit d'opinion.

Les paysans, déjà privés par les spéculateurs du droit de disposer librement de leurs produits, se voient menacés en outre du monopole étatiste et de la dictature bureaucratique. Les classes moyennes, frappées par la crise, frappées par la dévaluation, frappées par la hausse des prix, sont menacées d'une prolétarisation d'autant plus complète et d'une misère d'autant plus grande que le chômage ferme aux nouveaux prolétaires tout débouché jusque dans les professions manuelles.

Quelques avantages partiels conquis ici et là, les congés payés enfin institués, une « reprise » économique bien timide ne sauraient faire oublier aux Français d'aujourd'hui, et particulièrement aux jeunes Français, qu'ils ne trouveront, de quelque côté qu'ils se tournent, qu'une condition déchue dans une nation diminuée.

Les sacrifices pour rien

Voilà ce qu'ils ne pourront pas pardonner. Voilà ce que nous ne pourrons pas pardonner.

(Suite en dernière page)

LES CONSIGNES DE MONTREUIL

LES COMMUNISTES tenteront-ils bientôt leur coup de force ?..

M. MARX DORMOY contrôlerez-vous ces renseignements précis ?...

Pendant que Moscou cherche dans la presse de droite et dans les milieux politiques de droite, en France, des complices pour sa politique guerrière, les Soviets cherchent, d'autre part, à mettre sur pied, grâce au parti communiste français, une organisation armée prête à un coup de force insurrectionnel.

Au congrès de Montreuil, les chefs communistes ont tenu à rappeler que le parti était un parti de classe, c'est-à-dire un parti de lutte de classes, ce qui semble annoncer un nouveau changement de front du parti communiste, la politique « d'union de la nation française » n'ayant pas donné les résultats escomptés.

On sait, d'autre part, qu'une bonne partie des armes qui ont transité par la France et qui étaient destinées, en principe, aux gouvernementaux espagnols, sont restées sur notre territoire et ont servi à armer les troupes de choc communistes.

Les stocks d'armes ainsi constitués semblent avoir été considérables. En tous cas, on nous transmet à ce sujet des renseignements que nous croyons devoir mettre sous les yeux des autorités responsables. A elles de les vérifier.

Dans une réunion du Komintern, tenue le 18 octobre 1936, il aurait été décidé d'accorder une subvention de 25 millions de francs au parti communiste français pour l'achat d'armes.

Cette subvention aurait été accordée à la suite d'une proposition faite le 6 octobre par les camarades Thorez et Marty.

Le 24 octobre 1936, à la suite d'un ordre reçu de Moscou, le représentant commercial soviétique à Paris aurait ouvert un compte de 25 millions à la Banque du Crédit suisse à Zurich, au nom de M. Thorez.

Les agents chargés des achats d'armes auraient été, pour la Belgique, un Suisse habitant Anvers, W. Hartstein; pour la Hollande, l'armateur grec Pappadopoulos; pour la Suède, Johan Ericsson; pour la Suisse, R. Fluckiger, de Zurich.

Nous fournirons ultérieurement le détail des achats effectués par ces différents intermédiaires.

Ajoutons que, d'après un rapport en date du 22 décembre 1936, le nombre des armes actuellement possédées par le parti communiste serait de 120.000.

Et, si l'on veut découvrir l'emplacement des dépôts où ces armes sont abritées, on pourrait peut-être enquêter avec profit aux adresses suivantes :

A Annemasse, chez Blondel, restaurateur.
A Saint-Jean-Cap-Ferrat, villa Begonia.
A Nice, chez Ducoeur, au « Relais Fleuri », rue Notre-Dame.
A Marseille, 43, rue Forbin.
A Bordeaux, chez F. Morillon, garagiste, rue de la Croix-de-Seguy.
A Libourne, au garage Beauséjour.
A Perpignan, chez M. Palmade, armurier, rue du Maréchal-Foch, et chez M. Laffont, boulevard des Pyrénées.

Encore une fois, le dossier qui nous a été transmis contient peut-être des inexactitudes. Nous le livrons tel qu'il est aux vérifications nécessaires.

Mais, si nos renseignements sont exacts, il sera prouvé, une fois de plus, que Moscou organise, entretient et arme en France les troupes de choc de la guerre civile.

Et que fera alors le gouvernement de M. Blum, qui compte 72 communistes dans sa majorité parlementaire ?

René CAUBERTIER.

L'ALSACE-LORRAINE DEFEND SES LIBERTES

Leur combat

par Jean-Pierre MAXENCE

Les Alsaciens et les Lorrains ont mené et mènent la plus magnifique des luttes. Ils la font au nom de leur foi, ils la font au nom de leur dignité. Nous les saluons fraternellement. Mais leurs affaires sont leurs affaires. Il ne nous appartient pas d'y intervenir dans le détail. Ils sont assez courageux et assez forts pour imposer leur volonté à un gouvernement d'abjection, à un président du Conseil juif qui n'a pas les mêmes titres qu'eux à se réclamer, de père en fils, de génération en génération, de la civilisation française.

Ce que je voudrais dire seulement, c'est que le combat opiniâtre des Alsaciens et des Lorrains pour leurs libertés est un exemple pour les autres provinces françaises. Il ne s'agit point de séparatisme ! Il s'agit du respect des personnes. Il s'agit du respect dû aux groupes naturels qui font les races et les nations vivaces et fortes : familles, métiers, communes, provinces. Il s'agit, plus généralement, de manière plus universelle, du respect qu'un gouvernement de parlementaires et de chiens doit aux qualités si diverses des climats et des traditions qui composent une France durable. Centraliser, niveler, par là abaisser : telle est l'immonde devise du régime. Il importe que d'irréductibles résistances lui soient opposées. Que ces combats naissent chez les fils de ceux qui brisèrent toutes les tentations bismarckiennes, voilà qui est d'une insigne valeur. Mes camarades alsaciens, en défendant vos libertés et votre foi, ce sont les libertés et la foi de toutes les provinces françaises que vous défendez. Trop de lâchetés ailleurs et trop d'oppression démocratique nous ont parfois empêchés de le faire. Vous êtes les insurgés du moment, et pour les plus nobles, les plus féconds, les plus valables des motifs. Vous êtes nos maîtres dans le combat.

Car, et c'est ce que nous voulons faire entendre, dans chaque ville, chaque canton, chaque commune de France : nous ne nous sentons rien de commun avec ce régime de boue et de sang. Pour nous, désobéir aux lois est un devoir parce que les lois sont tyranniques et arbitraires; abattre nos maîtres est un devoir parce que nos maîtres sont de ceux qui ne tiennent leur pouvoir que de l'indignité; saper le régime présent est un devoir, parce que le saper c'est tuer le désordre et que pour créer un ordre acceptable il faut d'abord balayer le reste.

Je sais que vous n'êtes point de ceux pour qui l'agitation est une attitude vaine. Quand vous dites non, c'est avec calme, et votre volonté se fortifie de cette décision glacée. Je connais assez Schumann, par exemple, pour savoir que, s'il est un homme de foi, il n'est point un homme d'aventure. Mais nous vivons des temps où la défense de la plus ancienne foi, de la plus noble chrétienté, est une aventure.

Que nos camarades d'Alsace et de Lorraine acceptent donc le jeune salut de l'Insurgé aux combattants de la première et nécessaire insurrection des provinces françaises qui, parce qu'elles aiment l'unité, ne veulent point qu'elle se fasse étouffante, bureaucratique, niveleuse et abjecte.

×××

L'ALSACE unaninement DRESSEE

(De notre envoyé spécial **Robert Jourdan**)

«NEIN! HERR BLUM! NIEMALS!»
(manchette du *Elsaesser Kurier Freitag* den 12 Februar 1937.

Au souffle du rapide trouant la nuit, les points lumineux semblent fuir, éperdus.

Un jeu de plaques tournantes, d'aiguilles solides, le bruit se fait tonnerre. Une gare, violemment éclairée, jette dans le compartiment un bolide de clarté sitôt disparu.

1918-1937

Vingt ans d'injustices et d'insultes

par H. de REINACH

Ainsi, après dix-neuf ans de rattachement à la France, on est arrivé au triste résultat que l'Alsace soit une fois de plus obligée de rappeler la *France* au respect de sa parole. Lorsque nous disons « la France », c'est, en fait, plus exactement le « gouvernement français » que nous devrions dire, car c'est lui, le véritable parjure. Mais en droit, c'est bien la France entière qui est en cause, parce que l'engagement solennel de respecter nos libertés a été pris en 1915 par le généralissime Joffre et en janvier 1919 par le président Poincaré au nom de la France et non de quelque éphémère gouvernement.

Ceci situe de suite l'étendue du drame et ce qu'il a de profondément douloureux pour l'immense majorité des Alsaciens qui ne demandent qu'à vivre en bonne harmonie avec le reste de la France. Mais, hélas ! la fameuse distinction du « *pays réel* » et du « *pays légal* » est une monnaie qui n'a pas cours chez le simple. L'homme de chez nous qui ne connaît pas la vraie France — et comment la connaîtrait-il ? — la juge d'après ses représentants : donc gouvernement, fonctionnaires, compatriotes d'outre-Vosges établis en Alsace. Or, il a pu constater d'une manière générale jusqu'à présent, que tous les gouvernements qui se sont succédé n'ont, à peu d'exception près, pas compris, que les représentants locaux de ces gouvernements ne s'intéressaient guère à lui et d'ailleurs changeaient à chaque instant et que, par malheur, les Français des autres départements venant en Alsace comportaient trop souvent une fraction importante d'affairistes véreux venus là en exploiteurs. Comment dès lors s'étonner que le paysan, que l'ouvrier se dise parfois : « *C'est ça les Français ? Ils ne valent pas mieux que les Schwobes* ».

Aussi, nous les nationaux d'Alsace, avons-nous, dès le lendemain de l'Armistice, essayé de faire pénétrer dans l'esprit de la population la distinction entre la vraie France et la France officielle, mais nos efforts n'ont pas toujours été couronnés de succès. Et c'est précisément parce que nous savons que toute atteinte à nos libertés locales venant du gouvernement porte en même temps préjudice au prestige de la France que nous estimons de notre devoir d'être impitoyable envers tous ceux qui sont responsables de cet état de chose et cela dans l'intérêt même de l'unité française.

Et pour commencer, plus de monopole du patriotisme !

Dans les fourgons de l'armée française victorieuse faisant son entrée triomphale dans les villes de l'Alsace, heureuse et fière d'acclamer les vainqueurs, on a vu arriver des gens qui avaient passé la guerre en Suisse ou dans quelque coin de France, bien loin des tranchées et qui, devanciers du Front populaire, s'agitaient déjà en criant : « A nous toutes les places ! » Il n'y avait qu'eux qui connaissaient quelque chose aux affaires d'Alsace, ils s'insinuèrent dans tous les services du haut commissariat et se mirent à faire la chasse aux Boches et à alimenter les commissions de triage. Souvent, pour assouvir de petites vengeances ou évincer un concurrent futur, on expulsa de braves gens qui non seulement n'avaient rien à se reprocher, mais qui, quelquefois, avaient été jetés en prison par les Allemands pour francophilie ! Ah ! les vilains petits tripots auxquels on s'est livré, mais combien lucratifs !

(Suite en dernière page)

L'Insurgé, February 17, 1937, front page. Courtesy of Bibliothèque nationale de France.

This particular issue was almost entirely devoted to attacks on Blum, "the most baneful of the politicians we were fighting," as Monnier recalled years later.[153] The caricature materialized the horror felt by these far-right writers. It would have reminded *Insurgé* readers that in the face of antisemitic attacks, Blum had had to explain that he was truly French and that every citizen in France was, like him, the "son" of the nation.[154] In doing so, it stressed his alleged foreignness. In fact, the *Insurgé*'s editorial team—Maxence, Maulnier, Soupault, Blanchot, Haedens, and Richelet—published an insert "from six Frenchmen" who despised Blum and warned that he was responsible for the quasi-civil war raging in France.[155] To emphasize their point, a satirical version of the traditional folk song "La Carmagnole" (which they said had embodied the "revolt and hatred of those who are exploited") titled "La Blumignole" was offered to readers. Readers could sing that they "were an insurgent / of the Republic, of which Blum is the king / The pimp and his whore / we will get them."[156]

In the newspaper's pages, Blum was no longer the head of the left-wing coalition cabinet but the figment of far-right imagination, a fantastical figure coalescing all their fears and hatreds.[157] In their articles "Blum" was a corrupting agent of foreign powers: the capitalism whose "boots he licked"; communism, which was his "natural" state; and Germany, for whom, it was implied, he secretly worked.[158] He also embodied the evils of vulgarity and lack of style. He was foreign to a French culture that far-right critics wished to purify. For them he was neither French nor able to understand what made French civilization. How could any "national unity" come about around a man who did not possess an inch of "fiber of Frenchness"? asked Maxence.[159] Maxence had, the month before, called on brave men to "impose their will on a government of abjection, on a Jewish council president who can not claim for himself something which has been theirs from fathers to sons and generation to generation: French civilization."[160] "Blum" was the reminder of the disruption of the apparently "natural" transmission of French culture and traditions, which were essential for the nation—as they defined it—to emerge unscathed. "Blum" was the abject reminder of the fragility of the nation's boundaries and the perverted representation of the social body.

Their imagination of a nation compromised by external forces (socialism, communism), as well as internal dangers (impotent politicians, an illegitimate regime), and the nefarious consequences of modernity (capitalism, democracy) meant that the figure of the Jew had become the central actor of the nation's decadence and debasement, perverting the organic and natural relation that

PREMIERE ANNÉE. — N° 11. ★★★ PARAIT TOUS LES MERCREDIS 24 MARS 1937.

L'INSURGÉ

POLITIQUE ET SOCIAL

31, rue Caumartin, Paris-9e
Tél. : OPERA 29-51.

Le numéro : UN franc
C. C. P. 207.583. Paris

ASSASSINS, DÉMISSION...

Les victimes mystifiées

par Thierry MAULNIER

PLUS d'un ouvrier parisien est revenu pâle de honte, dimanche, de la cérémonie funèbre de Clichy.

On a vu souvent des politiciens exploiter des cadavres, se servir d'eux, les réquisitionner comme alliés politiques, s'en faire des tribunes ou des tremplins. On n'avait sans doute jamais vu escroquerie aussi cynique : les organisateurs et les instigateurs du massacre, les chefs de la manifestation et les chefs de la répression unis pour parader devant les cercueils.

Les morts ne savent pas se défendre, et l'on en abuse. Jamais pourtant des morts n'ont été plus magistralement dupés que les morts de Clichy, jamais des cadavres n'ont été victimes d'une escroquerie aussi scandaleuse : il a fallu atteindre MM. Auffray, Jouhaux, Thorez pour voir les morts servir de slogans publicitaires et de thèmes électoraux sur mesure.

Les manifestants de Clichy sont tombés parce qu'on leur avait menti : menti en leur présentant comme une menace fasciste une séance de cinéma ; menti en leur disant que tous ceux qui ne pensaient pas comme eux étaient des ennemis du peuple ; menti enfin en leur laissant croire qu'ils étaient les maîtres, et que tout leur était permis, pendant qu'on mobilisait la troupe pour tirer sur eux. On a menti dimanche encore, devant leurs cercueils : ils auront été mystifiés, ils auront été escroqués jusqu'au bout.

Dans la longue histoire des révolutions, il est assez rare de voir les mêmes hommes jeter au même instant dans la rue ceux qu'ils chargent de troubler l'ordre et ceux qu'ils chargent de le protéger ; il est assez rare de voir des manifestants fusillés par la police gouvernementale parce qu'ils ont obéi à l'appel lancé par le journal du chef du gouvernement : les chefs socialistes ont envoyé les manifestants à Clichy ; les chefs socialistes y ont envoyé les gardes mobiles. Le massacre a eu lieu sur rendez-vous.

(SUITE EN DERNIÈRE PAGE.)

DE LA C. G. T. A CLICHY

Quand les social-fusilleurs convoquent les frères des fusillés

Thorez, Jouhaux et Auffray ont osé parader devant le Peuple de Paris

A la porte Clignancourt, vers une heure l'équipe de l'*Insurgé* se retrouve près de la sortie du métro. La foule est dense. Nous sommes tous frappés par l'attitude [mé]caniquement morne des spectateurs. Les tâches sont distribuées : l'un de nous a un poste d'observation dans un appartement du boulevard Ornano, le second va filer sur Clichy, quant au troisième sa mission est la plus ingrate : il doit aller au devant du cortège et le remonter complètement en notant les incidents.

Ce sont nos notes, prises à la hâte, sous l'impression immédiate du moment, qui vont suivre.

Le cortège passe boulevard Ornano.

De la fenêtre où je suis, je domine la foule en attente. Mon impression du début se renforce : curiosité, sans plus. Les spectateurs sont venus là comme à un cortège ordinaire dans les rues de Paris. Fort peu d'insignes aux boutonnières. De-ci, de-là, des ilots de dix ou quinze inspecteurs en [ci]vil qui affectent de ne pas se dissimuler; c'est, du reste, le seul service d'ordre apparent.

Une rumeur vient de Paris, et soudain la tête du cortège débouche. J'observe les responsables de cette manœuvre de masse; la représentation parlementaire communiste est squelettique (une vingtaine de députés) les élus socialistes à peu près inexistants, mais ils ont tous un même visage apeuré et ennuyé. Je les regarde avec des jumelles :

Vaillant-Couturier essaye de hausser la tête; Jouhaux fume la pipe; Séverac, sans Brigitte, a l'air très isolé; Longuet, Paul Faure, Gaillard, se tassent pour se sentir moins seuls ; Cachin somnole en marchant; Thorez fait une moue très dictatoriale. Après eux vient la foule. Les hommes, les femmes défileront pendant plusieurs heures, mais absolument comme des fonctionnaires de la révolution en service commandé. J'ai vu l'enterrement de Barbusse, au moins là il y avait une mystique d'union, mais aujourd'hui la machine ne tourne pas rond... J'ai toujours plaisir à voir évoluer des masses, même pour des idées fausses, mais celles-là m'attristent, ce sont des moutons qui se pressent et qui ne sont même pas enragés. De-ci de-là, des groupes chantent une *Carmagnole* incomplète ou une *Internationale* anémique ; des cris de « Nous vengerons nos camarades ! » sont parfois assez bien rythmés... Pauvre Léon Blum qui n'êtes pas là pour voir comme cette foule vous aime !...

(SUITE EN DERNIÈRE PAGE.)

CAMARADES,

On fusille les uns.
On dissout les autres.

TOUS DEBOUT FACE AU RÉGIME!...

— Qui donc disait que je n'avais pas de sang français ?

HIER DU SANG, ET DEMAIN ?

par Jean-Pierre MAXENCE

I. DE BERGERY A L'INSURGÉ.

Gaston Bergery, qui a l'esprit critique développé et qui peut vous analyser une tragédie comme celle de Clichy avec l'aisance à demi cynique du conférencier à la mode, publie dans la Flèche *d'excellentes observations. En tout ce qu'elles ont de positif, on est prêt ici à les faire siennes. Que dis-je ? On les a devancées. L'édition spéciale de l'Insurgé disait déjà, quant à l'essentiel, ce que Bergery semblait découvrir deux jours plus tard. « Qui a tué ? Dans quelles conditions ? On peut espérer, écrit l'éditorialiste de la* Flèche, *que l'enquête l'établira. Pour aujourd'hui, je déclare que je n'en sais rien. Et tant que je ne le saurai pas, je me refuse à accuser d'assassinat les fascistes (qui peut-être n'y sont pour rien), la police (qui peut-être était en état de légitime défense) ou la masse populaire (qui avait été presque officiellement convoquée là). » Bergery voit juste mais manque de courage pour constater les évidences. A l'aide d'un peut-être ou d'un presque, il s'efforce de laisser passer la muscade tout en gardant l'allure d'un observateur intelligent. Nous ne l'avons pas attendu pour constater que les coupables n'étaient ni les membres du P. S. F., conviés à une paisible séance de cinéma, ni la police dont le rôle est d'assurer l'ordre, ni les travailleurs rassemblés devant la mairie à l'appel, mais oui, officiel, Bergery, du maire Auffray, du député Honel et du conseiller général Nalle. Cette mise hors de cause de Français trompés les uns et les autres était nécessaire. La* Flèche *l'a senti. On regrette pour elle et pour ses lecteurs qu'elle n'ait pu l'affirmer avec plus de franchise et de netteté.*

L'Insurgé, lui, l'a fait dès jeudi. Bergery ne trouvera pas dans notre édition spéciale une seule insulte, une seule attaque contre la foule dupée de Clichy. Sans doute, est-ce la raison pour laquelle, cette attitude le gênant, il nous attaque et nous accuse assez comiquement de faire « revivre l'abjection de certaines campagnes six-févriéristes ». Allons donc ! L'Huma, cynique et effrontée comme toujours, a pu désigner « les fascistes ». Nous nous sommes bien gardés, quant à nous, d'exciter nos amis contre les troupes communistes. Nous avons salué leurs morts, leurs pauvres morts qui sont nos frères. Il y a bien assez du gouvernement que soutient Bergery pour faire la sale besogne qui consiste à diviser les Français au profit des politiciens, à les dresser, membres du même corps, issus du même sang, les uns contre les autres alors qu'ils devraient se trouver tous unis face à un régime qui ne vit que de leurs divisions.

(Suite en deuxième page)

CATHOLIQUES

Contre le Capitalisme : OUI
Avec le Communisme : NON

La très importante, la décisive encyclique de Pie XI contre le communisme est nette. Toute collaboration des catholiques avec les communistes, athées et tenants d'un matérialisme, historique sinon métaphysique, est proscrite. Les Martin-Chauffier (de Vendredi) expliqueront cela à leurs lecteurs comme ils voudront. En sa pleine autorité, le chef de l'Eglise s'est prononcé. Il a motivé, expliqué, fortifié d'arguments, sa condamnation. Il sera, nous en sommes sûrs, entendu.

Que les partisans du libéralisme économique ne se hâtent point de prendre pour autant des allures de triomphe. En condamnant le communisme, Pie XI n'en dénonce pas moins les fautes lourdes du capitalisme, les erreurs foncières d'un régime où l'argent est roi.

Une doctrine sociale fondée d'abord sur la « justice », où la charité n'est que le couronnement de la justice, voilà celle que l'Eglise fait sienne. Elle n'est pas plus prête à pactiser avec les hontes et les scandales du régime présent, qu'à s'abandonner aux hontes et aux tyrannies niveleuses d'un régime marxiste envisagé comme futur.

L'Insurgé salue respectueusement cette encyclique libératrice. Il tient à souligner seulement qu'elle n'implique aucune reconnaissance des injustices actuelles, aucune louange adressée au paternalisme.

Les catholiques clairvoyants sauront reconnaître ceux qui, défendant la doctrine sociale qu'imposent la nature de l'homme et les conditions de la vie en société, défendent en même temps les valeurs catholiques.

Henri FALLIER.

L'Insurgé, March 24, 1937, front page. Courtesy of Bibliothèque nationale de France.

should exist between a citizen and his bounded community. It was the "Jew," that figure at once close and unassimilable, who was responsible for the passive impotence of the nation.[161] A Soupault caricature summed it up on June 25 as *L'Insurgé* commented upon the recent electoral results. While *L'Insurgé* explained that Doriot's defeat was not so much disappointment as further proof that "now even more, [we must] stand against the regime," Blum's resignation was given ample commentary in the editorials and in the drawing, which showed him dying in a coffin—an open bank vault.[162] "All" politicians were "rotten" and Blum's resignation, Maxence sarcastically wrote, was the occasion for a rather "melancholic funeral oration"; at least his tenure "as an imported Jew" had made visible the danger, corruption, and invasion of capitalism and foreign power.[163]

"Blum" was seen to be particularly dangerous because he was both an intellectual and a political representative, occupying the fields of literature and politics that far-right critics were intent on reclaiming. The denunciation of the Jew as "anti-artist" and foil to beauty and art was not a new occurrence. As art historian Mark Antliff has shown, Georges Sorel and Charles Maurras had commonly used that trope.[164] At the same time, "Blum" was both fascinating and repugnant, because he was either an "esthete"—decadent and effeminate—or a "hysterical" feminized figure (*Je Suis Partout* would also mine this gendered repertoire when portraying Jews).[165] For Monnier, "[his] long sickly sweet mare-like face with a muffled neighing, [and his] finely tuned elocution with growling inflexions all restrained me [in my anti-Jewish feelings] and even appealed to me. Because it was precisely this pleasure which worsened my hostility to the politician most dangerous for our country's future."[166] The repulsive pleasure was provoked by "Blum's" imagined femaleness. His feminized silhouette served as a reminder of the fragile masculinity they wanted to restore: neither woman nor man, he "gave the spectacle of an intelligence and culture perverted by the feminine nature of a great bourgeois woman [*grande bourgeoise*] who had escaped from the *Revue Blanche* and was trembling with emotion at the prospect of going to the people to appease his bad conscience."[167] Next to the hypervirile Communist Maurice Thorez, Blum embodied failed masculinity. Yet both tried to woo Marianne, the nation.[168]

"Blum" evoked a hysterical woman alien to the French people he was supposed to represent. With his "falsetto voice" and "cutely clenched fist," "his lacy cynicism, his nervous girl's tantrums that are spelled out with a hurt voice made him enunciate dismally irresponsible remarks."[169] Though feminized,

Blum's dangerously seductive appeal emanated from his power to lure proper French men into his clutches, thereby invoking the feared perversion of homosexual desire. Robert Brasillach gave *Combat* an impassioned letter addressed to "right-wing cuckolds" in which he explained that conservative politicians were just as despicable because cowardly. Their cowardice was the consequence of their inability to resist the seduction of "Blum." He described right-leaning Radical politician Henry Franklin-Bouillon as a man "obsessed by his own virility." It was obvious that "[Franklin-Bouillon] has accepted the denials that this oversexed gorilla [*gorille lubrique*] disdainfully granted him so that he can pretend to be a great man, an indefatigable male. When Blum returns, Franklin-Bouillon will fall in his arms rather than break his neck."[170] The "Jewish question" had found its embodiment in the frightening figure of "Blum," who perverted a proper masculine French citizenry. In *L'Insurgé*, antisemitism confirmed the need for insurgency and revolution.

Purifying the Nation: Some "Notes on Antisemitism"

Thierry Maulnier felt the "Jewish question" was significant enough to discuss in June 1938 in a long article published in *Combat*.[171] By then, *L'Insurgé* had folded due to lack of funds. Some of *Combat*'s most virulent journalists, Maurice Blanchot and Robert Brasillach, had left. Lucien Rebatet had edited a special issue of *Je Suis Partout* entirely devoted to the "Jewish problem" several months earlier in which the antisemitism was striking, even by the standards of traditional far-right and Maurrassian publications.[172] A few months after Blum's brief return as government head, Maulnier seemed to veer away from the kind of anti-Jewish rhetoric that he had participated in while at *L'Insurgé*. This article has been cited as evidence of his return to the fold of Maurrassian politics and to a public "split" from Brasillach, his friend and far-right companion, as well as from *Je Suis Partout*'s radical politics. Indeed, in this piece Maulnier wrote not in the tone of polemical invective but in the measured voice of the dispassionate and reasoned intellectual. On the surface, the essayist had left the polemicist behind.

Still, his "Notes on Antisemitism" seems to warrant more attention than it has been granted by historians. It was part of a series of three articles Maulnier penned in *Combat*, each titled "Notes on . . ." He had authored the first one in the second 1936 *Combat* issue "on Marxism," offering a critique of Marx, accusing him of "fetishizing" the social over "man."[173] In the piece he accused Marx of ignoring the true forces of history. Materialism could not explain everything: "gathering, organizing for one's defense, uniting through love-making, worrying about death" were social urges and should not be forgotten.[174] His piece on antisemitism came two years later, six months before his last "Notes," this time "on Fascism." In December 1938 he expressed disillusionment and criticism of Hitler and his regime, recognizing that "the great problem of the contemporary world is to organize the tremendous natural forces that man possesses for the first time in history in order [to bring about] a superior civilization and order."[175] But he chastised fascism's celebration of "instinct and violence" as the sole forces of history, just as he derided "authoritarian regimes censoring or burning books."[176] His condemnation was mostly focused on Nazism, and it was the Nazis' "antisemitic fury" that he berated (as well as fascist Italy's emphasis on marriage and reproduction as national duties).[177] It is important to note that here again, Maulnier began his article with his criticism of the Nazi regime's persecution of Jews. Antisemitism—that is, an obsessive focus on the nation defined *only* as biology and race—again was the main point of contention in his disagreement with Nazism (after Brasillach had publicly celebrated the "fascist spirit" in a series of three articles).[178]

In his June 1938 piece, Maulnier did not refute antisemitism but changed emphasis. He explained what he thought constituted "some of antisemitism's major characteristics, some of its justifications, and some of its dangers."[179] Couching his comments in abstract language, he first explained what he claimed should constitute antisemitism's strategic and philosophical uses, adding that he did not discard one or the other, as each could have its place. This was not a question of morality but of politics. Maulnier argued that antisemitism belonged to the realm of "myths" in the same manner that there was a "Freudian myth" and a "Marxist myth." But, he insisted, "the Jewish myth of antisemitism was an ancient one."[180] His article was ambiguous, with his silences and slippages just as telling as his assertions. Indeed, slipping from "myth" to "Jewish myth" when characterizing antisemitism implicitly displaced the burden and responsibility of antisemitic beliefs onto Jews—a well-known far-right cliché. His article did not refute antisemitism but only rejected a particular brand of it, which he framed within the context of his abandonment of insurgent politics. Furthermore, he asserted that antisemitism was a "myth" because it was based on two false yet related assumptions. On the one hand, it was based on a "vague yet profound and undeniable feeling of guilt: the Jew as a guilty race, as a morally inferior race." On the other hand, it relied on the "inferiority complex" experienced by the non-Jew in relation to the Jew: "The non-Jew would then always and everywhere be doomed to defeat when in the presence of the Jew."[181] This surprising psychological argument had the effect of reaffirming anti-Jewish rhetoric (and implicitly reminding readers of the many times Maulnier had called for a rejuvenation of a weakened French nationalism) while proclaiming to undo its logic. Similarly, his use of the singular "Jew" and "non-Jew" emphasized the ideological nature of these tropes, though all the while reiterating them.

Maulnier argued that antisemitism was primarily ideological, but, at the same time, he conceded that its ideological nature did not preclude it from being based in reality. Under the guise of his commitment to "realism" rather than "myth," he conceded that, in Western societies "Jews have a disproportionate influence and power compared to their numerical importance." He also explained that antisemitism's perennial existence had been possible because, "like communism, it provided an answer to *real* problems." The diagnosis had been correct. But, he clarified, the political remedy (communism, racial antisemitism) was misguided. To conclude, Maulnier reminded his readers that "this [criticism of the mythical nature of antisemitism] does not mean there is no Jewish problem."[182] Here, he implicitly recognized that there indeed did exist a "Jewish problem" (recognizing that invasion and contamination were not inventions) but insisted that the problem of Jewish presence and visibility within the national community should be thought through reasonably and rationally, in keeping with what constituted the French character, namely the ability to exercise reason.[183]

For Maulnier, it was not so much that antisemitism in itself was misguided as that it should be conceived of as a strategically useful model rather than a central motivation, or a totalizing discourse (as he accused Nazism of doing). The main issue was civilization, not ideology. He explained that the "Jewish question" could not be the sole driving ideological force of a nationalist politics, since it then only served as a mask for "reformism"—the symptom of parliamentary politics—produced an absurd politics, and, in its "vulgar" form, was "the refuge of many confusions."[184] In fact, Maulnier promoted here something resembling more the Maurrassian brand of antisemitism (*antisémitisme d'état*). As Brasillach would actually argue a year later, Maulnier called for an "*antisémitisme de raison*," but to different effect, since he refused any explicit appeal to a racial hierarchy.[185] This invocation of "reason" served different purposes. For Maulnier it meant not confusing the Jewish question, which was "historical," with its invocation as the sole origin of Western civilization's decadence. For him, an exclusive focus on Jewish domination and conspiracy evaded the central problem that was the true cause of decadence: the corrupt nature of the social body, the abject state of the nation, and the debasement brought about by capitalism, democracy, and the illusory quasi-religious embrace of totalitarian ideologies such as communism (even if, barely a year earlier, *L'Insurgé* had singled out Blum as the one who embodied abjection). He explained that, to French workers, "it did not matter whether [he] worked [for] M. Louis-Louis Dreyfus or rather for M. Renault or Michelin."[186] So, as Maulnier concluded, "the Jewish problem will find itself almost entirely resolved once the democratic State and mercantile society are abolished."[187] In 1938 Maulnier subsumed the "Jewish question" into the more pressing problems of the regime's illegitimacy, the corruption of capitalism, and the influence of socialism and communism in France. Antisemitism had not disappeared, but these other concerns took precedence.

Although Maulnier argued against the depiction of Jews as "demonic," "all-powerful," and "conspiratorial," he still subscribed to the traditional far-right and Maurrassian principle that Jews were foreign to the French nation. For him, it was a matter of avoiding the "domination of this *heterogeneous* element" that was ultimately "insurmountable."[188] All Jews were foreign and therefore unassimilable because they disrupted the harmony necessary for a unified nation. His position here contrasted with that of Action française, whose ideologues had always had a place for French Jews who were veterans of World War I. But for Maulnier, tainted with the oft-cited corruption of capitalism, democracy, and desire for a misguided revolution inspired by Marx, they could never belong.

Finally, according to Maulnier, a truly French antisemitism was neither "vulgar" nor German. It belonged to a French nationalist politics that still figured "the Jew" as that which threatened the national body and had to be expelled but that should concentrate on more pressing dangers. Maulnier's intimate belief was that French nationalism could not be founded within the realm of traditional parliamentary politics: in 1937 he and his companions had called for insurgency. In 1938, on nationalism, he advocated a "reasonable" position, a more moderate version of his revolutionary call which followed Maurras's injunctions but nonetheless never wavered from the commitment to a politics practiced outside of the regime, the law, and authority (as neither the Nazi regime nor

Je Suis Partout called for) that was embodied in a renewal of culture. In a 1938 essay Maulnier explained that obviously "the historic form of the nation is the only organized mode of existence of the human community in the West."[189] Restoring the plenitude of the nation meant preserving what made civilization. It meant thinking about the role of literature and, more especially, about how to formulate an aesthetics of politics that would contain such pervasive abjection and properly translate their fantasy of a whole social body, of a male subject made harmonious. In his mind, the privileged means to purification could be achieved through mastery of language and the restoration of French literature.[190]

Defining "Frenchness" as Aesthetics

How could the nation be reincarnated shorn of its abjection? How could the polity be embodied? The answer lay with literary figures who must engage in politics—a radically transformed politics. The enemies to be extirpated were materialism, communism, and capitalism because these forces threatened the boundaries and perverted the very nature of the French social body. Charles Mauban, one of *Combat*'s regular contributors, wrote: "It no longer suffices to know or even realize the political conditions of such a degenerate France, yet we must recognize that [France] must be rebuilt in each of us."[191] Those instances of degeneration could not simply be eradicated. Some form of regeneration was necessary. And for these young far-right intellectuals, "man" was a civilized creature and, as Maulnier had explained in one of his first published works, "civilization has been established through a long struggle against the nature of things."[192] Since the nation was depleted—a political issue—efforts to restore it involved not just revolution but a particular form of revolution that embodied French civilization—a cultural issue. Fantasies of the nation and of a male citizen were articulated around the ideas of culture, civilization, and literature.

Since politics and aesthetics were mutually dependent, aesthetics held a central place in the definition of a "new politics"—an indistinct and never defined category to which Young New Right critics nonetheless always appealed. They did not call for an aestheticization of politics but saw the aesthetic as the place for the political to be enacted. Neither should the aesthetic be politicized as such.[193] It went further, as they argued that the aesthetic must act as the site of regeneration and purity. This was necessary because they conceived of French citizenship as more than a question of political rights—rights they already possessed within the republican regime that they abhorred. French citizenship was made possible by the existence of a French civilization, in turn sustained by a culture that did not just emerge from republican schools but emanated from a particular French "essence." Culture was defined, following Maulnier, as the "means through which man dominates his masters, his circumstances, knows himself, and recognizes himself in what is essential about life."[194] The fate of Western (and European) civilization was at stake because these writers recognized that "beauty, cleanliness, and order obviously occup[ied] a special position among [its] requirements" and yet were now dwarfed by conflict and discontents.[195]

For them, "a civilized [man] was not just made up of a learned culture, but of a forgotten one, namely one incorporated into the intimacy of his being." And it was "this instinctive culture that must not disappear."[196] Culture and civilization were the products of both self-restraint and self-mastery, enabling the restoration of French masculinity.[197] It was clear to all that "culture is defined first and foremost as mastered (and dominated) culture."[198] The polysemous nature of the French word meaning "to dominate" reinforced the call for a masculine effort to master an idea coded as female. In the same way that an intellectual should be infused with culture but able to govern it, civilization was characterized by the "virile triumphs of the mind."[199] Maulnier defined the way culture should exist in his introduction to a critical monograph on Racine published in 1936. He explained:

> Racinian art is the most civilized because it is the most instinctive. Far from taking away from instinct in order to give back to intelligence, civilization represents a continuous enrichment of instinct and a constant addition to it. The civilized [man] is one for whom culture—that is the knowledge of the values and rules governing life—has become a life-style; he is a man whose entire being, and not just his intelligence, is shaped by his profound familiarity with beings, feelings and the very measures of man. [In short,] civilization educates intuition, [and] progressively incorporates the acquisitions of intelligence and sensibility from generation to generation.[200]

The aesthetics of a civilization depended on the cultural transmission from generation to generation: Maulnier held culture—and the capacity to produce the beautiful and the sublime—to be an undefinable yet essential possession that fathers passed on to sons in an unbroken filiation. For him, "inheritance is what is transmitted from fathers to sons, from the dead to the living, whether it be a biological, material, or cultural capital." He added, "It is therefore best honored by conservative thought for whom it constitutes continuity, the chain of generations, and is thus hated, or at least suspect in the eyes of revolutionary thought for whom it is the symbol—or worse, the instrument—of natural or social inequality."[201] A male genealogy of inherited taste and aesthetic appreciation alone guaranteed the distinctiveness of French civilization. Maulnier's belief in this conception of culture meant that as a far-right intellectual, he had to refuse democracy, socialism, communism, and reject Jews within the nation, since all conspired to uproot the filiation necessary for the survival of French culture.

In order to protect "this instinct of civilization, which, if not lost, is at least the first threatened for the present generations," Maulnier and his acolytes turned to literature as one of the privileged sites for cultural regeneration.[202] The realization in the wake of the postwar years that language was neither transparent nor immediate had gravely shaken the foundations for the possibility of a true culture.[203] A fantasy of wholeness was needed to oppose to the abject (the "Jew")—and this fantasy expressed itself in the desire to master culture and find its true essence in literature. They situated instinct not just in national culture (as *Je Suis Partout* would do) but more specifically in a fantasy of "literature." Literature offered a restorative space for the fragmented sense of self and alienation from the nation that these far-right critics experienced. They had identified the alienation of culture from politics and sought to reconcile the two: they were convinced that "in the aesthetic realm, in the political realm, the principles are the same."[204] This reflected Maulnier's fear of "internal turmoil" and his insistent return to the need for mastery, containment, and transcendence.

In the face of abjection, "literature," they hoped, would erase the vicissitudes of the divided subject. But only particular literary forms promised the fantasized return to a state before that unbearable division—which had been displaced onto the Jews and other internal enemies.[205] Historians and critics have noted Maulnier's particular love for a neoclassical aesthetics that for him—as for Maurras—held the greatest promise. As art historian Mark Antliff has aptly noted, "In the late 1930s Maulnier and the writers for *Combat* . . . like Sorel, . . . declared ethical violence to be beautiful and an expression of the sublime, and they likewise turned to Greek tragedy and classical civilization to discover the regenerative wellsprings of European culture."[206] Maulnier claimed that classical poetry and tragedy expressed the aesthetics that were capable of restoring the self and civilization to wholeness. He favored tragedy, especially Greek tragedy, as the most accomplished of literary forms. Only tragedy offered, in form and content, the possibility to transcend the contingencies of human life and thus embodied a universality of meaning. He held *Électre* to be a work that expressed the "ravages of the absolute."[207]

It was the seventeenth-century French playwright Jean Racine who, more than any other, epitomized literary achievement for Maulnier because "he unites within himself everything a civilization holds as irreplaceable, [and] that is most under attack, and whose remains we defend." In his works, Maulnier argued, Racine expressed "the essence and tragic immutability of man."[208] For that reason, "he is closest to us."[209] What made Racine the perfect epitome of civilization for Maulnier was the manner in which he achieved this. As literary scholar Mary Ann Frese Witt has noted, Racine was "'civilized' not because he represse[d] his violent instincts, but because he [gave] form to them."[210] It was the act of containment through language of the messy avatars of life, of man's instincts, and the violence that emerged that allowed the transcendence of abjection. That containment was made possible by a "severe" "rigor" and an "innate aptitude for the mastery of the most complex reality and the most burning fervor."[211] It was the perfect blend of Apollonian and Dionysian principles, of form and instinct, rigor and creativity, harnessed in one movement. Thus that harmonious blend produced "not the shapeless gangue of being" but something akin to "the incisiveness of the purest human metal."[212] These, Maulnier concluded, formed the "priceless treasures of Western culture" that his contemporaries must restore.[213] But Maulnier did not merely celebrate classicism in a nostalgic turn to a lost golden age. He was not just an anti-modern. His celebration also veered from Maurrassian classicism, as he was steeped in the literary turmoils and debates of his day. This became evident with the collection he published in 1939 that aimed to showcase the most striking representatives of French poetry.

If tragedy was favored by some as that which offered transcendence, for many of the Young New Right intellectuals poetic language itself represented the greatest form of literature, a genre able to produce a sense of the sublime, since poetic language was the only form allowing for solace and comfort. Poetry was described as the ultimate form of literature, for "a new civilization can emerge only in the light of poetry."[214] Again, Maulnier offered his reflections on the matter. His 1939 *Introduction à la poésie française* (Introduction to French Poetry) aimed to be a manifesto for the preservation of French culture, the definition of Frenchness, and the possibilities of the "rigorous order" of the poetic form—that most sublime form, according to him. Poetry exemplified the sublime because its "absolute intimacy coincided with the purest and most durable forms of language."[215] The register of purity and transcendence implied that poetry, in contrast to the abject features of French culture, offered an answer: it was a "purity filled with possibilities" and "crystal into which every man could gaze like Narcissus in order to love a figure unknown to himself."[216] In short, it offered the illusion of sameness unperturbed by the terrifying experience of individuation (castration, in psychoanalytic terms) and where attaining *jouissance* was believed possible—once difference was domesticated. Again, only certain poets could achieve this and Maulnier's selection did not just mirror Maurras's pantheon of beloved poets; it baffled some critics, especially his choice of sixteenth- and seventeenth-century authors. Next to Ronsard, d'Aubigné, Racine, and Corneille, Maulnier mentioned poetic works that Maurras had excluded from his own literary canon of Frenchness: some Romantics like Gérard de Nerval and Victor Hugo could be found. Maulnier also presented Baudelaire, Rimbaud, and Mallarmé and turned to Apollinaire, Valéry, and Cocteau.[217] Similarly, his narrative introduction devoted quite a few pages to surrealism as the one form of literary revolution he recognized but ultimately criticized. Strikingly, though, he ended his selection with Maurras himself.

The inclusion of Maurras was not innocent. This exposition of the best exemplars of French poetry was in fact a political act under the guise of aesthetic appreciation. Maulnier's own aesthetic choices allowed him to articulate a theory of literature that spoke of a particular conception of French taste, culture, and civilization—that is, of Frenchness. In his long introductory essay, Maulnier defined French poetry as the "assemblage of the most profound and most secret specificities."[218] Scholars have noted that he appeared to refute a narrowly nationalist vision of the French literary canon. He was not interested in finding commonalities among French poets as the means of defining something that was uniquely French. Yet he made a paradoxical argument: while he denied such an ideological operation, he devoted much of his essay to identifying some particular Frenchness that poetry translated. He argued that France's poetry, unlike that of England or Germany, tended to turn "not to mythology or history, but to an abstract and purified substance."[219] French poetry had always been concerned with constantly "purifying" itself and, as such, did suggest something about the French spirit.[220] It was not just that the "poetic act" was the "purest act of creation," but also that French poetry embodied a particular form of the sublime; this was why, he lamented in a brief interlude, France had lacked poets who "take up the responsibility of the nation and become the voice of the homeland," as Kipling had done for England and

D'Annunzio for Italy.[221] French civilization could be found in this "passion for purity."[222] For Maulnier, still in 1939, the aesthetics—in poetry—did function as a form of politics.

For Maulnier and his fellow intellectuals, only literature could provide a restorative peace in the face of the threats assailing the modern subject. It proved an especially auspicious arena for such restoration, as it allowed the (illusory) possibility of writing oneself as a political and intellectual subject. It is obvious upon reading *Combat* that, for them, the sublime emerged through the purity of form, enabling an aesthetics to emerge out of a knowledge that had been mastered.[223] Catholic literary critic René Vincent exclaimed in *Combat* that "style must rehabilitated," because "style is an expression of order."[224] Style and rigor were best embodied by literature. The performative nature of literature enabled the assumption of authorship through "aesthetic purification," the indispensable condition for an existence as a public figure of intellectual debates and a seeming—yet temporary—resolution to the alienation of the subject. The literary critic therefore held an especially significant place in this attempt to reconcile culture and politics. Jean-Pierre Maxence had laid out the role of the literary critic a few years earlier. He said "he" was

> an eternal man . . . that neither the University nor the State will manage to throttle nor get rid of. This man is hungry for beautiful fictions, he retains a taste for those myths that allow him to reach the deep recesses of intelligence; he possesses that sense of what makes great classical works, he can sense the ordered splendor from which beauty can escape time. He enters the subtle secrets that a delightful prudishness protects from the reach of fools.[225]

Being an intellectual therefore meant speaking both about culture (and especially literature) and politics. Only men acting as both political and literary critics could help define a different political order and restore the French nation: "Save the nation, save the nation's territorial, material and intellectual inheritance from possible invasion and increasing anarchy, remake a glorious and strong France."[226]

Conclusion

While they ultimately refused traditional antisemitism—a political solution—and "racist antisemitism"—a subjection to myth rather than reality—and proclaimed that only the aesthetic offered the much-needed "sublimating discourse" abolishing abjection, time, and historicity, the Young New Right could not articulate what their revolution would consist of.[227] They had proclaimed, in the second issue of *L'Insurgé*, that "a true revolution will renovate the broken thread of our history" and that this radical and complete overthrow "beyond the political and the social" would necessarily be "bitter and salubrious."[228] But that insurgent revolution, imagined in cultural and aesthetic terms, never fully materialized as politics. Having refused the road of conventional politics, they found that they could not translate their words into action, nor did they inaugurate a literary revolution. Their aesthetic choices had not substantially departed from those of their forefathers, Massis and Maurras. They merely returned to an all-too-familiar "classicism," even if inflected by contemporary concerns, and did not subvert style or content. Their fantasy was an impossible one that could never be enacted. Returning to wholeness unscathed by difference and the heterogeneity of modernity was a hopeless and empty desire. The Young New Right, though claiming novelty and youth, yearned for something forever lost. All they could do was to viciously denounce "their" Jewish enemy since that "true" and "authentic" France remained an unattainable myth. *L'Insurgé* died in October 1937, and the longed-for "new politics" born of literary sensibility never saw the light.

Combat outlasted the radical attempt at dissidence that *L'Insurgé* had been. But the Young New Right did not, in the next few years and until the outbreak of the war, echo the same violence nor find the same readership. The years 1938 and 1939 were devoted to familiar far-right themes, most strikingly to a far-right pacifism that warned in somber tones of the risks of an impending war. France's defeat and the emergence of the Vichy regime split the allegiances and friendships that had brought the Young New Right together. This time differences overrode "convergences" and affinities.[229]

Maulnier's trajectory is rather telling. He ultimately parted company with many of the more extreme and intransigent intellectuals of the far right. He returned to a more "conventional" far-right politics, writing in *L'Action Française*, devoting himself to theater, and, after 1945, contributing a regular chronicle to the conservative *Le Figaro*. Yet Maulnier seemed to have never fully renounced some of the fundamental principles that underlay his vision of the world in 1937. He never reneged on his anti-communism. In the post-Vichy years, he found society no longer haunted by the Jew, but he clung to a vision of the French nation that required imperial rule in order to affirm French civilization. Like others on the far right, he mobilized for the defense of "French

Algeria" and against Algerian independence.[230] Against the danger of decadence, he still maintained that nation and civilization were founded upon the liberatory promises of "literature" and guaranteed by the exercise of authority as the only condition allowing freedom to emerge: "Authority," he explained, "is not designed to bully or maim liberties for no reason, but to cure their insufficiencies, that is to help them bloom and survive."[231] Now an established right-wing figure, who received one of the most prestigious literary prizes in 1959 (Grand Prix de Littérature de l'Académie Française) and was elected to the French Academy in 1964, he spoke of the intellectual as the nonconformist and lucid prophet of his generation whose "judgments should be dictated by reason, and not passion, however generous that passion is."[232]

Above all, Maulnier still held that the intellectual should act within the public sphere of politics and literature because he alone could ensure that the truths needing to be told were indeed proclaimed loud and clear. For him,

> the intellectual—in its rightful meaning—is a man who chooses to question common sense and who accepts ready-made truths reluctantly. He knows reality demands a number of approaches that are often contradictory. He knows that the danger awaiting him in his quest for truth is what I might call conceptualization, [or] the dried up substitution of a pure idea for the content of lived experience.[233]

Ending his concise summary of the role of the intellectual, which echoed his many interwar articles, Maulnier wrote sternly: "Neither must he forget that as one devoted to the workings of intelligence, he may encounter some dangerous truths which may strike him as incompatible with his fellowmen's well-being, and that, at that moment, there will be for him a *cas de conscience*."[234] Forty years later, traces of his 1930s politics could still be found in his more "reasonable" conservatism. He had finally abandoned insurgency for the glories and comfort of theater and literature.

4

THE ABSENT AUTHOR

Maurice Blanchot and the Subjection of Politics

> If anything can save them [these moderates], if anything can save this country, it is the very violence of the disaster that will force French citizens to realize their own debasement and will bring out in them disgust for what they are.
>
> —Maurice Blanchot, *L'Insurgé*, 1937

When revered and "enigmatic" literary critic Maurice Blanchot passed away in 2003, numerous obituaries and reviews paid homage to the influential literary presence that had shaped the canon of the post-1945 literary world and whose traces could be found in the thought of Georges Bataille, Michel Foucault, and Jacques Derrida.[1] Blanchot's death was reported in words that stressed typically "blanchotian" themes: absence, silence, death, the impossibility of closure, the erasure of the author, and the role of literature in producing a possibility for "being." Obituaries and reviews, which frequently stressed how Blanchot's "biography was often no more than a bibliography," mentioned in passing his interwar journalistic and editorial work, alluding to the "taint" of some unspecified yet "scandalous" earlier political writings—a situation rendered more intriguing by the silence surrounding these throughout his life.[2] A journalist noted: "Blanchot's life was tainted by this initial 'fault,' his contribution to far-right publications during the 1930s. Their subsequent willful biographical omission was often interpreted as an evasion."[3] The question of Blanchot's politics has kept on returning, like the repressed that stubbornly resurfaces because it has never been fully worked through. It has haunted commentators who are eager to explain the shift in Blanchot's writings—from far-right journalist to champion of abstract literary criticism—and who call his particular ideological trajectory one of "radical refusal."

This "original taint" has elicited numerous debates among commentators and critics—though rarely among historians of that period. Recently, literary scholars have addressed Blanchot's political engagement more directly, especially with the publication of his postwar letters, articles, and chronicles on the subject of politics.[4] While more is being written on his interwar political chronicles, it is now known that, as noted Blanchot scholars Leslie Hill and Michael Holland Hill have said, "Blanchot after 1945 remained profoundly engaged, often in unexpected ways, in his epoch."[5] Why then return to the "scandal" haunting the figure of Blanchot? Whether youthful mistake, original sin, or shameful indifference, Blanchot's political and literary trajectory speaks to the complex and paradoxical nature of the 1930s, a period too often subsumed under the weight of the two world wars and the specter of Auschwitz—a specter Blanchot himself often referred to, taking his cue from philosopher Theodor Adorno, in order to affirm that "every story will now forever be before Auschwitz."[6] Maurice Blanchot has unfailingly been described as a mysterious and unique literary reference. Like that of the infamous novelist Louis-Ferdinand Céline, made scandalous by his vitriolic antisemitic pamphlets, Blanchot's work presents a particular conundrum for his readers: how might we explain, and make sense of an author who was once an unabashed far-right journalist and a great literary figure whose intellectual influence remains to this day? How do we account for the ways in which Blanchot's conservative nationalist "sentiments took their ugliest turn in his writing for *Combat* and *L'Insurgé* between 1936 and 1938"?[7] Those who have attempted to tackle this issue are still too often accused of being "polemical."[8] In fact, Blanchot's own trajectory embodies the inseparable relationship between aesthetics and politics, culture and ideology, that obsessed so many 1930s writers and critics, and that has yet to be fully historicized.

Blanchot remains mostly invisible to historians. While writings of the 1940s and the immediate postwar have been discussed and analyzed by literary critics, historians, especially those of 1930s politics and culture, remain largely silent on the issue.[9] Unlike several literary scholars, historians have mostly avoided a convincing and coherent narrative of Blanchot's political positions and literary achievements. Even while they concede that he played an important part in some of the period's magazines and newspapers—*Le Journal des Débats*, *Le Rempart*, *Aux Écoutes*, *Combat*, *L'Insurgé*—and "outbid his colleagues in sheer venom," he rarely appears as a prominent character in studies of the period.[10] As author and journalist, Blanchot does not easily correspond to the ready-made categories that have usually infused the intellectual and political history of twentieth-century France. Unlike identifiable characters such as the "Nazi dandy" Pierre Drieu La Rochelle, or the "Collaborator" Robert Brasillach, he cannot be located in a traditional political history whose paradigms provide little space for puzzling and complex figures, especially if they hold an uncontested place within the literary canon.[11] The case of Blanchot's interwar politics disrupts traditional (political) categories of history and the way historians address the seemingly transparent and self-evident relationship between aesthetics and politics. That particular political trajectory—from antisemitic far right to anticolonial left, as it has been told far too simply—in turn asks how we may historicize such figures and account for the ways literature and politics were intimately tied together in this decade and then resonated beyond it.[12]

Blanchot was especially emblematic of the Young New Right intellectual movement concerned with the restoration of "man" (the individual and the citizen) the social body, and the nation—all of which were perceived to be in crisis. Blanchot's interwar writings may therefore be read as attempts to address the urgent and pressing question of this "decentered self."[13] If the self was no abstract entity but needed to be embodied and properly sexed in order to provide a stable origin for the social body, how could the nation then be experienced as the emanation of every citizen? How might the nation—understood to be the (metropolitan) embodiment of civilization—be preserved in integrity and substance? How might unassimilable difference and heterogeneity be erased in order to restore the organic relationship between the nation and its citizens? Most of his 1930s journalism addressed that dilemma.[14]

Blanchot's youthful interwar writings were instrumental in shaping a discourse of the nation, its substance and borders, haunted by the figure of an "other," and in articulating an obsession with the way the subject can emerge undivided and in harmony with the social body—concerns that far-right writers like Thierry Maulnier, Jean-Pierre Maxence, and Jean de Fabrègues also addressed.[15] Politics and literature were the site where Blanchot worked through his possible answer to the crisis of subjectivity, self, and nation, and his relation to the difference which became associated with Jewishness. Like the Young New Right intellectuals he was close to (albeit for a few years only, in the late 1930s), he attempted then to find a resolution to a seemingly untenable political situation, that of interwar France perceived to be in the throes of a cultural and moral crisis. This enduring concern with otherness, difference, the sovereignty of the subject, and the impossibility of community provided themes that would preoccupy Blanchot throughout his entire career. While he returned to the questions after 1945, he would always do so obliquely, his writings tainted with shame and guilt after Auschwitz—the shame of his 1930s writings.

The Critical Impasse of Blanchot's Politics

Blanchot's 1930s and early 1940s writings have elicited controversial debates among commentators. These debates have echoed the scandals of the Heidegger and Paul de Man affairs as they confront the urgent questions that arise for those who must address the legacy of an incommensurable genocide and the manifest failure of modernity.[16] And these debates have, once again, had to pose the question of the meaning of a (philosophical and literary) canon, the relationship between politics and aesthetics, whether knowledge can remain outside of history, and how that relationship was envisaged in the twentieth century.[17] Rather than tracing Blanchot's writings within the confines of a genealogy of modernist and post-structuralist thought (an effect of dehistoricization), or stressing the "scandal" of his interwar political writings (an effect of simplistic overhistoricization), I argue that reading Blanchot historically means eschewing a defense of his interwar writings and emphasizing instead the particular ways in which his writings were produced within a fraught cultural and political moment, that of 1930s far-right endeavors to redefine the male subject, the social body, and the nation, and the ways the aesthetic realm of "literature" offered a *political* solution to these young far-right intellectuals.[18] It is imperative that we consider the important place of Blanchot's earlier writings in allowing for his postwar emergence as a presence haunted by otherness and Auschwitz. To reiterate his singularity and uniqueness ignores the historical contingency that produced his writings. Tracing a genealogy of his writings—not one concerned with the identification of a single origin to his literary ideas but instead one concerned with the different guises in which his obsessions reworked themselves—resituates his work within a history of reflections as to the place of the intellectual, the role of literature in the delineation of politics, and how we, contemporaries, might understand that relationship. Historicizing in this way does not deny Blanchot's "singular force and compelling originality" but asks how silence and displacement, rather than repression, have obscured a historical understanding of this literary figure.[19] Without providing a fictive unity to Blanchot the journalist and writer, it allows the identification of themes that he circled in the interwar years and the ways in which they were subsequently echoed throughout his postwar works.[20] There are no clear ruptures in Blanchot's thinking, but rather an incessant reworking of familiar themes, namely the possibility for the subject to come into being and its relation to otherness. (One might explore his committed anticolonial stance, opposition to de Gaulle, and enthusiasm for May '68 in light of his interwar concern for the nature of the French nation, opposition to the state's power, reflections on the substance of the law to found the individual and society, and call for radical refusal and insurgency.) Blanchot is both exemplary of the far-right group he belonged to and simultaneously fascinating for the ways in which he then negotiated his political positions after 1940. It is in the traces within his writings that historians may understand his political and aesthetic position and the ways he embodies the complexities of the twentieth century. Yet Blanchot's prose is rarely historicized, and Blanchot himself always refused to grant historicity to his writings. Not only have his interwar writings been decontextualized, but attention to the context in which they were produced has been repeatedly ignored—or simply misunderstood—by his readers.

Since Blanchot was never an uncomplicated apologist of antisemitism, analyzing the ways in which anti-Jewish sentiment reflected his understanding of the French nation demands a more nuanced reading of the work of politics as it may appear in both the form and the content of his 1930s journalism. The difficulty in speaking about Blanchot's politics has been best illustrated by the controversy surrounding the revelation by literary critic Jeffrey Mehlman in 1982 of Blanchot's antisemitism, which has, since then, been the subject of much debate and harsh criticism, despite its pertinence.[21] Still, for many critics, "that Blanchot has written some antisemitic sentences is undeniable." These antisemitic remarks are usually the same ones cited over and over in various studies, only to be quickly dismissed as irrelevant to his literary writings.[22] Blanchot himself never admitted to any antisemitic content nor any far-right ties, but alluded to his youthful texts in a letter to friend and critic Roger Laporte when he confessed, "People reproach me with good reason."[23] In fact, Blanchot never addressed his interwar writings except within the confines of personal correspondence to friends whom he asked to "bear witness" for him.[24] He never addressed such issues in his public writing—thereby denying any importance to this question which he symbolically relegated to the realm of private concerns.[25] That particular issue has thus systematically been treated, by Blanchot and critics alike, as marginal, a biographical curiosity. They are strategies exemplary of the desire to exculpate Blanchot as "great author" and, one might argue, preserve the literary canon.

To dismiss these infamous interwar utterances, biographical explanation has been cited more or less successfully, stressing his lifelong friendship with

Jewish philosopher Emmanuel Levinas. Similarly, his role as journalist and editor for Paul Lévy's conservative and satirical *Aux Écoutes* and *Le Rempart* is invoked to disprove any suspicion of antisemitism.[26] More importantly, Blanchot's role in saving Lévy from arrest in November 1940 and his help in hiding Levinas's wife and daughter in 1941—which were brought up by Lévy and Levinas rather than by Blanchot himself—are mentioned in order to exculpate him.[27] Too often, though, critics forget to mention that Blanchot contributed to *Le Rempart* and a few other publications alongside the usual coterie of young far-right intellectuals, from Jean-Pierre Maxence to Thierry Maulnier.[28] Critics have also claimed that he has been (unfairly) judged guilty "by association": writing in far-right newspapers such as *Combat* alongside openly far-right and antisemitic figures like Robert Brasillach, they argue, does not make him suspect, nor should it overshadow the significance of his thought,[29] especially since Blanchot has always strenuously invoked his dislike of Brasillach.[30] Similarly, critics minimize these antisemitic comments by emphasizing how limited they are. His biographer remarks that "only two" antisemitic remarks can be clearly identified.[31] One can observe a striking disingenuous literalness in critics' reading of Blanchot's "alleged" antisemitic remarks: in an otherwise excellent critical work on Blanchot, Leslie Hill writes:

> What is most startling of all about the accusation that Blanchot himself professed antisemitic views in the 1930s is that, to date, no evidence or any real substance has ever been produced to support it. At most, the charge rests on a particular interpretation of no more than four articles published by Blanchot between 1936 and 1937. In two of these cases . . . what is at issue are two blunt, even crudely polemical references to the reckless impatience—as Blanchot saw it at the time—of those Jewish émigrés to whom Blanchot refers, with peremptory violence as "unbridled Jews" . . . who, in 1936, wanted to declare immediate war on Hitler, irrespective of the chances of success or the human cost of such a policy. Elsewhere, there is a limited number of passages in *L'Insurgé* that it is possible to read as drawing to some measure on some of the standard themes of antisemitic invective . . . although, in the context in which the phrase appears, it is more immediately apparent that Blanchot is condemning Blum for his internationalism and support for the Soviet Union rather than make capital out of his Judaism.[32]

Hill's argument is characteristic of readings of Blanchot's journalistic writings: either invoking the weight of history or denying the burden of proof under the guise, once again, of historical faithfulness. Such literalness focuses on the actual presence of the word "Jew" in order to determine the probability of Blanchot's antisemitism. It explains his obsessive "hatred" of Léon Blum as a manifestation of his anti-communism (a common far-right passion in the 1930s) rather than considering these attacks as motivated by a desire to denounce French Jews, Jewishness, and Judaism—the embodiment of otherness and heterogeneity within the nation. It stresses the artificiality of rhetoric. Scholars explain that rhetorical flourishes and violence (or "excesses") were typical of the far right and therefore could hardly be taken at face value, nor seen as possessing any true content.[33] It minimizes whatever dubious remarks may have been made—almost accidentally—as a means of domesticating any attempt to complicate Blanchot's genealogy.

Stressing the limited presence of antisemitic comments reveals a narrow conception of the political and ignores the larger context in which Blanchot wrote. It also misreads the way politics and aesthetics were inseparable in Blanchot's vision of the world and underscored his interrogation into the meaning of literature and his search for an authorial self. Importantly, Blanchot did not write in a vacuum. His journalism was produced within the larger 1930s context of a "racial grammar," where references to Blum and Benda were not innocuous but were instead charged with a specific right-wing nationalist meaning.[34] National borders were a constant preoccupation, as was the presence of those deemed "other": foreigners, refugees, immigrants, but also colonial subjects. As the decade unfolded, Jewishness came to stand in for that otherness.[35] Not only did Blanchot occasionally and explicitly write disparagingly of Jews but, more importantly, the figure of the Jew came to symbolize in his journalistic prose the fraught relationship between the self and the nation, offering an explanation for the state of abjection he had identified. Counting the number of explicitly antisemitic words and references cannot be the sole measure of Blanchot's writings. We must read the themes, issues, and rhetorical gestures that he made within the context of his far-right journalism and ideology—and especially his contributions to *Combat* and *L'Insurgé*. The obsession with the "Jew" that appeared in 1937, especially after the Popular Front election, constituted the expression of a larger anxiety about the status of French citizen and subject motivating his interwar writings. Like his fellow far-right companions, Blanchot was concerned with the fate of the fragmented male subject. The question of his antisemitism cannot be historicized unless it is framed by an understanding of the ways in which the French nation and civilization were essential to this generation's definition of citizenship and a recognition of how the late 1930s marked a moment when most of these intellectuals focused their energies on the question of an unstable, abject subject whose fate might be resolved only by a turn to some form of aesthetics and radical revolution. Ultimately, though, in the face of abjection, the emergence of a fully autonomous being might be possible only through language. For Blanchot (as for Maulnier), literature enabled the disciplining of language (that which produces meaning), allowing the author to master a world in which the body and its vicissitudes could be erased, while the self could transcend its unstable nature and coherency could be given to the male subject.

Far-Right Journalism in the 1930s

When Blanchot became an active and prolific Parisian journalist and occasional literary critic, immersed in the world of the far-right press, his writings could hardly be singled out from those of the like-minded energetic intellectuals of the Young New Right. Like many other Young New Right writers, Blanchot belonged to a provincial bourgeois family. Born in 1907, he had studied philosophy and German in Strasbourg. His biographer suggests he probably then read Heidegger's philosophy in German. It was then that he met Jewish philosopher Emmanuel Levinas, who later recalled that they had become friends "in spite of [Blanchot's] political positions."[36] Blanchot moved to Paris in the early 1930s, where he briefly studied psychiatry and neurology at the Sainte-Anne hospital; he completed a philosophy thesis for the Sorbonne but soon became involved in one of the most promising far-right intellectual groups, in which he actively participated for the better part of the decade.

Blanchot joined the charismatic Thierry Maulnier, Catholic intellectual Jean de Fabrègues, and the iconoclastic Jean-Pierre Maxence. He first contributed to Jean de Fabrègues's *Réaction* in 1932 and, from 1933 to 1935, to its later incarnation, *La Revue du XXe Siècle*. Through his involvement in these rather obscure yet intellectually vibrant publications, Blanchot found his way to the heart of this group of young far-right intellectuals. He began writing short editorial pieces for the right-wing and nationalist *Journal des Débats Politiques et Littéraires*—where he would remain for the next twelve years (where Maxence was also a journalist)—and contributed to conservative newspapers like the satirical antiparliamentary and anticapitalist *Le Rempart*, owned by Paul Lévy—where he again wrote alongside Maulnier and Maxence.[37] Blanchot was therefore at once journalist, editor, and literary critic: he published both political and literary criticism, dividing his attention between reviews of fellow conservatives and far-right radicals and reflections on international politics.[38] But it was mostly in the Young New Right publications that Blanchot simultaneously and most fully developed his political voice *and* his literary voice—they, more often than not, echoed one another.

Blanchot had, since 1931, devoted himself to the denunciation of that which "uproot[ed] civilization and society," in keeping with that generation's obsession with attacking the forces of modernity.[39] The desire for a radical oppositional politics, which the Young New Right had inherited from Maurras's Action française, found its most glaring expression in Blanchot's contribution to two of the group's most prominent journalistic enterprises, the monthly intellectual magazine *Combat* and the 1937 polemical broadsheet *L'Insurgé*. Blanchot was a constant though not necessarily prolific contributor of political articles to *Combat* from February 1936 to December 1937. But *L'Insurgé* proved to be the place to which most of his energies would be devoted—albeit for a very short period—inaugurating weekly columns on both international and domestic affairs, as well as being the author of *L'Insurgé*'s only literary chronicle. It was the place where, according to a fellow *Insurgé* journalist, Blanchot was moved by "indignation" to become a "violent polemicist" who "never compromised."[40] Blanchot belonged to the editorial team and appeared prominently in the newspaper as one of its most powerful voices.

Blanchot set the tone in his inaugural contribution to *Combat*, in which he evoked the specter of revolt. It seemed obvious to the *Combat* journalists that in February 1936 "the inheritors of the post-war insurgents" needed more than "pious commemorations."[41] Like Maulnier and Maxence before him, in the face of corruption, incompetence, and cowardice Blanchot called for an unspecified revolt that involved breaking from traditional politics and bringing down the regime in the hope of a "true peace."[42] Blanchot's articles consistently denounced an illegitimate government, impoverished politics, an endangered culture, and an inauthentic nation "in the interest of revolt."[43] In this, Blanchot carried on the statements he had made in 1931 in the *Journal des Débats*, where he warned that a "government's bad politics helps revolution."[44] In 1936, he was no longer content to call for an indeterminate revolution. Most of his articles ended with a call to violence and insurrection—not literally "Terror," but the power of radical, oppositional, and external forces, that of true nonconformist "dissidents."[45]

To embrace insurgency, one had first to realize the dire ruins in which the French nation and its citizens found themselves, and then fight the "false ideas and dangerous passions" that were leading them astray.[46] Such was Blanchot's task. In so doing, he turned to the issues and vocabulary familiar to the far right, which other newspapers also peddled. He described a decadent France, whose culture was in danger of disappearing and whose political representatives lacked legitimacy and authority. His political chronicles systematically explained that decadence had irredeemably taken hold since the end of World War I.[47] Like many at *L'Action Française*, he indignantly mocked the parliamentary weakness of the Third Republic. On the question of French involvement in the Spanish conflict that dominated the news, he denounced the "comedy played to the French people by Communists before bewildered Radicals and terrified Socialists, which provides one of the most degrading spectacles one could imagine."[48] His articles, unsurprisingly, derided the warmongering of "foreign" Soviet Russia and the demise of the current "regime which had monopolized France and which has obstinately tended to serve anti-French interests."[49] He decried the state of the nation, which, for him, had lost its former prestige and dignity.

The motif of decadence, a classic far-right complaint, constituted the leitmotiv of his political chronicles, emphasizing the demise of French culture, the persistence of impotent politicians, and the need for a new social order. He relentlessly traced the descent of the French nation from "stupidity" to "decadence." Already in 1931, Blanchot had criticized what he deemed to be Mohandas Gandhi's "corrupt" and "foreign" spirituality in a barely veiled echo of Henri Massis's imperial defense of Western civilization against "Eastern" influences.[50] Blanchot was, however, increasingly lamenting France's loss of status as a grand European nation. His articles consistently displayed an interest in foreign affairs, international diplomacy, and France's role in Europe and the world, especially in the face of Hitler's policies and the wake of the Spanish Civil War. In fact, these topics formed the bulk of his *Combat* journalism. French decadence was obvious when one examined its foreign policy: he berated the "Franco-Soviet pact" as an "immense trick that exposes [France] to war."[51] After mocking those "moderate" politicians who were "both delighted and frightened by Hitler's monotonous howls—as they would be by rather loud obscenities," he warned that "stupidly admiring Franco while some are betraying the [French] nation" was "boring" and "rather disgusting."[52] He was "horrified" to witness both "the regime's inertia and French people's indifference to the fact that Germany is getting ready to rattle and undermine *our* empire with its colonial claims."[53] Blanchot repeatedly denounced the inability of ministers and politicians to revive and sustain a true French nationalism. The fate of the nation had never been so much at stake.

And like his fellow Young New Right contributors, Blanchot diverged from the traditional Maurrassian-inspired argument that still upheld the glory and reality of an authentic France as opposed to the artificial legal regime. That rhetoric on decadence had always evoked the illusory memory of a golden age in order to promise its readers the possibility of a restored future.[54] Blanchot, though, systematically and loudly argued that debasement was irreversible. Proof lay in the ways the regime and the nation were viewed by European neighbors. He explained that, contrary to many French people's beliefs, "the truth is rather different, as it is obvious that we are today one of the most despised and degraded people of the world."[55] Those who believed France could escape decadence were deluded.[56] Decadence affected everything: it was cultural, political, and social, tied together in the expression of the nation's decline and its members' disorientation.

Convinced of the irreversible effects of decadence, Blanchot inaugurated in his first *Insurgé* article a theme he had begun developing in *Combat*—the need for French people to finally see their nation for what it was, since this affected every single one of its citizens who remained "indifferent" and oblivious.[57] The structure of Blanchot's narrative was important: in those instances, he invoked a fate and burden he held in common with other French (male) citizens. He was also himself implicated in the decadent state that he berated. Blanchot thus warned his readers: "There is no greater danger for us than our decadence."[58] For him, "we will not have to darken our image, we will only have to see how others see us."[59] And, he maintained, there was nothing to be proud of. France was despicable and the French people should despise their nation for its current state. That meant they should also despise themselves. What was at stake was not decadence but its irreversibility symptomatic of the abjection of the nation: France had been made "unreal."[60]

Otherness and the Nation's Abjection

Blanchot both borrowed from and helped shape the Young New Right's rhetoric. His writings helped displace decadence, disgust, and abjection onto figures that were held to be both cause and consequence of the political and cultural impasse of French civilization. This displacement transpired in the ways in which he spoke of contemporary politics. He was most concerned with the reigning disorder of the world that had left politics "strangely confusing and worrisome."[61] The place of France within a world order especially preoccupied him. As a staunch proponent of anti-German French nationalism, Blanchot explained that he feared the unabashed anti-fascism that had, according to him, mistakenly led the French to vociferously condemn and oppose Hitler. Such a position—also derided by Maulnier—risked war with Germany and depleted any hope of providing substance to French nationalism. Even French colonies were at risk, a worrisome turn since they alone might restore the nation.[62] Those who were responsible were "revolutionaries and emigrant Jews [who] were ready to do anything to bring down Hitler and end all dictatorships."[63] In short, "Communists" and "Jews" were dictating France's foreign policy from within. Impotent politicians were guilty of sustaining this state of affairs, since they were unable to recognize the presence of such alien interests. They misused "the profound preoccupation seeking to maintain the country in its integrity."[64] The nation's wholeness and greatness were the crucial issue. In 1937, after almost a year of Popular Front government, he bemoaned the current "intellectual disorder and social breakdown."[65]

Underneath these familiar complaints, what Blanchot lamented was the "state of dissolution in which *we* find ourselves."[66] The decadence of the nation had materialized the loss of the social body's integrity. Dissolution meant that the individual could no longer exist: "One must realize that French opinion is currently being dissolved into a terrifying confusion."[67] The lack of French popular will or desire revealed the demise of national spirit. Frenchness—usually incarnated by the social body—was at stake, since "betrayal is no longer just external to our country, localized to some other rotten nation. It has penetrated more deeply. It has almost altered our substance."[68] That betrayal (presumably enacted by those neither truly nor authentically French) had not only penetrated the metaphorical body of the nation, revealing that the nation's boundaries could be easily traversed, but had contaminated what made up the nation, its very substance. Blanchot explained that, as a result of living "with a regime riddled with gangrene, France has been contaminated and lost any notion of what it is as well as the possibility of returning to what it must be."[69] The evocation of "contamination" and the rhetoric of disease were especially powerful. It had figured obsessively in Louis-Ferdinand Céline's bleak and pessimistic denunciation of modernity in his novel *Voyage au bout de la nuit*. It also figured in far-right vocabulary. Here, it further points to the organic nature of the nation while presuming that it had once existed as a pure, homogeneous, and untainted entity—a logic essential to the belief of far-right critics that France must be reinvented. Blanchot stayed within the familiar themes that the Young New Right expounded in the mid-1930s. What that meant for him was that "France no longer lives in the regime, the state, or mores." In Maurrassian fashion, he added it was now "neither legal . . . nor real."[70] It was "absent."[71]

The corruption of the social body and the contamination of the nation were terrifying prospects, as they revealed the fundamental fragility of the self—or how the subject was understood to exist socially. The self, according to far-right logic, was bound to the nation in an indissoluble manner. Young New Right writers had explained it often: nation and self were supposed to echo one another in unbroken harmony. But if the nation was compromised, would that not be experienced by every member of the nation? If the nation had once been "pure," what needed to be done in order to restore what had presumably been lost? For *L'Insurgé*, this was especially so after 1937, since the Popular Front visibly marked the difference and heterogeneity that allegedly characterized the nation. Blanchot's vision of a nation now enslaved, and his obsession with its "substance," which supposedly infused the being of every citizen, suggested that the subject's borders were constantly threatened. This led only to *abjection*, the favorite motif of the Young New Right and the theme most explicitly articulated by Blanchot. Abjection was not merely the affective response to a political situation. It held a metaphysical weight. It was obvious to these young men that there was "an imperative of demarcation that [was] subjectively experienced as abjection," since abjection—which, according to its theorist Julia Kristeva, is "above all ambiguity," that which troubles the illusion of unity and wholeness—acted as the reminder of the subject's impossibility, the fragility of its borders and one's unbearable lack in the face of the law.[72]

Like Maulnier, though perhaps even more starkly, Blanchot parted here with traditional Maurrassian politics as he expounded a vision of the French nation as irredeemably corrupted at its very core and explained that "we believe—because we are afraid to see the truth—that foreigners religiously make the distinction between the [French] regime and the nation. This would be most pleasant and convenient. But it is wrong."[73] France was not merely subjected to outside forces, but if the nation was tainted, French citizens' own identification with the social body meant that they themselves would also be contaminated and threatened by this pervasive abjection. Blanchot dedicated himself to the revelation of such a state in an *L'Insurgé* article devoted to "French abjection." Indeed, "we" are the abject, asserted Blanchot, because we agree to participate in an abject nation:

> As long as we have not understood this degradation, as long as we have not realized the disgust that we inevitably arouse in healthy nations, as long as we have not felt for ourselves the disdain we should have toward a nation that surrenders, there will be no hope of transforming France into anything else but a decadent state threatened by servitude.[74]

Paradoxically, it was not only that everyone was also contaminated in their very being but that one needed to "feel for oneself"—in short, experience in quasi-bodily terms—this state in order to realize what must be done. This problematic identification put the responsibility of such degradation on the shoulders of the French people themselves. There was no doubt, for Blanchot, that the "government had added its particular abjection to our own weakness."[75] Since the nation "no longer was," Blanchot insisted that "the French people" must surrender the illusion that "they are more than they really are." This delusion of political and cultural greatness inherited from a "historical pride" was merely a veil for the people's "passivity" and absolute "nothingness" and a "screen to their degradation."[76] No politics could escape the realization that they were no longer what they had been.

This all-encompassing and inescapable abjection meant that, for every citizen, the self was experienced as alien.[77] This alienation was experienced in bodily terms; it was not just metaphoric. Like other Young New Right intellectuals in *Combat* and *L'Insurgé*, Blanchot returned to the pervasive feelings of disgust and nausea. Did not abjection produce unbearable repugnance? After all, he explained, "We cannot look upon a people become insensitive to its conditions for living without nausea, as [that people] is incapable of sensing the abyss into which it is falling."[78] Time and time again, Blanchot repeated that he—and others—simply "thought this state of mind," namely the inability to face one's and the nation's abjection, "is disgusting."[79] As a result, he insisted that "everyone must be obsessed by the mirror of their shame."[80] Shame was indeed all-pervasive: it was the natural outcome of "French dishonor."[81] It emerged as the direct consequence of Blanchot's figuration of decadence in bodily terms. The irrepressible feelings of shame and disgust demanded a search for a stable identity, as French citizen and in relation to language in order to effect a "sense of stable contour."[82]

L'ABJECTION FRANÇAISE

REQUISITOIRE contre la France

UN RÉVOLUTIONNAIRE PEUREUX

Feu sur Léon Blum !

par Kléber HAEDENS

LE NOUVEAU MONDE

Ces Messieurs Dames

par Lucien FARNOUX-REYNAUD

L'AFFAIRE MORIZET

MOTS HISTORIQUES

A la POUBELLE «CONFESSIONS»!...

On embauche à la Jeune Garde...

La révolution des Soviets, c'est la mort des autres

LES TROIS ECHECS DE LA FRANCE...

A NOS CAMARADES QUI SERONT DEMAIN NOS ABONNES

NOUS VOULONS UNE FRANCE OU L'ON NE PUISSE PLUS DÉNOMBRER CHAQUE ANNÉE : 55 % D'INAPTES AU SERVICE MILITAIRE ET 25 % D'ILLETTRÉS.

"L'Abjection Française." *L'Insurgé*, January 13, 1937, p. 4. Courtesy of Bibliothèque nationale de France.

Antisemitism and the Mutilation of the Nation

How might borders be restored? Blanchot's conundrum was a contradictory one: it was because he fantasized that each Frenchman enjoyed an intimate connection with the nation that the contamination of the nation meant they felt abjection so acutely. The irrepressible feelings of shame and disgust demanded a way out of that which "disturbs identity, system, order" so as to effect a "sense of stable contour" that might be both embodied and bounded.[83] Since the nation had been violated, its nature tainted, shame, of course, inevitably emerged at the very moment of this realization. Identification with a perverted social body required that decadence be embodied if a political solution was to be found. Neither democracy, parliamentary regime, elected government, nor ideological alliance could allow a satisfactory alternative; and fascism was not a viable solution for Blanchot. Yet since abjection was unavoidable (the outcome of French people's identification with the nation), those young far-right intellectuals eager to proclaim radical dissidence needed another explanation. Abjection could not be located in the self: it had to be seen as outside, as other and fundamentally different. Abjection had to be found in "the place where [they were] not [but] which permitted [them] to be."[84] In keeping with far-right tradition and in reaction to recent events, abjection was displaced onto the figure of the "Jew." Blanchot substituted for a widespread abjection the fantasy of a single threat: Léon Blum. From corrupt and impotent politicians, Blanchot shifted to an indictment of Blum—whose prominence and visibility after May 1936 seemed only to confirm Blanchot's search for an origin and cause of abjection. According to one of his fellow journalists, Pierre Monnier, reminiscing almost fifty years later, "Never had Blum been judged with such disdain."[85] He added that Blanchot's political invective "executed [Blum] with a cold ferociousness."[86]

For if Blum had usurped the law, this meant that Blum—the repository of everything that these far-right intellectuals felt tainted by—had, in turn, caused their shame and disgust. In an article ruthlessly critical of the Popular Front, Blanchot asserted: "[We are] Blum's accomplices" (for allowing contamination and degradation to take place).[87] He also often reminded readers that it "is only fair that, until something new happens, Blum remains [both] the symbol and mouthpiece of that abject France we belong to."[88] Like other *Insurgé* writers, Blanchot recycled antisemitic tropes woven around the figure of "Léon Blum," as both cause and evidence of the fragile nature of the social body and symptomatic of an "absent France." Blum figured obsessively in Blanchot's *Insurgé* articles. As nation and self were synonymous, it had become obvious that "at the moment, France is Blum, everything that Blum does and says, we have to bear responsibility for, we wear its dishonor as if we had done it ourselves, as if we had said it ourselves."[89] Even further, he claimed, "There is in each of us an accomplice of Blum's betrayal and, a most horrible state, in us a second Blum or a second Viénot."[90] (The reference to Pierre Viénot was significant, for he was a Republican Socialist, undersecretary of foreign affairs and in charge of policy for the protectorates.) Blanchot insisted that "Blum was for the French people one of the main reasons for their humiliation."[91] France—and by extension every citizen—would reemerge only with the obliteration of Blum, that phantasmic figure who had polluted the essence of Frenchness.

The "Jewish problem" was even more dangerous, according to Blanchot, because it threatened the very status of France as a European nation. Blum oversaw the fate of the country and determined its policies. But he was also a foreign element. His presence only confirmed and revealed the nation's absence. Blanchot warned that since "Blum speaks in the name of France" and was "despised" by Nazi Germany, obviously "the Reich has displaced onto us its antipathy against Blum."[92] Blum metonymically signified those "Jewish forces" intent on generating social disorder within the nation. When Blanchot mentioned the grave danger of "Judeo-Bolshevism," he usually did so only in reference to Nazi Germany. Blum was therefore regarded as the origin of disorder inside and outside. Like many before him—such as Robert Brasillach, whom he disliked—Blanchot insisted on Blum's foreignness. Though Blum was French, in these newspapers Jewishness always meant foreignness. It was also the issue he most consistently evoked. That foreignness marked Blum as other, but also held the hope that abjection could be overcome: "Every moment and in all his interventions, [Blum] is so foreign to what France has been and to what [she] demands that he seemed to appear only to shame her for her degradation." Indeed, to Blanchot, the figure of Blum signified "a backward ideology, an old man's state of mind and a foreign race."[93] Blum represented all that should be opposed by a young generation of radical French far-right intellectuals, for Blum "was not even heir to the [French] civilization he defended."[94] That fact led to only one conclusion: "If being French means being united to Blum, then we are not good Frenchmen." In short, Blanchot wrote, they "did not want *that* France."[95] Blanchot's figuration of abjection through the language of antisemitism was neither original nor unique. It was in fact striking for the predictability of its arguments. Blanchot recycled clichés and tropes—those same clichés critics have said were merely rhetorical—but he did so with great verve and a powerful journalistic voice. It was that verve that made him a noticeable and important contributor to *Combat* and especially *L'Insurgé*.

Blanchot rarely attacked "Jews" as an undifferentiated group (as *L'Action Française* had done for years, and *Je Suis Partout* would do in its antisemitic special issue on "the Jews"), but it was the particular figure of the "Jew," most of all the imagined "Jewish intellectual," that he did attack relentlessly. The threat of Jewishness—that is, the embodiment of difference and the symbol of heterogeneity—was particularly trenchant when it touched upon questions of language, literature, and authorship. Blanchot firmly believed, as did Maulnier with him, that language was the foundation of culture, a culture understood by the far right to serve as the very substance of French civilization. Literature was the epitome of civilization for Blanchot and Maulnier, and they articulated particularly incisive critiques of those who they believed illegitimately practiced it and even contributed to its degradation. More specifically, Blanchot was critical of Julien Benda, who had been a favorite target of the far-right press for allegedly embodying the archetypal, modern intellectual Jew, and because of his argument regarding the role of the intellectual in politics.[96] Blanchot's reading of Benda—which did not directly refer to his "Jewishness" but implied it—refused to allow him a legitimate voice in the debate on the relationship between literature and politics. Indeed, "Benda had acquired with a certain audience the reputation of the kind of abstract character who defends the rights of pure reason with authority and an absolute contempt for human vicissitudes." The very fact that Benda was read at all was, in Blanchot's words, "a rather curious phenomenon."[97] Using familiar arguments regarding the cosmopolitan and nation-less Jew, Blanchot emphasized the way Jews made a travesty of language and, through such distortion, endangered French culture. Jews could only, as he claimed Benda did, "expertly falsify words." Blanchot further indicted Benda, arguing that he mirrored Blum, his "fellow Jew" (*correligionnaire*), emphasizing that Benda "thoroughly enjoys depicting Jews in a manner only imagined by the most intransigent of antisemites."[98]

These were the moments when Blanchot commonly resorted to the most conventional antisemitism: he claimed only Jews could recognize others "like themselves." His articles occasionally, though not consistently, resorted to the repertoire of gender that infused antisemitic rhetoric. He regularly singled out Blum for "his cosmopolitan instinct, far from virile temperament, [and] his taste for inconsistent rhetoric, [which] symbolize what the French people

[were] today."[99] Furthermore, such parody of an authentically French culture was obvious because "Blum" lacked the proper attributes of French masculinity. As a result, Blum could only mean an "absence of virility, a weakness unashamed of being weak, a self-conceit lacking in self-confidence."[100] Since Blum embodied the nation, every citizen would be contaminated. To add insult to injury, Blanchot sarcastically mused, Blum displayed an "atavistic"—thus necessarily effeminate—"sympathy" for Hitler—a manly leader. Instead, language needed to uphold the masculine citizen, not debase him. Blanchot concluded: "This is what there is in most Frenchmen's patriotism, [citizens] for whom France just confirms their selfishness and provides a veil to their debasement."[101] In the face of this, *L'Insurgé*'s task was indeed to tear down the veil.

Such remarks did not detract from the general tone of *L'Insurgé*. Their antisemitic content has, however, been the source of much debate. These pronouncements have also been given different explanations by Blanchot himself. Even if he did not deny his participation in far-right publications, he always contested accusations of antisemitism. He also never fully clarified his role in *L'Insurgé*. According to his biographer Christophe Bident, Blanchot explained that his departure from *Combat* and *L'Insurgé* had been precipitated by the fact that his texts were edited against his will (and, he added in a letter to another scholar, that his participation in *Combat* had been conditional upon Brasillach's absence).[102] In a 1977 letter to editor Maurice Nadeau, he explained that he had taken "steps . . . to close down *L'Insurgé* the moment it allowed an article with a hint of antisemitism to appear."[103] Yet that newspaper had "dabbled" in antisemitic rhetoric long before its demise at the end of 1937, a demise that most historians have asserted resulted from lack of funding. While it may never be possible to support or deny Blanchot's claims, the more important question lies in the ways in which his overall vision of the nation, the individual, and civilization unfolded and how Jewishness figured—albeit briefly—in his imagination of abjection and insurgency.

In early 1937, the only solution for Blanchot was to "shoot down this false France and replace her with an authentic France."[104] This was more than the conventional Maurrassian call to restore the "true" nation—in this case, an imperial nation-state that needed its colonies in order to "be present everywhere in the world."[105] The social body needed to be mutilated in order for this inauthentic regime to be expelled. A radical refusal would be enabled only through the violent rupture of separation—what some scholars have called a "logic of purification."[106] Mutilation evoked the possibility of recovering boundaries, as these "fantasies of dismemberment" would enable Blanchot to become a writer.[107] If the body was riddled with disgust, in the throes of abjection, then both the metaphorical body of the nation and the bodily self needed to be mutilated. Mutilation seemed the only way to purification—since restoring the nation was impossible, only that act would allow some form of regeneration. This metaphorical act was advocated by Maurice Blanchot on a page that, every week, exhorted its readers to "liberate France." In this article Blanchot explained that "there is no other way since the decay that characterizes this regime is becoming less separable from the nation, and it is becoming more hostile to it. The nation will only be able to free herself from it by detaching from herself what [the regime] has already corrupted in an exemplary mutilation."[108] He wrote: "The only way now to save our nation is to shoot down what best exemplifies its abjection."[109] Early on, Blanchot had indeed made the paradoxical argument that the French should experience the disdain others felt for them so that they could find the force to shoot down those "degraded beings" that governed them.[110] Self-hatred might lead to revolution. It was because Blanchot, like other far-right intellectuals, saw the regime, and this imaginary Jewish figure, as constitutive of the French national body that they needed to excise it in order to create an undivided state and emerge as autonomous citizens. The nation, he insisted, "was [yet] to come."[111]

The Self's Exile

In the mid-1930s, Blanchot's texts show him concerned with defining the conditions for a bounded sense of self. Mapping out the borders and the substance of the (male) subject was not just an ideological question—what it meant to be French—but also an ontological one. Nowhere was Blanchot's obsession with the unbearable conditions of abjection and the search for meaningful boundaries more vividly articulated than in a short text he wrote in 1936 but did not publish until 1951, "L'idylle." That abjection could be read as the symptom of anxiety in the face of the mark of sexual difference, the foundations for masculine identity and citizenship. "L'idylle" was one of the few overtly fictional texts that Blanchot wrote in the late 1930s and early 1940s (aside from his "novels").[112] While most have since taken Blanchot's word that "L'idylle" should be understood as the "prophetic" foreshadowing of Auschwitz (a point that he disputes two pages after having suggested it in the early 1980s essay following "L'idylle" and "Le dernier mot"), this short story in fact fictionalizes the radical alienation produced by totalitarian systems. Was this fictional text and those following a remarkable instance of the "metaphoric transpositions of political oppression"?[113] In 1936, what far-right critics like Blanchot attacked was not only Nazi "totalitarianism" but the totalitarian nature of the Soviet regime.[114] Communism was the most pressing danger for far-right critics then, since fascism, despite its excesses, still promised a seductive solution to the crisis of the modern world. As Blanchot wrote in his 1983 epilogue, "It happened in Auschwitz [and] it happened in the Gulag."[115] In light of Blanchot's mid-1930s obsessions, how might we understand this troubling and ambiguous short text? If read back to the year in which it was written, "L'idylle" may offer a somewhat different reading than Blanchot was willing to offer almost fifty years later when he reinterpreted his own fictional narratives, emphasizing the weight of the legacy and memory of Auschwitz. A contextual reading might show that this text offered a phantasmic rendering of the specter of abjection, and of the possibilities of being an individual freed from the alienation of modernity. It fictionalized Blanchot's agony over the possibility of a properly embodied and bounded self. It asked whether one could belong to a larger social order, whether a community (and a bounded and homogeneous nation) was at all possible. Jewishness arguably also figured in a muted manner, hinting at the work of difference within a community.[116] And it asked what demand sexual difference imposed on the self in order to allow citizenship—membership in a larger community.

"L'idylle" charts the fate of an apparently vagrant "stranger" who arrives at a hospice where he is at once welcomed, cared for, and imprisoned. While the "foreigner" (named Alexandre Akim by the institution director's wife) realizes he is no longer free and yearns for escape, he is told the institution allows neither freedom nor "communal life." Akim is told, "Here everyone lives helter-skelter with all the others, but there is no [possible] communal life."[117] No community is possible, yet all must live together. The meaning of these pronouncements is ambiguous. Is this a metaphor for all communities? Or is this a metaphor for the ways communities are corrupted when they are appropriated by a state that is always already oppressive, yet unavoidable? The question is about the relationships between the state (the hospice), the community (the collectivity of refugees), and the individual (Akim). In this story all the prisoners are "strangers." Like Akim, these men have been made nationless, and their relationships are characterized by a lack of "solidarity, everyone lived only for himself, and this promiscuity led to sly hatreds."[118] Is it the institution that makes them foreign or is foreignness, "strangeness to oneself" (in other words, abjection), a constitutive state of being that one can never escape? In the story, Akim's only possibility of return to freedom—and to his homeland—will come, he is told, if he marries, so he reluctantly accepts. The night before the wedding, as Akim wanders through the neighboring city, he is accused of having attempted to escape. He is punished by death through flogging.

Again in this story the questions of freedom, belonging, alienation, sexual difference, the body, and Jewishness constitute prominent motifs—as they had done in Blanchot's political articles. I suggest that it is the manner in which Jewishness and sexual difference were articulated, as unavoidable conditions of the individual and as that which generated foreignness, that we need to carefully examine.[119] Within this oppressive system, solidarity is made impossible through absurd labor and carefully delineated but unspoken rules—the individual is violently and unapologetically disciplined. Few individuals are named and all are subjected to the power of a mysterious and brutal law. Interestingly, of the few who are named, Akim notices a particularly deceitful prisoner, the only one given a name in the narration: Isaie Sitrok—a clear evocation of Jewishness and communism. Scholars have suggested that the name was an anagram of "Trotsky."[120] Sitrok is shown to be duplicitous, stealing money from his fellow inmates, and with "hideous traits."[121] Sitrok is a recurring figure in the text, exemplary of the degradation produced by this institution and one that Akim will especially despise. He is a barely veiled transcription of the repertoire of antisemitic characterization of "Bolshevik Jews." While Sitrok appears to be the product of the antisemitic imaginary, the main character—Akim—further complicates our reading of "L'idylle." Akim's own name echoes both the notion of the "first man," since it evokes Adam fallen from Eden, and more specifically, Lithuanian Jewish patronyms that Blanchot may have known.[122] If the character's name, "Akim," suggests Jewishness, that Jewishness is then tied to Akim's own state of foreignness. Further, Akim is named by others (the director's wife), hinting at the way otherness resides within oneself, is embodied by Jewishness, and is ascribed by others. In this story, it haunts the self, preventing boundedness and undivided harmony.

In parallel, one of the recurring themes, and Akim's obsession, is that of marriage—state-sanctioned heterosexual union.[123] Not only is the authority of the state symbolized by a married couple, the institution's director and his wife, but Akim's insistent curiosity will center on the question of the true nature of this marriage. Is the couple's idyllic bond fictive, or a mask for "deep and silent hatreds," as he is told? For heterosexuality is, in this story, tied to the law. One elderly man reminds Akim that in the case of the director and his wife:

> They made a fatal error. . . . They thought that love attracted them to one another when, in fact, they hated each other. Some signs made them feel that they were both tied to the same destiny. . . . How long did they fool each other? They woke up too late and discovered on their bodies the traces of their former intimacy where they could distinguish proof of their common fury; they had to carry on loving each other in order to continue hating each other.[124]

The system of heterosexuality is what produces literally "traces on their body": the impossibility of heterosexuality is inscribed upon the body—further emphasizing Blanchot's fictional and journalistic obsession with eradicating the burden of the body. In Blanchot's fiction of those years, the body is always rendered as suffering and beyond one's control.[125] Heterosexuality exists within marriage. Does marriage represent the possibility of happiness, an alternative to alienation and solitude? Marriage is mentioned by a variety of other characters in the story: a guard informs Akim that he was once married but "that women do not like his kind of job." The only way out of the institution is through "marriage." It represents the possibility of freedom and yet is always shown as failing (since the relationship of the director and his wife is always suspect). In many ways, the question of marriage drives the narrative, indeed propels the story itself and Akim's journey, and forms one of its most powerful motifs—a theme that critics, intent on reading the political in this story, have usually ignored. Marriage—heterosexual union and therefore the assumption of proper sexual difference—is here opposed to exile and foreignness. Since after World War I marriage had come to represent an "exemplary social and hence moral institution," it constituted the only possibility for one to become a rightful citizen of the polity and assume a bounded sense of self, away from the likes of nationless vagrants and Sitroks. It signified the literal and metaphorical domestication of the male individual because it enshrined morality and therefore civilization.[126] It is marriage that binds together the individual, the assumption of sexual difference, the renunciation of foreignness, and the social body as enshrined in the state.

Blanchot's short narrative circles around what appeared to be the unavoidability of one's exile and alienation that, fifty years later, he suggested not even marriage could eradicate: "The immigrant can try to naturalize, even through marriage, but he will always stay a migrant."[127] What might be the meaning of this interpretation offered by Blanchot himself? One is in exile, forever alienated from oneself, because one will always remain a stranger. Akim thus tells a new inmate that he will "learn that in this house, it is hard being a stranger/foreigner. You will also learn that it is difficult to stop being one." In fact, "even if you return to your home, you will begin a new exile."[128] But in the story, as in Blanchot's commentary decades later, ambiguity remained as to the origin of one's foreignness and whether it was imposed by others, embedded within oneself, or a state of being. Still, the story addressed the thorny question of belonging, citizenship, and community.

This impossibility of belonging is signified through the body—bodies that in this story are suffering, brutalized, erratic, and treacherous. Akim's body is always fragile: exhausted, famished, subjected to painful labor and brutalized. Akim is at different times feverish, suffocating, "delirious."[129] The lack of freedom and alienation of this totalitarian regime finds its ultimate expression in sadistic corporeal punishment: a long description of Akim's flogging, which will leave him "torn apart, humiliated, under the menace of being left to live in suffering so great that they will deprive him of life," and ultimately dead.[130] Here the answer is simple: there is no possibility of ever being freed from the vicissitudes of difference, alienation, solitude, and abjection. It seems, though, that a year later Blanchot began formulating a possible way out of abjection: not by fictionalizing it—this proved to be an impasse that he could not resolve—but through his turn to literature as critic and author.

From Intellectual to Author

How might Blanchot escape abjection? According to his theorization of the nature and role of literature, one needed to be an author.[131] Blanchot was not yet an "author" in the 1930s; he was a self-assured political journalist, an emerging literary critic, a tentative fiction writer, and an aspiring intellectual—in the same mold as some of his far-right companions, such as Thierry Maulnier.[132] Being an intellectual meant being a man of letters who was simultaneously engaged in the world of politics and art, both through individual acts and as the representative of a collective enterprise. After the Dreyfus Affair, it involved claiming a privileged position within the political world, one based upon a cultural legitimacy. The intellectual, as Blanchot explained decades later, was not "pure theoretician. He [was] between theory and practice."[133] Renouncing the status of "intellectual"—for whom "that which is remote matters to him just as much as that which is close, and more than himself" and which involved a public position—was decisive in Blanchot's desire to return to a harmonious and bounded subjectivity.[134] The assumption of authorship—that is, assuming the authority that allows one to speak—enabled him to disavow his far-right positions, and most importantly any antisemitic temptation. Being an author meant escaping the contingencies of the political, unlike the intellectual. But Blanchot never fully erased politics. As critics have pointed out, his interest in politics never really wavered. He submitted politics to the demand of literature.

Scholars have often dated what they term Blanchot's "abandonment" of politics to the demise of his career at *Combat* and *L'Insurgé* in late 1937, sometimes even insisting that his "retreat" did not take place until 1942. However, Blanchot did not so much abandon politics as harness it to literature. He abandoned political journalism and writing (he would speak of politics differently after that) and found in the position of disembodied "author" an escape from abjection and a symbolic space that gave consistency to his sense of self. This was not a sudden departure. Through the 1940s, Blanchot gradually shifted away from the political and worked his way toward what he imagined to be that pure space of literature. He had published fiction—*Thomas l'obscur* (1941), *Aminadab* (1942), *Le très-haut* (1948), and "Le dernier mot" (1935) and "L'idylle" (1936) (published together as a book in 1951)—but only occasionally returned to the "récit" as in, for instance, *L'arrêt de mort* (1948). Instead he dedicated himself after the war to the delineation of a philosophically inclined literary criticism and the reinvention of fictional narrative that he would become known for. Not until 1946 did he abandon publishing literary criticism in venues not entirely devoted to literature. He had continued writing a literary column for the *Journal des Débats* but ended his collaboration there in 1944.[135] After that, he contributed only to *L'Arche*, *Les Temps Modernes*, and, most significantly, to the review created by his friend Georges Bataille, *Critique*.[136] One might say that he finally became the postwar author that we now know only in 1949 with the publication of his first major work of literary criticism, *La part du feu*, a year after the publication of another attempt at a "novel," *Le très haut*.[137] The 1943 collection of literary essays, *Faux pas*, published by Gallimard, may not be considered an assertion of authorial legitimacy since it was actually a collection of texts already published: his literary chronicles from *Le Journal des Débats* as well as a few odd pieces (from *L'Insurgé* on Virginia Woolf, from *La Revue Française des Idées et des Oeuvres* on Lautréamont).[138] It signaled nonetheless his ambition to move away from journalism and toward literature only, not as novelist but as author. One may argue that once Blanchot abandoned public alignment with anything other than the literary, he completed the shift he had undertaken at the end of the 1930s. His brief involvement at Jeune France, a Vichy cultural organization that had attempted to rejuvenate culture, had also come to nothing.[139] Literary criticism was now his most visible and public activity.

La part du feu was an important moment in the evolution of Blanchot's relationship to literature. It addressed themes he had already addressed, but did so divorced from the contingencies of daily affairs and the urgency of dissidence and revolution. Its publication also corresponded to one of Blanchot's true "retreats" into solitude, from his Parisian home to his residence in Èze.[140] Already disavowed by some of his former far-right peers, he published in this collection an essay devoted to surrealism—the other avant-garde that the young far right had always seen as its misguided double in the 1930s. The essay reworked some of the topics touched upon in the preceding decade by Maulnier and others. Blanchot wrote: "Surrealists appeared to their contemporaries as those who destroy," and in this they displayed a "striking non-conformist violence."[141] Surrealism, he insisted, had offered a challenge to the Cartesian cogito that echoed contemporaneous attempts made by "German philosophy"—here presumably referring to Heidegger.[142] Blanchot praised surrealism for having "been haunted by this idea: that there is, that there must be in the making of man a moment where all difficulties dissolve, where antinomies no longer make sense, where knowledge provides mastery over things, where language is not discourse but reality itself without ceasing to be language's own reality, where man reaches the absolute."[143] He added, though, that they had ultimately failed. Maulnier had said as much in his 1939 *Introduction à la poésie française*. Just as other far-right critics had pointed out in the 1930s, Blanchot explained that surrealists did not possess the rigor and discipline necessary for such a radical endeavor.[144] In keeping with his interwar writing, Blanchot also devoted essays to Malraux and Gide—the great names of the period who had been the subject of so many chronicles in the far-right press and beyond. He also turned to those (Hölderlin, Mallarmé, Kafka, Char, and Nietzsche) who, from then on, infused his philosophical reflections on literature.

By blurring in his work the boundaries of fiction, criticism, essay, and philosophy, Blanchot could finally abandon all political journalism and activism (though not politics). Being an author allowed him to be intelligible as a subject: his devotion to literature—understood to operate as pure space—enabled him to encounter his reader and allowed for the erasure of the "threatening specter of abjection."[145] In the French Republic of Letters, authorship constituted a cultural and social space that legitimized one's work and cultural claims.[146] Through authorship, Blanchot was able to erase himself—an erasure and invisibility that subsequently became one of the principles of his ethics of writing and allowed for a disembodiment that he would maintain throughout his entire life.[147] Being an author meant negating the self while assuming the law of authority. In *La part du feu*, Blanchot articulated his fantasy of authorship: the author was now marked as an "indifferent, constraining, [and] empty place." Blanchot explained in *La part du feu*'s last essay, "Literature and the Right to Death," that "the writer is found and realized only through his work; before [the advent of his work], he is not only ignorant of who he is, but he is nothing."[148]

Throughout his postwar criticism, Blanchot nonetheless returned to the interwar years often portrayed as a symbolic moment of hope and literary and political experimentation. The 1930s had been a critical moment in his development as an *author*—allowing him to begin articulating his conception of literature—but it was precisely that formative moment that Blanchot erased. He had written a few literary reviews in the early 1930s, but it was at *L'Insurgé* that he devoted himself to a weekly literary chronicle.[149] He had begun defining there the kind of aesthetics that would ultimately free him from far-right politics. Yet after 1946, he remained ostensibly silent regarding his 1930s political and literary journalism. Some of his silences or omissions are glaring: Blanchot himself penned a letter in response to Mehlman's analysis of a 1942 article in *Le Journal des Débats*, in order to dispute the charge that he had been complicit with far-right politics. Blanchot vehemently denied any Maurrassian influence: "The fact remains that the name of Maurras is an indelible stain and an expression of dishonor."[150] Blanchot's earlier rhetoric of shame and disgust that in the 1930s had focused on the figure of "Blum" was now displaced onto the figure of Maurras, who represented the reminder of an impossible politics. He added: "I was never close to the man, during whatever period, and always kept my distance from the *Action Française*, even when Gide [himself] would call to see him out of curiosity."[151] The reference to Gide, though accurate, was not innocent: Gide exemplified the author who could be at once lucid in politics while selflessly committed to the work of literature (he had, after all, renounced communism). Indeed, Blanchot had referred to Maurras explicitly only once in his *Insurgé* political articles.[152] Still, Charles Maurras, who had been condemned in 1945 for collaboration with the enemy, was the symbol of

French dishonor in postwar France. Yet if Blanchot never entertained personal relations with the *Action Française* patriarch (unlike Maulnier, Brasillach, and Fabrègues) or was a member of the monarchist organization, he had in the 1930s actively participated in the dissident Maurrassian politics attempted by the Young New Right.[153]

Blanchot did not actually repress his past as far-right journalist. Nor did he deny it. Instead, he evaded its meaning by displacing the terms of his intellectual and political involvement. Displacement allowed him to shift the meaning of his past relations and deny the weight of his words through association and oblique realignment. He denied personal involvement with Maurras and *L'Action Française* before and during Vichy. But he never addressed the question of their intellectual influence. After all, for anyone involved in far-right politics, Maurras was unavoidable. That great far-right figure was the author to whom Blanchot had devoted the most reviews during his time as literary critic for *L'Insurgé*, reviews in which he explained that they allowed "that rare opportunity, regarding Charles Maurras, to taste a pleasure almost forbidden."[154] He had then gone on to say that "Maurras is the only one whom we can say has really and truly thought."[155] Maulnier, Brasillach, Fabrègues, and many others had written similar statements. Blanchot's reviews of Maurras's publications were entirely complimentary, reminding readers that "everything that M. Maurras has to teach us has an inestimable value."[156] Emphasizing the "beauty of what he produces" and the way he "invites man to a solitude in the face of the universe," Blanchot appeared to identify in Maurras a kindred spirit whose concerns mirrored his own, emphasizing his personal trajectory, utopian yearnings, and concern for the "life of the heart and the soul."[157] In a surprising reading of Maurrassian themes (echoing his own obsession more than that of Maurras), he suggested that his most enduring concern lay with the relation between self and other. Speaking of his conception of man, he argued in July 1937:

> There is in every being, an instinct of pure envy, a violence of friendship, an essential strength which relentlessly lead him to that other being and which, in order to attain what is outside of himself, drive him to achieve the most complete self-expression, to be carried far away by the highest tide, to quench his unshakeable thirst, and be forced to draw back from the mass of treasures by reaching beyond himself.[158]

Maurrassian literature, as Blanchot interpreted it in the interwar period, seemed to offer a vision of the self that was not haunted by abjection. Blanchot spoke then of "Maurrassian dialectics" as a metaphysics of being. In doing so, he evacuated any explicit politics from Maurras's writings and transformed him into a theorist whose reason illuminated contemporary thought.

In his *L'Insurgé* literary chronicle, Blanchot did not "read" Maurras as the far-right intellectual that he was but rather as an "author," focusing on his encounter with and translation of the form of language. Ironically, he was one of the few to have taken Maurras's aesthetics seriously, together with his belief in the beauty and French character of classicism that had informed his politics.[159] He evoked the "profound life" that underlay Maurras's writing: it was, according to Blanchot, the result of "a personal combination of words and movements, logic obeying those rhythms which drive too simple an idea to first force itself upon an arrogant language which resisted it." He added, "This was a rare combination. Abstraction triumphs only to acquire the power of an extreme sensitivity."[160] Blanchot's rendering and interpretation of Maurras's works was both ambivalent and ambiguous. He avoided the political question, a puzzling interpretation considering the Maurrassian emphasis "Politics First!" At the same time, he recognized Maurras's definitions of art and beauty (even if he avoided commenting on their content). Though praising him, Blanchot suggested that impenetrability characterized his thought, for there is "a secret Maurrassian sense of reason [that] like an unreadable star, becomes even more obscure as she displays a more beautiful and complete light."[161] Despite its offering an inadequate political model, Blanchot suggested that Maurras's thought should be influential, and he paid him homage. That early celebration, however, quickly disappeared from Blanchot's literary criticism.

In his effort, years later, to refute any suggestion of far-right involvement, Blanchot similarly relegated his participation in *Combat* and *L'Insurgé* to anecdote. He forcefully explained to a critic that he had "but few memories of *Combat*." However, he stressed that he specifically remembered being radically opposed to Robert Brasillach.[162] Once again, Blanchot displaced the nature of his involvement, emphasizing the personal as substitute and metonymy for the political:

> However, I recall that, having been in everything opposed to Brasillach who was himself entirely devoted to the cause of fascism and antisemitism, I had demanded from this magazine the assurance that Brasillach would not contribute to it, in order to become one of its contributors. The opposite was also true. Brasillach hated *Combat* because I had participated in it. [My] opposition to Brasillach and everything he represented has been a constant feature of mine.[163]

This is not to dispute Blanchot's own account (he was never close to Brasillach) but to note that his retroactive account of his journalistic production and its problematic politics served to uphold the myth of the uncompromising solitary figure he had fashioned after Vichy. By rearranging the terms of his involvement with *Combat*, Blanchot provided a comforting narrative evading the more difficult question of his own journalistic writings. Indeed, Blanchot and Brasillach actually simultaneously wrote in *Combat*, both providing an article per issue throughout its first year of existence until their departure the following year. Blanchot's subsequent withdrawal in 1937 corresponded to his increased involvement in *L'Insurgé*, while Brasillach, increasingly at odds with the *Combat* group, left to take up the editorship of *Je Suis Partout*. Again, in order to displace the question of the relationship between writing and politics, Blanchot—as he had done with regard to Maurras—refused to acknowledge personal relationships, as a means of disavowing any political intimacy and thus erasing the more slippery traces of his own far-right contributions. His emphatic denial of any association with Brasillach, "the Collaborator," signaled his desire to distance himself from the figure of an intellectual who was now the emblem of a generation gone astray, and of an infamous past to be eradicated. Personal memory replaced history, thereby erasing the political.

The Self and the Politics of Literature

Throughout these years, mapping out the conditions for a bounded self meant, for Blanchot, delineating the substance of the political and the shape of literature. At *L'Insurgé* he had been at once political pundit and literary reviewer—the two roles answered one another as they served to articulate his concern with abjection (in political articles) and its diagnosis and solution (in literary reviews). Exhibiting neither a double persona, "bilinguism," nor even "a schizophrenia that manifested itself in the conflicting tendencies of his political journalism and literary investigations," as some critics have claimed, Blanchot believed—like his fellow far-right writers—that politics and aesthetics were not separate and autonomous realms, and his own writings on the matter were inextricably related.[164] He penned his literary reviews under the rubric of "Civilization"—a page devoted to culture and art—while he mused on politics on the page titled "Liberate . . . France." Blanchot's horror at the nation's abjection, his denunciation of Blum's corruption, and his insistent call for a radical revolt were answered in his literary criticism. Over the course of 1937, he charted a vision of literature whose subversive potential could provide an escape from the untenable state of abjection. In *L'Insurgé*'s first January issue, he articulated his "indictment of France," while his literary chronicle explained how one could move "from revolution to literature."[165] His literary criticism explored how best to generate a culture that had been purged and regenerated. Since it was urgent to define the boundaries of the fragile male citizen, aesthetics—and literature especially—suggested how best to attain "perfection," a leitmotiv of Blanchot's writings.[166] The fate of the subject and nation that Blanchot lamented in his political commentaries was offered some form of salvation in the kind of literature he celebrated.

But negotiating the tense relationship between politics and literature was a complicated affair. In turning to literature, Blanchot enacted a paradoxical claim (one that preoccupied many authors in the 1930s): on the one hand, he wished for a literature divorced from the contingencies of the real; on the other, he refused a literature of "novels of ideas," where the literary was driven by external and political considerations. His intervention was hardly original, since it drew on the debates in the literary field since World War I about the ways the war had upset the possibilities of imagining the representation of reality.[167] This had also been a common accusation on the part of conservative and far-right critics regarding the Popular Front's investment in cultural affairs.[168] Blanchot implicitly refused the path taken by André Gide, who was portrayed as having abandoned the literary to embrace politics, while André Malraux had brought politics into the literary with works such as his celebrated 1933 *La condition humaine*. Blanchot castigated literary critics informed by political concerns, especially those left-wing critics who practiced a "trashy Marxism."[169] In contrast, he argued that his generation of far-right critics was not ideologically motivated and, accordingly, wrote in his first literary chronicle that he "hoped that no one will look for some horrifying excuse for politics in this chronicle concerned with books."[170] Instead, he claimed autonomy for literature—a necessary claim in those years when the novel was said to be "in crisis." It seemed both an imperative and a necessary demand on literature that, according to Blanchot, "[art]'s only purpose is to be in harmony with a command foreign to it." He added, "There is no greater corruption [for art] than, with impure passivity, to accept the work already done against a political system and a society."[171] Art, for him, should never resign itself to reflecting politics and should maintain within itself the imperious need to contest reality.

Despite his own claims, Blanchot the literary critic showed a keen sense of his audience. His *L'Insurgé* literary chronicles were not impervious to political concerns; indeed, they were infused by his political anxieties. While Blanchot showed a great appreciation of modernists—such as Virginia Woolf (whom he praised), Thomas Mann, and Rainer Maria Rilke—his criticism was generally applied to a rather conservative, even far-right, canon of authors, in keeping with the political world in which he was then immersed.[172] His was a rather predictable pantheon. He mostly reviewed right-wing authors and novelists. He spoke of Pierre Drieu La Rochelle's *Rêveuse bourgeoisie*, Marcel Jouhandeau's *Le saladier*, and Jacques Chardonne's *Romanesques*. He devoted enthusiastic pages to Catholic writer Paul Claudel and, most significantly, emblematic far-right figures like Georges Bernanos, Henry de Montherlant, Henri Massis, and Charles Maurras. He also positively reviewed the essays of personalist intellectual Denis de Rougemont on the decadence of contemporary culture and the fate of the intellectual—with whom Young New Right intellectuals had been in conversation earlier in the decade.

He insisted, though, that literature's submission to a "command foreign to it" should not be pure aestheticization—lest his refusal of politics be understood as such. He warned that the desire for a literature abstracted from the real—that is, aestheticized—had contributed to the demise of contemporary literature. He explained that "a number of writers, divorced from events, have considered literature as a refuge outside of chance and as an absolute where man is represented only by formal pleasures and aesthetic emotions." Pure aestheticism hardly constituted—and this, as early as 1930—an attractive possibility. Four years later, Blanchot attempted to define an aesthetic vision in which literature might serve as politics, offering a restorative and regenerative experience. Literature was to be not a refuge but an accomplishment. He argued that literature needed to be freed from material contingencies only to be more radically critical. It should retain its specificity, which he ascribed to its ability to embody the best of "man." In short, novelists must find a way out of base ideological motivation, so that "[they] extract from life not life itself but what can illuminate it, and what provides its own internal light."[173]

What could literature offer that politics had not? Blanchot imagined then that literature might offer a return to a state of being alleviated from the mark of (sexual) difference—that alienation and strangeness which had not found a resolution in fiction (as in "L'idylle"). And literature meant language. For Blanchot, in the throes of abjection, language could be molded: it alone could offer a respite to this unbearable state, so that for him, writing was a demand and literature the only possible site where the body was erased and the self realized.[174] Literature presented a possibility for *sublimation*, metaphorically generating that which offered an aesthetic resolution to abjection. One could reach a stable sense of self through sublimation in literature. This sublimation could transform (and thereby transcend the body) because it required the self-imposition of the rule of discipline; indeed, as Blanchot explained, literature requires "indifference," "pride," and "harshness."[175] The order generated by discipline in turn generated the boundedness yearned for by abject individuals. Blanchot had explained that "what . . . matters is the power of resistance that an author opposes to his work and the ease and licenses he has refused his work, the instincts he has mastered, the rigor he forced upon himself."[176] Blanchot assigned a privileged place to literature, as "art is [a novelist's] only weapon in his encounter with the absolute."[177] Literature allowed novelists to translate "the profound sentiment of things," as he claimed philosopher Alain had done. Here, Blanchot showed his independence as he gestured to Alain, who might otherwise have been dismissed, since he had also been known in the 1930s as a champion of anti-fascism and pacifism. Literature thus fantasized enabled aspiring authors like Blanchot to imagine escaping this untenable state of abjection, which they had, at some point, identified as emanating from the threat of "the Jew," especially since "Jews" like Blum and Benda corrupted language and literature. The only solution lay, for him, in the narrative resolution offered by literature. For Blanchot, in the throes of dissolution and abjection, the discipline of literature alone offered a respite, where body and self were finally both erased and realized.

Only certain types of literature could achieve this. It could play such a role as long as it did not succumb to the temptations that had befallen it in the last decade, most specifically by refusing the dangers of "realism" and "psychology," the twin heretical categories of Blanchotian criticism. Both were rooted in the material world and therefore subject to contamination and impurity, while what was required was transcendence.[178] Greatness was possible only when authors imagined a "fiction from which all psychology has been extricated."[179] Stories that "psychologized" offered only a surface because of their "glibness [and] banality under the veil of a seductive conception," while Blanchot yearned for a literature that provided substance and depth.[180] As he stressed in his 1933 review of Maxence's collection of essays on literature, "a certain domination of abstraction has made [writers] lose the taste for ideas; a certain realism has destroyed their sense of the real."[181] Blanchot refused simple abstraction (which he had earlier associated with Julien Benda), as it mirrored the base materialism of the real. Instead literature should be regenerative and promise disembodiment. According to Blanchot, who agreed with Maxence, realism implied simple and simplistic statements devoid of any effort for "the mind to meet the event."[182] Nor could the simple comforts of narrative coherence suffice. He often criticized works that displayed "too convoluted, and too abrupt a form, and which bored [their readers] with an excessively clumsy composition"; instead he celebrated authors, like Virginia Woolf, whose works were "novels without plot, without anecdote, and almost without characters."[183]

Literary form was essential to this enterprise, as it allowed for the "purity" of language to emerge.[184] Such was Blanchot's fantasy of the regenerative and transformative power of language, form, and literature. Only a certain purity of form could, according to his conception of literature, annihilate this pervasive sense of shame and untenable abjection, as it divorced the self from embodiment. Purity meant an abstract discipline that was not so much Maulnier's neoclassical aesthetics but allowed detachment from the messiness of the real. Literature could tame the divided subject through representation, characterized by a "certain indifference to vain matters."[185] Accordingly, he called for novels "extract[ing] from ideas and issues an almost pure movement and tension."[186] Over the course of his ten months at *L'Insurgé*, Blanchot therefore sought to define a literature that "extracts [its substance] from nothingness" and "where man is present."[187] He had laid out this vision in his programmatic statement in the first *L'Insurgé* issue, asking how literature could embody a revolutionary potential. It should not just be aestheticized or purely ideologically motivated. Thus, Blanchot defined what the boundaries of the political and literary should be. Literature alone could generate reality and literature alone could be revolutionary, since "only perfection is revolutionary." In fact,

> from these creative works emerges a truly revolutionary power. Their work is obscure and almost always unpredictable. But the hidden violence in which they last, the tension to which they force us, the move to liberation they make us desire or the perfection they lead us to, [all of these] are such that they act when we do not expect it, on a world we are unaware of.[188]

Literature was not mere escape nor safe haven; it offered a place of resolution—a narrative answer to abjection. By suggesting the possibility of transcending one's own mortality, literature meant that "it is in this perfect silence, in the emptiness replete with oneself, in the profound and infinitely perilous asylum, that man discovers himself and discovers the work with a feeling of fundamental anxiety, and in which is shaped the fate of a work of art."[189] The "substance" of literature was at stake in Blanchot's theorization of the literary. What mattered to him was the regenerative and restorative power of literature, which, when devoid of external considerations or futile attempts at realism, would help realize that "man's superior life in the products of art forces us to think how literature can be connected to some form of revolution."[190]

For Blanchot—unlike Maulnier and his far-right companions—pure literary form did not mean a return to some form of classicism as the embodiment of order and harmony. Instead, if literature offered the possibility of attaining liberation, it was through the particular self-discipline of the author. Again, authorship was bound to the possibility of a restorative purity:

> What matters more to [him] is that strength of opposition that is expressed in a creative work [*oeuvre*] and which is then assured of annihilating the power of other works or abolishing that piece of the ordinary real, as well as being assured of calling into existence other more powerful works, more powerful than itself, and determining a superior reality.[191]

Discipline would bring transcendence, which would, in turn, allow the self to emerge having resisted the "devouring nothingness of the world."[192] Instead of nothingness, the (abject) self could be given substance by those authors who (as he characterized Montherlant) have "master[ed their] steps over the abyss."[193] Authors might recover the substance that was now sorely lacking in a depleted nation and its abject citizens. Sublimation held the promise of freeing one from the vicissitudes of difference and heterogeneity. Such was Blanchot's theorization of literature—where literature would offer what the political had failed to do.

The Specter of Auschwitz: Memory and Shame

In a short essay published in the 1980s, *Les intellectuels en question*, Blanchot pondered the question of the role of the "intellectual." He, who had abandoned this position to appropriate that of an "absent author," interrogated the principles that made and determined an intellectual "because [himself, he] does not know what the term means."[194] Blanchot interrogated its meaning in an attempt to counteract Sartre's popularized understanding of the "engaged intellectual." Interestingly, he published this text shortly after the reprint of his mid-1930s short stories, "Le dernier mot" and "L'idylle," which appears far more ambiguous than one might assume upon reading it. As Blanchot meanders alongside the figures of Freud, Nietzsche, Levinas, Alain, Valéry, he also turns to interwar far-right literary and political figures such as Maurice Barrès and Léon Daudet, as well as his former foe, Léon Blum. This work, in fact, addresses the question of Blanchot's own interwar writings without ever doing so directly. It stands as an ambivalent essay that exemplifies his strategy of displacement and oblique realignment, as it leaves discernible traces for his readers to account for his former far-right and antisemitic past. While he makes no mention of his own involvement in the issue of Algerian independence (and only briefly mentions his participation in May '68), Blanchot dated—like many—the emergence of the figure and possibility of the intellectual to the infamous late-nineteenth-century Dreyfus Affair, which had so gravely shaken French society.[195]

From the Dreyfus Affair to the specter of Vichy, and propelled by his desire to follow Adorno's call for Auschwitz "never to repeat itself," Blanchot took the opportunity to reflect on Martin Heidegger's involvement with the Nazis. Blanchot did not formulate his harsh condemnation within his text: he deemed Heidegger's political claims "inexplicable and indefensible" in a footnote.[196] This is striking, as Blanchot rarely used footnotes, and here the footnote acts as a supplement haunting his text. More importantly, he wrote in this same textual supplement that "the more we ascribe importance to Heidegger's thinking, the more necessary it is to try to elucidate the meaning of his political involvement."[197] Considering the nature of Blanchot's own past as a far-right journalist, this might be read as an invitation to engage with the same kind of critical analysis he advocated in the case of Heidegger. Surprisingly, it also invited readers to see the political embedded in the aesthetic in ways that Blanchot had consistently refused after 1945. Blanchot confined his most explicit political and moral statements not to his text but to its margins, as a displaced commentary on his own thoughts and experience.

In a footnote again, Blanchot turned to his friend Georges Bataille's alleged flirtation with fascism—a strange insistence, since Bataille had never been close to any far-right intellectuals, but a clear response to accusations leveled at Bataille. Nor could he be suspected of having "dabbled" in antisemitism, even if he wrote on fascism. In this note, Blanchot did not address the temptation that fascism had been for many in the 1930s and even later (many, especially on the far right, had been seduced by fascism at some point, at least by Mussolini). Instead he correctly insisted that Bataille could not abide "the Nazi regime nor Pétain's regime or ideology (*famille, travail, patrie*)."[198] He avoided mentioning the interwar period, focusing only on the Vichy years. In Bataille's defense, Blanchot used the mode of witness rather than participant ("I can testify"). He justified this statement because of the urgency of time—indeed, "as, with years going by, witnesses of that time are becoming rare, and to let credit be given to such claims I know to be incontestably contrary to the truth."[199] Once again, exculpation was relegated to the margins of the text. Blanchot offered himself as moral witness (invoking the personal "I") to Bataille's purity while refusing to state a position in relation to two discredited phenomena—antisemitism and fascism—that actually haunted his own past. In doing this, he was simultaneously calling up the ghost of guilt while remaining silent about his own far-right involvement.

If, throughout this essay, Blanchot did indeed condemn antisemitism, which he termed "this ancient misery of thought" (thereby relating it to the archaic, that which does not belong to the modern), especially as it emerged around the Dreyfus Affair, he never mentioned its existence in the interwar years—a rather surprising silence considering its virulence then within the far-right press that he knew only too well.[200] He mentioned antisemitism in relation to the Nazi project that he termed Hitler's "furious antisemitism." That expression had been Maulnier's when he derided the Nazi regime in his late-1938 *Combat* article on fascism.[201] Could this be read as an echo of Blanchot's youthful politics in which Nazi anti-Jewish sentiment was derided because it espoused an irrational "racist antisemitism"? It is true that in the 1930s, Blanchot never wavered from his anti-German nationalism. Still, these omissions are glaring, especially in an essay whose subject matter is the relation of literature to politics and the meaning of an ethics of writing. Blanchot explained interwar political choices by referring to the war, the demise of democracies, economic difficulties, and the Spanish Civil War. In fact, as explanation for the seduction of fascism, he put forward arguments that sounded remarkably similar to those he and others had developed in *Combat* and *L'Insurgé*. Again echoing Thierry Maulnier's analysis in his 1938 article "Notes on Antisemitism" in which Maulnier had argued that French citizens should not succumb to the "Jewish myth"—nor the Communist one—Blanchot explained that it was the irrational pull of fascism that made it successful, "a society's need to once again open up to myths."[202] Slipping into the present tense to describe a democracy that "no longer shines" and that actually embodies "mediocrity, and whose economic difficulties brought about by the war, highlight its disastrous weaknesses," his harsh pronouncements on the democratic regime recalled his interwar analyses haranguing a corrupt and impotent regime that elicited only disgust.[203] His prose was still haunted by the figure of the "Jew"—"*le juif à la nuque raide*," as he had called the accused Captain Dreyfus.

Despite such slippery remembrance, Blanchot insisted that "from the Dreyfus Affair to Hitler and to Auschwitz, it has been confirmed that it was antisemitism (with racism and xenophobia) which has most forcefully revealed the intellectual to himself, namely, it is under this shape that the care for [the] *other* has forced him (or not) to get out of his creative solitude."[204] Blanchot's definition of the "intellectual" suggested that this position could never be separated from the temptation of antisemitism—Blanchot's own temptation when he had embraced radical oppositional far-right politics. One's relation to otherness was the question posed to the intellectual. And it was the failure of the 1930s *L'Insurgé* project that had propelled him to embrace the comforting, if painful, solitude of the author—a solitude, Blanchot hinted, forever evoked alongside shame, the shame that forever haunted him: "There is not a single day when, in the most vulnerable part of my memory, the recollection does not come back to me of these terrible words enshrined within [the poet] René Char's fragment: . . . [which] slap on the cracks of my face a red cast-iron smack."[205] Shame had replaced disgust. And to the occasionally misguided intellectual, Blanchot opposed the image of the solitary and detached author.

Of course, the image of a solitary author was a mythical construction. Blanchot never fully espoused the complete loneliness of the author. Nor did he disengage from politics. He was always involved in conversations with fellow thinkers and belonged to intellectual networks, from his correspondence with Emmanuel Levinas and Georges Bataille, to his exchange with editor Jean Paulhan.[206] Critics have often remarked on the ways in which *friendship*—a personal relation—figured as one of the central motifs of his work.[207] Bataille is a famous and important friend and intellectual companion to whom he repeatedly referred. Blanchot and Bataille met in 1940 and became very close friends, each often invoking the other's influence.[208] It is difficult to date Blanchot's early public acknowledgments of his intellectual friendship with Bataille, but he returned to it more and more over the course of his postwar literary criticism, while offering a defense of Bataille in his essay on intellectuals. It appears that Blanchot, in this way, reinterpreted his interwar intellectual and political path through the figure of Georges Bataille. Bataille's provocative insistence on the transgression of desire and law as the means to a different self allowed Blanchot to speak of utopian desires he had harbored but expressed in a radically different politics.[209] Most importantly, the appeal to transgression allowed Blanchot to reframe his espousal of far-right "dissidence" and reinterpret his enduring search for the meaning of otherness and community.

In his 1983 thoughts expressed in *La communauté inavouable* (The Unavowable Community), Blanchot spent much time showing how Bataille's 1936 attempts at political and ethical communities, enshrined in the groups/magazines *Acéphale* and *Contre-Attaque*, constituted radical utopian expressions.[210] These two groups, both initiated by Bataille, coincidentally mirrored Blanchot's own collaborative experiences, *Combat* and *L'Insurgé*. They were related enterprises (some of the same individuals contributed to both), and each corresponded to a more obscure and more transgressive experiment: just as *Acéphale* (the Headless) represented a more extreme and, according to Blanchot, more "absolute" attempt at a "human community," *L'Insurgé* (the Insurgent) had represented a more violent attempt at "dissident politics" in which Blanchot had called for revolution. This experiment showed how, for Blanchot, "each member of the community is not only all of the community, but the violent, disparate, splintered, impotent incarnation of a group of beings who, while tending to exist in their entirety, have as corollary the nothingness where they have already fallen."[211] Bataille's two groups and Blanchot's dual contributions embodied the separation of a reasonable and politically acceptable discourse—*Contre-Attaque*, *Combat*—that was at the same time disrupted by the experience of an almost irrational and willfully transgressive revolutionary practice—*Acéphale*, *L'Insurgé*, whose very titles evoked that marginal position and essential refusal of law and authority. Reading his past through his friend Georges Bataille enabled Blanchot to erase the more complicated political legacy he had to contend with—his own far-right positions and insistent invectives punctuated by an obsession with the corrupting "Jew"—which he had simultaneously abandoned and reworked in his literary writings.

The Historicity of Literature

Blanchot dehistoricized literature at the same time that he opened the way in his work for others to think of language as constitutive of subjectivity. His literary criticism developed the idea that the subject produced in literature was immune to the vicissitudes of history, and hence of political contingency, since "outside of decadence and renovation, a work of art becomes another work of art through a personal and incorruptible filiation."[212] One might suggest that Blanchot never tired of refining this early programmatic statement into a theory of literature "whose purpose," he had written in 1937, "has been to express man or the world, which belong to it so profoundly that [literature] remains almost indifferent to those vagaries which can befall him in his own universe."[213] Literature for him stood above politics and outside of history, reified in an abstract sphere. Literature was obviously not purely apolitical, but Blanchot argued that it must remain outside of the sphere of ideology: "What we basely call literature must be powerless considering a work which derives its meaning from something else than politics."[214] These principles, he insisted, must drive literary criticism. He wrote nothing less in his fragmentary text, *L'écriture du désastre* (The Writing of the Disaster) (which has been read as a reflection on the impossibility of writing after the disaster—the genocide of European Jews), when he explains that "writing, since it persists in a relation of irregularity with itself—and this with the utterly other—does not know what will become of itself politically: this is its intransitivity, its necessarily indirect relation to the political."[215]

The role of the author was essential to his conception of the literary, as one could not claim that "the man who has produced a work of art and the man who can be guessed at from this work of art" are one and the same man. They were irreducibly and radically different, separated by an "uncrossable abyss." Blanchot explained that the author "is merciless toward this being whose misfortunes, passion and joys provide him the mud with which he can only but shape perishable forms."[216] Yet, after 1945 and the shame generated by the discovery of the impossible disaster, that horrifying event that Auschwitz had been, guilt hovered around Blanchot's texts, alluding to his infamous past words. While Blanchot certainly never returned to his far-right beginnings, Jewishness kept on haunting his notion of "being," just as it had Akim in his 1936 short story. Turning to texts such as philosophers Jean-Luc Nancy's *La communauté desoeuvrée* (The Inoperative Community) and Emmanuel Levinas's reflection on the role of otherness in the constitution of being, Blanchot still held Jewishness as exemplary of modernity. Some critics have emphasized how his confrontation with the Shoah paradoxically "both acknowledges the historical manifestation of the Holocaust as a result of the project of modernity and privileges it as fundamentally singular, ahistorical, and unrepresentable."[217] Blanchot responded to texts articulating the Jew as modernity's limit and as that which had come to represent the dissolution of community.[218] While difference (in the form of Jewishness) still haunted him, for him only the author remained.

5

"NEGROID JEWS AGAINST WHITE MEN"

Louis-Ferdinand Céline and the Politics of Literature

Negroid Jews against White Men. Nothing more, nothing less.

—*L'école des cadavres*, 1938

When Louis-Ferdinand Céline's *Voyage au bout de la nuit* (Journey to the End of the Night) was published in 1932, it was an unmistakable sensation. In a period when the relationship between literature, culture, and politics consumed many, the book received almost unanimous praise across political lines. Some described the novel as "a violent dream [where] disgust is endlessly present."[1] In the Communist *L'Humanité*, one journalist described it as an "epic of despair, a confession where the lyrical mingles with satire." He thought it "sincere," "crude," "virulent," and above all "original."[2] In the conservative *Le Figaro*, another critic wrote that "aside from the Surrealists and Dadaists," few had expressed more violently the existential despair that preoccupied so many in these years.[3] Georges Bataille wrote that the novel's greatness lay in its exploration of death and misery.[4] Some, though, among the Young New Right were more circumspect. In *La Revue du Siècle*, they worried, of course, that Céline's "brutal" descriptions embodied nothing more than the "willful and exclusive search for baseness and garbage," and a stylistic affectation that "confused" contemporaries were deluded into embracing.[5] They added that Céline might not be that original, since his shocking verve was symptomatic of a decadent age. Few agreed with that assessment, however, and the novel was immensely popular.

Voyage au bout de la nuit struck a chord mostly because of the way it spoke of the experience of modernity. It offered a rather bleak vision of the world through the eyes of its hero, Ferdinand Bardamu, and did so in a manner that seemed novel, fresh, and perfectly in tune with its time. It was epic with a popular voice. Céline narrowly missed the prestigious Prix Goncourt in 1933. He was rejected at the last minute for the more conventional and less controversial *Les loups* by Guy Mazeline. But thanks to his dedicated editor, Robert Denoël, he was awarded the Prix Renaudot. The scandal of the Prix Goncourt actually proved a blessing, as the novel "sold more than 50,000 copies, with more than 5,000 newspapers and magazine articles devoted to it."[6] To add to the public fascination, Céline was an unusual figure on the interwar literary scene: he was a medical doctor by training and never fully left that profession. He was an Anglophone who had traveled to West Africa first in 1916–1917, then in 1925, and who had repeatedly visited the United States for personal and professional reasons. He did not belong to the Parisian literary establishment. Yet, after the success of *Voyage*, his subsequent works, which ranged from a play, *L'Église* (The Church) in 1933, to another epic novel, *Mort à crédit* (Death on the Installment Plan) in 1936, met with a more ambivalent reception, despite his editor's enduring enthusiasm and energy. Still, he was recognized as a formidable novelist by critics and authors as diverse as Léon Daudet, Jean-Paul Sartre, and Henry Miller.

Five years later, Céline claimed his readers' attention once again, this time for very different reasons. The publication of an extremely violent antisemitic pamphlet, *Bagatelles pour un massacre*, caused a huge controversy. It surprised many on the left, puzzled conservative nationalists, and delighted the younger intellectual far right. Most bemoaned its scatological register and others its obsession with nausea, disgust, and the obscene as the language of politics, though some explained that anti-Jewish sentiment was Céline's unfortunate hobby.[7] *Bagatelles* was the resounding and unapologetic articulation of a distinctively French racial antisemitism, offering readers fantasies of abject bodies, sexual perversion, and racial decadence. It was quickly followed, in 1938, by another pamphlet, *L'école des cadavres*, that did not relent in its obsessive denunciation of a Jewish threat corrupting bodies, the nation, and French civilization. Many did not know what to make of these pamphlets, and concluded, as Maurice Blanchot did decades later, that "Céline was a writer in the grip of delirium" and that "delirium [had] found expression in antisemitism."[8] That seemed to many at the time to be the only explanation.

After the success of *Voyage*, Céline's 1937 pamphlet *Bagatelles pour un massacre* baffled readers. It was hard to categorize, mingling fictional dialogues and scenes, ballet librettos, political essay, and newspaper extracts on the topic of nefarious Jewish influence. It was nonetheless a huge (and unexpected) commercial success.[9] Its main protagonist, named both "Ferdinand" (like *Voyage*'s hero) and "Céline" (like the author) seemed to make this book more barely veiled autobiography than fiction, or even political essay. Céline shamelessly borrowed and plagiarized numerous antisemitic texts and newspapers, while developing his unique literary style in the service of a virulent political text.[10] In *Bagatelles*, the "Negroid Jew" was the invisible colonizer who had corrupted the French male body and contaminated the metropolitan nation. The invasion that Céline denounced was portrayed as a sexual violation inflicted on French bodies. Jews were the sole origin, cause, and symptom of an overarching cultural decadence, biological degeneration, and loss of integrity of the French male body. It was that obsession with "the Jew" that horrified critics, seduced many on the far right, and inaugurated Céline's career as an unapologetic racial prophet.

Céline is now a celebrated icon of the French literary canon. His trajectory has since been the subject of myth and is still subject to speculation and controversy. After the publication of these two pamphlets, Céline found himself associated with the far-right pundits who had railed against the Popular Front, parliamentary democracy, and the decadence of modernity. While he never joined any political parties, his unabashed racist antisemitism, collaborationist activities, and self-proclaimed disgust with the French nation led to his inclusion at the end of the Vichy regime on the list of writers who had collaborated and must be "purged."[11] By then, though, Céline had fled France.[12] When he returned in 1951, he resumed publishing novels—*D'un château l'autre* (1957), *Nord* (1960), and *Guignols' Band II* (1964), among others—that have since come to be considered among the greatest he ever wrote. While now an uncontested part of the literary canon, Céline has always been haunted by the reputation engendered by these antisemitic pamphlets and his subsequent infamous escape from France.[13] This enduring controversy has obscured the fact that his literary endeavors throughout the 1930s were as much about defining the *racial* meaning of Frenchness as they were about deriding the decadence of Western civilization through the stories he told and the style he reinvented.

Céline's mid-1930s antisemitic writings are not included in his body of work (his widow has forbidden their reissue), and many literary critics and historians have argued that they are an anomaly in his literary career.[14] They fit uneasily with the canonical image of a great author, even one as unusual as Céline. The pamphlets have been an uncomfortable stain for those who have celebrated

Céline as one of the most distinctive and revolutionary voices to emerge on the French literary scene in the twentieth century. That unease is not unlike that which has followed Blanchot. As a result, Céline's politics have either been deemed irrelevant to his contribution to aesthetic novelty, merely the reflection of widely held beliefs in French popular culture at the time, or the unfortunate derivative of his unusual blend of anarchism, pacifism, and conservatism.[15] While biographers and historians have shown that Céline "was a life-long antisemite," still his fictional works have been separated from these more troublesome publications.[16] For a long time, and following the rigorous analysis of scholar Henri Godard, readers of Céline emphasized the distinction between his (poetic) style and (political) content in order to help elucidate the enigma of a literary author producing such problematic political texts.[17] More recently, critics have turned to Céline's biography and his personal correspondence for explanation of what appeared to have been a sudden embrace of a particularly "vulgar" and virulent antisemitism.[18]

In the mid-1990s, a number of literary critics began offering more-productive interpretations of Céline's political trajectory by taking seriously the ways in which Céline's antisemitic fantasies had emerged out of his own literary and aesthetic critique of modernity. Literary critic David Carroll's work has been exemplary in showing how "Céline . . . confirmed that anti-Semitism was an undeniable component of an ongoing French literary tradition, but he also placed anti-Semitism at the core of his own highly 'original' if not revolutionary literary-rhetorical legacy and thus made it an essential element of the modernist revolt against tradition as well."[19] Still others, such as Rosemary Scullion and Thomas Spears, showed how Céline's "turn to antisemitism" might be better explained by attention to his obsession with masculinity and heterosexual mastery, and his enduring fascination with female bodies.[20] These same critics have also noted the ways in which race figured prominently in the reactionary political vision offered by these polemical writings.[21] The wealth of studies on Céline points to the fact that he represents a particular conundrum, for he epitomizes the complex relationship of aesthetics and politics that has characterized the twentieth century especially when it comes to fascist, Nazi, racist, and antisemitic ideologies. Again, though, these interrogations and analyses have largely remained within the confines of literary history, literary criticism, and biography. It is as if Céline was not a serious object of analysis for political and intellectual history because of his unusual place within the canon, of what appears to be the "excessive" nature of his political ideas, and his literary style.

If he is categorized as a "right-wing literary anarchist," he has mostly been seen as the least representative and the most puzzling—because he was so rabidly antisemitic.[22] Rereading Céline within the context of the cultural discourses of difference and otherness in this decade suggests that we may need to take the political content of his pamphlets more seriously and examine not only how they resonated with his literary works but, more broadly, how they belonged to the intellectual and literary far right.

Though some critics have analyzed the fantasies of sex and gender traversing Céline's literature and others have pointed to a certain obsession with race, little attention has been paid to the ways in which he reconfigured both race *and* gender as the inseparable foundations of Frenchness, imagining a racialized masculinity.[23] Situating Céline's work within the larger historical context of the interwar years provides insight into the themes that infused his literary vision of the social and political. Framing his work in such a way allows historians to analyze how he reinvigorated conventional antisemitic and nationalist tropes. Some have noted, but few have analyzed, the relationship between "colonial ideology" and "modern antisemitism" in his fiction.[24] His virulent antisemitism must therefore be read with an eye to the colonial imaginary that sustained it and the obsession with a fragile heterosexual masculinity that drove his writings—in short, the distinctive discourse of nation and self that was articulated in those years, especially by conservative and far-right intellectuals. Céline's literary and political trajectory was symptomatic of the ways in which a gendered and racial discourse of civilization became an overarching cultural and political obsession in interwar France. Throughout his 1930s writings, he produced, as one critic has noted, an "elaborate construction of difference," echoing the terms of French cultural and political discourse.[25] A close reading of his most representative interwar texts shows how those obsessions unfolded and thus makes sense of these "aberrations." Like the intellectual far right, who both championed and ridiculed him, Céline's work was devoted to the restoration of a French masculinity deemed to be in crisis.

There is an evident thematic continuity between *Voyage* and *Bagatelles* that reveals how Céline's imagination of a racialized masculinity figured prominently in his works and infused his literary vision. Race appears to have been an obsession from the moment Céline began publishing in 1932. While most read *Voyage*, then and afterward, as the denunciation of "a society founded upon war, colonization, industrial labor, and inequality," it seems that it was biological and moral "degeneration" that supplied the underlying and consistent theme of Céline's works.[26] The vagaries of the interwar years allowed him to fantasize a fiction of "national regeneration," which he claimed was but an earnest and sincere *reaction* to the fundamental disorder of French society, which his narrator observed around him. The evolution of his writings therefore allows us to chart the ways in which Céline transformed this obsession into a fierce and unapologetic racialized antisemitism. Despite the convention of separating out the pamphlets from the literary works, both genres must be read together because they express a particular imagination of race, sex, and violence.[27] Céline, who was intent on challenging the legacy of modernity that was synonymous, for him, with race and blackness, urgently crafted a new idiom, that of racial antisemitism. He added his apocalyptic vision to the legacy of modernism whose aesthetics were far from immune from racial categories and where whiteness operated as the silent yet obsessive presence defining "modern man's alienation."[28] Race operated as the symptom, origin, and solution to the derelict state of his time. It was that which would eradicate the ill effects of modernity.

Céline conceived of the body as the site of political imagination. In his fictional text and in his pamphlets, he powerfully sexed and raced the "widespread fear [originating in the nineteenth century] that the energy of mind and body was dissipating under the strain of modernity."[29] Heterosexual masculinity was an enduring theme underlying Céline's fiction and pamphlets, in which he fictionalized questions about the precariousness of a masculine subjectivity dependent upon a notion of the "whole, organic, productive body" and which demanded that race delineate a proper masculinity.[30] His racist imagination obsessively focused on the male body as the solution to that abject self haunting the interwar period's far-right imaginary.[31] The fragile male body whose integrity had been perverted and undone must be reaffirmed. Unlike his contemporary Maurice Blanchot, who had attempted to erase the mark of the body and overcome the demand of sexual difference, the pamphleteer Céline attempted to restore a unified, whole, and embodied male subject. In his novels and pamphlets, Céline fictionalized the ways in which "race and sexuality [operated as] ordering mechanisms" of the French self.[32]

While *Voyage* represents Céline's first successful fictional attempt, *Bagatelles* is an important work to examine because, like the novel, it offers an aesthetics that is central to the political work of the pamphlet. What made *Bagatelles* so striking was the way in which it emerged out of a colonial and racist imaginary to become solely and entirely devoted to racial antisemitism. If *Voyage* perfectly fictionalized the Western imperial project of "subjugating, dominating, and regulating bodies and space," *Bagatelles* represented an attempt to overcome the racial contamination that pervaded metropolitan space.[33] In his pamphlet, Céline did not merely resort to the "lexicon of colonialism" but offered an antisemitic imaginary founded in the experience of colonization and racial thought.[34] Colonial imagination helped delineate a Frenchness that Céline, from 1937 onward, understood to be a "white Aryan category." The association of sexuality and race had long constituted the trope of antisemitic rhetoric and imagination.[35] Céline's pamphlets revealed how gender, sexuality, and race were constitutive of his vision of Frenchness articulated in a fantasy of abject bodies and national regeneration. His narrator, Ferdinand, had been driven in *Voyage* by fear and disgust, but in *Bagatelles*, anger and hate were unleashed.

Selfhood and the Martyrdom of Authorship

This vision was neither accident nor aberrant explosion. Céline himself never recanted, downplayed, or apologized for his texts. Instead, as literary scholar Philip Watts has shown, he never admitted guilt and systematically "disavowed" the taint of his antisemitism, arguing from 1946 onward that whatever he had written, he had done so out of patriotism and pacifism.[36] He wrote in the 1952 preface to *Voyage*: "Everything gets taken the wrong way." But this statement was quickly nuanced by his own confession that "I have been the cause of too much evil."[37] By 1952, Céline had suffered public and political shaming brought about by the end of the war and the demise of the Vichy regime. He had hastily fled Paris for Germany in 1944 where he found himself first in Baden-Baden, then in Sigmarigen in the midst of an exiled community of former French collaborationists and fascists such as *Je Suis Partout* journalists Lucien Rebatet and Pierre-Antoine Cousteau, as well as his friend Robert Le Vigan and prominent Vichy officials. (He later famously fictionalized this episode in *D'un château l'autre*, published in 1957, which was rather successful.) After escaping to Denmark, he was arrested by Danish authorities and imprisoned there. Tried in absentia in France in 1950, he was found guilty on February 21 of that same year. He was able to return to France only after his lenient sentencing and amnesty "as an ex-combatant of the 1914–18 war" in 1951.[38] Such a fate allowed Céline to claim unfair persecution and victimization. But this position—claimed for both the novels' author and their narrator—had always been a staple of his fiction. Indeed, Ferdinand—in both novels and pamphlets—was often portrayed as suffering from paranoid delusions, imagining his martyrdom at the hands of others, the unfortunate victim of an unkind world, and Céline still claimed as much in his first television interview in 1957.[39]

Yet it was paranoia that allowed Céline to accuse the world and, in 1937, all Jews, of being responsible for individual and collective degeneration. It was the trope of victimhood and the claim to madness that allowed him to logically unfold his antisemitic and racist arguments while at the same time claiming that "he"—as an author—had been misunderstood and therefore unfairly victimized. Already, in his 1941 short political text berating Jews, communism, and French defeat, *Les beaux draps*, readers had been told: "All that does not lie, is despised, tracked down, hunted down, thrown up, is hated to death."[40] Céline's 1952 preface to *Voyage*, written in the wake of his exile with other collaborationists and subsequent denunciation as a traitor to France, elaborated on this belief. It performed at once his victimization while blaming his (misguided) critics and readers. By hinting that his first novel was the authentic expression of a prophetic but martyred author, he suggested that *Bagatelles* (as well as the 1938 *L'école des cadavres* and the 1941 *Les beaux draps*) followed in that lineage and that his persecution had been unfair—the unrepentant position he would always maintain after 1945. As his narrator, Ferdinand, explained to his elusive and unreliable friend Robinson in *Voyage*: "A madman's thoughts are just the usual ideas of a human being, except that they're hermetically sealed inside his head."[41] Céline's pamphlets had made his madness only too visible to his readers. That madness was also what made readers and critics wonder whether they should take the pamphlets seriously or not.

Céline's complicated relationship to literary recognition, responsibility, and authorship alerts us to the ways in which he negotiated the demands of literary production with his own hygienist and racist vision of decadence and regeneration.[42] Indeed, from the very beginning of his career, Céline offered his reading public the "fiction of a double identity," where he was both author (under his pseudonym, Céline) and also Louis-Ferdinand Destouches, the small-time suburban doctor of the Parisian working classes.[43] This double positioning was further blurred by the systematic use of "Ferdinand" as the hero of both novels and pamphlets. Céline never claimed that any of his texts were autobiographical—even the pamphlets where the narrator was, for the first time, openly named "Céline"—yet he deliberately let his readers wonder about the subjective and autobiographical nature of his hero, Ferdinand, who could be all at once alter ego, pure fictional invention, and literary writing of the self.[44] Céline played on the confusion of *authorship* as his writings "transgresse[d] the traditional codes of categorization as 'autobiography.'"[45] It is in the performative function of narrator, author, and character that we can glean the ways in which those roles served to uphold his particular racial vision and enacted the contradictions and abjection of the male subject Céline was fictionalizing.

Nonetheless, the historicization of these pamphlets has not necessarily yielded convincing answers. Historians have argued that Céline set out to write his first vitriolic pamphlet, *Bagatelles*, in reaction to the 1937 Exposition universelle, where culture and politics came together under the tutelage of the Popular Front. The exposition had been regularly mocked by the far-right press as exemplifying the incompetence, corruption, and decadence of the Popular Front government. As one *L'Insurgé* contributor lamented, its construction "disfigured Paris."[46] *Je Suis Partout* railed that it was a "dishonor" to the French spirit and gave an "imperfect and misleading image" of France.[47] And, in *Bagatelles*, the exposition figured as the event that propelled the narration: it was, after all, the place where "Céline" tested his belief that all of French cultural institutions had been infested by Jews working to exclude Frenchmen like himself. It was a "magnificent and undeniable demonstration of that frenzied Jewish colonization."[48] While this explanation makes sense—and is offered by the author and narrator—identifying the pamphlet as the outcome of some *real* discontent experienced by Céline does not fully illuminate the ways in which the pamphlet was symptomatic of a long-standing racial vision already present in Céline's fiction. *Bagatelles* could not have been a surprise to those who were attentive to the concern with degeneration, civilization, and race in his earlier writings. Already, in 1933, barely a year after the success of *Voyage*, *L'Église* (which was met with a tepid reception) displayed a vocal obsession with Jewishness and race.[49] Like *Voyage*, *L'Église* is set in Africa, America, and a Parisian suburb. It features "Gologolo, Bardamu's young negro," as well as a Jewish administrator of the League of Nations, "Yudenzweck," and his Jewish colleague, "M. Mosaic."[50] It already prefigured what was to come. In fact, the pamphlet fit in the larger genealogy of Celinian themes: the racial content of class, the fate of "male desiring subjects," the centrality of this imaginary position in the articulation of rightful belonging to the metropolitan nation, and the need for displacement of the trauma of the war onto other bodies in order to contain degeneration and contamination. The pamphlets were therefore neither accident nor misguided disenchantment.

From *Voyage* to *Bagatelles*: The Race and Sex of Frenchness

I still raved quite a lot, but with a certain logic . . .

—*Voyage au bout de la nuit*

Céline has long been portrayed as the novelist of the working classes, providing a voice for the dispossessed, for those intent on challenging bourgeois morality, and for the anxieties generated by postwar modernity. As one far-right literary critic mused in a rather typical fashion, "Céline's quarrel is with the world at large, he knows the caddishness of the bourgeoisie, he knows the baseness of the proletariat."[51] And, more recently, a critic eloquently named him the "self-styled ethnographer of a downtrodden humanity."[52] Yet his adventure narrative and fictionalization of the ordinary owed much to the French authors who had in the previous decade published works denouncing the war, its experience, and its dehumanizing effects upon younger generations. Though he did not acknowledge it—aside from dedicating *Bagatelles* to Eugène Dabit, the author of *L'Hôtel du Nord*—Céline was part of this long genealogy of war literature that had become prominent in the interwar years with authors like Henri Barbusse and Pierre Mac Orlan (whom he knew).[53] Contemporary novelist Blaise Cendrars himself had noted the striking similarity of *Voyage* to his own *Moravagine*, published several years earlier, in which he had fictionalized "war, flight, America, life among the savages, madness, eroticism, suburbia, doctors, etc."[54] Céline himself announced in *Bagatelles* that Mac Orlan "had predicted everything, put it in music, thirty years ahead [of us]."[55] Similarly, Céline's first novel owes much to the trope of travel narratives that became popular in the 1920s and 1930s, in the wake of the development of tourism and ethnographic travel.[56] His depiction of Ferdinand's trials and tribulations in the United States also followed in the footsteps of right-wing authors Paul Morand and Georges Duhamel and their "American" novels.[57] Céline's vision found acclaim, however, because of the particular nature of his style, which unapologetically appropriated working-class slang and remade the very substance and structure of French language. As critic Henri Godard has noted, "Céline is more writer of popular French, than of slang and obscenity," and through that popular language, he seemed to have reinvented French literature.[58]

The shock caused by the publication of Céline's first novels lay in his use of the French language: his unabashed translation of the popular rhythms of spoken French, his complex use of registers of "obscenity and scatology," and "insults," in the service of epic narration, which, many have argued, he "successfully subverted."[59] In this respect, his was characteristic of the larger modernist experiments that had found expression especially in the British literary scene with authors such as Virginia Woolf, Ezra Pound, and T. S. Eliot.[60] "Modernism"—the literary movement—was also an idiom articulated through the language of race. In both content and form, modernism, as literary critics Edward Said and Fredric Jameson have shown, was implicated in the "structures of imperialism."[61] Little attention has been paid to the fact that Céline's vision similarly displayed that "post-realist modernist sensibility" that was *of* and *in imperialism*.[62] (Critics have often instead emphasized what appeared to be his scathing critique of French colonies and the settlers [*colons*] who lived there.) He always claimed that his "style" was like "jazz": authentic, unregulated, and instinctive—a style that, in the interwar years, was often associated with race and blackness and that shored up anxieties as to the meaning of French culture.[63] But in his fiction, he may have done so only to refute its association with "blackness" in an effort to redeem those white heterosexual male French bodies that had been assaulted and corrupted. Race and imperialism infused Céline's imagination.

Voyage au bout de la nuit tells the story of a young man, Ferdinand, who, having suffered the indignities and trauma of World War I, tries to find his way and travels to Africa and America. He attempts a variety of careers before settling down as a doctor in the Parisian working-class suburbs. *Voyage* is the epic, comic, and dark rendering of Ferdinand's trials and tribulations. The novel fictionalizes the inherent precariousness of masculine subjectivity through its play on style and space. While "class" seems to be the driving mode of Ferdinand's journey, it operates as a racial category. Under the guise of class, Ferdinand is concerned with the biological and anatomical nature of race. Class, capitalism, and materialism—the avowed themes of the novel—functions in relation to a racial vision of civilization. What is at stake in Ferdinand's quest is the degeneration of bodies, especially of French (and Western) bodies. That degeneration had been revealed as Ferdinand traveled to fantasized foreign spaces articulated as sites of racial identity. The conflation of class and race was hardly a new occurrence in Western literature and had found its most glaring articulation in the nineteenth century, whose obsessions involved the cultural production of the working classes—those "dangerous" classes—as racially inferior and degenerate. Following a long literary tradition, from Mary Shelley's 1816 *Frankenstein* to Émile Zola's 1885 *Germinal*, readers were offered visions of bourgeois anxieties regarding metropolitan working classes and colonial subjects. Though it has been read as a "satire of colonial society," *Voyage* thus offered a more ambiguous imaginary of bodies and modernity.[64]

Ferdinand's vision of the world involves the fear of transgression of racial boundaries, especially in relation to those colonial subjects who acted as reminders of a precarious French whiteness. In the tradition of late-nineteenth-century imperial novels, Céline offered, with his first novel, a foray into the "dark continent" that revealed the degeneration of white bodies, contaminated by the racial mingling occuring in Africa. *Voyage* revealed to its readers how the "civilized" had been made "savage." This was made evident to Ferdinand upon his arrival in an unnamed French African colony: he exclaimed that the experience of colonialism had been a "biological confession."[65] The narrator added: "Those blacks stink of their misery, their interminable vanities, and their repugnant resignation; actually, they're just like our poor people, except they have more children, less dirty washing, and less red wine."[66] *Voyage* portrayed Africans read through the prism of racialized class. The "toiling masses" that Ferdinand viewed only as a "hubbub of screeching, overexcited blacks" were nothing more than an instance of biological and racial degeneration—but one impossible to redeem and restore, unlike the metropolitan French working classes.[67]

Most of the degeneration observed in the colonies was merely a symptom of the ravages of modernity and its most outrageous expression—war. Céline's Ferdinand believes that inauthenticity was the mark of this postwar era; early in the novel he explains, "The little that had been left in 1914, people were ashamed of now. Everything you touched was phony, the sugar, the aeroplanes, the shoes, the jam, the photographs. . . . Everything you read, swallowed, sucked, admired, proclaimed, refuted, defended, was made up of hate-ridden myths and grinning masquerades, phony to the hilt."[68] War had revealed the fundamental artificiality of all that was modern and the horrific nature of what had first appeared to be an emblem of progress. Its deleterious consequences were everywhere, for the world had been turned upside down. Decadence and excess marked this postwar society where no space was left untouched by the transgression of proper boundaries. While Ferdinand wandered in Paris at night, all he could see was

> a hysterical bitch, you could see what she'd be like just by watching her cavorting in the dance hall of the Olympia. In that long cellar room. You could see her

> squinting out of a hundred mirrors, stamping her feet in the dust and despair to the music of a Negro-Judeo-Saxon band. Britishers and blacks, Levantines and Russians were everywhere, smoking and bellowing, military melancholics lined up on the red plush sofas.[69]

Sex and race were no longer contained.[70] That acute sense of chaos now unleashed in the places Ferdinand had called home was, after all, what had motivated the narrator's initial desire to leave the metropole and travel after he had returned from the war, a bitter, cynical, cowardly, and disillusioned veteran. Travel, the novel suggested, might help restore some pure, untainted, sense of self.

Strikingly, Ferdinand's trip to Africa revealed the protagonist's obsession with race and degeneracy, and illustrated how French masculinity had been endangered. Indeed, while Ferdinand proves eager to consume female bodies throughout the novel, his African stay is the only moment when he is rendered impotent. Once in Africa, Ferdinand could not engage in sex, though he was constantly surrounded by seemingly unstoppable sexual excesses and desires. Men were "assaulted" by African prostitutes who were likened to fierce and faceless "mosquitoes," colonial officers had let themselves go and vegetated under the care of their "black female companions," white women had seen their bodies softened and altered by the weather, and white men had lost all sense of propriety and restraint. Ferdinand's vision of Africa accorded with contemporary notions of colonial spaces as inherently dangerous to the Western constitution and inevitably inviting degeneration and contamination.[71] But the theme of purity appeared elsewhere in the novel: in America and in metropolitan France where "Arabs" lingered in cafés and seduced white women.[72] That the colony had contaminated the metropole—a fact made abundantly clear for Céline by the vogue for jazz, the presence of (African) black and (North African) Arab bodies within the Parisian cultural scene, as well as migrant workers, and the simultaneous fascination with and repulsion by all things African—fueled his anxiety regarding the integrity of white Western bodies that would be the subject of *Bagatelles*.[73] Again, in the pamphlet, it was the "experience" of race in Africa and at home that brought about the supposed "realization" of the abject, perverse, and inescapable rule of Jewishness, and Ferdinand's "conversion" to antisemitism.

Bagatelles pour un massacre: The Race of Jewishness

France is a Jewish colony, without any possibility of insurrection, discussion, or whispers.

—*Bagatelles pour un massacre*

Robert Brasillach explained in his 1941 memoir that for him and his friends, "Instinctual antisemitism had found [in 1937] its prophet in the shape of Louis-Ferdinand Céline." Brasillach claimed that Céline had "unleashed in *Bagatelles pour un massacre* a torrential work of joyous ferocity—it was most certainly excessive but with grand verve. No reasoning in this book, but only the "natives' revolt."[74] The natives—as Céline renamed French men—were revealed to have been subjected to a debasing and humiliating "Jewish colonialism," which had perverted all French individuals and corrupted what Céline deemed to be the racial essence of Frenchness. Racial degeneration had made Frenchness "pathetic and idiotic."[75] Brasillach concluded: "Its triumph was incredible."[76] His assessment barely came close to the surprising success and the subsequent controversy generated by the publication of Céline's 1937 antisemitic pamphlet. But his enthusiasm spoke to the way in which Céline manipulated race and gender to offer what he claimed was a much-needed distinctively French racial antisemitism.

In *Bagatelles*, readers were told that the alleged explicit origin of Ferdinand's fierce and unrelenting antisemitism lay in the refusal to publish his ballet librettos—themselves a device to get near desirable and seductive ballerinas—by Jewish financiers, critics, and theater owners.[77] Interestingly, the content of these ballets involved a hallucinatory fictionalization of the dangers of racial transgression brought about by the miscegenation and unbridled sexuality unleashed by the contamination of white Western bodies by African "savages." For the narrator Ferdinand did not just mention the rejection of his librettos. They literally framed the story of his tribulations at the hands of Jews. The librettos were palimpsests legitimating Ferdinand's unapologetic "conversion" to antisemitism.

One of Céline's three ballet librettos returns to the story recounted in *Paul and Virginie*, the widely read late-eighteenth-century novel by Bernardin de Saint-Pierre. As a Rousseauian demonstration of the purity of the state of nature, and set in the colony of Mauritius, Saint-Pierre's novel told of Paul and

Virginie, who, brought up far from the corruption of the metropole, lived in innocence and virtue, but whose love was finally thwarted by fate and human corruption.[78] Entitled "Scoundrel Paul. Brave Virginie," Céline's version offers a vision of gender, sex, and race intended to provide horrified delight to Parisian audiences. The libretto subverts the trope of eighteenth-century travel narratives, rendering their racial and sexual underpinnings only too visible, unveiling their fear of miscegenation and of excesses brought about by the European colonial experience.[79] It begins where the novel ended, with the shipwreck of Paul and Virginie on a remote tropical island where "savages" live.[80] While in the midst of a celebration with "tam-tam . . . music . . . furious dancing . . . lascivious . . . then jerky . . . exasperated . . . ," these "good savages" (identified as "negroes" and presumably echoing the slaves and maroons that appear in de Saint-Pierre's novel) give the two lovers a rejuvenating potion. While Virginie shuns it, Paul readily accepts, only to find himself perverted.[81] The potion unleashes his libidinal unconscious and he eagerly engages in "unnatural" relations with the native savages. Paul embodies the contemporary trope of the dangers believed to be haunting white colonial officers in tropical climates.[82] *Voyage* had already shown how the foreign and tropical climate of Africa led white men to allow themselves to be literally and metaphorically "unbuttoned," consumed by "alcoholism, malaria, [and] syphilis."[83] That motif was reproduced in the libretto.

The climax of the ballet comes when both protagonists, accompanied by these same "savages," return to the metropole and unleash a scene of orgiastic frenzy reminiscent of the popular representations of jazz nights, where black men and white women engaged in sexually suggestive dances all night long.[84] Here, the excessive sexual perversions and crazy music of the "savages" both frighten and seduce "young French men and young French women."[85] Proper bourgeois heterosexual moral codes have been undone by the mysterious potion and the presence of foreign racial bodies. Virginie is made jealous by Paul's unrestrained dance with Mirella, another virginal young French woman who has now succumbed to the effects of the potion and "lasciviously" embraces Paul. Upon seeing this, Virginie drinks the potion herself and becomes "defiant and mocking." She "rips off her clothes, and dances with even greater impetuous energy, more provocatively [than Mirella], and lewdness." As Mirella witnesses Paul returning to Virginie, she shoots her. The scene ends with Paul crying by Virginie's side, while the "devilish machine" of an American train, "The Fulmicoach . . . with a man playing the trumpet at its helm" enters the scene and leads the "enthusiastic" crowd offstage.[86] The sound of the train's arrival, Céline specifies, is "in the style of jazz."[87] The libretto is thus bookended by a movement similar to the one undertaken in *Voyage*: from the colony to the metropole. In both cases, the fantasy of "America" as the ominous marker of technology and industrialization intervenes in that movement.

The ballet libretto in its phantasmic fictionalization of racial and sexual contamination used one trope, which had first emerged in *Voyage*. In *Bagatelles*, it was the symbol of racial and sexual disorder: the particular insistent sound of the African "tam-tam." Céline's recurrent use of the tam-tam is interesting in that it had also been a staple of descriptions of the newly popular jazz music performances that were all the rage in Paris, which, according to many contemporary commentators, could be defined by the use of drums and improvisation. References to tam-tams would have been familiar to readers who were aware of the popular "bal Nègre" of the rue Blomet and the performances of Josephine Baker.[88] It was even said by an interwar critic to possess an "infernal rhythm."[89] In fact, Céline's descriptions of tam-tam and dancing strikingly echo the ways in which jazz concert halls and nightclubs were depicted by critics in the interwar years. The tam-tam figures prominently in the African scenes of *Voyage*, providing the background to Ferdinand's own descent into madness in the jungle. It always becomes louder in the African nights as African women, mosquitoes, and the darkness of the night assault Ferdinand's body, just as the drums assault his senses. For Ferdinand, Africa means "the big black night of the hot countries, with its brutal tom-tom heart that always beats too fast."[90] The "tam-tam" was also what provided the libretto its rhythm and signified the absolute orgiastic nature of the lovers' encounter with the "tribe" of "negroes."[91] It haunts the characters and resonates within French metropolitan space. Throughout the pamphlet, it was also a recurring theme, this time signifying the racial nature of Jewishness perverting French bodies. It evoked the inauthentic, perverted, and suspect nature of Jews and Jewish influence in France. Céline explains that, very simply, "the semite, who is truly a negro, is a perpetual beast in tam-tam."[92] The tam-tam acted as the literal reminder of the plight of that "idiot of a native French man."[93] While in *Voyage* the "biological" experience of race could still be contained within the (African) colony, in *Bagatelles* there was neither respite nor escape. Jewishness had pervaded everything: contamination and dissolution now infused every aspect of metropolitan life.

Céline thus harnessed colonial racist rhetoric in order to affirm that Jews exemplified racial perversion—as antisemites did when they spoke of the "Oriental" nature of Jews. While the "blackness" of the Jew—a common antisemitic rhetorical device—served to emphasize the unnaturalness of Jewishness, it also showed the racial nature of the danger.[94] The racialization of Jewishness had emerged in "nineteenth-century race discourse, [in which] race was inscribed in every element of the body and soul, mind and sexuality, temperament and ability," and that belief characterized Céline's portrayal of Jews.[95] Jewishness was suspect because it metonymically embodied all that was (racially) non-Western, and therefore outside the bounds of civilization. The Western man must fear the most from the "Jewish race" because it was irredeemably tainted by miscegenation. This was anxiously articulated in *Bagatelles*, where, we were told, the "Jews are hybrid."[96] They were the product of an unnatural Afro-Asian miscegenation since they were "the garbage of Africa, the garbage of Asia."[97] This hybrid category produced only "Negroid Judaïzation"—a perversion of both the social body of the nation and the French male body.[98] In fact, Céline veered little from this racial vision, and in his 1941 pamphlet directly linked Jews to the former French colony of Haiti—site of the first "black revolution"—again associating blackness and Jewishness. He explained that "there is a [Toussaint] L'Ouverture in every Jew. Me, I would send them all over there, to Saint-Domingue, the Caribbean; that would be a good environment for them, they would finally see what a communism between cousins looks like since they are no longer interested in Palestine."[99] Using the older colonial name rather than its contemporary one, and emphasizing familial kinship, Céline shored up visions of violence, revolt, and insurrection by impure racial others.

Only an appeal to race could make sense of the decadence that had taken place since the traumatic experience of the Great War and had, for Céline, been confirmed by the rise of the Popular Front and of communism, involvement in the Spanish Civil War, and the Exposition universelle that opened in Paris in 1937. Céline's narrator raged, why should it be that "after so many Frenchmen of the soil having died under enemy bullets in Flanders or at Verdun, we should now be inundated by ten thousand yids [who are] all so *couscous*, deathly racist and insatiable?"[100] Race therefore made sense of modernity—war, industrialization, technology—and decadence. It acted as that driving principle of civilization. It explained how France, once a great imperial nation-state, now stood like its former colonized subjects: enslaved, oppressed, and humiliated. As Céline asserted, "The natives are bled out, frozen, shoved aside, subdued . . . with this new oriental rush of at least a million civil servants with their little ones . . . , a pockmarked caravan of Asian hordes."[101] The colonizer had become the colonized. Céline insisted on this theme and always maintained that French people should now recognize that they were oppressed natives. In fact, he added in his second attempt at pamphleteering, in 1938:

> We—native Frenchmen [*français de souche*]—are subjugated, bullied, oppressed, cuckold, ripped off, demeaned. [We are] at once and vividly, admirably, relentless, frantically, fastidiously even, ridiculed. Tirelessly and perpetually [ridiculed] by our careerist racial brothers [who are] freemasons, [and] Jews' willing dogs, [who] gorge at any garbage especially Jewish rubbish . . . lost to Jewish whistles.[102]

France was represented as a nation under assault, a soil held hostage by foreign individuals—implicitly reaffirming the Barrèsian relationship of French citizens to the metropolitan French soil—and now in the throes of a foreign invasion. The whole world of Asians, "Orientals," Africans was pouring into France. France was not only "a colony of international Jewish power," but especially since the Popular Front, "yid colonization had shown itself to be more and more impatient, tyrannical, sensitive, intransigent."[103] *Bagatelles*' Ferdinand ruefully explains after having denounced the ways in which "Mister Blum holds in his Jewish hands [Frenchmen's] means of living, . . . their reason for being," that "this is how things happen in Africa. But, on this side, in France, we are the *bicots*."[104] Here, Céline's use of the common racist insult designating North Africans indicated that French were "natives" held in contempt by foreign Jews. Following Ferdinand's logic, the conclusion became obvious: "With [Blum's] hordes conquering this country, [and] subduing the natives," French citizens could only realize that "Jews are our master, here, over there, in Russia, in England, in America, everywhere!"[105] Such colonization was not just metaphoric but meant that "in a Jewish world, the 'white man' can only be manual laborer or soldier, the intellectual must be Jewish."[106] The world had been turned upside down, and as a result, Ferdinand's contemporaries had been "thoroughly judaïzed and negrified."[107] This implied that the French people were now nothing more than a "slave herd."[108] Most horrifying was, as Ferdinand explained it, "colonization by Negroid Jews [which] embodies the worst of moral and physical abjections."[109] Frenchmen had been made into abject and passive victims; and it was this abjection that made visible the demise of Frenchness.

Claiming that France had been subjected to an unnatural "Jewish colonization" implied that French metropolitan citizens were akin to *natives*—an indigenous people rendered decadent through subjection. Céline's rhetoric further emphasized the racial nature of those "natively" French. While Jews were a "hybrid race," it was undeniable that Frenchness was also a racial category. *Bagatelles*' narrator could be read seamlessly slipping between native, white, and Frenchman. More strikingly, it was Céline's systematic usage of the term "Aryan" that would have struck his readers—especially since it unabashedly evoked Nazi racial policies and terminology at a time when even those on the far right were divided over Nazi antisemitism and what some termed its enthusiasm for "racial myths." Through the rhetoric of colonization, Céline racialized the content of the category "Aryan," which figured systematically and obsessively in his pamphlet. Céline had first mentioned the category in the introductory pages of *Bagatelles* and, as the text unfolded, he used the term interchangeably to refer to Western men, French men, and all those who were not Jewish.[110] He insistently referred to those who were "racially French."[111] Being "Aryan" was an essence, not an attribute that could be lost—as evidenced by his use of the noun rather than the adjective.

What seemed to obsess Céline especially was that after the decadence of the last few years and the unrelenting foreign invasion by Jews, "Aryans" had lost any "sense of racial self-help."[112] That "racial solidarity" was indicative of a civilization that had not been tainted by otherness. Its loss meant that "any communal mystical sense" had disappeared.[113] What made French people especially abject was the fact that they did not even rebel against Jews and other racial others. Céline bemoaned the situation whereby "as soon as a native reveals himself . . . the others of that same race are outraged, lynching is no3t far away. . . . In penal colonies, the worst abuses are exercised by inmates themselves . . . they are a thousand times more cruel between themselves." Enslavement had produced that division and lack of "racial solidarity" because, according to Céline, "those racial brothers are well trained." He added, "[The Aryan] now understands only the Jew . . . what comes out of the Jewish sewer . . . he relishes it, he is delighted by it . . . and nothing else. . . . Aryans, the French especially, now live and breathe under the sign of envy, of mutual and complete hatred, of a fanatical and absolute slander."[114] In a logic not dissimilar to that of the Young New Right, it was not just the nation which was under assault but French citizens themselves, who had been corrupted and now lived in complete ignorance of the extent of their abjection. Consumed by self-hatred and an inability to recognize what needed to be done, Frenchmen had forgotten the truth of their "racial essence": Céline lamented, "The white man, the French especially, hates everything that reminds him of his race."[115] Yet his pamphlet showed that this was what must be done.

This realization motivated the pamphlet's narrator. *Bagatelles* offered a number of commentaries on the ways in which racial degeneration required a different politics. In the pamphlet Céline has his friend the Montmartre artist Popol (a fictionalization of Céline's friend the artist Gen Paul) tell Ferdinand that the only way to denounce and counter this omnipotent Jewish rule over French territory, culture, and politics was to claim the position of oppressed and persecuted. After one of Ferdinand's rants against "Jewish power," Popol exclaims: "If I were you, I would become a free-mason . . . that is quite a baptism for an Aryan! It would cleanse you a little but . . . it would make you a little black . . . to be white is no longer what rules in France . . . it is 'blackening' that you need. The future belongs to the 'negroes'!"[116] The denunciation of racial corruption and the recognition of one's colonized status in turn offered the readers of Céline's pamphlets a way to comprehend what needed to be done. It, in fact, legitimated the very existence of the pamphlets offered as prophetic kernels of truth, which needed to be revealed in order for social and political regeneration to occur.

The tone became even more urgent a year later in *L'école des cadavres*. As Céline explained, "democracies [are] Aryan masses who have been domesticated, ransomed, vinegared, divided, tricked, bewildered, [but also] hypnotized, depersonalized, trained to absurdly hate the fraternal by Jews eager to plunder."[117] Now the novelist turned political pundit. There was only one political solution and that was rebellion against the invasion. He thus asserted: "For now, in Germany, in Italy, in Russia, in fact almost everywhere, the Jew discovers a resistance to his will." That resistance was the necessary and urgent racial antisemitism that he termed "a certain Aryan racism."[118] He had hinted at it toward the end of *Bagatelles*, explaining he "would prefer twelve Hitlers to one omnipotent Blum."[119] Antisemitism was a question of race. It had to fashion politics because it alone would allow for the eradication of biological degeneration and the recovery of the mastery that was foundational to racialized French masculinity.

Impure Male Bodies

> That the body regains [its] *joie de vivre*, finds its pleasure again, its rhythm, the verve it had forfeited, the charms of its flight. . . . The mind will surely follow! . . . For the mind means a perfect body, and first a mystical line, the supple detour of a gesture, a message from the soul.
>
> *Bagatelles pour un massacre*

Céline's antisemitic vision expressed itself in the language of obscenity, sexual transgression, and bodily abjection. As many critics have noted, the fate of bodies consumed the novelist. *Voyage* had already offered racialized imaginings of female and male bodies since, as its protagonist had exclaimed, "[a] body always tells the truth, that's why it's usually depressing and disgusting to look at."[120] *Voyage* had portrayed its main character as a man who simultaneously was consumed with unsatisfied desire for enticing female bodies and viewed women as only either "sluts" or "domestic at heart."[121] His relentless desire to possess female bodies was directed only at those who were not degenerate or contaminated. In France, Ferdinand has an adventure with an American nurse, Lola, whose "pure American body" delights him.[122] However, as a colonial civil servant, he never engages in sexual relationships while in Africa (unlike in France and America), where both black female bodies—shown to be impure—and white female bodies—shown to have degenerated under the influence of the tropical climate—prove repulsive. Upon his return to metropolitan France and as a doctor in Paris's working-class suburbs, he finds himself again horrified, repulsed, but also strangely fascinated by the degenerate working-class female bodies he is called upon to take care of. In contrast to the "erotico-mystical admiration" that Ferdinand experiences in front of "absolutely and undeniably beautiful women" in New York, his poor female patients in Paris are but orifices, body parts, and excretions eliciting in him apathy, indifference, and disgust.[123] When visiting a female patient who has undergone a botched abortion, Ferdinand remarks: "I couldn't see anything in her vagina. Blood clots. A glug-glug between her legs like in the decapitated colonel's neck in the war."[124] The analogy with the deathly war-inflicted wounds that Ferdinand had witnessed was hardly a coincidence, for it evokes here the absolute absurdity and yet incontrovertible fact of degeneration brought about by the miserable conditions of modernity—war and industrialization. The abject condition of these instances of failed motherhood reveals how the metropolitan space has been contaminated and rendered sterile in his fantasy of social and national degeneration.

In contrast to *Voyage*'s narrative of abject female bodies that Ferdinand either yearns for or finds repulsive, *Bagatelles* allowed Céline to focus on the male body as the site of invasion, assault, perversion, and loss of integrity. In *Bagatelles*, bodies literally signify the decadence of French civilization. Western civilization had been lost, for

> the Western man [is] like a primate, stubborn, a drunk, a fake and a cuckold. He is a born-slave for Jews, all ready for them, rendered stupid by primary school with all their words and then with alcohol, later again he is emasculated by compulsory education . . . to be sure he will never recover, never get back his music, will never sing again.[125]

By the mid-1930s, Céline claimed that the Western male body no longer epitomized civilization: it was inauthentic and subject to the ills of alcoholism and a lack of rationality. Republican education had perverted the allegedly authentic Frenchman and, under the rule of Jewishness, had proved unable to regulate appropriately the social, instead encouraging moral degeneration. Heterosexual masculinity had been fundamentally undone.

Bagatelles thus articulated an "aesthetics and politics of the body."[126] The male body was an unstable construction through which Céline expressed his horror of modernity and compulsion for eroticized violence. The degradation of the flesh brought about by modernity (male bodies had been split, dislocated, and dismembered by the experience of the war) was translated into a threat to the autonomous male self from women, racial others, and Jews. Céline lamented, "For us poor pre-war Frenchmen, precarious survivors of '14, [we] are obviously deemed the most debased of a tired alcoholic race, finished, despicable, overwhelmingly detestable to the point of death, by the Jews."[127] *Bagatelles* offered a narrative of the precarious identity of the male French citizen, highlighting its contradictions and tensions. As historian Carolyn Dean has noted in relation to the interwar French cultural imagination, authors like Céline symptomatically articulated "the social body's metaphorical masculinity and its possible sexual violation."[128] That violation was minutely described by Céline. But the abjection it entailed was also displaced onto the bodies of those deemed different (and which were also repugnant and disgusting), and thus irreducibly foreign to Frenchness.

A pornographic vision of the body organized around the lexicon of gender, race, and sexuality sustained Céline's imagination. Obsessively, the pamphlet echoed the postwar realization that "the scarred and mutilated body of the disabled soldier [had become] a privileged site of the fantasy of national recuperation."[129] That fantasy of restoration and "phallic mastery," as critic Rosemarie Scullion has termed it, infused *Bagatelles*' racist antisemitism.[130] Céline's obsession not only fantasized "the Jew's body" but focused around the troubling issue of the bodily integrity of the "Aryan" man. Only an exclusionary and normative body could effectively symbolize the ideal of "modern virility."[131] As critic Thomas Spears has noted, *Bagatelles* offered virility in response to fantasized emasculation, violation, and feminization.[132] The pamphlet thus charted the conditions for the reconstruction of a French male body, untouched by the devastating effects of modernity—war, industrialization, urbanization, mechanization—that its author identified with "the Jew."

The fantasy of a "Jewish body" served an important function in antisemitic texts.[133] Like many other French interwar antisemites, Céline offered fantasies of Jewish bodies characterized by their lack of proper boundaries and propensity to perversion. What was presented as terrifying in his antisemitic prose was precisely the imagination of "the Jew's" alleged absence of substance, his unboundedness and formlessness that, at the same time, encompassed his perverse emasculating force. The Jew's body was first and foremost threatening because it was imagined as lacking in biological and physical substance, in flesh, blood, and organs. The Jew's "emptiness" threatened to engulf, swallowing everything up, for, as Céline explained in *Bagatelles*, "they come along in masses, completely camouflaged, all sinuous, all supple."[134] The fantasized figure of the "Jew" acted in Céline's texts as that "imaginary uncanniness and real threat . . . beckoning to [him] and ending up engulfing [him]."[135] It was this essential lack of substance evoking a lack of borders in all bodies that enabled "him" to take over, contaminate, and taint non-Jewish male bodies. Céline exclaimed that we "have to be an arse like an Aryan not to have seen all these obvious characteristics of the Jewishness that possesses us, that encircles us, crushes us, and bleeds us in every possible and unimaginable manner."[136] Such presence was more than mere "invasion": it involved bodily contamination and penetration. Paradoxically, Céline claimed that the very contamination experienced by non-Jewish bodies was not evidence of their weakness or lack of firm and proper boundaries—a lack within—but pointed to the power of the Jew. "Céline," his narrator, described fellow French citizens as endlessly "drafting, cheating, ducking before what is essential: the Jew." He added, "They merely come close to the truth: the Jew."[137] The sheer repetition of "the Jew" reinforced the image of a presence that was everywhere. Through its omnipotent and unbounded presence, "the Jew" dissolved the very boundaries of French masculinity, for it was the "most uncompromising parasite, most voracious, most likely to dissolve: the Jew!"[138]

It was therefore no surprise that one of the leitmotivs in the pamphlet was dissolution (of borders, of bodies), as it would be for the journalists of *Je Suis Partout*, who enthusiastically embraced his 1937 pamphlet. It also formed the recurring theme for a number of far-right and antisemitic interwar thinkers eager to find resolution for a decentered and precarious male subject at a time when "all the criteria defining what makes a self and what gives it legitimacy were perceived as having dissolved."[139] Céline often invoked that threat. He warned that "the Aryan is going to be dissolved."[140] The use of the passive construction in French only served to emphasize what was going to be done to him. He insisted that the one who has been "Judaized, is shrinking, evaporating, eluding. . . . Nobody left."[141] The Jewish dissolution of the "Aryan" body was signified through the endless appearance and naming of Jewish individuals, "from the most insignificant Jewish painter, Jewish pianist, Jewish banker, Jewish star, Jewish thief, Jewish author, Jewish book, Jewish play, Jewish song . . . to the perfection of Jewish tyranny."[142] The cause of the dissolution of the Aryan character and disappearance of Western civilization had only one origin, the Jewish presence that he reviled.[143] He cried that there was "nothing but them . . . everything for them. . . . Always and everywhere!"[144] The Célinian category of "the Jew" metaphorically signified all that was corrupt, vile, and threatening to the physical, symbolic, and social body.[145] Céline could not describe what that imagined Jewish body was made of because it was, for him, everywhere and nowhere, formless and unbounded. For him, everything happened because of "these wandering Jews, my friend, these world citizens! . . . They empty your balls and your head, they rip you off, they suck your blood."[146]

The formless, unbounded, and parasitic "Jew's body" was fetishized as difference. Jewish bodies were never represented as a whole but signified through body parts—nose, foot, penis—in keeping with a long tradition of antisemitic iconography.[147] Those fetishized Jewish body parts acted as reminders of racial difference. They literally and visibly embodied that which was not French. The Frenchman, in Ferdinand's eyes, was reduced to the state of flesh and meat under Jewish feet.[148] A Jewish mouth drowned Frenchmen with a repulsive viscous mass of persuasive words.[149] And Léon Blum, a familiar object of antisemitic hatred in 1937, "owns in his hands all [Frenchmen's] means of existence."[150] In fact, his speech and style are mocked for embodying that "Oriental" disposition for moral and sexual deviousness: "Ah! See how he writes our Bloum! See how intelligent he is! Ah! The Orient! With a big and long prick . . . ! Very yid-like!"[151] Céline repeatedly bemoaned the fact that "Jews are not ashamed of their Jewish race, quite the contrary, for God's sake! . . . And not ashamed of circumcision!"[152] Circumcision was the physical inscription of the body of difference and race and separated Jews from others. Indeed, Céline said he feared Jews because "until the end of times, the Jew will crucify us in order to avenge his foreskin."[153] It symbolically marked the lack that characterized racial difference and that encompassed the unbearable threat of dissolution of the self for Céline.[154] Céline thus claimed in *Bagatelles* that "if Einstein wasn't a yid, if Bergson weren't cut, if Proust were only from Britanny, if Freud did not have the mark. . . . We wouldn't mention any of them."[155] Even culture was determined by racial identity, and Jewishness disqualified those authors and thinkers from being included in the canon of Western civilization. His obsession with the haunting and contaminating presence of the Jewish body meant that in order to eradicate this danger, Jews should be exterminated "to the last Jew left, prick included."[156]

French masculinity was, in response, located in a sexualized body whose integrity was threatened by the emasculating (and impure because already castrated) Jewish phallus. The figure of the Jew was seen to be both lacking and powerful. He was feminized, a "eunuch," while at other times given the power to emasculate "Aryan" male bodies.[157] Céline asserted that Jews owned Aryan men's pleasure—something that could be achieved through language. *Bagatelles* showed "Céline" claiming he had witnessed this firsthand as he listened to his boss, the Jewish civil servant and diplomat Yubelblatt, recounting how he had convinced politicians and civil servants to embrace his ideas. Yubelblatt, Céline said, won people over because "[he] knows the way to make them come" and "[he] provides to all this chit-chatting a kind of 'ejaculatory' quality." In fact, Yubelblatt is presented as almost sexually enacting what he described. He embodies the sinister, insidious corrupting and potent Jewish male. Yubelblatt explains that

> when they hear such a well-defined text, miraculously arrived to them [. . .] . . . they surrender, they "adopt" it! . . . with such joy! Ejaculating as best they can . . . the orgasm! They relax . . . they forgive themselves . . . they stroke themselves . . . they relish it . . . they congratulate each other . . . vanity does

> the rest . . . they immediately convince each other . . . that they have managed to come by themselves. . . . Myself, I don't linger there, I disappear, I erase myself . . . I leave them to their effusions. I have said nothing . . . I have done nothing . . . I always have them to myself.[158]

The act of listening to this account is also shown to have tainted Céline himself, rendered him passive in response to the power of these Jewish words. There is at this point an ambiguous slippage: narrator, author, and reader are conflated so that all become passive recipients of the "ebullition of words" of Yubelblatt's lecture.[159] Céline has been silenced by "the Jew." As a result, he wrote that now "[he] wrote like a Jew." His ability to write had been perverted as "[he] went circumlocuting." "Circum" evoked—in reference to circumcision—the castration of the one who speaks, the *locuteur*. The narrator, and by extension the reader, had now been corrupted, miscegenated. Everything that was "tainted" by Jewishness found itself feminized and devirilized.

In fact, Céline systematically depicted a male body that had been assaulted. In *Bagatelles*' imaginary of virile heterosexuality, the male body had had to surrender its essential maleness as every orifice it possessed was subjected to the "Jewish colonizing fury."[160] Céline the character thus exclaimed as he explained that at least Hitler did not lie like Jews did, that when it came to Jews, "we no longer know what we take in our mouth, a cock or bottle."[161] *Bagatelles* displayed a striking obsession with the violation of "Aryan" male bodies by Jewish bodies—always portrayed as unnatural. The invisibility and omnipotence of Jews was such that anyone who resisted would nonetheless experience some form of violation at the hands of Jews. Céline warned that "were you to venture even the smallest word against the great yid invasion, [this would mean] the colonization of your buttocks, for all of you."[162] Here, Céline insisted on the sexual nature of this colonization. His vocabulary called up images of sexual violence and rape (which were already present in *Voyage*), while his prose offered very graphic descriptions of sexual encounters (between faceless and anonymous Jews and powerless and strangely willing unnamed Aryan men and women). The pamphlet sees Céline berating his fellow Frenchmen, clamoring that "when your Jewish masters will next time order you to proudly lick with your tongue the crevices of their balls . . . to suck hard on their prick . . . not to harm your stomach, surely you will find even more impetuous ways to express your delight." He abruptly concluded: "I can hear you [moaning] from right here."[163] Throughout the pamphlet, it seems that there was a particular pleasure elicited for Céline—and, maybe, for his readers—in describing so intently that which was supposed to be the most disgusting and horrifying.

Returning to his obsession with the racial nature of such contamination, he explained: "The 'Racial myth,' well that's for us! The prejudiced lie! To shove it up our arses! So that our buttocks are well and wide opened! While they bugger us, they revel in it."[164] This was a particularly favorite motif, for again, Céline had a protagonist ask in his pamphlet: "Mr. The Jew, when precisely will you want me to pull down my pants? Will you be so kind as to bugger me?"[165] In this heterosexual economy, sodomy represented the most abject violation. It was the ultimate colonization: as Céline reminded his reader, "colonization 'from inside' was the most degrading, the most vile colonization." Even worse, he wrote, "colonization by Negroid Jews is the worst of all moral and physical abjections."[166] Sodomy became a shorthand for (the fear of) homosexuality, which was synonymous with perversion for many interwar conservative and far-right critics.

Insisting on the degenerative effects of homosexual perversion, in turn, highlighted the disorder unleashed by heterosexual deviance. Heterosexual masculinity was endangered by the propensity Céline ascribed to "Aryan women [who] don't use reason, these cuties follow their instinct, their belly."[167] Women could not be trusted to resist the seduction of "Oriental" Jews. The male "Aryan" body was, for Céline, literally killed off by the unnatural sexual relationships between French women and Jewish men. The alleged sexual unfaithfulness of French women on the home front who had betrayed good soldiers was a recurrent cliché of interwar fictional production, fueling Céline's own fantasies.[168] He offered the apocalyptic vision of deviant and orgiastic sexual acts taking place over the bodies of French men—in a description that echoed the orgy scenes in his ballet libretto:

> Woman, especially the French one, adores frizzies, Abyssinians, they have some quite amazing dicks! They are so vicious, so affectionate! They understand women so well! . . . Oh, this Orientalism! It is something else. . . . Cuckolds of the trenches, poor "kosher" meat, you will not be forgotten! You will be pumped, snapped, swallowed, melted into the Jewish victory. . . . [T]hey will have sex on your tombs, your beloved wives with yids. They will come to your carnages, puke on Sundays, fuck on your martyrdom.[169]

Invoking all at once the trope of black male sexuality, Jewish seduction, and violence, Céline portrayed women as the conduit to devirilization, miscegenation, and contamination. Even American women—who had been the subject of Ferdinand's admiration in *Voyage*—are accused of loving nothing more than "sodomy with negroes" and "marriage with Jews."[170] Céline thus declared: "Woman is a born betraying bitch . . . as much as the Jew is a born crook."[171] Céline's obsession was the sexual and corporeal corruption of French women by Jewish men. In his pamphlet, women had no individual existence (aside from his Russian guide, Nathalie). They were never granted names or faces but existed only as a multitude of dehumanized, corrupt, and decaying female bodies. In a hospital, he saw only "bloodless, scraggy, crawling" female bodies.[172] He portrayed them as always already "infected" and "contaminated" by Jewish men. Female bodies were already "naturally" repulsive, and had now been made irreversibly so through the taint of Jewishness.

The insistent invocation of Jewish (sexual and bodily) invasion—tainting female bodies and corrupting male bodies—allowed Céline to remind his readers that this was a political issue. He had explained in his pamphlet that "the Western man represents the ideal fool, wrapped up, completely open to the Jews . . . to the confusing, prophesying dialectic of the Jew,"[173] only to conclude that he had been humiliated and made passive because, "ideologically, the Aryan is a cuckold."[174] This was hardly a surprise, according to Céline's phantasmic imaginary, for it was the fate of a nation that had lost what had made it great. Just like Jean-Pierre Maxence, who had described in his memoirs a nation that, under the rule of inept politicians, had become nothing more than "Europe's whore [*putain*]," who surrendered "without any resistance," at every meeting, Céline wrote that "France is a female nation, always good at [selling herself]."[175] His political register, unlike Maxence's, used the language of sex and race to express his indignation; to him it was obvious that "at the time of the negro. Jew in her arse, that's her happiness, he will kill her off, that's his role."[176] Racial identity had become an urgent political issue, one that involved self and nation. He summed it up simply by declaring that, now, in France, there was only "Negroid Jews against White Men. Nothing more, nothing less."[177]

The Aryan's Fetish

It seemed that the regeneration of virile masculinity—a seemingly impossible enterprise considering the pervasiveness of racialized contamination that Céline claimed had taken place—could still be achieved. Virility demanded the assertion of male heterosexual desire around "female desired objects."[178] Only properly directed masculine desire provided the underpinning for racial purity. For, as Ferdinand in *Voyage* bluntly explains upon meeting his former American lover, Lola, "Where there's a luxurious body there's always a possibility of rape, of a direct, violent breaking and entering into the heart of wealth and luxury, with no fear of having to return the loot."[179] The violent assertion of male heterosexual desire founded Western racial identity. The (white Anglo-Saxon) female body alone offered the possibility of such restoration. For its readers, *Bagatelles* performed what seems to be driving Céline's narrators, namely the belief that a voyeuristic gaze and a fetishistic relationship with female bodies may hold the promise of a way out of the abjection of pervasive Jewish colonization and racial contamination, and a means of ultimately recovering a potent heterosexual masculinity.[180]

If mastery and self-discipline were the required qualities for French heterosexual masculinity, these were also at once precarious and always subject to collapse. That instability had, after all, inspired many of the Young New Right intellectuals' interrogations of the self. Céline's prose fictionalized the need to overcome such inherent instability. In *Voyage*, Ferdinand finds comfort only in women's bodies—bodies to be relished, enjoyed, and that provide him pleasure. But he still experiences the loss of sexual potency once subject to racial contamination in Africa—the only space where he does not engage in a sexual act, instead insisting upon the absolute disgust and repulsion elicited by degenerate white and black female bodies. *Bagatelles* always portrays Ferdinand in conversation with men, in discussions about masculinity, and no female characters ever appear in his narrative (aside from the Russian guide Nathalie, who tries to seduce him to no avail).[181] But what emerges is the desire to consume the bodies of ballerinas, who come to be the only objects of Ferdinand's voyeuristic desire. Whereas *Voyage*'s Ferdinand still finds comfort in the "divine leg-owners" he admires in New York City, and in the "erotic promiscuity of those splendid, welcoming creatures," the Detroit prostitutes that help "restore his soul," *Bagatelles* offers a narrator incapable of consummating his desire.[182] As in Africa, where he is rendered impotent by racial contamination, in *Bagatelles*, Jewish colonization, invasion, and penetration render Ferdinand incapable of asserting his all-consuming desire. Only voyeurism and fetishism produce the necessary sublimation that allows escape from the abjection that he experiences.

In Céline's world, a properly racialized male body was one whose integrity and boundaries had been restored and that was no longer under assault. It erased possible violations by redirecting a naturalized heterosexual desire onto a female object. Here, only the disciplined and bounded female body of the ballet dancer offered the promise of restoration of heterosexual masculinity. The female figure of the ballerina embodied a traditional form of femininity that was antithetical to the "New Woman" of postwar modernity.[183] While the "garçonne" refused to display conventional markers of femininity and suggested androgyny with her hipless, breastless, and formless body, the ballerina was at once muscular and adorned with the signs of femininity. The ballet dancer also embodied yearned-for order, restraint, hierarchy, and borders. She was not the unruly and "wild" dancer of the "Revue Nègre," dancing suggestively to the sound of jazz, as Josephine Baker had famously done. As Rosemarie Scullion has remarked, Céline's ballet librettos fictionalized an "essentialized view of the female body" constructed as "a delectable surface to which [Ferdinand's] gaze is obsessively drawn."[184] The ballet dancer's body was the only one that elicited from Céline's narrator almost romantic exclamations—radically at odds with the descriptions of abject and disgusting bodies that otherwise populated the pamphlet. Ferdinand thus mused in a conversation with Gutman that

> in a dancer's leg, the world, its waves, all its rhythms, its craziness, its wishes are inscribed! . . . Never written! The most subtle poem! . . . So moving! . . . Everything! An incredible poem, warm and fragile like the moving balance of a ballerina's leg perfectly aligned. . . . Life takes hold of them, so pure . . . takes them away . . . with the slightest move, I want to lose myself with them. . . . The whole life . . . shivering . . . undulating . . . [. . .] They [the ballerinas] are calling me! . . . I am no longer myself . . . I surrender myself . . . [. . .] I want to crumble down, collapse, fade away, go up in smoke, become cloud . . . into an arabesque . . . into the nothingness . . . into the mirage's fountains . . . I want to die from the most beautiful.[185]

Céline suggests that the beauty in the movement of ballerinas' legs is akin to the beauty that emerges from the sublimation of language undertaken in poetry. The female body was fragmented by this male gaze—her leg was especially beautiful and enticing—and aestheticized for male consumption. She was molded into a "pure" aesthetic object that could be possessed. Indeed, it is through the "[female] body's [brutal and painful] transformation into art" that the male body could be recomposed.[186] The fetishization of the female body, especially dancers' legs, produced the sublimation found in the sacred and the realm of purity.

But this pure aesthetic pleasure also emerged from the contemplation of healthy, muscular, feminine bodies that contrasted with the degenerate, perverted, and repulsive bodies that inhabited *Bagatelles*. Those female bodies must properly embody normative gender roles in order to allow for the virile masculinity of the narrator to assert itself: a harmonious social body could emerge if "female difference within a presumed heterosexual order" was "incorporated."[187] Only the "idealized" figure of the ballerina restored the virility of French masculinity. The pleasure of masculine fetishistic voyeurism offered the fantasy of "stabiliz[ing] masculinity."[188] This pleasure emerged not from experience—as it did in *Voyage*—but from the act of male spectatorship. As he engages in such voyeuristic gazing, Céline "crumble[s] down, collapse[s], fade[s] away, go[es] up in smoke, become[s] cloud . . . into an arabesque . . . into the nothingness . . . into the mirage's fountains . . . ," evoking the dissolution of the masculine self. But this dissolution was different from the one Céline described Frenchmen experiencing when subjected to racial contamination at the hands of fantasized Jews. This feeling of dissolution was restorative, as it redirected the French male citizen's desire.[189] It provided the pleasure necessary for the narrator so that he could find and achieve wholeness in "nothingness." These female bodies were objects of desire and devoid of any subjectivity. They were there only to be consumed phantasmically. Céline confessed to Gutman that he had developed "an almost absolutely tyrannical taste for these ballet dancers."[190]

In this heterosexual economy, the French man restored his masculinity and control through the fetishizing and predatory gaze of the male voyeur. This, Céline readily acknowledged, was essential to his own sense of identity: for "changing anything to [his] state of anonymous voyeur would be an unfaithfulness that [he] will undoubtedly die of."[191] It was the act of looking that enabled Céline to restore control. This male gaze was associated with that of a predator. For "hidden by some heavy curtain . . . he has no desire to reveal himself personally . . . he would only like to observe in the greatest secret those cute darlings [. . .] as one admires sacred objects at church."[192] Consuming pure and properly gendered female bodies allowed Céline to move from abjection to the sacred. It was no surprise that both the ballet libretto and Céline's lust for female ballet dancers prefaced *Bagatelles* and provided its avowed origin. The female body must be manipulated, molded, and disciplined for proper heterosexual masculinity to be reaffirmed and escape racial abjection.[193]

Conclusion

The intimate relationship between race, sexuality, culture, and politics drove Céline's narrative vision. His works offered racialized heteronormativity as the place for a fantasy of regeneration. Yet the "pornographic aesthetics of race" that infused his texts did not always influence the reception of his works.[194] When *Voyage* was published, few critics observed and commented on the racialization at work in the narrator's trials and tribulations. *Voyage* told the tale of Ferdinand's travels to Africa and America, which stood as rich phantasmic sites where European male subjectivity simultaneously confronted, reinvented, and reaffirmed itself in the face of possible contamination and the need for violent mastery. Yet the novel was almost unanimously celebrated by critics and authors across the political spectrum, who saw in it a pessimistic yet prophetic commentary on postwar France.

French critics and readers, in the early 1930s, had been willing to ignore the violent racialization of gendered bodies that formed Céline's obsession. That position became untenable with the publication of *Bagatelles*, whose form defied genres, and whose content troubled many. Gide famously thought it a satire while Rebatet embraced it. *Bagatelles*, and *L'école des cadavres* a year later, received a more divided reception, puzzling critics and requiring greater explanation as to what could account for a supposedly sudden shift in tone and content.[195] As I have argued, *Bagatelles* did not represent a sudden departure from Céline's earlier fictionalization, but was seen as such because French critics and readers had been willing to ignore and accept the racialization of gendered bodies that formed Céline's enduring obsession and that was already at work in his first novel. In the same manner, it was the ways in which race, sexuality, culture, and bodies were fictionalized in Céline's antisemitic pamphlets that determined the reception he encountered among far-right intellectuals.

The reception of *Bagatelles* among that group was as divided as it was in the literary scene at large. Céline's "conversion" to antisemitism was not sufficient to make him a welcome author in the literary canon that the far right upheld and celebrated. Instead, critics and intellectuals such as Léon Daudet, Thierry Maulnier, and Robert Brasillach responded to Céline's "pornographic aesthetics of race" according to the ways in which his vision confirmed their own understanding of the relationships between nation, bodies, and race. What critics, especially those on the far right, were often troubled by and critical of was not Céline's racial vision, even less his antisemitism—whose legitimacy was not questioned—but the manner in which he unfolded it, the form it took, and the ways in which it seemed excessive. Céline disrupted the conventions of political imagination and rhetoric. For many far-right critics, Céline's antisemitism proved impossible to embrace because it "had gone too far" and, in *Bagatelles*, appeared as the product of a deranged and paranoid mind. Céline thus hardly embodied a desirable kind of rational and reasonable political discourse.

The Young New Right rejected the racial vision that Céline offered because it revealed an obsession with an abject body that only the category of race could overcome. This imaginary erased the nation in favor of an idiom of sex and race that sat uncomfortably with their own far-right nationalism. Céline's aesthetics were embodied in his style—focusing on the low, the base, the abject—which was radically at odds with the aesthetics of order and purity that intellectuals like Maulnier, Fabrègues, and Blanchot were calling for throughout that decade. Céline's "scatological style" was hardly exemplary of the kind of purification they were intent on bringing about.[196] Whereas critics like Blanchot argued for sublimation through the rigor and discipline of language to eradicate the mark of sexual difference and erase the pervasive abjection they experienced, Céline appeared to them as one who instead let language loose and reveled in the abject, one for whom only the reaffirmation of male heterosexuality upon other fetishized bodies would prove satisfying. Blanchot never reviewed Céline's novels or pamphlets—a telling silence—though he was busy writing his weekly *L'Insurgé* literary chronicle in 1937 when debates raged over the publication of *Bagatelles*. Catholic Young New Right critic René Vincent berated *Bagatelles*' "incontinent style," its "obscene images" and "delirious subjectivism" that were so remote from that "great" antisemitic author Drumont.[197] He ironically surmised that the "personality's frantic dissociation, latent freudism," and "filthy" language displayed by the pamphlet pointed to Céline's own Jewishness, since they were the characteristics of modernity. Céline therefore exemplified to Young New Right critics a perverse and misguided example of how much the novel—that quintessential modern form—had degenerated.[198]

If Céline's fictionalization of "filth," "defilement," "suffering," and "horror" seemed repulsive to Young New Right critics, it was also because his answer to the conundrum posed by the abjection of the nation found an answer only in the category of race—a single-minded vision that, again, was at odds with the ways in which they envisaged the political solution to such anxieties.[199] Reaffirming Western, and especially French, civilization demanded in the Young

New Right's imaginary an "aesthetics of separation" where racial contamination was kept at bay and contained within the colonies, thus allowing for the (metropolitan) nation to emerge untainted.[200] Additionally, they argued antisemitism could not be the sole driving force of a new politics. Céline instead tore the veil and showed how any belief in escaping such contamination—especially when it came to the question of Jewish "invasion" and "influence"—was a delusion. All his politics were subsumed by his antisemitic vision of the world. This kind of affirmation could only be refused by the Young New Right. As Vincent observed in his 1939 review of *L'école des cadavres*, "upon his apocalyptic rendering, Louis-Ferdinand Céline foreshadows the disappearance of France and Frenchmen."[201] Finally, Céline's obsession with "Aryanness" denied the very specificity and boundaries of Frenchness, for it offered a racialization that denied a specifically French nationalism able to recover French civilization through purification.

Yet Céline's pamphlets were celebrated by another group of far-right critics and intellectuals, that of the far-right newspaper *Je Suis Partout*, now under the editorial guidance of novelist Robert Brasillach. Rebatet—who became one of Céline's greatest fans—wrote that "they were reciting [and] proclaiming" this pamphlet.[202] He defended what he called Céline's possibly excessive but "strange genius of garbage." He concluded, "For crazy years, what better painter than a madman?"[203] Two months later, *Je Suis Partout* published long extracts of the pamphlet, alongside a striking (and antisemitic) caricature by Ralph Soupault.[204] This was the same issue in which Rebatet authored an entire page on "political immigrants," asking whether "one could avoid pogroms" in the face of the invasion of "German Jewry from Moscow."[205] The last extract stated: "We live now under Jewish fascism." Ominously, they quoted Céline's clamoring that the "Jew is a born-dictator [who is] far worse than Mussolini. Democracy was always nothing more than the screen for Jewish dictatorship."[206] The image showed a young, bemused-looking World War I soldier gazing into the distance. Behind him, a repugnant and fat "Jew" sat on bags of money holding a beautiful naked woman in each arm. Soupault, who had brought to life *L'Insurgé*'s obsessions, now translated Céline's fantasies for the newspapers' readers.

If Céline's abject bodies and racial obsessions made him a difficult author to appropriate and "defend," one might wonder how he became the champion that the young far-right journalists of *Je Suis Partout* made their own. Céline himself did not, as author, publicly align himself with any political group until

JE SUIS PARTOUT

LES HOMMES ET LES IDÉES

LA CRITIQUE

UN ROMAN ÉTRANGER

MORCEAUX CHOISIS

« BAGATELLES POUR UN MASSACRE »

LE LIVRE DE LA SEMAINE

« BAGATELLES POUR UN MASSACRE »

par Louis-Ferdinand CELINE

LES MÉMOIRES DE WINSTON CHURCHILL

PARLEMENTARISME ANGLAIS ET FRANÇAIS

LA GUERRE JUIVE

GRAND PRIX du Cercle Littéraire

Suzanne Frémont

AU DELA DU VOILE

JACQUES PÉRICARD

LE SOLDAT DE VERDUN

au courant

3 fr. 50

"Les Hommes et les Idées." *Je Suis Partout*, March 4, 1938, p. 8. Courtesy of Bibliothèque nationale de France.

the Vichy years.[207] In fact, many critics have pointed out that while Lucien Rebabet was a sincere and enthusiastic reader (whose own 1942 *Les décombres* was a barely veiled attempt at replicating a certain Célinian vision), Céline's "scatological vision" and "pornographic aesthetics" may have not been as easy for Robert Brasillach to embrace. He had been a reluctant reader of *Voyage au bout de la nuit*, and his own homoerotic imaginary was at odds with Céline's fictionalization of the fantasy of a masterful and virile heterosexual body that derided any homoerotic aesthetics.[208] What *Je Suis Partout* embraced in Céline was the apocalyptic vision of the way French bodies had been contaminated and perverted. His vision was a "nostalgic" one, like theirs, yearning for lost boundaries.[209] And while they refused the necessary reveling in abjection that Céline forced upon his readers, they were able to do so by turning to fascism, the only political aesthetics and ideological commitment that, to them, offered the promise of sublimation out of abjection.

6

THE RACE OF FASCISM

Je Suis Partout, Race, and Culture

> In any case they are here, and of course they are young: some of them have suffered from the war, others from their nations' revolutions, all have suffered from the crisis. They know what their nation is, its past, they believe in its future. . . . They want a pure nation, a pure history, a pure race.
>
> —Robert Brasillach, *Je Suis Partout*, 1938

In May 1936, the antisemitic cultural critic Lucien Rebatet reviewed a "fascist film" intended, he claimed, to showcase the "imperial task of European powers."[1] Rebatet explained that he had expected to see an "abundance of exotic images, exemplars of methodical, intelligent, and humane colonization," but found only a rather dull cinematographic exercise that failed to reveal what should have been the film's true purpose: to show "the calm and alive figure of fascism at work." It is hardly a coincidence that Rebatet's review of "a fascist film" was preceded by a scathing indictment of a "Soviet film" that he deemed "of unbelievable Semitism." This release, Rebatet railed, was yet another glaring instance of the "Jewish propaganda which was now making its way in newspapers and entertainment."[2] For Rebatet, cinema was the quintessential modern art form: it embodied "the ability to convey the joy and feeling of a huge crowd . . . with only a few images."[3] This, he explained in 1938, was what Leni Riefenstahl had done so brilliantly in her film of the 1936 Berlin Olympic games. He praised her aesthetics, which offered "crescendos of sensations" and expertly showed "virile efforts" and how the games had been the "great dream of all the races."[4] Those assertions on race, culture, and fascism were typical of *Je Suis Partout*. In the 1930s, *Je Suis Partout* promoted a racialized Frenchness whose boundaries were mapped through the simultaneous and necessary subjection of colonized subjects (abroad in the empire), which allowed the denunciation and verbal persecution of French Jews (within the nation). In answer to the dilemma of the postwar self that had obsessed them in the early part of the decade, *Je Suis Partout* spent much of the late 1930s yearning for what it imagined to be France's lost boundaries. This nostalgic yearning determined these writers and journalists' articulation of a racial antisemitism sustained by proud colonial commitment, which, in turn, structured their intellectual, political, and cultural imagining of the world.

Je Suis Partout has been most remembered for its collaborationist position during the Vichy years as well as for the rhetorical violence it displayed in the late 1930s: to many historians, its "murderous passion remains to this day unexplainable."[5] Its history has been told as the history of a fascist newspaper—one of the rare instances of French intellectuals embracing fascism, its ideology and aesthetics—whose writers found both hope and a model in the resounding and seemingly unstoppable success of Hitler's Nazi regime. However, the attention (rightfully) paid to their delineation of a "French fascism" has tended to obscure the place that antisemitism held in the political visions of these men. It has usually been considered to be too "crude" or "vulgar" to warrant further analysis. Additionally, aside from one rigorous but politically indulgent study, *Je Suis Partout* has not been the subject of any sustained exploration.[6] Only its most prominent contributors—usually Robert Brasillach and Lucien Rebatet—have been featured in monographs because of the role they played during the Occupation. Yet those works divorce these intellectuals from the intellectual and political world in which they wrote. These singular figures dominate, rather than being seen as symptomatic of, a discourse that they helped to define and articulate in this newspaper throughout the 1930s. Their obsession with "the Jew" and their reinvention of French antisemitism was in fact not supplemental to their fascism, but formed the "ideological backbone" of their conception of French citizens. Antisemitic imagination translated a particular—gendered and raced—vision of the world that subsequently fueled their political choices and attachments. But reading *Je Suis Partout* as fascist *and* antisemitic (which means considering these two ideological positions as somewhat distinct from one another) has repressed the logic at work in the delineation of a male and virile far-right politics. Instead, by tracing the ways in which these far-right intellectuals were committed to the eradication of "Blum" and relied on rule over colonized "natives" to provide mastery and control, we may shed light on the debates concerning French fascism

While a number of Young New Right intellectuals inaugurated in 1936 their own magazine, *Combat*, *Je Suis Partout* garnered visibility in the same year as one of France's leading far-right publications. Created in 1930, it was then not yet the full-fledged instrument of that younger generation moving away from *Combat*. But it was already developing the kind of ideological platform that men like Brasillach, Rebatet, Cousteau, and Blond made their own and later radicalized. In 1936 its editorial committee proclaimed that it would now devote itself to bringing about the demise of the Popular Front, and the noxious communist and Jewish influence that had caused the corruption of the nation. Throughout the 1930s, *Je Suis Partout* became known for its open embrace of fascist regimes across Europe, its violent denunciation of French politics at home and abroad, and its violent antisemitism. In the wake of the "failed days of February 1934," the accession to power of the Popular Front, the Spanish Civil War, and the growing "bolchevization of Europe," these journalists and intellectuals produced an increasingly violent rhetoric, insulting, denouncing, and berating the politicians and intellectuals they deemed to constitute the "anti-France."[7] Its editor, Pierre Gaxotte, explained in June 1936, "France is finished; but its demise will allow [it] to be reborn. Many things can be broken, but this fall will embody, for the best ones, an emancipation." Against the incarnation of the nation whose end he predicted, he opposed the emergence of the true and untainted France they were committed to restoring.[8] In opposition to the socialist rule of the Popular Front, he laid out *Je Suis Partout*'s program:

> France will wake up. France is waking up. But to deserve victory, we need to fight everywhere and all of the time. We need to resist. We need to fight back. . . . We need to be ready. To be strong, to be firm. . . . There are those who think and those who follow. There are the French men of France and there are the others. . . . We need to fight. We need to fight knowing what we want. The past is dead. . . . We are fighting for a national revolution in order to restore health, strength, and happiness to France. We are fighting for the people because we come from the people. We are fighting for the nation. For its greatness . . . for order against anarchy, for justice, against civil war, for union against the truncheon, for happiness against misery, for light against filth, for youth against those who are dying.[9]

Gaxotte's repetitions and short sentences emphasize the urgency of the situation: as he mentions "Frenchmen" before moving to a generalizable "we," he typically creates a binary opposition which allows him to define the terms of far-right political struggle associating the nation with happiness, in ways that invoke order, justice, youth, and unity—a far-right cliché that *Je Suis Partout* mined most effectively. As the heirs to *L'Action Française*, and in parallel to the Young New Right endeavors, *Je Suis Partout* journalists practiced an extremely violent political rhetoric, which, "in 1936 and 1937 had [for them] represented the golden age of invective."[10] As Brasillach himself recalled in 1941, these few years epitomized "one of the craziest times that France experienced [and] probably the most harmful." But, he explained, this was also what had allowed them to emerge as a new self-conscious generation of intellectuals committed to radical oppositional politics.[11]

As intellectuals concerned with the crisis of the subject and the boundaries of the community like their peers at *Combat*, *Je Suis Partout*'s young journalists were obsessed with the dissolution of the nation and its citizens. The borders of the national community were threatened, made porous by the assault, both from within and from without, of elements irreducibly foreign to the "true" character of France. They saw their era to be a decadent, perverted, and unstable one, a degradation made manifest by the existence of a democratic regime they deemed not only illegitimate but antithetical to French history. Republican principles had failed to protect against the dangers of unbridled capitalism; it had allowed the invasion of communist ideas; most significantly, the commitment to "assimilation"—which had been one of the fundamental principles of the republican universalism inherited from the Enlightenment, and had subsequently been explicitly embraced by left-wing politics—had allowed, in their mind, the most dangerous individuals to live within the nation and invade it from outside: Jews.[12] *Je Suis Partout* called for the emergence of a "new" nationalism, led by oppositional critics—the young intellectuals of the far right—who would restore "a pure nation, a pure history, a pure race."[13] While their political critique of decadence kept within the terms of Maurrassian thought, it was their obsession with dissolution (rather than abjection) that infused their exclusively racial and colonial imagination of Frenchness. Their conception of French citizenship could be defined only through the reaffirmation of a masculine, bounded, and antisemitic individual, who should be infused with an innate sense of the nation's history and civilization.

Je Suis Partout, and its most prominent contributors—Robert Brasillach, Lucien Rebatet, Pierre-Antoine Cousteau, and the "elders," Pierre Gaxotte, Pierre Villette (otherwise known as "Dorsay"), André Bellessort, and Jean-Jacques Brousson—became the champions of a masculine definition of a fascist and antisemitic nationalism and the drafting of a new "virile politics."[14] Unlike their fellow writers at *Combat* and *L'Insurgé*, they were not concerned with abjection and its manifestations: it might be the occasional characteristic of politicians or individuals they reviled—such as the Communist regime they deemed "abject"—but for them, the essence of the nation and its citizens was never contaminated by a pervasive state of abjection. In this, they mostly kept to a Maurrassian political vision. What preoccupied them was fantasies of dissolution and corruption. Those fantasies underscored their claim to "restoring" a racially embodied and bounded masculinity. They defined the contours of the rightful Frenchman in opposition to republican, parliamentary politics. The Frenchman's identity depended on his place within a French community defined by order and harmonious functioning, which was, in turn, guaranteed by authoritarian institutions. Culture, which they conceived of as the expression of art, mores, and social practices, held a central place in providing substance to French identity and citizenship.[15]

For them, the Popular Front government inaugurated in June 1936 made real the threat of the national community's dissolution: not only were borders porous, but the substance of the nation was in danger of dissolution. In the hands of Socialist politicians, far-right critics felt that their nation would be irredeemably transformed into a undifferentiated whole where citizens existed without any firm attachment to the community. The national community itself would no longer retain its place, standing, and influence within the larger (but politically unstable) European and world order. In response to assimilation and undifferentiation, the exclusion of Jews enabled the reestablishment of order, hierarchy, and difference within the national community and throughout the empire, a difference (or heterogeneity) unified by a distinctive culture and tradition. As scholar Pierre Birnbaum has shown, French "political antisemitism" had a long tradition of identifying Jews with industrialization, modernity, and secularization and berating the fact that "citizens [had] become, at least in the public sphere, identical in every respect."[16] Frenchness was not just a matter of formal rights—after all, the Jews they singled out in their articles were French citizens—but a matter of instinct, tradition, and culture. Frenchness, they argued, was therefore radically distinct from Jewishness and, in 1938, this required a racialized conception of the political community.

Je Suis Partout's relentless obsession with a mythical "Jewish" danger and invasion—both internal and external—formed the centerpiece of its antisemitic rhetoric. Predictably, its contributors figured "Jews" as the repository of all evils afflicting French society; it was Jews who had stolen the substance of citizenship. The nation had been lost: it constituted, in their writings, the focus of their denunciation of the contemporary political order and drove their desire to eradicate the pervasive Jewishness—signifying disorder—of French society.[17] In their own eyes, their position within the French citizenry, as intellectuals and men of letters—men infused with the greatness of culture—allowed them to speak to the realm of politics.

In order to produce themselves as politically engaged intellectuals and men of letters, they made a fantasized masculinity the foundation of their imagination of the nation and its boundaries. Their particular vision of a new political, social, and sexual order depended upon the reaffirmation of a heterosexual and virile masculine subject, and this, in turn, required the disavowal of the "threat" of homosexuality (at least in public political discourse), which was understood as effeminate, furtive, and unregulated. Because "homosexuality"—as deviant perversion—haunted the borders of their masculine world while always threatening to erupt from within, they had to constantly reiterate the need for a heterosexual social world, bound by the celebration of masculinity and "proper" gender roles.[18] *Je Suis Partout*'s writers told tales of homosocial friendship and restored virility. They called for a fraternity of manly intellectual brothers who could save the nation through their oppositional force. French masculinity, they believed, should not only be manly but, through its boundedness, should also exemplify virility. In the years following Blum's accession to power, they called for the eradication of "Blum," the embodiment of all corruption, and, with him, the proliferating faceless Jews who had transformed the very essence of the nation. "Blum," and his Jewish acolytes, personified the perversion of the rightful gendered and sexual order of French society. Under the guise of manly seduction, as less than a man—a feminized incarnation of the ills of modernity—and potential homosexual threat, he had tainted "Marianne," the symbolic female incarnation of the nation. A return to a "normal" order therefore meant the reappropriation of French culture, its takeover by men who could speak in the name of the nation, and the reaffirmation of a properly bounded citizenship.

The Figure of the Fascist and Antisemitic "Homosexual"

The "accusation" of homosexuality has marked the history of *Je Suis Partout* and of those French intellectuals involved in collaborationist relations with German occupying forces during the Vichy years. The trope of homosexuality had long been mobilized by both left and right to discredit, denounce, or exclude those perceived to have endangered French politics, culture, and society. In the 1930s, homosexuality had been redefined as a pornographic instance, that which marked those who could not and did not belong to the community. As the diametrical opposite of the reproductive demand of the heterosexual family, it was perceived by numerous cultural critics and social hygienists to embody one of the most potent threats to the health of the nation and the integrity of the social body.[19] Ironically, or perhaps predictably, "homosexuality" also became the narrative device used to explain and criticize French fascists' treason. Conceived as an especially deviant practice and nature, homosexuality was equated with fascism (it had already appeared in 1930s anti-fascist discourse), and fascism was presumed, in post-1945 France, to have been the expression of a repressed homosexuality and perverse homoerotic desire.[20] This was especially the case for many of the *Je Suis Partout* journalists, concerning whom the suggestion of homosexuality has been a staple invoked by contemporaries, critics, and historians: homosexuality served to discredit them and make them into unacceptable men and citizens.

Robert Brasillach, whose unheroic fate and execution transformed him into a tragic figure, has been a particular site for the articulations of such arguments and tropes.[21] As his friend and fellow far-right intellectual Thierry Maulnier explained, Brasillach's execution in February 1945 meant that his passion for youth and poetry were therefore frozen in time and "made incorruptible."[22] Once executed, Brasillach forever remained the emblem of a far-right celebration of youthful masculinity infused with nostalgic and poetic sentimentality. He was the "Romantic Fascist."[23] This is where the always present danger of homosexual desire was invoked. In Brasillach's trial, the prosecution suggested that he had been guilty of sleeping with Germans, a metaphorical charge that feminized him, while tainting him with the charge of homosexuality—an "accusation" that barred him from claiming to be a "man," and by association, from being "truly French." Here, his perverse desires were said to have led him politically astray. To have been a collaborator and thus committed treason implied a lack of proper manliness and a deviant character. This charge, made by prosecutor Marcel Reboul, was most famously reiterated by Jean-Paul Sartre in his *Situations III* article "What Is a Collaborator?" A collaborator, according to Sartre, was not a proper man since "he" had been seduced by the deceptive and dangerous forces of Nazism.[24] Brasillach was thus "cast . . . as a man seeking to be sodomized by a German occupier."[25] Homosexuality was both origin and sign of suspicious and "pathological" politics. Paradoxically, the bluntness of Sartre's rhetorical charge directly echoed the repeated accusations that *Je Suis Partout* made during the 1930s against the Jewish corruption of the female body of the nation. It indirectly reiterated some far-right clichés regarding the decadence of the "crazy years" during which homosexuality, androgyny, jazz, and surrealism were said to have corrupted the character of the nation. It also reworked Louis-Ferdinand Céline's own imagination of French male bodies colonized, sodomized, and perverted by Jewish men in his 1937 antisemitic pamphlet, *Bagatelles pour un massacre*.

The terms of the troubled and heated post-Vichy discussions of the status of the intellectual and his relation to politics echoed what had constituted the obsession of far-right writers during the 1930s: how could one be a "man" in times of "crisis"? And what made a manly intellectual? During Brasillach's trial, if prosecutor Reboul evoked "a crisis of masculinity" to explain fascist intellectuals and Vichy collaborationism, it was because the proper nature of a French masculinity had, since the end of the First World War, constituted one of the central concerns of French culture.[26] For many critics during the Épuration trials that began in late 1944 against those guilty of collaboration, Brasillach could not be representative of a masculine politics and intellect.

Homosexuality was a trope of 1930s antisemitic discursive productions of the fantasized "Jew," and it was also mobilized in post-Vichy descriptions of French collaborators and far-right intellectuals. However, critics' attention to this question, although pointing to the way accusations of homosexuality circulated in post-1945 France, have too often unwittingly reproduced this metaphorical charge rather than critically engaging with how such discursive production operated to define who would rightfully be a French citizen.[27] They have engaged in conversations that ponder the question of the "true" sexual orientation of some of these men—often implied to mean a repressed or latent homosexuality. By focusing on the potentially titillating details of biographical explanation, some critics have not addressed the ways in which sexuality and gender functioned within far-right intellectuals' production of themselves, the world, and their object of hatred. One critic has indeed remarked, "Brasillach's sexuality has long been the subject of speculation."[28] Literary scholar Alice Kaplan has explained that the charge of homosexuality invoked against Brasillach has been for her "the most difficult to analyze."[29] Recognizing that "the 'accusation' of homosexuality haunt[ed] him up to and during his trial," she nonetheless explains that "the particular current of Nazi masculinity in Brasillach's writing suggests that his fascism may have been sparked and nourished by homoerotic feeling."[30] For Kaplan, Brasillach's attraction to fascism "seems to have been his way of living out a certain kind of homoerotic longing."[31] Despite her disclaimers, Kaplan does not explore how, for instance, novelists Louis-Ferdinand Céline and Pierre Drieu La Rochelle's private disparaging comments regarding the young far-right novelist emanated from their own espousal of a virile and heterosexual masculinity that they took pains to enact in their writings. These war veterans believed in the need to restore a normative heterosexual masculinity that served as the test-limit for their imagination of French politics and culture.[32] Although Kaplan points out how the relationship between fascism and homoeroticism is always presumed in Brasillach's case, her own account reproduces that particular assumption.[33] The association made between homosexuality, antisemitism, and fascism has been an enduring one.

Lucien Rebatet, another prominent *Je Suis Partout* journalist (who was imprisoned in the early 1950s after having fled to Sigmarigen with a number of collaborationists), has similarly been a figure whose ideological commitment has been explained by his sexual orientation. In his biography and elsewhere, he is portrayed as a man obsessed with the precarious state of his own masculinity, in the throes of an identity crisis brought about by the absence of a properly manly father—his father had not been mobilized during the Great War, a fact allegedly experienced as "shameful" by Rebatet. Paternal authority—and therefore the power of the law to found the individual—had failed him and produced an inadequate and thus deviant masculinity. His biographer also asserted that he suffered from an "inferiority complex" caused by his lack of manly physical attributes: he has insisted upon Rebatet's anxiety about his deficiency in physical manliness, and explained his concern with securing his masculinity as resulting from the trauma of a Jesuit education, youthful homosexual affairs, and a traumatic romantic rejection by a young woman.[34] Rebatet's obsession with virility is explained as the symptomatic manifestation of an inability to express an "unavowable homosexuality." Once again, the figure of Rebatet has provided, according to his biographer and historians, the model of a closeted homosexuality channeled into antisemitic obsessions and fascist attraction. The specter of racism and antisemitism is not interrogated but done away with by a simple explanation: sexual repression produces a hatred of the "other."[35] Here, vulgar psychoanalytic categories have helped sustain biographical arguments that, in turn, obscure the ways gender and sexuality constituted central terms of far-right and *Je Suis Partout* writers' imaginary.

Psychobiographical analyses have thus told the story of young men trapped in the throes of unresolved oedipal relationships, yearning for fathers they had lost. Rebatet is now "the parricide fascist." He has typically been described as being driven by a feeling of inferiority, a man "with a weak and little-structured personality, little-assured of his virility, [who] needed a strong model with which to identify." For his critics, Rebatet had found a "father-figure" who could recognize his masculine self in the far-right authoritarian Charles "Maurras [and] then . . . Hitler."[36] Rebatet's insistence on virility throughout his polemical and autobiographical writings is thus seen "to illustrate the Freudian hypothesis that the castration complex constitutes the unconscious root of [his] antisemitism."[37] These biographical arguments have reproduced the dubious equation of homosexuality—as a deviant practice—with a "pathological" ideological commitment.[38] Rather than interpreting the ways in which men like Rebatet articulated their politics, sexuality is seen as connected to ideology, and fascism is read as a psychological condition.

Instead of searching for a category—homosexuality—that might stand in as origin or explanation for political choices, we must take more seriously the ways in which the tropes of heterosexual deviance, sexual perversion, and abject homosexuality helped mark the bounds of the male citizen and the meaning of public letters in French history. The political community was defined, in far-right writings, through the prism of gender and sexuality in order to determine who would rightfully belong to the French nation. These categories of difference became central to a discourse of exclusion obsessed with heterogeneity and dissolution. We may therefore interpret Rebatet's enthusiasm for Céline not as the displacement of a repressed homosexuality but as a recognition that Céline's knotting together of gender, race, and sexuality in a fantasy of degeneration and abjection echoed Rebatet's own "virile politics" and beyond him, those of *Je Suis Partout*.[39] Through the delineation of norms, morality, and character, sexuality operated as the privileged prism for European twentieth-century nationalism, which fed many French critics' concerns in the 1930s.[40] For those opposed to the right, homosexuality "explained" the attraction of some to antisemitic and fascist ideology, while for the far right, antipathy to perverse homosexuality and gendered deviances helped translate their obsession with (sexual) difference—an obsession that was articulated through the fantasized figure of the Jew.

Je Suis Partout: Friendship and Violence

In 1930, *Je Suis Partout*'s editor announced the birth of a new "great [political and literary] weekly newspaper of world affairs" that would devote itself to informing its readers about the state of the world. From its inception in 1930, *Je Suis Partout* was led by École normale supérieure graduate, Maurrassian historian, and former secretary to Charles Maurras Pierre Gaxotte, who acted as editor in chief and mentor to many of these young far-right critics. Gaxotte had been a contributor to *Candide* and was in charge of the Historical Studies series for the publisher Fayard, which asked him to oversee the creation of this newspaper.[41] Under his editorship, *Je Suis Partout* moved away from being a heterogeneous collection of articles by former Maurrassian, far-right, and politically moderate contributors and became the privileged space for expression by young critics eager to radicalize Maurras's positions and distance themselves from the Young New Right. Gaxotte encouraged these contributors to find their own voice.[42] On the eve of 1938, a front-page insert proclaimed: "*Je Suis Partout* is not like any other paper." Alongside a list of all its journalists throughout the world, it confidently asserted that those who "are against Marxism and social conservatism. Against war and French degradation. Against anarchy and despotism . . . must read *Je Suis partout*."[43]

Originally, the newspaper differed little from the traditional and very successful far-right publications that had inspired it. As its owner, the conservative publishing house Fayard viewed it as the complement to one of its leading newspapers, *Candide*. According to Rebatet, *Je Suis Partout* had originally been conceived to "be the right-wing version of the Bolshevik newspaper *Lu* which offered every week a voluminous review of the foreign press, [and] a kind of younger brother to *Candide* which would be more serious and more fluent" in contemporary affairs.[44] Gaxotte was a direct transplant from *Candide*, and many of its contributors migrated from the safety of *Candide* and *L'Action Française* to the pages of *Je Suis Partout*. Despite the similarity in format and relatively uneventful beginnings, *Je Suis Partout* developed its own distinct identity, as well as a faithful readership ranging from 45,000 to 80,000 between 1930 and 1939.[45] In 1939, it could compete with the conservative *Le Figaro*, whose circulation was closer to 80,000, while the Communist *L'Humanité* sold 350,000 issues the same year.[46] The newspaper had many lives, twice disappearing, in 1936 and 1941, yet always resurrecting itself and displaying a surprising longevity. It gradually evolved into the polemical, fiercely antisemitic, and violent publication it became known as, finding its "true voice" after the Popular Front election, and surpassing (in violent language) in 1938 and 1939 even the newspaper that had for so long influenced the right, Maurras's *L'Action Française*.[47]

By 1939, *Je Suis Partout* incarnated one of the most prominent antisemitic voices in print. As one historian has shown, it was identified as one of the most prominent newspapers (that was not attached to a party or a political organization) involved in "anti-Jewish propaganda" by a secret police report. It had become "one of the [interwar period's] forums for a triumphant antisemitism."[48] *Je Suis Partout*'s identity was rooted in vociferous and unabashedly violent far-right oppositional politics.

At first, *Je Suis Partout* seemed but one more voice in the cacophony of rhetorical violence characterizing most of the far-right press. This increasing animosity led several governments to turn to legislative means in an attempt to restrain the virulence that far-right journalists displayed in attacking their political opponents. It was not unusual for a far-right newspaper to be prosecuted for defamation or encouraging hatred: Charles Maurras had been imprisoned for six months in 1936 for calling for the assassination of politicians he deemed traitors, while *L'Insurgé*'s editorial team also prosecuted for a front page that had accused Blum of assassinating the French people. But it was the tragic end to the Salengro affair that vindicated the government's efforts to rein in this verbal violence. A defamation campaign against Lille mayor and minister of the interior Roger Salengro was launched by *L'Action Française* in 1936. It was systematically relayed by *Gringoire* and provided the impetus for one of the government's first attempts to issue a law intended to curb the polemical violence of the press. *Gringoire*'s editor, anti-republican and xenophobic polemicist Henri Béraud, had (falsely) accused Salengro of having deserted during World War I and having offered to betray the country by relaying information to the Germans. *Gringoire*'s campaign against Salengro was relentless, calling him a traitor, coward, and deserter despite undeniable evidence of his innocence. Four days after being cleared by a war council and the parliament in November 1936, Salengro committed suicide.[49] *Je Suis Partout* was therefore not alone in its rhetorical violence and slander tactics; both were common among far-right newspapers. Still, *Je Suis Partout* gradually emerged as one of the far-right press's most radical voices, above and beyond other far-right publications in tone, content, and politics, and in 1937 it took a turn toward greater violence.

This turn was made possible only when its younger journalists were able to "take over" the newspaper, which, once freed from external constraints, allowed the unleashing of their political violence and the radicalization of their positions. After six years of relative success, and in the wake of the Popular Front victory in May 1936, *Je Suis Partout*'s financial backer, Fayard, decided to shut down what it saw as a potentially politically embarrassing venture and announced the demise of the newspaper.[50] The decision was a political and strategic one, brought on by the publisher's desire to keep a low profile in the face of a newly elected left-wing government. Fayard's choice to end *Je Suis Partout* rather than *Candide* may point to the politicized nature of *Je Suis Partout*. Its journalists, however, energized by the battles they saw ahead of them and outraged at the thought of ending *Je Suis Partout*'s life, decided to take over and become its owners and partners, as well as contributors. Invoking their "sacrifice," they announced that "*Je Suis Partout*'s contributors would rather deprive themselves and give up a third of their salaries than let their newspaper disappear."[51] Since they now lived "in complete fiction," the newspaper offered a home in a world that had become *unreal*.[52] It was their refuge in a disorienting, horrifying, and uncanny world.

Against the current alienating character of the nation, *Je Suis Partout* provided the comfort of male friendship knit together by a revulsion for difference. Special issues, such as the one imagined by Robert Brasillach three months after the demise of the first Popular Front government led by Léon Blum, were "devised in a friendly fashion by the editorial team, . . . infused by a communal doctrine, will, and struggle."[53] They argued that a community of spirit and political will sustained their journalism, and they conceived of writing as an eminently political act. For them, it was obvious in 1936 that "*Je Suis Partout* cannot die at the very moment when Blum promises prosperity, happiness, wealth, and good health to the French nation."[54] They argued that they alone embodied truth, disinterested objectivity, and impartial lucidity. In one article, they disingenuously claimed to be "a newspaper [devoted] to criticism, observation, and study."[55] They described themselves as both the intellectual elite and lonely prophets in a decadent world. They "were everywhere," and they argued that they alone could unveil the truth of modern corrupt society because they "were FREE": *Je Suis Partout* explained in the first week of 1937 that it was "a true cooperative . . . united in the defense of the same ideas."[56] That common ideological commitment characterized the newspaper and was enabled by the constitution of a young and eager group of far-right critics who took full control of it. Gaxotte relinquished his editorship—though not his front-page column—to the benefit of his up-and-coming protégé, the novelist and literary critic Robert Brasillach.[57] Unlike the Young New Right and its eagerness to create a new voice in print, Brasillach and his friends reinvented far-right politics from within.

The "soviet," as they ironically called it, was constituted of such men as Lucien Rebatet, Pierre-Antoine Cousteau, Alain Laubreaux, Georges Blond, Claude Jeantet, and other, less prominent contributors.[58] Its history was a tale of male friendship where, "above the city and [their] youth, [they] wove a friendly and communal world of ideas, sentiments, predictions, and memories."[59] Acutely aware that *Je Suis Partout* represented the expression of "their friendship and love for life," a male brotherhood cemented their ideological commitment.[60] In the words of one of its contributors, they were a new generation: indeed, if, in 1936, "we see a young right of both national and social spirit emerge, clearly opposed to the blind and insensitive forces of capitalism, it is because these young men have reacted against the insolent pretense that claims all idealism is absent from those in France who hold a pen."[61] To be a young far-right intellectual in 1930s France meant to fight with one's own words, wielding the pen as they would weapons in war.

Like their far-right companions at *L'Insurgé*, they were a diverse collection of literary critics, polemicists, aspiring novelists and intellectuals, and men come to journalism as a substitute for political activism. By 1937, when he took over from Gaxotte, Brasillach was already known as the author of impressionist novels, a rather dashing figure of French literary criticism and an emerging name in the world of far-right publications. He had garnered a certain notoriety with his first article, provocatively titled "Oraison funèbre pour M. Gide" (Funeral Sermon for Gide), which was followed by his famous declaration in 1931 that "the post-war era has ended."[62] Lucien Rebatet and Pierre-Antoine Cousteau were two of the most prominent polemicists among the *Je Suis Partout* "soviet." Rebatet had begun his career in the far-right press as film critic under the pseudonym François Vinneuil. He had contributed only film reviews to Maurras's cherished newspaper, but after beginning a regular stint at *Je Suis Partout* in 1933, he found his voice in its pages and became one of its leading political commentators. Rebatet's specialty ranged from xenophobia to antisemitism; he penned a series of articles titled "Foreigners in France" and oversaw the writing of *Je Suis Partout*'s special issues "on the Jews."[63] He also played a central role in the evolution of the newspaper, but never gave up his weekly film critique.

Pierre-Antoine Cousteau, another alumnus of the prestigious Louis-le-Grand lycée, had come to journalism after several years of mediocre jobs and failed business ventures in the United States; he was appointed "specialist" of questions dealing with the United States and Russia, and took over in 1934 as one of the leading commentators on the Spanish Civil War.[64] In the background, Claude Roy and Georges Blond, who were also both involved in *Combat*, penned articles on literature, Roy inaugurating a series on the fate of "young literature" in 1937 and Blond writing a weekly column, "Les blessés de l'esprit," regularly castigating the French press and any form of political consensus. If Roy always remained a discreet figure in *Je Suis Partout*, Blond, a "young man whose hair gracefully decorate[d] his intelligent forehead" and a budding novelist, was most notable for his anti-feminist and racist assertions. But to his fellow racist and antisemitic nationalist Alain Laubreaux, those were "reasonable passions [which] could be seen blazing in his eyes."[65]

Je Suis Partout's content was characterized by its thematic pages ranging from "Men and Ideas," "Around the World," and "Elsewhere" to pages focused on individual countries like England or the United States—indeed, the newspaper prided itself on being the only one of its kind displaying an entire page devoted to colonial affairs under the telling title "*Our* Empire." That page became a regular feature in 1936 and appeared once a month to enlighten metropolitan readers as to the state of *their* colonies. The page on Nazi Germany was written by Claude Jeantet from 1930 until the newspaper's demise in the early 1940s. He was one of the few journalists whose career began and ended with *Je Suis Partout* and whose journalism coincided with a sustained political activism. With his brother, Gabriel, he had split from the Action française organization in 1931 and began pursuing a journalistic career. His brother became a committed far-right activist, and both joined Doriot's Parti populaire français and became members of the short-lived and infamous secret terrorist-like La Cagoule organization.[66]

These young men were joined by seasoned veterans, such as Jean-Jacques Brousson, former secretary to novelist Anatole France whose vitriolic articles never relented in their fierce antisemitic rhetoric inherited from the Dreyfus Affair. Bernard de Vaulx—another well-known signature of *L'Action Française*, *Candide*, and *Ric et Jac*—contributed numerous literary chronicles, while Pierre Daye, another name familiar to readers of *Candide* and *Gringoire*, and lieutenant of the Belgian fascist organization Rex, kept *Je Suis Partout* informed on the success of Rex's fascist leader, Léon Degrelle.[67] The only other journalist to have written in the newspaper from beginning to end was Pierre Villette, who, under the pseudonym Dorsay, published a weekly front-page commentary on parliamentary affairs (and did so until 1944), the "game of people and political parties." Those were among the few, yet significant, names in the pages of the newspaper. In fact, contrary to the common portrayal of *Je Suis Partout* as a rather "vulgar" publication, it offered an impressive array of contributors that included prominent authors like Marcel Aymé, who provided some of his writings, Jacques Bainville, Henry Bordeaux, and even the well-known Martinican novelist René Maran, who wrote from 1936 to early 1937.[68]

In keeping with far-right journalistic tone, the weekly publication favored irony, pastiche, parody, and satire. Its sarcastic texts were complemented by a wide range of caricatures that helped readers decipher the significant issues at stake. The respected Hermann-Paul penned front-page caricatures, often evoking the matronly Marianne in the throes of confusion when faced with brutish Communists and a dangerously seductive "Blum."[69] Ralph Soupault started providing drawings toward the end of 1937 when *L'Insurgé* folded.[70] Still, *Je Suis Partout*'s young journalists parted ways with *Combat* and *L'Insurgé*, since Catholic right-wing intellectuals hardly figured as *Je Suis Partout*'s "founding fathers." While Georges Bernanos had overseen the birth of *Combat* and was featured in the pages of this far-right magazine with "notes" of his own, he was never included in *Je Suis Partout*'s pantheon of "great men." The influence of Catholic authors was marginal in this weekly newspaper. The nationalist writer Maurice Barrès was only occasionally mentioned, despite his undeniable but subterranean influence.

Unsurprisingly, the most prominent reference was Charles Maurras, whose name was regularly invoked with respect and deference. His articles were published on the front page, and his influence was often praised.[71] For the thirtieth anniversary of the birth of the newspaper *L'Action Française*, Gaxotte penned a front-page article in which he told readers that Maurras "is right. He has always been right." He explained they still admired him and found him to be "the MASTER, the one who has shown us the way," because "since the beginning of this century, he has demonstrated the stupidity of democracy, of liberalism and its natural son, socialism."[72] Such praise was common among far-right pundits. Not only had Maurras diagnosed the nation's ills but, for Brasillach, his political organization had been the only one to "officially embrace antisemitism."[73] Their repeated homages to Maurrassian thought—despite a growing disagreement regarding their position toward Nazi Germany—meant the editorial group followed Maurras's famous motto, "Politics first!" and devoted themselves to reflections on the regime, nationalism, and European and international affairs. While the Young New Right came together around the question of the abject state of the nation, *Je Suis Partout* critics were obsessed with the French nation as a bounded nation—rid of decay, putrefaction, and rot—within a larger European, colonial, and world order where Frenchness was preserved.

Politics, Dissolution, and the "Jewish Republic"

In February 1934, *Je Suis Partout* journalists railed against the government's "repression" of the February riots. Those events ultimately confirmed the urgency of the problem: for them, one needed to realize that corruption was irrefutable. It was especially, now, "everywhere and first in France: the nation and the regime."[74] Their editorials and articles were devoted to pointing out and denouncing the dissolution that characterized the French nation and its government. The terms of their political critique—which borrowed and followed Maurras's injunction that the republican and democratic regime was inauthentic and artificial—were increasingly focused on a decadence that seemed to have reached everywhere and everything. They attacked democracy, capitalism, socialism, and communism. They decried the nation's degradation, the citizens' passivity, and the corruption of culture. They reinvested these conventional far-right themes with a virulence and vocabulary that seemed, as the decade unfolded, to exceed even the violence of Action française. The 1936 election of the Popular Front, the Spanish Civil War, and the vagaries of diplomacy with Nazi Germany only served as external proofs of what they feared most. The effects of the decadence and dissolution that they imagined were, in their writings, displaced onto those who were deemed its authors, namely Jews—who could then be blamed for the chaos within the nation.

Disorder, of course, was the outcome of the inauthentic rule of law that had not followed "the real country," as Maurras was fond of reminding his followers. Gaxotte and his acolytes incessantly denounced democracy, which in their eyes was a perversion of the natural order. By allowing infinite representation, an excess of individualism, and popular politics, democracy denied the laws of history: "Just as nature is horrified by emptiness, democracy's profound essence is that of instability"[75] Democratic regimes perverted "nature," which meant that "[they] naturally tend toward the worst. That is [their] profound law."[76] Such a regime produced chaos and instability because it allowed electoral representation to dictate the fate of the government and the country. That chaos, in turn, undermined the true character of the French nation, ill-suited to "either soviet or fascist dictatorship" (the excessive rule of order) but needing a politics based on "authority and order" (a harmonious expression of order).[77] In 1938, Georges Blond observed that "rather than becoming more and more aware, the citizen [in a democratic regime] becomes more and more demented."[78] He added somewhat sarcastically, "Who is to blame if reality is not democratic, if the nature of things, our body and nervous system's reactions to invention are not democratic?"[79] The disjuncture between the "legal country"—the democratic regime—and the "true country"—the nation—created a tension within French society that *Je Suis Partout* journalists argued was the origin of France's decadence as a European nation. This fundamental "contradiction" disrupted the long history of French civilization and obviously generated the corrupt governments they hated.[80] Moreover, in the current European context, they argued that France was being wrongly degraded and underestimated because of its regime—an argument they had in common with *Combat* and *L'Insurgé* and that resonated forcefully in the latter half of the decade. They argued, rather typically, that one of the Popular Front's worst curses had been "to have linked the fate of France to that of democracy, so that all the blows suffered by the democratic regime seem to be suffered by France itself."[81] The nation was wounded in its very heart. France had been lost. It was "lacking."[82] Such was the leitmotiv of Gaxotte, Brasillach, Rebatet, and their collaborators.

Furthermore, French society had been made fragile by the tense and insecure economic situation, which, they felt, governments had proved useless in addressing. Still preoccupied by the aftereffects of the Depression of 1929, which had hit France late but hard, they recognized the necessity for a substantial economic recovery, the end of unemployment, and the curtailing of unbridled capitalism practiced by the "200 families." Their economic analyses, which were often featured on the front page, followed that rhetoric of decadence. On the surface, *Je Suis Partout* exhibited a sustained concern for French workers, though in doing so, it was far less adamant in its anti-bourgeois rhetoric and its commitment to the resolution of socioeconomic issues through syndicalism than were Maulnier and others at *Combat* and *L'Insurgé*. These attacks nonetheless helped shore up the publication's denunciation of both capitalism and communism and its affirmation that only the nation—conceived as a harmonious, hierarchically bounded whole—mattered. Gaxotte and Dorsay were quick to point out that, contrary to the popular Marxist analyses of their day,

France was not a class-based society. They claimed the French worker was a "realist" and not an ideologue eager to unite with workers across nations.[83] Instead, they explained, had it not been for a socialist government, the French people—and especially the working classes—would never have embraced class politics. They had been duped out of fear. Gaxotte wrote that "in truth, [he] referred to 'the proletariat' without really believing in that word and just to do like everyone else. [He] did not like this expression because it seems to confuse minds rather than clarify."[84] By insisting on the recognition of class politics, the Popular Front had driven a wedge in French society, because it pitted French citizens against one another.

The issue was not economic—that is, materialist, in far-right terms—but, above all, political. Editorialist Pierre Gaxotte noted: "There can be no technical remedy to an ill which is political."[85] Articles endlessly decried the "political decomposition" that beset the nation. After 1936, their authors wrote, it had become obvious that "rot was spreading as the number and significance of the rotten men increased."[86] Such putrefaction—a leitmotiv in the first ten years of *Je Suis Partout*'s existence—had later been brought to life by the Socialist government, an avatar made possible by the republican regime undermining the essence of the "true nation." They never explained what had come first: the decay of the nation allowing such a deviant regime to take over or a perverted regime that caused the decay of nation. Instead, they resorted to a rhetoric of illness and disease inherited from Maurrassian ideology in order to speak of the national body politic. Again, in a discussion of the new Popular Front government, Gaxotte asserted that "ills are not disappearing, wounds are not healing, and the cure is no longer effective." For him, the "national union" called for by so many politicians was but a "poultice without effect on this cancer."[87] To these far-right nationalists, it was obvious that "France is like a sick person."[88] Since the "disease has shown itself to be such a contagious condition," Dorsay wrote in the wake of the fall of the Chautemps government, which had replaced Blum in June 1937, "France needs men who are alive, in good health, happy and optimistic." Indeed, "good health implies in the one who possesses it the ability to react against this disease."[89] They claimed that they alone could diagnose the situation.[90]

The immediate cause of such ills could, according to them, be easily identified: it lay in the Socialist government, which, in May 1936, held the fate of the nation in its hands. They considered socialism to be alien to French character, even more so since it seemed to be only an avatar for communism; and Communists had been members of the Popular Front coalition (even though they refused to participate in the newly elected Socialist government). They considered French Communists to be conspirators in disguise, always plotting to take over and govern for Stalin, who was a "revolutionary" and sought to cause revolution "everywhere."[91] Such alleged danger justified their obsession with Communist Russia, since the widespread June 1936 strikes seemed to confirm the government's ineptitude, democracy's tendency to chaos, while providing a taste of the disorder to come if the government remained in left-wing, Socialist—and therefore Communist—hands. To witness such alien forces in power was unbearable. This justified their incessant coverage of "Soviet affairs"; as they explained, "What takes place in the USSR cannot leave *Je Suis Partout* journalists indifferent."[92] Their anti-communism was visceral. It should be especially so, they clamored, because left-wing political movements were nothing more than a front for a far more dangerous force, that of "Judeo-Bolshevism."

"Judeo-Bolshevism" was the accusation most commonly leveled at those considered foreign to the French nation. In 1937, one journalist explained that "people no longer shout 'soviets everywhere!' but whisper 'Jews everywhere!'"[93] A reading of *Je Suis Partout* from 1936 onward illustrates the intertwining of the rhetoric of xenophobia, anti-communism, and antisemitism. It was common practice for *Je Suis Partout* to describe Jews as quietly invading France, unbeknownst to unsuspecting French citizens and benevolent Socialist politicians. The conventional theme of "invasion" was central to their anxiety concerning national boundaries. That fear of foreign invasion obviously did not reflect the realities and complexities of French immigration and refugee policy. It reflected the fantasies of staunch nationalists and far-right activists and regularly circulated throughout the 1930s. Despite the fact that "by the mid-1920s, France had become the most important destination for immigrants in the entire industrialized world," and that the country, in the words of historian Vicki Caron, had been since 1933 a "major haven for German and Central European refugees" (many of whom were Jewish), the French government had, in 1934 and 1935, "cracked down" on both immigrants and refugees.[94] But these anxieties never diminished for *Je Suis Partout*. In the wake of the Popular Front's policies, its journalists felt that "we have remained the most stupidly faithful to the principle of open door when the whole of Europe is vomiting its parasites and human garbage."[95] As a result, they felt that everywhere they turned, they witnessed the signs of such foreign invasion—a theme that, Vicki Caron points out, was no longer the prerogative of the far right.[96] But within the pages of the far-right newspaper, that threat of invasion was especially dangerous because it was a "Jewish invasion." France, as they experienced it, was now the site of unbridled and uncontrollable racial heterogeneity. Disarray was everywhere within the nation.

The "confusion" brought about by foreign Jewish influence was made visible by the "confusion" now characterizing the metropole. "Foreignness" and "Jewishness" were interchangeable terms for them and infused their apocalyptic vision of a nation and culture being undone. Cousteau wrote that during Popular Front gatherings and demonstrations, Paris offered a vision of "a civil war in laces," where culture had been contaminated and disorder reigned. This was especially evident in popular cultural activities such as cinema. He observed that those queuing up to watch a newly released Russian film were "smelly women carefully bundled up in expensive furs." These (presumably) Jewish women were accompanied by over-groomed and athletic young men, and also by some "oriental and effete dandies with hair that is too nappy and who represent the pride of the Popular Front's Negroid intelligentsia."[97] For Cousteau and his peers, the cosmopolitanism and "negrophilia" of the 1920s had only wreaked havoc upon French civilization by allowing the ascendance of "unassimilable" Jews. Parisian public spaces were overrun by distasteful women and deviant male youths whose foreignness, like Blum's, was signified by their association with "Marxism," perverted gender roles, and primitive character. Cousteau used here the clichés typical of subsequent far-right accounts of the Popular Front regime: bourgeois women, insensitive to the plight of the French people, were the living emblem of selfish luxury, and their bodies revealed their racial origin. Cousteau's wrath was especially directed at those "oriental" androgynous dandies whose masculinity and sexuality were, for him, obviously questionable and who acted as the champions of the necessarily foreign—that is, Jewish—Popular Front intellectuals. Culture had been undone, politics was in turmoil, and civilization had been corrupted. Typically, Cousteau held that any public expression of communism was nothing more than the expression of an international Jewish conspiracy.[98] For the authors of *Je Suis Partout*, it was not anti-communism *and* antisemitism that formed the cornerstones of their oppositional politics, but Jewishness under the guise of communism that horrified them. Pierre Gaxotte had said as much in January 1936: "Marxism was [Blum's] homeland and birth certificate."[99] As the caricature illustrating Rebatet's article on the "Jewish [Russian] revolution" stated, "The proletarian was the socialist slave of the Jew" in Soviet Russia.[100]

Because of the chaos brought upon the French culture, "Judeo-Bolshevism" was always to be denounced. Their explanation was very simple. Communism—that is, Marxism under another name—was a Jewish invention. They did not offer an economic analysis—as some Young New Right intellectuals attempted, for example, Maulnier in devoting a chapter to Marx in his 1938 essay on nationalism—and barely a political one. They constantly spoke of the "Jewish origins" of communism's great reference: Marx. Gaxotte told his readers that "Marx was neither historian, nor sociologist, nor economist [but] was a rabbi let loose in history, economy, and sociology." Marx could therefore hardly be a serious intellectual reference since "his work was that of a theologian. He had translated Hegel into numbers and dates, into religion and prophecy." As a man "infused with the metaphysics characteristic of his originary training, [Marx] could not observe phenomena like a scholar." Instead of drafting a theory of society, Gaxotte affirmed, "he has tried to find the essence of things, [and] the indestructible metaphysical realities, so similar to themselves and that sustain themselves without alteration, in the manner of Plato who had defined the 'ideas' hidden behind the fleeting game of appearances."[101] Marx made false and illusory promises because he was of Jewish descent.[102]

As a result, they explained, they could no longer claim the French nation as their own because of its corruption by Jews: "France had become permeable because of its [Jewish] leader's [Marxist] ideology."[103] The nation's borders were threatened not only by a foreign invasion from outside but also from within, by the emergence of republican and left-wing politics and the public visibility of Jewish citizens. The law of the republican regime could not found their claim to Frenchness nor could it allow them to be full French citizens. Corruption of the republican regime had brought about the dissolution of the social body. "Freedom" under a republican regime meant "subjection" because it was impossible to be a fully autonomous citizen under the regime currently ruling France.[104] And that subjection meant enslavement to a "Jew." Once Blum had been elected to power, the origin of decadence became all too evident: it was the "Jew." In fact, as Cousteau asserted, it was obvious that "M. Blum's legal France constitutes an object of anxiety or horror in all of civilized Europe."[105] In order to reestablish Frenchness, they argued, they "needed to redo France." Indeed, "this is the most urgent task. . . . France's decadence has become too visible to be ignored. If the cause [of this decadence] is maintained, we will pay with the consequences: war, defeat."[106] The survival of the nation depended upon their dedicated antisemitic ideas.

"Blum" and French Antisemitism: A Question of Race

As *Je Suis Partout* watched with horror, the Popular Front came to power in June 1936, and Dorsay asked whether "Blum's accession to power will wake up the Jewish question."[107] With a Jewish politician now at the head of the government, *Je Suis Partout* resurrected the notion that the Jews were the cause of antisemitism. As was common for antisemites, they relished insisting that *they* were not driven by hate, but that Jews themselves had elicited this hatred. The burden of responsibility lay on Jew themselves—a fact that noted literary critic and respected *académicien* André Bellessort explained:

> Our antisemitism, which is by the way entirely theoretical—ask Germany . . . what true antisemitism is about—has awakened Jews' own Semitism and has given them an even stronger sense [of themselves], were it not for the fact that they had been the first ones to put forward, at any opportunity and in their own literature, their own ethnic difference.

He added: "A thinker like Bernard Lazare, a lawyer such as Blum do more harm to the Jewish cause than thousands of antisemites."[108] Anti-Jewish sentiment was therefore not a political reaction, they argued, but the instinctive, necessary, and natural reaction experienced by any reasonable French citizen. Robert Brasillach summed up *Je Suis Partout*'s position in a forceful front-page editorial: "The Blum government's accession to power aroused a movement that had been almost unknown in France since the Dreyfus Affair: namely antisemitism."[109] References to that other foundational moment for French antisemitic intellectuals—the late-nineteenth-century Dreyfus Affair—allowed them to insist on the urgency of the situation in 1936. Indeed, "this was no longer the benevolent era of the Dreyfus Affair when, encouraged by their anticlericalism, a number of ignorant and respectable French people had embraced [the Jewish cause]. Since then, Jews have made their way."[110] Dorsay, in 1938, still railed that antisemitism, in the twentieth century and in its French incarnation, was a different—and more urgent—matter: "Antisemitism, as we conceived [it,] was not a matter of opposition to religion."[111] He exclaimed they were not that "stupid" or that "intolerant." But what they could not abide, he insisted, was that "elements that are foreign to us because of their blood and their heredity persist and are determined to govern us!"[112]

The idea that Jewishness was irreducibly distinct from Frenchness and unassimilable to French society increasingly prevailed—in contrast to Maurras and Daudet, who had always had a place for the World War I French Jewish veterans who had proved their attachment to the French nation with their personal sacrifice. After all, even Daudet had claimed, in 1933, that those who were "racially Jewish but French by heart [and] have fought or worked for long for France" were not the same as Blum.[113] For *Je Suis Partout* journalists, *all* Jews without exception must be excluded from the nation. Although they recognized that some—though not many, they insisted—Jews had fought for France, they had done so as colonial subjects and so did not act out of earnest patriotic sentiment. They had defended a "soil which has welcomed them" but not one which was their own.[114] Brasillach further clarified *Je Suis Partout*'s position: "The Frenchman is obviously instinctively antisemitic but he does not like to be seen to be persecuting innocent people for vague tales of origins." However, he added, "Blum [had] taught him that antisemitism was truly different."[115] Instinct harnessed by reason characterized French antisemitism. Theirs was, they claimed, a rational and reasonable response to the invasion and corruption that Jews had initiated—in order to define the national community through race. Defining a racialized imagination of the community did not, they insisted, require embracing a eugenicist and scientific racial ideology. Following the nationalist tradition articulated by Maurice Barrès, far-right intellectuals held that the French nation was not a pure racial entity. From *Combat* to *Je Suis Partout*, most insisted that they refused Gobineau's legacy that had been so readily adopted by Nazi ideology and instead adamantly defined their own antisemitism in contrast to a German "racist" version developed through the prism of racial purity. They believed the French nation was made of different individuals held together by culture, tradition, and civilization. Still, their idea of the nation relied on a racialized understanding of Jewishness and of "culture."[116]

Novelist Marcel Jouhandeau—a well-respected literary figure—defined it most clearly in a 1936 article on *Je Suis Partout*'s literary page. Jouhandeau, who published an antisemitic pamphlet the following year titled *Le péril juif* (The Jewish Threat), explained:

> We, Frenchmen, are clearly not a race. France is a combination of heterogeneous elements: it is a nation. As a result, the Jew is physiologically remarkably organized to battle a people whose unity is purely virtual. [The Jew] is a strong and inassimilable element who slides himself among weak and dispersed elements, like a sickness quietly attacking us from everywhere all at once; not only are we not defending ourselves, but we are unaware we should be defending ourselves. When the Jew fights, driven by his knowledge of what he wants and

> where he is going, we do not even know what we are losing, nor what he is gaining. . . . [W]e are talking of something else here: this is race, and the most terrible race of all, the harshest of all; France has fallen to this lion's race with a jackal's heart.[117]

Intent on drafting a racial definition of the meaning of Frenchness, *Je Suis Partout* insisted, as would Céline, that Jews had colonized France: French people were akin to natives. For Cousteau, "The Jews—who are irreducible nationalists—uttered in their own language with a serene lack of discretion those revolutionary calls that they deemed unnecessary to translate for those pigs of Frenchmen, for the natives."[118] As a consequence, "this nation's individuality has been endangered."[119] If Frenchmen were now natives—an unbearable thought since it dissolved the boundaries between French citizens and their colonial subjects whom they considered the "true natives"—then *Je Suis Partout* needed to embrace the call Céline had uttered in his antisemitic pamphlet concerning the "revolt of [those French] indigenous people."[120] Antisemitism was the only rational response to the fact that, as Jouhandeau wrote, "at night, we are disfigured, we are mutilated, we are slaughtered."[121] The danger was insidious, but undeniable. In this way, far-right critics could thus argue that *all* Jews, irrespective of national origin, were foreign to the French nation.

As in the pages of *L'Insurgé*, the figure of Jewish Socialist leader Léon Blum provided a focus for their attacks. Just as Xavier Vallat had famously done in the Chamber of Deputies, Dorsay exclaimed that, shockingly, "for the first time in the history of France, an Israelite has been called to power."[122] Blum held power and made a claim to French culture—both of which were especially horrifying. In their writings, "Blum" had become a figure larger than life, embodying all ills and evils at once—war, revolution, communism, capitalism, parliamentary democracy, and modernity. *Je Suis Partout* never ceased attacking him, even after he resigned from his position as head of the government in June 1937. His successor, Radical politician Camille Chautemps, was considered ignorant, stupid, and incompetent, but he never elicited the same kind of hateful rhetoric. The indignation and horror of *Je Suis Partout* journalists were just as virulent in 1938, when Blum came back to power for his second tenure. How could the French people not see the effects Blum had on their nation?

> And this French people which does not move, carries on going to the bistro or the cinema, reading *Paris-Soir* or listening to Brossolette, this amorphous, debased, degraded people who does not understand that it is disgraced and

> insulted; that the Blum government is both a national humiliation and an international provocation, that has made it the brunt of the world's mockery. Not one paving-stone has been thrown. Not one minister has been slapped. And not one "news" organ has let out a cry for help.[123]

"Blum" was therefore both the cause and the symptom of the decadent state of the nation. "Blum" as he was imagined by *Je Suis Partout* journalists personified Céline's complaint that "the Jew" is the "most uncompromising parasite, most voracious, most likely to dissolve! The Jew!"[124] As Gaxotte had complained: "It was Him, again Him, always Him."[125]

Unsurprisingly, "Blum" appeared obsessively in their writings because he represented the gender and sexual disorder that far-right intellectuals wanted to undo. One of the great causes of anxiety had indeed been the disorder wrought in the social body, the simultaneous erasure and dissolution of sexual difference, and the perversion of the proper definitions of masculinity and femininity that for far-right critics corresponded to a specifically French arrangement of society and provided its underpinning. The figure of "Blum" provided the site where differences between men and women were revealed to be unstable. It was not that "Blum" conflated both male and female qualities (the accusation of "hermaphroditism" appeared only once in *Je Suis Partout*).[126] Anguish was provoked because "Blum" could, in their minds, embody either masculinity or femininity, thereby transgressing the proper sexual and gendered order of the social body. The danger emanated from his embodiment of effeminacy, the specter of deviant homosexuality, and excessive heterosexual desire.

It was irrefutable that "Blum," as they saw him, was different from "us Frenchmen."[127] He embodied that difference in his physical appearance. His foreignness lay in the fact that he was literally marked as different in his own body: Dorsay asked whether "he was a man like all others." He answered that Léon Blum "has been marked at birth with an indelible sign," which explained the "natural instinct [that] he had developed in the heat of the last few years' political events."[128] The indelible mark that obsessed far-right intellectuals, infused with a Catholic tradition, was the mark of circumcision (an obsession that never figured prominently in the Young New Right's writings). Just as for Céline, who had, in *Bagatelles pour un massacre*, obsessively returned to the fact of circumcision as the literal inscription on a Jewish body of his absolute and irreducible difference, it also figured as the symbolic reminder of the unassimilable difference and nature of Jews. Brousson reminded his readers that "there is an impassable abyss—that probably came from those ritual mutilations—between the circumcised and the uncircumcised."[129] Circumcision, for these intellectuals, revealed the Jew's unmanly character: lack characterized the male Jewish body.

The figure of Blum was dangerous because he was not a "real" and "proper" man. French masculinity should be infused with manliness, a quality Blum was shown to be incapable of possessing. In caricatures and articles, Blum was systematically portrayed as both feminized and effeminate. While the association of effeminacy and Jewishness had a long history, it took on a particular force for *Je Suis Partout* authors eager to intervene in cultural and political debates and identify the origin of the decadence they wished to undo.[130] He was the reminder of the fragile masculinity they wanted to restore. He embodied the feminized intellectual and was therefore both fascinating and repugnant, offering a "burlesque and disgusting spectacle."[131] Interestingly, in their accounts, there was often a repulsive pleasure provoked by Blum's imagined femininity: his femininity could seduce, against one's instincts, but the realization of that seductive power provoked an uncontrollable revulsion. Journalist Georges Blond observed that during one of Blum's public appearances, "everyone around [him] was swept through with delight and exaltation by the spectacle of Léon Blum's dance," while he found himself "taken by a physical discomfort," and asked, "How can one stand the spectacle of [Blum's] trance-like state without shuddering?"[132] For him, that seductive body elicited only "physical illness." In another instance, Rebatet commented that, while "Blum was blowing kisses to the crowd," he disliked these "feminine perversions."[133] The effeminacy inherent in Jewishness was emblematic of "feminine perversion."[134]

"Blum" was often described as a hysterical woman, with writers frequently mentioning his "female" or "falsetto" voice with "precious accents" and "coquettish gestures."[135] Here, hysterical femininity—nervousness, impulsiveness, unbridled passion—was the opposite of manly reason. He was the only politician who was described as a prostitute, seduced by the brutish yet manly French Communist leader, Maurice Thorez. Blum was the syphilitic prostitute in the hands of his Communist pimp, the "handsome Maurice."[136] As a "woman," "Blum" represented the decadence of modernity.

Through his feminization, Blum evoked the danger of a feminizing homosexuality, which was, for these far-right intellectuals who were obsessed with virility, absolutely unthinkable. A Jewish man could not embody manliness or virility, often coded as heterosexual. Instead, he was shown willing to seduce foreign leaders, epitomizing the dual threat of seduction and perversion. It was a cliché of their writing to point out, as Rebatet often did, that Blum was "like a decadent ephebe of the 1890s."[137] As the emblem of sexual deviance, male homosexuality appeared, for many interwar far-right critics, to be the repository of the forces corrupting the nation, invoking degradation and perversion. Their description of homosexuality was haunted especially by the figure of André Gide, who had long appeared in *Je Suis Partout*'s pantheon of deviance. According to Cousteau in an interview with nationalist and conservative author Gonzague Truc, Gide was "an artist of incredible *seduction*." Truc added that in order to recognize his literary greatness, one needed to "close one's eyes to the taste for perversion that Gide takes delight in."[138] It was precisely that "taste for perversion" which could be found in Blum, whose cultural prestige as an author—on the topic of sex and marriage, no less—made him suspect. Perversion, as the main defining characteristic of homosexuality, was perceived to be constitutive of Jewishness and of the French Socialist leader's body and personality.

But "Blum" did not just appear as feminized, effeminate, or homosexual deviant. He especially embodied a perverse sexual threat to the nation, usually portrayed under the guise of the female figure of "Marianne."[139] He was portrayed raping Marianne, leading her astray, lying to her as a heartless seducer would. The formless and sinuous "Léon Blum" held a mysterious and irrepressible sexual power over French women, who were bewitched by his appearance: "He likes to be comforted and held by experienced women," explained Brasillach.[140] His instinct was to seduce because, as Rebatet described him, he was "mealy-mouthed, undulating, whispering and incredibly exotic."[141] In their minds, French women—naturally weak-minded and in need of male guidance—could not help themselves and succumbed to Blum's charm, perversion, and insinuating words. It was his actual foreignness—the difference of circumcision—which made him attractive. Though paradoxical (that which was unacceptable was precisely what attracted women), this argument actually reflected *Je Suis Partout*'s gender politics. Rebatet insisted that Blum's attractiveness was especially true for the Socialist "regime's female chattel," Parisian women.[142] Blum's different gendered incarnations transgressed the acceptable boundaries of the metaphorical social body and of the French male citizens' identity.

"Blum's" irrepressible power—and threat—therefore lay in his ability to both disrupt and embody a gendered and sexed identity that was antithetical to Frenchness as *Je Suis Partout* defined it. Sarcastic and recurrent references in its pages to "citizen Blum" emphasized that alien character.[143] "Blum's" ability to embody the dissolution of sexual difference explained the hold he possessed on French society, the "messianic pride" he displayed in his leadership, greatness, and exercise of power.[144] *Je Suis Partout* journalists said, in 1937, that they were "barely exaggerating. Indeed, Blum practically holds absolute power in France. And he uses it to undo France."[145] The undoing of France needed to be fought so that the culture of French civilization could be preserved:

> Jews have nothing left to envy: they hold the supreme power, that is Power in short. . . . By that I mean the soul of this country. They have power over it, a power that is their own and that they transform into something prestigious and magical; and it is because I feel this so violently that I can no longer sleep: that I wonder what wakes me up at night and drives me to shout on the ramparts as if what I am meant to protect was being slaughtered.[146]

As Jouhandeau experienced it, the survival of the French man was at stake here.

The Pleasures of the Colonial Sublime

To restore French civilization and culture—the foundations of the French nation—these writers and intellectuals built on their antisemitic vision in order to re-imagine a bounded nation—whose very boundedness depended upon their mastery of borders. Since the self and the nation were held together in a sacred relationship, the boundedness of the metropolitan nation required not only the purification of the national body but the enactment of control and possession over the greater borders of the French empire as well as an uncanny ability to gaze at and master what was outside of (metropolitan) France. *Je Suis Partout* did so through reporting on its journalists' incessant travels outside of France, and their obsessive commentaries on colonial territories. The newspaper was especially striking for its concern with international and colonial politics. It featured pages on Nazi Germany and Fascist Italy, in features titled "Elsewhere," "Everywhere," and "Around the World." These were not just the offerings of a politically minded newspaper but gave the illusion of omnipotent ubiquity—the ability to cross and recross boundaries just as it denounced the dissolution of its own social body. The newspaper's title itself—*I Am Everywhere*—promised such masterful ubiquity—always coded as masculine, since those writing, traveling, and consuming were always men, bound together in a metaphorical fraternity undisrupted by feminine presence.[147]

Je Suis Partout was premised upon the illusion that its journalists, akin to ethnographers, really were disseminated everywhere in the world as special correspondents and reported on what they saw. The truth was that they never actually left their Parisian offices except for holidays. In this, they mirrored the colonial explorers and ethnographers, such as Michel Leiris, who had in the previous decade captured the public imagination with tales of exotic travel and fearless adventure. The 1931 Colonial Exposition had been immensely popular, welcoming thousands of visitors reveling in the delights of supposedly "authentic" villages populated by those "natives" whom France benevolently ruled.[148] *Je Suis Partout* readers could therefore safely and comfortably consume this exoticism in the confines of Parisian cafés.

Frenchness depended upon control and possession, and the page titled "*Our* Empire" reminded *Je Suis Partout* readers of this necessity. That page was usually authored by journalists specializing in "colonial affairs" (rather than the usual coterie of regular contributors) or was simply anonymous. Among its regular contributors were the Martinican-born novelist René Maran, who had received the prestigious Prix Goncourt in 1921 for his "true Negro novel," *Batouala*, and also wrote in *Candide*.[149] Maran was known for his "reformist critique" of French colonialism, and his articles (appearing weekly in 1933 and 1936–37) on economic and political issues did not fundamentally challenge France's civilizing mission.[150] It is also interesting to note that "Marius Ary Leblond"—the pseudonym of two prominent writers, Georges Athénas and Aimé Merlo from the island of Réunion—also wrote for this page. Another assiduous journalist was Georges Roux, who had been writing exclusively on French Africa, the "Middle-East," the "Near East," and "Franco-Arab relations" since 1931.[151] According to some of these contributors and the newspaper at large, the colonies were the required underpinnings of French citizenship; as Maran himself stated in an article otherwise critical of colonization and "integral racism," "France did not distinguish between its legitimate sons and its adopted children."[152] Roux summed it up when he explained that in order to keep chaos and disorder at bay, "it is necessary to find a form of collaboration between French and Algerian Muslims under the aegis of the tricolor flag where respect for French primacy is upheld."[153] Their "Greater France" was tied together by indissoluble ties of affection and duty. Such an intimate—but still hierarchical—relationship is what *Je Suis Partout* journalists yearned for and what should be restored

N° 292. — 27 JUIN 1936. JE SUIS PARTOUT 5

NOTRE EMPIRE

La Guyane française et l'exploitation aurifère

Un placer à la Guyane

René MARAN.

Le problème du riz en Cochinchine

Retour de la rizerie (Dessins de Charles ROISEAU.)

René LEGAL.

Joie et douleur au pays du soleil

Scènes de la vie martiniquaise

Antillaise

Type indigène

DEUX NOVEMBRE

Paulette NARDAL.

Les intérêts français en péril dans le Proche-Orient

Robert VEYSSIÉ.

"Notre Empire." *Je Suis Partout*, June 27, 1936, p. 9. Courtesy of Bibliothèque nationale de France.

in France itself. The order and hierarchy of the French empire guaranteed the greatness of the French nation. As one journalist commented in the face of Nazi Germany's pretensions to colonial territories,

> A Frenchman cannot ignore [the following]:
>
> 1. that France is a whole, that is not narrowly constrained by a geographical configuration and that every one of its parts which constitute what we call an "empire" are indispensable to the life and strength of the nation, as well as to its economic balance and prosperity.
>
> 2. that, unless one is an accomplice to those sellers or thieves of French substance, we cannot agree to giving up colonial territories just because of the fallacious excuse of "finally being in peace."[154]

The French nation and civilization depended upon the permanence of its empire. France's imperial fate was neither marginal nor unimportant. It was central to their nationalist and antisemitic claims.

In *Je Suis Partout*, the colonies were the nostalgic site of a harmonious pleasure and the joys of rule. While one commentator lamented the faded glories of Chandernagore, one of the "remnants of the great French empire in the Indies," Leblond celebrated the idyllic and sensuous natives of the island of Réunion, whose existence, he argued, should not be disrupted by the impersonal destruction of mindless modern tourism.[155] Another critic explained that the "absence of a French Kipling" did not mean that France was devoid of imperial sensibility.[156] Yet another article, whose tone departed somewhat from the usual musings, enticed readers to discover "joy and suffering under the sun: scenes of Martiniquan life."[157] Strikingly (though this may not have been obvious to *Je Suis Partout* readers), it was authored by the Martinican intellectual and editor of *La Revue du Monde Noir* Paulette Nardal, who played an important role in the emergence of the *négritude* movement. She was also the only woman to write for this page.[158] The article's critique of French colonialism was, however, muted by the evocation of a past long gone, which was given (a different) tone in other articles. In this piece, Nardal described the exotic spectacle of a carnival in Martinique. She mused that "these men and women really play at recreating for amused spectators what was a tragic past. [Is this mere] detachment? Carelessness? It is, after all, nothing but the past." It was, she reminded readers, "Christian civilization [that] has transformed the Negro sorcerer into the devil."[159] Nardal published only two articles in *Je Suis Partout* and the critique embedded in them was, both times, framed and overshadowed by the aesthetic exoticization that characterized this

N° 275. — 29 FEVRIER 1936. JE SUIS PARTOUT 5

NOTRE EMPIRE

L'Afrique Occidentale a rétabli ses finances

Femme aux calebasses (Soudan)
(Bois gravé de Ch. BOIRAU)

Notable Ouoloff (Dakar)
(dessin de Ch. BOIRAU)

Robert DELAVIGNETTE

Jeune fille Bobo (ancienne Haute-Volta). (dessin de Ch. BOIRAU)

LE BAGNE ET LA MISE EN VALEUR DE LA GUYANE

Piroguiers sur la Sanaga (Cameroun)
(Bois gravé de Ch. BOIRAU)

René MARAN.

Une des belles filles de l'Empire

Coiffure de femme Toucouleure du Soudan.
(Bois gravé de Ch. BOIRAU)

Robert WETSSIE.

La formation des agitateurs communistes en Indochine

J.-L. D'AIGNOT.

"Notre Empire." *Je Suis Partout*, February 29, 1936, p. 5. Courtesy of Bibliothèque nationale de France.

section. While Nardal ended her article by quoting the Martinican poet Gilbert Gratiant (a meaningful citation on a page celebrating colonies), an illustration showed an "indigenous type" as if one were in a museum, while another drawing showed an "Antillean woman" on the beach.[160]

To add to the vicarious delight of empire, this colonial page regularly offered ethnographic travel narratives showcasing the sceneries and peoples of Algeria, or "Morocco, island of peace."[161] Even when discussing colonial politics, economic difficulties, or "native" discontent, they insisted on the sensory delights of these territories. In a series of articles devoted to Algeria, chronicler Jean Paillard lamented that he "did not understand why there was not more tourism in the beautiful country of Algeria." After all, it had it all: "daily maritime and air connections, excellent roads, pleasant hotels that were often first-class . . . charming beaches, winter sports in the Atlas . . . unforgettable oasis in the South . . . a varied countryside everywhere [that] was sometimes wild and bare, but more often incomparably rich and colourful."[162] Descriptions like these inevitably prefaced discussions regarding the political fate of the colony, here a discussion of the undesirability of the Blum-Viollette project—a proposal that offered to extend French citizenship to a select number of elite Algerian Muslims (approximately 20,000, who were either civil servants, members of the military, or degree holders) while allowing them to follow Islamic law.[163] Still, the pleasure elicited in these articles was always one that approached some kind of unbearable *jouissance*. As Paillard had stated, "Seeing Algiers emerge from the sea remains one of these sumptuous joys that fill a traveler's life forever, to the point of dulling any future pleasures."[164]

Mastery also expressed itself aesthetically. Strikingly, pages on the imperial adventure were adorned not with satirical caricatures of politics but with exotic, almost photographic drawings of African or Algerian families, in stark and evocative black and white. Painterly representations often featured aestheticized portraits of native women. Scenes illustrated the articles devoted to forays of journalists into the heart of the French empire. These allowed the pleasures of an ethnographic gaze as happy and inarticulate "natives" reassured metropolitan readers of their ability to conquer and embody civilization. (It was the only page in the newspaper that featured such aesthetics.) *Je Suis Partout*'s utopian vision of exotic spaces populated by gentle and docile native subjects symbolically affirmed racial mastery and control in the service of the restoration of French civilization. And that was what needed to be preserved.

It is notable that *Je Suis Partout* insisted on the luxury and delights offered by exotic colonial spaces to illustrate its desire for the boundedness of the self, for since the late nineteenth century, French hygienists and civil servants had warned against the potentially debilitating and contaminating effects on French bodies of such foreign environments and climates.[165] This ability to contaminate and corrupt had formed the staple of Louis-Ferdinand Céline's depiction of Bardamu's trials and tribulations as a colonial civil servant in West Africa. But rarely did *Je Suis Partout* mention disease or fatigue—those remained in the background.[166] Since the racial contamination and weakening of bodies was nonetheless always to be feared, the control forced upon unnamed and undifferentiated "natives" as described in *Je Suis Partout*'s colonial pages was what provided individuality to French citizens. After all, one journalist claimed, "the ability for colonization is a fundamentally Latin virtue" even if sometimes exercised a bit too brutally.[167] In far-right nationalist rhetoric, French civilization especially had been made great because of its Latin origins. The figure of the unnamed native offered these far-right intellectuals a seeming resolution to potential disorder. It acted as a mirror confirming the borders of the self. Because it was tenuous and illusory, the sensuous pleasure and peaceful harmony offered by the colonies needed to be constantly reaffirmed.

Such an ethnographic gaze contrasted greatly with the newspaper's front pages devoted to domestic politics. These were littered with angry and vitriolic denunciations of the government, proclaiming that "for the first time, a messianic Jew was now in power."[168] While colonized territories offered soothing and restorative comfort, a site of harmony and order with their "swaying palm trees," "plentiful resources," and "peaceful natives," France was the site of a heroic and vital struggle for the souls of its embattled male citizens. Those aesthetically pleasing colonial motifs and illustrations—directly influenced by the "colonial craze" for all things African and foreign, which had beset France in the 1920s and had been celebrated in the 1931 Colonial Exposition—contrasted with the freakish caricatures of "ugly" and repulsive Jews that began appearing in the newspaper in late 1937.

Though they occasionally called for a reform of colonial rule, the writers in *Je Suis Partout* asserted that only order and authority could preserve the French empire. In the 1930s, they warned of the decadence that prevailed in metropolitan France and was seeping into the colonies. This was because of the artificial and disruptive nature of the democratic regime, and its latest incarnation, the Popular Front. In an article on the future of Guyana, one journalist—who actually began by mentioning a pioneer who had been antisemitic—said that Guyana was indeed "an ancient French territory, maybe older than Lorraine."[169] But, he ominously continued, "since '89, Guyana had received [only] two notable gifts from the metropole: the abolition of slavery, which has brought about its material ruin . . . and universal suffrage, which has spread havoc [*chienlit*]." The result was undeniable and figured as the avowed motivation behind many articles in 1937 and 1938, with claims that "this noble country is completely decrepit and decadent."[170] Again invocations of the perverse effects of Popular Front rule upon the colonies served as a shorthand for a much graver danger.

In fact, if there was disorder and chaos, it was because of the impure and disruptive presence of Jews in the colonies. *Je Suis Partout* journalists warned that the foreign figure of the "Jew" through invasion and contamination—and since the 1871 Crémieux decree that had "naturalized" Jews living in Algeria, a French colony since 1830—was corrupting the hierarchy that separated French citizens and their racial inferiors. Division had been introduced into an otherwise racially ordered space; in his description of North Africa, Roux opposed to a "forgetful," "improvident," "careless," "religious," "reserved," primitive "Arab who lived only in the present" (and was wisely guided by the French), the "money-grabbing," "naturally impudent" Jew always ready to invade.[171] Jewish invasion was always to be feared, and the example of Madagascar was used to illustrate the point. One journalist pointed out that Polish Jewish workers—an instance of doubly "foreign" immigration—should not be brought over to the island as agricultural laborers. This project was profoundly misguided and if "Madagascar were a settler colony, it should be populated by those metropolitan French who are unemployed."[172] A striking caricature emphasized the point a few months later. While an African statue stood at the right side of the drawing, one could see Jews arriving at the island on a boat, ready to "invade."[173] This "unnatural" invasion would bring out not only French antisemitism but the "old indigenous antisemitic tradition" that could wake up at any time if nothing was done to prevent this "incredible Jewish invasion."[174] A staple of colonial articles warned that Algerian riots like those of the early 1930s could erupt again in 1936, for it would be very easy to reanimate "[Algerians'] congenital antisemitism to the point of paroxysm."[175] According to *Je Suis Partout*, the Jewish moneylenders "proliferating in the Algerian *bled* [countryside]" would inevitably awake these uncivilized natives' instinctive hatred for Jews.[176] The argument was remarkably identical two years later, when Georges Roux asked whether "French Africa had become a Jewish Kingdom."[177] This time, his article was not featured on the colonial page but appeared on the newly created page on "Israel." Because the French nation was allowing Jews to enter it, to corrupt it, and had done so since republicans had ruled France, the model that French colonialists presented in their domination of colonial subjects could not be fully realized.

Je Suis Partout's portrayal of colonies and colonial subjects—downplaying any form of political activism or social unrest and dissatisfaction, while ascribing any disorder to "native" antisemitism—was somewhat disingenuous, since in the 1930s French colonies were hardly peaceful sites of benevolent paternal rule over grateful subjects. The interwar years had witnessed the emergence of "anti-colonial nativist and nationalist" movements as well as riots and protests across French colonial territories.[178] Articles devoted to the French empire tended to downplay these events. When they did discuss discontent, riots, and the possibility of nationalist insurrection and revolution, they usually laid the blame on the illegitimate republican and left-wing government. For instance, Georges Roux warned, "It is possible that this new government will bring an external war upon us. It may be likely that it will bring us to the brink of a French civil war, [but] it is certain that it is going to cause an Algerian civil war."[179] Still, the articles usually appeared amid writings celebrating the joys and exotic pleasures provided by the colonies. They nonetheless demonstrated the pervasive anxiety created by the inherent divisive influence of Jews as well as Communists within colonial territories. These anxieties emerged not so much around French Caribbean, African, and Asian colonies as around North African territories, and Algeria specifically, which was regularly featured from 1936 to 1938. Algeria was a particular cause of concern because, unlike other North African territories where, one journalist explained, "a sinister blend of Marxism and pan-Islamism bubbles under these turbans that owe everything to France," "Algeria already somewhat embodied the face of France."[180]

Beginning in 1937, *Je Suis Partout* inaugurated a series of articles destined to investigate "anti-French movements in the colonies." One of the forces that encouraged rebellion against French rule was the pervasive influence of communism. As Roux warned, "Our imperial work is undermined by the communist virus."[181] This was worrisome because, "in Europe, the Communist Party preaches the brotherhood of the peoples. In Africa, it excites racial hatred, encourages Arab nationalism, and exploits antisemitism."[182] Communism was especially disruptive since it had come in the wake of the infamous

1936 Blum-Viollette project offering to extend French citizenship to some elite Algerian Muslims. Such initiatives threatened to undo the proper ordering of the empire. This, these far-right journalists explained, would wreak havoc upon the colonial hierarchy and encourage Muslim nationalists who were "anti-French."[183] Communist influence could now run free because Blum's Socialist government proved itself unable and unwilling to protect and preserve the French imperial legacy. Those policies would undo the "natural" order and hierarchy of the French empire. *Je Suis Partout* supported the French settlers protesting such reforms. As Gaxotte had already warned in May 1936, Blum's "government will undoubtedly provide guns to the natives so that they kill the colonizers [*colons*]."[184] Roux returned to this topic several times, always predicting "the end of the French empire." He announced that "French domination in North Africa will have lasted from 1830 to 1938. It started under the aegis of the old monarchy, and it will have ended under the Popular Front."[185] As he concluded, "If one had wanted the loss of our empire and premeditated the nation's ruin, one would not act any differently."[186]

From "Instinct" to a Legal Status for the Jews

In order to enact such control, *Je Suis Partout* translated its racial obsession into a political argument against equality, denying the history of emancipation that had characterized the state since the French Revolution. In 1791, the French state had been the first European nation to emancipate its Jewish inhabitants, granting them full "citizenship" and thereby ending a historical legacy of minority status.[187] It was precisely because subsequent republican regimes and their institutions had been open to Jews that these intellectuals must revolt against republican democracy. *Je Suis Partout* thus denounced the illegitimacy of the republican regime by pointing to its inability to protect the great French imperial nation against Jewish invasion. It reminded readers that "one of the first initiatives" of the current republican regime had been to enact the Crémieux decree in 1871, thus allowing Jews to inhabit the French empire and, by extension, undermine it. One article (presumably written by Rebatet) claimed that, more than sixty years later, in 1937, not only had a Jew—Léon Blum—come to be prime minister but it was evident that "the Jews were the origin of all the troubles in *our* North Africa." It asserted, as the newspaper had done repeatedly since 1937, that "one of the strongest feelings of the Arab or the Berber is their horror of the Jew."[188] Robert Brasillach thus justified *Je Suis Partout*'s urgency in addressing the Jewish question by reminding his readers that "all peoples," from "the Romans" to the "Arabs," and "European nations," had been hostile to Jews.[189] Two years earlier, Brasillach had already explained that the time might have come for a "lesser France"—a play on the imperial notion of the "Greater France"—in order to prevent the naturalization of Jews who were "foreign" to France. For anyone with "common sense," it was time to "protect the French race."[190] Another journalist added that in the face of the Popular Front's destructive policies, metropolitan French should remember that it was the French colonizers (*colons*) who were true "subtle and virile heroes," just as Charles Maurras had been.[191] If nothing was done to counter Jewish rule and invasion, then, for instance, "the French of Algeria will revolt," cried Georges Roux.[192] For *Je Suis Partout*, it was time to act against French Jews.

But this was not to be the unfettered violence of pogroms exhibited by "less civilized" nations and occasionally displayed by "unruly Arab Muslims." Disorderly violence was, according to *Je Suis Partout*, antithetical to the French national character (both reasonable and reasoned) and needed to be contained. Its journalists therefore turned to the law to establish the French (racialized) citizen by advocating in 1939 not oppositional insurgency as the Young New Right had done but a separate legal status for the Jews.[193] Only the imposition of such a law would enable the end of dissolution and allow the emergence of a "New Man." It was the law that had symbolically and politically maintained the distinction between French citizens and colonial subjects, and only the law could distinguish between rightful French citizens and Jewish individuals deemed foreign. Against a long tradition of wrongheaded republican assimilation, French Jews needed to be defined legally as aliens without rights or privileges in the nation and its colonies. The law would thus reaffirm the boundaries of "Greater France."

French citizens, *Je Suis Partout* argued, should take inspiration from their Muslim subjects, who were "naturally antisemitic."[194] The series of articles on Algeria that appeared in the spring of 1938 constantly reminded readers that "Algeria is antisemitic"[195] *Je Suis Partout* argued that the Jewish presence had both created and awakened a "native" hatred of Jews. If even unruly and irrational colonial subjects—in this case, Algerian Muslims who might one day become French—showed they rejected Jews, then the French needed to show "the solution" to the problem. The French ruled the colonies because they—unlike colonized subjects—had the ability to exercise reason and law; Jews should, as a rule, be expelled from the national and colonial body. The empire thus haunted the nation and, as such, helped show what should be done in France.[196] One journalist maintained that, indeed, "one of the colonizer's first dut[ies] . . . is to respect his subject's feelings."[197] Peace and order in the empire thus required that anti-Jewish sentiment be translated into concrete legal action both in the colonies and at home. Following this logic, *Je Suis Partout* argued in 1939 for the immediate and unequivocal imposition of a racial status for French Jews in order to separate out these "monkeys"—as Brasillach called them—from true Frenchmen.[198]

Rebatet explained in his 1942 best seller *Les décombres* (The Ruins) that the "*Je Suis Partout* team was, within the nation, one of the few healthy and vigorous cells able to fight against the virus."[199] In the latter half of the 1930s, one of *Je Suis Partout*'s most cherished topics was the "Jewish question"—something that Thierry Maulnier would deplore in *Combat*. Whether it be Brousson, Blond, Brasillach, or Jeantet, it seemed every journalist felt a pressing need to address this issue. Rebatet's articles on "political refugees in France," which he began in 1938, served as a thinly disguised justification for writings on Jewish influence, power, and invasion of Europe, and how France was affected. Rebatet justified such lengthy investigation by the urgency of the situation: while he recognized the benefits brought by a foreign workforce to the country's economic health, he was concerned by the "danger that these exotic additions that proved reluctant to any assimilation represented for the integrity of [his] race."[200] Most significantly, *Je Suis Partout* inaugurated a new era for the far-right press when it published two special issues entirely devoted to the "Jewish question," in April 1938 and February 1939. While the first issue, advertised as "incredible, impartial and informed," investigated the nature and position of "Jews" throughout the world, the second issue focused on "Jews and France" and insisted upon the historical specificity of French antisemitism.[201] Authored entirely by polemicist Lucien Rebatet, the 1939 special issue was so successful that it had to be reissued.

Almost two years after Blum's resignation from the government, *Je Suis Partout* claimed that, more than ever, antisemitism was resurfacing with greater force in France:

> Antisemitism is being born again in France. It has touched parts of the country and segments of the population that, until now, seemed the most indifferent to such concerns. As journalists who have for a long time made the Jewish question their priority in thinking about the regime . . . we have witnessed this almost daily.[202]

NEUVIEME ANNEE. — N° 388. — VENDREDI 15 AVRIL 1938. NUMERO SPECIAL Le numéro : 1 fr. 25

JE SUIS PARTOUT

21, RUE MARGUERIN, 11. — PARIS (14e) Téléphone : Gobelins 60.24

Le grand hebdomadaire de la vie mondiale

Rédacteur en chef : ROBERT BRASILLACH

Que vous aimiez ou non les Juifs, vous devez savoir ce qu'ils sont. Informez-vous en lisant ce numéro rigoureusement objectif.

LES JUIFS

Les articles et les textes qui composent ce numéro ont été écrits ou rassemblés par Lucien REBATET

LA QUESTION JUIVE

— C'était si mal commode de nous téléphoner parmi tant d'autres Lévy que j'ai pris le nom de comte de Champaubert !

Robert BRASILLACH.

VENDREDI SAINT

— Ah! Blum, tout augmente, où sont les 30 deniers de ton ancêtre?

LES JUIFS ET L'ALLEMAGNE

L'émancipation des Juifs allemands

— SUITE EN 2e PAGE —

"Les Juifs." *Je Suis Partout*, special issue, April 15, 1938, front page. Courtesy of Bibliothèque nationale de France.

In 1938, what had been denounced in the colonies was now happening at home. France had become the "refuge for German Jewry"; since 1933, "it stank of the ghetto!"[203] In the face of these imagined dangers, there was only one sane and "normal" reaction: antisemitism. Robert Brasillach explained in 1938 that "whether you want it or not, France rules over seventy millions of white, yellow, black, Muslim, converted, fetishistic, civilized, barbarian men who do not have a single idea in common, except one: they do not like the Jews."[204] Antisemitism in 1938 could therefore no longer be theoretical but "was born out of simple experience."[205] France was not alone in having experienced anti-Jewish hatred: "every people has been antisemitic."[206] Antisemitism was thus "not a German invention but a French tradition."[207]

It was therefore necessary to "address the question without any prejudice." The problem appeared to be simple. As Brasillach laid it out: "What are the Jews? They are foreigners." Jewishness was not a question of religion, but a question of race, especially since Brasillach reminded most of the French people that Jews were neither faithful nor religious: "The Jews are a nation."[208] It was "inconsiderate assimilation which has produced antisemitism." Brasillach added that republican assimiliationist policies have failed since "they have not prevailed against the race."[209] Jews "falsify our history, make our opinion."[210] They had endangered the empire, corrupted the nation, and made it impossible ever to achieve a harmonious society.

What was the newspaper's purpose in drafting a special issue on the Jews in 1938? Brasillach answered in his editorial that "[they] hope this issue will help discern the motivation behind this instinctive reaction [antisemitism] and will transform it into a reasonable decision."[211] Far-right critics had, since 1936, argued that their anti-Jewish hatred was a matter of "instinct," a visceral and uncontrollable "gut reaction." Translating "instinct" into "reason" constituted *Je Suis Partout*'s aim in drafting a French antisemitism, because, they argued, their political vision needed to appeal to a distinct French characteristic—the ability to be rational—unlike Hitler, who they explained had appealed to "myth," a characteristic more attractive to the German people, who were prone to "mysticism" and whose nation was "morally archaic."[212] The marriage of instinct and reason was distinctively French, unlike the situation in "Oriental" or Eastern European countries, which, Brasillach asserted, unnecessarily resorted to pogroms and persecutions as a result of their "anarchical character and the lack of confidence people felt in the greatness of their nation."[213] Unlike these less civilized nations, Brasillach insisted, France had different aims. He explained it forcefully: "We do not want to kill anyone. We do not wish to organize pogroms." Obviously, this was also a rhetorical justification enabling the definition of a specifically French position—Brasillach and Rebatet had often insisted that their antisemitism was not "racist" like the Nazi version; neither were they xenophobic, they repeatedly claimed, despite their calls against the alleged threats of foreign immigration.[214] Brasillach reiterated what he held to be French nationalists' position in 1939 in his editorial to the second special issue on the Jews: neither persecution nor pogrom. There was only one way to solve this problem: "The best way to prevent the unforeseeable reactions of instinctive antisemitism is to organize an antisemitism of reason," a reasoned and reasonable antisemitism.[215]

Je Suis Partout called for radical action: a legal status for the Jews. Its writers appealed to the power of the law to redefine the boundaries of the nation in order to protect French people and exclude those who were deemed foreign even if they possessed French citizenship. The power of the law enshrined French reason and enabled the restoration of French citizenship: law established the subject because it enabled the transformation of instinct into reason. This was a necessary step, especially since until that time, Rebatet argued, the "law has proved to be brazenly unequal. It has been exclusively judeophile."[216] Yet this certainly did not imply that law should be abandoned. Paradoxically, the weapons to be used first against the Jews were actually already in place: Rebatet proclaimed that first, whatever legislation already existed should in fact be enforced rather than ignored when it came to foreign, naturalized individuals and undesirable political refugees—all of whom were Jews in Rebatet's mind.[217] In 1938, *Je Suis Partout* proposed a status legislating the conditions under which all individuals deemed Jewish could reside in France and those already French could be excluded from the national community: the French state "needs to consider all Jews originating from foreign nations as foreigners and oppose their naturalization with the severest of dams." This means "considering long-established Jews as a minority with a [special] status which would protect them at the same time as it protects us from them." Such a legal status provided the "only means to ensure without violence national peace and the absolute independence of French soil."[218] A year later, *Je Suis Partout*'s position had not changed. Even more than before, Brasillach reiterated what needed to be done: a legal status designed to distinguish and exclude all Jewish individuals—irrespective of their citizenship status—in order to restore the nation and its French character. This would not be difficult since, Brasillach said, "everyone knows what a Jew is."[219]

The Culture of French Fascism

The law helped preserve the distinctiveness of French civilization, and that distinctiveness was to be found in culture. Political battles were also and especially waged in the realm of culture as far-right intellectuals recognized that culture could serve as politics. To define culture had become especially urgent in the late 1930s because far-right intellectuals felt they needed to oppose the "revolutionary intellectuals" who illegitimately invoked the homeland and the French people in order to claim "national cultural values" against the forces of the right and fascism.[220] The Popular Front, they maintained, had "replaced naïve poets, scrupulous novelists and humanist writers with political scoundrels."[221] The struggle against decadence—restoring French virility—should be fought just as ardently outside the political arena.

Left-wing intellectuals especially had to be uncovered for the mystifying lies they kept on telling the French people: they epitomized a form of masculinity that far-right critics argued did not embody the Frenchness they yearned for. Alongside the figures of André Gide—associated with homosexuality—and Julien Benda—associated with Jewishness—the figure of novelist André Malraux came to represent the ills of a socialist-inspired and anti-fascist manliness. Brasillach therefore often returned to the topic of André Malraux's status in French politics and culture. While allowing Malraux some intellectual credibility and literary value, Brasillach repeatedly referred to the "diabolical sensuality and intelligence" of Malraux's "partly illegible and hazy novels." He explained that these half-formed and imperfect works served only to promote the type of masculine heroism that Brasillach felt consisted more in a love of blood and death than in "true heroism."[222] In Brasillach's mind, Malraux was an "adventurer" briefly involved in the world of letters rather than a true intellectual.[223] Malraux's works were those of "an activist and a partisan" whose attempt to draw sympathy to the Spanish Republican cause had produced a "fragmented and spasmodic art."[224] French manliness should be measured and balanced, not eager and zealous. *Je Suis Partout* accused antifascist intellectuals of a suspect "eagerness" when they fought against European fascist threats. Brasillach was especially intent on delegitimizing Malraux, who had garnered attention through his highly public involvement with the Republican forces against Franco's Phalangist troops in the Spanish Civil War. In contrast, Brasillach celebrated the virile qualities of Belgian fascist leader Léon Degrelle.

To make matters worse, intellectuals' sense of their role had been muddled by the presence and visibility of those who spoke in the name of Frenchness and to whom *Je Suis Partout* denied any legitimacy: this meant denying Jewish intellectuals' right to participate in the public sphere. Not only was Victor Basch, the French head of the League of the Rights of Man mocked, but Julien Benda, the author of the 1927 essay on intellectuals' role, was also singled out for attack. Ten years after his first, much-debated essay, Benda published a memoir, titled *La jeunesse d'un clerc* (An Intellectual's Youth). Benda's claim to the position of man of letters was of course contested by *Je Suis Partout* critics, as it was by the far right in general: his was an overblown claim where "through the publication of aborted and convoluted books, Benda has consecrated himself an intellectual."[225] Again, the trope of "convoluted thought" as synonymous with Jewishness—already put forth by *Combat*—reappeared. For Brousson, a Dreyfus Affair veteran and longtime Action française supporter, Benda's Jewishness canceled any claims he made to being an intellectual. He insisted that "as long as France will be France, an intellectual will mean something clear, but not [something] slimy, Byzantine, and so narrowly-defined." His indignation was palpable as he asked "how such a Jew could pretend to be an intellectual."[226] Jews like Benda only entertained a perverse relationship to the French language: even if "vanquished by the most categorical arguments, he will be able to invent whatever sophism."[227] Even Blond described Benda with particular venom. He expressed his horror at this "amazing insect with a man's name" who "gets out of his hole crying, 'I am a Jew! I am a Jew! I am a Jew!'" Benda "botches citations and with his small agile legs, which he has dipped in ink, begins tracing very regular sentences."[228] Benda represented the worst in literary journalism, an "obscene puppet" masquerading as an intellectual.[229] Today with public letters under the rule of Blum, a "former intellectual on holiday," they concluded, "the intellectual has become a poor and pathetic man."[230]

The intellectual, according to *Je Suis Partout*, could be a full participant in the Republic of Letters only if he felt culture and understood it in an organic way. His role consisted not in displaying an abstract sum of knowledge nor in overanalyzing issues and debates but in acting as the receptacle of cultural ideas and aesthetic value. Brasillach believed, as did his mentor Gaxotte, that in tracing a "true portrait of France," one must understand first and foremost that culture was "'something else' first."[231] Culture implied an aspiration to and a respect for beauty, its indispensable underpinning, but this should not be an aesthetic ideal divorced from natural sensibility. He asserted, "One can imagine a people that would be illiterate and also be a cultured people."[232] Like Maulnier, he argued that culture relied on tradition and, in turn, embodied a distinctive French character:

> All the elements that have made our country what it is today must form our culture; French culture cannot be redone unless it has been made perceptible to everyone as the fairytale is made perceptible to the child; because French culture can not be remade—no more than any other country's culture—without its history, its true legendary character, and its poetry being born again first. French culture cannot be remade without re-creating this diffuse metaphysics that we need after bread: we need to reassert the conditions necessary for bread, and reassert the conditions necessary for life and the greatness of France. But in order to reassert these conditions, we must first begin to understand.[233]

After the basic need for biological survival, what mattered most was the culture that had made the nation, a culture felt, sensed, and experienced rather than explained, analyzed, and formalized. This was an idea particularly dear to Brasillach. He explained that "a people's culture is not to know more or less a sum of things: let's leave these illusory conceptions to Soviet Russia or America. But it means establishing a vast wave of symbols that is immediately understandable, it means understanding oneself."[234] Culture was therefore instinctive and enabled the self to find its true expression in the individual, and the individual to identify with his fellow citizens and with the nation as a whole. So, as an anonymous journalist wrote, "Our national tradition is so widely human that anything that narrows the heart and obscures intelligence prevents us from being fully and completely French."[235]

Brasillach insisted that such a conception was neither Romantic nor a romanticized version of the past. Instead, it meant a deep and unbroken connection with what Léon Daudet had termed the "diffuse metaphysics" of a nation, an innate knowledge (*savoir*) that Brasillach opposed to abstract knowledge (*apprendre*).[236] This metaphysics should be expressed in a national poetic language, since "there is no great nation without a national poetics."[237] Poetic language had long been considered to provide an unmediated access to truth and beauty, and to be the expression of one's true soul. It was also praised by Maurras and Maulnier. In his writings, Brasillach saw poetic language—exemplified in the form and genre of poetry—as the privileged access to the truth of the nation. Brasillach's own status as novelist and literary critic bolstered his claim. As a longtime *Je Suis Partout* chronicler, Brasillach produced literary criticism that was appealing not just because it had driven him to oppose "the genre of literature that been so fashionable in the postwar years" but because it was sustained by "the echoes [and] resonances which spring throughout from the fact that, in sight of those human conflicts evoked by books, a critic is a soul who senses the sparkles of his dreams, regrets, and hopes live again."[238] According to this conception of culture, literature, and national character, the literary critic could therefore act as a prophet to his decadent age, since he alone could articulate the "intimate and naïve relation [he held] with the great forces of nature."[239]

Brasillach's obsession with youth, Greek aesthetics, and male friendship underscored his ideas concerning literature, culture, and civilization. Yet one of the primary ways in which he enacted the reestablishment of a rightful masculinity and harmonious culture found its expression not so much in his fiction as in his weekly column to a fictitious interlocutor, Angèle. Brasillach's column *Lettre à une provinciale* (Letter to a Provincial Woman) began in June 1936 in the wake of the Popular Front May victory.[240] It revealed the subterranean obsession he had displayed throughout his literary career with the celebrated author André Gide. Brasillach had penned his first published article in 1930 as a eulogy to Gide: a scandalous act since Gide was alive and still writing. As a young aspiring intellectual, Brasillach had asserted his authorial independence by positioning himself against the literary canon embodied in the figure of Gide. His *Je Suis Partout* column was also a recognizable pastiche of Gide's famous "note to Angèle" (and maybe a reference to the philosopher Pascal, author of the essays titled "The Provincials," especially celebrated for their biting and witty style).[241] The themes were not explicitly political but rather concerned culture as it was being produced, harnessed, and devised in the Popular Front years, ranging from leisure to vacations, tourism, cinema, theater, consumerism, train ticket prices, the 1937 Exposition universelle, and the cultural politics of left-wing intellectuals.

Brasillach's opening sentence was always punctuated with the polite reference to "my dear Angèle," whom he addressed directly, thus inviting the reader to be privy to an intimate correspondence made public in the pages of his newspaper.[242] His address to his "dear Angèle" allowed him to pose as the one possessing, displaying, and dispensing knowledge. He did so using a purposely ironic tone. In his first column, Brasillach said that "since [she] did not read newspapers," he was "responding to [her] request to be informed on contemporary events." He lamented the fact that, when she did read, according to his paternalistic view, she read either frivolous women's magazines or some socialist-oriented newspapers.[243] Among books that might be of interest to her, he especially recommended Maurras's latest publication, "one of the most beautiful [texts] he may have ever written."[244] He wrote that "since he knew her to be of a rather independent mind, [he] thought this book might interest [her]"; it was a small Italian pamphlet that Brasillach claimed to have picked up in Italy and that asked whether "France would become fascist."[245] The tone of confidence allowed Brasillach to weave his favorite political themes into this imaginary conversation. Most of all, it reaffirmed him in his position as male citizen and intellectual, holder of knowledge, and both involved in and informed about the public (and Parisian) world of politics.

Angèle, according to Brasillach's oblique descriptions, was a heterosexual married woman, "a good housewife" with children, leading a quiet middle-class life in the province.[246] Indeed, only heterosexual women, contained within the economy of marriage and reproductive politics (acting as the counterpoint to a masterful masculine virility), were visible in far-right discourse. She was a "beautiful Jacobine" but, in 1937, held "resolutely democratic opinions," which Brasillach hinted might the product of her ignorance and naiveté.[247] Indeed, he began one column admitting that Angèle found herself "worried by the fate of the Republic and the regime it had given itself."[248] But he found her arguments to be premised on her "cunning femininity," so inseparable from her position as a woman within the private world of intimacy and family life.[249] His choice of female interlocutor was no accident: in 1936, women did not enjoy political rights (such as the right to vote) and would not do so until after World War II. By writing to Angèle, Brasillach could therefore produce a world in which women were contained within the private world of family and their proper role as patriotic mothers—an especially pressing necessity for the men who had watched, disgusted, when Blum had appointed women to positions of power in the Popular Front government. Since she was "reasonable," however, Brasillach wondered, "Could [she] not be told the truth?"[250] Brasillach's role was to translate culture and politics for her so that she could *see* the nation, the regime, and its politicians for what they were. But in doing so, he also depicted a female character who embodied the most traditional aspects of femininity, as conceived by his own misogynist imagination. Brasillach's "letters" were often couched in a reassuring if patronizing tone, for Angèle was easily scared; for instance, he reassured her that the Belgian fascist leader Léon Degrelle was not the fearsome character she had heard of. His evocation of Degrelle was especially meaningful, for Belgian fascism promised the possibility of restoring an imperial fascist nation (Belgium proudly held on to its African colonies).[251] And like Mussolini and Italian fascism, Degrelle epitomized a proud and heroic masculinity that *Je Suis Partout* had celebrated in a 1936 special issue.[252] "Angèle" was "pleasant" and "charming" but naive, illogical, following fancies and fashions rather than rationality and reason. She could not be trusted in politics. Brasillach wrote that he could see "the charming illogical nature of [her] heart and mind," which had driven her to welcome the Popular Front while nonetheless being seduced by charismatic leaders that she secretly admired.[253]

French women were also constantly under the threat of seduction by the Jew. "Angèle," like many other French women, Brasillach suggested, was not immune to the sinuous seduction of Blum. He wrote that as a young woman once drawn to Blum's youthful reflections on marriage—which had scandalously argued for independent female sexual experience before marriage—"[she] was a tender soul, and surely will quiver with joy when [she] learn[s] that Blum had once written poetry."[254] Such female weakness was encouraged by the fact that Blum, as depicted by Brasillach, "loves to be nursed and comforted in the arms of expert women."[255] Women were thus depicted as weak but also prone to lascivious behavior and therefore needing to be reined in by familial paternal authority. Furthermore, women could exist only as objects of exchange between men within the public world of letters and politics, as Brasillach demonstrated with his epistolary writings to "Angèle." Through his correspondence to her, he fashioned an imaginary relation with Gide, which helped him further assert himself as a male intellectual.

But as months went on, and the government seemed to remain in power, Brasillach increasingly used his column to express himself "on things dear to his heart but that do not appear to be so to everybody else's heart," namely this "universal and despicable consent to defeat" that he witnessed among his fellow citizens, and what he found to be the French people's indifference to the corruption of the regime and the decadence of French civilization.[256] He professed that he was a nationalist who could not abide partisan battles and whose only concern was the truth. His columns became more overtly political in 1938. With "Angèle," he had created a fictional character who could experience the feelings of horror and incredulity that any "commonsense" average French individual should experience in the face of Popular Front rule. In another letter where he mused over the fate of Spain, he—again—complained about the fate of the French nation, which because it "did not have a [real and legitimate] government," was at the mercy of other European nations. He exhorted Angèle to join him and sarcastically concluded, "We have to hurry and at least request the status of protectorate."[257]

Brasillach's fantasy of a fascist masculinity thus found expression in his various writings on politics and culture, and in his conception of the role of the French intellectual. His appeal to instinct, feeling, and reason, however, was translated in a different manner after his execution for treason. Brasillach's ideological commitment had been infused with a sense of the central importance of culture and the role of nostalgia, poetry, and youth. After 1945, his friends, fellow far-right writers, and critics explained his embrace of antisemitism as a political tool and his attraction to fascism as the product of his novelistic sensibility rather than an engagement with politics. Maurice Bardèche, his longtime friend and brother-in-law, not only denied that his actions could be understood within the realm of politics but reiterated classic antisemitic rhetoric by arguing that Brasillach's had been the only rational and commonsense response.[258] Henri Massis explained that Brasillach's ideas had emerged not out of a political doctrine but from a sentimental education—here directly reproducing the terms through which Brasillach had defined his involvement as intellectual in his 1941 youthful memoir, *Notre avant-guerre*.[259] In explaining Brasillach's embrace of antisemitism and fascism, critics artificially divorced his literary persona from his political writings (in ways similar to Céline) and failed to address the ways in which Brasillach's conception of the role of culture and literature was central to his definition of a new politics. It was precisely his position as intellectual and author that allowed him to stake a claim in the politics of his day.

Conclusion

Brasillach has been held to be exemplary of *Je Suis Partout*'s politics. His vision of a bounded, gendered, and raced nation illuminates the ways in which he, and his fellow journalists, moved further away from Maurrassian politics, distanced themselves from the Young New Right, and ultimately embraced a uniquely French fascism. In 1939, Brasillach brought Rebatet's 1936 juxtaposition of fascism, antisemitism, colonialism, and anti-communism to its logical conclusion. The law that *Je Suis Partout* called for in the late 1930s, which would disenfranchise French Jews, would not be a republican law; it had to be a law of a different nature, one that would bind the nation together, its citizens and subjects. It needed to be the law of a strong authoritarian state founded upon race.

These racial imaginings led them to argue—in the case of *Je Suis Partout*—for a French fascism and to proclaim—in the case of Céline, the pamphleteer championed by *Je Suis Partout*—"Better Hitler than Blum." Only a turn to fascism—the promise of a sublime aesthetics—would, they believed, provide a remedy for the decadence, dissolution, and lack of depth that characterized "modern man." Fascism, in a French manner, offered the possibility of systematizing an "instinctual antisemitism" into a rational legislative effort that would allow the restorative binding together of the nation and its citizens. Fascism was a "virile" politics promising the restoration of masculine privilege and authority. Fascism alone would help preserve the empire untouched as the racial origin and foundation of French masculinity. Restoring boundaries was a racial enterprise, and fascism promised mastery over these boundaries.

CONCLUSION

Traces

Far-right intellectuals experienced varying fates with the demise of the Vichy regime, in part determined by their trajectory during the "Dark Years." Few retreated from politics.[1] However, traces of their intense journalistic production of the 1930s can be found in the public positions they took in the 1950s and 1960s, nowhere more strikingly than around the question of the Algerian war and the need for France to embrace decolonization. If antisemitism was somewhat muted after 1945, it never really disappeared from their political trajectory, even as the far-right nationalism they expounded was now explicitly reconfigured around the question of the French empire. Historian Henry Rousso first noted how some of the postwar debates (such as those concerning the Algerian war) were debates about the mobilization of the memory and "political legacy" of the Vichy years.[2] Again, the role of intellectuals in politics was an issue, especially, in the words of historian James Le Sueur, in the case of the "French-Algerian War" that became a "crucible for intellectuals."[3] In this way, the situations of Blanchot, Maulnier, and Céline are symptomatic of the vagaries of intellectual involvement.

Critics have often (favorably) commented on Blanchot's retreat from public involvement in politics, a retreat that he only occasionally suspended for specific issues, most notably the Algerian war and the petition that came to symbolize intellectuals' anticolonial opposition and commitment to human rights.[4] The

"Manifeste des 121," published in 1960, was a document that brought together 121 intellectuals, scholars, and thinkers and argued against the war in Algeria, calling for a "right to rebellion [*insoumission*]" in protest of the torture and violence committed in the name of the French nation against Algerian nationalists and civilians. It is now well known that Blanchot, along with Dyonis Mascolo, played a central role in the drafting of this petition.[5] This discovery has allowed critics to argue that Blanchot, haunted by the knowledge of the Shoah, moved from the radical right to the radical left. I want to suggest a slightly different interpretation, which, while not denying the ways in which Blanchot redeemed his earlier involvement in far-right politics, nonetheless suggests more of a continuity that reframes what appears on the surface to be a "political reversal."

Given that Blanchot was one of the authors of the "Manifeste," two themes are especially striking in that they seem to echo some of his youthful political imaginary. The urgent emphasis in the "Manifeste" on the need to disobey the state and the official rule of law in the name of a higher cause, here the cause of Algerian independence, mirrors the Young New Right's commitment to insurgency in the face of the injustice of illegitimate and arbitrary law and authority—in the 1930s embodied by the parliamentary regime. Indeed, the call for insurgency—conceived as an irrepressible demand in the face of arbitrary law—is a theme to which Blanchot often returned in his political writings.[6] Moreover, Blanchot's commitment to a bounded nation can be said to have been reshaped into his commitment to decolonization. In November 1937, he had claimed that it was urgent and necessary to "preserve the integrity of the [national] territory." Similarly, committing to anticolonialism functioned as a means of restoring a national territory (here, Algerian), while at the same time disavowing a (French) nationalism that was too narrow because it was claimed at the expense of others. For the claim made was that Algeria's own sovereignty must be recognized lest a divisive war erupt. Obviously, there is no reason to doubt the sincerity of Blanchot's commitment to an anticolonial human rights discourse. But in light of the Young New Right's belief that France's colonized subjects were not French and could not be assimilated into Frenchness and that a nation must be whole, the call for Algerian independence arguably operated as the recasting of that earlier theorization of the nation. Blanchot now refused the nation's imperial logic, but his political refusal may have been haunted by the memory of earlier obsessions he had renounced.

While Blanchot expiated his past, Thierry Maulnier, once his fellow traveler, turned staunchly conservative and remained, after 1945, wedded to the idea of an authoritarian and nationalist state. In keeping with his earlier belief in the greatness of Western civilization, Maulnier (and, unsurprisingly, Massis) was one of the signatories of the petition that came out in *Le Figaro* in response to the "Manifeste des 121." This petition supported "French Algeria." There is little information to suggest that Maulnier had any more involvement than merely signing the petition. But his presence in the pages of *Le Figaro*, his election to the Académie française, and the few political writings he authored in the 1950s and 1960s suggest that while abandoning his earlier Maurrassian far-right identity, he embraced a right-wing authoritarian anti-communism devoted to the preservation of a great imperial France, beacon of civilization. Since the Vichy years, he had also insistently argued for the "autonomy" of literature from contingent considerations—such as the political.[7] This time Maulnier was no longer an insurgent but firmly conservative—like those he had always mocked in the 1930s.

For Pierre Monnier, the far-right activist and *L'Insurgé* journalist, the 1930s remained the symbol of a utopian politics that had, for a brief time, held the promise of a radically different social, political, and cultural order. Monnier and his fellow far-right journalists had felt a particular urgency in drafting a colonial and antisemitic nationalist politics that would eradicate the decadence, crisis, and corruption of interwar France. Writing his memoirs almost fifty years later, Monnier explained that he wanted to "serve truth," which required "doing these men justice without either congratulating or blaming them in the name of rules or laws that were not theirs."[8] Monnier contested history's judgment of that period and of the role and influence of far-right intellectuals. He had, for instance, sent a letter to the judicial authorities who were prosecuting Céline (whom he never ceased admiring) in absentia in the 1950s for collaboration, in order to try and defend him against "unjust" accusations. Monnier never apologized, justified, or renounced his former political involvement with both the newspaper *L'Insurgé* and the secret political organization La Cagoule. In his memoirs, he suggested that he had been a privileged witness and had recorded these memories as a testimony to history where "[he] told lived events and experienced feelings when they happened . . . and without shifting them according to the knowledge of facts that occurred afterwards."[9] As *Je Suis Partout*'s former editor and a self-titled historian, Pierre Gaxotte had once written, "The past is vast and messy. Telling a story means choosing and simplifying."[10] This is what Monnier did.

Gaxotte's maxim became the motto of far-right intellectuals in the post-1945 era as they negotiated the taint and, for some, the shame of their former involvement. Many—like Lucien Rebatet and Pierre-Antoine Cousteau—never renounced their virulent politics; and, while some—like Thierry Maulnier, who became a respected Académie française member and conservative pundit—managed to blind their public to their previous antisemitic and anti-republican politics, most enjoyed far less prominent but nonetheless fairly respectable literary careers in far-right circles in the 1950s and 1960s.[11] Rebatet continued writing (unsuccessful) novels and even authored *Une histoire de la musique* (A History of Music) in 1969. He carried on writing for the far-right press, such as *Rivarol*. In his journalism, the figure of the "Arab" soon replaced the reviled and abject figure of the "Jew" (though he always remained antisemitic).[12] His infamous pamphlet *Les décombres* was reissued posthumously in 1976, with some of its most vicious passages expunged, under the title *Les mémoires d'un fasciste* (A Fascist's Memoirs) by publisher Jean-Jacques Pauvert. Maurice Bardèche, a very minor figure in 1930s far-right circles and an academic, became the official guardian of his brother-in-law's, Robert Brasillach's, memory. After having published a revisionist attack on the existence of the Holocaust, he granted American scholar Alice Kaplan an interview in 1982, during which it became clear that his political opinions had never wavered; they were merely "misunderstood" by contemporary critics too eager to judge and condemn. According to him, these criticisms testified to the "excesses that came with the victory in 1945 [that] were excesses of Jewish inspiration [. . . leading] to the current catastrophe—that is to say, the destruction of Europe."[13] Again, blame for political vagaries was laid upon Jews, as it had been in the 1930s. While not all far-right intellectuals retained their political ideals intact and untainted by the tragic realization of the horrors of the Holocaust—Maulnier and especially Blanchot are examples to oppose to men like Rebatet, Bardèche, Céline, and Monnier—the one common feature that can be found, even after the *épuration* and the demand for accountability that emerged in France in the 1970s, is their fierce anti-communism, which allowed many of them to reemerge as more traditional conservative critics in the 1950s and 1960s.[14] Race and gender also continued to figure as privileged instances of difference, and in the wake of the Algerian war, the theme of French masculinity often resurfaced around the fantasized figure of the "Arab."

Recounting the ways these intellectuals reemerged on the literary and political scene after 1945 is beyond the scope of this project.[15] But tracing the ways in which figures like Maurice Blanchot or Louis-Ferdinand Céline themselves attempted to control how they would be read matters to historians who are intent on deciphering the complex ways in which 1930s far-right intellectuals articulated a vision of the nation that haunts the politics of French history.[16] The "aftereffects" of the 1930s, as one scholar has termed these, are still to be accounted for, and demand modes of reading that depart from a literal understanding of the expression of exclusionary discourses of gender, race, and sexuality, and of the operations of identity, culture, and politics.

Some Historiographical Debates

As I have shown, the intellectual far right articulated a distinctive fantasy of the nation. The nation was, for them, something lost that must be recovered. This fantasy was symptomatic of the threats unleashed by modernity against a normative masculinity that was foundational to their vision of French citizenship. These intellectuals articulated a reactionary politics that was all at once antisemitic, racist, and colonial and that they argued called for an aesthetics in response to the profound "abjection" they experienced in the interwar period. In contrast to previous far-right thinkers like Charles Maurras and Henri Massis, or even contemporary far-right leaders such as Colonel de La Rocque, Jacques Doriot, or Marcel Déat, who bemoaned decadence and disorder, they produced a discourse driven by an obsession with abjection, disgust, dissolution, and degeneration. The "abjection" they talked about and constantly returned to was said to be caused and embodied by uncontained threats that seemed to have undone the nation from within. The threats were those who were considered to be aberrant members of the community, first and foremost Jews, but also those considered deviant (homosexuals) as well as those whose presence was necessary in order to uphold order and hierarchy (colonial subjects). In short, throughout the 1930s, the intellectual far right attempted to map the conditions for normative conceptions of the male body, of heterosexual virile masculinity, and of a racialized notion of Frenchness. Those themes were at the heart of the far-right and fascist writings that these men produced in the interwar period.

These themes have been explored by historians and literary scholars, usually, however, within only one frame of analysis (considering gender, or sexuality, or race), or by divorcing these intellectuals from their larger context (considering them only in relation to their far-right forefathers). I have suggested a different, synthetic reading that may shed light on the familiar issues of French fascism, antisemitism, and citizenship by addressing the remaining gaps in the historiography (despite the many works on the matter). These gaps and silences have, as a result, determined how we evaluate and understand today the place and contributions that these far-right intellectuals made then.

The topic of French fascism and of the far right, traditionally the preserve of political history, has been well mined and remains an enduring point of discussion and debate for historians.[17] The publication of Zeev Sternhell's *Neither Right nor Left* in the 1980s (a term he borrowed directly from the writers he examined) caused a controversy that resonates to this day.[18] Sternhell did not merely assert, against conventional wisdom, that French fascism had existed. He insisted that its roots could be found in a left-wing discourse that blended with nationalism and that had been present much earlier than most were willing to acknowledge. He pointed to Georges Sorel as one of these early pioneers. But he also, strikingly, explored Thierry Maulnier's own role in articulating more than a fascination with fascism. While Sternhell has been criticized for overvaluing (and therefore flattening out and dehistoricizing) the circulation of ideas, other historians have argued for an attention to "fascist" social practices. Robert Soucy has deemed a "social history of fascism" more productive that escapes the dilemmas of settling once and for all on the definitional category of fascism. Historian Robert Paxton has emphasized focusing on "how Fascism worked," rather than only on its words and texts.[19] While French historians such as Philippe Burrin have recently approached the topic in a complex and nuanced manner, the question of how to define and identify fascist movements and intellectuals is still an open one.[20] The implicit opposition between action and words that more or less structures these debates has not been challenged by a more nuanced understanding of discourse. Even Paul Mazgaj, a historian of the French far right whose work takes seriously both action and words (as well as culture and politics), subscribes to this division.[21] Unsurprisingly, and despite the insightful analysis by Roger Griffin of the *palingenetic* logic structuring these ideological visions that took seriously the rhetoric of decadence and regeneration, attention to the relationship of politics and aesthetics has usually not been the main focus.[22]

On the other hand, though a focus on aesthetics is not entirely new, and has recently enjoyed renewed interest, it has mostly been the work of scholars outside of history. Much insightful work has been done around the question of "fascist modernism," interrogating, in the wake of Walter Benjamin's reflections and Theodor Adorno's challenge, the complex and fascinating manner in which after World War I the cultural and aesthetic movement of modernism intersected with and generated a fascist aesthetics of the nation.[23] Italian fascism, and its relationship with futurism, has especially lent itself to provocative explorations that have highlighted the complex and ambiguous ways in which modernism and fascism, in the words of Roger Griffin, possessed a "profound kinship."[24] In the case of France, a serious and rigorous body of work began emerging in the 1990s, offering incisive new insights into that particular aspect of the interwar intellectual far right. Literary scholars have productively furthered some of Sternhell's observations by taking seriously the aesthetic claims made by these far-right intellectuals and authors. David Carroll's study *French Literary Fascism* exemplifies this movement.[25] Carroll's impressive work forcefully and convincingly makes a case for the need to examine the "literary forms that fascism and anti-Semitism took in France."[26] His analysis of Maurras, Brasillach, Maulnier, Céline, Drieu La Rochelle, and Rebatet demonstrates how their politics found a corollary in a particular vision of culture and a firmly entrenched belief that literature had a place in their vision of revolution and regeneration. He shows how a "Fascist aesthetics of the body" (for Drieu La Rochelle) and a "poetics of race" (for Céline) emerged. It is therefore hardly a coincidence that Thierry Maulnier—usually set aside, or thought to be "too intellectual"—is a persistent object of study, for in many ways he articulated the complexities and ambiguities of the far right, its distinctiveness (as opposed to the older generations), and concern with both politics and aesthetics. Indeed, focusing on Maulnier, art historian Mark Antliff's analysis of the synthesis of aesthetics and violence has persuasively demonstrated how an "avant-garde fascism" did emerge and how we might take its claims seriously.[27] His work shows how attention to the "fusion of politics and aesthetics" might shed light on the ideological underpinnings of the young intellectual far right.

Despite their conceptual sophistication, these analyses have not fully made their way into the historiographical canon on the French far right and on fascism. While engaging the rhetoric and aesthetic vision in the texts of these intellectuals, they have tended to focus on individual figures—Brasillach or Maulnier, for instance—in ways that divorce the figures from their immediate historical context and, especially, from the larger political and cultural network in which they were involved.[28] Carroll, for instance, while offering powerful analysis of "literary fascists," examines mostly their published texts and little of their journalistic writings. He reads texts from the 1930s and 1940s as if little had changed.[29] These intellectuals were not just authors but were at once writers, novelists, journalists, essayists, chroniclers, and even conference organizers. In contrast to the recent wave of French historians and sociologists, like Gisèle

Sapiro, Nicolas Kessler, Antonin Guyader, and Hervé Serry, who have jettisoned grand narratives for minute and impressively detailed empirical studies, literary theorists have offered discussions of disembodied literary figures.[30] While the distinction I draw does not attend to the differences among these scholars, it reflects the ways in which disciplinary assumptions—on how to "do" history or literature—still inflect this particular topic.

It is undeniable, however, that this distinction no longer holds fast. In the wake of extremely productive late-twentieth-century scholarship, historians are now attending more carefully to the manner in which politics and aesthetics must be considered in thinking about the intellectual far right. Paul Mazgaj's ambitious, thorough, and rigorous study, *Imagining Fascism*, may be the first English-language history that delves into the "cultural politics" of the young intellectual far right. While Nicolas Kessler's political history remains firmly within a historiographical tradition that stresses the intellectual far right's Maurrassian origins, Mazgaj takes seriously their claim to being "engaged writers" and the ways in which they attempted to "articulate a French-style fascism." He also attends to the vagaries of their trajectories and influences.[31] Mazgaj's analysis of these writers' "heady mix of militant generationalism and intransigent nationalism" highlights how their political claim to regeneration and renewal also involved culture and should be understood within a larger "civilizational" obsession.[32] Still, Mazgaj's consideration of their "cultural politics" looks at culture—broadly understood—and spends little time on their literary endeavors—in either form or content—and aesthetic aspirations. The very minor role that Maurice Blanchot plays in his narrative—despite his importance to both *Combat* and especially *L'Insurgé*—is indicative of his relative indifference to this matter.[33] Again, there is little engagement with the work of literary theorists, despite his avowed interest in the subject matter. Yet the claim of these intellectuals that they were not aestheticizing politics nor politicizing the aesthetic, but offering something else, must be interrogated.[34]

A similar gap has characterized works on French antisemitism. For this young generation of far-right intellectuals, antisemitism was neither an irrational choice nor a pragmatic ideology; it spoke to (and answered) their preoccupation with the nature of the male self and citizen. I show that it held a central place in their delineation of the (imperial) nation-state. Specifically, I argue that within the intellectual genealogy I have constructed, antisemitism was not a mere additive to a particular fascist vision of the nation but foundational to their nostalgic yearning for a presumed lost nation. Antisemitic fantasies of aberrant and abhorrent Jewish figures stood in as both cause and symptom of a nation that had been depleted and corrupt and therefore could no longer provide substance and identity to its male citizens (now de-virilized). Additionally, I show how this interwar French antisemitism was mapped through and within the larger context of a civilizational discourse defining French citizens in relation to abject figures deemed foreign (namely Jews and immigrants) and inferior (colonized subjects).

Antisemitism has a long history in France. Yet it would be a grave mistake to chart the history of contemporary France as one beset by antisemitism portrayed as an unchanging and ahistorical phenomenon, merely "the furious repetition of a cultural stereotype" that reemerges in times of "crisis" in order to provide a "scapegoat" for the ills besetting the nation.[35] Instead, it becomes especially important to chart the very contingency of the conditions in which antisemitism manifested itself and the ways in which it was articulated. Postcolonial theorist Homi Bhabha has explained, "'The Jew' stands for that experience of a lethal modernity" which, he points out, has been "shared by histories of slavery and colonialism."[36] As a symbol of modernity and its contradictions, "the Jew" as that phantasmic figure haunting the republican French state has indeed often served to draft an exclusionary and bounded nation. However, in the twentieth century, one might argue that as the quintessential symptom of the experience of modernity, antisemitism may be understood not as yet another instance of the vagaries of nationalism but as radically embedded and constituted through the experience of race, colonialism, and the constitution of the nation-state first and foremost as an imperial nation-state.

Since the groundbreaking work of postcolonial theory, historians have mined the archive to reveal how imperialism was not a phenomenon separate from the metropolitan state but rather constituted both the experience and the imagination of nation and infused the metropole in ways that were ignored. Yet histories of antisemitism and colonialism have remained within separate fields, acknowledging each other's insights—that culture and race served to violently exclude, persecute, and manage specific categories of people in the name of Western civilization—yet not necessarily interrogating how both were embedded. Indeed, scholars have written "as if [antisemitism and colonial racism] exist in hermetically sealed historical settings."[37] In the case of France, colonialism and racism are seen as parallel to antisemitism, where that pathological obsession with the Jew emerges as a metropolitan manifestation, in juxtaposition to what may occur in colonial territories. If theorists have analyzed how racial theories in the nineteenth and twentieth centuries often juxtaposed the "Jew" and the "black" as figures of repulsion and contamination, historians have still not fully mined these insights in theorizing the genealogy of French citizenship: noted historian of migration Gérard Noiriel has claimed that both "'anti-semitism' and 'racism' are ideologies and political programs born at the end of the nineteenth century with the development of immigration and colonization," hinting at the ways in which they need to be thought together rather than side by side.[38] Even then, antisemitism is not theorized but subsumed within a larger history of xenophobia (and often, as in this case, gender and sexuality—though categories of difference—are also ignored). Even when the "continuity between colonial ideology and modern anti-Semitism" is noted, little elaboration follows.[39] This study has challenged that assumption by exploring how the nation was imagined and defined through the simultaneous imagination of the relationship between metropolitan French, colonial subjects, and Jewish citizens.

If we take historians' insights seriously and understand the colonial racism that undergirded Western imperialism, how might we understand antisemitism differently? As Laura Ann Stoler has argued in regard to racism and its colonial artifacts, there is in racism "a tension between rupture and recuperation," so that "racism always appears renewed and new at the same time."[40] Antisemitism also functions as a repeatedly reinvented tradition. Since "the savage, the primitive, the colonized" operated as "reference points of difference, critique and desire" in the "making of European bourgeois identity," how might they have functioned to inflect and infuse the discursive production of anti-Jewish sentiment and politics?[41] This matters especially as we try to elucidate what "paved the road to Vichy."[42] If, for instance, as Brett Berliner has insightfully explained, "representations of the exotic *nègre* formed part of the French social imagination and helped define and stabilize French identity during the interwar years," then how are we to understand the reformulation of the "Jew" in the French cultural and social imaginary in those same years?[43] If race and colonialism determined the boundaries of Frenchness, may we understand the place ascribed to "the Jew" as one framed by these concerns? In fact, since "the Jew" signifies a "multitude of incommensurable categories," historicizing its particular incarnation seems urgent.[44]

Finally, historians of the far right and of fascism in France have surprisingly remained oblivious to the ways gender and sexuality inflected understandings of the self, the nation, and citizenship. That absence is baffling, not least for its seeming indifference to the rich theorization and historicization undertaken by feminist and gender historians. It ignores the insights that George Mosse first pioneered on the relationship between masculinity and nationalism.[45] It also ignores the work that has productively interrogated the ways gender, sexuality, and race functioned in Italian fascism and German Nazism. For many, the publication in the late 1970s of Klaus Theweleit's *Male Fantasies* represents a groundbreaking moment. In his two-volume psychoanalytically inflected study, Theweleit offered a serious engagement with the ways "fantasies" structured the Freikorps's ideological, cultural, and intellectual relation to the world. These fantasies mapped a masculine desire haunted by the dangerous forces of "effeminacy, unhealthiness, criminality, Jewishness—all of which existed together under the umbrella of 'Bolshevism.'"[46] Theweleit argued that this discourse of manliness relied on a horror of that identified as unbounded, viscous, abject—female bodies especially—which expressed itself in a rhetoric of virility and the exercise of violence. While suggestive, Theweleit's work has remained inspirational rather than foundational. Its overly formalistic and essentialist theorization has been criticized by historians intent on exploring *how* gender and sexuality were deployed in the service of fascist and Nazi ideologies. To argue that these men's fantasies were the outcome of a "narcissistic wound" seemed to ignore the historical—and therefore contingent—nature of their ideas.[47] Still, scholars have begun analyzing the ways, for some as in the Italian context, a "fantasy of the social body as an organic whole" was, in the wake of World War I, expressed through a rhetoric of virility. As Barbara Spackman has shown, the Italian fascist rhetoric of virility that she identified in Mussolini, Marinetti, and D'Annunzio, "lined with nationalism," was defined "against femininity, homosexuality and Bolshevik internationalism."[48] More recently, historians of Nazi Germany such as Dagmar Herzog have explored how "sexual politics functioned as a main locus for the recurrent reconstructions of memory and meanings of Nazism."[49] Following Foucault, she demonstrates how, far from being peripheral, sex was at the heart of Nazi racial policies (repressive and deadly for some, emancipatory for others) and has endured in the ways the legacy of Nazism was negotiated, erased, displaced, and invoked in Germany until the 1990s. Herzog's work is exemplary in its attention to the discursive production of these categories, and has opened the door for sustained analyses of Nazi Germany and the Holocaust.[50]

In the French context, scholars such as Francine Muel-Dreyfus and Miranda Pollard have demonstrated how the Vichy regime's policies were driven by a conservative vision of the gendered and sexual arrangement of French society that celebrated a triumphant manliness, called for the domestication of femininity through motherhood and heterosexuality, and translated order, authority, and nationalism through the "mobilization of gender."[51] National identity and imagined communities have been defined through prevailing ideas of gender and race, as the work of Karen Adler on Liberation France's reconstruction efforts rigorously demonstrates.[52] Yet, despite the fact that these visions did not suddenly emerge in 1940 but had been circulating in the interwar years, as Mary-Louise Roberts and Carolyn Dean have shown, work on this earlier period is still largely absent, especially in relation to the French far right.[53] This is partly the result of disciplinary assumptions. The varied and rich political history on the French right and far right has usually remained impervious to the scholarship of gender.[54] Similarly, intellectual history—in general, and for France specifically—has been slow in understanding how the inclusion of gender was not the mere addition of an object of study but changed the very methodological assumptions that might undergird such questions.[55]

Memories

The interwar period, and especially the French far right, has not been the subject of much fictionalization, unlike the Vichy years.[56] So we must turn to Littell's *Les bienveillantes* as the most recent (fictional rather than scholarly) attempt to elucidate the relationship of identity and politics, aesthetics and ideology, fascism and antisemitism, sexuality and race. Reviewers have emphasized the erudite construction of this novel, with its "Aeschylean title" referring to "the Furies of Greek mythology" and tragedy—and to the remark made by Primo Levi in *The Drowned and the Saved*.[57] Rather than denouncing the novel for its "pornography of violence," French and American critics have mostly explained it as being part of a genealogy of "literature of transgression." This is the argument of award-winning critic Daniel Mendelsohn.[58] Historian Samuel Moyn, while more circumspect regarding the graphic violence and sex in the novel, has instead pointed to its remapping of Theweleit's argument regarding "male fantasies."

In fact, there has been a return on the part of reviewers and commentators to the interwar work of authors like Georges Bataille and Maurice Blanchot to help interpret Littell's fictionalization. Despite Mendelsohn's claim that *Les bienveillantes* echoes Bataille's 1928 *Story of the Eye*, where "pleasurable fulfilment . . . is pursued in a series of increasingly severe transgressions that paradoxically reaffirms rather than obliterates the limit placed on desire," Littell's novel is hardly akin to the infamous work of Georges Bataille, despite the author's avowed debt to Bataille and Blanchot's post-1945 work.[59] The novel's rhetorical gestures may be more a reflection of the gaps and silences around the French far right than a transposition of transgression. Mendelsohn notes Aue's reading of Blanchot in the novel but only to point to the intertextual reference implied by Littell, since the collection of essays to which Aue refers—the 1943 *Faux Pas*—contains an essay titled "The Myth of Orestes."[60] He ignores the question of Aue's choice of Blanchot precisely because, we are told, Aue knew his 1930s articles in far-right newspapers. Mendelsohn praises the manner in which Littell renders "abjection" as a means to "break new taboos in order to make us think about evil."[61] Indeed, Littell's portrayal of Aue seems the perfect illustration of Julia Kristeva's explanation that "the abject is perverse because it neither gives up nor assumes a prohibition, a rule, or a law; but turns them aside, misleads, corrupts; uses them, takes advantage of them, the better to deny them."[62] But, again, Kristeva's own powerful theorization of abjection—just like Mendelsohn's reference—relies not just on psychoanalytic concepts but also on Georges Bataille's own essay on abjection, which he published in the interwar years.

One of the enduring problems in portraying this period and its dilemmas has been how not to reiterate the very categories and ideas that were produced at this particularly fraught moment. While reviewers have turned to authors of the interwar years—Bataille, Blanchot—to explain Littell's novel, the author himself has, in his portrait of a character that is "outside of morality," reproduced one of the most enduring and reactionary tropes that often characterize attempts to elucidate the nature of Nazi morality: namely the equation that is made between sexual "perversion" and transgression as metonym for amorality or perverse morality.[63] Aue, the Nazi who is to "stand in for Nazism as a whole," is portrayed as a "homosexual" (in the sense of Michel Foucault's "species") whose dubious moral detachment finds expression in the "perverse" delights he discovers in graphically narrated illicit gay sex in the dark back streets of Berlin, dingy apartments, and suspicious and somber corners during his European travels.[64] He revels in the abject, as Kristeva defines it. Aue's (perverse) enjoyment of bodily fluids—shit, piss, blood, semen—whose body often escapes him, taken by desire, or fraught with sickness, nausea, vomiting that leave him incapacitated, revels in what is considered debased, degrading, and uncivilized, all the while being the perfect product of European civilization and culture. I would contend that the depiction of Aue as a perverse homosexual, his incestuous desire for his sister, and the brutal murder of his hated mother and stepfather can be read not so much as symptomatic of Greek tragedy structure or even fantasies of "feminine dissolution" (as Moyn has aptly noted) but as symptomatic of this long-standing troping of "perverse sexuality" as both cause and consequence of Nazism.[65] Rather than offering an unusual and daring encounter with amorality, Littell offers a fictionalization of the very themes that have haunted problematic portrayals of Nazism, fascism, and antisemitism and that have come to permeate popular culture and even academic accounts.

The silence surrounding this aspect of the novel (which makes *Les bienveillantes* less of a transgressive novelty than some would wish) as well as the anger unleashed at it—with accusations of voyeurism and pornography—have obscured how much our imagination of Nazi (and, in the case of France, far-right) morality is embedded in a language of gender and sexuality, which, in turn, gives substance to the racial and antisemitic fantasies sustaining this vision of the world.[66] As Dagmar Herzog has shown, the popular clichés surrounding this period have centered on "fascism as decadent; fascism as intrinsically homoerotic; fascism as femininity gone awry; Adolf Hitler's gender-bending as the key to his ability to seduce a nation; and fascism (or even the Holocaust itself) as the titillating backdrop for hard-core pornographic fantasies."[67] These stereotypes still endure. In many ways, the same can be said of the French fascists and far-right authors that I have analyzed in this book.

A more insistent problem that has emerged out of this enduring troping is the silence it produces around the fact that these fantasies of abjection, dissolution, and perversion figure in the interwar far-right authors' own politics and aesthetics. Their desire for an undifferentiated self and a whole nation relied on fantasized notions of racialized and gendered Frenchness that have yet to be fully explored. Littell's novel has not brought out a revisiting of France's own past engagement in antisemitism, colonialism, and fascism, and the ways in which these were imbricated. Doing so is urgent and would illuminate how gender, race, and sexuality have historically operated in the unfolding of French politics, culture, and literature.

REFERENCE MATTER

NOTES

INTRODUCTION

1. The controversy has mostly centered on whether one could write a novel whose central character was a Nazi officer, both guilty and witness to the Shoah. This novel, written in the first person as a "memoir," follows a young officer, Maximilien Aue (who is also of French descent), in his rise through the ranks of the Nazi regime, to Stalingrad, the Eastern Front, Auschwitz, and Hungary. Aue witnesses the work of the Einsatzgruppen and of the death factories. Even more striking, Aue's personal life proves to be just as much the topic of the novel. The novel ends with the brutal murder by Aue of his mother. Many critics have praised the novel's impeccable research, the way it renders in fictional prose the latest findings and insights of historians of the Holocaust. Claude Lanzmann, author of the world-famous 1985 documentary *Shoah*, commented that the novel was "faultlessly erudite." Yet he wondered whether the author's rendition of the main character's trajectory through those dark years—expressed through "disgust, vomiting, incredible diarrheas, sexual perversions, and metaphysical reflections"—might not actually relish and play on a certain fascination with death and horror. Most French critics praised the novel, however, and much of the controversy focused on the question of the novel's style; Etchegoin, "Claude Lanzmann." Intellectual historian Samuel Moyn has also commented in a recent review that "Littell is rather impressively up to date"; "A Nazi Zelig." The novel's reception varied outside France: a *New York Times* book critic calls it an "odious stunt"; Kakutani, "Unrepentant and Telling Stories of Horrors Untellable."

2. Littell, *Les bienveillantes*, 464. (Throughout this book, all translations from the French are mine unless otherwise noted.)

3. Ibid., 466, 465. Material in this introduction and in Chapter 6 appeared in Sanos, "Fascist Fantasies of Perversion and Abjection."

4. On this issue, see the excellent analysis provided by Dean, *Fragility of Empathy*, 106–34. A few reviewers have commented on Littell's reliance on Klaus Theweleit's theory of aggressive bounded masculinity in the throes of misogynist desire for his portrayal of Aue. See especially Moyn, who notes the desire for "feminine dissolution" that pervades the novel; "A Nazi Zelig." See also Dominick LaCapra's critique of Littell's text, which, he argues, "act[s] out phantasms rather than situate them in a manner that offers critical perspective on them," and where "erotic excesses" are equated to "genocidal ex-

cesses"; "Historical and Literary Approaches," 76, 80; Dean, *Fragility of Empathy*, 108. See also Andrew Hewitt's important work on the association of fascism and homosexuality, *Political Inversions*, esp. 38–78 and 245–85, and my Conclusion.

5. This has been well documented. The association first began with Sartre's indictment of Brasillach as a collaborator. On this issue, see Kaplan, *Reproductions of Banality*, and Kaplan, *The Collaborator;* see also Hewitt, *Political Inversions*; Dean, *Fragility of Empathy*, 108–11.

6. Littell, *Les bienveillantes*, 470.

7. Ibid., 462.

8. Ibid., 470.

9. Ibid., 471.

10. Ibid., 460. We are not told whether these "pre-war writings" were Blanchot's violent political articles or the literary reviews he had begun authoring, both at the short-lived polemical newspaper *L'Insurgé*. LaCapra notes Littell's own reference to Bataille and Blanchot, which he does not explicate; "Historical and Literary Approaches," 74–75.

11. That characterization was already present in works such as Liliana Cavani's scandalous 1974 film *The Night Porter*, in which deviant heterosexuality, sadomasochism, and perverse homosexuality structure the narrative. See Frost, *Sex Drives*, in which she discusses a number of French authors (Georges Bataille, Vercors, Jean Genet, and Marguerite Duras) and notes: "Homosexuality is often pathologized . . . as sadomasochism," which indeed characterizes Littell's novel; 99.

12. Littell, *Les bienveillantes*, 471.

13. Dean, *Fragility of Empathy*, 107.

14. The novel was awarded the Prix Goncourt and the Prix de l'Académie française.

15. I have translated "Jeune Droite" as "Young New Right," unlike Paul Mazgaj, who refers to the "Young Right" in *Imagining Fascism*. While the translation I use is admittedly clumsier, it attends to the fact that *jeune* refers to both novelty and youth—two themes that this intellectual group claimed.

16. Historians have taken this split at face value. I discuss some of the distinctive features of this historiography in my conclusion.

17. I situate my work alongside recent and diverse historical studies that view this period with an eye to challenging the binaries (left vs. right), separations (metropole and colony), and conventions (analyzing Catholics separately from other political formations) that have infused our understanding of the interwar years and the Popular Front era. See, for instance, Wilder, *The French Imperial Nation-State*; Wardaugh, *In Pursuit of the People*; Geroulanos, *An Atheism That Is Not Humanist*; and Nord, *France's New Deal*.

18. Dean, "'The Open Secret'" 159.

19. Hewitt, *Fascist Modernism*, 5.

20. Rancière has written extensively on the topic; see his *Aesthetics and Its Discontents*; *Politics of Aesthetics*; and *The Aesthetic Unconscious*. For an excellent and insightful philosophical reflection on the issue, see Michaud, *Cult of Art in Nazi Germany*.

21. Rancière, *The Aesthetic Unconscious*, 4–5.

22. Rancière, *Aesthetics and Its Discontents*, 25.

23. See Benjamin, "L'oeuvre d'art à l'ère de sa reproductibilité technique (première version, 1935)," 110–13; and "L'oeuvre d'art à l'époque de sa reproductibilité technique (dernière version de 1939)," 313–16.

24. Most literary scholars remain within the confines of the literary canon and usually focus on the most well known of these far-right figures. For instance, little attention is paid to Jean-Pierre Maxence, Jean de Fabrègues, Pierre-Antoine Cousteau, or Pierre Monnier, despite their important roles in these networks and newspapers.

25. This has, in turn, determined my choice not to include Pierre Drieu La Rochelle, who was older and a war veteran. More importantly, his literature did not offer an aesthetics the way these intellectuals attempted to. In that I depart from David Carroll's pioneering work *French Literary Fascism*, which sees Drieu La Rochelle as exemplary of "literary fascism." I elaborate on his argument that in the case of these writers, "literature and art are considered to represent nothing less than the truth of politics"; 11. On the other hand, I included Céline because his aesthetic vision was embraced and appropriated by *Je Suis Partout*. Céline's pamphlets were a matter of debate for these intellectuals precisely because of the ways in which his antisemitic fantasies spoke to their imagination of how gender and race undergirded their fantasy of Frenchness.

26. In this, I borrow from historian of the French far right Paul Mazgaj, who has paid attention to that dimension of these intellectuals' political discourse, in *Imagining Fascism*.

27. See the works of Joan Wallach Scott, *Only Paradoxes to Offer* and *Parité!* There is a rich historiography on the issue, especially around the French Revolution. See Hunt, *Family Romance and the French Revolution*; Landes, *Visualizing the Nation*; Riot-Sarcey, *La démocratie à l'épreuve des femmes*; and Fraisse, *Muse de la raison*, among others.

28. See Kessler, *Histoire politique*; Sapiro, *La guerre des écrivains*; and, more recently, Mazgaj, *Imagining Fascism*.

29. Some have reflected on the ways masculinity figures in the discourse of the intellectual far right. In *Reproductions of Banality*, literary scholar Alice Y. Kaplan offers a reading of Rebatet and Brasillach's pre-oedipal "fascist desire" inspired by Theweleit. Predictably, the intellectual most often analyzed is Pierre Drieu La Rochelle, especially his 1939 novel, *Gilles*. See, for instance, Carroll, *French Literary Fascism*, 147–70. Richard Golsan and Melanie Hawthorne have edited a collection, *Gender and Fascism in Modern France*, that, aside from one article by Andrew Hewitt on Sartre and Genet, considers mostly women. Monographic studies have appeared on Louis-Ferdinand Céline by literary scholars Rosemarie Scullion and Thomas Spears. Only one study exists of *Je Suis Partout*'s gendered ideology during the Vichy years: Tumblety, "Revenge of the Fascist Knights."

30. See Gilman, *Difference and Pathology*, and Gilman, *The Jew's Body*.

31. The imbrication of race, gender, and sexuality in French antisemitic discourse has been noted by historians like Stephen Wilson and Pierre Birnbaum, while Christopher Forth has impressively analyzed the complex ways in which it was deployed during an infamous moment of French history, the Dreyfus Affair; Wilson, *Ideology and Expe-*

rience; Pierre Birnbaum devotes one chapter of *Un mythe politique* to the topic; Forth, *The Dreyfus Affair*. More recently, historians have explored the ways these tropes functioned in canonical texts; see, for instance, Jonathan Judaken's analysis, "The Queer Jew."

32. Roberts, *Civilization Without Sexes*; Dean, *The Frail Social Body*; Surkis, "Enemies Within."

33. For theorizations of gender and sexuality, see Butler, *Bodies That Matter*; and Butler and Scott, eds., *Feminists Theorize the Political*. Though they are not as often read in the American context, French feminist theorists such as Christine Delphy, Nicole Claude-Matthieu, and Colette Guillaumin have offered their "materialist" theorization of sexual difference. See Delphy, *L'ennemi principal*; and *Classer, Dominer*. More recently, in a different theoretical vein that considers gender, race, and colonialism in imaginaries of the French nation, see Dorlin, *La matrice de la race*. In the wake of postcolonial studies, Ann Laura Stoler has called for the recognition of the imbrication of gender, sexuality, and race in imperialism and nationalism, in both *Carnal Knowledge and Imperial Power* and *Race and the Education of Desire*.

34. Nye, *Masculinity and Male Codes of Honor in Modern France*. On masculinity and nationalism, see Mosse, *The Image of Man*.

35. Surkis, *Sexing the Citizen*.

36. Forth, *The Dreyfus Affair*, 22. See also Birnbaum, *Un mythe politique*.

37. On this, see Forth, *The Dreyfus Affair*, 67–102.

38. Céline, *Journey*, 70.

39. On the central role of sexual difference, gender, and sexuality in the anxieties of postwar France, and in defining civilization and citizenship, see both Dean, *The Frail Social Body*, and Roberts, *Civilization Without Sexes*.

40. Maulnier, *La crise est dans l'homme*.

41. Maurice Blanchot, "Lectures de l'Insurgé: *Réflexions sur la force* par Alphonse Sèche, Éditions de France," *L'Insurgé* (March 17, 1937), 3.

42. The definitional debate has a long history. My purpose is not to presume these intellectuals' fascism but to interrogate how they turned to what they understood to be fascism and to shed some light on their attraction to it.

43. Kristeva, *Powers of Horror*; Butler, *Bodies That Matter*; Agamben, *Homo Sacer*.

44. Kristeva, *Powers of Horror*, 2.

45. Bataille, "L'abjection et les formes misérables," 219.

46. Ibid., 220.

CHAPTER 1

1. Thierry Maulnier, "Il faut reconquérir notre univers," *Combat* (June 1936), 3–4.

2. Maulnier, *La crise est dans l'homme*; Maulnier, *Les mythes socialistes*; Francis, Maulnier, and Maxence, *Demain la France*.

3. For an account of the early journalistic and political involvement of these "nonconformist" intellectuals, see the classic study by Loubet del Bayle, *Les non-conformistes des années 30*, 30, 38; see also the rigorously researched study by Nicolas Kessler, *Histoire politique*.

4. This is René Vincent's expression; "Aimer sa jeunesse," *La Revue du XXe Siècle* (March–April 1935), 35.

5. Jean de Fabrègues, "Manifeste," *Réaction pour l'Ordre* (April 5, 1930), 1.

6. Vincent, "Aimer sa jeunesse," 35–36.

7. For example, see Maxence, *Histoire de dix ans*, and Maulnier, *La crise est dans l'homme.*

8. Jean de Fabrègues, "Le sens de notre effort," *La Revue du XXe Siècle* (March–April 1935), 2.

9. Maxence accuses Raymond Poincaré of having inflicted this upon France and of having been unable to find viable solutions to France's financial crisis; *Histoire de dix ans*, 110.

10. Greater attention has been paid to the ways in which gender, sexuality, race, and empire figured and circulated in French interwar culture. See, for instance, Roberts, *Civilization Without Sexes*; Dean, *The Frail Social Body*; Wilder, *The French Imperial Nation-State*; Camiscioli, *Reproducing the French Race*; Ezra, *The Colonial Unconscious*; and tangentially, but no less importantly for the period, Edwards, *Practice of Diaspora.*

11. This is the convention used by most historians; see, for instance, Dard, *Le rendez-vous manqué*, 126; also Raimond, *Éloge et critique de la modernité.*

12. Brasillach, *Notre avant-guerre*, 62–64, 110–21.

13. On the relationship of French fascists with cinema, see Kaplan, *Reproductions of Banality*. On Brasillach as "Romantic Fascist," see Mazgaj, "Ce mal de siècle."

14. Maxence, *Histoire de dix ans*, 96, 74.

15. Ibid., 74.

16. Ibid., 177.

17. Jean Le Marchand, "L'âge du cinéma," *Combat* (January 10, 1935), 11.

18. Brasillach, *Notre avant-guerre*, 173–74.

19. Jackson, *Making Jazz French*, 71.

20. Lucien Farnoux-Reynaud, "L'époque du jazz-band," *Le Gaulois*, March 6, 1926, cited in ibid.

21. On the reception and interpretation of jazz in the interwar years, see Matthew Jordan's *Le jazz*, which very carefully traces the anxieties that this musical form (as well as the orchestras, nightclubs, and dance forms that came with it) elicited and the variety of responses to it.

22. Archer-Straw, *Negrophilia*, 159–77. See also Stovall, *Paris Noir*; Ezra, *The Colonial Unconscious*; Berliner, *Ambivalent Desire.*

23. See Jennifer Anne Boittin's evocative tracing of these "cosmopolitan" Parisian spaces, *Colonial Metropolis*, 77. For an overview of African and African-American influences (and their conflation) on French art and entertainment, see Blake, *Le tumulte noir.*

24. Maxence does not specifically mention the phenomenon of "negrophilia," but his discussion of that period in his memoirs refers frequently to the ways in which new "fads" misled those who wanted to rejuvenate French culture; *Histoire de dix ans*, 46.

25. Leiris, *L'âge d'homme*, 161.

26. Jean de Fabrègues, "Rencontres de générations," *Réaction pour l'Ordre* (January–February 1932), 28.

27. Wilder, *The French Imperial Nation-State*, 28.

28. Saint-Domingue and its slave rebellion, which led to the constitution of the Republic of Haiti, has haunted French historical memory and colonial discourse in often marginalized yet meaningful ways. For a narrative that captures the impact of the slave uprising, see Dubois, *Avengers of the New World*. On the issue of the memory of Saint-Domingue, see Trouillot, *Silencing the Past*. On the figure of the "mulatto woman," see Garraway, *The Libertine Colony*.

29. See Boittin, *Colonial Metropolis*, esp. ch. 1, "Josephine Baker: Colonial Woman," 1–36.

30. Maxence, *Histoire de dix ans*, 29.

31. On this issue and the interwar era as a "unique moment in terms of the representation of the space of the nation," see Panchasi, "'Fortress France,'" 479.

32. On policy efforts in French West Africa—whose conceptual framework fails to interrogate the "double bind" that, according to Gary Wilder, was constitutive of Republican ideology—see Conklin, *A Mission to Civilize*. For a more nuanced analysis, see Wilder, *The French Imperial Nation-State*.

33. Wilder, *The French Imperial Nation-State*, 27–28. See also Boittin, *Colonial Metropolis*; on colonial workers, see Stovall, "The Color Line Behind the Lines."

34. On the question of the "refugee crisis," see the excellent work by Caron, *Uneasy Asylum*. On the ways in which citizenship was embodied and immigration, see Camiscioli, *Reproducing the French Race*. On how "foreign male bodies" also embodied "sexual and somatic threats," see Surkis, "Enemies Within," 109.

35. Louis-Ferdinand Céline, preface to the 1952 Gallimard edition, *Journey to the End of the Night* (New York: New Directions, 2006).

36. Maxence, *Histoire de dix ans*, 32.

37. Brasillach, *Notre avant-guerre*, 199.

38. Ibid., 200–208, 209.

39. Maxence, *Histoire de dix ans*, 85.

40. Ibid., 85–86.

41. Maxence, "Le cas André Gide," ibid., 146–49. See also Maulnier, *La crise est dans l'homme*, 121.

42. Émile Vaast, "Querelle de générations," *Réaction* (January–February 1932), 16. Émile Vaast was the pseudonym of Émile Béchet, cited in Kessler, *Histoire politique*, 184.

43. Maxence, *Histoire de dix ans*, 178.

44. Ibid., 177. On Massis, see *La guerre de trente ans*, x.

45. Maulnier, *La crise est dans l'homme*, 246.

46. Maxence, *Histoire de dix ans*, 178.

47. Carolyn J. Dean argues that this search constituted George Bataille's and Jacques Lacan's theoretical projects; *The Self and Its Pleasures*, 3. I follow Dean in her exposition that the "decentered self" is a "historically and culturally specific" production that finds its expression in the interwar period; ibid., 1.

48. On the historically specific engagements in the question of the "self," see Seigel, *The Idea of the Self*, esp. 469–507.

49. On genealogies of nineteenth-century French intellectual attempts to trace and define the conditions for selfhood, see Goldstein, *The Post-Revolutionary Self*.

50. Dean, *The Self and Its Pleasures*, 3.

51. This is the issue that Stefanos Geroulanos explores and traces, while he identifies the "origin" of post-1945 radical intellectual remappings in these interwar questions and queries; *An Atheism That Is Not Humanist*, 5.

52. Tonnet-Lacroix, *La littérature française*, 106.

53. Bernstein, *La France des années 30*, 79.

54. See Jolles, "The Tactile Turn."

55. For a brief overview, see Geroulanos, *An Atheism That Is Not Humanist*, 100–129. On Maritain's relationship to modernity, politics, and "the Jewish Question," see the nuanced and rigorous study by Richard Crane, *Passion of Israel*.

56. Maxence, *Histoire de dix ans*, 76.

57. Maulnier, *La crise est dans l'homme*, 13.

58. On the evolution and dissemination of psychoanalysis in France, see Elisabeth Roudinesco, *Histoire de la psychanalyse en France*, esp. 1:269–431 and 2:19–161.

59. See his writings on society, *Écrits posthumes*, vol. 2 of *Oeuvres complètes*. See also Surya, *Georges Bataille*.

60. Pagès, *Les fictions du politique*, 311. While still studying medicine, Céline read some of Freud's works and came to believe that the unconscious played an essential role in health. See Gibault, *Céline*, 86. See also Alméras, *Les idées de Céline*, 71, 98. According to Dean, who explains that the reception and absorption of psychoanalysis was a contested issue in interwar France, Céline's adoption of psychoanalytic principles was therefore unusual, especially for a doctor concerned with public hygiene; *The Self and Its Pleasures*, 11–57.

61. Hewitt, *Life of Céline*, 127.

62. Brasillach, *Notre avant-guerre*, 47.

63. This position was held by those who wrote at *Combat*, like Jean de Fabrègues, who in 1935 claimed that "Freudism" was misguided though intuitively correct in what it had uncovered; "Lettre à l'abonné, à l'ami, au lecteur d'occasion," *La Revue du XXe Siècle* (February 1935), 1.

64. Maxence, *Histoire de dix ans*, 82–83.

65. Jean de Fabrègues, "Indépendence? Oui, sauf de la vérité," *Combat* (February 1936), 4–5.

66. For a brief but informative overview of the energy and variety of Catholic culture and activism in those years, see Nord, "Catholic Culture in Interwar France."

67. Maulnier, "Il faut reconquérir notre univers," *Combat* (June 1936), 3.

68. Far-right intellectuals were wrapped up in the terms of contemporary debates and were similarly obsessed with the relationship between subjectivity and seeing. For instance, literary critic Maurice Blanchot's interwar journalistic texts and his own specular conception of the world strikingly echoed other texts of the period, such as

psychoanalyst Jacques Lacan's 1936 article on the "mirror stage." Blanchot, like Lacan, had been trained in psychiatry at Sainte-Anne hospital, where, his biographer suggests, they may have met—a speculative point. However, tracing the cultural background to the emergence of psychoanalysis and the interwar conception of "seeing" as constitutive of subjectivity is beyond the scope of this book. See Bident, *Maurice Blanchot*, 29; see also Jay, *Downcast Eyes*, and Roudinesco, *Jacques Lacan*.

69. Roudinesco, *Jacques Lacan*, 149.

70. Maulnier, *Les mythes socialistes*, 18.

71. Jean de Fabrègues, Robert Francis, Jean-Pierre Maxence, and Thierry Maulnier, "Une politique vivante," *La Revue du XXe Siècle*, no. 3 (January 1935), 3. Those early magazines, *Réaction pour l'Ordre*, *La Revue du Siècle*, and *La Revue du XXe Siècle*, were still situated within a Catholic nexus that also included *La Revue Universelle*, directed by Jacques Bainville and Henri Massis, where Jacques Maritain regularly contributed. Some historians have suggested that these arguments (and these magazines) epitomize more of a religious outlook than a political one. While it is true that the early 1930s "non-conformist" movement was concerned with "spiritual renewal," I argue that, in the case of far-right intellectuals, rather than emphasize one (the religious) at the expense of the other (political) or vice versa, we need to consider the ways in which these terms were part of a larger cultural concern with the self, the individual, and male subjectivity. On the "non-conformists," see Loubet del Bayle, *Les non-conformistes des années 30*; also Guyader, *La revue idées, 1941–1944*, 46–49. On an emphasis on the religious, see Dard, *Le rendez-vous manqué*, 124–26. This is also Kessler's argument in *Histoire politique*. Paul Mazgaj rightly emphasizes how, for some young far-right intellectuals like Maxence, early magazines such as *Revue Française* were designed within a broad commitment to "Christian Humanism . . . rather than narrow confessional grounds"; *Imagining Fascism*, 96, 58–67.

72. Surkis, *Sexing the Citizen*, 1–16.

73. Georges Verdeil, "Entre l'individu et l'état: Les corps sociaux," *La Revue du XXe Siècle*, no. 3 (January 1935), 32.

74. Maulnier, *Mythes socialistes*, 20.

75. On Marianne as political allegory, see Agulhon, *Marianne au pouvoir*.

76. Maulnier, *Mythes socialistes*, 43.

77. Maulnier, *La crise est dans l'homme*, 185.

78. As historian Carolyn Dean has noted, the sexual was reaffirmed as the site of political and social boundary marking and policing. See Dean, *The Frail Social Body*; see also Surkis, "Enemies Within," 103–22.

79. On the ways in which gender was central to the understanding of change in the postwar cultural discourse of civilization, see Roberts, *Civilization Without Sexes*, 5.

80. Ibid., 45.

81. For an overall account of the way the three figures of the "modern woman," the "mother," and the "single woman" articulated a postwar "discourse on female identity," see ibid., 5. On the obsession with masculinity and "devirilization," see the overview provided by Surkis, "Enemies Within," 103–22.

82. Leiris, *L'âge d'homme*, 141. Italics are mine.

83. Surkis, "Enemies Within," 104. A similar obsession emerged in interwar Britain, where, as historian Susan Kent, in *Making Peace*, has argued, gender and sexuality provided the prism through which British men and women understood the experience of war. Kent shows how this had a decisive effect on British feminists' claims to political legitimacy. On the cultural, social, and political effects of the violence of World War I, see her excellent *Aftershocks*.

84. Dean, *The Frail Social Body*, 3.

85. René Vincent, "L'après-guerre s'embourgeoise," *Réaction pour l'Ordre* (January–February 1932), 20.

86. Thierry Maulnier, "Témoignage pour l'évidence," *Réaction pour l'Ordre* (January–February 1932), 13.

87. Massis, *Maurras et notre temps*, 98.

88. Gide, *Corydon*, 149–54. There had already been two versions of *Corydon*, one published in 1911 with only twelve copies, and one in 1920 with only twenty-one copies.

89. Massis, *Dix ans après*, 95.

90. Brasillach, *Notre avant-guerre*, 127.

91. "Dissociation" and "fragmentation" are recurring themes and expressions in both *Combat* and *L'Insurgé*. For an example of this rhetoric, tying these themes to the emergence of political ideologies trading in "myths" (fascism, communism, racism), and an argument for the need to restore unity, wholeness, and harmony, see Maulnier, "Il faut reconquérir notre univers," 3–4.

92. Maxence, *Histoire de dix ans*, 76–77.

93. Dean, *The Frail Social Body*, 142, 159; on the circulation of these arguments among the antifascist left, see Meyers, "Feminizing Fascist Men."

94. Brasillach, *Notre avant-guerre*, 11–12.

95. Dean, *The Frail Social Body*, 13.

96. On how "gender" constituted a central cultural and social term for the understanding of the transformations that affected French society after World War I, see Roberts, whose expression I borrow; *Civilization Without Sexes*, vii.

97. Marcel Arland, "Le masque de l'après-guerre," *Réaction pour l'Ordre* (January–February 1932), 2. This article appears in a special issue of *Réaction* devoted to the question of "the end of our postwar era," in the wake of Brasillach's article in *Candide*. It was reprinted in Massis's collection of essays on the state of postwar literature, *Dix ans après*, 117–23.

98. Massis, *Maurras et notre temps*, 253.

99. Ibid., 253. His description directly echoes Brasillach's own account: Massis's reminiscences, published thirty years later, often borrow from the memoirs of his protégé—from Brasillach or from articles published in those years.

100. Jacques de Broze, "Essai sur la notion d'etat," *La Revue du XXe Siècle*, no. 3 (January 1935), 18.

101. Fabrègues, "Manifeste," 1.

102. The author asserts this by referring to Robert Francis, Jean-Pierre Maxence, and Thierry Maulnier's 1934 *Demain la France* as an example of "lucid analysis"; ibid.

103. On the relationship of Catholic thinkers to politics, and to Maurrassian ideas and practices in the 1920s and 1930s, as well as Jacques Maritain's leading role, see the excellent study by Hervé Serry, *Naissance de l'intellectuel catholique.*

104. Jacques Maritain was one of the great proponents and champions of "Thomism," a spiritual philosophy based on the writings and teachings of Saint Thomas; for an overview, see Auzépy-Chavagnac, *Jean de Fabrègues et la Jeune Droite Catholique.* See also Crane, *Passion of Israel.*

105. Emmanuel Mounier, mission statement to the first issue of *Esprit* (1932), cited in Berstein, *La France des années trente*, 96. Mounier became the champion of a particularly militant left-wing Catholicism in the second half of the 1930s, which influenced his subsequent choice to "resist" during the Vichy regime.

106. Borchert, *Encyclopedia of Philosophy*, 233. On the early development of this new personalist generation, see Kessler, *Histoire politique*, 230–33; and on the ideological divide that emerged between Mounier and Fabrègues, 242–49.

107. Maulnier, *La crise est dans l'homme*, 185.

108. Fabrègues, "Manifeste," 1.

109. Jean de Fabrègues, "Revue des revues," *Réaction* (February 1931), 4.

110. Massis, *Défense de l'Occident*, 205.

111. Dean, *The Frail Social Body*, 2–24. On this "anti-modern spiritual renewal," see Raimond, *Éloge et critique de la modernité*, 119–44.

112. Marcel Desrois, "L'individu et la personalité," *La Revue du Siècle* (February 1934), 36.

113. Maxence, *Histoire de dix ans*, 102.

114. Massis, *Dix ans après*, 68, 93.

115. Maulnier, "Témoignage pour l'évidence," 13.

116. Vincent, "L'après-guerre s'embourgeoise," 20.

117. Maulnier, *La crise est dans l'homme*, 7.

118. Maxence, *Histoire de dix ans*, 77.

119. Brasillach, *Notre avant-guerre*, 51.

120. Foster, *Compulsive Beauty*, xiii.

121. Therese Lichtenstein makes this point in reference to surrealists' photographs of Paris; "The City in Twilight," in *Twilight Visions*, 1; on the surrealists' relationship with mass print culture, see Walz, *Pulp Surrealism.*

122. There is an extensive bibliography concerning the surrealist movement. See especially Audoin, *Les surréalistes*; Caws, *The Surrealist Look*; and the already cited Foster, *Compulsive Beauty*, among others. On surrealists' political involvement, see Short, "Politics of Surrealism."

123. Cited in Foster, *Compulsive Beauty*, 20.

124. Spiteri and LaCoss, introduction to *Surrealism, Politics, and Culture*, 6.

125. I follow Foster's analysis of surrealists; *Compulsive Beauty*, xix, 9, 13.

126. Bellmer was known to the French surrealists and exiled himself in France, following Nazi attacks on his work; ibid., 102. Foster argues that Bellmer's dolls offer "an immanent critique of the fascist conception of the body"; ibid., 110.

127. Ibid., esp. chs. 2–5. Kristeva argues, following Freud, that the uncanny and the abject are related; *Powers of Horror*, 1–32.

128. Thierry Maulnier, "La Vie Littéraire: Les dangers de l'innocence," *L'Action Française* (June 1, 1933), 3.

129. Ibid.

130. Maulnier, *La crise est dans l'homme*, 147.

131. Fabrègues, "Le sens de notre effort," 2.

132. Maulnier, "Les dangers de l'innocence," 3.

133. Maxence, *Histoire de dix ans*, 195.

134. Fabrègues, "Le sens de notre effort," 7.

135. For an excellent analysis of the overall realization and concern, amid republican critics, social hygienists, and theorists such as Émile Durkheim, of the need to redefine a self-governing and bounded heterosexual (republican) masculinity, see Surkis, *Sexing the Citizen*. Surkis's work provides the context (and backdrop to these issues) in which these far-right critics produced their definition of a masculine bounded and exclusionary self.

136. Maxence, *Histoire de dix ans*, 16.

137. On the cultural politics of the Popular Front era, see Andrew and Ungar, *Popular Front Paris and the Poetics of Culture*. For a thorough and insightful analysis that examines these attempts across political lines, see Jessica Wardaugh's *In Pursuit of the People*.

138. Louis Aragon, cited in Jackson, *The Popular Front in France*, 119.

139. For a discussion of the cultural battles raging throughout the 1930s on who had the right to speak in the name of "the people," see Wardaugh, *In Pursuit of the People*.

140. Maxence, *Histoire de dix ans*, 78.

141. The rupture between the 1920s and the 1930s was not, however, as great as was imagined then and as has been described since. See Tonnet-Lacroix, *La littérature française*, 5.

142. Massis, *Dix ans après*, 10.

143. Tonnet-Lacroix, *La littérature française*, 4–10.

144. Naturalism expressed an ideological and aesthetic position that was actively criticized by right-wing critics since it was viewed as having corrupted the foundations of literature and having betrayed its true purpose. On this question, see Raimond, *La crise du roman*.

145. Tonnet-Lacroix, *La littérature française*, 22.

146. Schalk, "*La trahison des clercs*"; Benda, *La jeunesse d'un clerc*.

147. Tonnet-Lacroix, *La littérature française*, 18–20.

148. For circulation figures, see ibid., 19.

149. Ibid., 18.

150. Massis, *Dix ans après*, 91.

151. Loubet del Bayle, *Les non-conformistes des années 30*, has described this "nonconformist" discourse and movement. These young far-right writers hardly belonged to such a tradition, since they had emerged from a well-known and influential far-right

genealogy, but they introduced and narrated themselves as such. Véronique Auzépy-Chavagnac argues for the existence of a "Jeune Droite catholique," as she focuses on the figure of Jean de Fabrègues; *Jean de Fabrègues et la Jeune Droite Catholique*. But Kessler's depiction of a "Jeune Droite conservatrice" is more accurate; *Histoire politique*.

152. Robert Brasillach, "La fin de l'après-guerre," *Candide* (August 27–September 24, 1931). Brasillach, who confessed in his 1941 memoir to having used the expression coined by one of his fellow students, had first expressed this in a review of Pierre Drieu La Rochelle's *Feu follet* in *L'Action Française*; see his account in *Notre avant-guerre*, 135–36. I am paraphrasing Kessler, *Histoire politique*, 149.

153. See Robert Brasillach's account, *Notre avant-guerre*, 136. This sense of a "different age emerging," often reiterated by far-right critics, must be nuanced, however, as a number of them nostalgically recalled such feelings in memoirs often written decades later.

154. Mazgaj takes the "generational prism" as central to his analysis of the Young Right; *Imagining Fascism* 13, 17–19.

155. See Loubet del Bayle, *Les non-conformistes des années 30*, 121–52, 327–81.

156. Maxence, *Histoire de dix ans*, 14.

157. Ibid., 99.

158. The rhetoric of "crisis" is not only a staple of the writings of far-right intellectuals. It has rarely been interrogated by historians who often similarly describe the 1930s as a time of "crisis." As an example of historical analysis that questions the deployment of the notion of "crisis," see Surkis, *Sexing the Citizen*, 11–12. For an example of crisis rhetoric, see Maxence, *Histoire de dix ans*.

159. Maulnier, *La crise est dans l'homme*, 233.

160. Levenson, *The Cambridge Companion to Modernism*, 5.

CHAPTER 2

1. I borrow the expression "languages of decadence and renewal" from the title of historian Paul Mazgaj's first chapter, which is devoted to those who influenced this emerging far right. Mazgaj explicitly frames his reading with Robert Wohl's notion of "generation." Mazgaj's emphasis, in his very thoughtful and ambitious study, on this "generational" identity does not stress how this rhetoric was itself self-consciously manufactured by these intellectuals in order to distance themselves from the political legacy that had shaped their vision and obscures the ways in which they belonged to the larger context of the 1930s, to which surrealists and others also belonged. See Mazgaj, *Imagining Fascism*.

2. Jean de Fabrègues, "Rencontre de générations," *Réaction pour l'Ordre* (February 1, 1932), 26.

3. In order to distinguish between the political organization and the newspaper, since they have the same name, the newspaper name will appear in italics.

4. On the emergence of the notion of "intellectual" around the Dreyfus Affair, see Ory and Sirinelli, *Les intellectuels en France de l'Affaire Dreyfus*. There is a rich historiography on the topic; see, among others, Bonnaud-Lamotte and Rispail, *Intellectuel(s) des années trente*; Sirinelli, *Intellectuels et passions françaises*; Charle, *Naissance des "intellec-*

tuels"; Judt, *Past Imperfect*; Jennings, *Intellectuals in Twentieth-Century France*; Prochasson and Rasmussen, *Au nom de la patrie*; Hanna, *Mobilization of Intellect*; Sapiro, *La guerre des écrivains*; Winock, *Le siècle des intellectuels*.

5. In this I follow Mazgaj, who is one of the few to have rightly identified and analyzed the role Henri Massis played in helping "bridge the generational gap"; *Imagining Fascism*, 56–78. To date, his study is the most sensitive to the different contexts in which the young far right emerged. But rather than insisting on this generational shift, which Mazgaj takes as his framework of analysis, I show how they both departed from their intellectual forefathers while simultaneous reinventing and rejuvenating from within a formative intellectual and political influence. The strategies of legitimacy (within the social field of "intellectual politics"), which historical sociologist Gisèle Sapiro has so carefully charted, are therefore important: it is noteworthy that both the Young New Right and the group of intellectuals associated with *Je Suis Partout* rarely mentioned either Daudet or Massis explicitly. But they constantly paid tribute to Maurras. Nonetheless, that silence may tell us about these strategies of legitimation and authorship rather than speaking to the actual influence Maurras exercised. For instance, *La Revue Universelle*, coedited by Henri Massis, was also a venue in which a number of young far-right intellectuals wrote. On strategies of legitimacy and respectability, see Sapiro, *La guerre des écrivains*.

6. Of all these young intellectuals, literary critic Maurice Blanchot remained an exception to this generational recognition of Maurras's influence. Although Blanchot began his career within the fold of far-right-leaning newspapers, he never admitted—or even contested, especially much later in his life—any influence by Charles Maurras. Yet Maurras's place as a towering figure of the far right overall—whether embraced or later abandoned—cannot be ignored.

7. Fabrègues, *Charles Maurras*, 11.

8. Brasillach, *Notre avant-guerre*, 121.

9. Anonymous editorial, "Pour le jubilé littéraire de Charles Maurras," *Combat* (April 1936), 14. Similarly, the influential right-wing literary publication *La Revue Universelle* also published a special issue on January 1, 1937, celebrating Maurras's "jubilé littéraire," cited in Huguenin, *À l'école de l'Action française*, 328.

10. Robert Brasillach, "Charles Maurras devant le monde nouveau," *Je Suis Partout* (November 7, 1936), front page. Brasillach's celebration of Maurras introduced his first article on *Je Suis Partout*'s front page.

11. See, for instance, the issue in which they celebrate Maurras's ideological "purity"; Robert Brasillach, "Charles Maurras ou le héros," *Je Suis Partout* (June 10, 1938); René Vincent, "Croquis pour un portrait de Charles Maurras," *Combat* (July 1938), 13–14.

12. Brasillach, *Notre avant-guerre*, 42.

13. Fabrègues, *Charles Maurras*, 11.

14. Vincent, "Croquis pour un portrait," 13. On Maurras's denunciation of Romanticism, revolution, and Rousseau, see David Carroll, one of the rare critics to have taken seriously the aesthetic foundations of Maurras's politics; *French Literary Fascism*, 74–75. Bruno Goyet also argues in *Charles Maurras* that politics have overshadowed scholars' assessment of Maurras's literary ambitions.

15. Vincent, "Croquis pour un portrait," 13.

16. Weber, *L'Action française*, vii. Weber's study remains to this day the most rigorous and comprehensive examination of Maurras's organization. On Maurras's relationship with Catholic intellectuals, see also Serry, *Naissance de l'intellectuel catholique*.

17. Capitan Peter, *Charles Maurras*, 17: Capitan Peter's analysis relies exclusively on Maurras's writings from the late nineteenth century and the 1910s–1920s. She very briefly examines the 1930s and the Vichy years, in her epilogue only.

18. This is the argument advanced by Renard, *L'Action française et la vie littéraire (1931–1944)*, 10.

19. Monnier, *À l'ombre des têtes molles*, 17.

20. Raoul Girardet, "L'héritage de l'Action française," *Revue Française de Science Politique* (October–December 1957), cited in Huguenin, *À l'école de l'Action française*, 503. The term *école* simultaneously suggests a training ground and a systematic body of thought (*école de pensée*), rightly capturing the full range of influence of this organization.

21. He added, "the intellectual youth especially," and his hospitality toward young recruits was legendary. Maurras, *Poètes*, 89.

22. On Daudet's 1927 arrest for defamation, prison stay, and escape to Belgium, as well as Maurras's 1936 arrest, see Weber, *L'Action française*, 301–9, 426–27.

23. Massis, *Maurras et notre temps*, 207; I borrow the expression from Mazgaj, *Imagining Fascism*, 46; on Massis and Maurras, see his brief overview, ibid., 46–49.

24. Rebatet, *Les décombres*, 20.

25. Massis, *Maurras et notre temps*, 207.

26. For a detailed and vivid history of the organization, see Weber, *L'Action française*, 6. For a historiographical overview of studies of Action française, see Goyet, *Charles Maurras*, 101–43.

27. Weber, *L'Action française*, 26.

28. Capitan Peter, *Charles Maurras*, 41.

29. Léon Daudet, "La peste socialiste et la gangrène démocratique," *L'Action Française* (April 26, 1933).

30. Maurras, *Romantisme et révolution*, 4.

31. Weber, *L'Action française*, 260.

32. Ibid., 233–37. See also Kessler, *Histoire politique*, 84; Goyet, *Charles Maurras*, 31–42.

33. On the ways in which prominent Catholic intellectuals like Jacques Maritain negotiated this affair, see Serry, *Naissance de l'intellectuel catholique*.

34. Weber, *L'Action française*, 341.

35. Capitan Peter, *Charles Maurras*, 20.

36. Louis Bourget, "L'universelle affirmation du 'politique d'abord,'" *L'Action Française* (April 22, 1933).

37. Vincent, "Croquis pour un portrait," 14. The question of Maurras's fascism has been a source of debate among historians, following the influence of Eugen Weber's work, the French historical school, and the Sternhell controversy; on this debate, see Goyet, *Charles Maurras*, 117–33.

38. Léon Daudet, "Hitler et l'oeuvre de Briand," *L'Action Française* (February 1, 1933).

39. Léon Daudet, "Le 1er janvier à l'Action française," *L'Action Française* (January 1, 1936).

40. Daudet, *Bréviaire du journalisme*, 85.

41. Maurras, *Romantisme et révolution*, 1.

42. Capitan Peter, *Charles Maurras*, 78.

43. Mosse, *Toward the Final Solution*, 13, 15. See also Kleeblatt, *The Dreyfus Affair*.

44. Anonymous, "La dissolution du Reichstag," *L'Action Française* (February 2, 1933).

45. Vincent, "Croquis pour un portrait," 13.

46. Charles Maurras, "La politique: Juifs d'Allemagne," *L'Action Française* (March 3, 1933).

47. Charles Maurras, "La politique," *L'Action Française* (January 3, 1934).

48. Monnier, *À l'ombre des têtes molles*, 42.

49. Monnier, like many of the new generation of far-right critics in the 1930s, cited Maurras's hatred of Germany as a motive for his disagreement and subsequent split with the great Action française leader; see ibid., 109.

50. For an example of this, see the last section in Maurras, *Le pape, la guerre et la paix*.

51. Monnier, *À l'ombre des têtes molles*, 42.

52. Maurras, *Le romantisme féminin*, 88.

53. For instance, see Maurras, *Poètes*; *Barbarie et Poésie*; and the posthumously published *Maîtres et témoins de ma vie d'esprit*.

54. Carroll, *French Literary Fascism*, 83.

55. Maurras, *Le romantisme féminin*, 19.

56. Maurras, *Romantisme et révolution*, 2; *Poètes*, 47.

57. Maurras, *Le romantisme féminin*, 144, 147.

58. Ibid., 148.

59. In French, Maurras's language evokes both ideas, just as the word *étrange* refers to both "strange" and "foreign"; ibid., 166. Carroll has noted the gendering of the nation in this characterization of the nation but argues that the French nation represented, for Maurras, a "masculine ideal"—a reading that flattens the ways in which gender and race functioned in far-right rhetoric from Maurras to Maulnier and Brasillach. Carroll, *French Literary Fascism*, 79–80.

60. Monnier, *À l'ombre des têtes molles*, 28.

61. Brasillach, "Charles Maurras devant le monde nouveau."

62. Ibid.

63. Although a number of studies of Maurras have been published, a careful analysis of the intellectual and political influence and legacy of Léon Daudet is long overdue, as he usually appears only as Maurras's acolyte, when his influence seems to have been greater than acknowledged—if indirectly—even if he was never mentioned by the critics of the Young New Right, who generally referred to the more glorious names of Charles Maurras and Henri Massis. Their accounts have very much shaped subsequent studies of Action française, both the movement and the newspaper. See the preface to

Daudet's collected writings by Bernard Oudin in Daudet, *Souvenirs et polémiques*; also Broche, *Léon Daudet, le dernier imprécateur*; Marque, *Léon Daudet*; Vatré, *Léon Daudet ou le libre réactionnaire*. One exception to this "misrecognition" of Daudet's influence is Guyader, *La revue idées, 1941–1944*, 35.

64. On this topic, see *Bréviaire du journalisme*, published after "forty-five years of journalism and twenty-nine of daily editorials," in which Daudet explains his conception of journalism; 9.

65. Massis, *Maurras et notre temps*, 234.

66. This is a common description among historians of Daudet. Oudin, preface, *Souvenirs et polémiques*, ii.

67. Kléber Haedens, preface to Daudet, *Souvenirs littéraires*, 5. For an account of Haedens's career, see Montety, *Salut à Kléber Haedens*.

68. Daudet, *Bréviaire du journalisme*, 89.

69. Cited in Massis, *Maurras et notre temps*, 233; Daudet, cited in Oudin, preface, *Souvenirs littéraires*, v.

70. Both men had dabbled in literature, but Daudet proved to be a mediocre novelist. His most famous novel, a biting satire of the medical world titled *Les morticoles*, was published in 1894, but no other, despite his prolific output, has survived for posterity. Massis, *Maurras et notre temps*, 151.

71. Léon Daudet, *L'Action Française* (March 28, 1936).

72. Daudet, *Bréviaire du journalisme*, 18.

73. Ibid., 79, 115.

74. Ibid., 119, 210.

75. André Bellessort, "La critique: *Les universaux* de Léon Daudet," *Je Suis Partout* (February 15, 1936), 9.

76. This was the title of Maurras's article: "La politique: Doutes et questions," *L'Action Française* (1930–1939).

77. Capitan Peter, *Charles Maurras*, 78.

78. Bellessort, "La critique," 9.

79. Vatré, *Léon Daudet ou le libre réactionnaire*, 91–93.

80. Mme Léon Daudet, "Propagande 1936," *L'Action Française* (January 15, 1936), front page.

81. Daudet, *Bréviaire du journalisme*, 121, 213.

82. Monnier, *À l'ombre des têtes molles*, 20.

83. Mazgaj rightly argues that Massis was central to the emergence of the Young New Right and "discovered" them; *Imagining Fascism*, 57, and esp. 56–78.

84. Foureau, "*La Revue Universelle* (1920–1940)," 4.

85. Ibid., 39. Foureau explains that it was this concern with Western civilization that would drive Massis to become actively engaged in the Algerian War, where he would side with defenders of French Algeria—and refuse the possibility of the dismantling of France's imperial purpose and destiny. There is indeed a striking continuity in Massis's commitment to imperialism and obsession with Western civilization.

86. Sapiro, *La guerre des écrivains*, 132. On Massis's public interventions in the Republic of Letters, see Sirinelli, *Intellectuels et passions françaises*.

87. Massis, *Défense de l'Occident*, 1.

88. Ibid., 2, 7.

89. Ibid., 11, 16.

90. Ibid., 8.

91. Ibid., 136–40, 140, 137, 136.

92. Ibid., 4, 5, 143.

93. Ibid., 200.

94. Ibid., 115, 113, 71–74.

95. Ibid., 19.

96. Ibid., 42.

97. Ibid., 11. Massis opens his essay with warning of this impending danger.

98. Ibid., 14.

99. Cited in Sirinelli, *Intellectuels et passions françaises*, 50–51. On the issue of imperialism, see also Foureau, "*La Revue Universelle* (1920–1940)," 40.

100. Sirinelli, *Intellectuels et passions françaises*, 51.

101. Massis, *Défense de l'Occident*, 206.

102. Mazgaj, *Imagining Fascism*, 56–57, 70–71. On Massis's influence, see also Kessler, *Histoire politique*, 35–60.

103. Maxence, *Histoire de dix ans*, 150.

104. Massis, *La guerre de trente ans*, 75.

105. In this I differ from David Carroll, who, while having offered the first thoughtful and astute analysis of the relationship between aesthetics and politics among these "literary fascists," adopts a reading of this relationship that does not sufficiently stress the reworkings fashioned by the young intellectual far right. Carroll examines individual authors rather than networks of conversations and affinities and the nuanced ways in which they differed; *French Literary Fascism*.

106. Brasillach, *Notre avant-guerre*, 46.

107. Ibid., 160.

108. Monnier, *À l'ombre des têtes molles*, 18.

109. René Vincent, "Aimer notre jeunesse," *La Revue du XXe Siècle* (March–April 1935), 39.

110. Though some, like Olivier Dard, emphasize that Maulnier remained a staunch monarchist, based upon his sustained contributions to *Le Courrier Royal*, where he supported a return to the French monarchy (a fact that Kessler also noted); *Le rendez-vous manqué*, 221–22.

111. Gisèle Sapiro has similarly noted that during the Vichy collaborationist years, *Je Suis Partout* "wished itself to be the 'revolutionary' and 'avant-gardist' pole of intellectual collaborationism," an attitude that had already emerged throughout the 1930s; *La guerre des écrivains*, 39.

112. Maxence, *Histoire de dix ans*, 216. In terms of a "generational concern" with a "new" politics, see Loubet del Bayle, *Les non-conformistes des années 30*. Loubet del

Bayle, however, is more concerned with the conservative right and the Catholic left and ends his analysis in 1935. Paul Mazgaj makes a similar critique in *Imagining Fascism*, 17. I argue that a substantial radicalization occurs in 1937, having emerged in the wake of February 1934 and crystallized around the Popular Front.

113. Loubet del Bayle, *Les non-conformistes*, 37–38.

114. Georges Bernanos, "Messages aux jeunes français," *Réaction pour l'Ordre* (April 5, 1930), 4–7; Émile Vaast, "Bernanos," *Réaction pour l'Ordre* (May 1931), 12.

115. Jean de Fabrègues, "Manifeste," *Réaction pour l'Ordre* (April 5, 1930), 3.

116. Kessler, *Histoire politique*, 17.

117. Jean de Fabrègues, Robert Francis, Jean-Pierre Maxence, and Thierry Maulnier, "Une politique vivante," *La Revue du XXe Siècle*, no. 3 (January 1935), 3.

118. Loubet del Bayle, *Les non-conformistes*, 30–31.

119. Auzépy-Chavagnac, *Jean de Fabrègues*, 406; see also Montety, *Thierry Maulnier*.

120. See particularly Verdès-Leroux, *Refus et violences*. This is especially the case with a certain tradition of French political and intellectual history; see Loubet del Bayle, *Les non-conformistes*; more recently, albeit to a lesser extent, see Kessler, *Histoire politique*.

121. For instance, Maxence recalls in his memoirs when he worked at *Le Rempart*, edited by Paul Lévy, in the spring of 1933, alongside Thierry Maulnier and Maurice Blanchot; *Histoire de dix ans*, 290–91. For details on their involvement and the emergence of this group, see Kessler, *Histoire politique*, and Mazgaj, *Imagining Fascism*.

122. Thierry Maulnier, "Témoignage pour l'évidence," *Réaction pour l'Ordre* (January–February 1932), 10–14.

123. Jean-Pierre Maxence, "Bernanos ou la fidélité totale," *Réaction pour l'Ordre* (May 1931), 17–19. Following a trial, Pierre Godmé changed his pseudonym, adding "Pierre" (Jean-Pierre Maxence).

124. Thierry Maulnier, "Nietszche" (April 1933); and Maurice Blanchot, "Chronique de France" (May 1933), among others.

125. Blond was José Lupin's childhood friend and had failed the École normale supérieure entrance exam. As they were beginning their journalistic careers, he was working for the publishing house Fayard. See Brasillach, *Notre avant-guerre*, 98.

126. Jean de Fabrègues, "*La Revue du XXe Siècle* et la presse," *La Revue du XXe Siècle* (March–April 1935), 79–80.

127. Pierre Monnier was a young far-right activist who later joined the infamous underground political organization La Cagoule. He also wrote under the pseudonym Maurice Grandchamp and proved to be one of the most committed to *L'Insurgé*, whose creation he claimed to have initiated. See his memoirs, *À l'ombre des têtes molles*. Monnier never abandoned his far-right politics and subsequently published a virulent defense of Louis-Ferdinand Céline's antisemitic pamphlets, *Céline et les têtes molles*.

128. Claude Orland (Claude Roy), "Où va la jeune littérature? Charles Mauban," *Je Suis Partout* (August 13, 1937), 8.

129. Robert Francis, "Le roman, terre du miracle," *Je Suis Partout* (May 22, 1937), 8.

130. Pierre Gaxotte, "Destin de la France," *Combat* (April 1937), 8.

131. In his 1937 "Lettre à une provinciale" chronicle, Brasillach announced that

Maulnier was scheduled to take part in the inaugural conference that *Je Suis Partout* was organizing; "Lettre à une provinciale: La première conférence de *Je Suis Partout*," *Je Suis Partout* (November 11, 1937), 3. In 1941, Maulnier took over as *Je Suis Partout*'s editor in chief in order to ensure its continuing publication. See Dioudonnat, "*Je Suis Partout*."

132. René Vincent, "Robert Brasillach, *L'enfant de la nuit*," *La Revue du XXe Siècle* (January 1935), 69.

133. A fact commented upon by many biographers; see Massis, *Maurras et notre temps*; Brasillach, *Notre avant-guerre*; and Montety, *Thierry Maulnier*. "Convergence" is a term often used by some of these men, from Maulnier to Monnier.

134. Jean de Fabrègues, "Lettre à l'abonné, à l'ami, au lecteur d'occasion," *La Revue du XXe Siècle* (February 1935), 2.

135. Brasillach, *Notre avant-guerre*, 15.

136. Robert Brasillach has recounted their École normale supérieure years in *Notre avant-guerre*.

137. Rubenstein, *What's Left?*, 15.

138. Other prestigious alumni included Raymond Aron, Georges Canguilhem, Paul Nizan, and Maurice Merleau-Ponty. See Sirinelli, "Annexe 1," in *Génération intellectuelle*, 647–59.

139. See Brasillach's account, *Notre avant-guerre*, 27–30.

140. Rubenstein argues that this right-wing tradition and "the presence of rightist *normaliens* is either ignored or seen as an aberration." Indeed, Sirinelli's magisterial study of the institution, *Génération intellectuelle*, focused only on its pacifist, Communist, and socialist currents and proponents. Unfortunately, Rubenstein's analysis shows little attention to the historical context in which this generation emerged and relies on the umbrella term of "rightist"; *What's Left?*, 13.

141. Montety, *Thierry Maulnier*. See also Sirinelli, *Génération intellectuelle*; Brasillach, *Notre avant-guerre*, 20.

142. Brasillach, *Notre avant-guerre*, 21–23. Sirinelli's study confirms Brasillach's portrait of Bellessort as a rather unusual and nonconformist figure—for *both* his politics and his interest in foreign countries—in this institution; Sirinelli, *Génération intellectuelle*, 76–78.

143. For instance, "Both Maulnier and Brasillach . . . worked with Fortunat Strowski (who wrote for right-wing journals in the 1930s and 1940s) as their thesis director"; see Rubenstein, *What's Left?*, 38. See also Brasillach's account, *Notre avant-guerre*, 119.

144. The newspaper *Je Suis Partout* became a favored choice for many of these young, educated men, once again contradicting the image it has been given by historians as a rather crude political press organ: Claude Jeantet, who was both a young Maurrassian and later in charge of *Je Suis Partout*'s page on Germany, was not an ENS graduate but an alumni of the prestigious Lycée Louis-le-Grand, where Maulnier and Brasillach had gone; Sirinelli, *Génération intellectuelle*, 71.

145. Rubenstein, *What's Left?*, 38.

146. Auzépy-Chavagnac, *Jean de Fabrègues*; Bident, *Maurice Blanchot*.

147. Maxence is said to have brought many of them together at *L'Insurgé* in 1937; Brasillach, *Notre avant-guerre*, 152.

148. Maxence, *Histoire de dix ans*, 103.

149. Monnier, *À l'ombre des têtes molles*, 206.

150. Formerly a contributor to *Candide* and *L'Action Française*, Pierre Gaxotte was *Je Suis Partout*'s editor in chief until Brasillach replaced him. Pierre Gaxotte, "Conversations: Sur le destin de la France," *Combat* (April 1937), 8–9.

151. Fabrègues, "Lettre à l'abonné," 3.

152. Maxence, *Histoire de dix ans*, 103.

153. For this, see Dard, *Le rendez-vous manqué*; Loubet del Bayle, *Les non-conformistes*; Kessler, *Histoire politique*; Mazgaj, *Imagining Fascism*; Verdès-Leroux, *Refus et violences.*

154. Jackson, *The Popular Front in France*, 1.

155. Ibid., 6; for an overview, see also Serge Berstein, *La France des années trente*, 58–77. These right-wing, nationalist, and far-right organizations were referred to as *ligues*. See Millman, *La question juive.*

156. Léon Daudet, "Les pourris de la Chambre. Les braves gens de Paris," *L'Action Française* (January 13, 1934).

157. Berstein, *Le 6 février 1934*, 90.

158. Louis-Ferdinand Céline, "Contre la dictature des voleurs! Tous ce soir, devant la Chambre!" *L'Action Française* (January 22, 1934), front-page editorial.

159. Daudet, "Les pourris de la Chambre."

160. "À bas les voleurs," *L'Action Française* (January 7, 1934) and *L'Action Française* (January 9, 1934); "Contre les voleurs! Pour l'honneur français," *L'Action Française* (January 12, 1934); "Contre la dictature des voleurs," *L'Action Française* (January 22, 1934); "Contre les parlementaires voleurs," *L'Action Française* (January 23, 1934); "Dehors les voleurs," *L'Action Française* (January 27, 1934); "Contre les voleurs, tous ces soir devant la chambre," *L'Action Française* (February 6, 1934); "Après les voleurs, les assassins. Paris couvert de sang," *L'Action Française* (February 7, 1934).

161. Brasillach, *Notre avant-guerre*, 177.

162. Maurice Blanchot, "La politique: La fin du 6 février," *Combat* (February 1935), 10.

163. Ibid.

164. Maxence, *Histoire de dix ans*, 281, 282.

165. Blanchot, "La politique," 10.

166. Brasillach, *Notre avant-guerre*, 198.

167. Maxence, *Histoire de dix ans*, 250.

168. Ibid.

169. Ibid.

170. This was the explanatory model used by the officials in charge of the "commission d'enquête chargée de rechercher les causes et les origines des évènements du 6 février 1934," an eleven-volume parliamentary report commissioned only a few days after the riots; cited in Berstein, *Le 6 février 1934*, 11, 19. Jackson notes: "Any study of the origins of the Popular Front must begin on 6 February 1934. . . . The riots were merely a symptom of the crisis of French democracy"; *The Popular Front in France*, 17.

171. Parliamentary report, cited in Berstein, *Le 6 février 1934*, 19.

172. Brasillach, *Notre avant-guerre*, 5.

173. Monnier, *À l'ombre des têtes molles*, 127.

174. Mme Léon Daudet, "Propagande 1936."

175. Claude Roy, "Les faits," *La Revue du XXe Siècle* (May–June 1935), 80.

176. Brasillach, *Notre avant-guerre*, 230.

CHAPTER 3

1. Maulnier, *Mythes socialistes*, 15. Material in this chapter appeared in Sanos, "'From Revolution to Literature.'"

2. Maulnier, *Mythes socialistes*, 32.

3. Thierry Maulnier, "Il faut reconquérir la France," *L'Insurgé* (January 13, 1937), front page.

4. Thierry Maulnier, "On veut pousser la France à la guerre," *L'Insurgé* (June 2, 1937), front page; "À bas la guerre!" *L'Insurgé* (June 2, 1937), 8.

5. Thierry Maulnier, "Sortirons-nous de l'abjection française?" *Combat* (November 1936), 6.

6. Thierry Maulnier, "Pas de réconciliation sans révolution," *L'Insurgé* (January 27, 1937), front page.

7. Thierry Maulnier, "Un régime ennemi des arts," *Combat* (April 1936), 5.

8. This is the position of political historian Nicolas Kessler, who insists upon *L'Insurgé*'s "isolated allusions" in a footnote on only one page of his four-hundred-page monograph. His is a rather surprising dismissal considering the extensive and rigorous nature of his study of the Young New Right, but such analysis nonetheless reflects the assumptions behind historians' understanding of far-right intellectuals' networks and positions in the 1930s; *Histoire politique*, 398–99, 379, 379 n. 3.

9. Ibid., 379. See also Paul Mazgaj's study of the Young New Right, which emphasizes their fascism and sees their antisemitism as secondary, as opposed to the "strident antisemitism" of *Je Suis Partout*; *Imagining Fascism*, 119, 183.

10. Maulnier, *Au-delà du nationalisme*.

11. On this notion, which pervades most of the Young New Right's writings, see ibid., esp. 224–37.

12. Maurice Blanchot, "On demande des dissidents," *Combat* (December 1937), 20.

13. Monnier, *À l'ombre des têtes molles*, 70.

14. Jean de Fabrègues, "Manifeste," *Réaction pour l'Ordre* (April 5, 1930), 2.

15. Jean de Fabrègues, "Lettre à André Chamson sur le nationalisme," *Réaction pour l'Ordre* (May 5, 1930), 39.

16. Francis, Maulnier, and Maxence, *Demain la France*, 189.

17. Monnier, *À l'ombre des têtes molles*, 89.

18. Historians have sometimes commented on what they perceive to be the "impotence" and inability of these far-right intellectuals to bring to fruition the criticisms they leveled in print. This, I argue, is a misreading of the kind of political involvement they called for. They rarely conceived of themselves as political activists (aside from men like Pierre Monnier, who never thought of himself as an "intellectual"), and their attempts at political involvement were few, tentative, and short-lived, often ending in disillusion-

ment. Ultimately, this refusal of the messy compromises of political activism may be one of the reasons they were rather critical of Drieu La Rochelle. See Dard, *Le rendez-vous manqué*, 222–27; Kessler, *Histoire politique*, 369–71; for a concise and synthetic summary, see Majgaz, *Imagining Fascism*, 171, 192–97. On Solidarité française and the PPF, see Soucy, *French Fascism*, 59–103, 204–79; and Burrin, *La dérive fasciste*.

19. Francis, Maulnier, and Maxence, *Demain la France*, 18.

20. Jean Loisy, "Tartuffe est à gauche," *Combat* (February 1936), 8–9.

21. *Combat*'s editors, Maulnier and Fabrègues (presumably the authors of the editorial), were specifically referring to the response of left-wing intellectuals to conservative Catholic writer Henri Massis's petition "Intellectuals for European Peace and the Defense of the West," signed by most of the figures of the far right in October 1935 (Henri Béraud, Robert Brasillach, Alphonse de Chateaubriand, Léon Daudet, Pierre Drieu La Rochelle, Pierre Gaxotte, Jean de Fabrègues, Bernard Faÿ, Thierry Maulnier, Charles Maurras, Jean-Pierre Maxence, Henry de Monfreid, and André Rousseaux, among others); Sirinelli, *Intellectuels et passions françaises*, 92–93.

22. Anonymous editorial, *Combat* (January 10, 1937), 2.

23. Ibid.

24. Ibid.

25. Monnier, *À l'ombre des têtes molles*, 104. Brasillach and Massis also praised Maulnier for his ability to reason and produce clear and forceful (political) analyses; in Robert Brasillach, *Notre avant-guerre*; Massis, *Maurras et notre temps*.

26. Montety, *Thierry Maulnier*, 106, 110.

27. Anonymous editorial, "Sentimentalité politique, la passion personnelle ou les haines de classe?" *Combat* (January 10, 1936), 2.

28. Ibid. Newspapers were predominantly more successful in Paris than in the rest of France in terms of circulation. There was also a clear "slide toward the right" during those years; Bellanger et al., *Histoire générale*, 457.

29. Georges Blond, "Liberté de presse?" *Combat* (January 10, 1936), 7–8.

30. Robert Brasillach, "Un vieux gaulois," *Combat* (April 1936), 10.

31. Georges Blond criticized the contemporary press for its dependence on advertisements, in "Liberté de presse?" Unlike more traditional far-right newspapers, neither *Combat* nor *L'Insurgé* benefited from advertisements. But *L'Insurgé*'s financial backing has always been a source of debate. Its shareholders were the editors, Maulnier, Maxence, and Blanchot. It was also financed by Lesieur vegetable-oil company owner Jacques Lemaigre-Dubreuil, who also funded Jean Filliol and Eugène Deloncle, leaders of the terrorist far-right organization La Cagoule. Because the newspaper took over a space formerly occupied by that organization, ties have always been suspected, but never fully elucidated. On this, see Bident, *Maurice Blanchot*, 92; Dard, *Le rendez-vous manqué*, 229–30 n. 4; Kessler, *Histoire politique*, 374–75, 384–85; Montety, *Thierry Maulnier*, 127; Soucy, *French Fascism*, 46–53; Weber, *L'Action française*, 437–43.

32. See *L'Insurgé*, issues March 17 and March 24, 1937.

33. Claude Roy on Thierry Maulnier, review: "Où va la jeune littérature? Thierry Maulnier," *Je Suis Partout* (July 23, 1937), 8.

34. Maxence, *Histoire de dix ans*, 17.

35. On the relationship between culture and politics in the Young New Right, see Mazgaj, *Imagining Fascism*, 79–103. But Mazgaj, like literary scholar David Carroll, considers "culture" writ large (though Carroll pays more attention to antisemitism and Maulnier's aesthetics). See Carroll, *French Literary Fascism*.

36. Editorial, *Combat* (January 1939), 3.

37. Maurice Grandchamp, "Lecteurs de *L'Insurgé*, à l'oeuvre dans vos syndicats," *L'Insurgé* (March 3, 1937), 2.

38. Personal letter to his mother, January 25, 1936, cited in Montety, *Thierry Maulnier*, 117.

39. Insert on the relationship between *L'Insurgé* and *Combat*, where a rather disingenuous claim concerning their independence from one another appears—a blatantly false claim; Jean de Fabrègues and Thierry Maulnier, *Combat* (February 1937), 2.

40. Editorial, *Combat* (January 1939), 3.

41. Vincent was, with Fabrègues, the main architect and founder of the Vichy newspaper *Idées*, which was explicitly designed in the same spirit—and format—as *Combat*. Cited in Guyader, *La revue "Idées," 1940–1944*, 70.

42. Monnier, *À l'ombre des têtes molles*, 157.

43. Ibid., 156.

44. Monnier privileges Maulnier's role, as he was himself politically closer to Maulnier than to the ultra-Catholic Fabrègues; ibid., 155.

45. Ibid., 156.

46. Brasillach, *Notre avant-guerre*, 240; Monnier, *À l'ombre des têtes molles*, 159.

47. Monnier, *À l'ombre des têtes molles*, 159.

48. Editorial, *Combat* (January 10, 1936), 2.

49. Wardaugh, *In Pursuit of the People*, 56–150.

50. The newspaper actually used color (usually blue or red); Kessler, *Histoire politique*, 376. Soupault, "Le 6 février 1934," *L'Insurgé* (February 10, 1937). Ralph Soupault worked for a number of far-right publications, including *Je Suis Partout* and *L'Action Française*. His style was both instantly recognizable and inimitable, rather innovative in its use of color, texture, and lines, and, according to Kaplan, inspired by a futurist aesthetics, a project that had at some point inspired and interested Soupault; Kaplan, *Reproductions of Banality*, 88–90. On caricatures, see also Marie-Anne Mattard-Bonucci, "L'image, figure majeure du discours antisémite?" *Vingtième siècle: Revue d'histoire* 72 (October–December 2001): 27–39. This feature of *L'Insurgé* is striking enough that most scholars on Blanchot's writings mention the "Blum with menorah" or "Blum dripping with blood" caricatures. See Bident, *Maurice Blanchot*, 92; Kessler, *Histoire politique*, 379; Mesnard, *Maurice Blanchot*, 32; Wolin, *The Seduction of Unreason*, 198–99.

51. Among the most famous of these cartoonists were Jean Sennep (whose caricatures appeared in *Candide* and, occasionally in *Je Suis Partout*), Ralph Soupault, René Georges Hermann-Paul, and Delongrave.

52. On this idea, see Žižek, *Plague of Fantasies*. Opinions differ as to the nature and reputation of *Combat*: "pamphlet-like" for Kessler (who quotes Thierry Maulnier), more

sophisticated for Verdès-Leroux, while Sternhell described *L'Insurgé* as "neo-fascist." Kessler, *Histoire politique*, 339; Verdès-Leroux, *Refus et violences*, 23; Sternhell, *Neither Right nor Left*, 371.

53. Monnier, *À l'ombre des têtes molles*, 192. His memoirs focus more on *L'Insurgé*, a venture in which he was very much involved, and which coincided with his activism in La Cagoule, rather than on *Combat*, which was designed for a more "intellectual" audience. Similarly, Robert Brasillach barely mentions *L'Insurgé*, whose short life span in 1937 corresponds to his gradual retreat from *Combat* and greater involvement in *Je Suis Partout*, in *Notre avant-guerre*, 222.

54. Fabrègues, and those close to him—René Vincent, for instance—did not participate in the *L'Insurgé* experiment, which was too radical for them and removed from their interest in a renewal of a Catholic vision of society. Fabrègues was much more involved with those groups that Loubet del Bayle has associated with the "non-conformists"; Fabrègues engaged in many print conversations with Catholic philosopher and founder of *Esprit* Emmanel Mounier. See *Revue du Siècle*, *Revue du XXe Siècle*, and his biography by Auzépy-Chavagnac, *Jean de Fabrègues*.

55. On the origins of the newspaper, Monnier recalled that it was designed to be more populist and to "reach a wider audience"; *À l'ombre des têtes molles*, 191–95.

56. Ibid., 153. Aside from Kessler, for a faithful account of *L'Insurgé*'s politics, see Mazgaj, *Imagining Fascism*, 158–81. Rage is the trope used to describe this newspaper: Paul Sérant has asserted that "the most zealous and enraged *Combat* contributors found themselves writing in *L'Insurgé*"; *Les dissidents de l'Action française*, 125. Kessler calls its hostility to communism "hysterical"; *Histoire politique*, 381. A study of *L'Insurgé* is still lacking. Most historians and literary critics turn to it but do not examine it in depth. Steven Ungar's incisive study of Maurice Blanchot's political writings offers no such reading. Neither does Kessler's otherwise excellent overview of the Young New Right, is rather brief in a very detailed and rigorous work. Finally, Zeev Sternhell, who has argued that Thierry Maulnier should indeed be considered a French Fascist, has not examined this newspaper, only *Combat*, and mistakenly attributed its editorship as the sole responsibility of Jean-Pierre Maxence. See Kessler, *Histoire politique*, 375–88; Mazgaj, *Imagining Fascism*, 170–71; Sternhell, *Neither Right nor Left*, 371, 383n; Ungar, *Scandal and Aftereffect*.

57. Robert Brasillach, "Lettre à une provinciale: En suivant les orphéons," *Je Suis Partout* (May 15, 1937), 3.

58. Ibid. The "excesses" that Brasillach mentions may refer either to the headlines lamenting the abjection of the French nation and its people or to its close attention to social and economic issues.

59. Ibid.

60. On this, see Žižek, *Plague of Fantasies*.

61. Dominique Bertin (pseudonym for Thierry Maulnier), "Nous voulons des agitateurs," *L'Insurgé* (January 13, 1937), front page, and Bertin, "Nous restons victorieux," *L'Insurgé* (January 20, 1937), front page. On the creation of a fictional "public" that defines a legitimate politics through print practices, see Warner, *Letters of the Republic*, and Warner, *Publics and Counterpublics*.

62. Daudet, *Bréviaire du journalisme*, 46.

63. Maurice Blanchot, "La politique: La fin du 6 février," *Combat* (February 1936), 10.

64. Monnier, *À l'ombre des têtes molles*, 196.

65. Thierry Maulnier, "Désobéissance aux lois," *Combat* (January 1937), 3.

66. Thierry Maulnier, "Les deux violences," *Combat* (February 1936), 6.

67. Thierry Maulnier, "Pour une politique de la France," *Combat* (January 1939), 6.

68. Thierry Maulnier, "Témoignage pour l'évidence," *Réaction pour l'Ordre* (January–February 1932), 12.

69. Émile Vaast, "Défense de la France," *Réaction pour l'Ordre* (March 1931), 14.

70. Fabrègues, "Manifeste," 2.

71. See Sternhell, *Neither Right nor Left*, 258. Kessler notes that a "veritable flood of disgust pours out of [*L'Insurgé*'s] pages"; *Histoire politique*, 378.

72. For instance, see Jean Loisy, "Exposition 1937: Paris n'aura pas d'acropole," *L'Insurgé* (January 13, 1937), 5. On the recurring nature of the idea of decadence, see Bernheimer, *Decadent Subjects*; Frétigné and Jankowiak, *La décadence dans la culture et la pensée politique*. The prevalence of "decadence" in interwar far-right thinking has been amply demonstrated, most notably by historian Michel Winock, who has examined novelist Drieu La Rochelle's obsession with decadence and its transformation into the "fascist parable" *Gilles*, published in 1939 and reprinted uncut in 1942; see "Une parabole fasciste: *Gilles* de Drieu La Rochelle," in Winock, *Nationalisme, antisémitisme, et fascisme en France*, 346–73.

73. Sander Gilman, cited in Bernheimer, *Decadent Subjects*, 5.

74. See Slavoj Žižek's discussion of the "narrative occlusion of antagonism"; *Plague of Fantasies*, 10–13.

75. Maulnier, "Sortirons-nous de l'abjection française?" 5.

76. Thierry Maulnier, "Nous ne voulons plus être humiliés," *L'Insurgé* (February 17, 1937), front page.

77. Ibid.

78. Maurice Blanchot, "Nous, les complices de Blum," *L'Insurgé* (January 20, 1937), 5. See Carolyn J. Dean on the social body perceived to be "porous" in the interwar period; *The Frail Social Body*.

79. Maulnier, "Pas de réconciliation sans révolution," front page.

80. René Vincent, "Un noir vaut bien un blanc," *Combat* (July 1938), 10. Vincent also admiringly approved of the beauty of Leni Riefenstahl's propaganda films on the 1936 Berlin Olympics; "*Les dieux du stade* et *Jeunesse olympique*," *Combat* (October 1938), 4.

81. Editorial, "Une France qui nous dégoûte," *Combat* (April 1936), 3.

82. Georges Blond, "Procès de la famille," *Combat* (June 1936), 7; Blond, "L'impartialité contre l'intelligence," *Combat* (October 1936), 3.

83. Editorial, "Une France qui nous dégoûte," 3.

84. Jean Framet, "Ceux qui ruinent les français," *L'Insurgé* (March 17, 1937), 7.

85. "On tue la France . . . mais on promet des portefeuilles," *L'Insurgé* (February 24, 1937), 6.

86. Editorial, "Une France qui nous dégoûte"; Brasillach, "Un vieux gaulois," 10.

87. Headline: "À bas le régime abject!" *L'Action Française* (February 5, 1934), front page; Léon Daudet, "Bande de traîtres, de voleurs, d'assassins," *L'Action Française* (January 7, 1934), front page.

88. Charles Maurras, *L'Action Française* (July 7, 1934), front page.

89. Jean-Pierre Maxence, "À bas l'union nationale! Autour des gens qui ont ruiné, trahi, dupé les français," *L'Insurgé* (March 17, 1937), front page; Thierry Maulnier, "Les victimes mystifiées," *L'Insurgé* (March 24, 1937), front page.

90. Jean-Pierre Maxence, "Les radicaux, les modérés et les trusts préparent UN NOUVEAU MINISTÈRE. On y retrouvera tous les pourris . . ." *L'Insurgé* (January 13, 1937), front page.

91. Jean-Pierre Maxence, "Hier du sang, et demain?" *L'Insurgé* (March 24, 1937), 2. See Berstein, *La France des années trente*, 132; Wardaugh, *In Search of the People*, 188–95.

92. Pierre Danlor, "À la poubelle: Confessions," *L'Insurgé* (January 13, 1937), 9.

93. Anonymous editorial, *Combat* (January 1936), 2.

94. Thierry Maulnier, "Notes sur le marxisme," *Combat* (March 1936), 5–6.

95. Maulnier, "Désobéissance aux lois," 3.

96. For Jacqueline Rose, "the claim to possession seems to lay bare its unconscious undercurrents, its own peculiar vulnerability, and its dangers, with such exemplary clarity and such disturbing force"; *States of Fantasy*, 7.

97. Maulnier, "Désobéissance aux lois," 2. What is interesting is the repetition of the word "nation"—not just adjectives, in order to reinforce the "odious" sentiment of France no longer being its own self.

98. Thierry Maulnier, "Il faut choisir: le régime ou l'empire," *L'Insurgé* (March 17, 1937), front page.

99. Brasillach, "Un vieux gaulois," 10.

100. Maulnier, "Sortirons-nous de l'abjection française?" 5.

101. Kristeva, *Powers of Horror*, 2.

102. Maxence, "Les radicaux, les modérés et les trusts."

103. Monnier, *À l'ombre des têtes molles*, 199.

104. Ibid., 207. See also Mazgaj, *Imagining Fascism*, 174–76.

105. I thank Jennifer S. Milligan for pointing this out to me.

106. See Montety's account, *Thierry Maulnier*; Sérant, *Les dissidents de l'Action française*, 212–13; Kessler, *Histoire politique*, 356–57—which rely on Massis's own recollections.

107. Maulnier, "Sortirons-nous de l'abjection française?" 5.

108. Maurice Blanchot, "Réquisitoire contre la France," *L'Insurgé* (January 13, 1937), 4.

109. Charles Mauban, "De la fierté," *Combat* (July 1937), 4.

110. Maulnier, "Il faut reconquérir notre univers," 3.

111. Maulnier, "Désopeissance aux lois," 3. The process of abjection is not one that can be identified outside of oneself but actually transforms the one who identifies it into an abject individual, thereby necessitating some form of normative containment; see Kristeva, *Powers of Horror*, 22.

112. Maulnier, "Il faut reconquérir notre univers," 3.
113. Thierry Maulnier, "Le communisme, ce fantôme," *L'Insurgé* (March 3, 1937), front page.
114. Ibid.
115. Ibid.
116. Émile Vaast, "Rapports du pays légal et du pays réel," *Combat* (January 1936), 9.
117. Maulnier, "Le communisme, ce fantôme."
118. Maurice Blanchot, "Terrorisme, méthode de salut public," *Combat* (July 1936), 8.
119. Maulnier, "Les deux violences." On Maulnier and Sorelian violence, see Antliff, *Avant-Garde Fascism*, 203–46.
120. T.M. (Thierry Maulnier), "Le seul combat possible," *Combat* (June 1936), 5.
121. Maulnier, "Les deux violences."
122. On the logic of disruption, see Lear, *Open-Minded.*
123. Maulnier, "Notes sur le marxisme," 5.
124. Maulnier, "Il faut reconquérir notre univers," 3–4.
125. Maulnier, "Notes sur le marxisme," 5.
126. Anonymous editorial, *Combat* (January 1936), 2.
127. Maulnier, "Les deux violences," 6.
128. Maulnier, "Désobéissance aux lois," 3.
129. Kristeva, *Powers of Horror*, 7.
130. For a discussion of the way the body relates to the writing and imagination of a nation, see Smith, *The Gender of History*, 30; Kristeva, *Powers of Horror*, 4.
131. Jean-Pierre Maxence, "Hier du sang, et demain?" *L'Insurgé* (March 24, 1937), 2.
132. Butler, *Bodies That Matter.*
133. Grosz, "Julia Kristeva," 197.
134. Thierry Maulnier, "Non, M. Blum n'est pas digne!" *L'Insurgé* (March 10, 1937), front page.
135. Monnier, *À l'ombre des têtes molles*, 131. Antisemitism in both *Combat* and *L'Insurgé* is usually played down by critics. Even Nicolas Kessler, who has written a very rigorous study of this "group," devotes a mere five pages to the question. He writes in a footnote that their antisemitism was incomparable to that of *L'Action Française* and could therefore be but of little importance. But if one is to emphasize *L'Action Française* as training ground and major intellectual influence, the question of what they retained of *L'Action Française* antisemitism needs to be addressed. See *Histoire politique*, 379.
136. Georges Blond, "Histoires morales," *Combat* (March 1936), 8.
137. Insert, "Lucien Rebatet, en relisant Drumont," *Combat* (March 1936), 2.
138. "Textes à relire: Drumont," *Combat* (January 1938), 8–9.
139. Anonymous insert, "Portraits de *L'Insurgé*" (January 13, 1937), front page.
140. Monnier, *À l'ombre des têtes molles*, 269. As noted earlier, Monnier had to tone down his account in the face of possible accusations of antisemitism; but it must be remembered that he never renounced his former far-right ideology, as demonstrated in his spirited defense of Céline's antisemitic pamphlets. See also his *Céline et les têtes molles.*

141. Thierry Maulnier, "Les français improvisés," *L'Insurgé* (February 10, 1937), 8.

142. Lucien Farnoux-Reynaud, "Le nouveau monde: Les hommes de nulle part . . . ," *L'Insurgé* (March, 24, 1937), 7.

143. Ibid.

144. Ibid.

145. Brasillach, "Un vieux gaulois," 10.

146. Caricatures decreased after July 1937, coincidentally after Blum's resignation in June 1937. When they resumed, they were far less aesthetically striking and more conventional, probably because Soupault seems to have stopped contributing to *L'Insurgé*. He seems to have moved to *Je Suis Partout*, where his caricatures appeared from 1938 on. It is obvious that "Blum" provided the *Insurgé* editorial team with its favorite and richest object of attacks, as subsequent caricatures do not have the apocalyptic verve of Soupault's drawings. For examples of front-page caricatures of Blum, see *L'Insurgé*, February 10 and 17; every issue for the month of March, April 21, May 1, and June 25.

147. Ralph Soupault, "Bismarck," *L'Insurgé* (February 17, 1937), front page.

148. Ralph Soupault, "Draveil 1937: Provocation au meurtre en Tunisie"; "Blum nous inculpe, MERCI," *L'Insurgé* (March 10, 1937), front page.

149. On the motif of "true France," see Lebovics, *True France*.

150. Monnier, *À l'ombre des têtes molles*, 254.

151. Ralph Soupault, "Qui disait que je n'avais pas de sang francais?" *L'Insurgé* (March 24, 1937), front page. This particular caricature is also striking in that Blum's figure echoes the dangerous vampiric creature fictionalized by German artist F. W. Murnau in his 1922 film *Nosferatu*; on this, see Tatar, *Lustmord*, 41–61.

152. Kléber Haedens, "Blum-Thiers," *L'Insurgé* (March 24, 1937), 6.

153. Monnier, *À l'ombre des têtes molles*, 130.

154. Blum had often been obliged to reiterate and insist on his French citizenship, in response to the mounting antisemitic attacks that were hurled at him, and this even within the parliamentary house. In a famous anecdote, Xavier Vallat had exclaimed upon learning of Blum's election: "This old gallo-roman country is ruled by a Jew." The far right always claimed he was a recent immigrant, recently naturalized, even claiming at some point that he had really been born "Karfunkelstein." Blum had been forced to publicly say that he "was Jewish AND French." See Jackson, *The Popular Front in France*, 250–52; Weber, *Action française*, 415.

155. This insert was in response to their indictment for "incitement to murder and violence"; Jean-Pierre Maxence, Thierry Maulnier, Ralph Soupault, Maurice Blanchot, Kléber Haedens, Guy Richelet, "Léon Blum, vous étiez prévenu," *L'Insurgé* (March 24, 1947), 3.

156. "La Blumignole," *L'Insurgé* (March 24, 1937), 6.

157. On the operation of ideological fantasy, see Žižek, *Plague of Fantasies*.

158. Headline, "Blum social-bourgeois lèche les bottes du capitalisme et nous inculpe," *L'Insurgé* (March 10, 1937), 3.

159. Jean-Pierre Maxence, "À bas l'union nationale! Autour des gens qui ont ruiné, trahi, dupé les français," *L'Insurgé* (March 17, 1937), front page.

160. Jean-Pierre Maxence, "L'Alsace-Lorraine défend ses libertés," *L'Insurgé* (February 17, 1937), front page. Notice the construction ending with "French civilization," thereby resonating with greater force.

161. Maurice Blanchot, "La France, condamnée à tort," *L'Insurgé* (May 12, 1937), 6. Kristeva, *Powers of Horror*, 1.

162. Ralph Soupault, "Mort sans crédit;" headline: "Plus que jamais debout contre le régime. Après Blum, Chautemps, demain un autre. Tous des pourris. Blum abattu, Doriot battu, une seule leçon. Rien à tenter sur le plan parlementaire: La révolution nécessaire . . . ," *L'Insurgé* (June 25, 1937), front page.

163. Jean-Pierre Maxence, "Assez de chantages électoraux: les vrais problèmes se règlent ailleurs. Électoralement battu, Doriot peut vaincre dans le pays," *L'Insurgé* (June 25, 1937), front page.

164. See Antliff, *Avant-Garde Fascism*, esp. 63–110.

165. For instance, Maxence describes Blum as an "anarchical and sated esthete," in "À bas l'union nationale," 6.

166. Monnier, *À l'ombre des têtes molles*, 131.

167. Ibid., 53.

168. Ralph Soupault, "Faîtes payer les riches!" *L'Insurgé* (July 7, 1937), front page.

169. Monnier, *À l'ombre des têtes molles*, 54, 131, 53–54.

170. Robert Brasillach, "Lettre aux cocus de droite," *Combat* (March 1936), 4.

171. Thierry Maulnier, "Notes sur l'antisémitisme," *Combat* (June 1938), 5–7.

172. "Les juifs," special issue, *Je Suis Partout* (April 15, 1938).

173. Maulnier, "Notes sur le marxisme," 5.

174. Ibid., 5.

175. Thierry Maulnier, "Notes sur le fascisme," *Combat* (December 1938), 3–4.

176. Ibid., 4.

177. Ibid., 3.

178. Robert Brasillach, "Introduction à l'esprit fasciste," *Je Suis Partout* (June 24, 1938); "Introduction à l'esprit fasciste, II. Comment se forment les mythes," *Je Suis Partout* (July 1, 1938); "Introduction à l'esprit fasciste, III. Un type humain nouveau," *Je Suis Partout* (July 8, 1938). Maulnier had always been more critical of Hitler than of Mussolini.

179. Maulnier, "Notes sur l'antisémitisme," 5.

180. Ibid.

181. Ibid. These beliefs, he explained, were asserted in some of the most violently anti-Jewish pamphlets that had recently been published, presumably a reference to Louis-Ferdinand Céline's antisemitic pamphlets, *Bagatelles pour un massacre* (1937) and *L'école des cadavres* (1938). Both had been praised by Rebatet and Brasillach in *Je Suis Partout* but criticized by René Vincent in *Combat*.

182. Maulnier, "Notes sur l'antisémitisme," 5.

183. Maulnier, as did Robert Brasillach in his editorials to the *Je Suis Partout* special issues on the Jews, invokes "reason" in order to justify antisemitism. However, the content of the two men's positions differed.

184. Maulnier, "Notes sur l'antisémitisme," 5.

185. Maulnier and Brasillach parted on the meaning they ascribed to the notion of a reasoned and reasonable antisemitism. Brasillach held a racialized understanding of antisemitism. Mostly this hinged on their understanding of the nature of French antisemitism, as opposed to what they termed German "racist antisemitism."

186. Maulnier, "Notes sur l'antisémitisme," 5.

187. Ibid.

188. Maulnier, "Notes sur l'antisémitisme," 5, 6.

189. Maulnier, *Au-delà du nationalisme*, 9.

190. According to psychoanalysis, language structures the subject who is constituted through lack. Defining the individual (or "man") thus necessarily involves the privileged space of language, namely literature. On contemporary inquiries into the meaning of "man," see Gerounalos, *An Atheism That Is Not Humanist*.

191. Charles Mauban, "De la fierté," *Combat* (July 1937), 4. The sentence construction is very evocative: it begins with "a degenerate France," and emphasis is put on the "we" [as Frenchmen], which appears twice.

192. Maulnier, *La crise est dans l'homme*, 95.

193. On this issue, see Carroll, who argues that we should think of the interwar far right's strategy as one of "aesthetics-as-ideology"; *French Literary Fascism*, 6; and Antliff's insightful analysis, *Avant-Garde Fascism*, 227–28.

194. Maulnier, *La crise est dans l'homme*, 47.

195. This was the impetus behind Sigmund Freud's inquiry into the "nature" of civilization published in 1937, an intellectual inquiry made urgent by what he had witnessed with the Great War and prior to his exile to England; *Civilization and Its Discontents*, 45.

196. Maulnier, *Racine*, 26.

197. This claim seems to be contradictory to their claim that they are transgressing the boundaries of acceptable understanding of the language of politics and being subversive.

198. Thierry Maulnier, "Progrès et culture," *Combat* (February 1937), 4.

199. Claude Orland (Claude Roy), "Les faits: Plaisirs de la France," *Combat* (June 1936), 15.

200. Maulnier, *Racine*, 25.

201. Maulnier, "Héritage," in *Le sens des mots*, 103.

202. Ibid.

203. Éliane Tonnet-Lacroix argues that this inaugurated a moment of crisis of confidence in literature and its role; *La littérature française*, 26–28.

204. Jean Loisy, "La politique et les arts," *La Revue du XXe Siècle* (May–June 1935), 28–29.

205. Their logic thus suggests a fantasized return to the pre-oedipal, which, in psychoanalysis, precedes the ineluctable imposition of castration, namely of individuation. Following Kristeva, the abject is a reminder of that division; *Powers of Horror*, 5, 7, 13–15.

206. Antliff, *Avant-Garde Fascism*, 250.

207. Thierry Maulnier, "*Électre* et la critique," *Je Suis Partout* (June 5, 1937), 8.

208. Maulnier, *Racine*, 11.

209. Ibid., 9.

210. Witt, *The Search for Modern Tragedy*, 145. Similarly, Brasillach celebrated the poet Virgil.

211. Maulnier, *Racine*, 22.

212. Ibid., 23, 26.

213. Ibid., 27.

214. Francis de Miomandre, "Réflexions sur la poésie," *L'Insurgé* (February 17, 1937), 7. Antliff has similarly pointed to the ways in which Maulnier and his fellow journalists at *Combat* crafted a "palingenetic definition of classicism," which helped attain a "revolutionary sublime"; *Avant-Garde Fascism*, 241, 206.

215. Maulnier, *Introduction à la poésie française*, 11. Maulnier seems to have been inspired by, or modeled his narrative introduction on, the style of Maurice Blanchot's literary chronicles, and cites Heidegger in the opening pages.

216. Maulnier, *Introduction à la poésie française*, 12.

217. Maurras had celebrated only Verlaine, and harshly dismissed Rimbaud, who had "corrupted him." While Maulnier did include Péguy, his selection indicated a greater independence of aesthetic appreciation, reminiscent of Daudet's own aesthetic eclecticism, rather than Maurras's narrow classicism. For the complete list, see ibid., 362–64.

218. Ibid., 10.

219. Ibid., 43.

220. Ibid., 50.

221. Ibid., 22, 40.

222. Ibid., 55, 57.

223. Maulnier, "Progrès et culture," 4.

224. René Vincent, "Réhabilitons le style," *Combat* (July 1937), 13.

225. Jean-Pierre Maxence, "Condition temporelle de la critique," *La Revue du XXe Siècle* (March–April 1935), 15.

226. Maulnier, "Le communisme, ce fantôme," 3.

227. Kristeva, *Powers of Horror*, 7.

228. Dominique Bertin (pseudonym for Thierry Maulnier), "Nous restons victorieux," *L'Insurgé* (January 20, 1937), 3.

229. For an elaboration of Young New Right intellectuals' trajectories beyond 1939, see Kessler, *Histoire politique*; Mazgaj, *Imagining Fascism*; Sapiro, *La guerre des écrivains*.

230. This was also Massis's position. On this, see Montety, *Thierry Maulnier*, 293–301.

231. Maulnier, "Autorité," in *Le sens des mots*, 25. On his defense of anticommunism, see "Anticommunisme," 13.

232. Maulnier, "Intellectuel," in *Le sens des mots*, 124; Montety, *Thierry Maulnier*, 321–23.

233. Maulnier, "Intellectuel," in *Le sens des mots*, 123–24.

234. Ibid.

CHAPTER 4

1. This is evident in the scholarly production that takes Blanchot as a departure point for a deconstructionist philosophy of literature, language, and religion. See, for instance, Hart and Hartman, *The Power of Contestation*; Hart, *The Dark Gaze*; Hall, Nelson, and Vardoulakis, *After Blanchot.*

2. Johnson, "Obituary: Maurice Blanchot"; Loret, "Blanchot s'efface." No intellectual biography of Maurice Blanchot had been published until the thoroughly researched and rigorous *Maurice Blanchot*, by Christophe Bident. The title of this chapter is taken from Michel Foucault's characterization of Blanchot as an author "absent from his own texts[:] absent because of the marvelous force of their existence"; 550, in "La pensée du dehors," *Critique* 229 (June 1966), cited in Foucault, *Dits et écrits*, 546–67.

3. Loret, "Blanchot s'efface."

4. See the important publication of Blanchot's post-1945 political writings, *Écrits politiques, 1953–1993*, as well as the 2007 issue reprinting extracts of letters on the topic of his interwar engagement with the far right; Hill and Holland, eds., "Blanchot's Epoch." For one of the earliest expositions of Blanchot's lifelong projects and writings, see Bident, *Maurice Blanchot*; see, more recently, the collection published from a conference organized by the Association des amis de Maurice Blanchot, which includes talks by Étienne Balibar, Christophe Bident, Kevin Hart, Leslie Hill, Michael Holland, and Jean-Luc Nancy, *Blanchot dans son siècle.*

5. Hill and Holland, introduction to "Blanchot's Epoch." For an article that makes the similar claim that Blanchot never really "retreated" from politics, see Hill, "'Not in Our Name.'"

6. Blanchot, *Après-Coup*, 99. Blanchot's recurring reference to Auschwitz has led critics to turn to his interrogation of literature and being as a means of engaging with the question of the crisis of representation produced by the Holocaust—often to great effect; see, for instance, Bernard-Donals and Glezjer, *Between Witness and Testimony*; and Sampath, "Time's Impossibility."

7. Ethan Kleinberg devotes a chapter to Blanchot's far-right politics and relationship to literature, rightly arguing that his politics then can be understood as an attempt to resolve the question of a "nation in crisis from within" and exploring Blanchot's similarities and divergences from Heidegger. I part somewhat with Kleinberg's analysis of Blanchot's interwar writings, for by not fully interrogating the very terms of Blanchot's texts, I contend, it does not sufficiently question the tropes characterizing most work on this issue while dehistoricizing the context of Blanchot's nationalism. Kleinberg, *Generation Existential*, 210–12.

8. That is, for instance, Leslie Hill's rather harsh characterization of the works of Steven Ungar, Philippe Mesnard, Jeffrey Mehlman, and Richard Wolin. Yet these scholars' arguments are not all the same: while Wolin's avowed purpose is to uncover the fascist temptations and seductions of a number of twentieth-century critics and philosophers (like Bataille and Blanchot), Ungar and Mesnard have offered valuable insights as to ways of reading Blanchot's interwar politics and taking this topic as a serious subject of inquiry; Hill, "'Not in Our Name,'" 143.

9. Historian Eugen Weber was the first to mention Blanchot's involvement in the interwar far-right press, in *L'Action française*. Zeev Sternhell mentions Blanchot only in passing, in *Neither Right nor Left*. More recently, Blanchot appears in Nicolas Kessler's extensive study of the Young New Right, *Histoire politique*. Literary scholars have also now begun taking seriously the issue of Blanchot's political and literary writings in the 1930s, offering a more nuanced consideration of the relationship of politics and aesthetics (even if, again, Blanchot is not fully "historicized"); see Yasuhara, "Maurice Blanchot dans les années 1930"; Olpez, "The Political Share of Literature." See also a recent review by Daniel Uhrig, commenting on the publication of Blanchot's political writings, who calls for a more thorough and careful archivally based reading of Blanchot's 1930s texts, beyond "superficiality" and "partiality"; Uhrig, "Maurice Blanchot, Political Writings, 1953–1993."

10. This is, for instance, the case of Paul Mazgaj, whose synthetic and rigorous overview of the Young New Right does not further explore Blanchot's role and writings; *Imagining Fascism*, 173.

11. Those are the titles of intellectual biographies: Desanti, *Drieu La Rochelle*; Kaplan, *The Collaborator*.

12. Philippe Burrin has explored how political allegiances shifted in the 1930s, as in the case of Jacques Doriot, who went from left to right (while some, like Blanchot and Claude Roy, went from right to left with the experience of the war); *La dérive fasciste*.

13. I follow Carolyn J. Dean's characterization of one of the fundamental issues of the interwar period; *The Self and Its Pleasures*.

14. Even Hill agrees that Blanchot's foremost preoccupation then was "the nation of France itself"; "'Not in Our Name,'" 145.

15. My reading echoes while also parting ways with Kleinberg's, which reads Blanchot's obsession with the French nation as "[taking] the form of an extreme Cartesianism in which the nation became the cogito," where "France was the ultimate 'I,'" where Blanchot wished to maintain the nation as "the ultimate controlling subject"; Kleinberg, *Generation Existential*, 210, 212, 213.

16. Blanchot's commitment and involvement in the interwar far-right milieu has been mentioned in passing over the years: Philippe Lacoue-Labarthe, for instance, a critic of Heidegger, mentions Blanchot in an article addressing the question of Martin Heidegger's Nazi allegiance; see Lacoue-Labarthe, "Neither Accident nor Mistake." Yet the issue has never been explored at length except in the case of Jeffrey Mehlman, who, in order to provide a (moral) indictment and denunciation of Blanchot's writings, proved intent on stressing the scandal of his 1930s writings; *Legacies of Antisemitism in France*.

17. For an analysis of de Man's "collaborationist scandal" that does not exculpate him, see Felman, "After the Apocalypse."

18. I therefore situate my work at odds with that of intellectual historian Richard Wolin (though we address the same subject matter), who is intent on uncovering in Blanchot and others (often canonical references of postmodernism and post-structuralism) a structural "romance" with fascism; see Wolin, *The Seduction of Unreason*, esp.

187–219. For an example of the productive ways in which the historicization of the literary and philosophical canon's great figures can shed light on an author's concerns, see Baring, "Liberalism and the Algerian War," and also Samuel Moyn, who aims "to restore contingency to [philosopher] Levinas's trajectory" in order to refute teleological accounts of his philosophy; Moyn, *Origins of the Other*.

19. Hill, *Blanchot*, 4. My work owes much to Steven Ungar's provocative study, and to his astute insights regarding the place of "displacement," "the politics of abjection," and the role of dehistoricization in Blanchot's 1930s writings. My purpose is to further these insights and properly historicize Blanchot, a task that Ungar, a literary critic, did not undertake. See *Scandal and Aftereffect*.

20. For very interesting analyses of the question of Blanchot's politics that have been central to my understanding of Blanchot, see Ungar, *Scandal and Aftereffect*, 123; and Mesnard, *Maurice Blanchot*.

21. They have been presented by Jeffrey Mehlman himself in both of his works containing articles on Blanchot: *Legacies of Anti-Semitism in France* and *Genealogies of the Text*. Mehlman's work has been crucial in bringing this question to light. But within the French literary world he has become a figure akin to that of controversial intellectual historian Zeev Sternhell. He has been rebuked and derided for his apparent desire to identify some incontrovertible antisemitism in Blanchot's writings. However, as Philippe Mesnard has noted, while we may recognize that Mehlman's "intuition" was correct, his analysis remains arbitrary and ahistorical, often overstating the case for the political taint of Blanchot's writings. For Mehlman, "Blanchot at *Combat*" is, like his textual forefathers Édouard Drumont and Georges Bernanos, unmistakably antisemitic. Through a selective and partial reading of Blanchot's journalistic pieces at *Combat* and *Le Journal des Débats*, he further claims that Blanchot embodied a specific form of French fascism. Blanchot, as described by Mehlman, is a polemical and fierce figure, but one whose ambiguous trajectory and obsessions with the boundaries of the self are too quickly erased. I argue that Blanchot cannot be made into an uncomplicated apologist for antisemitism. Mehlman's description is based solely on Sternhell's only citation of Blanchot. In *Genealogies of the Text*, Blanchot has been transformed from "antisemitic" to "fascist" without any explanation for that particular rhetorical move. Mehlman has been accused of acting like a "prosecutor"; see Verdès-Leroux, *Refus et violences*, 17; Mesnard, *Maurice Blanchot*, 40. Mehlman is also excoriated by Deborah Hess, who catalogs all his factual errors and what she calls his deliberate "rhetorical tricks." But, aside from plausible readings of Blanchot's 1930s and 1940s fiction, Hess does not provide any substantial analysis; *Politics and Literature*, esp. 61–114.

22. Loret, "Blanchot s'efface." This emphasis on "a certain antisemitism" is also noted by Mesnard; *Maurice Blanchot*, 39.

23. Loret, "Ces textes que, avec raison, on me reproche," in "Blanchot s'efface." Notice how the evocation of reproach—using the impersonal construction "one" while inserting "with reason" in the middle of the sentence—at once denies and affirms.

24. See, for instance, Maurice Blanchot, "Letter to Maurice Nadeau" (April 21, 1977), cited in Hill, *Paragraph*, 19.

25. He has commented only a few times on this question, every time in the format of a personal letter: one was a letter written to his friend Roger Laporte and read aloud at a conference in response to Mehlman's piece. Another was mentioned by Deborah Hess in response to her inquiries; *Politics and Literature*, 265. Another was reprinted with comments in a collection of essays; Gill, *Maurice Blanchot*. Finally, in 2007, Leslie Hill and Michael Holland reprinted letters he had sent to Raymond Bellour and Maurice Nadeau on the topic in 2007; Hill and Holland, "Blanchot's Epoch," 15–19.

26. Hess, *Politics and Literature*, 241.

27. Bident, *Maurice Blanchot*, 156; Mesnard, *Maurice Blanchot*, 43; Kleinberg, *Generation Existential*, 247. In relation to his intellectual and political trajectory, critics have also invoked Blanchot's experience of narrowly escaping execution during the war, narrated (as fiction, not autobiography) in *L'instant de ma mort*.

28. This is mentioned by Jean-Pierre Maxence himself, who praises Paul Lévy for the absolute freedom he allowed all of them; *Histoire de dix ans*, 290–91.

29. See Haase and Large, *Maurice Blanchot*, 4–6; and Hill, *Blanchot*, 37. Kleinberg, *Generation Existential*, 211–12.

30. Blanchot, "Letter to Maurice Nadeau" (April 21, 1977), 18; see also the letter to the author (August 20, 1983), cited in a footnote by Diane Rubenstein; *What's Left?*, 187.

31. Bident, *Maurice Blanchot*, 96.

32. Hill, *Blanchot*, 36–37.

33. Bident argues that Blanchot's antisemitism was only a rhetorical tool, a "*lapsus controlé*"; *Maurice Blanchot*, 96. Hess argues that "Blanchot was certainly guilty of sins of rhetoric, but not of fascism nor of anti-Semitism"; *Politics and Literature*, 11.

34. Intellectual Julien Benda, for instance, had always constituted one of the prime targets of the antisemitic far-right press, such as *L'Action Française* and *Je Suis Partout*. Speaking of him in derogatory tones was within this antisemitic genealogy, and even in literary debates. See Capitan Peter, *Charles Maurras*.

35. On this topic, see Caron, *Uneasy Asylum*; Schor, *L'opinion française*; and the suggestions made by Camiscioli, *Reproducing the French Race*.

36. Bident, *Maurice Blanchot*, 37, 38.

37. Blanchot began his journalistic career with a literary review published in the conservative and monarchist *La Revue Universelle*, in January 1931, in Bident, *Maurice Blanchot*, 60; see also Loubet del Bayle, *Les non-conformistes des années 30*, 60. He published a front-page article, "Comment s'emparer du pouvoir?" in *Le Journal des Débats* on August 18, 1931. My analysis relies mostly on the Young New Right's publications that Blanchot contributed to. I do not examine his writings in *Aux Écoutes*, *Le Rempart*, or *Le Journal des Débats*, as I suggest that, as for Maulnier, *Combat* and *L'Insurgé* represented an attempt at dissident journalism and politics in ways that other newspapers did not and could not.

38. In *Réaction pour l'Ordre*, *Revue du Siècle*, and then *Revue du XXe Siècle*, Blanchot contributed both literary reviews and political chronicles: regarding literature; "Nouvelle querelle des anciens et des modernes," *Réaction* (April–May 1932), 11–16; "Positions," *La Revue du Siècle* (October 1933), 75–77. His political chronicles slightly

outweighed his literary critiques; "Morale et Politique," *La Revue du Siècle* (May 1933), 60–65; "La démocratie et les relations franco-allemandes," *La Revue du XXe Siècle* (February 1935), 56–59; and "Le dérèglement de la diplomatie française," *La Revue du XXe Siècle* (May–June 1935), 53–57.

39. Those were the terms used by Blanchot in a review critical of writers who, he argued, pointed to material causes as the sole origin of modernity; "Nouvelle querelle des anciens et des modernes."

40. Pierre Monnier is one of the few far-right companions of these years, also involved in *L'Insurgé*, who has commented on Blanchot's journalistic writings—comments made possible by the fact that Monnier was neither an intellectual nor involved in literature after 1945 and never renounced his earlier political commitments; *À l'ombre des têtes molles*, 224.

41. Maurice Blanchot, "La politique: La fin du 6 février," *Combat* (February 1935), 10.

42. Maurice Blanchot, "La guerre pour rien," *Combat* (March 1936), 10–11.

43. Blanchot, "La politique," 10.

44. The article is signed "M.B."; "Comment s'emparer du pouvoir," *Le Journal des Débats* (August 18, 1931), front page.

45. Blanchot ended his contributions to *Combat* with an article clamoring for a "true dissidence": "On demande des dissidents," *Combat* (December 1937), 11. Many critics have debated Blanchot's use of the word "terror," discussing what he meant by a call for "terrorism" in his article "Le terrorisme, méthode de salut public," *Combat* (July 1936), 8. See, for instance, literary scholar James Swenson's insightful discussion, in which he emphasizes the metaphorical nature of Blanchot's call for terrorism, "Revolutionary Sentences (in Law, Death, Community)." However, if one takes Blanchot's call for terrorism in the context of his journalism rather than by itself, then the failed February protest, calls for riots, and radical oppositional politics, though not necessarily a call to terrorism, I argue, hint at the metaphorical violence of Blanchot's prose.

46. Blanchot, "La démocratie et les relations franco-allemandes," 56.

47. Most of Blanchot's political chronicles contain a reference to the state of decadence that has taken hold "in the last fifteen years," as he wrote in 1935, or "for the last eighteen years," in 1937; *La Revue du XXe Siècle* (February 1935); *La Revue du XXe Siècle* (May–June 1935); "Réquisitoire contre la France," *L'Insurgé* (January 13, 1937); "Blum, notre planche de salut," *L'Insurgé* (January 27, 1937); "Notre première ennemie," *L'Insurgé* (February 3, 1937); "Le déshonneur français," *L'Insurgé* (February 24, 1937); "M. Delbos paiera," *L'Insurgé* (March 10, 1937); "Le temps de la guerre," *L'Insurgé* (March 17, 1937).

48. Maurice Blanchot, "La grande passion des modérés," *Combat* (November 1936), 3.

49. Maurice Blanchot, "Nous les complices de Blum," *L'Insurgé* (January 20, 1937), 6.

50. I have not been able to read the original article that his biographer claimed may have been the first one Blanchot ever authored as a journalist, but it is reviewed and extensively quoted (as was often the practice in the 1930s press) in *Le Journal des Débats* (August 29, 1931), 4.

51. Blanchot, "La guerre pour rien," 10.

52. Blanchot, "La grande passion des modérés," 3.

53. Maurice Blanchot, "La crise qui va s'ouvrir," *L'Insurgé* (February 10, 1937), 4.

54. For an analysis of the motif of decadence, see Michel Winock, "Une parabole fasciste: 'Gilles' de Drieu La Rochelle," in *Nationalisme, antisémitisme, et fascisme en France*, 346–73.

55. Blanchot, "Réquisitoire contre la France," 4.

56. Blanchot, "La crise qui va s'ouvrir," 4.

57. Ibid.

58. Maurice Blanchot, "Blum, notre planche de salut," *L'Insurgé* (January 27, 1937), 4 (my italics).

59. Blanchot, "Réquisitoire contre la France," 4.

60. Maurice Blanchot, "La France, nation à venir," *Combat* (November 1937), 3.

61. Blanchot, "La guerre pour rien," 10–11.

62. Blanchot, "La crise qui va s'ouvrir," 4.

63. Maurice Blanchot, "Après le coup de force germanique," *Combat* (April 1936), 11.

64. Blanchot, "Nous les complices de Blum," 4.

65. Maurice Blanchot, "Les lectures de l'Insurgé: *Réflexions sur la force*, par Alphonse Sèche, Editions de France," *L'Insurgé* (March 17, 1937), 3.

66. Blanchot, "Nous les complices de Blum," 4 (my italics).

67. Ibid.

68. Ibid.

69. Maurice Blanchot, "L'impasse," *L'Insurgé* (February 17, 1937), 4.

70. Blanchot, "La France, nation à venir," 3.

71. Ibid., 4.

72. Kristeva, *Powers of Horror*, 23. As Judith Butler has explained, in order for the subject to come into being, there needs to be the "formation of an ego—a bounded sense of self"; *Bodies That Matter*, 58.

73. Blanchot, "Réquisitoire contre la France," 4.

74. Ibid.

75. Blanchot, "Blum, Notre planche de salut," 4.

76. Blanchot, "La France, nation à venir," 3; Maurice Blanchot, "Ce qu'ils appellent patriotisme," *L'Insurgé* (March 3, 1937), 4.

77. The ego, that is the self, is experienced as alien, as not one's own since it is the place for the other's desire. Alienation thus founds the subject, a fearful idea to these far-right writers, which they regularly mention. See Jacques Lacan, "Le stade du miroir comme formateur de la fonction du Je," in *Écrits 1*; and "Subversion du sujet et dialectique du désir dans l'inconscient freudien," in *Écrits 2*.

78. Blanchot, "La crise qui va s'ouvrir," 4.

79. Blanchot, "La grande passion des modérés," 3.

80. Maurice Blanchot, "M. Delbos a raison," *L'Insurgé* (April 21, 1937), 4.

81. Blanchot, "Le déshonneur français," 6.

82. Judith Butler asserts that "the bodily ego [provides] a sense of stable contour"; *Bodies That Matter*, 14.

83. Kristeva, *Powers of Horror*, 4; Butler, *Bodies That Matter*, 14.

84. Kristeva, *Powers of Horror*, 3.

85. Monnier, *À l'ombre des têtes molles*, 224.

86. Monnier's use of military language reinforces the sense of violence he ascribes to Blanchot's writings; ibid., 159.

87. Blanchot, "Nous les complices de Blum," 4.

88. Blanchot, "Réquisitoire contre la France," 4.

89. Ibid.

90. Blanchot, "Nous les complices de Blum," 4.

91. Maurice Blanchot, "Les français et le couronnement," *L'Insurgé* (May 19, 1937), 3.

92. Blanchot, "Blum, notre planche de salut," 4.

93. Ibid. This is usually the one quote cited by Blanchot critics as a means of simultaneously gesturing to and denying his antisemitism.

94. Ibid.

95. Maurice Blanchot, "Blum provoque la guerre," *L'Insurgé* (March 31, 1937), 3.

96. Benda, *La trahison des clercs*; Benda, *La jeunesse d'un clerc*.

97. Maurice Blanchot, "Lectures de l'Insurgé: *La jeunesse d'un clerc*, par Julien Benda, NRF," *L'Insurgé* (February 10, 1937), 5.

98. Ibid.

99. Blanchot, " M. Delbos a raison," 4.

100. Blanchot, "Ce qu'ils appellent patriotisme," 4.

101. Ibid.

102. Bident, *Maurice Blanchot*, 101; Rubenstein, *What's Left?*, 187 n. 72; Hess, *Politics and Literature*, 240.

103. Blanchot, "Letter to Maurice Nadeau," 19.

104. Blanchot, "La crise qui va s'ouvrir," 4.

105. Ibid.

106. Bident argues that Blanchot's antisemitism was nothing more than a manifestation of this logic; *Maurice Blanchot*, 96.

107. Such exemplary mutilation was then thought to be foundational to the subject—castration—as Jacques Lacan himself also explained in his 1938 article on the family, in which he suggested that mutilation indeed evoked "fantasies of dismemberment," which echoed the many literary and testimonial translations of experiences of the First World War.

108. Blanchot, "L'impasse," *L'Insurgé* (February 17, 1937), 4.

109. Blanchot, "M. Delbos a raison," 4.

110. Blanchot, "Nous les complices de Blum," 4.

111. Blanchot, "La France, nation à venir," 3–4. This article concerns the government's foreign affairs and colonial policy.

112. This story was published along with "Le dernier mot," written in 1935 as *Le ressassement éternel* (Paris: Éditions de Minuit, 1951). In its 1983 reprint, which contains an additional essay, Blanchot calls it a "récit," in *Après coup, précédé par le ressassement éternel*, 92. This is an ambiguous term in Blanchot's work that, after 1954, characterizes a narrative that is conceptually distinct from a novel. On Blanchot's articulation of the

notion of "récit," see Just, "The Politics of the Novel and Maurice Blanchot's Theory of the *Récit*, 1954–1964."

113. Hess, *Politics and Literature*, 7. After having suggested that his short fiction spoke of the "veiled barbarism" that found its expression in the useless labor required in concentration camps, Blanchot explains that this story should not be reduced to a historical reading—contemporary or retrospective; *Après-Coup*, 95–96.

114. I follow Deborah Hess's analysis and agree with her reading, but my interest lies in the way the body, sexual difference, and therefore again the possibility of a bounded masculine self is here the central, if subterranean, issue. See Hess, *Politics and Literature*, 139–52.

115. Blanchot himself suggests the "prophetic" nature of this story; *Après-Coup*, 94, 95–96.

116. Mesnard argues that this text is a meditation on foreignness and is structured through the figure of the foreigner; *Maurice Blanchot*, 63.

117. Blanchot, *L'idylle*, 11.

118. Ibid., 34.

119. Some scholars have touched upon this issue: Bident, *Maurice Blanchot*, 127–37; Yasuhara, "Maurice Blanchot dans les années 1930," 297–309.

120. Bident recognizes that this suggests his "Jewishness"; he further suggests this might be an anagram of Trotsky but stops short of stating that it might refer to the familiar threat of "Judeo-Bolchevism." He instead argues that "Jewish presence is minor" in this story; *Maurice Blanchot*, 133. In a story where few names are explicitly used, one might notice the relationship generated by Blanchot among identity, otherness, and Jewishness. Similarly, as many critics have noted, Blanchot chose Aminadab as the title and narrator's name for his 1942 novel *Aminadab*. Critics have usually explained that he used the name of Emmanuel Levinas's younger brother, who died prematurely in a concentration camp.

121. Blanchot, *L'idylle*, 19.

122. I thank Janet Wagner for her insights on this issue. See Beider, *Dictionary of Jewish Surnames*, 274, 277.

123. I follow Judith Surkis's argument regarding the role of conjugal heterosexual marriage in normalizing a precarious masculinity; *Sexing the Citizen*.

124. Blanchot, *L'idylle*, 28.

125. See, for instance, Blanchot, *Thomas l'obscur*; Blanchot, *Aminadab*.

126. On French discourse regarding conjugal marriage, masculinity, and morality, see Surkis, *Sexing the Citizen*. In a similar vein, on the role of sexuality in the imagination of ethics, politics, and community in Germany and Central Europe, see Matysik, *Reforming the Moral Subject*.

127. Though Blanchot also stresses that "exile is neither psychological nor ontological"; *L'idylle*, 95.

128. Ibid., 41, 42.

129. Ibid., 50, 51, 43.

130. Ibid., 53.

131. On authorship, see Foucault, "Qu'est-ce qu'un auteur?" in *Dits et écrits, 1954–1975*, 817–49.

132. Bident, *Maurice Blanchot*, 91.

133. Blanchot's own words, almost fifty years later, in the essay *Les intellectuels en question*. There is extensive literature on the question of "the intellectual" in French history and culture, most notably around the Dreyfus Affair and the Algerian war of independence.

134. Ibid., 14.

135. Bident, *Maurice Blanchot*, 181–99. Those have been recently published as a collection: Blanchot, *Chroniques littéraires* (ed. Christophe Bident).

136. I am not arguing that politics do not appear outside of political chronicles.

137. Hill has argued that *Le très-haut* signals not "disengagement" but an "urgent political novel about politics." This may be the case; I am emphasizing here the form his writings took—avowedly about politics or not—and the ways Blanchot occupied the position of author, as opposed to that of political journalist; "'Not in Our Name,'" 144. On the politics of this novel, see Stoekl, *Politics, Writing, Mutilation*, 25–31.

138. I rely, for this reading, on Bident's charting of Blanchot's writing and publication in the 1940s and 1940s; see *Maurice Blanchot*, 224–27.

139. Jeune France lasted only two years, from 1940 to 1942. Philip Nord explains that its purpose was the "regeneration of French culture in an era of moral decay," and it also included Claude Roy and Jean de Fabrègues (in Lyon); Nord, "Pierre Schaeffer and *Jeune France*," 685, 692. See also Bident, *Maurice Blanchot*, 158–67.

140. Bident, *Maurice Blanchot*, 301.

141. Ibid., 297 n. 3. Maurice Blanchot, "Réflexions sur le surréalisme," 91.

142. Blanchot, "Réflexions sur le surréalisme," 91. On Blanchot and Heidegger, see Kleinberg, *Generation Existential*, 209–44.

143. Blanchot, "Réflexions sur le surréalisme," 91.

144. Ibid.," 101–2.

145. Butler, *Bodies That Matter*, 9.

146. On this, see Bourdieu, *Rules of Art*; for a historical study of this principle, see Sapiro, *La guerre des écrivains*.

147. Blanchot notoriously refused to have any photographs of himself released and consistently rejected requests for interviews.

148. Maurice Blanchot, "La littérature et le droit à la mort," in *La part du feu*, 296.

149. See also Yasuhara, "Maurice Blanchot dans les années 1930," 128–71.

150. Blanchot, letter to Roger Laporte, December 24, 1992, in Gill, *Maurice Blanchot*, 209–10.

151. Ibid.

152. Maurice Blanchot, "La seule manière d'être français," *L'Insurgé* (June 16, 1937), 4.

153. Blanchot, letter to Maurice Nadeau (1977), 18.

154. Maurice Blanchot, "Les lectures de l'Insurgé: *La dentelle du rempart*, par Charles Maurras, Grasset," *L'Insurgé* (February 24, 1937), 5.

155. Maurice Blanchot, "Les lectures de l'Insurgé: *Penser avec les mains*, par Denis de Rougemont, Albin Michel," *L'Insurgé* (January 27, 1937), 5.

156. Maurice Blanchot, "Les lectures de l'Insurgé: *Les vergers sur la mer*, Flammarion; *Mes idées politiques*, par Charles Maurras, Fayard," *L'Insurgé* (July 28, 1937), 5.

157. Blanchot, "Les lectures: *Les vergers sur la mer*," 5.

158. Ibid. (my italics).

159. Maurras's aesthetics are rarely considered when it comes to understanding the relationship—in his case as in those of Blanchot, Maulnier, and Brasillach—of aesthetics and politics; see Barko, *L'esthétique littéraire de Charles Maurras*.

160. Blanchot, "Les lectures: *La dentelle*," 5.

161. Ibid.

162. Blanchot, cited in a footnote, from a letter to the author, August 20, 1983, in Rubenstein, *What's Left?*, 187. See also letter to Maurice Nadeau, 18.

163. Blanchot, cited in a footnote, from a letter to the author, August 20, 1983, in Rubenstein, *What's Left?*, 187.

164. Mesnard argues that Blanchot practiced "bilingual writing"; *Maurice Blanchot*, 53. The theme of "duality" is a recurrent explanatory trope. See Verdès-Leroux, "homme double," *Refus et violences*, 19; Hill, "his relation to politics a dual one," *Blanchot*, 29. Hill, especially, argues for two languages fundamentally distinct from one another, 29. Kleinberg further reiterates this notion; *Generation Existential*, 214. Only recently have arguments been made regarding the intimate relationship between politics and literature in those years; see the rigorous study by Yasuhara, "Maurice Blanchot dans les années 1930"; and Yasuhara, "De la révolution à la littérature." Even Hill has somewhat shifted his earlier position; "'Not in Our Name.'"

165. Blanchot, "Réquisitoire contre la France"; and "De la révolution à la littérature," *L'Insurgé* (January 13, 1937), 6.

166. This recurring theme has been noted by Yasuhara, who insists, though, that Blanchot had a "tendency" to idealize political concepts. We part on our respective analyses of the role of literature in relation to politics; "Maurice Blanchot dans les années 1930," 126.

167. On this question, see Marineau, "Le concept d'aventure dans la prose narrative française du vingtième siècle"; also Hanna, *Mobilization of Intellect*.

168. See Jackson, *The Popular Front in France*, 113–30; Wardaugh, *In Pursuit of the People*, 56–73, 151–82.

169. Blanchot, "De la révolution à la littérature," 3.

170. Ibid.

171. Ibid.

172. Blanchot never reviewed Louis-Ferdinand Céline, despite the resonance, scandal, and controversies he had caused. This glaring absence makes sense insofar as Céline did not easily fit the aesthetics articulated by the Young New Right. One can also surmise that Céline would not be of interest to Blanchot since his novels and pamphlets fictionalized an abject body while Blanchot himself was preoccupied with liberatory disembodiment.

173. Maurice Blanchot, "Lectures de l'Insurgé: *Le magasin des travestis*, par G. Reyer, NRF; *Zobain*, par Raymond Guérin, NRF," *L'Insurgé* (February 17, 1937), 5. I am not,

however, commenting on Blanchot's post-1945 theorization of literature, a project that is obviously beyond the scope of this book and that others have tackled masterfully.

174. See Blanchot, *L'espace littéraire*; but also some excellent literary criticism in Gill, *Maurice Blanchot*.

175. Blanchot, "De la révolution à la littérature," 3.

176. Ibid.

177. Maurice Blanchot, "Lectures de l'Insurgé: *Nouvelle Histoire de Mouchette*, par George Bernanos, Plon," *L'Insurgé* (June 16, 1937), 5.

178. The meaning given to transcendence by Blanchot differs from the conception offered by Maulnier, though some, like Yasuhara, argue that it is not transcendence that Blanchot calls for.

179. Maurice Blanchot, "Lectures de l'Insurgé: *Les vagues*, par Virginia Woolf, Stock." *L'Insurgé* (September 9, 1937), 5.

180. Maurice Blanchot, "Lectures de l'Insurgé: *Maldagne*, par Hubert Chatelon, Librairie Gallimard," *L'Insurgé* (April 7, 1937), 5; "Lectures de l'Insurgé: *La maison au bord du monde*, par Jean Guirec, Albin Michel; *La rue du Chat-qui-pêche*, par Jolan Foldes, Albin Michel," *L'Insurgé* (May 19, 1937), 5.

181. Maurice Blanchot, "Les livres: Positions," *La Revue du Siècle* (October 1933), 75.

182. Ibid. 75–77.

183. Maurice Blanchot, "Lectures de l'Insurgé: *Sangs*, par Louise Hervieu, Denoël et Steele," *L'Insurgé* (January 20, 1937), 5; "Lectures: *Les vagues*," 5.

184. Blanchot will be concerned throughout his entire life with the ways in which language can translate the conditions of being, from *récits* to novels, or partial, fragmented writing, which he experimented with later in his life.

185. Blanchot, "De la révolution à la littérature," 3.

186. Maurice Blanchot praises the book he reviews in such terms; "Lectures: *Penser avec les mains*," 5.

187. Maurice Blanchot, "Lectures de l'Insurgé: *Le saladier*, par Marcel Jouhandeau, Librairie Gallimard," *L'Insurgé* (March 3, 1937), 5; "Lectures: *La maison au bord du monde*," 5.

188. Blanchot, " De la révolution à la littérature," 3.

189. Maurice Blanchot, "Lectures de l'Insurgé: *Lettre à un jeune poète*, par Rainer Maria Rilke, Grasset . . . ," *L'Insurgé* (August 25, 1937), 5.

190. Blanchot, "De la révolution à la littérature," 3.

191. Ibid.

192. Maurice Blanchot, "Les lectures de l'Insurgé: *Journal*, par Francois Mauriac, Grasset," *L'Insurgé* (May 26, 1937), 5.

193. Maurice Blanchot, "Les lectures de l'Insurgé: *Le démon du bien*, par Henry de Montherlant, Grasset," *L'Insurgé* (July 21, 1937), 5.

194. Blanchot, *Les intellectuels en question*, 11.

195. This is a remarkable omission considering his participation in the *Manifeste des 121* (and subsequent failed attempt at some transnational intellectual resistance), which he mentions only once, toward the end of this text; *Les intellectuels en question*, 58. See

Éric Hoppenot, "Avertissement," in Blanchot, *Écrits politiques*, 8–11. His biographer frames this text as part of Blanchot's general 1980s "moment of autobiographical unveiling," which, he argues, reveals Blanchot's concerns with testimony, memory, and accountability. On this, see Bident, *Maurice Blanchot*, 558–71.

196. Blanchot, *Les intellectuels en question*, 11.

197. Ibid., 10.

198. Ibid., 41. Scholars have also interrogated Bataille's fascination with fascism. See, for instance, Frost, *Sex Drives*, 59–79; Wolin, *The Seduction of Unreason*, 153–86; Falasca-Zamponi, "A Left Sacred or a Sacred Left?"

199. Blanchot, *Les intellectuels en question*, 41. The very structure of the sentence in French deliberately relegates the "I" of the author to its latter part and ends with that word in order for it to resonate, yet not be upfront, "truth."

200. Ibid., 37. Strikingly, this is the opportunity for Blanchot's biographer to write most clearly regarding Blanchot's antisemitism: "It is indeed antisemitism that has revealed Blanchot to himself not without some clashes [*non sans contrariétés*], in the infinite exigency of the arrival of the Other, the Absolute Other"; Bident, *Maurice Blanchot*, 566.

201. Thierry Maulnier, "Notes sur le fascisme," *Combat* (December 1938), 3.

202. Blanchot, *Les intellectuels en question*, 46.

203. Ibid., 47. Blanchot here actually switches from the present perfect to the present in the course of his description of the interwar French political situation.

204. Ibid., 52.

205. Ibid., 59. Deborah Hess argues that Blanchot's regret for articles liable to misinterpretation because of their "ironic mode" proves that he was absolutely not antisemitic. However, her claim relies on a rigid binary that does not attend to the complexity of the issue. It is in this sense that Blanchot differs from the case of Louis-Ferdinand Céline; see Hess, *Politics and Literature*, 14. Levinas himself wrote: "[Blanchot] has journeyed through a very personal evolution where he never compromised with himself"; cited in Bident, *Maurice Blanchot*, 38.

206. On Paulhan and Blanchot's literary and political "relationship," see Jenny, "Paulhan, Blanchot, and 'Le 14 juillet.'"

207. Blanchot has often, and at length, mentioned his long-lasting and important friendships, which have inspired his literary work, from Emmanuel Lévinas to René Char, Dionys Mascolo, and Robert Antelme, among others. See Bident, *Maurice Blanchot*.

208. See Michel Surya's biography, *Georges Bataille*. Critics have usually mentioned Blanchot's first reading of Nietzsche as the result of Bataille's influence. However, few have noted that Blanchot knew and wrote alongside Thierry Maulnier in the early 1930s and that Maulnier was then well known for his knowledge of Nietzsche—presumably unusual for a far-right journalist—since he had published an essay on Nietzsche in 1925.

209. On Bataille and the self, see Dean, *The Self and Its Pleasures*, esp. chaps. 5–7.

210. Blanchot, *La communauté inavouable*, 26–30.

211. Ibid., 28.

212. Blanchot, "De la révolution à la littérature," 3.

213. Ibid.

214. Ibid.

215. Blanchot, *Writing of the Disaster*, 78 (my italics). On Blanchot's postwar thought on freedom, see Gerounalos, *An Atheism That Is Not Humanist*, 251–67.

216. Blanchot, "Les lectures de l'Insurgé: *Journal*," 5.

217. Kleinberg, *Generation Existential*, 215. On Blanchot's relation to Judaism in his post-1945 thought (nonetheless disputing the presence of any antisemitism in Blanchot's work both before and after the war), see Hammerschlag, *The Figural Jew*, 166–200.

218. Scholars (such as Dominick LaCapra) have noted how "Jewishness" has indeed functioned in postmodern thought as that which signifies the inherent limits of modernity since it has come to work in the history of Western metaphysics as that which reveals its own failings. Yet, in the case of Blanchot, who had begun his career as a far-right journalist, that fetishistic obsession with Jewishness may come to carry a different meaning. See, for instance, Silverman, "Re-figuring the Jew in France."

CHAPTER 5

1. Lucien Wahl, *L'Information* (October 28, 1932), in Derval, *70 Critiques*, 15.

2. Jean Fréville, *L'Humanité* (December 19, 1932), in Derval, *70 Critiques*, 93.

3. André Rousseaux, *Le Figaro* (December 10, 1932), in Derval, *70 Critiques*, 68.

4. Georges Bataille, *La Critique Sociale* (January 1933), in Derval, *70 Critiques*, 117.

5. Jacques Victor de Laprade, "Le cas Céline," *La Revue du Siècle* (April 1933), 70, 71. A few months later, Émile Vaast also derided the manner in which pacifists had embraced this novel; "La révolte de Bardamu," *La Revue du Siècle* (September 1933), 74–75.

6. Hewitt, *Life of Céline*, 112–13. This excellent and impeccably researched biography charts the vagaries of Céline's life and career.

7. See Derval, *L'accueil critique*.

8. Maurice Blanchot, "Letter to Raymond Bellour" (1966), in Hill and Holland, "Blanchot's Epoch," 16.

9. Hewitt, *Life of Céline*, 171. Only recently have scholars begun emphasizing the need to take seriously the ballet librettos inserted in the pamphlet; see Dutoit, "Poetic Propaganda," esp. 155–97.

10. On Céline's borrowings and plagiarism, see the impressive work done by Alice Yaeger Kaplan, *Relevé des sources et citations dans "Bagatelles."*

11. He did publish a third pamphlet, *Les beaux draps*, in 1941. People paid little attention to this one because of its pessimistic tone. On Céline's relationship with conservative and far-right figures in the 1930s and the Vichy years, see Gibault, *Céline*, 179, 260, 282–83, 289, 296–97, and Hewitt, *Life of Céline*. On Céline's trial and his response, see Watts, *Allegories of the Purge*, 140–86.

12. Hewitt, *Life of Céline*, 225–56.

13. On the vagaries of Céline's postwar literary reputation, see Hewitt, "The Success of the *Monstre Sacré*."

14. Lucette Destouches explained that she had done so because they "came to life in a particular historical context, and at a particular moment" and " no longer need to exist"; Véronique Robert with Lucette Destouches, *Céline secret*, 128.

15. This last position is the one offered by Hewitt in his nuanced and thoughtful biography, *Life of Céline*. Against the few who have taken Céline's politics seriously (such as Philippe Alméras and Yves Pagès, among others), most well-known readers of Céline tend to stress the aesthetics over the political. This is especially the case for Godard, *Poétique de Céline*, and Kristeva, *Powers of Horror*.

16. See, for instance, Solomon, "Céline on the 1937 Paris Exposition Universelle as Jewish Conspiracy," 71. See also Gibault, *Céline*; Hewitt, *Life of Céline*; and Émile Brami's recent biography, *Céline*, which—unusually—mostly cites Céline's own writings as a way of fictionalizing his life.

17. This characterizes the analysis of Céline's most preeminent expert, Henri Godard, in *Poétique de Céline*. Kristeva argues that the pamphlets should be read *alongside* the fiction; *Powers of Horror*, 174.

18. Even critics who have analyzed the themes of race and antisemitism in Céline's works tend to turn to biography and "private" or unpublished writings to elucidate this issue. See, for instance, Alméras, *Les idées de Céline*; Séébold, *Essai de situation des pamphlets de Louis-Ferdinand Céline*, 108–9.

19. Carroll, *French Literary Fascism*, 173.

20. Scullion, "Choreographing Sexual Difference"; Spears, "Virility and the Jewish 'Invasion' in Céline's Pamphlets"; Forrest, "The (Con)Quest of the Other." But these do not examine the interplay with race. Godard acknowledges race but downplays its importance; *Poétique de Céline*, 186, 206, 200.

21. See Scullion, "Style, Subversion, Modernity."

22. Even Scullion, who has, so far, authored the most incisive work on Céline, variously analyzing how gender, race, and nation are articulated in his work, calls him an "extremist"; ibid., 181, 185. See Richard, *L'anarchisme*; Pagès, *Les fictions du politique*. For a rigorous and thorough examination of the structure, references, rhetoric, and immediate context of *Bagatelles* by a literary scholar, see Tettamanzi, *Esthétique de l'outrance*.

23. Éric Séébold also makes the point that race constituted Céline's enduring obsession, but his short essay unfortunately hardly elaborates or historicizes; *Essai de situation des pamphlets de Louis-Ferdinand Céline*, 108–9. Similarly, Philippe Alméras has powerfully argued for the presence of race and racism throughout Céline's entire life and works. But, in doing so, he uses biographical and private correspondence, whereas I am interested in the discursive effects of Céline's texts. Alméras, who rightly identifies the inseparability of Céline's ideology and literary poetics, notes rather than investigates the structure of Céline's antisemitism; *Les idées de Céline*.

24. For instance, Scullion, "Style, Subversion, Modernity," 185.

25. Ibid., 190.

26. While arguing, like many before him, that *Voyage* is a novel denouncing colonization, Godard does concede that "degeneration" constitutes an enduring theme and that, in the face of a degeneration that Céline bemoans, he wishes to "restore a former order of things in its mythical purity." However, like Kristeva, he refutes its centrality and suggests it might be the misguided but "natural reaction" of an author "judging national identity in danger"; *Poétique de Céline*, 186, 206, 200.

27. Kristeva rightly points out that "isolating [the pamphlets] from the whole of his writings constitutes a defensive claim on the part of the left or right," an insight that I take as my point of departure. She adds that "the pamphlets provide the phantasmatic substratum on which . . . the novelistic works were built." However, this is not merely "an ideological stance," as she insists, but an interpretative framework produced by the disciplinary demand of literature and history; *Powers of Horror*, 174. For an astute critique of Céline's own invocation of "style" as a strategy to dismiss the problematic political content of his pamphlets (and Kristeva's somewhat mimetic gesture), see Carroll, *French Literary Fascism*, 171–95. On degeneracy and masculinity, see Surkis, "Enemies Within."

28. On the imperial racialization at work in Western aesthetics, see Said, *Culture and Imperialism*, and Mercer, *Cosmopolitan Modernisms*, among others.

29. Rabinbach, *The Human Motor*, 6.

30. Panchasi, "Reconstructions," 110.

31. On abjection, see Sanos, "From Revolution to Literature." On the bodily imaginary at work in *Voyage*, see Destrual, "Le corps s'écrit."

32. Stoler, *Race and the Education of Desire*, 9.

33. Said, *Culture and Imperialism*, 3–61.

34. Solomon, "Céline on the 1937 Paris Exposition Universelle as Jewish Conspiracy," 73.

35. Gilman, *The Jew's Body*; Mosse, *Nationalism and Sexuality*; Garb and Nochlin, *The Jew in the Text*; Birnbaum, *Un mythe politique*, esp. 196–236.

36. On the role of the metaphor of the "body" and use of the trope of victim, see Watts, *Allegories of the Purge*, 140–63.

37. Céline, preface to the 1952 Gallimard edition, *Journey to the End of the Night*, 1.

38. Hewitt, *Life of Céline*, 253–54. The presiding judge did not realize that Destouches was the infamous novelist Céline.

39. Interview with Pierre Dumayet, "Lectures pour Tous" (RTF, 1957), in *Céline vivant*.

40. Céline, *Les beaux draps*, 26.

41. Céline, *Journey*, 357.

42. On authorship as a social and cultural position, one that brings the "author" into being, see Foucault, "Qu'est-ce qu'un auteur?"

43. On the negotiations of authorship, see the very insightful work by Roussin, *Misère de la littérature, terreur de l'histoire*, 25. On the use of "Ferdinand" throughout Céline's works of fiction, see also Godard, *Poétique de Céline*, 286–95.

44. Spears, "Céline and 'Autofictional' First-Person Narration," 363.

45. Ibid., 357.

46. Dominique Aury, "Exposition du Front Populaire: Paris défiguré," *L'Insurgé* (April 7, 1937), 2.

47. Lucien Bernard, "L'architecture de l'Exposition déshonore l'art français," *L'Insurgé* (May 26, 1937), 8; Thierry Maulnier, "Cherchez ailleurs l'exposition," *L'Insurgé* (May 26, 1937), 7.

48. Céline, *Bagatelles*, 125.

49. This point is made, among others, by Marks, *Marrano as Metaphor*, 70–84. On Céline and the 1937 Exposition universelle, see Solomon, "Céline and the 1937 Paris Exposition Universelle as Jewish Conspiracy," 60–87; and Dutoit, "Poetic Propaganda," 31–92—though we part company on our interpretation of the pamphlet and the continuity of Céline's ideas.

50. Céline, *L'Église*, 66, 124.

51. Robert Brasillach, "On Rereading *Journey*," *La Révolution Nationale* (September 25, 1943), cited in Stanford, *Céline and His Critics*, 49.

52. Loselle, "Traveling in the Work of Louis-Ferdinand Céline," 96.

53. On the genealogy of "war literature" and a recovery of the work of novelist Pierre Mac Orlan (who can be seen as a precursor to Céline), see Marineau, "Le concept d'aventure dans la prose narrative française du vingtième siècle," 219–322.

54. Bochner, "Blaise Without War."

55. Céline, *Bagatelles*, 216.

56. On travel and tourism as tropes, thematic structures, and critique of modernity, see Loselle's astute and thoughtful study "Traveling in the Work of Louis-Ferdinand Céline," esp. 20–106, where Loselle demonstrates how Céline's first novel owed much to the visions authored by conservative writers Paul Morand and Georges Duhamel. See also Loselle, *History's Double*. On travel and tourism as colonial enterprises, see Barrel, "Death on the Nile"; Furlough, "Une leçon de choses."

57. Hewitt, *Life of Céline*, 63.

58. Godard, *Poétique de Céline*, 71.

59. Ibid., 71, 167. Much of Godard's study is devoted to recovering what he argues to be Céline's innovative re-creation of the French language and the aesthetics of his novelistic writing.

60. Michael Levenson explains that their work has been described as embodying common obsessions: "The recurring act of fragmenting unities (unities of character or plot or pictorial space or lyric form), the use of mythic paradigms, the refusal of norms of beauty, the willingness to make radical linguistic experiments, all often inspired by the resolve (in Eliot's phrase) to startle and disturb the public"—all of which can also be used for Céline; Levenson, *The Cambridge Companion to Modernism*, 3.

61. Said, *Orientalism*, and especially *Culture and Imperialism*. Jameson, "Modernism and Imperialism," 44, 54; on the ways in which race functioned in the very stylistic and linguistic innovations of Anglo-American modernists (especially Ezra Pound, T. S. Eliot, and Gertrude Stein, among others) and a reconsideration of the decisive role of African American culture and literature in this canonical aesthetics, see North, *The Dialect of Modernism*.

62. Said, *Culture and Imperialism*, 188. Some critics have acknowledged the insistent presence of "colonial ideology" in Céline's writings, but they confine it to his description of his trip to Africa, where, we are told, he expressed a depiction of Africa "through the cultural filter of those who wrote about the colonies," from Pierre Loti to Rudyard Kipling and Joseph Conrad. See, for instance, Hewitt, *Life of Céline*, 37.

63. On the ways in which "race and musical style became a central way of thinking

about jazz music during the 1920s and 1930s," see Jackson, *Making Jazz French*, 25. On jazz and anxieties regarding French culture, see Jordan, *Le jazz.*

64. On this, see Mitterand, "Nègres et négriers."

65. Céline, *Journey*, 95.

66. Ibid., 121.

67. Ibid., 119.

68. Ibid., 44–45.

69. Ibid., 59.

70. On the ways in which gender constituted a marker of social order in the interwar years, see Mary Louise Roberts, who explains that "gender was central to how change was understood in the post-war decade"; *Civilization Without Sexes*, 4–5; Dean, *The Frail Social Body*; Forrest, "The (Con)Quest of the Other," 120–39.

71. On the discursive articulation of bodies, empire, and geography, see the excellent study by Jennings, *Curing the Colonizers.*

72. Céline, *Journey*, 270–74.

73. On "interwar Paris as a colonial space" where "the specter of 'empire'"—through the presence of colonial migrants, anti-imperialist, and feminist artists and intellectuals—"guided the self-identification of its residents as well as their social and political interactions," see Boittin, *Colonial Metropolis*, xiv–xv.

74. Brasillach, *Notre avant-guerre*, 245.

75. Céline, *Bagatelles*, 45.

76. Brasillach, *Notre avant-guerre*, 245.

77. Céline, *Bagatelles*, 28–29.

78. This short story was published in 1788: slaves are good and obedient, and while the main characters live in an idealized setting, they are threatened by the corruption of Parisian society. Saint-Pierre, *Paul et Virginie.*

79. On the ways in which late-eighteenth-century literature fictionalized anxieties regarding creolization and racial boundaries and articulated incestuous fantasies of familial kinship, see Garraway, *The Libertine Colony.*

80. Céline, *Bagatelles*, 30.

81. Ibid.

82. Jennings, *Curing the Colonizers*, 8–39.

83. Céline, *Journey*, 98.

84. Céline, *Bagatelles*, 39. On the politics of jazz dancing, see Jordan, *Le jazz*, 67–72.

85. Céline, *Bagatelles*, 38–39.

86. Ibid. On the ways America figured in the interwar French cultural imagination—most notably around an obsession with the "future"—see Panchasi, *Future Tense.* On jazz and modernity, see Jordan, *Le jazz*, 94–98.

87. Céline, *Bagatelles*, 39.

88. The libretto strikingly mines many of the themes and tropes of *l'art nègre* that influenced so many in those years. On this, see Blake, *Le Tumulte Noir*; on jazz, its cultural meaning and reception in France, see Jackson, *Making Jazz French*, esp. 27–32, 40–46, 71–103; also Jordan, *Le jazz.*

89. Jackson, *Making Jazz French*, 78.

90. Céline, *Journey*, 112, 108.

91. Céline, *Bagatelles*, 31, 37.

92. Ibid., 186. Céline specifically refers to the "African tam-tam" he heard in Cameroon and that he can now hear in metropolitan France; ibid., 203. His account strikingly echoes his description of Bardamu in Africa in *Voyage*.

93. The original reads: "pauvre simple con d'indigène français"—a phrase that recurs throughout the pamphlet; Céline, *Bagatelles*, 45.

94. On the blackness of the "Jew" in antisemitic rhetoric, see Gilman, *The Jew's Body*, 171–74. On the "Orientalization" of the Jews, see Malchow, *Gothic Images of Race*, esp. 149–65. On the "ambivalence" of the figure of the Jew in Western racial thought, see Cheyette, "Neither Black nor White."

95. Brown, "Tolerance and Equality," 20.

96. Céline, *Bagatelles*, 191–92. See also Séébold, *Essai de situation des pamphlets de Louis-Ferdinand Céline*, 54.

97. Céline, *Bagatelles*, 47. Stoler, *Race and the Education of Desire*, 7–9, 11.

98. Céline, *Bagatelles*, 173.

99. Ibid., 113.

100. Ibid., 58.

101. Ibid., 77.

102. Céline, *L'école des cadavres*, 31.

103. Céline, *Bagatelles*, 131, 268.

104. Ibid., 97.

105. Ibid., 97, 49.

106. Ibid., 131.

107. Ibid., 187. On the trope of black male sexuality articulated around "a masculine fantasy of mastery and control," see Mercer, "Reading Racial Fetishism," 311.

108. Céline, *Bagatelles*, 67.

109. Ibid., 97.

110. The noun is mentioned fairly early on for a four-hundred-page work; ibid., 49–51.

111. Céline specifically uses the term "Français de race"; ibid., 243, 250.

112. Ibid., 67.

113. Ibid. Céline uses the term "Aryan" in both *Bagatelles* and *L'école des cadavres*, but not in *Les beaux draps*, which, despite antisemitic references, focuses more on communism, the French defeat, and relation with Nazi Germany.

114. Céline, *Bagatelles*, 67.

115. Ibid., 68.

116. Ibid., 58.

117. Céline, *L'école des cadavres*, 25.

118. Ibid., 28.

119. Céline, *Bagatelles*, 318.

120. Céline, *Journey*, 233. On the delineation of a feminine ideal and the gendering of the social body in Céline's fiction, see Forrest, "The (Con)Quest of the Other," 120–39.

121. Céline, *Journey*, 64.

122. Ibid., 44.

123. Ibid., 259.

124. Ibid., 224. The descriptions of female bodies in this manner echo, as Philippe Roussin has remarked, the thesis that Louis-Ferdinand Céline had authored at the beginning of his medical career, *La vie et l'oeuvre de Philippe Ignace Semmelweiss* (1924). Roussin argues that Céline weaves together in his exploration of the work of Dr. Semmelweiss the themes of sex and death; *Misère de la littérature*, 51–54. Few critics have systematically analyzed the ways in which female bodies figure in Céline's fiction and pamphlets. Hewitt, for instance, remarks briefly that, as one critic has pointed out, female bodies can both provide "plastic beauty" and also act as "agents of death" and decomposition, but he does not elaborate; *Life of Céline*, 52.

125. Céline, *Bagatelles*, 59.

126. I use David Carroll's expression in relation to Drieu La Rochelle's fascism. However, Carroll does not consider the issue of gender and sexual difference as one that is intrinsically concerned with the mapping of an "antisemitic body"; Carroll, *French Literary Fascism*, 160. On *Voyage* similarly offering an "imaginary of the health and sick body" that is also gendered, see Destrual, "Le corps s'écrit," 66.

127. Céline, *Bagatelles*, 97.

128. Dean, *The Frail Social Body*, 16.

129. Panchasi, "Reconstructions," 110.

130. Scullion, introduction to *Céline and the Politics of Difference*, 7.

131. Mosse, *The Image of Man*, 14.

132. Spears argues, as I do, for a reading of Céline's pamphlets as driven by an obsessional concern with virile masculinity, and situating the fantasized and racialized figure of the Jew within this logic. While he eloquently offers an analysis of the relationship between sexuality and Céline's writing, noting the "virilized call for arms Céline issues in his pamphlets," the association between Jews and blacks, the haunting danger of sodomy, and the desire for "phallic power," Spears turns to a biographical explanation. For him—as for many others as well—such texts show "an obvious persecution complex" and "blustering machismo." While we identify similar themes, I differ in my understanding of Céline's fantasies, as I argue that they are situated within a larger French interwar cultural discourse of gender, race, and sexuality; Spears, "Virility and the Jewish 'Invasion' in Céline's Pamphlets," 117, 99, 110, 111, 109, 104, 110.

133. On the cultural and political fantasies of Jewish bodies, see Gilman, *The Jew's Body*.

134. Céline, *Bagatelles*, 156.

135. Kristeva, *Powers of Horror*, 4.

136. Céline, *Bagatelles*, 129.

137. Ibid., 49.

138. Ibid., 127.

139. Dean, *The Self and Its Pleasures*, 3.
140. Céline, *Bagatelles*, 156.
141. Ibid., 226.
142. Ibid., 125.
143. Ibid., 14.
144. Ibid., 27.
145. Ibid., 49.
146. Ibid., 57.
147. On French antisemitic iconography, see, for instance, Kleeblatt, *The Dreyfus Affair*. See also Birnbaum, *Un mythe politique* and *"La France aux français."*
148. Céline, *Bagatelles*, 53. Gilman charts how such rhetorical tropes were articulated and disseminated throughout the nineteenth century, especially through medical literature; see Gilman, *The Jew's Body*, 38–59.
149. Céline, *Bagatelles*, 98–117.
150. Ibid., 97.
151. Ibid., 241.
152. Ibid., 129.
153. Ibid., 132.
154. Circumcision directly evokes castration. On the role of the phallus, castration, and fantasy in the constitution of subjectivity and identity, see Jacques Lacan, *Écrits 1*, especially "La signification du phallus," 103–15, and "Subversion du sujet et dialectique du désir dans l'inconscient freudien," 151–91. See also Miller, *Lacan*.
155. Céline, *Bagatelles*, 66.
156. This sentence indeed concludes not only the paragraph but this section devoted to the Jews and the massacres of World War I; ibid., 95.
157. There is a constant oscillation between these two positions; ibid., 170.
158. Ibid., 106.
159. Ibid., 107.
160. Ibid., 121.
161. Ibid., 83. The French word (*chandelle*, candle), could mean either a rifle or a wine bottle, or it could refer to mucus in nineteenth-century slang. I have chosen the reference to liquid, though that translation may be debatable. Lorédan Larchey, *Dictionnaire de l'argot parisien* (Paris: Les Éditions de Paris, 1996), 85.
162. Céline, *Bagatelles*, 62.
163. Ibid., 71.
164. Ibid., 129.
165. Ibid., 61.
166. Ibid., 97. Kristeva, Spears, and others have noted and commented on the obsession with sodomy and homosexuality that pervades Céline's pamphlets. See Kristeva, *Powers of Horror*, 183–84; Spears, "Virility and Jewish 'Invasion' in Céline's Pamphlets," 111–14.
167. Céline, *Bagatelles*, 326.
168. Roberts, *Civilization Without Sexes*, 37–41.
169. Céline, *Bagatelles*, 89.

170. Ibid., 275.

171. Ibid., 89.

172. Ibid., 120–21.

173. Ibid., 114.

174. Ibid., 128.

175. Maxence, *Histoire de dix ans*, 114. I have imperfectly translated Céline's words: "La France est une nation femelle, toujours bonne à tourner morue"; *Bagatelles*, 243. This formulation is almost identical to what Céline declared in a 1934 letter to a friend in which he explained, "France is an old female [*femelle*] who is emptying herself like these women, in Africa, whose periods last weeks. It's that repulsive hemorrhage"; cited in Alméras, *Les idées de Céline*, 105 (my translation).

176. Céline, *Bagatelles*, 243.

177. Céline, *L'école des cadavres*, 25.

178. Stoler, *Race and the Education of Desire*, 15.

179. Céline, *Journey*, 183.

180. See Forrest's very astute reading of the ways in which voyeurism structures Ferdinand's heterosexual male desire in *Voyage*, more specifically in relation to American female bodies; "The (Con)Quest of the Other," 120–39. On Céline's voyeurism and fetishism, see Scullion, "Choreographing Sexual Difference."

181. Céline, *Bagatelles*, 47.

182. Céline, *Journey*, 170, 195.

183. Céline, *Bagatelles*, 40. Scullion explains how ballet obsessed Céline; "Choreographing Sexual Difference," 140, 150–52. For the figure of the New Woman, see Roberts, *Civilization Without Sexes*, 76.

184. Scullion's reading of the articulation of gender, sexuality, and masculinity in Céline's texts rightly points to his unabashed heteronormative and masculinist vision. However, Scullion turns to Céline's letters as evidence of this vision. As others have commented, this vision can be found in his published works. Scullion, "Choreographing Sexual Difference," 141, 142.

185. Céline, *Bagatelles*, 12.

186. Solomon-Godeau, "The Legs of the Countess," 289. On the violence masked in producing aesthetic pleasure in ballet, see also Scullion, "Choreographing Sexual Difference." Dutoit argues that "Ferdinand's erotic desires seem to be elicited by a nostalgia for a mystical whole, one that entails the death of individual self"; "Poetic Propaganda," 163.

187. Brown, "Tolerance and Equality," 35.

188. I follow Scullion's analysis in this respect but insist upon the racialized heteronormativity inherent in Céline's vision—which, in its tension between the abject and the sacred, echoes Georges Bataille. Scullion, "Choreographing Sexual Difference," 157, 161.

189. On the ways in which (ideological) fantasies sustain social identity, see Žižek, *Plague of Fantasies*.

190. Céline, *Bagatelles*, 12.

191. Louis-Ferdinand Céline, "Lettre, 1938," cited in Alméras, *Lettres des années noires*, 12.

192. Céline, *Bagatelles*, 13.

193. Scullion, “Choreographing Sexual Difference,” 144–46.

194. This is Ann Laura Stoler’s expression; *Race and the Education of Desire*, 184.

195. Céline’s second novel, *Mort à crédit*, published in 1936, was not as successful as hoped and found a mixed reception. This was followed by the publication of his first political pamphlet, *Mea culpa*, at the end of the same year. On this, see Gibault, *Céline*, 118–29. See Derval’s insightful introduction, *L’accueil critique*, 7–33.

196. René Vincent, “Louis-Ferdinand Céline: *L’école des cadavres*,” *Combat* (January 1939), 14.

197. René Vincent, “Les aveux du juif Céline,” *Combat* (March 1938), 13.

198. Ibid., 13.

199. Those are the terms used by Kristeva in her essay on abjection, which focuses on Céline’s particular vision. Kristeva has been rightly criticized for her exclusive focus on Céline’s aesthetics at the expense of any consideration of the political content of his abject vision. See *Powers of Horror*.

200. I am borrowing Edward Said’s expression; *Culture and Imperialism*, 129.

201. Vincent, “Louis-Ferdinand Céline,” 14.

202. Lucien Rebatet, “‘Bagatelles pour un massacre,’” *Je Suis Partout* (January 21, 1938), 8.

203. Ibid.

204. Louis-Ferdinand Céline, “Morceaux choisis: ‘Bagatelles pour un Massacre,’” *Je Suis Partout* (March 4, 1938), 8.

205. Lucien Rebatet, “Les émigrés politiques: Peut-on éviter les pogroms?” *Je Suis Partout* (March 4, 1938), 4.

206. Céline, *Bagatelles pour un Massacre*, 8.

207. On this topic, see Alméras, *Les idées de Céline*, esp. 161–252; and Gibault, *Céline*, 221–304.

208. As some critics have noted, Brasillach was ambivalent in his reception of *Bagatelles*, but he did ultimately welcome Céline as part of *Je Suis Partout*’s pantheon of authors. Both Brasillach and Rebatet took their distance from Céline when he published *L’école des cadavres* in 1938. Indeed, it was not as well received as his first pamphlet and did not sell well. Hewitt, *Life of Céline*, 113, 178; see also Scullion, “Style, Subversion, Modernity,” 184, 271 n. 29.

209. This nostalgia is also noted by Scullion; “Style, Subversion, Modernity,” 192.

CHAPTER 6

1. François Vinneuil (pseudonym of Lucien Rebatet), “Le Cinéma: Un film soviétique: *Frontière*; Un film fasciste: *Vérités sur l’Italie*,” *Je Suis Partout* (May 23, 1936), 4. Hereafter cited as *JSP*.

2. Ibid.; Dorsay, “Au-delà de l’expérience Blum,” *JSP* (May 30, 1936), front page.

3. François Vinneuil, “Le film de l’Olympiade 1936,” *JSP* (July 8, 1938), 9.

4. Ibid.

5. Jeannine Verdès-Leroux actually asserts that their ideological stand remains “un-

explainable," but she is one of the very few historians to recognize the centrality of antisemitism to *Je Suis Partout*'s ideological positions; *Refus et violences*, 24.

6. Pierre-Marie Dioudonnat's study remains the only one to date. It is empirically rigorous but more "recovery" than analysis: he dismisses accusations of fascism and antisemitism by arguing that the newspaper merely displayed an "extreme form of nationalism." He explains its turn to fascism as the expression of a "metaphysical anguish." It is important to note that this study was published by La Table Ronde, a right-wing publishing house set up by Thierry Maulnier and others after 1945. See Dioudonnat, *"Je Suis Partout,"* 7–8.

7. Dorsay, "Le jeu des hommes et des partis," *JSP* (January 4, 1936), 2.

8. Pierre Gaxotte, "Chacun doit se situer: Oui il faut des réformes," *JSP* (June 27, 1936), front page.

9. Pierre Gaxotte, "Ils seront vaincus mais il faut se battre," *JSP* (July 4, 1936), front page.

10. This a posteriori description came from one of *Je Suis Partout*'s most virulent journalists, Lucien Rebatet; *Les décombres*, 52.

11. In his 1941 memoirs, Robert Brasillach pointed to 1936 as the originary moment for the French far right's revelation and embrace of fascism; despite his retrospective description, 1936 undoubtedly constituted a foundational moment for *Je Suis Partout* journalists; *Notre avant-guerre*, 233.

12. On this history of French Jews, assimilation, and universalism, see Hyman, *The Jews of Modern France*.

13. Brasillach, "Introduction à l'esprit fasciste: III. Un type humain nouveau," *JSP* (July 8, 1938), 3. This article was part of a series of three successive columns, titled "Lettre à une provinciale," that Brasillach devoted to the question of fascism.

14. The contributors mentioned have been identified according to the significance of their journalistic writings, presence, and the content of their articles. For a fully detailed and complete list of the many *Je Suis Partout* collaborators—occasional and regular—see Pierre-Marie Dioudonnat, *Les 700 rédacteurs de "Je Suis Partout."* I owe this expression to Judith Surkis.

15. One of the first insightful studies on this question was David Carroll's *French Literary Fascism*. But Carroll does not examine how *Je Suis Partout* participated in this particular movement, focusing only on the figure of novelist Robert Brasillach.

16. Birnbaum, *Un mythe politique*, 15.

17. Renata Salecl explains that the nation, in such discourses, functions as "traumatic elements around [which] fantasies are interlaced." It is conceived as something that "always returns . . . articulat[ing] the fantasy structure which serves as support to ethnic hatred"; 418. According to her, those are fantasies of an Other stealing one's enjoyment; "National Identity and Socialist Moral Majority," 418–24. On fantasy, see Žižek, *Plague of Fantasies*.

18. The issue that preoccupied these men was first and foremost how virility might be restored (a concern shared by "gay men [who] wished to renew and regenerate virility," according to Carolyn Dean) and is to be situated within a larger cultural discourse on the nature of the category of homosexuality. See Dean, *The Frail Social Body*, 162.

On the reaffirmation of "proper" gender roles, especially focusing on the redemptive power of motherhood, in the postwar years, see Roberts, *Civilization Without Sexes*. On masculinity and nationalism, see the seminal work of George Mosse, *The Image of Man*.

19. See Carolyn Dean's analysis of the cultural redefinition of "sexuality" in interwar France, *The Frail Social Body*. On the history of homosexuality as a category of abjection—and its association with Jewishness—see also Dean, "'The Open Secret.'"

20. The association of fascism and homosexuality has been analyzed by Hewitt, *Political Inversions*; by Dean, *Fragility of Empathy*; and, within the context of a post-1945 German discourse equating Nazism to sexual repression, by Herzog, *Sex After Fascism*. On the ways in which that association was already at work in the 1930s, especially from the anti-fascist left, see Meyers, "Feminizing Fascist Men."

21. See Carroll, *French Literary Fascism*, and his discussion of Klaus Theweleit's theory of fascist masculinity, 148–59.

22. Thierry Maulnier, "L'oeuvre critique," 67, in Sipriot, *Robert Brasillach et la génération perdue*.

23. On the ways this portrayal—manufactured by far-right writers themselves in the wake of his execution—has helped depoliticize Brasillach, see Mazgaj, "Ce mal de siècle."

24. Sartre, "Qu'est-ce qu'un collaborateur?" in *Situations III*. As historians have rightly explained, Sartre's depiction of collaborators as less than "proper" men because they were tainted with the accusation of homosexuality also meant that Vichy collaborators were no longer considered French: sexuality in post-1945 France served to symbolically exclude individuals from the bounds of the French citizenry, thus participating in the production of the enduring myth that Vichy—and its supporters considered to be traitors—had not been a French initiative but was forced upon the "real France" by a German occupier that had thus violated the national character. On the ways gender and sexuality were central to Sartre's analysis of antisemitism and collaboration, see Judaken, "The Queer Jew"; on Sartre's relationship to Jewishness, see Judaken, *Jean-Paul Sartre and the Jewish Question*.

25. Watts, *Allegories of the Purge*, 31.

26. Kaplan, *The Collaborator*, 164; on the French obsession with masculinity in the post–World War I years, see Roberts, *Civilization Without Sexes*; Panchasi, "Reconstructions."

27. Jonathan Judaken makes a similar point about how antisemitic images can be deployed even by those fighting it and explains that gender played a central role in that deployment; "The Queer Jew," 47, 57.

28. Watts, *Allegories of the Purge*, 31.

29. Kaplan, *The Collaborator*, xii.

30. Ibid., 7.

31. Ibid., 7.

32. Kaplan explains: "Whatever the reality of his sexual life, Brasillach's writing suggests a homoerotic attraction to the rituals of fascism," a rhetorical disclaimer, since the question of Brasillach's homosexuality is one of the first questions she discusses in her introduction. She repeatedly refers to Brasillach's prose as marred by an unabashed

admiration for the power of friendship and love between men and a certain sentimentality, which signifies, in her prose, a particular tendency to homoeroticism; ibid., 8. This especially resurfaces in her previous study of "fascist intellectuals"; *Reproductions of Banality.*

33. Kaplan, *The Collaborator*, 7–8, 239–40. The question is not whether Brasillach was truly homosexual or not but how those categories helped define the self, the citizen, and the nation and circulated in these texts. Like Meyers, I am not interested in bringing fascist or far-right intellectuals "out of the closet" but in examining, as he put it, the "cultural work" performed by the ways in which gender, sexuality, and race are imbricated and articulated in the writings of these men. For an analysis of the relationships between homosexuality, fascism, and antisemitism (in relation to another interwar novelist, Marcel Jouhandeau, who also contributed to *JSP*), see Eribon, *Hérésies.*

34. Belot, *Lucien Rebatet.*

35. Birnbaum himself falls prey to such a description when speaking of novelist Drieu La Rochelle; *Un mythe politique*, 229.

36. This is rather typical of accounts of Rebatet's ideological commitment; Gaussen, "Maurras et Lucien Rebatet," 16. See also Belot, *Lucien Rebatet.*

37. Belot, *Lucien Rebatet*, 88; for an exposition of the themes and issues in Rebatet's novel, a thinly disguised autobiography published in 1952, see Ifri, *Les deux étendards.* Even though Rebatet began publishing again in the 1950s, he remained bitter because of the lack of success of the novel that he had hoped would rescue him from the shame of his past as a polemical pamphleteer.

38. On this, see Dean, *Fragility of Empathy*, 107.

39. There has surprisingly been little work on this question in *Je Suis Partout*, except Tumblety, "Revenge of the Fascist Knights."

40. On this issue, see Mosse, *Nationalism and Sexuality*; Mosse, *The Image of Man*; and Dean, *The Frail Social Body*, in which she demonstrates that "sexuality was central in shaping who was and was not included in the category 'French,'" in interwar France through the metaphorical delineation of the social body; 15.

41. Dioudonnat, *"Je Suis Partout,"* 29–34.

42. Gaxotte's role in encouraging and allowing for these young far-right intellectuals to "emerge" has been underestimated by historians. Indeed, his influence and the role he played in these men's lives as mentor can be witnessed in a Brasillach article devoted to Gaxotte, "Portrait de la France," *JSP* (January 30, 1937), but also in the violence unleashed against Gaxotte by most *Je Suis Partout* journalists (Rebatet, Cousteau, Laubreaux) in the 1940s when he decided to disavow their politics and distance himself from them. Cousteau and Rebatet's prison memoirs also illustrate the sense of betrayal they experienced. See Cousteau and Rebatet, *Dialogues de "vaincus."*

43. Similar inserts can be found throughout 1937. Insert, *Je Suis Partout* (December 31, 1938), front page.

44. Rebatet, *Les décombres*, 41.

45. See Dioudonnat, *"Je Suis Partout,"* for further details.

46. Those are figures for March 1939; Bellanger et al., *Histoire générale*, 511.

47. Reading *JSP* confirms Dioudonnat's description of its evolution as incremental. Dioudonnat correctly writes that "[*JSP*] never suffered any brutal transformation: it evolved in barely noticeable variations, discreet changes and little-apparent breaks"; *"Je Suis Partout,"* 7–8.

48. Sapiro, *La guerre des écrivains,* 39. The police report is no longer available in the police archives but was reprinted in Kingston, *Anti-Semitism in France During the 1930s,* 11–74.

49. Berstein, *La France des années trente,* 130. See also Jackson, *The Popular Front in France.*

50. See Dioudonnat, *"Je Suis Partout."*

51. Anonymous insert, *JSP* (May 16, 1936), front page.

52. Dorsay, "Après le coup d'état radical," *JSP* (January 25, 1936), front page.

53. Pierre Gaxotte, "Quinze mois de Front Populaire," in "Le Front Populaire," special issue, *JSP* (September 24, 1937), front page.

54. Anonymous insert, *JSP*, front page

55. Dorsay, "Après le coup d'état radical," 2.

56. Anonymous insert, "Ce qu'est *Je Suis Partout*," *JSP* (January 2, 1937), 2. The same insert appeared on December 31, 1937.

57. He had originally offered the position to Lucien Rebatet, who refused it, thus revealing that Gaxotte was certainly not adverse to a radicalization of *JSP* politics, since Rebatet was, alongside Cousteau, one of its most viciously conservative contributors; Dioudonnat, *"Je Suis Partout,"* 125.

58. Rebatet famously described the *JSP* group as a "soviet," emphasizing their tight-knit and collegial atmosphere; *Les décombres*, 43.

59. Brasillach, *Notre avant-guerre*, 90. Of course, one should take into account Brasillach's own propensity for nostalgia and romanticization of a particular instance of male friendship which he upheld as dearest to him and which inevitably shaped the way he recounted, in 1941, the emergence of their journalistic venture. Indeed, he added that this experience "was a rare and beautiful thing"; ibid.

60. Ibid., 274.

61. Dorsay, "Où sont maintenant les vraies forces?" *JSP* (February 22, 1936), 2.

62. Robert Brasillach, "Oraison funèbre pour M. Gide," *La Revue Française* (November 30, 1930); "La fin de l'après-guerre," *Candide* (August 27–September 24, 1931).

63. Lucien Rebatet, "Les Juifs," special issue, *JSP* (April 15, 1938); "Les Juifs et la France," special issue, *JSP* (February 17, 1939).

64. Cousteau also penned "The Soviets' Russia," special issue, *JSP* (April 4, 1936); see Dioudonnat, *"Je Suis Partout,"* 65–66.

65. Alain Laubreaux, "Sur la scène: Jeu de massacre," *JSP* (January 28, 1938), 9.

66. Monnier, *À l'ombre des têtes molles*, 90. Gabriel Jeantet, like many of the *JSP* journalists, never ceased his far-right activities and can be traced after 1945 through the 1970s as an active member of marginal far-right organizations. See Weber, *L'Action française*, 436–43.

67. See Dioudonnat, *Les 700 rédacteurs de "Je Suis Partout."*

68. On exact dates of their contributions, see ibid.

69. On the role of caricature in emphasizing and disseminating the content of newspapers, see Matard-Bonucci, "L'image." See also Galimi, "Une internationale antisémite des images?"

70. He penned a caricature of Blum that strikingly recalled his front-page drawings for *L'Insurgé*, but generally only illustrated book reviews; *JSP* (July 1, 1938), 9.

71. Charles Maurras, "L'état français," *JSP* (January 7, 1938); *Je Suis Partout* regularly featured Maurras's thought and writings throughout its existence.

72. Pierre Gaxotte, "Pour les 30 ans de *L'Action Française*, souvenirs sur Charles Maurras par trois de ses anciens secrétaires, Pierre Gaxotte, Louis Michaut, Bernard de Vaulx," *JSP* (April 1, 1938), front page.

73. Robert Brasillach, "La question juive," in "Les juifs," special issue, *JSP* (April 15, 1938), front page.

74. This is the title of Gaxotte's editorial, "Partout et d'abord en France: La nation et le régime," *JSP* (February 10, 1934), front page.

75. Pierre Gaxotte, "La Grande Loi: Pas d'ennemis à gauche!" *JSP* (May 2, 1936), front page.

76. Ibid.

77. Pierre Gaxotte, "Manque de France," *JSP* (January 7, 1938), front page.

78. Georges Blond, "Les conquêtes de la science: Plus on est de fous," *JSP* (January 21, 1938), 2.

79. Ibid.

80. In his weekly column, "Le jeu des hommes et des partis," Dorsay speaks of the "contradiction" between "legal country" and "true country"; *JSP* (January 11, 1936), front page.

81. Gaxotte, "Manque de France," front page.

82. "Lacking France" was one of the most recurring themes of Gaxotte's editorials; see ibid. The register of the hollowness of the nation is one that circulated throughout most of these far-right periodicals; for *Combat*, France was "absent."

83. Dorsay, "Le jeu des hommes et des partis: Travailleurs de toutes les classes unissez-vous! Il faut se battre maintenant quand on veut travailler," *JSP* (January 14, 1938), front page.

84. Pierre Gaxotte, "Ces vieux n'ont donc pas d'enfants?" *JSP* (February 11, 1938), front page.

85. Pierre Gaxotte, "Il n'y a pas de remède technique à un mal qui est politique," *JSP* (March 13, 1937), front page.

86. Pierre Gaxotte, "Premier regard sur la métaphysique socialiste," *JSP* (January 13, 1934), front page.

87. Pierre Gaxotte, "Le cataplasme de l'union nationale," *JSP* (February 29, 1936), front page.

88. Dorsay, "Le jeu des hommes et des partis: Sur quel côté le malade va-t-il se tourner?" *JSP* (April 18, 1936). Note that, in contrast to the Young New Right claiming in

the pages of its own newspaper that France was indeed sick, corrupt, abject, for *Je Suis Partout*, France was "like" a sick person.

89. Dorsay, "Le jeu des hommes et des partis: Il paraît que nous avons un gouvernement!" *JSP* (January 21, 1938), front page.

90. Dorsay, "Le jeu des hommes et des partis: Le vrai visage de la France," *JSP* (March 21, 1936), front page.

91. Pierre-Antoine Cousteau, Editorial, in "La Russie des Soviets," special issue, *JSP* (April 4, 1936), front page.

92. Ibid.

93. Jean-Jacques Brousson, "Le retour de l'enfant prodigue (1)," *JSP* (March 13, 1937), 8.

94. Camiscioli, *Reproducing the French Race*, 1; Vicki Caron identifies two moments of policy "crackdown," in 1934–35 and 1938, in *Uneasy Asylum*, 1, 43–50. On immigration in the 1930s, and French people's and politicians' perceptions of the "Refugee Question," see also Noiriel, *Le creuset français*.

95. Lucien Rebatet, "Les émigrés politiques en France," *JSP* (January 28, 1938), front page.

96. Caron, *Uneasy Asylum*, 65–66.

97. Pierre-Antoine Cousteau, "Pour épater les bourgeois: La guerre civile en dentelles," *JSP* (January 4, 1936), 5.

98. Pierre-Antoine Cousteau, "Tous au mur dimanche! La garden party dans la nécropole, choses vues," *JSP* (May 30, 1936), 3.

99. Pierre Gaxotte, "Le danger de 1936: L'alliance russe," *JSP* (January 4, 1936), front page.

100. Lucien Rebatet, "Les juifs dans la révolution," in "Les Juifs," special issue, *JSP* (April 15, 1938), 3.

101. Gaxotte, "Premier regard sur la métaphysique socialiste," *JSP* (January 13, 1934), front page.

102. Claude Jeantet often refers to Marx's "Jewish origins," which he explains that Nazi Germans have, according to him, rightly uncovered; "En zig-zag à travers le Reich," *JSP* (January 4, 1936), 11.

103. Claude Jeantet, "Un rapprochement franco-allemand est-il encore possible?" *JSP* (May 23, 1936), 5.

104. Pierre Gaxotte, "La bêtise n'aurait donc plus de limites?" *JSP* (May 29, 1937), front page.

105. Pierre-Antoine Cousteau, "La guerre hispano-soviétique," *JSP* (August 22, 1936), front page.

106. Pierre Gaxotte, "Pour un rétablissement français," *JSP* (March 14, 1936), front page.

107. Dorsay, "La lutte des hommes et de partis: Sous le règne des paradoxes," *JSP* (May 16, 1936), front page.

108. André Bellessort, "La critique: Léon Blum vu par Marcel Thiébaut," *JSP* (September 10, 1937), 8.

109. Brasillach, "La question juive," in "Les Juifs," special issue, *JSP* (April 15, 1938), front page.

110. Lucien Rebatet, "Juifs et Catholiques," *JSP* (April 1, 1938), 8.

111. Dorsay, "Le juif Mandel fait partie du conseil supérieur de la défense nationale: La mobilisation n'est pas la guerre!" *JSP* (May 20, 1938), front page.

112. Ibid.

113. Léon Daudet, "Un juif qui sème l'antisémitisme," *L'Action Française* (October 11, 1933).

114. Brasillach, "La question juive."

115. This is an oft-cited claim made by Brasillach that has too often been misread as showing that he was not a proponent of racial antisemitism; *Notre avant-guerre*, 244.

116. "Race" was a term often invoked in 1930s France: Léon Blum himself, for instance, had declared in response to antisemitic attacks that he was both French and of the Jewish race; the use of the term "race" did not necessarily mean it possessed a racial content; but *Je Suis Partout* was distinctive in that it increasingly infused its understanding of "race" with a racialized understanding of (Jewish) identity, which, in turn, allowed it to define the nation in specific ways.

117. Marcel Jouhandeau, "Vous prendrez possession du pays," *JSP* (July 30, 1937), 8.

118. Cousteau, "Tous au mur, dimanche!" 3.

119. Jouhandeau, "Vous prendrez possession du pays," 8.

120. *Je Suis Partout* often invoked Céline's expression in direct reference to his 1937 antisemitic work, *Bagatelles pour un massacre*; Pierre-Antoine Cousteau, "Tour d'horizon," *JSP* (January 28, 1938), 3.

121. Jouhandeau, "Vous prendrez possession du pays," 8.

122. Dorsay, "Le jeu des hommes et des partis: Au-delà de l'expérience Blum," *JSP* (May 30, 1936), front page.

123. Pierre-Antoine Cousteau, "Tour d'horizon," *JSP* (March 18, 1938), 4.

124. Céline, *Bagatelles pour un massacre*, 127.

125. Pierre Gaxotte, "Le mécanisme révolutionnaire," *JSP* (May 16, 1936), front page.

126. Lucien Rebatet described Léon Blum as "the hermaphrodite" only once; "Les attractions de Luna-Park, choses vues par Lucien Rebatet," *JSP* (May 12, 1937), 5. This distinction is significant because historians have often attempted to use the notion of hermaphroditism to explain the particular obsession with gender and sex that far-right antisemites displayed. See Birnbaum, *Un mythe politique*, 196–236.

127. Jean-Jacques Brousson, "Blum et le savetier," *JSP* (February 27, 1937), 8.

128. Dorsay, "La tragi-comédie du jour: M. Blum a la haine de la patrie," *JSP* (February 27, 1937), 2.

129. Jean-Jacques Brousson, "Rétablissez l'édit de Nantes en faveur des chrétiens," *JSP* (February 20, 1937), 8.

130. On the discursive production of the male Jewish body in late-nineteenth-century France, see Forth, *The Dreyfus Affair*.

131. Rebatet, "Les attractions de Luna-Park," 5.

132. Georges Blond, "Léon Blum ou la plainte," in "Le Front Populaire," special issue, *JSP* (September 24, 1937), front page.

133. Rebatet, "Les attractions de Luna-Park," 5.

134. Ibid.

135. Ibid.; Pierre-Antoine Cousteau, "3 h. à la SFIO: Le prophète prophétise le beau fixe," *JSP* (June 6, 1936); Pierre Gaxotte, "Discours et propagande," *JSP* (April 25, 1936), front page.

136. Jean Meillonnas, "Après le meeting du Vel d'Hiv': La mobilisation communiste contre M. Blum," *JSP* (March 13, 1937), 2.

137. Rebatet, "Les attractions de Luna-Park," 5. On the "protean" nature of the category of male homosexuality in the interwar years, see Dean, *The Frail Social Body*, esp. 130–72; on "masculinism" in early "homosexual emancipatory thought," see Hewitt, *Political Inversions*, 79–129.

138. Pierre-Antoine Cousteau, citing Gonzague Truc, "Entretien avec M. Gonzague Truc: Arbitre infortuné des duels littéraires," *JSP* (June 9, 1934), 4.

139. Dating from the French Revolution, the French republic had been represented as a woman, Marianne—mostly in republican imagery. For French far-right critics in the 1930s, "Marianne" indifferently referred to the Republic (in caricatures) or the Nation; but more often than not, in *Je Suis Partout*, those invocations were meant to refer to the "nation." See Agulhon, *Marianne au pouvoir*.

140. Robert Brasillach, "Lettre à une provinciale: En lisant Léon Blum," *JSP* (May 22, 1937), 3.

141. Rebatet, "Les attractions de Luna-Park," 5.

142. Lucien Rebatet, "L'escroquerie de l'Exposition, choses vues par Lucien Rebatet," *JSP* (May 29, 1937), 5.

143. References to "citizen Blum" can be found especially in the writings of two of *Je Suis Partout*'s most vicious antisemites, Jean-Jacques Brousson and Lucien Rebatet. See Brousson, "Le juvenat," *JSP* (August 29, 1936), 8; Rebatet, "L'escroquerie de l'Exposition," 5, and "Les attractions de Luna Park," 5.

144. Jean Meillonnas, "Le front de la liberté," *JSP* (April 10, 1937), 3.

145. Dorsay, "La tragédie du jour: Francais! Vous laisserez-vous suicider?" *JSP* (February 20, 1937), 2.

146. Jouhandeau, "Vous prendrez possession du pays," 8.

147. The most vivid portrayals of such "fraternal" trips by the *JSP* "brotherly gang" reveling in its homosociability can be found in Brasillach's memoir, *Notre avant-guerre*.

148. On the 1931 Colonial Exposition, see Lebovics, *True France*, esp. 51–97. See also Ezra, *The Colonial Unconscious*.

149. Maran was celebrated by Léopold Sédar Senghor as a precursor to "Négritude" despite his reformist positions. See the biographical notice provided by Dioudonnat, *Les 700 rédacteurs de "Je Suis Partout,"* 61.

150. Maran had, at times, complained about financial difficulties, which may have motivated his journalism at *Je Suis Partout* (he had lost his post as colonial administrator because of his novel). Still, his articles remained rather devoid of political pro-

nouncements even as they highlighted the "colonial crisis" affecting Guyana and other territories. He proved less timid when it came to Algeria and antisemitism. See Wilder, *The French Imperial Nation-State*, 162–66; for an analysis of the novel and overview of his relationship to black internationalism, and involvement in the interwar intellectual scene, see Edwards, *The Practice of Diaspora*, 69–119; and Conklin, "Who Speaks for Africa?"

151. Dioudonnat, *Les 700 rédacteurs de "Je Suis Partout,"* 79.

152. His article begins by explaining that "at the beginning, colonialism is legalized arbitrariness and founded upon might translated into law," but then he distinguishes between forms of colonialism and racism and, while berating the racism of Spengler and Gobineau, absolves France of these "crimes"; René Maran, "Pour la propagande française aux États-Unis et en Amérique Latine: Autour d'une nomination de gouverneur," *JSP* (January 9, 1937), 6.

153. Georges Roux, "La poudrière algérienne," *JSP* (July 2, 1937), 5.

154. Robert Veyssié, "Ce que la France a fait pour le Togo et le Cameroun," *JSP* (April 25, 1936), 11.

155. Marcel Carret, "Impressions de Chandernagor," and Marius Ary-Leblond, "Le tourisme et la Réunion," *JSP* (May 30, 1936), 9.

156. Henri Menjaud, "La littérature coloniale," *JSP* (March 28, 1936), 5.

157. Paulette Nardal, "Joie et douleur au pays du soleil: Scènes de la vie martiniquaise," *JSP* (June 27, 1936), 10.

158. The second article was published as part of the series "Anti-French Movements in the Colonies": Paulette Nardal, "Aux Antilles: Les communistes profitent de la crise pour provoquer des troubles dans nos plus anciennes colonies," *JSP* (July 16, 1937), 6. For a brief and very evocative overview of Nardal's role in interwar Paris and her anticolonial and internationalist politics, see Edwards, *The Practice of Diaspora*, 119–86, and Boittin, *Colonial Metropolis*, 133–39. Nardal, who with her sisters organized a literary salon attended by most African American and Négritude intellectuals during the interwar years, also wrote "literature for the colonial administration, promoting tourism," upon her return to Martinique; see Sharpley-Whiting, *Négritude Women*, 18.

159. Nardal, "Joie et douleur au pays du soleil," 10.

160. Ibid.

161. B. Simionesco, ". . . Choses vues à Oran," *JSP* (May 22, 1937), front page; Georges Roux, "Le Maroc, îlot de paix," *JSP* (May 22, 1937), 5.

162. Jean Paillard, "L'Algérie dominion? (2)," *JSP* (May 13, 1938), 5.

163. Jackson, *The Popular Front in France*, 154–58.

164. Jean Paillard, "L'Algérie dominion? (1)," *JSP* (May 6, 1938), 5.

165. Jennings, *Curing the Colonizers*.

166. For instance, this is but one brief sentence in a very long article: René Maran, "La Guyane Française et l'exploitation aurifère," *JSP* (June 27, 1936), 10.

167. Paillard, "L'Algérie dominion? (1)," 5.

168. Dorsay, "Sous le règne du paradoxe," *JSP* (May 16, 1936), front page.

169. Jacques Perret, "Illustration de la Guyane et défense du bagne," *JSP* (April 1, 1938), 5.

170. Ibid.

171. Georges Roux, "L'Afrique française, royaume juif?" *JSP* (August 12, 1938), 4.

172. A. Querillac, "L'emigration étrangère n'a rien à faire à Madagascar," *JSP* (May 13, 1938), 5.

173. Caricature, *JSP* (July 1, 1938), 5.

174. Roux, "L'Afrique française, royaume juif?" 4.

175. René Maran, "Les émeutes algériennes," *JSP* (August 1, 1936), 4. A series of articles reiterate this argument: Anonymous, "À travers l'Algérie," *JSP* (August 1, 1936), 4; Anonymous, "L'Algérie menacée," *JSP* (September 1, 1937), 3; Georges Roux, "Notre empire en péril de mort: L'Afrique du Nord à la veille de la révolte," *JSP* (March 20, 1937), front page; Roux, "La poudrière algérienne," 5.

176. Maran, "Les émeutes algériennes," 4. For an analysis of an instance of Algerian riots, see Cole, "Antisémitisme et situation coloniale."

177. Roux, "L'Afrique française, royaume juif?" 4.

178. Wilder, "Unthinking French History," 28. See Lebovics, *True France*, 93–134.

179. Georges Roux, "Le ministère actuel: C'est la fin de l'empire français," *JSP* (March 18, 1938), 5.

180. Simionesco, ". . . Choses vues à Oran."

181. Roux, "Notre empire en péril de mort," 5.

182. Deputé Paul Sarin, "Le communisme en Afrique du Nord," *JSP* (August 1, 1936), 4.

183. Anonymous, "L'Algérie menacée," 3.

184. Pierre Gaxotte, "Tandis que M. Blum accouche d'un ministère," *JSP* (May 30, 1936), front page.

185. Roux, "Le ministère actuel," 5.

186. Roux, "Notre empire en péril de mort," 5.

187. See Hyman, *The Jews of Modern France*; Benbassa, *Histoire des Juifs en France*.

188. Anonymous, "Les juifs et l'empire français," in "Les juifs," special issue, *JSP* (April 15, 1938), 9. On the arguments that emerged around the question of French citizenship regarding Algerian Jews and Muslims, see Shepard, *The Invention of Decolonization*, esp. 169–82.

189. Brasillach, "La question juive," 9.

190. In typical fashion, Brasillach claimed he was not "xenophobic," and concluded that it was time for the French, in the face of such invasion, to ask for their own "reservation" as the "Indians" had done in the United States; "Lettre à une provinciale: Pour une moins grande France," *JSP* (November 21, 1936), 3.

191. Jean Paillard, "L'Algérie dominion? (3)," *JSP* (May 20, 1938), 5.

192. Roux, "Le ministère actuel," 5.

193. Rebatet had proposed this in his 1938 special issue, but the piece's title was more tentative and buried in the back of the issue, rather than on the front page: Lucien Rebatet, "Esquisse de quelques conclusions," *JSP* (April, 15, 1938), 9.

194. Anonymous, "L'Algérie menacée," 3.

195. Paillard, "L'Algérie dominion?" 5.

196. On the conceptual and political inseparability of empire and nation and the necessity of seeing the nation as produced through the empire, see Burton, introduction to *After the Imperial Turn*, 1–26.

197. Anonymous, "Les juifs et l'empire français," 9.

198. This was the result of Brasillach's pun necessitated by the recent implementation of the 1938 Marchandeau Law designed to curb vitriolic newspaper attacks (or "hate speech"): Brasillach thus called not for antisemitism but "ANTISI*É*MITISME" (a play on the word *simiesque*, which means monkey-like) and likening Jews to monkeys that needed to be subjected to the forces of civilization; Robert Brasillach, "Lettre à une provinciale: La question singe. Il nous faut organiser un antisiémitisme d'état et de raison," *JSP* (March 31, 1939), front page.

199. Rebatet, *Les décombres*, 52 (my italics).

200. Lucien Rebatet, "Les émigrés politiques en France," *JSP* (January 28, 1938), front page.

201. "Les Juifs," special issue, *JSP* (April 15, 1938); "Les Juifs et la France," special issue, *JSP* (February 17, 1939).

202. Lucien Rebatet, "Juifs et Catholiques," *JSP* (April 1, 1938), 8.

203. Lucien Rebatet, "Les émigrés politiques en France: Les communistes italiens," *JSP* (February 11, 1938), 5.

204. Brasillach, "La question juive," front page.

205. Lucien Rebatet, "Les émigrés politiques: Peut-on éviter les pogroms?" *JSP* (March 4, 1938), 4.

206. Brasillach, "La question juive," front page

207. Robert Brasillach, "Les français devant les juifs," *JSP* special issue, "Les juifs et la France" (February 17, 1939), front page.

208. Brasillach, "La question juive," front page; Brasillach, "Les français devant les Juifs," front page.

209. Brasillach, "La question juive," front page

210. Marcel Jouhandeau, "Réponse ouverte à M. René Schwob," *JSP* (January 14, 1938), 8.

211. Brasillach, "La question juive," front page.

212. See Claude Jeantet's articles, "En zig-zag à travers le Reich," *JSP* (1936–38). This charge echoes Henri Massis's civilizational rhetoric.

213. Dorsay, "Le ministère franco-russe veut la guerre!" *JSP* (February 4, 1938), 2; Brasillach, "Les français devant les Juifs," front page.

214. Rebatet even explained that he could not be xenophobic since he had married a "foreigner." His wife was Romanian. See his "autobiography," *Les décombres*.

215. Brasillach, "La question juive," front page (my italics).

216. Lucien Rebatet, "Les émigrés politiques en France: Les russes blancs succomberont-ils aux manoeuvres des Soviets?" *JSP* (January 28, 1938), 5.

217. Rebatet, "Les émigrés politiques: Peut-on éviter les pogroms?" 5.

218. Brasillach, "La question juive," front page.

219. Brasillach, "Les français devant les Juifs," front page.

220. This point is made by Massis in *Maurras et notre temps*, 299, as a means of justifying this contestation; but here again he points to 1936, as Brasillach had done, as the foundational moment for a fascist awakening,

221. Jean-Jacques Brousson, "Voilà pourquoi nous sommes adhérents," *JSP* (March 27, 1937), 8.

222. Robert Brasillach, "Lettre à une provinciale: Allo, Malraux?" *JSP* (January 2, 1937), 3.

223. Robert Brasillach, "Lettre à une provinciale: Le colonel Malraux soutient le moral de l'arrière," *JSP* (January 16, 1937), 3.

224. Gabriel Brunet, "Un art émietté et convulsif," in "L'Espoir," *JSP* (January 14, 1938), 8.

225. Brousson, "La jeunesse d'un clerc?" 8.

226. Ibid.

227. Lucien Rebatet, "Un semeur d'antisémitisme: M. Benda," *JSP* (February 18, 1938), 8.

228. Georges Blond, "Les blessés de l'esprit: Je pense donc je fuis," *JSP* (March 20, 1937), 2.

229. Robert Brasillach, "La fin de l'après-guerre: Vieilles maisons, vieux papiers," *JSP* (January 14, 1938), 8.

230. Brousson, "Le retour de l'enfant prodigue (1)," 8.

231. Brasillach, "Portrait de la France," front page, 6.

232. Ibid., 6.

233. Ibid., front page.

234. Ibid.

235. This particular assertion was made within the context of a discussion regarding the state of education, a topic of acute importance in the cultural battles that were being waged in France at the time. That topic had been a favorite of Kléber Haedens in both *Je Suis Partout* and *L'Insurgé*. Le professeur, "Chronique universitaire: Culture et formation civique," *JSP* (March 24, 1934), 2.

236. Brasillach, "Portrait de la France," front page.

237. Brasillach, "Il n'y a pas de grand pays sans cette poésie nationale"; ibid.

238. Gabriel Brunet, "Robert Brasillach," *JSP* (January 1, 1936), 8.

239. Gabriel Brunet, on describing the characteristics of Brasillach's literary criticism, said that he possessed a "sens très vif d'un contact intime et naïf avec les grandes forces de la nature"; in "La Critique: Robert Brasillach, *Portraits*," *JSP* (January 11, 1936), 9.

240. For an analysis of Brasillach's nostalgic "aesthetic fascism," see Witt, *The Search for Modern Tragedy*.

241. This was also an attack on what was considered to be the French literary establishment, since Gide was one of the most famous contributors to the respected literary magazine, the *NRF*. Brasillach occasionally refers to Gide "sending sweet notes to" Angèle, and "having ACCUSTOMED [Angèle] to rather sophisticated discussions,"

or mentions Gide "being moved by the fact the Angèle of his youth might have other interlocutors than him," in, respectively, "Lettre à une provinciale: Les marchands de poireaux," *JSP* (July 25, 1936), 4; and "Lettre à une provinciale: Êtes-vous pour le Louvre ou pour la danse du ventre?" *JSP* (February 27, 1937), 3; "Lettre à une provinciale: Art et technique," *JSP* (May 1, 1937), 3; "Lettre à une provinciale: Propos sur un poète russe," *JSP* (February 13, 1937), 3. On the strategies used by authors and intellectuals to insert themselves within the literary field, see Bourdieu, *Rules of Art*.

242. Brasillach, "Lettre à une provinciale: Voyage dans la lune," *JSP* (June 13, 1936), 2.

243. Brasillach, "Lettre à une provinciale: Loisirs, délices et orgues," *JSP* (July 4, 1936), 4.

244. Brasillach, "Lettre à une provinciale: Jean Cassou, Prix de la Renaissance," *JSP* (June 27, 1936), 3; "Lettre à une provinciale: En attendant le marché aux puces," *JSP* (January 23, 1937), 3; "Lettre à une provinciale: Charles Maurras est sorti de prison," *JSP* (July 9, 1937), 3.

245. Brasillach, "Lettre à une provinciale: Un portrait italien de la France," *JSP* (April 3, 1937), 3.

246. Brasillach, "Lettre à une provinciale: Savez-vous planter les choux?" *JSP* (October 3, 1936), 3.

247. Ibid.

248. Brasillach, "Lettre à une provinciale: Histoires vraies," *JSP* (July 11, 1936), 4.

249. Brasillach, "Lettre à une provinciale: M. Le Trouhadec saisi par la morale," *JSP* (March 10, 1937), 3.

250. Brasillach, "Lettre à une provinciale: L'étranger aime-t-il la France?" *JSP* (October 17, 1936), 3.

251. I thank Todd Shepard for this reminder.

252. *JSP* special issue "Qu'est-ce-que Rex?" (October 24, 1936).

253. Robert Brasillach, "Lettre à une provinciale: Visite à Léon Degrelle," *JSP* (June 6, 1936), front page.

254. Brasillach, "Vous êtes une âme tendre, ma chère Angèle, et vous ne découvrirez pas sans frémir de joie que M. Blum jadis écrît des poèmes," in "Lettre à une provinciale: En lisant Léon Blum," 3.

255. Ibid.

256. Brasillach, "Lettre à une provinciale: Quand demandera-t-on l'extradition d'André Malraux?" *JSP* (January 16, 1937), 3. This is the tone most characteristic of his column after 1937.

257. Brasillach, "Lettre à une provinciale: En attendant les camions des tueurs," *JSP* (August 8, 1936), 2.

258. This is no surprise, as Bardèche, who has been in charge of the Brasillach archives and patrimony since his death, is a notorious far-right intellectual figure (and former academic known for his work on Proust) who never renounced his commitment to far-right ideas, which he had, however, never expressed publicly in the 1930s, and became well known after 1945 through his revisionist positions; Maurice Bardèche, "Une autre image de Brasillach," in Sipriot, *Robert Brasillach et la génération perdue*, 213–21.

259. For a summary of the myth of Brasillach's "Romantic fascism," see Mazgaj, "Ce mal de siècle."

CONCLUSION

1. But some, like Jean-Pierre Maxence, who had been imprisoned in Germany, took up different lives. Maxence moved to Switzerland and founded an institute for Thomist studies, devoting his life to Catholicism until his death in 1956. This is the information provided by his son, who also wrote in a brief preface to the second edition of his father's "chronicle of the 1930s," that he and his mother, Hélène Colomb—who had also been a contributor to *L'Insurgé*—had helped hide Jewish children during the Occupation years. It would be very difficult to verify such a claim but, as is common to far-right journalists, personal action is usually invoked to disprove the charge of ideologically motivated antisemitism. See Jean-Luc Maxence, preface to second edition of Jean-Pierre Maxence, *Histoire de dix ans*, 8.

2. Rousso's pioneering study famously pointed to the inability of French people and historians to deal with the less wholesome aspects of the past. His model (which relies on popular psychoanalytic notions: neurosis, repression, acting out, etc.) has recently been revisited. He also pointed to the resurgence of far-right antisemitism at the very moment when a "Jewish memory" of Vichy emerged in the 1970s. Rousso, *Le syndrome de Vichy*, 93–95, 155–94; see also Golsan, "The Legacy of World War II in France."

3. Le Sueur, *Uncivil War*, 3.

4. For an overview of Blanchot's post-1945 political writings, see Blanchot, *Écrits politiques 1953–1993*; for a summary of Blanchot's postwar activities, see Bident, *Maurice Blanchot.*

5. On Blanchot's role, see Bident, *Maurice Blanchot*, 391–402.

6. See, for instance, Hill, "'Not in Our Name.'" Mesnard argues that, for Blanchot, only General Charles De Gaulle, who was then president, will suffer the same wrath as Blum once did; *Maurice Blanchot*, 33.

7. On this issue and these debates, see Sapiro, *La guerre des écrivains*.

8. Monnier, *À l'ombre des têtes molles*, 11.

9. Ibid., 10.

10. Pierre Gaxotte, "Rêveries sur la grandeur française," *JSP* (January 16, 1937), 3.

11. Montety, *Thierry Maulnier*. See, for instance, Cousteau and Rebatet, *Dialogues de "vaincus."*

12. Historian Todd Shepard has recently shown how far-right journalists, in their accounts regarding the events of May '68, (including Rebatet), articulated a discourse of virility, which took as the central focus of their denunciation of recent political events the Algerian as deviant and corrupting figure; in "L'extrême-droite et 'Mai 68.'"

13. Maurice Bardèche published his revisionist pamphlet *Nuremberg ou la terre promise* in 1948; see his interview, in Kaplan, *Reproductions of Banality*, 177–78.

14. See Thierry Maulnier's entry on communism in his "dictionary," where he echoes his 1930s attacks; "Communisme," in *Le sens des mots*, 34.

15. On French intellectuals after 1945, see Judt, *Past Imperfect*; Winock, *Le siècle des intellectuels*; Sapiro, *La guerre des écrivains*.

16. On this, see Rousso, *Le syndrome de Vichy*; for a nuanced and interesting discussion, see literary critic Steven Ungar's *Scandal and Aftereffect*.

17. On fascism, see the very useful and comprehensive overview provided in Robert Paxton's bibliographic essay *The Anatomy of Fascism*, 221–49.

18. Sternhell, *Ni droite ni gauche*. It was first published in English three years later.

19. Soucy, *French Fascism*, 10; Paxton, *The Anatomy of Fascism*, xi. For an excellent summary of the historiography, see Paul Mazgaj's introduction to *Imagining Fascism*, 13–34. See also Soucy's introduction to *French Fascism*, 1–25; and Matthew Affron and Mark Antliff's introduction to *Fascist Visions*, 3–24.

20. See Burrin, *La dérive fasciste*.

21. He explains that paying attention to the young far right's political "behavior" and not just their "ideological stances" and "vehement diatribes" provides a different understanding of the debate on this group's fascism; *Imagining Fascism*, 33.

22. Griffin, *The Nature of Fascism*.

23. See the excellent work done by Hewitt, *Fascist Modernism*, and Griffin, *Modernism and Fascism*.

24. Griffin, *Modernism and Fascism*, 1. In addition to the work of Emilio Gentile and Walter Adamson, see Blum, *The Other Modernism*; Falasca-Zamponi, *Fascist Spectacle*; Ben-Ghiat, *Fascist Modernities*; Witt, *The Search for Modern Tragedy*.

25. Kaplan, *Reproductions of Banality*; Golsan, *Fascism, Aesthetics, and Culture*; Ungar, *Scandal and Its Aftereffects*; Affron and Antliff, *Fascist Visions*.

26. Carroll, *French Literary Fascism*, 5.

27. Antliff, *Avant-Garde Fascism*.

28. For engaging works that fall into this category, see the works of Alice Kaplan, David Carroll, and Steven Ungar, as well as those of both Rosemarie Scullion and Thomas Spears on Céline.

29. This is Carroll's main weakness, and it is especially problematic in the case of Rebatet, who was mostly a journalist until the publication of *Les décombres* in 1942—the main text Carroll refers to. Similarly, neither Brasillach's nor Maulnier's extensive journalistic writings are considered. His otherwise astute analysis ends up being a rather selective reading of their texts, divorced from their actual historical production and without any context that might illuminate the shifts in their thinking.

30. Sapiro, *La guerre des écrivains*; Kessler, *Histoire politique*; Serry, *Naissance de l'intellectuel catholique*; Guyader, *La revue idées, 1941–1944*. To these, one might add the insights offered by the recent excellent social histories of the French right, the Faisceau, Croix de Feu, and the Parti social français, by Passmore, *From Liberalism to Fascism*; Kennedy, *Reconciling France Against Democracy*; and Kalman, *The Extreme Right in Interwar France*.

31. Mazgaj, *Imagining Fascism*, 15.

32. Mazgaj is rightly critical of Loubet del Bayle and of Kessler's refusal to consider the fascination that fascism held for this group. Some important figures—like Brasil-

lach—fall by the wayside of this narrative after 1934; *Imagining Fascism*, 14, 21–22, and 279 n. 19.

33. Though that indifference is also a choice Mazgaj made, as he knew that examining Blanchot involved a different set of questions, notably on the literary field, which were not the explicit theme of his book. I thank Paul Mazgaj for our exchange on the matter.

34. On Walter Benjamin's insight, which many scholars have borrowed to analyze fascism, see Benjamin, "L'oeuvre d'art à l'époque de sa reproduction technique," 140–71. Mary Ann Frese Witt offers an analysis of what she terms their "aesthetic fascism" and examines Maulnier's and Brasillach's celebration of tragedy as a form of politics. Her analysis is compelling but, once again, pays too little attention to historical context; *The Search for Modern Tragedy*, 135–89.

35. Bhabha, "Joking Aside," xv.

36. Ibid.

37. Bryan Cheyette and Laura Marcus, "Some Methodological Anxieties," in Cheyette and Marcus, *Modernity, Culture, and "the Jew,"* 2.

38. Noiriel, *Immigration, antisémitisme et racisme*. This ambitious study is a synthetic overview especially concerned with the ways in which individual "instinctive reactions [relied on such ideologies] to transform them into public discourses"; 9. For a recent instance of work that takes different manifestations of antisemitism within a colonial framework seriously, and here in colonial Algeria, see Cole, "Antisémitisme et situation coloniale pendant l'entre-deux-guerres en Algérie." Indeed, as I have shown with *Je Suis Partout*, French far-right antisemitism articulated itself both through a colonial imaginary and always with an eye to what was happening in the colonies, Algeria especially.

39. See, for instance, Scullion, "Style, Subversion, Modernity," 184.

40. Stoler, *Race and the Education of Desire*, 89. Recent historical studies have rectified this: attention to the epistemological constitution of republican categories of citizenship through the lexicon of culture and race have been especially well illuminated, by Todd Shepard, for instance, who shows how, in the wake of the Algerian war of independence, the French government espoused decolonization through the simultaneous "reintegration" of Algerian Jews within the rule of metropolitan Jew. This "reintegration" was articulated through the exclusion of all Algerian Muslims from Frenchness. This argument thus solidified the discursive construction of "Muslim" as being fundamentally unassimilable to French citizenship. See Shepard, *The Invention of Decolonization*.

41. Stoler, *Race and the Education of Desire*, 7, 5.

42. I am borrowing from Vicki Caron, in "Prelude to Vichy" and "The Antisemitic Revival in France in the 1930s." Caron's work has been seminal: she has shown how antisemitism must be framed by the larger context of migration and the reformulation of national boundaries, an uneven process throughout the 1930s, when the republican state alternately welcomed and tried to control the flux of (Jewish) refugees feeling the increasing persecution of the Nazi regime; see Caron, *Uneasy Asylum*.

43. Berliner, *Ambivalent Desire*, 7.

44. Cheyette and Marcus, "Some Methodological Anxieties."

45. Mosse, *Nationalism and Sexuality*; Mosse, *The Image of Man*.

46. Theweleit, *Male Fantasies*, vol. 2, *Male Bodies*, 13.

47. This is not to dismiss the use of psychoanalytic theory or categories for historical analysis. It is Theweleit's use of these—within the context of a Deleuzian notion of desire—that has been criticized, for it failed to address important questions, while "naturalizing" what he described in problematic ways.

48. Spackman, *Fascist Virilities*, xv, xiii. In a similar vein, on "literary texts that imagine fascism as a libidinal phenomenon," see Frost, *Sex Drives*; and for a critique of turns to "narcissism" and other "misuses" of (Freudian) psychoanalytic models, see Hewitt, *Political Inversions*.

49. Herzog, *Sex after Fascism*, 1. Her work can be located at the intersection of studies inspired by Michel Foucault's theorization of sexuality and German and Jewish women's historiography.

50. See, for instance, Herzog, *Sexuality and German Fascism*. Recently, works on women during the Holocaust, as well as gender, sexuality, and violence, have challenged and enriched conventional historiography. See, for instance, Ofer and Weitzman, *Women in the Holocaust*, and Herzog, *Brutality and Desire*.

51. Muel-Dreyfus, *Vichy et l'éternel féminin*; Pollard, *Reign of Virtue*.

52. Adler, *Jews and Gender in Liberation France*.

53. Roberts, *Civilization Without Sexes*; Dean, *The Frail Social Body*; Meyers, "Feminizing Fascist Men."

54. This is strikingly the case with what might be termed the "Sciences-Po" school of political history, which has dominated the field, from René Rémond to Michel Winock and Jean-François Sirinelli. Recent works exhibit the same indifference, despite the French and American scholarship on women, gender, and politics.

55. See my essay "The Subject and the World of Difference," reviewing two recent publications (by Judith Surkis and Tracie Matysik) that exemplify the productive ways in which the consideration of gender and sexuality has furthered the objects and methods of intellectual history.

56. While Louis-Ferdinand Céline continues to be the subject of essays and biographies, Maurice Blanchot has evaded any incursion into his life. To this day, only one biography exists. Angie David's recent biography of Dominique Aury (who was Jean Paulhan's lover and authored the early 1950s scandalous short pornographic novel *Histoire d'O*, but was also a translator, Thierry Maulnier's lover, and Maurice Blanchot's close friend) received impressive critical success and the Prix Goncourt de la Biographie. The editor did not include any bibliographic apparatus, a problematic choice considering that the biography relied extensively on historians' accounts that she never cites, as well as archival sources that have been, previously, unavailable to historians.

57. See Mendelsohn, "Transgression," 18; Moyn, "A Nazi Zelig."

58. Mendelsohn writes: "And so, rather than using the graphic details of violence and sex simply (and naively) to shock his reader in a superficial way, the violence, the 'pornography of violence' even, are consciously evoked, given their baroquely nightmar-

ish details, in order to heighten the 'impression of the sacrilegious'—not to somehow defend Aue because he is outside of morality, but to show us, horribly, what a life outside of morality looks, feels, sounds, and smells like"; "Transgression," 21.

59. LaCapra, "Historical and Literary Approaches." For an example of the intellectual debt Littell owes Blanchot, see his short piece on Blanchot, reading, and authorship, originally published in the *NRF*, that can be accessed on a recently created scholarly site devoted to Blanchot, *Espace Maurice Blanchot*; Littell, "Lire?" For a very insightful reading of Bataille's story that takes fantasy and desire seriously in order to read Bataille's fantasies of transgression, see Brower, "Story of the Eye."

60. Mendelsohn, "Transgression," 21.

61. Ibid.

62. Kristeva, *Powers of Horror*, 15.

63. Mendelsohn, "Transgression," 21.

64. Littell's portrayal strikingly echoes the representations and tropes that emerged in Weimar Germany and were articulated around the public German obsession with sexual murder. See the excellent study by Maria Tatar, *Lustmord*. The characterization is Samuel Moyn's; "A Nazi Zelig."

65. I thank Samuel Moyn for our exchange on the matter.

66. Carolyn Dean has also analyzed how anxieties regarding the failure of empathy demonstrated by the Nazi project and those who were complicit with it have been explained in reference to the sexual repression of latent homosexuality and the deviance of overt homosexual desire. See Dean, *The Fragility of Empathy*, 106–34.

67. Herzog, *Sex After Fascism*, 11.

BIBLIOGRAPHY

PRIMARY SOURCES

L'Action Française: L'organe du nationalisme intégral
Candide
Combat
Gringoire
L'Insurgé Politique et Social
Je Suis Partout: Le grand hebdomadaire de la vie mondiale
Réaction pour l'Ordre
La Revue du Siècle
La Revue du XXe Siècle

Benda, Julien. *La trahison des clercs*. Paris: Gallimard, 1927.
———. *La jeunesse d'un clerc*. Paris: Gallimard, 1937.
Benjamin, Walter. "L'oeuvre d'art à l'ère de sa reproductibilité technique (première version, 1935)." In *Oeuvres* III, 67–113. Paris: Gallimard, 2000.
———. "L'oeuvre d'art à l'époque de sa reproductibilité technique (dernière version de 1939)." In *Oeuvres* III, 269–316. Paris: Gallimard, 2000.
Blanchot, Maurice. *Thomas l'obscur*. Paris: Gallimard, 1941.
———. *Aminadab*. Paris: Gallimard, 1942.
———. *Comment la littérature est-elle possible?* Paris: J. Corti, 1942.
———. *Faux pas*. Paris: Gallimard, 1943.
———. *L'arrêt de mort*. Paris: Gallimard, 1948.
———. *La part du feu*. Paris: Gallimard, 1949.
———. "Réflexions sur le surréalisme." In *La part du feu*. Paris: Gallimard, 1949.
———. *L'espace littéraire*. Paris: Gallimard, 1955.
———. *L'écriture du désastre*. Paris: Gallimard, 1980.
———. *Après-Coup (précédé par Le ressassement éternel)*. Paris: Éditions de Minuit, 1983.
———. *La communauté inavouable*. Paris: Éditions de Minuit, 1983.
———. *Michel Foucault tel que je l'imagine*. Paris: Fata Morgana, 1986.
———. *L'instant de ma mort*. Paris: Fata Morgana, 1994.

———. *Writing of the Disaster*. Lincoln: University of Nebraska Press, 1995.

———. *Les intellectuels en question*. Paris: Farrago, 2000.

———. *Chroniques littéraires du 'Journal des Débats,' Avril 1941–Août 1944*. Edited by Christophe Bident. Paris: Gallimard, 2007.

———. *Écrits politiques, 1953–1993*. Edited by Éric Hoppenot. Paris: Gallimard, 2008.

Blond, Georges. *Journal d'un imprudent*. Paris: Fayard, 1936.

Brasillach, Robert. *Notre avant-guerre*. Paris: Plon, 1941.

Céline, Louis-Ferdinand. *Voyage au bout de la nuit*. Paris: Denoël, 1932.

———. *Mort à crédit*. Paris: Denoël, 1936.

———. *Bagatelles pour un massacre*. Paris: Denoël, 1937.

———. *L'école des cadavres*. Paris: Denoël, 1938.

———. *Les beaux draps*. Paris: Nouvelles Éditions Françaises, 1941.

———. *L'Église*. Paris: Gallimard, 1952.

———. *Journey to the End of the Night*. New York: New Directions, 2006.

Cousteau, Pierre-Antoine. *L'Amérique juive*. Paris: Les Éditions de France, 1942.

———. *En ce temps-là*. Paris: Diffusion/La Librairie française, 1959.

Cousteau, Pierre-Antoine, and Lucien Rebatet. *Dialogues de "vaincus" (prison de Clairvaux, Janvier–Décembre 1950)*. Edited by Robert Belot. Paris: Berg International, 1999.

Daudet, Léon. *Bréviaire du journalisme*. Paris: Gallimard-NRF, 1936.

———. *Mes idées esthétiques*. Paris: Fayard, 1939.

———. *Souvenirs littéraires*. Paris: Grasset, 1968.

———. *Souvenirs et polémiques*. Paris: Robert Laffont, 1992.

Fabrègues, Jean de, Robert Francis, Jean-Pierre Maxence, and Thierry Maulnier. *Charles Maurras et son Action française*. Paris: Librairie Académique Perrin, 1966.

Francis, Robert, Thierry Maulnier, and Jean-Pierre Maxence. *Demain la France*. Paris: Éditions Grasset, 1934.

Freud, Sigmund. *Civilization and Its Discontents*. New York: Norton, 1961.

Gide, André. *Corydon: Quatre dialogues socratiques*. Paris: Gallimard, 1924.

Heidegger, Martin. "The Origins of the Work of Art" (1936). In *Basic Writings*, 139–211. New York: HarperCollins, 1993.

Jouhandeau, Marcel. *Le Saladier*. Paris: Gallimard, 1936.

———. *Le péril juif*. Paris: Sorlot, 1937.

———. *De l'abjection*. Paris: Gallimard, 1939.

Leiris, Michel. *L'âge d'homme (précédé de: De la littérature considérée comme une tauromachie)*. Paris: Gallimard, 1939.

Massis, Henri. *Défense de l'Occident*. Paris: Plon, 1927.

———. *Réflexions sur l'art du roman*. Paris: Plon, 1927.

———. *Dix ans après. Réflexions sur la littérature d'après-guerre*. Paris: Desclée de Brouwer, 1932.

———. *La guerre de trente ans: Destin d'un âge, 1909–1939*. Paris: Plon, 1940.
———. *Les idées restent*. Lyon: H. Lardanchet, 1941.
———. *Maurras et notre temps: Entretiens et souvenirs*. Paris: Plon, 1961.
Maulnier, Thierry. *Nietzsche*. Paris: Gallimard, 1925.
———. *La crise est dans l'homme*. Paris: Librairie de la Revue Française–Alexis Rédier, 1932.
———. *Les mythes socialistes*. Paris: Gallimard, 1936.
———. *Racine*. Paris: Gallimard, 1936. 2nd ed., 1988.
———. *Au-delà du nationalisme*. Paris: Gallimard, 1938.
———. *Introduction à la poésie française*. Paris: Gallimard, 1939.
———. *La France, la guerre et la paix*. Paris: H. Lardanchet, 1942.
———. *Le sens des mots*. Paris: Flammarion, 1976.
Maurras, Charles. *Le pape, la guerre et la paix*. Paris: Nouvelle Librairie Nationale, 1917.
———. *Romantisme et révolution*. Paris: Nouvelle Librairie Nationale, 1922.
———. *Poètes*. Paris: Le Divan, 1923.
———. *Barbarie et poésie*. Paris: Nouvelle Librairie Nationale, 1925.
———. *Le romantisme féminin*. Paris: A la cité des livres, 1927.
———. *Maîtres et témoins de ma vie d'esprit: Barrès, Mistral, France, Verlaine, Moréas*. Paris: Flammarion, 1954.
———. *Critique et poésie*. Paris: Librairie Académique Perrin, 1968.
Maxence, Jean-Pierre. *Histoire de dix ans, 1927–1937: Chronique des années trente*. Paris: Gallimard, 1939; 2nd ed., Monaco: Editions du Rocher, 2005.
Monnier, Pierre. *À l'ombre des têtes molles*. Paris: La Table Ronde, 1987.
———. *Céline et les têtes molles*. Bruxelles: Le Bulletin Célinien, 1998.
Rebatet, Lucien. *Les décombres*. Paris: Denoël, 1942.
———. *Céline soi-même*. Paris: Van Bagaden, 1987.
Roy, Claude. *Moi je: Essai d'autobiographie*. Paris: Gallimard, 1969.
Saint-Pierre, Bernardin de. *Paul et Virginie*. First published 1788. Paris: Gallimard, 2004.
Sartre, Jean-Paul. *Situations III*. Paris: Gallimard, 1949.

SELECTED SECONDARY SOURCES

Adler, K. H. *Jews and Gender in Liberation France*. Cambridge: Cambridge University Press, 2003.
Affron, Matthew, and Mark Antliff, eds. *Fascist Visions: Art and Ideology in France and Italy*. Princeton, NJ: Princeton University Press, 1997.
Agamben, Giorgio. *Homo Sacer: Sovereign Power and Bare Life*. Stanford, CA: Stanford University Press, 1998.
Agulhon, Maurice. *Marianne au pouvoir: L'imagerie et la symbolique républicaines de 1880 à 1914*. Paris: Flammarion, 1992.
Alméras, Philippe. *Les idées de Céline*. Paris: Berg International, 1992.

——. *Je suis le bouc: Céline et l'antisémitisme*. Paris: Denoël, 2000.

——, ed. *Lettres des années noires*. Paris: Berg, 1994.

Andrew, Dudley, and Steven Ungar. *Popular Front Paris and the Poetics of Culture*. Cambridge, MA: Harvard University Press, 2005.

Antliff, Mark. *Avant-Garde Fascism: The Mobilization of Myth, Art, and Culture in France, 1909–1939*. Durham, NC: Duke University Press, 2007.

Apter, Emily, and William Pietz, eds. *Fetishism as Cultural Discourse*. Ithaca, NY: Cornell University Press, 1993.

——. "French Colonial Studies and Post-Colonial Theory." *SubStance* 24, no. 1/2, issue 76/77: France's Identity Crises (1995): 169–80.

Archer-Straw, Petrine. *Negrophilia: Avant-Garde Paris and Black Culture in the 1920s*. New York: Thames and Hudson, 2000.

Arendt, Hannah. *Sur l'antisémitisme*. Paris: Seuil, 1973.

Arnold, Edward, ed. *The Development of the Radical Right in France: From Boulanger to Le Pen*. London: Macmillan, 2000.

Audoin, Philippe. *Les surréalistes*. Paris: Seuil, 1973.

Auzépy-Chavagnac, Véronique. *Jean de Fabrègues et la Jeune Droite Catholique: Aux sources de la Révolution Nationale*. Villeneuve-d'Asq: Presses Universitaires du Septentrion, 2002.

Azéma, Jean-Pierre, and François Bédarida. *La France des années noires*. Paris: Seuil, 1993.

Baring, Edward. "Liberalism and the Algerian War: The Case of Jacques Derrida." *Critical Inquiry* 36 (Winter 2010): 239–61.

Barko, Ivan. *L'esthétique littéraire de Charles Maurras*. Paris: Droz, 1961.

Barrel, John. "Death on the Nile: Fantasy and the Literature of Tourism, 1840–60." In *Cultures of Empire: Colonizers in Britain and the Empire in the Nineteenth and Twentieth Centuries*, edited by Catherine Hall, 187–206. New York: Routledge, 2000.

Barthes, Roland. *Le plaisir du texte*. Paris: Seuil, 1973.

Bataille, Georges. "L'abjection et les formes misérables." In *Écrits posthumes, 1922–1940*. Vol. 2 of *Oeuvres complètes*, 217–21. Paris: Gallimard, 1970.

——. *Écrits posthumes, 1922–1940*. Vol. 2 of *Oeuvres complètes*, 217–21. Paris: Gallimard, 1970.

Bayles, Janette Kay. "Figuring the Abject: Politics, Aesthetics, and the Crisis of National Identity in Interwar French Literature and Cinema." PhD diss., University of Iowa, 1999.

Beale, Marjorie. *The Modernist Enterprise: French Elites and the Threat to Modernity, 1900–1940*. Stanford, CA: Stanford University Press, 1999.

Beider, Alexander. *A Dictionary of Jewish Surnames from the Russian Empire*. Teaneck, NJ: Avotaynu, 1993.

Bellanger, Claude, Jacques Godechot, Pierre Guiral, and Fernand Terrou. *Histoire générale de la presse française*. Vol. 3, *1871–1940*. Paris: Presses Universitaires de France, 1972.

Belot, Robert. *Lucien Rebatet: Un itinéraire fasciste*. Paris: Seuil, 1994.

Ben-Ghiat, Ruth. *Fascist Modernities: Italy, 1922–1945*. Berkeley: University of California Press, 2001.

Benbassa, Esther. *Histoire des juifs de France*. Paris: Seuil, 1997.

Berezin, Mabel. *Making the Fascist Self: The Political Culture of Interwar Italy*. Ithaca, NY: Cornell University Press, 1997.

Berliner, Brett. *Ambivalent Desire: The Exotic Black Other in Jazz-Age France*. Amherst: University of Massachusetts Press, 2002.

Bernard-Donals, Michel, and Richard Glezjer. *Between Witness and Testimony: The Holocaust and the Limits of Representation*. Albany: SUNY Press, 2001.

Bernheimer, Charles. *Decadent Subjects: The Idea of Decadence in Art, Literature, Philosophy, and Culture of the* Fin de Siècle *in Europe*. Baltimore: Johns Hopkins University Press, 2002.

Berstein, Serge. *Le 6 février 1934*. Paris: Gallimard, 1975.

———. *La France des années 30*. 2nd ed. Paris: Armand Colin, 1993.

Bhabha, Homi. "Joking Aside: The Idea of a Self-Critical Community." Foreword to *Modernity, Culture, and the Jew*, edited by Bryan Cheyette and Laura Marcus, xv–xx. Stanford, CA: Stanford University Press, 1998.

Bident, Christophe. *Maurice Blanchot, partenaire invisible: Essai biographique*. Paris: Champ Vallon, 1998.

Birnbaum, Pierre. *"La France aux français": Histoire des haines nationalistes*. Paris: Seuil, 1994.

———. *Un mythe politique: La "république juive," de Léon Blum à Pierre Mendès France*. Paris: Gallimard, 1995.

———. *Le moment antisémite: Un tour de la France en 1898*. Paris: Fayard, 1998.

Blake, Jody. *Le tumulte noir: Modernist Art and Popular Entertainment in Jazz-Age Paris, 1900–1930*. University Park: Pennsylvania State University Press, 2003.

Blanchot dans son siècle (Association des Amis de Maurice Blanchot, textes rassemblés). Lyon: Éditions Paragon, 2009.

Blondiaux, Isabelle. *Une écriture psychotique: Louis-Ferdinand Céline*. Paris: Nizet, 1985.

Blum, Cinzia Sartini. *The Other Modernism: F. T. Marinetti's Futurist Fiction of Power*. Berkeley: University of California Press, 1996.

Bochner, Jay. "Blaise Without War: The War on Anarchy in Blaise Cendrars' *Moravagine*." *Modernism/Modernity* 2, no. 2 (April 1995): 49–62.

Boittin, Jennifer Anne. *Colonial Metropolis: The Urban Grounds of Anti-Imperialism and Feminism in Interwar Paris*. Lincoln: University of Nebraska Press, 2010.

Bonnaud-Lamotte, Danielle, and Jean-Luc Rispail, eds. *Intellectuels(s) des années trente: Entre le rêve et l'action*. Paris: Éditions du CNRS, 1989.

Borchert, Donald M., ed. *Encyclopedia of Philosophy*. 2nd ed. New York: Macmillan, 2005.

Bounan, Michel. *L'art de Céline et son temps*. Paris: Éditions Allia, 1998.

Bourdieu, Pierre. *Questions de sociologie*. Paris: Éditions de Minuit, 1984.

———. *The Rules of Art: Genesis and Structure of the Literary Field*. Stanford, CA: Stanford University Press, 1996.

Brami, Emile. *Céline*. Paris: Éditions Écritures, 2003.

Broche, François. *Léon Daudet, le dernier imprécateur*. Paris: Robert Laffont, 1992.

Brower, Brady. "Story of the Eye: Fantasy of the Orgy and Its Limit." *American Imago* 59, no. 1 (2002): 73–89.

Brown, Wendy. "Tolerance and Equality: 'The Jewish Question' and 'the Woman Question.'" In *Feminism and the Shifting Boundaries of the Private Sphere*, edited by Debra Keats and Joan W. Scott, 15–42. Urbana: University of Illinois Press, 2004.

Burrin, Philippe. *La dérive fasciste: Doriot, Déat, Bergery, 1933–1935*. Paris: Seuil, 1986.

Burton, Antoinette, ed. *After the Imperial Turn: Thinking With and Through the Nation*. Durham, NC: Duke University Press, 2003.

Butler, Judith. *Bodies That Matter: On the Discursive Limits of "Sex."* New York: Routledge, 1993.

———. *Excitable Speech: A Politics of the Performative*. New York: Routledge, 1997.

Butler, Judith, and Joan W. Scott, eds. *Feminists Theorize the Political*. New York: Routledge, 1992.

Byrnes, Robert. *Antisemitism in Modern France*. New Brunswick, NJ: Rutgers University Press, 1950.

Camiscioli, Elisa. *Reproducing the French Race: Immigration, Intimacy, and Embodiment in the Early Twentieth Century*. Durham, NC: Duke University Press, 2009.

Capitan Peter, Colette. *Charles Maurras et l'idéologie d'Action Française: Étude sociologique d'une pensée de droite*. Paris: Seuil, 1972.

Caron, Vicki. "Prelude to Vichy: France and the Jewish Refugees in the Era of Appeasement." *Journal of Contemporary History* 20, no. 1 (January 1985): 157–76.

———. "The Antisemitic Revival in France in the 1930s: The Socioeconomic Dimension Reconsidered." *Journal of Modern History* 70, no. 1 (March 1998): 240–73.

———. *Uneasy Asylum: France and the Jewish Refugee Crisis, 1933–1942*. Stanford, CA: Stanford University Press, 1999.

Carroll, David. *French Literary Fascism: Nationalism, Anti-Semitism, and the Ideology of Culture*. Princeton, NJ: Princeton University Press, 1995.

Caws, Mary Ann. *The Surrealist Look: An Erotics of Encounter*. Cambridge, MA: MIT Press, 1997.

Céline vivant: Entretiens—Biographie. Paris: INA/Éditions Montparnasse, 2007.

Charle, Christophe. *Naissance des "intellectuels," 1880–1900*. Paris: Éditions de Minuit, 1990.

Cheyette, Bryan. "Neither Black nor White: The Figure of 'the Jew' in Imperial British Literature." In *The Jew in the Text: Modernity and the Construction of Identity*, edited by Tamar Garb and Linda Nochlin, 31–41. London: Thames and Hudson, 1995.

Cheyette, Bryan, and Laura Marcus, eds. *Modernity, Culture, and "the Jew."* Stanford, CA: Stanford University Press, 1998.

Clarke, Jackie. "Imagined Productive Communities: Industrial Rationalisation and Cultural Crisis in 1930s France." *Modern and Contemporary France* 8, no. 3 (2000): 345–57.

———. "Engineering a New Order in the 1930s: The Case of Jean Coutrot." *French Historical Studies* 24, no. 1 (Winter 2001): 63–86.

Cole, Joshua. "Antisémitisme et situation coloniale dans l'entre-deux-guerres en Algérie: Les émeutes antijuives de Constantine (Août 1934)." *Vingtième Siècle*, no. 108 (October–December 2010): 3–23.

Conklin, Alice. *A Mission to Civilize: The Republican Idea of Empire in France and West Africa, 1895–1930*. Stanford, CA: Stanford University Press, 1997.

———. "Who Speaks for Africa? The René Maran–Blaise Diagne Trial in 1920s Paris." In *The Color of Liberty: Histories of Race in France*, edited by Sue Peabody and Tyler Stovall, 2–37. Durham, NC: Duke University Press, 2003.

Conley, Tom, and Steven Ungar, eds. *Identity Papers: Contested Nationhood in Twentieth-Century France*. Minneapolis: University of Minnesota Press, 1996.

Crane, Richard. *Passion of Israel: Jacques Maritain, Catholic Conscience, and the Holocaust*. Scranton, PA: University of Scranton Press, 2010.

Dard, Olivier. *Le rendez-vous manqué des relèves des années 30*. Paris: Presses Universitaires de France, 2002.

Dauphin, Jean-Pierre, and Henri Godard, eds. *Céline et l'actualité littéraire, 1932–1957*. Paris: Gallimard, 1976.

David, Angie. *Dominique Aury*. Paris: Éditions Léo Scheer, 2006.

Dean, Carolyn. *The Self and Its Pleasures: Bataille, Lacan, and the History of the Decentered Subject*. Ithaca, NY: Cornell University Press, 1992.

———. *The Frail Social Body: Pornography, Homosexuality, and Other Fantasies in Interwar France*. Berkeley: University of California Press, 2000.

———. *The Fragility of Empathy After the Holocaust*. Ithaca, NY: Cornell University Press, 2004.

———. "'The Open Secret': Affect, and the History of Sexuality." In *Sexuality at the Fin-de-siècle: The Makings of a "Central Problem,"* edited by Peter Cryle and Christopher Forth, 156–67. Newark: University of Delaware Press, 2008.

Deane, Seamus, ed. *Nationalism, Colonialism, and Literature*. Minneapolis: University of Minnesota Press, 1990.

Delphy, Christine. *Classer, dominer: Qui sont les "autres"?* Paris: La Fabrique, 2008.

———. *L'ennemi principal*. Vol. 2: *Penser le genre*. Paris: Éditions Syllepse, 2009.

Derval, André, ed. *70 Critiques de 'Voyage au bout de la nuit,' 1932–1935*. Paris: IMEC Éditions, 1993.

———. *L'accueil critique de 'Bagatelles pour un massacre.'* Paris: Éditions Écritures, 2010.

Desanti, Dominique. *Drieu La Rochelle: Du dandy au Nazi*. Paris: Flammarion, 1978.

Destrual, Philippe. "Le corps s'écrit: Somatique du *Voyage au bout de la nuit*." In Céline, *Voyage au bout de la nuit*, edited by Alain Cresciucci, 55–70. Paris: Klincksieck, 1993.

Dioudonnat, Pierre-Marie. *"Je Suis Partout," 1930–1944: Les maurrassiens devant la tentation fasciste*. Paris: La Table Ronde, 1973.

———. *Les 700 rédacteurs de "Je Suis Partout" 1930–1944: Dictionnaire des écrivains et journalistes qui ont collaboré au "grand hebdomadaire de la vie mondiale" devenu le principal organe du fascisme français*. Paris: Sedopols, 1993.

Dorlin, Elsa. *La matrice de la race: Généalogie sexuelle et coloniale de la nation française*. Paris: La Découverte, 2009.

Dubois, Laurent. *Avengers of the New World: The Story of the Haitian Revolution*. Cambridge, MA: Belknap Press of Harvard University Press, 2005.

Dupeux, Georges. *Le Front Populaire et les élections de 1936*. Paris: A. Colin, 1959.

Dutoit, Anne-Catherine. "Poetic Propaganda: Aesthetics and Politics in Céline's *Bagatelles pour un massacre*." PhD diss., Columbia University, 2009.

Edwards, Brent Hayes. *The Practice of Diaspora: Literature, Translation, and the Rise of Black Internationalism*. Cambridge, MA: Harvard University Press, 2003.

Eksteins, Modris. *Rites of Spring: The Great War and the Birth of the Modern Age*. Boston: Houghton Mifflin, 1989.

Eribon, Didier. *Héresies: Essais sur la théorie de la sexualité*. Paris: Fayard, 2003.

Etchegoin, Marie-France. "Claude Lanzmann juge *Les Bienveillantes*." *Le Nouvel Observateur*, September 21, 2006.

Ezra, Elisabeth. *The Colonial Unconscious: Race and Culture in Interwar France*. Ithaca, NY: Cornell University Press, 2000.

Falasca-Zamponi, Simonetta. *Fascist Spectacle: The Aesthetics of Power in Mussolini's Italy*. Berkeley: University of California Press, 2000.

———. "A Left Sacred or a Sacred Left? The Collège de Sociologie, Fascism, and Political Culture in Interwar France." *South Central Review* 23, no. 1 (Spring 2006): 40–54.

Felman, Shoshana. "After the Apocalypse: Paul de Man and the Fall to Silence." In Shoshana Felman and Dori Laub, *Testimony: Crises of Witnessing in Literature, Psychoanalysis, and History*, 120–64. London and New York: Routledge, 1992.

———, ed. *Literature and Psychoanalysis: The Question of Reading: Otherwise*. Baltimore: Johns Hopkins University Press, 1982.

Fohlen, Claude. *La France de l'entre-deux-guerres, 1917–1939*. Paris: Casterman, 1966.

Forrest, Jennifer. "The (Con)Quest of the Other in *Voyage au bout de la nuit*." In *Céline and the Politics of Difference*, edited by Rosemarie Scullion et al., 120–39. Hanover, NH: University Press of New England, 1995.

Forth, Christopher. "Nietzsche, Decadence, and Regeneration in France, 1891–1895." *Journal of the History of Ideas* 54, no. 1 (January 1993): 97–117.

———. *The Dreyfus Affair and the Crisis of French Manhood.* Baltimore: Johns Hopkins University Press, 2004.

Forth, Christopher, and Bertrand Taithe, eds. *French Masculinities: History, Politics, Culture.* New York: Palgrave Macmillan, 2007.

Foster, Hal. *Compulsive Beauty.* Cambridge, MA: MIT Press, 1993.

Foucault, Michel. *La pensée du dehors.* Paris: Fata Morgana, 1986.

———. *Dits et écrits.* Vol. 1, *1954–1975.* Paris: Gallimard, 2001.

Foureau, Christine. "*La Revue Universelle* (1920–1940): Aux origines intellectuelles du pétainisme." PhD diss., Princeton University, 1999.

Fraisse, Geneviève. *Muse de la raison: Démocratie et exclusion des femmes.* Paris: Flammarion, 1995.

Frétigné, Jean-Yves, and François Jankowiak, eds. *La décadence dans la culture et la pensée politique: Espagne, France et Italie (XVIIIe–XXe siècle).* Paris: École Française de Rome, 2008.

Frost, Laura. *Sex Drives: Fantasies of Fascism in Literary Modernism.* Ithaca, NY: Cornell University Press, 2002.

Furlough, Ellen. "Une leçon de choses: Tourism, Empire, and the Nation in Interwar France." *French Historical Studies* 25, no. 3 (Summer 2002): 441–73.

Galimi, Valeria. "Une internationale antisémite des images? *Je Suis Partout* et le cas des caricatures." In *Antisémythes: L'image des juifs entre culture et politique (1848–1939)*, edited by Marie-Anne Matard-Bonucci, 427–37. Paris: Nouveau Monde Éditions, 2005.

Garb, Tamar, and Linda Nochlin, eds. *The Jew in the Text: Modernity and the Construction of Identity.* London: Thames and Hudson, 1995.

Garraway, Doris. *The Libertine Colony: Creolization in the Early French Caribbean.* Durham, NC: Duke University Press, 2005.

Gaussen, Frédéric. "Maurras et Lucien Rebatet, le fasciste parricide." *Le Monde*, May 3, 2000.

Geroulanos, Stefanos. *An Atheism That Is Not Humanist Emerges in French Thought.* Stanford, CA: Stanford University Press, 2010.

Gibault, François. *Céline.* Vol. 2, *1932–1944: Délires et persécutions.* Paris: Mercure de France, 1985.

Gill, Carolyn Bailey, ed. *Maurice Blanchot: The Demand of Writing.* London and New York: Routledge, 1996.

Gilman, Sander. *Difference and Pathology: Stereotypes of Sexuality, Race, and Madness.* Ithaca, NY: Cornell University Press, 1985.

———. *The Jew's Body.* New York: Routledge, 1991.

Gilman, Sander, and Steven Katz, eds. *Anti-Semitism in Times of Crisis.* New York: New York University Press, 1991.

Godard, Henri. *Poétique de Céline.* Paris: Gallimard-NRF, 1985.

———. *Céline scandale.* Paris: Gallimard, 1994.

Goldstein, Jan. *The Post-Revolutionary Self: Politics and Psyche in France, 1750–1850.* Cambridge, MA: Harvard University Press, 2005.

Golsan, Richard. "The Legacy of World War II in France: Mapping the Discourses of Memory." In *The Politics of Memory in Postwar Europe*, edited by Richard Ned Lebow, Wulf Kansteiner, and Claudio Fogu, 73–101. Durham, NC: Duke University Press, 2006.

———, ed. *Fascism, Aesthetics, and Culture.* Hanover, NH: University Press of New England, 1992.

Golsan, Richard, and Melanie Hawthorne, eds. *Gender and Fascism in Modern France.* Hanover, NH: University Press of New England, 1997.

Goyet, Bruno. *Charles Maurras.* Paris: Presses de la Fondation Nationale des Sciences Politiques, 2000.

Green, Mary Jean. *Fiction in the Historical Present: French Writers and the Thirties.* Hanover, NH: University Press of New England, 1986.

Griffin, Roger. *The Nature of Fascism.* New York: Routledge, 1993.

———. *Modernism and Fascism: The Sense of a Beginning Under Mussolini and Hitler.* New York: Palgrave Macmillan, 2007.

Grosz, Elizabeth. "Julia Kristeva." In *Feminism and Psychoanalysis*, edited by Elizabeth Wright, 194–200. Oxford: Blackwell, 1992.

Guyader, Antonin. *La revue Idées, 1941–1944: Des non-conformistes en révolution nationale.* Paris: L'Harmattan, 2006.

Haase, Ullrich, and William Large. *Maurice Blanchot.* London: Routledge, 2001.

Hall, Catherine, ed. *Cultures of Empire: Colonizers in Britain and the Empire in the Nineteenth and Twentieth Centuries.* New York: Routledge, 2000.

Hammerschlag, Sarah. *The Figural Jew: Politics and Identity in Postwar French Thought.* Chicago: University of Chicago Press, 2010

Hanna, Martha. *The Mobilization of Intellect: French Scholars and Writers During the Great War.* Cambridge, MA: Harvard University Press, 1996.

Hart, Kevin. *The Dark Gaze: Maurice Blanchot and the Sacred.* Chicago: University of Chicago Press, 2004.

Hart, Kevin, and Geoffrey Hartman, eds. *The Power of Contestation: Perspectives on Maurice Blanchot.* Baltimore: Johns Hopkins University Press, 2004.

Herzog, Dagmar. *Intimacy and Exclusion: Religious Politics in Pre-Revolutionary Baden.* Princeton, NJ: Princeton University Press, 1996.

———. *Sex After Fascism: Memory and Morality in Twentieth-Century Germany.* Princeton, NJ: Princeton University Press, 2005.

———, ed. *Sexuality and German Fascism.* New York: Berghahn Books, 2004.

———, ed. *Brutality and Desire: War and Sexuality in Europe's Twentieth Century.* New York: Palgrave Macmillan, 2009.

Hess, Deborah. *Politics and Literature: The Case of Maurice Blanchot.* New York: Peter Lang, 1999.

Hewitt, Andrew. *Fascist Modernism: Aesthetics, Politics, and the Avant-Garde*. Stanford, CA: Stanford University Press, 1993.

———. *Political Inversions: Homosexuality, Fascism, and the Modernist Imaginary*. Stanford, CA: Stanford University Press, 1996.

Hewitt, Nicholas. *"Les maladies du siècle": The Image of Malaise in French Fiction and Thought in the Inter-War Years*. Hull, UK: Hull University Press, 1988.

———. *The Life of Céline: A Critical Biography*. Oxford: Blackwell, 1999.

———. "The Success of the *Monstre Sacré* in Postwar France." *SubStance* 23, no. 3 (2003): 29–42.

Hill, Leslie. *Blanchot: Extreme Contemporary*. London and New York: Routledge, 1997.

———. "'Not in Our Name': Blanchot, Politics, the Neuter." Special issue, *Paragraph* 30, no. 3 (2007): 141–59.

Hill, Leslie, and Michael Holland, eds. "Blanchot's Epoch." Special issue, *Paragraph* 30, no. 3 (2007).

Hill, Leslie, Brian Nelson, and Dimitris Vardoulakis, eds. *After Blanchot: Literature, Criticism, Philosophy*. Newark: University of Delaware Press, 2006.

Hobsbawn, Eric, and Terence Ranger, eds. *The Invention of Tradition*. Cambridge: Cambridge University Press, 1983.

Huguenin, François. *À l'école de l'Action française: Un siècle de vie intellectuelle*. Paris: J. C. Lattès, 1998.

Hunt, Lynn. *The Family Romance and the French Revolution*. Berkeley: University of California Press, 1993.

Hyman, Paula. *From Dreyfus to Vichy: The Remaking of French Jewry, 1906–1939*. New York: Columbia University Press, 1979.

———. *The Jews of Modern France*. Berkeley: University of California Press, 1998.

Ifri, Pascal. *Les deux étendards: Dossier d'un chef-d'oeuvre maudit*. Lausanne: Éditions l'âge d'homme, 2001.

Jackson, Jeffrey H. *Making Jazz French: Music and Modern Life in Interwar Paris*. Durham, NC: Duke University Press, 2003.

Jackson, Julian. *The Popular Front in France: Defending Democracy, 1934–1938*. Cambridge: Cambridge University Press, 1988.

———. *The Dark Years, 1940–1944*. Oxford: Oxford University Press, 2001.

Jameson, Fredric. "Modernism and Imperialism." In *Nationalism, Colonialism, and Literature*, edited by Seamus Deane, 43–66. Minneapolis: University of Minnesota Press, 1990.

Jay, Martin. "'The Aesthetic Ideology' as Ideology: Or What Does It Mean to Aestheticize Politics?" In *Force Fields: Between Intellectual History and Cultural Critique*, 71–83. New York: Routledge, 1992.

———. *Downcast Eyes: The Denigration of Vision in Twentieth-Century French Thought*. Berkeley: University of California Press, 1994.

Jennings, Eric T. *Curing the Colonizers: Hydrotherapy, Climatology, and French Colonial Spas*. Durham, NC: Duke University Press, 2006.

Jennings, Jeremy, ed. *Intellectuals in Twentieth-Century France: Mandarins and Samurais*. London: Macmillan, 1993.

Jenny, Laurent. "Paulhan, Blanchot, and 'Le 14 Juillet.'" *Yale French Studies* 106 (2004): 125–39.

Johnson, Douglas. "Obituary: Maurice Blanchot: Enigmatic French Writer Committed to the Virtues of Silence and Abstraction." *The Guardian*, March 1, 2003.

Jolles, Adam. "The Tactile Turn: Envisioning a Postcolonial Aesthetics in France." *Yale French Studies* 109 (2006): 17–38.

Jordan, Matthew. *Le jazz: Jazz and French Cultural Identity*. Urbana: University of Illinois Press, 2010.

Judaken, Jonathan. "The Queer Jew: Gender, Sexuality, and Jean-Paul Sartre's Anti-Antisemitism." *Patterns of Prejudice* 33, no. 3 (July 1999): 45–63.

———. *Jean-Paul Sartre and the Jewish Question: Anti-Antisemitism and the Politics of the French Intellectual*. Lincoln: University of Nebraska Press, 2009.

Judt, Tony. *Past Imperfect: French Intellectuals, 1944–1956*. Berkeley: University of California Press, 1992.

Julius, Anthony. *T. S. Eliot, Anti-Semitism, and Literary Form*. Cambridge: Cambridge University Press, 1995.

Just, Daniel. "The Politics of the Novel and Maurice Blanchot's Theory of the *Récit*, 1954–1964." *French Forum* 33, nos. 1–2 (Winter/Spring 2008): 121–39.

Kakutani, Michiko. "Unrepentant and Telling Stories of Horrors Untellable." *New York Times*, February 23, 2009.

Kalman, Samuel. "Reconsidering Fascist Anti-Semitism and Xenophobia in 1920s France: The Doctrinal Contribution of Georges Valois and the Faisceau." *French History* 16, no. 3 (Fall 2002): 345–65.

———. *The Extreme Right in Interwar France: The Faisceau and the Croix de Feu*. Burlington, VT: Ashgate, 2008.

Kaplan, Alice. *Reproductions of Banality: Fascism, Literature, and French Intellectual Life*. Minneapolis: University of Minnesota Press, 1986.

———. *Relevé des sources et citations dans 'Bagatelles pour un massacre.'* Paris: Éditions du Lérot, 1987.

———. *The Collaborator: The Trial and Execution of Robert Brasillach*. Chicago: University of Chicago Press, 2000.

Kemal, Salim, and Ivan Gaskell, eds. *Politics and Aesthetics in the Arts*. Cambridge: Cambridge University Press, 2000.

Kennedy, Sean. *Reconciling France Against Democracy: The Croix de Feu and the Parti Social Français, 1927–1945*. Montreal: McGill-Queen's University Press, 2007.

Kent, Susan. *Making Peace: The Reconstruction of Gender in Interwar Britain.* Princeton, NJ: Princeton University Press, 1993.

———. *Aftershocks: The Politics of Trauma in Britain, 1918–1931.* New York: Palgrave Macmillan, 2009.

Kern, Steven. *The Culture of Time and Space, 1880–1918.* Cambridge, MA: Harvard University Press, 1986.

Kessler, Nicolas. *Histoire politique de la Jeune Droite (1929–1942): Une révolution conservatrice à la française.* Paris: L'Harmattan, 2001.

Khanna, Ranjana. *Dark Continents: Psychoanalysis and Colonialism.* Durham, NC: Duke University Press, 2003.

Kingston, Paul. *Anti-Semitism in France During the 1930s: Organisations, Personalities, and Propaganda.* Hull, UK: University of Hull Press, 1983.

Kleeblatt, Norman, ed. *The Dreyfus Affair: Art, Truth, and Justice.* Berkeley: University of California Press, 1987.

Kleinberg, Ethan. *Generation Existential: Heidegger's Philosophy in France, 1927–1961.* Ithaca, NY: Cornell University Press, 2005.

Kristeva, Julia. *Powers of Horror: An Essay on Abjection.* New York: Columbia University Press, 1982.

Lacan, Jacques. *Écrits 1.* Paris: Seuil, 1966.

———. *Écrits 2.* Paris: Seuil, 1972.

———. *Les quatre concepts fondamentaux de la psychanalyse.* Paris: Seuil, 1973.

LaCapra, Dominick. "Intellectual History and Its Ways." *American Historical Review* 97, no. 2 (April 1992): 425–39.

———. "Historical and Literary Approaches to the 'Final Solution': Saul Friedländer and Jonathan Littell." *History and Theory* 50 (February 2011): 71–97.

Lacoue-Labarthe, Philippe. "Neither Accident nor Mistake." *Critical Inquiry* 15, no. 2 (Winter 1989): 481–84.

Landes, Joan. *Visualizing the Nation: Gender, Representation, and Revolution in Eighteenth-Century France.* Ithaca, NY: Cornell University Press, 2003.

Lang, Berel. *Heidegger's Silences.* Ithaca, NY: Cornell University Press, 1996.

Laporte, Roger. *A l'extrême pointe: Proust, Bataille, Blanchot.* Paris: P.O.L., 1998.

Laval, Michel. *Brasillach ou la tentation du clerc.* Paris: Hachette, 1972.

Lear, Jonathan. *Open-Minded: Working Out the Logic of the Soul.* Cambridge, MA: Harvard University Press, 1998.

Lebovics, Herman. *True France: The Wars over Cultural Identity.* Ithaca, NY: Cornell University Press, 1992.

Leroy, Géraldi, and Anne Roche. *Les écrivains et le Front Populaire.* Paris: Presses de la Fondation Nationale des Sciences Politiques, 1986.

Le Sueur, James. *Uncivil War: Intellectuals and Identity Politics During the Decolonization of Algeria.* 2nd ed. Lincoln: University of Nebraska Press, 2005.

Levenson, Michael, ed. *The Cambridge Companion to Modernism*. Cambridge: Cambridge University Press, 1999.

Levinson, Jerrold, ed. *Aesthetics and Ethics: Essays at the Intersection*. Cambridge: Cambridge University Press, 1998.

Lichtenstein, Therese, ed. *Twilight Visions: Surrealism and Paris*. Berkeley: University of California Press, 2009.

Lindenberg, Daniel. *Les années souterraines, 1937–1947*. Paris: La Découverte, 1990.

Littell, Jonathan. *Les bienveillantes*. Paris: Gallimard, 2006.

———. "Lire?" *Espace Maurice Blanchot*. http://www.blanchot.fr/fr/index.php?option=com_content&task=view&id=201&Itemid=40. Accessed December 4, 2011.

Loret, Eric. "Blanchot s'efface: Le plus secret des écrivains français est mort chez lui, près de Paris, à 95 ans." *Libération*, February 24, 2003.

Loselle, Andrea. "Traveling in the Work of Louis-Ferdinand Céline." PhD diss., Columbia University, 1990.

———. "Bardamu's American Dream: Censorship and Prostitution." *South Atlantic Quarterly* 93, no. 2 (Spring 1994): 225–42.

———. *History's Double: Cultural Tourism in Twentieth-Century Writing*. New York: St Martin's Press, 1997.

Loubet del Bayle, Jean-Louis. *Les non-conformistes des années 30: Une tentative de renouvellement de la pensée politique française*. Paris: Seuil, 1969.

Luce, Stanford L., ed. and trans. *Céline and His Critics: Scandals and Paradox*. Saratoga, CA: Anma Libri, 1986.

Malchow, Howard. *Gothic Images of Race in Nineteenth-Century Britain*. Stanford, CA: Stanford University Press, 1996.

Marineau, Hélène. "Le concept d'aventure dans la prose narrative française du vingtième siècle." PhD diss., Rutgers University / Université de Paris VIII–Vincennes, 2007.

Marks, Elaine. *Marrano as Metaphor: The Jewish Presence in French Writing*. New York: Columbia University Press, 1996.

Marque, Jean-Noël. *Léon Daudet*. Paris: Fayard, 1971.

Marrus, Michael, and Robert Paxton. *Vichy et les juifs*. Paris: Calmann-Lévy, 1981.

Matard-Bonucci, Marie-Anne. "L'image, figure majeure du discours antisémite?" *Vingtième siècle: Revue d'histoire* 72 (October–December 2001): 27–39.

———, ed. *Antisémythes: L'image des juifs entre culture et politique (1848–1939)*. Paris: Nouveau Monde Éditions, 2005.

Matard-Bonucci, Marie-Anne, and Pierre Milza, eds. *L'homme nouveau dans l'Europe fasciste (1922–1945): Entre dictature et totalitarisme*. Paris: Fayard, 2004.

Matysik, Tracie. *Reforming the Moral Subject: Ethics and Sexuality in Central Europe, 1890–1930*. Ithaca, NY: Cornell University Press, 2008.

"Maurice Blanchot." Special issue, *Critique* 229 (1966).

Mazgaj, Paul. "The Origins of the French Radical Right: A Historiographical Essay." *French Historical Studies* 15, no. 2 (Fall 1987): 287–315.

———. "Ce mal de siècle: The 'Romantic' Fascism of Robert Brasillach." *Historical Reflections / Réflexions Historiques* 23, no. 1 (1997): 49–72.

———. "Engagement and the French Nationalist Right: The Case of the Jeune Droite." *European History Quarterly* 32, no. 2 (April 2002): 207–32.

———. *Imagining Fascism: The Cultural Politics of the French Young Right, 1930–1945*. Newark: University of Delaware Press, 2007.

Mehlman, Jeffrey. *Legacies of Anti-Semitism in France*. Minneapolis: University of Minnesota Press, 1983.

———. *Genealogies of the Text: Literature, Psychoanalysis, and Politics in Modern France*. Cambridge: Cambridge University Press, 1995.

Mendelsohn, Daniel. "Transgression." *New York Review of Books*, March 26, 2009.

Mercer, Kobena. "Reading Racial Fetishism: The Photographs of Robert Mapplethorpe." In *Fetishism as Cultural Discourse*, edited by Emily Apter and William Pietz, 311. Ithaca: Cornell University Press, 1993.

———, ed. *Cosmopolitan Modernisms*. Cambridge, MA: MIT Press, 2005.

Mesnard, Philippe. *Maurice Blanchot: Le sujet de l'engagement*. Paris: L'Harmattan, 1996.

Meyers, Mark. "Feminizing Fascist Men: Crowd Psychology, Gender, and Sexuality in French Antifascism, 1929–1945." *French Historical Studies* 29, no. 1 (Winter 2006): 109–42.

Michaud, Eric. *The Cult of Art in Nazi Germany*. Stanford, CA: Stanford University Press, 2004.

Miller, Gérard, ed. *Lacan*. Paris: Bordas, 1987.

Millman, Richard. *La question juive entre les deux guerres: Ligues de droite et antisémitisme en France*. Paris: Armand Colin, 1992.

Mitterand, Henri. "Nègres et négriers dans le *Voyage au bout de la nuit*." In Céline, *Voyage au bout de la nuit*, edited by Alain Cresciucci, 165–173. Paris: Klincksieck, 1993.

Montety, Etienne de. *Thierry Maulnier: Biographie*. Paris: Julliard, 1994.

———. *Salut à Kléber Haedens*. Paris: Grasset, 1996.

Mosse, George. *Nationalism and Sexuality: Middle-Class Morality and Sexual Norms in Modern Europe*. Madison: University of Wisconsin Press, 1985.

———. *Toward the Final Solution: A History of European Racism*. 2nd ed. New York: Howard Fertig, 1985.

———. *The Image of Man: The Creation of Modern Masculinity*. New York: Oxford University Press, 1996.

Moyn, Samuel. *Origins of the Other: Emmanuel Lévinas Between Revelation and Ethics*. Ithaca, NY: Cornell University Press, 2005.

———. "A Nazi Zelig." *The Nation*, March 4, 2009.

Muel-Dreyfus, Francine. *Vichy et l'éternel féminin. Contribution à une sociologie politique de l'ordre des corps*. Paris: Seuil, 1998.

Noiriel, Gérard. *Le creuset français: Histoire de l'immigration, XIXe–XXe siècles*. Paris: Seuil, 1988.

———. *Les origines républicaines de Vichy*. Paris: Hachette Littératures, 1999.

———. *Immigration, antisémitisme, et racisme en France (XIXe–XXe siècle): Discours publics, humiliations privées*. Paris: Fayard, 2007.

Nord, Philip. "Catholic Culture in Interwar France." *French Politics, Culture, and Society* 21, no. 3 (Fall 2003): 1–20.

———. "Pierre Schaeffer and *Jeune France*: Cultural Politics in the Vichy Years." *French Historical Studies* 30, no. 4 (Fall 2007): 685–709.

———. *France's New Deal: From the Thirties to the Postwar Era*. Princeton, NJ: Princeton University Press, 2010.

North, Michael. *The Dialect of Modernism: Race, Language, and Twentieth-Century Literature*. New York: Oxford University Press, 1990.

Nye, Robert. *Masculinity and Male Codes of Honor in Modern France*. Berkeley: University of California Press, 1998.

Ofer, Dalia, and Lenore Weitzman, eds. *Women in the Holocaust*. New Haven, CT: Yale University Press, 1999.

Olpez, Hannes. "The Political Share of Literature: Maurice Blanchot, 1931–1937." *Paragraph* 33, no. 1 (March 2010): 70–89.

Ory, Pascal, and Jean-François Sirinelli. *Les intellectuels en France de l'Affaire Dreyfus à nos jours*. Paris: Librairie Armand Colin, 1992.

Pagès, Yves. *Les fictions du politique chez Louis-Ferdinand Céline*. Paris: Seuil-L'Univers Historique, 1994.

Panchasi, Roxanne. "Reconstructions: Prosthetics and the Rehabilitation of the Male Body in World War One France." *Differences* 7, no. 3 (Fall 1995): 109–21.

———. "'Fortress France': Protecting the Nation and Its Bodies, 1918–1940." *Historical Reflections / Réflexions Historiques* 33, no. 3 (2007): 475–504.

———. *Future Tense: The Culture of Anticipation in France Between the Wars*. Ithaca, NY: Cornell University Press, 2009.

Passmore, Kevin. *From Liberalism to Fascism: The Right in a French Province, 1928–1939*. Cambridge: Cambridge University Press, 1997.

Paxton, Robert, *The Anatomy of Fascism*. New York: Knopf, 2004.

Peabody, Sue, and Tyler Stovall, eds. *The Color of Liberty: Histories of Race in France*. Durham, NC: Duke University Press, 2003.

Peterson, Lars. "The Age of the Weekly: Contesting Culture in the *hebdomadaires politico-littéraires* (1933–1940)." PhD diss., University of Iowa, 2003.

Pollard, Miranda. *Reign of Virtue: Mobilizing Gender in Vichy France*. Chicago: University of Chicago Press, 1998.

Prochasson, Christophe, and Anne Rasmussen. *Au nom de la patrie: Les intellectuels et la première guerre mondiale, 1910–1919*. Paris: La Découverte, 1996.

Rabinbach, Anson. *The Human Motor: Energy, Fatigue, and the Origins of Modernity*. Berkeley: University of California Press, 1992.

Raimond, Michel. *La crise du roman: Des lendemains du naturalisme aux années vingt*. 5th ed. Paris: José Corti, 1993.

———. *Éloge et critique de la modernité: De la première à la deuxième guerre mondiale*. Paris: Presses Universitaires de France, 2000.

Rancière, Jacques. *Les noms de l'histoire: Essai de poétique du savoir*. Paris: Le Seuil, 1992.

———. *Le partage du sensible: Esthétique et politique*. Paris: La Fabrique, 2000.

———. *Aesthetics and Its Discontents*. Cambridge: Polity Press, 2004.

———. *The Politics of Aesthetics: The Distribution of the Sensible*. New York: Continuum, 2006.

———. *The Aesthetic Unconscious*. Cambridge: Polity Press, 2009.

Renard, Paul. *L'Action française et la vie littéraire (1931–1944)*. Lille: Presses Universitaires du Septentrion, 2003.

Reynolds, Siân. *France Between the Wars: Gender and Politics*. London: Routledge, 1996.

Richard, François. *L'anarchisme de droite dans la littérature contemporaine*. Paris: Presses Universitaires de France, 1988.

Riot-Sarcey, Michèle. *La démocratie à l'épreuve des femmes: Trois figures critiques du pouvoir, 1830–1848*. Paris: Albin Michel, 1993.

Robert, Véronique, with Lucette Destouches. *Céline secret*. Paris: Grasset, 2001.

Roberts, Mary Louise. *Civilization Without Sexes: Reconstructing Gender in Postwar France, 1917–1927*. Chicago: University of Chicago Press, 1994.

Rose, Jacqueline. *States of Fantasy*. The Clarendon Lectures. New York: Oxford University Press, 1996.

Roudinesco, Elisabeth. *Jacques Lacan: Esquisse d'une vie, histoire d'un système de pensée*. Paris: Fayard, 1993.

———. *Histoire de la psychanalyse en France*. Vol. 1, *1885–1939*. Paris: Fayard, 1994.

———. *Histoire de la psychanalyse en France*. Vol. 2, *1925–1985*. Paris: Fayard, 1994.

Roussin, Philippe. *Misère de la littérature, terreur de l'histoire: Céline et la littérature contemporaine*. Paris: Gallimard, 2005.

Rousso, Henry. *Le syndrome de Vichy de 1944 à nos jours*. 2nd ed. Paris: Seuil, 1990.

Rubenstein, Diane. *What's Left? The École Normale Supérieure and the Right*. Madison: University of Wisconsin Press, 1990.

Said, Edward. *Culture and Imperialism*. New York: Vintage, 1993.

———. *Orientalism: Western Conceptions of the Orient*. London: Penguin Books, 1995.

Salecl, Renata. "National Identity and Socialist Moral Majority." In *Becoming National. A Reader*, edited by Geoff Eley and Ronald Grigor Suny, 418–24. New York: Oxford University Press, 1996.

Sampath, Raj. "Time's Impossibility: The Holocaust and the Historicity of History." In *Contemporary Portrayals of Auschwitz,* edited by Alan Rosenberg, James R. Watson, and Detlef Linke, 283–93. Amherst, MA: Humanity Books, 2000.

Sanos, Sandrine. "'From Revolution to Literature': The Political Aesthetics of the Young New Right, 1936–1937." *Contemporary French and Francophone Studies: Sites* 10, no. 1 (January 2006): 85–95.

———. "Fascist Fantasies of Perversion and Abjection: Race, Gender, and Sexuality in the Interwar Far-Right." *Proceedings of the 2009 Western Society for French History* 37 (Fall 2010): 1–17. http://quod.lib.umich.edu/w/wsfh/volumes.html.

———. "The Subject and the World of Difference." *Modern Intellectual History* 8, no. 1 (April 2011): 1–13.

Sapiro, Gisèle. "Académie Française et Académie Goncourt dans les années '40: Fonction et fonctionnement des institutions de la vie littéraire en période de crise nationale." *Texte et histoire littéraire* 12 (1992): 151–97.

———. *La guerre des écrivains, 1940–1953*. Paris: Fayard, 1999.

Sarocchi, Jean. *Julien Benda: Portrait d'un intellectuel.* Paris: A.-G. Nizet, 1968.

Sartre, Jean-Paul. *Anti-Semite and Jew.* New York: Schocken, 1960.

Schalk, David. "*La trahison des clercs*—1927 and Later." *French Historical Studies* 7, no. 2 (Fall 1971): 245–63.

———. "Professors as Watchdogs: Paul Nizan's Theory of the Intellectual and Politics." *Journal of the History of Ideas* 34, no. 1 (January–March 1973): 79–96.

Schor, Ralph. *L'opinion française et les étrangers en France, 1919–1939*. Paris: Publications de la Sorbonne, 1980.

———. *L'antisémitisme en France pendant les années trente: Prélude à Vichy*. Brussels: Éditions Complexe, 1991.

Scott, Joan W. *Only Paradoxes to Offer: French Feminists and the Rights of Man*. Cambridge, MA: Harvard University Press, 1997.

———. *Parité! Sexual Equality and the Crisis of French Universalism*. Chicago: University of Chicago Press, 2005.

Scullion, Rosemarie. "Style, Subversion, Modernity: L.-F. Céline's Anti-Semitic Pamphlets." In *Fascism, Aesthetics, and Culture*, edited by Richard Golsan, 179–97. Hanover, NH: University Press of New England, 1992.

———. "Choreographing Sexual Difference: Ballet and Gender in Céline." In *Céline and the Politics of Difference*, edited by Rosemarie Scullion et al., 140–68. Hanover, NH: University Press of New England, 1995.

Scullion, Rosemarie, Philip H. Solomon, and Thomas C. Spear, eds. *Céline and the Politics of Difference*. Hanover, NH: University Press of New England, 1995.

Séébold, Éric. *Essai de situation des pamphlets de Louis-Ferdinand Céline*. Paris: Éditions du Lérot, 1985.

Seigel, Jerrold. *The Idea of the Self: Thought and Experience in Western Europe Since the Seventeenth Century*. New York: Cambridge University Press, 2005.

Sérant, Paul. *Les dissidents de l'Action française*. Paris: Copernic, 1978.

Serry, Hervé. *Naissance de l'intellectuel catholique*. Paris: La Découverte, 2004.

Sharpley-Whiting, Denean T. *Négritude Women*. Minneapolis: University of Minnesota Press, 2002.

Shepard, Todd. *The Invention of Decolonization: Algeria and the Remaking of France*. Ithaca, NY: Cornell University Press, 2006.

———. "L'extrême-droite et 'Mai 68': Une obsession d'Algérie et de virilité." *Clio: Histoire, Femmes, et Société* 29 (Spring 2009): 35–55.

Shepherdson, Charles. *Vital Signs: Nature, Culture, and Psychoanalysis*. New York: Routledge, 2000.

Short, Robert. "The Politics of Surrealism, 1920–36." In *Surrealism, Politics, and Culture*, edited by Raymond Spiteri and Donald LaCoss, 18–36. New York: Ashgate, 2003.

Silverman, Max. "Re-Figuring the Jew in France." In *Modernity, Culture, and the Jew*, edited by Bryan Cheyette and Laura Marcus, 197–210. Stanford, CA: Stanford University Press, 1998.

Sipriot, Pierre, ed. *Robert Brasillach et la génération perdue*. Paris: Éditions du Rocher, 1987.

Sirinelli, Jean-François. *Génération intellectuelle: Khâgneux et normaliens dans l'entre-deux-guerres*. Paris: Fayard, 1988.

———. *Intellectuels et passions françaises: Manifestes et pétitions au XXe siècle*. Paris: Fayard, 1990.

Slavin, David. *Colonial Cinema and Imperial France, 1919–1939: White Blind Spots, Male Fantasies, Settler Myths*. Baltimore: Johns Hopkins University Press, 2001.

Smith, Bonnie. *The Gender of History: Men, Women, and Historical Practice*. Cambridge, MA: Harvard University Press, 1998.

Solomon, Philip H. "Céline on the 1937 Paris Exposition Universelle as Jewish Conspiracy." In *Identity Papers: Contested Nationhood in Twentieth-Century France*, edited by Steven Ungar and Tom Conley, 66–87. Minneapolis: University of Minnesota Press, 1996.

Solomon-Godeau, Abigail. "The Legs of the Countess." In *Fetishism as Cultural Discourse*, edited by Emily Apter and William Pietz. Ithaca, NY: Cornell University Press, 1993.

Soucy, Robert. *French Fascism: The Second Wave, 1933–1939*. New Haven: Yale University Press, 1995.

Spackman, Barbara. *Fascist Virilities: Rhetoric, Ideology, and Social Fantasy in Italy*. Minneapolis: University of Minnesota Press, 1996.

Spears, Thomas C. "Céline and 'Autofictional' First-Person Narration." *Studies in the Novel* 23, no. 3 (Fall 1991): 357–70.

———. "Virility and the Jewish 'Invasion' in Céline's Pamphlets." In *Céline and the Politics of Difference*, edited by Rosemarie Scullion et al., 98–119. Hanover, NH: University Press of New England, 1995.

Spiteri, Raymond, and Donald LaCoss, eds. *Surrealism, Politics, and Culture*. New York: Ashgate, 2003.

Sternhell, Zeev. *Maurice Barrès et le nationalisme français*. Paris: A. Colin, 1972.

———. *Ni droite ni gauche: L'idéologie fasciste en France*. Paris: Éditions du Seuil, 1983.

———. *Neither Right nor Left: Fascist Ideology in France*. Translated by David Maisel. Princeton, NJ: Princeton University Press, 1996.

Sthème de Jubécourt, Gérard. *Robert Brasillach: Critique littéraire*. Lausanne: Association des Amis de Robert Brasillach, 1972.

Stoekl, Allan. *Politics, Writing, Mutilation: The Cases of Bataille, Blanchot, Roussel, Leiris, and Ponge*. Minneapolis: University of Minnesota Press, 1985.

Stoler, Ann Laura. *Race and the Education of Desire: Foucault's "History of Sexuality" and the Colonial Order of Things*. Durham, NC: Duke University Press, 1995.

———. *Carnal Knowledge and Imperial Power: Race and the Intimate in Colonial Rule*. 2nd ed. Berkeley: University of California Press, 2010.

Stovall, Tyler. "The Color Line Behind the Lines: Racial Violence in France During the Great War." *American Historical Review* 103, no. 3 (June 1998): 737–69.

———. *Paris Noir: African Americans in the City of Light*. New York: Mariner Books, 1998.

Surkis, Judith. *Sexing the Citizen: Morality and Masculinity in France, 1870–1920*. Ithaca, NY: Cornell University Press, 2006.

———. "Enemies Within: Venereal Disease and the Defense of French Masculinity Between the Wars." In *French Masculinities: History, Culture, and Politics*, edited by Christopher Forth and Bertrand Taithe, 103–22. New York: Palgrave Macmillan, 2007.

Surya, Michel. *Georges Bataille: La mort à l'oeuvre*. Paris: Éditions Garamont, 1987.

Swenson, James. "Revolutionary Sentences (in Law, Death, Community)." In "The Place of Maurice Blanchot," edited by Thomas Pepper. Special issue, *Yale French Studies* 93 (1998): 11–29.

Taguieff, Pierre-André, Grégoire Kauffmann, and Michaël Lenoire, eds. *L'antisémitisme de plume, 1940–1944: Études et documents*. Paris: Berg, 1999.

———. *La nouvelle judéophobie*. Paris: Les Mille et Une Nuits, 2002.

Tatar, Maria. *Lustmord: Sexual Murder in Weimar Germany*. Princeton, NJ: Princeton University Press, 1995.

Tettamanzi, Régis. *Esthétique de l'outrance: Idéologie et stylistique dans les pamphlets de L.-F. Céline*. Paris: Éditions du Lérot, 1999.

Theweleit, Klaus. *Male Fantasies*. Vol. 1, *Women, Floods, Bodies, History*. Cambridge: Cambridge University Press, 1987.

———. *Male Fantasies*. Vol. 2, *Male Bodies: Psychoanalyzing the White Terror*. Minneapolis: University of Minnesota Press, 1989.

Tison-Braun, Micheline. *La crise de l'humanisme: Le conflit de l'individu et de la société dans la littérature française moderne*. Vol. 2, *1914–1939*. Paris: Nizet, 1967.

Toda, Michel. *Henri Massis: Un témoin de la droite intellectuelle*. Paris: La Table Ronde, 1987.

Tonnet-Lacroix, Éliane. *Après-guerre et sensibilités littéraires (1919–1924)*. Paris: Publications de la Sorbonne, 1991.

———. *La littérature française de l'entre-deux-guerres, 1919–1939*. Paris: Nathan, 1993.

Trouillot, Michel-Rolph. *Silencing the Past: Power and the Production of History*. Boston: Beacon Press, 1995.

Tumblety, Joan. "Revenge of the Fascist Knights: Masculine Identities in *Je Suis Partout*, 1940–1944." *Modern and Contemporary France* 7, no. 1 (1999): 11–20.

Uhrig, Daniel. "Maurice Blanchot, Political Writings, 1953–1993." *H-France Review* 11, no. 187 (August 2011): 1–10.

Ungar, Steven. *Scandal and Aftereffect: Blanchot and France Since 1930*. Minneapolis: University of Minnesota Press, 1995.

Vatré, Eric. *Léon Daudet ou le libre réactionnaire*. Paris: Éditions France-Empire, 1987.

Verdès-Leroux, Jeannine. *Refus et violences: Politique et littérature à l'extrême-droite des années trente aux retombées de la Libération*. Paris: Gallimard, 1996.

Virtanen, Reino. "Nietzsche and the Action Française: Nietzsche's Significance for French Rightist Thought." *Journal of the History of Ideas* 11, no. 2 (April 1950): 191–214.

Walz, Robin. *Pulp Surrealism: Insolent Popular Culture in Early Twentieth-Century Paris*. Berkeley: University of California Press, 2000.

Wardaugh, Jessica. *In Pursuit of the People: Political Culture in France, 1934–9*. London: Palgrave Macmillan, 2009.

Warner, Michael. *The Letters of the Republic: Publication and the Public Sphere in Eighteenth-Century America*. Cambridge, MA: Harvard University Press, 1990.

———. *Publics and Counterpublics*. New York: Zone Books, 2002.

Watts, Philip. *Allegories of the Purge: How Literature Responded to the Postwar Trials of Writers and Intellectuals in France*. Stanford, CA: Stanford University Press, 1998.

Weber, Eugen. *L'Action française*. Paris: Fayard, 1985.

———. *The Hollow Years: France in the 1930s*. New York: Norton, 1994.

White, Hayden. *Tropics of Discourse: Essays in Cultural Criticism*. Baltimore: Johns Hopkins University Press, 1978.

Wiener, Martin. "Treating 'Historical' Sources as Literary Texts: Literary Historicism and Modern British History." *Journal of Modern History* 70 (September 1998): 619–38.

Wilder, Gary. "Unthinking French History: Colonial Studies Beyond National Identity." In *After the Imperial Turn: Thinking With and Through the Nation*, edited by Antoinette Burton, 125–43. Durham, NC: Duke University Press, 2003.

———. *The French Imperial Nation-State: Négritude and Colonial Humanism Between the Two World Wars*. Chicago: University of Chicago Press, 2005.

Wilson, Stephen. *Ideology and Experience: Anti-Semitism in France at the Time of the Dreyfus Affair*. 2nd ed. New York: Littman Library of Jewish Civilization, 2007.

Winock, Michel. *Nationalisme, antisémitisme, et fascisme en France*. Paris: Seuil, 1990.

———. *Le siècle des intellectuels*. Paris: Seuil, 1997.

Wistrich. Robert. *Antisemitism: The Longest Hatred*. London: Thames, 1991.

Witt, Mary Ann Frese. *The Search for Modern Tragedy: Aesthetic Fascism in Italy and France*. Ithaca, NY: Cornell University Press, 2001.

Wohl, Robert. *The Generation of 1914*. Cambridge, MA: Harvard University Press, 1979.

Wolin, Richard, ed. *The Heidegger Controversy: A Critical Reader*. New York: Columbia University Press, 1991.

———. *The Seduction of Unreason: The Intellectual Romance with Fascism from Nietzsche to Postmodernism*. Princeton, NJ: Princeton University Press, 2004.

Yasuhara, Shinichiro. "'De la révolution à la littérature': La genèse de la critique littéraire de Maurice Blanchot dans les années 30." *Études de Langue et Littérature Françaises* 87 (2005): 96–114.

———. "Maurice Blanchot dans les années 1930: La dissidence politique et la perfection littéraire." PhD diss., Université Paris VIII–Vincennes, 2006.

Zagdanski, Stéphane. *Céline seul: Essai*. Paris: Gallimard, 1993.

———. *De l'antisémitisme*. Paris: Julliard, 1995.

Žižek, Slavoj. *The Sublime Object of Ideology*. New York: Verso, 1989.

———. *The Plague of Fantasies*. New York: Verso, 1997.

INDEX

Page numbers in italic indicate illustrations.

Abjection: aesthetics and, 2, 4, 6, 14; antisemitism and, 77; Blanchot and, 128–31, 133–34, 137, 141, 150; and the body, 2, 12–14, 131; and citizenship, 76, 92, 95–96; crisis and, 13–14; defined, 4; fascism and, 12; historicization of, 13; *L'Insurgé* and, 85; intellectual far right and, 3, 4, 13–14, 75–76, 249; *Je Suis Partout* and, 197–98; Jews and, 98–99; literature and, 112; in Littell's *Les bienveillantes*, 1–3, 257; of the nation, 89–98, 174–77; otherness and, 133; political function of, 90, 133; psychoanalytic conception of, 290n205; and the self, 13, 95–96, 98, 130–31, 286n111; surrealism and, 36

"abjection Française, L'," *L'Insurgé*, 94–95, *132*

Acéphale (Headless) [magazine], 156

Action française, 3, 92, 95, 109, 126, 208, 210; as antecedent to 1930s far right, 44; antisemitism of, 51–53; Blanchot on, 144; Catholicism and, 50; demonstrations of, 19; and February days, 71; founding of, 49; ideology of, 49–55; influence of, 46–49, 51; and nationalism, 42, 49–55

Action Française, L' (newspaper), 15, 32, 46–48, 51–52, 54–55, 57, 58, 62–63, 71–73, 77, 79, 87, 116, 127, 135, 204, 205, 208, 209, 287n135, 292n9

Adler, Karen, 256

Adorno, Theodor, 119, 153, 250

Aesthetics: abjection and, 2, 4, 6, 14; of colonialism, 227; Frenchness as, 110–15; Maurras and, 53–54; perversion associated with, 2; politics and, 4–8, 37–40, 110, 147–48; scholarship on, 250–52; and the self, 24–25; solutions offered by, 6. *See also* Literature

Aesthetics of hate, 4, 6

Africa. *See* Black culture; Colonialism

African art, 20

Agamben, Giorgio, 13

Alain (pseudonym of Émile-Auguste Chartier), 150, 153

Algeria (colonial), 116–17, 223, 227, 229–32, 321–22n150, 329n38

Algerian War of Independence, 117, 153, 245–48, 276n85, 329n40

Alienation, and formation of the self, 297n77

Alméras, Philippe, 305n15, 305n18, 305n23

America. *See* United States

Antelme, Robert, 303n207

Antisemitism: abjection and, 77; Action française and, 51–53; of Arabs, Muslims, and North Africans, 229–32; Blanchot and, 122–24, 133–37, 139, 154, 157, 294n21, 295n33, 303n205; of Brasillach, 100, 216–17, 231–33, 235–36, 243, 324n198; and capitalism, 99; of Céline, 119, 159–93, 201, 218–19, 278n127, 287n140, 289n181; and civilization, 52–53; colonialism and, 8, 229–33, 253–54; of Daudet, 55, 57; French, 52, 78, 108–9, 195, 217, 229, 233, 235–36, 252–53; gender and, 9; German, 52, 217, 235–36; instinctual, 171, 217, 235; of intellectual far right, 77–78; *Je Suis Partout* and, 194–244; Jews blamed for, 216;

Antisemitism (*continued*): Maulnier on, 106–9, 154; of Maurras, 52–53; nationalism and, 51–53, 78, 99, 109, 124–25; native/congenital, 229–32; in periodicals, 287n135; political, 198; and purification, 106–10; race and, 52, 159, 163, 177, 195, 217, 236, 290n185; rational, 108–9, 217, 232–33, 235–36; scholarship on, 252–54; sexuality and, 160, 162–64; universality of, 232, 235; of Young New Right, 77–78, 99. *See also* Jews and Jewishness
Antliff, Mark, 105, 112, 251, 291n214
Apollinaire, Guillaume, 20
Aragon, Louis, 35
Arche, L' (journal), 142
Arland, Marcel, 30, 31
Aryan, 164, 176–77, 180–85, 191, 309n113. *See also* Race
Asia. *See* Eastern civilization
Athénas, Georges. *See* Leblond, Marius Ary
Aury, Dominique, 330n56
Auschwitz, 119–21, 137, 138, 153, 157, 292n6
Authenticity, 53, 136, 169. *See also* "legal" country vs. "real" country
Authorship: Blanchot and, 141–47, 152, 155, 157; Céline and, 165–66; intellectuals and, 80–81
Aux Écoutes (Attentive and Suspicious Listener) [magazine], 66, 119, 123
Auzépy-Chavagnac, Véronique, 272n151
Avant-garde: far-right, 34–37, 81–88; surrealism and, 34–35
Aymé, Marcel, 209

Bainville, Jacques, 51, 55, 58, 209, 268n71
Baker, Josephine, 20–21, 30, 173, 187
Barbarism, 50, 53
Barbusse, Henri, 167
Bardèche, Maurice, 19, 34, 68, 70, 243, 248, 326n258
Barrès, Maurice, 24, 25, 39, 87, 153, 209, 217
Basch, Victor, 238
Bataille, Georges, 13, 118, 142, 153–56, 158, 256; and psychoanalysis, 25–26; and the self, 266n47; *Story of the Eye*, 256–57
Belgium, 241–42
Bellessort, André, 69, 197, 216, 279n142
Bellmer, Hans, 36, 270n126
Benda, Julien, 39, 40, 80, 124, 135, 150, 237–38, 295n34; *La jeunesse d'un clerc* (An Intellectual's Youth), 238
Benjamin, Walter, 7, 250
Béraud, Henri, 69, 205, 282n21
Berl, Emmanuel, 38
Berliner, Brett, 254
Bernanos, Georges, 38, 56, 64, 66, 79, 149, 209
Bhabha, Homi, 253
Bident, Christophe, 136, 292n2, 295n33, 299n120
Birnbaum, Pierre, 198, 263n31
Black culture, 19–21, 168, 170–74, 214
Blanchot, Maurice, 2, 63, 69, 118–57, 256–57, 330n56; and abjection, 13, 96, 128–31, 133–34, 137, 141, 150; and antisemitism, 122–24, 133–37, 139, 154, 157, 294n21, 295n33, 303n205; and authorship, 141–47, 152, 155, 157; and autonomy of the aesthetic, 5–6; background of, 125; and Bataille, 153–56; on Blum, 103, 133–36; and the body, 140–41; Brasillach and, 123, 134, 136, 146–47; Céline and, 159, 190, 301n159; *La communauté inavouable* (The Unavowable Community), 156; and crisis, 11; on decadence, 127–28; and disgust, 91; and dissidence, 78, 88, 126, 296n45; *L'écriture du désastre* (The Writing of the Disaster), 157; *Faux pas*, 142; and February days, 72; and foreign affairs, 127, 129; friendships of, 155, 303n207; and Gide, 143, 144, 148; "L'idylle," 137–41, 149, 299n120; influence of, 118; influences on, 144–45, 273n6; *Les intellectuals en question*, 152–54; interwar writings of, 5–6, 118–57; and language, 125, 135, 149, 151, 302n184; and literature, 135, 141–52; and Maurras, 144–46; and the nation, 120, 124; near-execution of, 295n27; *La part du feu*, 142–44; and periodicals, 66, 67, 87, 106, 125–26, 252, 282n31, 292n9, 295n37, 295n38; and politics, 41, 118–57, 245–46, 284n56, 293n12; in postwar era, 245–46; on role of intellectuals, 88, 152–55; and seeing, 267n68; and the self, 120, 137–41; self-presentation

of, 122, 144–47, 153–56, 295n25, 300n147, 302n195; and terrorism, 97, 296n45; and Young New Right, 120, 125–28, 145
Blond, Georges: background of, 1, 16, 69, 278n125; on Benda, 238; on Blum, 220; and disgust, 91; on Jewish question, 233; and periodicals, 66, 67, 87, 196, 207–8; and politics, 41, 211; on the press-advertising relationship, 282n31; on role of intellectuals, 81
Blum, Léon, 29, 44, 55, 75–76, 78, 85, 92, 94, 95, 98–101, 103, 105–6, 109, 123–24, 133–36, 153, 175, 177, 182, 196, 199, 205, 206, 215–22, 231, 238, 241–42, 244, 288n146, 288n151, 288n154, 320n116, 320n126
Blum-Viollette project, 227, 231
Body: abjection and, 2, 12–14, 131; antisemitism and, 101; Blanchot and, 140–41; of Blum, 219; Céline and, 163, 178–85; Céline on female, 184–88, 310n124; and decadence, 179; Jewish, 180–82, 219–20; male, 179–85; masculine, 9–10; mutilation of, 136–37, 298n107; social, 6, 7, 10, 27–30, 33, 89–94, 96, 109–10, 120–21, 129–30, 133, 136–37, 179, 219
Bonald, Louis de, 47
Bordeaux, Henry, 209
Borders and boundaries: abjection and, 98; anxiety about, 7, 9–11, 21, 23, 29, 91, 124, 130, 195, 197, 213, 222; of bodies, 180–81; of the citizen, 148; of Frenchness, 191, 194–95; *Je Suis Partout* and, 210; Jewish transgression of, 180–81, 215; legal protection of, 232, 236; of masculinity, 24, 181, 186; of the public, 38, 44; racial, 169, 186, 194; restoration of, 97, 133; of the self, 24, 36, 228
Boundaries. *See* Borders and boundaries
Bourgeoisie: class anxieties of, 169; corruption and decadence of, 18; and sexuality, 172; threats to, 30
Brami, Émile, 305n16
Brancusi, Constantin, 20
Brasillach, Robert, 1–3, 12, 15, 16, 80, 194, 282n21; antisemitism of, 100, 216–17, 231–33, 235–36, 243, 324n198; Blanchot and, 123, 134, 136, 146–47; on Blum, 106, 221, 242; *Les cadets de l'Alcazar* (with Massis), 62; and Céline, 189, 193, 313n208; and cinema, 18–19; and collaboration, 65, 119, 200, 262n5; on culture, 238–42; on decadence, 30; execution of, 200, 243; and fascism, 107, 200–202, 243–44; and February days, 72–73; and Gide, 30, 240, 242, 325n241; and homosexuality, 200–202, 315n32, 316n33; influences on, 61, 68–70; on Jewish question, 233, 235–36; *Lettre à un provinciale* (Letter to a Provincial Woman), 240–43; literary criticism of, 40, 239–40, 251; on Malraux, 237; on masculinity, 237; Maulnier's parting from, 78, 106, 290n185; on Maurras, 46, 54–55; memoir of, 18, 22, 171, 243, 314n11; *Notre avant-guerre*, 18, 243; and periodicals, 63–67, 87, 106, 191, 196, 207, 284n53; and politics, 41, 197; in postwar era, 65; on the press, 81; and psychoanalysis, 26; social ties of, 68; and surrealism, 34; and tourism, 22; and virility, 93
Breton, André, 35
Briand, Aristide, 95
Britain, 269n83
Brousson, Jean-Jacques, 197, 208, 219, 233, 238
Bucard, Marcel, 79
Burrin, Philippe, 250, 293n12
Butler, Judith, 13, 264n33

La Cagoule, 208, 247, 282n31, 284n53
Cahiers, Les (Notebooks) [magazine], 16, 64, 69
Caillaux, Joseph, 95
Camelots du roi, 51, 63
Candide (newspaper), 40, 41, 66, 81, 85, 204, 206, 208, 223
Capitalism: and antisemitism, 99; idealism and, 76; and individualism, 31, 33; Jews associated with, 109; opposition to, 18, 31, 43, 76, 99, 110, 197, 211
Capitan Peter, Collete, 274n17
Caricatures, 85, 100–101, 288n146
Caron, Vicki, 213, 329n42
Carroll, David, 53, 161, 263n25, 263n29, 273n14, 277n105, 310n126, 314n15, 328n29; *French Literary Fascism*, 251

Catholicism: and abjection, 94; and Action française, 50; fragility of, 29–30; and intellectual far right, 58, 268n71; *Je Suis Partout* little influenced by, 209; and the self, 25, 26, 32–33, 41
Catholic nationalism, 3, 5
Cavani, Liliana, *The Night Porter*, 262n11
Céline, Louis-Ferdinand (pseudonym of Louis-Ferdinand Destouches), 1, 38, 56, 158–93, 244, 251, 263n25, 306n38; and abjection, 13; antisemitism of, 119, 159–93, 201, 218–19, 278n127, 287n140, 289n181; and authorship, 165–66; and autonomy of the aesthetic, 5–6; background of, 159; *Bagatelles pour un massacre*, 159–60, 163–64, 166–67, 171–87, 189–90, 201, 219, 289n181; ballet librettos of, 171–73, 187; *Les beaux draps*, 165, 304n11, 309n113; Blanchot and, 159, 190, 301n172; and the body, 163, 178–85; and class, 167–68; and colonialism/imperialism, 162–64, 168–93, 228, 307n62; and disease rhetoric, 129; *D'un château l'autre*, 160, 164; *L'école des cadavres*, 159, 177, 189, 289n181, 313n208; *L'Église* (The Church), 159, 166; and Freud, 25–26, 267n60; *Guignols' Band II*, 160; influences on, 167; interwar writings of, 5–6; and language, 167–68, 190; madness of, 164–65; and masculinity, 162–63, 179–88, 201, 202; *Mea culpa*, 313n195; and modernity, 158, 163, 169–70, 178; *Mort à crédit* (Death on the Installment Plan), 26, 159, 313n195; *Nord*, 160; and periodicals, 83; and politics, 160–62; and race, 160–93; Rebatet and, 189, 191, 193, 203, 313n208; reputation of, 160, 164; self-presentation of, 164; as victim, 164–65; *Voyage au bout de la nuit* (Journey to the End of the Night), 10, 21–22, 38, 56, 129, 158–59, 162–65, 167–70, 172, 173, 178, 186, 189, 193; Young New Right and, 190–91
Cendrars, Blaise, *Moravagine*, 167
Char, René, 143, 155, 303n207
Chardonne, Jacques, *Romanesques*, 149
Chateaubriand, Alphonse de, 282n21
Chautemps, Camille, 101, 212, 218
Chenut, Christian, 64
Chiappe, Jean, 71
Cinema, 18–19, 194, 214
Circumcision, 182–83, 219–21, 311n154
Citizenship: abjection and, 76, 92, 95–96; for Algerians, 227, 231, 329n40; Blum and, 288n154; cultural element of, 4, 110–11; individualism and, 33; of Jews, 229, 231–32, 236, 329n40; masculinity and, 8–11, 28; natural relationship of, to the nation, 98, 103, 105
Civilization: antisemitism and, 52–53; blackness in relation to Western, 20–21; culture and, 111–12; Frenchness and, 62, 76, 77, 89; Freud on, 290n195; intellectual far right and, 8, 42; Massis and, 58–62, 77, 127, 276n85; nationhood and, 110; race and, 77–78, 169; Western, 20–21, 58–62, 76, 111, 127, 174, 179, 181, 276n85
Class: Céline and, 167–68; France and, 211–12; race and, 168–69
Classicism, 6, 112–13, 291n214
Claudel, Paul, 149; *Le partage de midi*, 70
Claude-Matthieu, Nicole, 264n33
Clichy riots (1937), 92, 101
Cocteau, Jean, 38
Cole, Joshua, 329n38
Collaboration: Brasillach and, 65, 119, 200, 262n5; Cousteau and, 65; *Je Suis Partout* and, 195, 277n111; Maurras and, 144–45; Rebatet and, 65, 202; Sartre on, 200, 315n23
Colomb, Hélène, 327n1
Colonial Exposition (1931), 21, 25, 61, 223, 228
Colonialism: aesthetics of, 227; and antisemitism, 8, 229–33, 253–54; Céline and, 162–64, 168–93, 307n62; communism and, 230–31; and difference, 21; Frenchness and, 61, 223, 225, 228–31; and health, 228; intellectuals' opposition to, 245–47; in interwar years, 308n73; *Je Suis Partout* and, 196, 208, 222–31; Jews and, 229–32; native opposition to, 230–31; pleasures of, 225, 227; scholarship on, 253–54; and the self, 25. *See also* Imperialism
Combat (Struggle) [magazine], 3, 4, 15, 16, 46, 64–67, 77, 78–83, *84*, 87, 90–93, 95–96,

99–100, 106, 110, 115, 116, 119, 123, 124, 126–28, 135, 136, 146–47, 154, 156, 196, 197, 208, 209, 211, 233, 238, 252, 282n21, 282n31, 283n41, 283n52, 284n53, 287n135, 291n214, 295n37, 296n45
Comité de vigilance des intellectuels antifascistes (Anti-Fascist Intellectuals' Watchdog Committee), 71
Communism: in the colonies, 230–31; and culture, 37; and February days, 71; Gide and, 23, 39; Jewishness and, 214–15; opposition to, 39, 93, 94, 96, 110, 138, 174, 196, 211–12, 214; surrealism and, 35
Communist Party, 37
Congress for World Peace (1932), 23
Contre-Attaque (magazine), 156
Corruption and decadence: of bourgeoisie, 18; far right preoccupation with, 11, 13–15, 17–18; Gide and, 23
Cousin, Victor, 24
Cousteau, Pierre-Antoine, 2, 3, 16, 263n24; antisemitism of, 218; and collaboration, 65; on Gide, 221; influences on, 61; and periodicals, 196, 207–8; and politics, 41, 197, 214, 215; in postwar era, 65, 164, 248
Crémieux decree (1871), 229, 231
Crisis: abjection and, 13–14; background on, 15–18; intellectual far right and, 4, 11, 23–24, 272n158; of masculinity, 28, 162, 179–85, 201; Maulnier and, 15–16, 89; of modernity, 23; of the self, 24
Critique (journal), 142
Croix de feu, 71, 72, 76
Culture: civilization and, 111–12; conflicts over, 37–38; Daudet on, 55–58, 239; French, 76, 237–43; *Je Suis Partout* and, 198, 237–43; literature and, 112–15; Maulnier on, 111–15; Popular Front and, 148, 166, 237, 240

Dabit, Eugène, *L'hôtel du nord*, 38, 167
Daladier, Édouard, 71
D'Annunzio, Gabriele, 115, 255
Dard, Olivier, 277n110
Daudet, Alphonse, 55
Daudet, Léon, 26, 40, 282n21; and *L'Action Française*, 51, 55, 57; antisemitism of, 55, 57; Blanchot and, 153; and Céline, 159, 189; cultural criticism of, 55–58, 239; and February days, 71–72; influence of, 45, 47, 48, 55–58, 68, 273n5, 275n63; and Jews, 217; and journalism, 57; and literature, 55–57, 88, 276n70; *Les Morticoles*, 276n70
David, Angie, 330n56
Daye, Pierre, 208
Dean, Carolyn, 2, 6, 24, 29, 179, 256, 264n33, 266n47, 267n60, 268n78, 314n18, 331n66
Déat, Marcel, 249
Decadence: anxiety about, 90; Blanchot on, 127; the body and, 179; bourgeoisie and, 18; Eastern civilization as source of, 59–61; French Revolution as source of, 49; as interwar theme, 11–16, 285n72; Jews as source of, 51, 94, 99, 160, 210, 215; Maulnier and, 13, 15–16
De Gaulle, Charles, 122, 327n6
Degeneration, 160, 162–63, 165–66, 168–70, 305n26
Degradation, 90–91
Degrelle, Léon, 208, 237, 241–42
Delarue-Mardrus, Lucie, 54
Delebecque, Jean, 55
Deloncle, Eugène, 282n31
Delongrave, 283n51
Delphy, Christine, 264n33
De Man, Paul, 121
Democracy: and individualism, 31, 33; Jews associated with, 109, 191; left-wing defense of, 71; opposition to, 18, 31, 43, 49–50, 79, 83, 92, 154, 197, 210–11
Denoël, Robert, 159
Denoël and Steele, 38
Derrida, Jacques, 118
Desrois, Marcel, 33
Destouches, Lucette, 160, 304n14
Deviance: anxiety about, 29–30; homosexuality as, 30; and masculinity, 28–29
Dioudonnat, Pierre-Marie, 314n6, 317n47
Discipline, 25, 36. *See also* Order
Disease, rhetoric of, 129, 212, 233
Disgust. *See* Abjection
Disorder, 11, 16–17, 27, 29, 32–33, 36, 44, 60, 79, 89, 93, 129, 134, 163, 173, 199, 210, 219, 228–30. *See also* Order

Dissidence, 78–81, 126
Dissociation, 269n91
Dissolution, 13–14, 181, 188, 197–98, 210
Doriot, Jacques, 79, 105, 208, 249, 293n12
Dorsay. *See* Villette, Pierre
Dreyfus, Alfred, 45, 49, 155
Dreyfus, Louis-Louis, 100
Dreyfus Affair, 10, 37, 39, 44–45, 46, 49, 51–52, 55, 57, 141, 153, 154, 208, 216
Drieu La Rochelle, Pierre, 41, 119, 202, 251, 263n25, 282n18, 282n21, 285n72; *Gilles*, 285n72; *Rêveuse bourgeoisie*, 149
Drumont, Edouard, 99; *La fin d'un monde*, 99; *La France juive*, 51, 57, 99
Duchamp, Marcel, 35
Duhamel, Georges, 167, 307n56
Durkheim, Émile, 24

Eastern civilization, 59–61, 182, 236
Eastern Europe, 236
École normale supérieure (ENS), 68–69, 279n140
Economy, 211
Eliot, T. S., 168
Éluard, Paul, 35
Enlightenment, 197
Epuration trials, 201, 248
Equality, 231
Ernst, Max, 35
Esprit (Thought) [journal], 32, 33
Ethiopia, 61
Ethnography, 21, 223, 227–28
Étudiant Français, L', 63
Etudiants d'Action fracçaise, 51
Exotic, the, 19–21, 194, 221, 223. 225, 227–28, 233, 254
Exposition universelle (1937), 166, 174

Fabrègues, Jean de, 3, 69, 70, 263n24; *Christianisme et Civilisations* (Christianity and Civilizations), 65; and *Combat*, 15; and dissidence, 79; on individualism, 31–32; influence of, 64; on jazz, 20; and Jeune France, 300n139; on Maurras, 46, 47; on modernity, 16; and the nation, 120; and New Humanism, 44; and periodicals, 63–67, 83, 85, 125, 284n54; and politics, 41, 79; in postwar era, 65; on role of intellectuals, 282n21; and the self, 26, 33; and surrealism, 36
Farnoux-Reynaud, Lucien, 19
Far-right intellectuals. *See* Intellectual far right
Fascism: abjection and, 12; Belgian, 241–42; Blanchot on, 153; Brasillach and, 107, 200–202, 243–44; criticisms of, 107; homosexuality associated with, 1–3, 200, 202, 203, 258; intellectual far right and, 12–14; Italian, 250–51; *Je Suis Partout* and, 195–96; masculinity associated with, 1–3, 242; Maurras and, 50–51, 274n37; newspaper of, 3–4; and order, 96–98; scholarship on, 250
Faÿ, Bernard, 282n21
Fayard publishing house, 40, 204, 206
February days (1934), 43–44, 70–74, 85, 88, 196, 210
Figaro, Le (newspaper), 116, 158, 204, 247
Filliol, Jean, 282n31
Fontenoy, Jean, 79
Foreigners and the foreign: anxiety over invasion of, 175–77, 179–80, 185–86, 191, 198, 213–15, 229–30; attitudes toward, 49; in Blanchot's "L'idylle," 138–41; Blum as instance of, 219, 221; and Frenchness, 100; *Je Suis Partout* and, 213; Jewishness and, 109, 134, 139, 214, 216–17, 232, 235, 236; prevalence of, 213; Romanticism and, 54. *See also* Immigrants; Otherness
Forrest, Jennifer, 305n20, 312n180
Forth, Christopher, 10, 263n31
Foster, Hal, 35–36, 270n126
Foucault, Michel, 118, 255, 257, 292n2
Foureau, Christine, 58, 276n85
Fragmentation, 13, 24–26, 30, 35, 269n91
France. *See* Nationalism and the nation
France, Anatole, 208
Francis, Robert, 26, 66, 67
Franciste movement, 79
Franco, Francisco, 127, 237
Franklin-Bouillon, Henry, 106
Freemasons, 49
Frenchness: as aesthetics, 110–15; ancestry and, 100; Blanchot on, 129; Céline on, 164, 171; and civilization, 62, 76, 77,

89; and colonialism/imperialism, 61, 223, 225, 228–31; culture as locus of, 76, 237–43; defining, 37, 41–42; intellectual far right and, 10–12, 64; *Je Suis Partout* and, 197, 198; loss of, 93; race and, 176–77, 217–18, 229, 232. *See also* Marianne (symbol of France)
French Revolution, 49–50, 54, 231
Freud, Sigmund, 25–26, 35, 153, 267n60, 290n195
Friendship: Blanchot and, 155, 303n207; of *Je Suis Partout*'s contributors, 206–7
Frost, Laura, 262n11
Fulgur (magazine), 68

Gandhi, Mohandas, 60, 127
Gaudy, Georges, 55
Gaxotte, Pierre, 67, 69, 70, 196, 197, 204, 206, 209–12, 215, 219, 231, 238, 247, 280n150, 282n21, 316n42
Gen Paul (given name, Eugène Paul), 177
Gender: antisemitism and, 9, 219–22; Blum and, 105–6, 135–36, 219–22; in interwar years, 308n70; Jewishness and, 135–36, 219–22; literature and, 30–31; politics and, 8–11; scholarship on, 254–56; and self-society relationship, 28–29. *See also* Heterosexuality; Homosexuality; Masculinity; Women
Germany: antisemitism of, 52, 217, 235; attitudes toward, 52–53, 60, 275n49
Geroulanos, Stefanos, 267n51
Gide, André: Blanchot and, 143, 144, 148; Brasillach and, 30, 240, 242, 325n241; and Céline's *Bagatelles*, 189; and communism, 23, 39; *Corydon*, 29, 30, 269n88; criticisms of, 23, 29–30, 37, 237; as deviant, 221; influence of, 22–23, 29–30; and the novel, 38; public disputes of, 40
Gilman, Sander, 9, 311n148
Girardet, Raoul, 48
Giraudoux, Jean, 38, 69
Gobineau, Joseph Arthur de, 52, 61, 217
Godard, Henri, 160, 167, 305n15, 305n17, 305n20, 305n26, 307n59
Godmé, Pierre. *See* Maxence, Jean-Pierre
Golsan, Richard, 263n29
Goyet, Bruno, 273n14
Grandchamp, Maurice (pseudonym of Pierre Monnier), 278n127. *See* Monnier, Pierre
Grand Prix de la Critique, 81
Grand Prix de Littérature de l'Académie Française, 59, 117
Gratiant, Gilbert, 227
Gravier, François, 67, 87
Great War, 17, 39, 52, 59, 109, 174
Greek tragedy, 112–13
Griffin, Roger, 250, 250–51
Gringoire (newspaper), 40, 69, 81, 85, 205, 208
Guéhenno, Jean, 38
Guillaumin, Colette, 264n33
Guyader, Antonin, 252
Guyana, 228–29

Haedens, Kléber, 56, 67, 101, 103, 325n235
Haiti, 20–21, 174, 266n28
Hawthorne, Melanie, 263n29
Hegel, G. W. F., 215
Heidegger, Martin, 121, 125, 143, 153
Hermann-Paul, René Georges, 209, 283n51
Hermaphrodism, 219, 320n126
Herriot, Édouard, 95, 100
Herzog, Dagmar, 255, 258, 330n49
Hess, Deborah, 294n21, 295n33, 303n205
Heterosexuality: Céline and, 161–63, 168, 172, 179, 183–88; normative, 28–29, 139–40, 172, 199
Hewitt, Andrew, 7, 263n29, 305n15
Hill, Leslie, 119, 123, 292n8, 300n137
Hill, Michael Holland, 119
Historiography of interwar years, 249–56
Hitler, Adolf, 41, 44, 52, 92, 107, 127, 129, 136, 154, 177, 183, 203, 235, 244, 258
Hölderlin, Friedrich, 143
Holocaust, 248, 255, 258. *See also* Auschwitz
"Hommes et les Idées, Less" *Je Suis Partout*, *192*
Homosexuality: in Céline's work, 183–84; as denunciation, 199–201, 203; as deviant, 30, 199, 221; fascism associated with, 1–3, 200, 202, 203, 258; intellectual far right and, 1–3, 201; *Je Suis Partout* and, 200; Jewishness associated with, 220–21; and sadomasochism, 262n11

Humanité, L', (newspaper), 158, 204
Idealism, 75–76, 92

Idées (newspaper), 283n41
Immigrants, 100, 213. *See also* Foreigners and the foreign
Imperialism: defense of, 61, 276n85; France's failures at, 90; modernism and, 168; scholarship on, 253–54. *See also* Colonialism
Individualism: criticisms of, 31–33; modernity and, 32–33
Insurgé, L' (The Insurgent) [newspaper], 16, 19, 64, 66–67, 69, 75, 77, 79, 81–82, 85, *86*, 87–88, 91–96, 99–101, *102*, 103, *104*, 105, 106, 109, 116, 119, 124, 126, 128, 130–31, *132*, 133–36, 142, 144–49, 151, 154, 156, 166, 190, 197, 205, 209, 211, 247, 252, 281n8, 282n31, 283n39, 284n53, 284n54, 284n56, 287n135, 295n37
Insurgency, 76–77, 88, 96–97, 99, 115–16, 127, 246
Integral nationalism, 33, 42, 47, 51–52
Intellectual far right: and abjection, 3, 4, 13–14, 75–76, 249; antisemitism of, 77–78; attractions of modernity for, 18–19; and authorship, 80–81; background on, 3–6; common conceptions of, 1–3; crisis perceived by, 4, 11, 23–24, 272n158; Daudet's influence on, 55–58; dissendent and oppositional stance of, 43–44; educational backgrounds of, 68–70; emergence of new (1930s), 62–70; and fascism, 12–14; galvanizing events for, 43–44; goals of, 43; historiographical debates about, 249–56; and homosexuality, 1–3, 201; ideological underpinnings of, 4–5, 43, 62–70; influences on, 44–64, 68–69, 88, 273n5; intellectual adversaries of, 135, 237–38; and literature, 7–8; and masculinity, 9–10; masculinity and, 263n29; Massis's influence on, 58–62; Maurras's influence on, 49–55; nationalism of, 9–12; and perversion, 1–3; political engagement of, 37, 79–80, 281n18; in postwar era, 245–49; as revolutionaries, 81–88, 96–97, 115–16; role of, 80–81, 117, 152–55, 201, 237–38, 245, 282n21; and the self, 10, 25–26; social ties within, 67–68; surrealism in relation to, 34–37; two groups of, 3–5, 8, 64–67, 77–78, 116. *See also* Young New Right
Intellectuals, Jewish and left-wing, 135, 237–38
Interwar years: colonialism in, 308n73; cultural context of, 17–24; gender in, 308n70; newspapers and magazines in, 39–40; race as concept in, 320n116; scholarship on, 249–56; the self in, 24–34
Invasion, fears of, 175–77, 179–80, 185–86, 191, 198, 213–15, 229–30

Jackson, Jeffrey, 19
Jackson, Julian, 37
Jameson, Fredric, 168
Jazz, 19, 20, 168, 170, 172–73, 265n21
Jeantet, Claude, 207–8, 233, 279n144, 319n102
Jeantet, Gabriel, 208, 317n66
Je Suis Partout (I Am Everywhere) [newspaper], 2, 3–4, 16, 18, 40, 46, 64–67, 69, 77–78, 105, 106, 109, 135, 147, 166, 181, 191, *192*, 193, 194–244, *224*, *226*, *234*, 277n111, 278n131, 279n144, 284n53, 288n146, 313n208, 314n6, 317n47
Jeune Droite (Young New Right), 3, 262n15, 272n151. *See also* Young New Right
Jeune France, 143, 300n139
Jeunesses patriotes, 71
Jewish question/problem, 52, 77, 106–9, 134, 232, 233, *234*, 235
Jews and Jewishness: abjection and, 98–99; barbarism of, 61; Blum as representative of, 75, 78, 85, 99, 133–34, 215, 218–20; bodies of, 180–82, 219–20; citizenship of, 229, 231–32, 236, 329n40; in the colonies, 229–32; and communism, 214–15; decadence of, 51, 94, 99, 160, 210, 215; fantasies of, 98–106, 180; as foreign, 109, 134, 139, 214, 216–17, 232, 235, 236; and gender, 135–36, 219–22; homosexuality associated with, 220–21; intellectuals among, 135, 238; and language, 135; legal status of, 232–33, 236, 243; and modernity, 157, 253, 304n218; and the nation, 124–25; as opposed to art and beauty, 105; otherness and, 124,

133–34; and race, 173–74, 235; and sexuality, 9–10; as threat, 49, 85, 98–106, 109, 133, 135, 159–60, 166, 173–75, 180–81, 197–99, 213–14, 217–18, 222, 229–30. *See also* Antisemitism; Dreyfus Affair
Jordan, Matthew, 265n21
Jouhandeau, Marcel, 217–18, 222; *Le péril juif* (The Jewish Threat), 217; *Le saladier*, 149
Journal des Débats, Le (Journal of Debates), 66, 119, 125–26, 142, 144
Journalism, 57, 125–28
Judaken, Jonathan, 315n27
Judeo-Bolshevism, 134, 213, 215
"Juifs, Les" *Je Suis Partout*, 234

Kafka, Franz, 143
Kaplan, Alice Y., 201–2, 248, 263n29, 315n32
Kent, Susan, 269n83
Kessler, Nicolas, 252, 272n151, 281n8, 283n52, 284n56, 287n135, 292n9, 328n32
Kipling, Rudyard, 114
Kleinberg, Ethan, 292n7, 293n15
Kristeva, Julia, 13, 130, 257, 305n15, 305n17, 306n27, 313n199

Lacan, Jacques, 26, 266n47, 267n68, 298n107
LaCapra, Dominick, 261n4, 304n218
Lacoue-Labarthe, Philippe, 293n16
Language: Blanchot and, 125, 135, 149, 151, 302n184; Céline and, 167–68, 190; Jews and, 135; Maulnier and, 125, 135; Maurras and, 54; and the self, 125, 290n190
Lanzmann, Claude, 261n1
Laporte, Roger, 122
La Rocque, François de, 72, 79, 92, 249
Larpent, Colonel, 55
Laubreaux, Alain, 207–8
Lautréamont, Isidore-Lucien Ducasse, Comte de, 142
Law, Jewish status under, 232–33, 236, 243
Lazare, Bernard, 216
Leblond, Marius Ary (pseudonym of Georges Athénas and Aimé Merlo), 223, 225
"legal" country vs. "real" country, 49, 91, 128, 130, 211
Leiris, Michel, 20, 28, 223
Lemaigre-Dubreuil, Jacques, 282n31
Le Marchand, Jean, 67, 79
Le Sueur, James, 245
Levenson, Michael, 307n60
Levi, Primo, 256
Le Vigan, Robert, 164
Levinas, Emmanuel, 123, 125, 153, 155, 157, 299n120, 303n205, 303n207
Lévy, Paul, 123, 125, 278n121
Lichtenstein, Therese, 270n121
Literature: abjection and, 112; autonomy of, 5, 39, 148, 156–57, 247; Blanchot and, 135, 141–52; conflicts over, 37–39; and culture, 112–15; Daudet and, 55–57, 276n70; far-right criticisms of, 31; and gender/sexuality, 30–31; Gide and, 22–23; intellectual far right and, 7–8; market for, 38; Maulnier and, 38, 135, 291n217; Maurras and, 56; politics and, 5, 39, 147–52, 157; and purity, 151–52; revolutionary character of, 151–52; scholarship on, 251–52; and the self, 149–50, 156–57; styles of, 6. *See also* Aesthetics; Poetry
Littell, Jonathan, *Les bienveillantes*, 1–3, 256–58, 261n1, 261n4
Loisy, Jean, 66, 67, 87
Loselle, Andrea, 307n56
Loubet del Bayle, Jean-Louis, 271n151, 277n112, 284n54, 328n32
Louis-le-Grand *lycée*, 68–69, 279n144
Lu (newspaper), 204
Lupin, José, 66, 68, 278n125

Mac Orlan, Pierre, 167, 307n53
Magazines. *See* Newspapers and magazines
Maistre, Joseph de, 47
Mallarmé, Stéphane, 143
Malraux, André, 30, 38, 143, 237; *La condition humaine*, 38, 148
Malvy, Louis-Jean, 95
Man. *See* Self
"Manifeste des 121," 245–47
Mann, Thomas, 149
Maran, René, 209, 223, 321n149, 321n150
Margueritte, Victor, *La garçonne*, 30
Marianne (magazine), 40

Marianne (symbol of France), 27, 53, 105, 199, 209, 221, 321n139
Marinetti, Filippo Tommaso, 255
Maritain, Jacques, 25, 32, 41, 68, 268n71, 270n104
Marriage, 29, 107, 139–40, 221, 242
Marx, Karl, 93, 106–7, 109, 215, 319n102
Marxism, 92–93, 96–98, 106–7, 148, 211, 214, 215, 230
Mascolo, Dionys, 246, 303n207
Masculinity: Blum lacking in, 219–21; Brasillach on, 237; Céline and, 162–63, 179–88, 201, 202; citizenship and, 8–11, 28; conceptions of, 10; crisis of, 28, 162, 179–85, 201; and deviance, 28–29; fascism associated with, 1–3, 242; French heterosexual, 184–88; intellectual far right and, 9–10, 263n29, 271n135; in interwar years, 10–11; *Je Suis Partout* and, 199, 222–23; left-wing, 237; nationalism and, 10; restoration of, 11; scholarship on, 255. *See also* Gender
Massis, Henri, 149, 249, 268n71, 282n21; on Action française, 48; on Brasillach, 243; *Les cadets de l'Alcazar* (with Brasillach), 62; and civilization, 58–62, 77, 127, 276n85; and crisis, 23; on Daudet, 56; on decadence, 33–34; and Gide, 29, 40; influence of, 45, 58–62, 68, 273n5; on literature, 38; on Maurras, 56; reminiscences of, 269n99; and the self, 31, 32, 33–34
Materialism: criticisms of, 32–33, 75–76, 92, 110; in literature, 150; socialism as, 76
Matin, Le (newspaper), 40
Mauban, Charles, 110
Maulnier, Thierry (pseudonym of Jacques Talagrand), 1, 3, 6, 25, 75, 117, 314n6; and abjection, 13, 95; and aesthetics, 251; anti-communism of, 93; on antisemitism, 106–9, 154, 233; background on, 15–16; on Blum, 103; on Brasillach, 200; Brasillach's parting from, 78, 106, 290n185; and Céline, 189; and civilization, 89, 110; and crisis, 11, 15–16, 23–24, 75, 89; on culture, 111–15; on decadence, 29, 34, 90; on degradation, 90; and dissidence, 88; and fascism, 250, 284n56; on Frenchness, 93, 100; and Hitler, 129, 154; influences on, 61, 69–70; on insurgency, 76, 97; *Introduction à la poésie française*, 113; on Jews, 77, 99; and language, 125, 135; and literature, 38, 135, 251, 291n217; on Marxism, 106–7, 215; as monarchist, 277n110; and the nation, 120; on order, 97–98; and periodicals, 15, 63–67, 82, 83, 85, 123, 125, 278n131, 282n31; and politics, 41, 80, 116; in postwar era, 65, 117, 246–48; and psychoanalysis, 26; on role of intellectuals, 117, 282n21; and the self, 26–27, 32–33, 92–93; social ties of, 68; and surrealism, 34, 36, 143; and virility, 8, 42; writing of, 80–81
Mauriac, François, *Les anges noirs*, 40
Maurras, Charles, 1, 249, 282n21; and Action française, 15, 36, 46–55; and *L'Action Française*, 57; anti-democratic sentiments of, 49–50, 92; anti-German sentiment of, 52–53, 275n49; antisemitism of, 52–53, 105; Blanchot and, 144–46, 149; and collaboration, 144–45; criticisms of, 72, 79; and fascism, 50–51, 274n37; and February days, 72; imprisonment of, 205; influence of, 45–49, 51, 54–55, 68–69, 97, 126, 144–46, 273n5, 273n6; *Je Suis Partout* and, 209; and Jews, 216–17; and literature, 56, 251, 291n217, 301n159; nationalism of, 51–53, 210; Rebatet and, 203; *Romantisme et révolution*, 49; secretaries to, 63, 69, 204
Maurrassian nationalism, 3, 5, 45, 50–54, 83, 95
Maxence, Jean-Pierre (pseudonym of Pierre Godmé), 1, 3, 15, 16, 20, 22, 43, 150, 263n24, 265n9, 282n21; on abjection, 94, 98; on Blum, 103, 105; and cinema, 19; and crisis, 23; and disgust, 91; and dissidence, 81–82, 88; and February days, 72; influence of, 64; influences on, 70; and literature, 23, 115; memoirs of, 23, 38, 62, 91, 185, 265n24; and the nation, 120; and periodicals, 64, 66, 67, 69–70, 85, 123, 125, 282n31; and politics, 41, 79–80; in postwar era, 327n1; pseudonym of, 64, 278n123; and the self, 25, 26; and surrealism, 34
May 1968 demonstrations, 122, 153, 327n12
Mazeline, Guy, *Les Loups*, 159

Mazgaj, Paul, 62, 250, 262n15, 263n26, 272n1, 272n154, 273n5, 277n112, 281n9, 328n32, 329n33; *Imagining Fascism*, 252
Mehlman, Jeffrey, 122, 144, 292n8, 293n16, 294n21
Mendelsohn, Daniel, 256–57
Merlo, Aimé. *See* Leblond, Marius Ary
Mesnard, Philippe, 292n8, 294n21, 327n6
Métèques. *See* Foreigners and the foreign
Meyers, Mark, 316n33
Miller, Henry, 159
Modernism, 6, 168
Modernity: anxiety about, 16–17; attractions of, 18–24; Céline and, 158, 163, 169–70, 178; cinema and, 194; criticisms of, 59, 82; individualism and, 32–33; intellectual far right and, 82; Jewishness and, 157, 253, 304n218; race and, 163, 168, 174; war as expression of, 169, 174, 178
Monfreid, Henry de, 282n21
Monnier, Pierre, 16, 70, 263n24; on abjection, 94; on Action française, 54; and antisemitism, 287n140; on Blanchot, 296n40, 298n86; on Blum, 103, 105, 133; *Céline et les têtes molles*, 278n127; and dissidence, 78–79, 79; and February days, 73; on Maurras, 275n49; memoirs of, 79, 247, 284n53; and periodicals, 63, 67, 83, 284n53; and politics, 281n18; in postwar era, 247–48, 278n127
Montherlant, Henry de, 149, 152
Morand, Paul, 167, 307n56
Mosse, George, 255
Mounier, Emmanuel, 32–33, 41, 270n105, 284n54
Moyn, Samuel, 256, 261n1, 261n4
Muel-Dreyfus, Francine, 255
Murnau, F. W., 288n151
Museum of Modern Art, New York City, 19
Music, 19, 20
Muslims, 227, 231, 232, 329n40
Mussolini, Benito, 44, 59, 61, 153, 191, 242, 255
Mutilation, 136–37, 298n107

Nadeau, Maurice, 136
Nancy, Jean-Luc, 157
Narcissism, 26–27
Nardal, Paulette, 225, 227, 322n158
Nationalism and the nation: abjection and, 89–98, 174–77; Action française and, 42, 47–55; and antisemitism, 51–53, 78, 99, 109, 124–25; Blanchot and, 120, 124; boundaries of, 21–22; and civilization, 110; in the colonies, 230–31; and gender, 28; integral nationalism, 33, 42, 47, 51–52; of intellectual far right, 9–12; masculinity and, 10; Massis and, 58–62; Maurrassian, 3, 5, 45, 50–54, 83, 95; nineteenth-century, 47; and race, 4; and the self, 11, 27, 33, 130; threats to, 11, 49. *See also* Frenchness; Marianne (symbol of France)
Naturalism, 271n144
Nazism: and antisemitism, 107–9, 154; attitudes toward, 176; collaboration with, 200; common conceptions of, 2, 257–58; France compared to, 77; Heidegger and, 153; *Je Suis Partout* and, 208, 210; sexuality and, 255, 257–58; totalitarianism of, 138
Négritude movement, 225, 321n149
Negrophilia, 19–20, 214, 265n24
Neoclassicism, 112
New Humanism, 44
New order, 17, 41
Newspapers and magazines, 39–40, 63–67, 81–88, 205, 282n28, 282n31
New Woman, 28
Nietzsche, Friedrich, 66, 69, 143, 153, 303n208
Noailles, Anna, Countess of, 54
Noiriel, Gérard, 254, 329n38
Non-conformism, 32, 34, 41, 43, 58, 69, 70, 117, 268n71, 271n151, 284n54
Nord, Philip, 300n139
Northern Africa. *See* Colonialism
"Notre Empire," *Je Suis Partout*, 224, 226
Nouvelle Revue Française, La (New French Journal), 22–23, 40
Novel, the, 39
Nye, Robert, 10

Order, 25, 47, 49, 56, 64, 96–98, 115, 190, 199, 211, 228–29. *See also* Discipline; Disorder; New order
Orient. *See* Eastern civilization

Orland, Claude (pseudonym of Claude Roy), 66. *See* Roy, Claude
Otherness: abjection and, 133; intellectuals and, 155; Jews and, 124, 133–34; in 1930s discourse, 124. *See also* Foreigners and the foreign

Pagès, Yves, 305n15
Paillard, Jean, 227
Panassié, Hugues, 87
Paris, 20
Paris Commune (1871), 88
Paris-Soir (newspaper), 40
Parliamentary government, 109, 127
Parti populaire français (PPF), 79, 208
Parti social français (PSF), 79, 92
Pascal, Blaise, 240
Paul, Gen. *See* Gen Paul
Paul-Boncour, Joseph, 95, 100
Paulhan, Jean, 155
Pauvert, Jean-Jacques, 248
Paxton, Robert, 250
Péguy, Charles, 291n217
Periodicals. *See* Newspapers and magazines
Personalism, 31–34, 41, 43
Perversion: aesthetics associated with, 2; homosexuality as, 221; intellectual far right and, 1–3; in interwar years, 28–29; Nazism and, 257–58
Pétain, Henri-Philippe, 153
Picabia, Francis, 20
Picasso, Pablo, 20
Plato, 215
Poetry, 53–54, 113–14, 239. *See also* Literature
Poincaré, Raymond, 265n9
Politics: Action française and, 50; aesthetics and, 4–8, 37–40, 110, 147–48; gender and, 8–11; intellectual far right and, 37, 79–80; literature and, 5, 39, 147–52, 157; Young New Right and, 79–80
Pollard, Miranda, 255
Popular Front: and black culture, 214; and colonialism, 231; and culture, 148, 166, 237, 240; demise of first government of, 206; emergence of, 15, 37, 71, 73; far right opposition to, 44, 75, 76, 79, 81, 95, 124, 129, 130, 160, 166, 174, 196, 198, 210, 211, 212; as sign of abjection, 94; stereotypes of, 214
Pound, Ezra, 168
Prix Goncourt, 38, 57, 159, 223
Prix Renaudot, 38, 159
Protestants, 49
Proust, Marcel, 38, 56
Psychoanalysis: and abjection, 290n205; Céline and, 267n60; historiographical use of, 255, 330n47; and the self, 11, 25–26; surrealism and, 35
Psychology, in literature, 150
Pujo, Maurice, 49
Purity and purification: aesthetics as means to, 4; Blanchot and, 136; in Céline's work, 170; far right desire for, 14, 89, 95, 97, 103, 130, 190; the Jewish question/problem and, 107–10; literature and, 151–52

Race: antisemitism and, 52, 159, 163, 177, 195, 217, 236, 290n185; Céline and, 160–93; civilization and, 77–78, 169; class and, 167–68; equality and, 91; and Frenchness, 176–77, 217–18, 229, 232; in interwar years, 320n116; *Je Suis Partout* and, 194–244; Jewishness and, 173, 235; and modernity, 163, 168, 174; nationalism and, 4; scholarship on, 253–54
Racine, Jean, 81, 111, 113
Rancière, Jacques, 1, 7
Réaction pour l'Ordre (Reaction for Order) [magazine], 16, 64, 65, 67, 79, 89, 125, 268n71
Realism: epistemological and political, 75, 92, 97, 108; in literature, 150–51
Reason, as basis for French antisemitism, 108–9, 217, 232–33, 235–36
Rebatet, Lucien, 1–3, 16, 214, 251, 328n29; on Action française, 48; antisemitism of, 99, 106, 231, 233, 236, 248; on Blum, 220–21, 320n126; and Céline, 189, 191, 193, 203, 313n208; and cinema, 18; and collaboration, 65, 202; *Les décombres*, 2, 193, 233, 248; and fascism, 194, 202–3; and homosexuality, 202–3; on Jewish question, 233; marriage of, 324n214; *Les mémoires d'un fasciste* (A Fascist's Memoirs), 248; and

music, 19; and periodicals, 63, 67, 196, 207, 248, 317n57; and politics, 41, 197; in postwar era, 65, 164, 248
Reboul, Marcel, 200–201
Refugees, 213
Régnier, Madame de, 54
Rémond, René, 330n54
Rempart, Le (newspaper), 119, 123, 125, 278n121
Republicanism: opposition to, 31, 49–50, 55, 56, 92, 94, 197, 212, 215, 231; and social regulation, 27; universalism of, 197
Restoration: of France, 110, 115, 129–30, 199; inadequacy of, 95, 137; intellectual far right's calls for, 43–44; through literature, 112, 115, 149, 152; of masculinity, 11, 111, 186–88, 198; of the self, 28; of social order, 29, 97–98
Revolution. *See* Insurgency
Revue du Siècle, La (Journal of the Century), 16, 31, 64, 66, 158, 268n71
Revue du XXe Siècle, La (Journal of the Twentieth Century), 26–27, 64, 66, 67, 82, 125, 268n71
Revue Française, La (The French Journal), 16, 64, 142
Revue Universelle, La (Universal Journal), 32, 58, 62, 63, 268n71
Rex, 208
Ric et Jac (newspaper), 208
Richelet, Guy, 70, 103
Riefenstahl, Leni, 18, 194, 285n80
Rilke, Rainer Maria, 149
Rimbaud, Arthur, 291n217
Rivarol (newspaper), 248
Roberts, Mary Louise, 256, 264n33, 308n70; *Femme Moderne*, 30
Romanticism, 24, 36, 47, 53–54
Rougemont, Denis de, 149
Rousseau, Jean-Jacques, 47
Rousseaux, André, 282n21
Roussin, Philippe, 310n124
Rousso, Henry, 245, 327n2
Roux, Georges, 223, 229–32
Roy, Claude, 40, 66, 67, 74, 87, 208, 293n12, 300n139
Rubenstein, Diane, 279n140
Said, Edward, 168
Saillenfest, Jean, 66, 67, 87
Saint-Domingue, 266n28. *See also* Haiti
Saint-Pierre, Bernardin de, *Paul and Virginie*, 171–72
Salecl, Renata, 314n17
Salengro, Roger, 205
Salleron, Louis, 67
Sapiro, Gisèle, 251–52, 273n5, 277n111
Sartre, Jean-Paul, 152, 159, 200–201, 262n5, 315n23; "What Is a Collaborator?" 200
Scholarship, 5, 7–9, 263n24
Scholarship, on interwar years, 249–56
Scott, Joan Wallach, 264n33
Scullion, Rosemarie, 161, 180, 187, 263n29, 305n20, 305n22, 312n184
Séébold, Éric, 305n23
Seeing, 267n68
Self: abjection and, 13, 95–96, 98, 130–31, 286n111; aesthetics and, 24–25; alienation and, 297n77; Blanchot and, 120, 137–41; borders of, 24, 36, 228; colonialism and, 228; conceptions of, 10–11; fragile and fragmented, 24–26, 29; and gender, 28–29; individualism and, 31–32; intellectual far right and, 10, 25–26; in interwar years, 10–11, 24–34; language and, 125, 290n190; literature and, 149–50, 156–57; narcissism of, 26–27; the nation and, 11, 27, 33, 130; political regulation of, 27; restoration of, 28; society in relation to, 28, 32–33, 92–93, 121–22, 138–41; surrealism and, 34–37
Semmelweiss, Philippe Ignace, 310n124
Senghor, Léopold Sédar, 321n149
Sennep, Jean, 283n51
Sérant, Paul, 284n56
Serry, Hervé, 252, 270n103
Sexual difference: anxiety about, 26, 28, 30–31, 219; in Blanchot's "L'idylle," 139–40; intellectual far right and, 9; the self and, 13
Sexuality: in Blanchot's "L'idylle," 139–40; bourgeoisie and, 172; in Céline's work, 160, 162–64, 170–73; French male, 183–85; Jewishness and, 9–10; literature and, 30–31; Nazism and, 255, 257–58; scholarship on, 254–56; in Vichy regime, 315n23. *See also* Heterosexuality; Homosexuality

Shame, 155
Shelley, Mary, *Frankenstein*, 169
Shepard, Todd, 327n12, 329n40
Sicard, Maurice-Yvan, 79
Sirinelli, Jean-François, 279n140, 330n54
Socialism: materialism and, 32, 76; opposition to, 49, 76, 94, 99, 212–13
Society: restoration of, 29; self in relation to, 28, 32–33, 121–22, 138–41; social body, 6, 7, 10, 27–30, 33, 89–94, 96, 109–10, 120–21, 129–30, 133, 136–37, 179, 219
Solidarité française, 71, 79
Sorbonne, 69
Sorel, Georges, 97, 105, 112, 250
Soucy, Robert, 250
Soupault, Philippe, 35
Soupault, Ralph, 85, 101, 103, 105, 191, 209, 283n50, 283n51, 288n146, 288n151
Soviet Union, 23, 127, 138, 194, 213, 239
Spackman, Barbara, 255
Spanish Civil War, 15, 39, 44, 62, 85, 127, 174, 196, 210, 237
Spears, Thomas, 161, 180, 263n29, 305n20, 310n132
Spengler, Oswald, *The Decline of the West*, 60
Stalin, Joseph, 85, 213
Stavisky, Alexandre, 71, 100
Stavisky affair, 71–72
Sternhell, Zeev, 251, 283n52, 284n56, 292n9, 294n21; *Neither Right nor Left*, 250
Stoler, Ann Laura, 254, 264n33
Strowski, Fortunat, 279n143
Subjectivity. *See* Self
Sublime, 2, 6, 13, 14, 111–15
Surkis, Judith, 271n135
Surrealism: Blanchot on, 143; and gender/sexuality, 30; intellectual far right in relation to, 34–37; and masculinity, 28; principles of, 34–35; and psychoanalysis, 35; and the self, 11, 25, 34–37
Swenson, James, 296n45

La Table Ronde, 314n6
Tagore, Rabindranath, 60
Talagrand, Jacques. *See* Maulnier, Thierry
Tam-tam, 172–73
Tanguy, Yves, 35
Temps Modernes, Les (journal), 142
Terrorism, 97, 296n45
Theweleit, Klaus, 256, 261n4, 330n47; *Male Fantasies*, 255
Third Republic, 50, 71–72, 96, 127
Thomism, 270n104
Thorez, Maurice, 105, 220
Totalitarianism, 138
Tragedy, 112–13
Travel and tourism, 22, 222–23, 225, 227
Truc, Gonzague, 221
TSF radio, 19

Uncanny, the, 35–36
Unconscious, the, 25–26
Ungar, Steven, 284n56, 292n8, 294n19
United States, 19, 173, 239

Vaast, Émile, 66, 67, 89
Valéry, Paul, 38, 153
Vallat, Xavier, 218, 288n154
Vallès, Jules, 88
Vaugeois, Henri, 49
Vaulx, Bernard de, 208
Vendredi (magazine), 40
Verdeil, Georges, 27
Verdès-Leroux, Jeannine, 283n52, 294n21, 313n5
Verlaine, Paul, 291n217
Vichy regime, 116, 160, 164, 195, 245, 255, 315n23
Viénot, Pierre, 134
Villette, Pierre (pseudonym: Dorsay), 197, 208–9, 211–12, 216, 218–19
Vincent, René, 16; and Céline, 190–91; on film, 285n80; influences on, 63; on literature, 115; and masculinity, 29; on Maurras, 46, 52; and music, 19; and periodicals, 64, 66, 67, 82, 283n41, 284n54; on race, 91
Virility: Blum lacking in, 105–6, 135–36, 220–21; Brasillach and, 93, 237; Céline and, 180, 183–86, 188; Italian fascism and, 255; Maulnier and, 8, 42; as political value, 10, 195, 197, 199, 202; Rebatet and, 202–3; restoration of, 25, 36, 314n18; scholarship on, 255

Vivien, Renée, 54

Watts, Philip, 164
Weber, Eugen, 47, 50, 274n16, 292n9
Western civilization, 20–21, 58–62, 76, 111, 127, 174, 179, 181, 276n85
Wilson, Stephen, 263n31
Winock, Michel, 285n72, 330n54
Witt, Mary Ann Frese, 113, 329n34
Wohl, Robert, 272n1
Wolin, Richard, 292n8, 293n18
Women: in Blum's government, 241; in Céline's work, 184–88, 310n124; far right's view of, 221, 240–42; in interwar years, 28; political rights withheld from, 241; Romanticism and, 54. *See also* Gender
Woolf, Virginia, 142, 149, 151, 168
World War I. *See* Great War

Young New Right: and abjection, 90, 95–96; anti-communism of, 93; antisemitism of, 77–78, 99; Blanchot and, 120, 125–28, 145; and Céline, 190–91; defined, 4, 262n15; emergence of, 46, 62–70; and personalism, 33; and poetry, 113–14; political engagement of, 79–80, 110; as revolutionaries, 81–88, 115–16; and the self, 120, 130. *See also* Intellectual far right

Zola, Émile, 56; *Germinal*, 169
Zouzou (film), 20